PTL

PTL

The Rise and Fall of Jim and Tammy Faye Bakker's Evangelical Empire

JOHN WIGGER

To David,
with warmest regards,
John

OXFORD
UNIVERSITY PRESS

OXFORD
UNIVERSITY PRESS

Oxford University Press is a department of the University of Oxford. It furthers the University's objective of excellence in research, scholarship, and education by publishing worldwide. Oxford is a registered trade mark of Oxford University Press in the UK and certain other countries.

Published in the United States of America by Oxford University Press
198 Madison Avenue, New York, NY 10016, United States of America.

CIP data is on file at the Library of Congress
ISBN 978–0–19–937971–2

1 3 5 7 9 8 6 4 2

Printed by Edwards Brothers Malloy, United States of America

For Melodie, Hannah, Allison, Natalie, and Emma

Contents

Acknowledgments

MANY FRIENDS HELPED to make this book possible. Thanks to my current and former graduate students: Brandon Flint, Hunter Hampton, Josh McMullen, Josh Rice, Jonathan Root, Luke Schleif, T. J. Tomlin, Darin Tuck, Jenny Wiard, and Cassie Yacovazzi. They formed the wonderfully generous and supportive community in which this book took shape and their careful reading of draft after draft made it much better. Extra thanks to Jonathan Root, who worked for me as a research assistant and whose own scholarship on the prosperity gospel helped me to understand its nuances. Thanks to my colleagues John Frymire, Jonathan Sperber, and Steve Watts, who listened to me drone on about this project for years and still had the patience to read the final draft and offer their wisdom. Thanks as well to Kate Bowler, Barry Hankins, and Phil Sinitiere, who graciously read the final manuscript and offered their expert advice, and to Mark DeMoss, Dan Foster, Armin Mattes, Ben Park, and Randall Stephens, who commented on various chapters. Melinda Lockwood became my executive assistant when I became department chair in 2013. Since then she has far exceeded her job description to help me track down sources and arrange interviews, always in the most cheerful and professional manner imaginable. It was worth becoming chair just for her assistance. Thanks to Maria David of the *Charlotte Observer* who graciously helped me find sources and photos. Thanks also to my brilliant agent, Colleen Mohyde, and my wonderful editor at Oxford, Cynthia Read.

The University of Missouri Research Council funded portions of the research for this book, as did the Kinder Institute on Constitutional Democracy at the University of Missouri.

I conducted scores of interviews for this book, the majority of them on the record. Thanks to those who were willing to talk with me, particularly since the ministry ended in disappointment for most of them. Their contributions added immeasurably to the story and are evident throughout the text and in the notes. I am also grateful to the Flower Pentecostal Heritage Center at the Assemblies of God headquarters in Springfield, Missouri, and in particular to the center's director, Darrin Rodgers, and its reference archivist, Glenn Gohr. In addition to its extensive collection of print sources, the Flower Center provided access to the PTL videos that they have digitized so far.

I am indebted to the fine work of the many reporters at the *Charlotte Observer*, who diligently wrote about PTL during the 1970s and 1980s, and in particular to Charles E. Shepard, who also wrote a Pulitzer Prize winning book about the ministry, *Forgiven: The Rise and Fall of Jim Bakker and the PTL Ministry*, published in 1989. Shepard and I take different approaches to writing about the ministry, but I am immensely grateful to have had his book available to help make sense of the many twists and turns in the story.

Thanks to my brother, Bill, his wife, Mindy, and their children, Julia and Alex, for welcoming me into their home when I traveled to North Carolina. Staying with them made these trips so much more enjoyable. As always, I am most deeply grateful to my family, most especially my lovely wife, Melodie, who believed at the beginning, and to my wonderful and talented daughters, Hannah, Allison, Natalie, and Emma, of whom I am endlessly proud.

PTL

Introduction

ON A CRISP Carolina morning in January 1987, Jim Bakker stood before a crowd of supporters and prepared to break ground on the Crystal Palace Ministry Center. It was his biggest project to date as head of PTL, the television and theme park empire that he and his wife, Tammy Faye, had launched in 1974 in Charlotte, North Carolina. PTL was an acronym for Praise the Lord or People That Love. Critics rendered it Pass the Loot or Pay the Lady, an allusion to Tammy Faye, famous for her outrageous makeup. The date, January 2, was no accident. It was Bakker's birthday and the day he usually chose to launch major projects. Intended as a replica of London's famed nineteenth-century Crystal Palace, Bakker's version called for a glass structure 916 feet long and 420 feet wide. The complex would enclose 1.25 million square feet, including a 30,000-seat auditorium and a 5,000-seat television studio, at a cost of $100 million. It would be the largest church in the world.[1]

At the time Bakker's confidence did not strike many observers as entirely unwarranted. He had started PTL thirteen years earlier with half a dozen employees and some makeshift television equipment in a former furniture store. By 1986 PTL had grown into a worldwide ministry with 2,500 employees, revenues of $129 million a year, and a 2,300-acre theme park and ministry center called Heritage USA. During 1986 six million people visited Heritage USA, making it the third-most visited attraction in the United States, after Disneyland and Disney World. PTL's satellite network included more than 1,300 cable systems and reached into fourteen million homes in the United States. The ministry's programs were seen in as many as forty nations around the world, making Bakker an international celebrity and opening up enormous fundraising potential.

When Bakker broke ground on the Crystal Palace center, Heritage USA already had a five-hundred-room hotel, the Heritage Grand Hotel, with another five-hundred-room hotel, the Heritage Grand Towers, nearing completion alongside it. The complex had one of the largest waterparks in America, a state-of-the-art television studio, half a dozen restaurants, a miniature railroad to shuttle visitors around the park, an enclosed shopping mall attached to the Heritage Grand, a petting zoo, horseback riding trails, paddleboats, tennis courts, miniature golf, a home for unwed mothers, a home for disabled children known as Kevin's House, and several condominium and housing developments. Plans called for adding a thirty-one-story glass condominium tower to the Crystal Palace complex, an eighteen-hole golf course lined by $1 billion in condominiums, a village called Old Jerusalem with its own two-hundred-room hotel, and a variety of other lodging, including bunkhouses, country mansions, and campgrounds. Heritage USA was as much an all-inclusive community as it was a theme park. Bakker hoped that it would eventually have thirty-thousand full-time residents. He assured his audience that the best was yet to come.

Two and a half months later, on March 19, 1987, Jim Bakker resigned in disgrace from PTL after his December 1980 sexual encounter with Jessica Hahn in a Florida hotel room became public. Hahn described Bakker forcing himself on her in an article in *Playboy*, while he claimed that she was a professional who knew "all the tricks of the trade." In the wake of the Hahn revelation, stories appeared about Bakker's involvement in gay relationships and visits to prostitutes, sometimes wearing a blond wig as a disguise. A decade later, in 1996, Bakker revealed that he had been sexually abused from age eleven until he was in high school by an adult man from his church, leaving him with a confused sexual identity and a deep sense of guilt and inferiority. The memories became "ghosts" that "swarmed through my thoughts" at vulnerable moments.[2]

The 1987 scandal was initially about sex, but it soon turned to money after it was discovered that PTL had paid Hahn and her representatives $265,000 in hush money. When he resigned, Bakker turned the ministry over to fundamentalist preacher Jerry Falwell. He and his team quickly discovered that PTL was $65 million in debt and bleeding money at a rate of $2 million a month. That summer workers boarded up the unfinished Towers Hotel, which never opened. Falwell and his entire staff left PTL in October 1987, less than seven months after he took charge of the ministry. When he took over, Falwell praised PTL as "one of the major miracle ministries of this century. I doubt there's ever been anything like it in the

2,000-year history of the church." When he left he declared that Bakker had turned PTL into a "scab and cancer on the face of Christianity," a disaster unparalleled in the last 2,000 years. By then PTL was already in bankruptcy, headed for liquidation.[3]

Two years later, in 1989, Bakker went on trial for wire and mail fraud, accused of overselling "lifetime partnerships" to Heritage USA and misusing the money donated for its construction. The trial unfolded in a circus-like atmosphere before US District Judge Robert "Maximum Bob" Potter. A witness collapsed on the stand and Bakker himself had a psychological breakdown, crawling under his lawyer's couch as federal marshals came to get him. He was convicted and initially sentenced to forty-five years in prison, serving nearly five years before his release. For millions who watched the scandal unfold in the press and on television, PTL and the Bakkers became a national symbol of the excesses of the 1980s and the greed of televangelists in particular.

IN BOTH ITS rise and fall, PTL demonstrates the power of religion to connect with American culture. The creation of PTL and Heritage USA followed a well-established trajectory in American evangelicalism as it evolved from field preaching, to camp meetings, to big tent revivals, to radio and television. George Whitefield, the famous evangelist of the Great Awakening, became colonial America's first celebrity, delivering dramatic sermons outdoors to tens of thousands at a time when America's largest cities numbered fewer than forty thousand people.[4] Camp meetings, pioneered by the Methodists in the early nineteenth century, invited the faithful to bring their wagons and tents, sometimes by the thousands, and gather in a festive atmosphere for preaching, worship, prayer, and fellowship. The theatrical nature of camp meetings, with their nighttime preaching under the somber glow of torches, accompanied by the shrieks and groans of seekers, only added to their appeal.

In the late nineteenth and early twentieth centuries, Billy Sunday, a former professional baseball player, and other big-tent evangelists combined religion and mass entertainment in ways that drew millions annually to their revivals. Their tents could transform almost any public space into the site of a crusade, and they appeared regularly on the front pages of America's newspapers. Over the course of his career, which reached its height in the pre-World War I years, Sunday preached to more than one hundred million people, converting more than a million of them. Aimee Semple McPherson preached in tents early in her career before moving to Los Angeles and building a megachurch, Angelus Temple. In 1924 she started her own radio station, a technologically advanced 500-watt facility that cost $25,000. With few stations to compete against at the time, her broadcasts could be heard for thousands of miles. For all of their theological conservatism, evangelicals have often pushed the envelope of communication technology, driven by the imperative to proclaim the gospel to the ends of the earth. Bakker's use of television was part of a long line of innovation, a heritage that dared religious entrepreneurs to think big.[5]

Bakker's breakthrough innovation was the Christian talk show. Oral Roberts, Billy Graham, Archbishop Fulton Sheen, and Kathryn Kuhlman pioneered religious broadcasting in the 1950s and 1960s. But their programs mostly looked like a church service, classroom lecture, or crusade, concepts developed before cameras were a consideration. Bakker envisioned a new "formula" better suited for television, initially modeled after the *Tonight Show* with Johnny Carson. Bakker pioneered the Christian talk show format in the 1960s and early 1970s, first with Pat Robertson at the Christian Broadcasting Network (CBN) in Virginia Beach and then Paul Crouch at the Trinity Broadcasting Network (TBN) in southern California. At PTL Jim and Tammy created their own unique style, often doing two hours or more of live, unscripted television a day in front of a studio audience. Viewers came to believe that they were a part of PTL's mission and the drama of Jim and Tammy's personal life. The Bakkers became their friends, and PTL their extended family.

At its best, the television show was a crossroad where evangelical religion and American pop culture met. Everyone who was anyone among evangelicals eventually appeared on the show, including Colonel Sanders, Little Richard, former Black Panther Eldridge Cleaver, Watergate figure Chuck Colson, Apollo astronaut James Irwin, Ruth Carter Stapleton, *Hustler* magazine publisher Larry Flynt, Maria Von Trapp of *Sound of Music* fame, singer Pat Boone, actors Efrem Zimbalist Jr., Dean Jones, Mr. T, Dale Evans and Roy Rogers, World Heavyweight boxing champion George Foreman, NBA Hall of Famer Jerry Lucas, and bodybuilder Lou Ferrigno. Among the celebrity preachers who appeared on the show were Oral Roberts, Robert Schuller, Norman Vincent Peale, Mother Angelica, Marilyn Hickey, and Paul Yongii Cho (now known as David Yongii Cho), pastor of the world's largest church in Korea. The theme that held it all together was the desire to engage broadly.

It was more than entertainment. When Jim and Tammy and their guests prayed, viewers reached out their hands toward their televisions and prayed along at home. For many, PTL seemed more relevant than their local church. They watched the show to learn the meaning of the scriptures and the condition of the church around the world, but they also tuned in for candid discussions about sex, marriage, parenting, substance abuse, diet and exercise, and dealing with depression and other psychological problems. What the show lacked in polish it often made up for in spontaneity and unfiltered candor, particularly from Tammy. At times she had her own show aimed specifically at women, the last of which was called *Tammy's House Party*. PTL's television programs attracted a broad range of viewers of varying ages from across the United States. By the mid-1980s more PTL "partners," the term the ministry used for its supporters, lived in California than any other state.

PTL's second innovation under Bakker was the satellite network, launched in 1978. ESPN did not begin satellite transmission until late 1979, more than a year after PTL.[6] Only HBO and Ted Turner's station in Atlanta beat PTL into space. The satellite network beamed Christian programming into millions of homes twenty-four hours a day, allowing PTL to create a range of its own programming and sell airtime to other ministries.

The enormous fundraising potential of the satellite network enabled Bakker to initiate a third innovation, creating a Christian Disneyland in the rolling hills along the border between North and South Carolina. Heritage USA was unlike anything else in America—part community, part church ministry, part vacation resort. But it cost more than even the television money could support. In the fall of 1983 Bakker came up with what seemed like the perfect solution. In exchange for a contribution of $1,000, "lifetime partners" would receive four days and three nights free lodging at the Heritage Grand Hotel every year for the rest of their lives. It seemed too good to be true and it was. Bakker soon expanded the partnership program to fund a wave of construction that continually pushed the ministry beyond its means. PTL was nearly always broke, leveraged to the point of collapse.

Almost all of the money went into Heritage USA, a place that Bakker's followers absolutely loved. From 1984 to 1987 they bought more than 150,000 lifetime partnerships with the expectation of enjoying all that the park had to offer. Heritage USA provided Christian families a place to relax and have a good time, while also attending worship services and a variety of seminars, workshops, dinner theater performances, and concerts. Many also worked as phone counselors via hundreds of lines strung throughout the park, some that they could access from their RVs or campers parked in the campground. Among Heritage USA's most popular recreational attractions was the $13 million waterpark. Its signature ride, the 163-foot long Typhoon, propelled swimmers up to 30 miles per hour before they plunged into the pool at the bottom. The waterpark also featured a football-field sized wave pool and a sand beach with 1,400 pieces of beach furniture. For PTL's partners, the dizzying pace of activity and growth only seemed to confirm that God was on their side. Along the way many made lifelong friends, mended broken lives, and saw miracles. Heritage USA was "the most beautiful place in all the world," said one lifetime partner. "It was just a little bit of heaven here on earth."[7]

Underpinning PTL's rise was a set of theological ideas clustered around faith and the abundant life, often called the prosperity gospel, which blended easily with post-World War II affluence. Bakker's conception of faith called on believers to take risks and extend themselves beyond their resources, counting on God to provide. When it came to money, for those with enough faith God employed a "special math" that did not rely on "facts," Bakker said. Like other prosperity preachers, he claimed that believers could speak almost anything into existence, a concept sometimes called "name it and claim it," or "blab it and grab it." "Don't pray, 'Lord, Your will be done,' when you are praying for health or wealth. You already know it is God's will for you to have those things," Bakker told his audience. "When you want a new car, just claim it. Pray specifically; tell God what kind you want, and be sure to specify what options and what color you want too!"[8] At its best, faith understood in this way inspired believers to take chances and think big. At its worst, it fostered an alternate reality that could shade into fantasy and denial. At PTL, it did both.

As Pentecostals gained a new level of affluence in the 1970s and 1980s, and as they joined forces with charismatics, who adopted Pentecostal beliefs but remained in their mainline Protestant and Catholic churches, therapeutic well-being and self-fulfillment became central to Bakker's message. "To think that God doesn't want your life to be rich, exciting and full of adventure is the greatest lie that I know," he wrote in *Eight Keys to Success*, published in 1980. No good thing in this life was beyond the reach of those who truly believed, Bakker told his audience. "God wants you to be happy. God wants you to be rich. God wants you to prosper, even as your soul prospers."[9]

Jim and Tammy practiced what they preached. By the mid-1980s they enjoyed a lifestyle of conspicuous extravagance. They used PTL money to buy a 10,000-square-foot home near Heritage USA, a condo on the Florida coast, and vacation homes in Palm Springs and Gatlinburg, Tennessee. They traveled with an entourage, flew first class or chartered jets, bought luxury cars, boats, and expensive clothes, and showed off their wealth in nouveau riche style. To their supporters, Jim and Tammy represented something new on the American religious landscape. They were Pentecostals who had made it, TV stars in an era when television defined American popular culture. From 1984 to 1987 the Bakkers' total compensation from PTL was $4.7 million. The desire to experience all that consumer culture had to offer was a powerful link between the Bakkers and their audience.

The story of PTL defies the notion that the evangelical resurgence in the 1970s and 1980s was primarily about the rise of fundamentalism and the Religious Right in politics. Jim and Tammy only cared about politics for its celebrity appeal. Before the 1980 presidential election Jim Bakker flew on Air Force One with President Carter, visited the White House, and taped an interview with Ronald Reagan, but declined to endorse either candidate. PTL was more Pentecostal than fundamentalist. Pentecostals have a better sense of how a culture feels than how a society works. Pentecostalism tends to be more therapeutic and lacks the militancy of fundamentalism, which is why Bakker closed his television shows by smiling into the camera and saying, "God loves you, he really does."

I interviewed more than fifty people for this book, everyone from Alan Dershowitz to Jessica Hahn. I first met Hahn at a deli off Mulholland Drive in Los Angeles, the kind of place with Porsches and Ferraris in the parking lot and people I knew I should recognize inside. I have also incorporated testimony from the criminal trials of Jim Bakker and his associates, David and James Taggart, along with other sources. The story that emerges, particularly from my interviews with former PTLers, is of a ministry started by a small group of energetic young believers, mostly in their twenties and thirties, who felt sure that God had called them to change the world through television. That meant they had to be big, which meant big money. In the 1980s Bakker used that money to change the direction of the ministry, shifting the focus from television to Heritage USA, from evangelism to a Christian version of the good life. In the process many of the original staff quit, disillusioned by the corruption they saw creeping into the ministry. Yet PTL continued to grow, supported by hundreds of thousands of followers drawn to its combination of faith and cultural relevancy. It was church with a waterpark, revival in the comfort of a luxury hotel, preachers who were television stars.

Then it all fell apart.

I

The DJ and the Queen

JIM BAKKER GREW up in Muskegon Heights and Muskegon, Michigan, where he graduated from high school. His father, Raleigh, worked as a machinist in the Sealed Power Corporation's piston ring plant for forty-two and a half years. Though he always had a steady job and made a decent living, Jim grew up thinking, "We lived in poverty." In fact, the Bakkers, like many Pentecostals, participated in the wave of prosperity that swept over the nation in the post-World War II years. Their first house on Sanford Street in Muskegon Heights was made of cement block and painted orange, like a pumpkin. They later moved to a house in more fashionable Muskegon and then, when Jim as about fifteen, to a former lumber-era mansion on Webster Avenue. It was "a beautiful home," with a "grand player piano" in the living room, according to one of Jim's high school friends, Sandy Tyers. Raleigh "loved to drive in style," according to another childhood friend of Jim's. He preferred Cadillacs, which he bought used. When televisions first became popular in the mid-1950s, Raleigh bought one over the objections of his wife. To most Pentecostals, secular television represented an extension of movies and the theater, both gateways to vice, if not hell. Raleigh was more tolerant. As much as any other consumer product of the time, television defined the good life, a message that Jim internalized early on. Like everyone else, his favorite show was *I Love Lucy*. When Jim needed a tape recorder for a speech class at school, his father spent "several hundred dollars" on the best reel-to-reel model he could find.[1]

Bakker's insecurities growing up had less to do with family finances than his distant relationship with his parents, Raleigh and Furnia, who were never particularly nurturing. Bakker was born premature and left at the hospital in an incubator after his mother went home. A heating element burned his foot, lengthening his stay. Even after he came home, "Mom and Dad considered me so fragile that they didn't allow my brothers and sister to even breathe on me." As a young child he "never experienced the sensation of my family members' touch," Bakker later wrote. As he matured, his "stern, Dutch family" rarely showed much affection. His father once washed his mouth out with Palmolive soap for saying "Gee whiz," and his mother "emphasized fastidious standards of cleanliness." Sandy Tyers was often at the Bakkers' home for dinner and other occasions but did not remember Furnia saying "more than ten words in all the years that I knew them." She was what people at the time called high-strung. "I was starved for physical touch and attention," Bakker writes.[2]

His hunger for affirmation was filled in part by his grandmother Irmilda Irwin. He spent hours at her house. "She was the one person in my life against whom I never remember feeling even a tinge of resentment," Bakker later recalled. "There was something about the way she lived and loved that made you feel special. It was something that I didn't see in the lives of many folks who called themselves followers of Jesus." Including his parents, whom he rarely wrote about with such intimacy or conviction. When Bakker completed his first large-scale building project in 1976, Heritage Village, he placed a large portrait of his grandmother in the main building. There was no similar tribute to his parents. Despite his grandmother's support, there really was no substitute for the lack of approval that Bakker felt at home.

The one thing Bakker had in common with his parents was church. Bakker's grandfather, Joe Bakker, had been one of the original organizers of Central Assembly of God, where the family still attended. Joe was a stern and bitter man who was hard on his wife and children. Most of the family regarded him as a "bad seed," according to Jim's cousin George Bakker.[3]

The church often failed to provide the comfort that Bakker lacked at home. As a child he was terrified by a three-foot tall picture of a human eye that hung on the wall of his Sunday school room as he and the other children sang, "His eye is watching you, you, you." It left him with the impression that "the big 'eye' was always looking and He would get you if you were bad." Not only did Pentecostals not go to the movies, they were not supposed to dance, bowl, play cards, shoot pool, or listen to rock 'n' roll. At Central Assembly the young people sat in an addition off the main sanctuary, out of sight of their parents. During service Jim and his friends, including his cousin George Bakker and Sandy Tyers, would sneak out a back door and go across the street to a drugstore that had a soda fountain. There they would listen to Fats Domino on the jukebox, careful to slip back into church before the service ended. The tension between church and culture formed a central axis of Bakker's life, as it did for millions of young people of his generation. Everything he did at PTL was to some degree an attempt to reconcile the Pentecostalism of his youth with all that post-war American culture, driven by affluence, entertainment, and consumerism, had to offer.[4]

Bakker's childhood also harbored a dark secret, one that he kept even from his family through everything that happened at PTL. As he tells it in his post-prison autobiography, when Bakker was about eleven years old a young man from his church who was in his late twenties or early thirties approached him one Sunday night after church and asked if he would like to go to a drive-in for a hamburger. Lonely as he was, Bakker was "awed that this adult would want me." The man (Bakker calls him Russell) was a member of the church, so Bakker's parents were not concerned. At the restaurant the man "gave me his undivided attention. I felt wonderfully special," Bakker writes. After they ate, the man drove "to the edge of town" and kept going. They drove down a "deserted dirt road" and stopped. The man assured Bakker that everything was okay as he unzipped Bakker's jeans and began to fondle him. "I felt almost proud that Russell would give me so much attention. I thought, *So this is what having a buddy is all about! This must be what the big guys do,*" Bakker writes. He describes the man as kind and reassuring. "Many people assume that child molesters beat their victims into submitting to their desires. I am convinced the exact opposite is true in most cases. The molester gives the child the love, attention, self-esteem, or kindness that the child may not be getting from his or her family and friends."

After that, the man became "a frequent figure" in Bakker's life. He took Bakker to "isolated construction sites," or simply "stopped along the road somewhere." When Bakker mowed his lawn the man took him "up to his bedroom and molested me." "I allowed Russell to do whatever he wanted to do to me and I tried to comply with his requests because he lavished attention and caring touches on me," Bakker writes. He was the perfect victim: "shy, not too likely to talk, especially reluctant to talk in a group setting, and yet . . . I could keep up appearances; I could maintain a public persona even when I was falling apart internally." By high school the man had "faded from the scene," but of course he was never far from Bakker's mind.

Like many victims, for years Bakker wondered if somehow it was his fault, if "I had brought it on myself." He also worried that "there was a part of me that was not heterosexual, but homosexual." He certainly could not tell anyone in his 1950s church, knowing the shame that it would bring on his family. Not until he went to prison in 1990 did Bakker, by his own account, open up to a psychologist, Dr. Daniel Foster, and confront "how my sexual identity had been confused by my childhood experiences." Throughout his ministry the issue of Bakker's sexuality lurked behind the scenes, a shadow glimpsed only in passing.[5]

Bakker's experience of abuse and reaction to it are all too typical. Child sexual abuse has been called an international pandemic, partially hidden by massive underreporting. Estimates of the prevalence of child sexual abuse in the United States vary widely, but generally fall in the range of 25–30 percent for girls and 8–13 percent for boys. Abusers are usually not strangers, but acquaintances whom the child knows, as was the case with Bakker. More often than not, abusers use coaxing rather than physical force to engage children, insinuating themselves into their victims' lives through family, religious, and social connections. Offenders often appear friendly and concerned, generous and trustworthy, a deception made easier in the presence of emotionally distant parents. The abuse can produce a range of symptoms, including anxiety, depression, loss of self-esteem, difficulty interacting with others in social or interpersonal settings, sexual dysfunction, continuation of the victim-perpetrator cycle, and learning impairment, often reflected in difficulty at school. Many victims never tell anyone out of embarrassment or fear of punishment and rejection. For a child growing up in a distant family, where this sort of thing could never be discussed, the result was devastating. "The lifelong impact and the fear of exposure I felt as a result of being molested as a child cannot be told too emphatically," Bakker later wrote. Years later, whenever he walked onto a television studio set, the "ghosts" of his childhood abuse lurked in the wings. "Especially frightening were the worries that someday, someone was going to stand up in one of our PTL audiences, and announce, 'I know something about you, Jim Bakker.' "[6]

Teachers told Jim's parents that he was a "slow learner." "He liked school, but he couldn't learn—not at first," his father later recounted. "He was terrible in spelling, even though we drilled and drilled." Bakker eventually had to repeat his senior year of high school before he could graduate. While never academically gifted, he nevertheless found an identity for himself in high school. At Muskegon High, a young teacher, Bill Harrison, who taught English, journalism, and photography, encouraged Bakker's creativity. Under Harrison's guidance Bakker found that he had a range of talents in organizing and promoting events. He joined the photography club and the school newspaper, eventually becoming editor. Using his tape recorder, he DJ'd at a photography club dance, discovered he liked it, and began spinning records for other clubs' dances.[7]

In the fall of 1956 Bakker directed a fifteen-act vaudeville-style variety show as a fundraiser for the school newspaper. Headlining the show, which took place on December 20, was Marlene Kinnucan, who reprised a "Miss Elvis Presley" act she had recently performed on Steve Allen's *Tonight Show* on NBC. Also featured were pantomimes, singing, a piano solo, a French horn quartet, a "Mambo Cambo," a pseudo-German comic band, a Marilyn Monroe impersonator, a comic reading, and Charleston dancers. The show sold out and was so popular it became an annual event.[8]

Bakker directed the show for the next two years. The 1957 version starred Shirley Swanson, Miss Michigan 1956, and a cast of two hundred in twenty-five acts. Kinnucan was back with her Elvis routine, as were the Charleston dancers by popular demand. After the show, four hundred kids descended on the Bakkers' home, the old lumber mansion on Webster Avenue, for a party. Bakker was thrilled beyond belief. "I was in the limelight completely—the center of attention. . . . I was obsessed with popularity and would do almost anything to get it," he later wrote.[9]

By the end of high school Jim had become more comfortable with who he was. He always "had an angle" and "did things with a flair that no other kid that age did," according to his cousin, George Bakker. Most of the boys at their high school were into sports or hunting, but Jim chose a different path. His high school girlfriend, Sally Wickerink, remembers him as a "lovely guy" who, like her, dreamed of escaping their papermill town. Jim often found George a date so that he and Sally could double date with George, who had a car. They went to movies, down to the lakeshore, or out for pizza, a new thing in Muskegon at the time.[10]

Classmates did not see Bakker as lonely and insecure, the way he later remembered himself. In his yearbook photos he looks confident and well dressed. One student who was too shy to talk to Bakker at the time later remembered him as "one of the most popular boys in our class. . . . He was into everything." Another student remembered him as "real energetic and a promoter" without "any religious leanings at all." Under "Ambition" in his senior yearbook Bakker wrote, "To do the best possible in everything I do," not the words of someone who expects to fail. (The young women whose photos appear on either side of Bakker's listed their ambitions as "to be a model" and "to live in a trailer." Odds are one of them succeeded.) His teacher, Bill Harrison, remembered Bakker as "very ambitious and excited and somewhat excitable, a promoter, thoroughly involved with what he was doing. He always acted as if he had a mission. He was a good kid." "I used to say I wanted to make him a rock-and-roll singer," added Harrison. "He had the looks, style, everything. We could have gone a long way." Bakker couldn't sing, but other than that, Harrison had it just about right.[11]

The turning point in his religious life, as Bakker later remembered it, was when he ran over three-year-old Jimmy Summerfield. Bakker had just dropped off Sandy Tyers at her home and was pulling up to church on a snowy Sunday night. He was driving his father's '52 Cadillac with his cousin George in the seat next to him when he felt a bump. The boy had slid down a snow bank in front of the car. The front tire rolled over his chest, crushing his collarbone and puncturing a lung. At first Bakker despaired that the boy might die, but miraculously he survived without debilitating injuries. The miracle of Summerfield's recovery, Bakker would later say, convinced him to attend Bible College.[12]

Bakker retold the Jimmy Summerfield story throughout his career, but not always exactly as it happened. In his first autobiography, published in 1976, he implied that the accident occurred during his senior year of high school, leading him to quit DJing at school dances, read his Bible more seriously, and set his course for Bible College after graduation. In fact, the accident happened on December 16, 1956, two years before Bakker's final year of high school, when he was sixteen. For the next two years he continued to produce the school variety show, work on the school paper, and develop his love for show business and entertainment. Running over Jimmy Summerfield was undoubtedly a shocking experience, but it did not immediately transform Bakker's life.[13]

To the surprise of many who knew him, by the summer of 1959 Bakker had decided to attend North Central Bible College in Minneapolis, rather than pursue journalism as Harrison had urged him to do. For a Pentecostal from the upper Midwest, North Central was a logical choice. North Central Bible Institute, as it was originally called, opened on October 1, 1930, with twenty-six students under the auspices of the North Central District of the Assemblies of God church. With over two hundred students by the fall of 1936, the school moved to the former Asbury Hospital at 910 Elliot Avenue. In 1955 the Institute changed to a four-year program, awarding its first bachelor's degrees to eight students the following year. The name was changed to North Central Bible College in April 1957, two years before Bakker arrived.[14]

North Central's development mirrored the growing sophistication of the Assemblies of God. Organized in Hot Springs, Arkansas, in 1914, the Assemblies of God was part of the first wave of the worldwide Pentecostal revival. Pentecostalism's origins defy easy explanation. It took shape in the late nineteenth and early twentieth centuries from a wide variety of radical holiness groups, most of which had their roots in Methodism. They believed that Jesus was coming soon and that God intended to restore to believers the spiritual power of the first-century church in these perilous last days. Where the New Testament church had sprouted to life under the "early rain" of the spirit, holiness people saw themselves as nurtured by the "latter rain" before the final harvest and the end of time.[15]

The name Pentecostal comes from an event recorded in the book of Acts. In this account, after his resurrection Jesus appeared to his disciples and promised that they would "receive power, after that the Holy Ghost is come upon you." Later, as the disciples were gathered together in Jerusalem during Pentecost, the Jewish Feast of Weeks, "suddenly there came a sound from heaven as of a rushing mighty wind, and it filled all the house where they were sitting. And there appeared unto them cloven tongues like as of fire, and it sat upon each of them. And they were all filled with the Holy Ghost, and began to speak with other tongues, as the Spirit gave them utterance."[16] Most churches have historically concluded that this experience was unique to the first-century disciples, but Pentecostals argued that it had only been neglected. The fire was still available, if only believers would seek it.

Most accounts date the start of Pentecostalism to the Azusa Street revival in Los Angeles in April 1906. William Seymour, a black holiness preacher, brought the new Pentecostal message to Los Angeles after learning it from another holiness preacher, Charles Parham. Born in Iowa in 1873, Parham suffered a steady stream of illnesses as a child and young man. He preached for a few years as a Methodist (though he was never ordained) before leaving the church because he believed it had abandoned holiness for respectability. After crisscrossing the United States visiting fringe holiness groups, Parham opened the Bethel Bible College in Topeka, Kansas, in October 1900. Though the school only operated for a few months, it was here that one of his students, Agnes Ozman, first spoke in tongues (also known as glossolalia). Parham and his followers concluded that the ability to instantly speak foreign languages would allow missionaries to evangelize the world without having to learn the languages, sparking a world-wide revival that would usher in Christ's second coming.[17]

In December 1905, Parham moved to Houston, Texas, where he opened another Bible school to teach his new understanding of the connection between Baptism in the Holy Spirit and speaking in tongues. One of his first students was William Seymour, the son of former slaves, born on the Louisiana Gulf Coast in 1870. Seymour grew up in a Catholic home and lost one eye to smallpox shortly after moving to Indianapolis in 1895. There he worked as a waiter and converted to Methodism before joining the Evening Light Saints, a radical holiness group. In 1903 Seymour moved to Houston, where he attended a holiness church led by Lucy Farrow, a niece of Frederick Douglass and former slave, who also worked as a cook and nanny to support herself. Farrow urged Seymour to attend Parham's school shortly after it opened. To abide by Texas's segregation laws, Seymour sat outside the classroom door to hear Parham teach. After six weeks, Seymour received a call to preach at a holiness mission in Los Angeles, arriving on February 22, 1906.[18]

Things did not begin well in Los Angeles. Seymour was promptly locked out of the holiness church that had invited him because the pastor, Julia Hutchins, disagreed with his new theology on baptism in the Holy Spirit. At that point Seymour himself had not yet spoken in tongues, but he was determined to press on. With nowhere else to go he moved his meetings to the home of Richard and Ruth Asberry on nearby North Bonnie Brae Street. There, on April 9, Seymour and a number of others finally received the Baptism in the Holy Spirit with speaking in tongues. The news brought crowds of onlookers who soon overflowed into the street. As the numbers grew, the meeting moved to a former African Methodist Episcopal church, which had recently been used as a tenement house, stable, and warehouse, at 312 Azusa Street.[19]

Under the headline, "Weird Babel of Tongues," the *Los Angeles Daily Times* announced the revival in a front-page article on April 18, 1906, less than a week after the Azusa Street meetings began. "Breathing strange utterances and mouthing a creed which it would seem no sane mortal could understand, the newest religious sect has started in Los Angeles," declared the *Times*.

> Meetings are held in a tumble-down shack on Azusa Street, near San Pedro street, and the devotees of the weird doctrine practice the most fanatical rites, preach the wildest theories and work themselves into a state of mad excitement in their peculiar zeal.

> Colored people and a sprinkling of whites compose the congregation, and night is made hideous in the neighborhood by the howlings of the worshippers, who spend hours swaying forth and back in a nerve-racking attitude of prayer and supplication. They claim to have "the gift of tongues," and to be able to comprehend the babel.[20]

The *Times* coverage set the tone for most Americans' interpretation of Pentecostalism for the next half century. Pentecostals were widely perceived as ignorant fanatics, partly because of their practice of speaking in tongues, but also because of the movement's interracial composition and the prominence of female leaders (the same would be true at PTL under Bakker). It was perceived as a religion of the poor and dispossessed, meeting in storefront churches and in tumble-down buildings across the tracks, where decent people rarely ventured. Pentecostalism was exactly what scholars and cultural opinion shapers of the mid-twentieth century had in mind when they declared that modernity could not help but sweep away religious superstition. In all likelihood, as historian Grant Wacker argues, Pentecostals more broadly reflected middle America in terms of their occupations and economic status than most Americans realized. But not until after World War II, really the 1970s, would they finally gain a wider measure of social acceptance. Most of the young people who helped Bakker start PTL knew what it was to grow up in a church that others laughed at.[21]

The Azusa revival continued for three years, with thousands visiting from across the United States and other parts of the world. Sunday meetings swelled to as many as 1,500. The mission began printing a newspaper, *Apostolic Faith,* in September 1906, eventually printing more than a dozen editions through May 1908. By that time, it had reported on Pentecostal outpourings in scores of American cities and in China, Liberia, South Africa, India, England, Wales, Ireland, Sweden, Norway, Denmark, Germany, Mexico, Canada, Australia, and Hawaii. Within three years, the Azusa Street revival had spread to more than forty countries. Pentecostalism was anything but a strictly Bible Belt phenomenon. Frank Bartleman, an independent holiness preacher, joined the revival when it first moved to Azusa Street. He claimed to have written more than five hundred articles for the holiness press and to have received "no less then five hundred personal letters . . . in the early Azusa days, from leading church workers, preachers and teachers, all over the world, inquiring anxiously about the revival." The newspaper and extensive correspondence networks demonstrate what would become a persistent theme among Pentecostals: the ability to creatively communicate their message with little money or institutional support. Used to operating on a shoestring, they made it up as they went along.[22]

Azusa Street did not create Pentecostalism by itself, but after it nothing would ever be the same. Within a decade an astonishing number of new Pentecostal churches and independent organizations sprang up across the United States, including the Assemblies of God, the church Jim Bakker grew up in. Still, Pentecostals remained invisible to most Americans, spreading unevenly across the American landscape. When Sinclair Lewis wrote *Elmer Gantry* in 1926, he chose to portray Gantry as a Methodist and Baptist rather than a Pentecostal, presumably because the latter were not yet prominent enough to make them an inviting target. In 1941 the Assemblies of God headquarters in Springfield, Missouri, employed only 125 people. Bakker's generation changed that. By 1987 the Springfield headquarters had more than one thousand employees. Today the Assemblies of God has more than fifty million adherents worldwide.[23]

At North Central, Bakker became involved in the same kinds of activities he had excelled at in high school. By his second year he was co-editor of the school newspaper, the *Northern Light*. The yearbook photo of the staff shows Bakker sitting at the center of a table, looking confident and at ease, surrounded by a staff of eight young women, with his co-editor standing behind him. That November Bakker also acted in a school "missionary play" entitled "The Return of Chandra." The plot revolved around a young man from India who comes to America to study medicine. Once here he becomes disillusioned with the Christians he meets and gives up "all thoughts of religion," according to a preview in the *Northern Light*. Readers were urged to attend and find out if Chandra rediscovers his faith and returns to the church, though the title left little doubt.[24]

Bakker also began attending an independent Pentecostal church, the Minneapolis Evangelistic Auditorium (MEA), run by a husband and wife team of Assemblies of God preachers, Russell and Fern Olson. The MEA met in a former theater, built in 1920 as a silent movie and vaudeville house, located at 1405 Nicollet Avenue, about a mile from North Central. By all accounts, Fern was the more dynamic speaker of the two, with a big singing voice and an outgoing, flamboyant manner. She represented a long tradition of female preaching in holiness and Pentecostal churches that stretched back into the nineteenth century. Russell Olson also preached, hosted a local radio show, and taught homiletics at North Central.

It was at the MEA that Bakker finally received the Baptism in the Holy Spirit, with speaking in tongues, a rite of passage for all Pentecostals. At the close of a meeting Russell Olson asked anyone who wanted to "receive the Holy Spirit," to come forward. "Without even thinking," Bakker responded. "'Lord,' I said in desperation, 'I give up.' The moment I spoke those words, the Lord baptized me with the Holy Spirit and immediately I began speaking in a language I hadn't learned. For what seemed like hours I was lost with God," Bakker later recounted. Though he had attended an Assemblies of God church all his life, it was not until he broke free of his parents and his childhood home that he fully embraced the faith for himself. This newfound spiritual fervor carried over to his life at North Central, where Bakker described himself as a "Holy Joe."[25]

When he returned to Muskegon that December, Bakker and his high school girlfriend Sally Wickerink went out one last time. Bakker told her that he wanted to become a television preacher, with a wife who was "an equal partner" in ministry, perhaps reflecting his experiences with Fern Olson. He and Sally, who was not a member of Bakker's church, went their separate ways. George Bakker, who had always thought that Jim and Sally would get married, was surprised. But by then George had lost faith in the message of their church.[26]

Bakker's experiences at North Central and MEA gave him a new sense of direction. He looks confident and poised, even smug, in his sophomore yearbook photo. His hair is swept back stylishly, and his suit looks sharp. His future wife Tammy looks surprisingly plain by comparison in her photo that same year (her first at North Central), with no hint of the makeup for which she would later be famous. Not surprising considering where she came from.[27]

Tammy LaValley grew up in a house without indoor plumbing in International Falls, Minnesota. She was the oldest of eight children, two born before her parents divorced when she was about three, and six born after her mother remarried. Their house had three small bedrooms upstairs, one downstairs, a small living room connected to a dining room, and a kitchen, with an outhouse in back. The house was heated by an oil stove in the living room. Tammy's childhood friend, Nancy Helland, remembers that Tammy's family "didn't have any money and they lived in a squalid brown house." To get to Tammy's room you had to climb a "tiny narrow staircase . . . almost like a ladder." The chaos of growing up in a large family in a small house without much money shaped Tammy's childhood memories. "Saturday night at our house was just a riot because that was when we got our baths," she later wrote. Her mother would heat water on the stove and pour it into a galvanized tub. They all had to use the same water, with the "cleanest ones" going first. While they bathed her mother would make fudge and tune the radio to Saturday night *National Barn Dance*.

Tammy's home was in a gritty working-class neighborhood, a place of "splendid squalor," as one former resident remembers. Most of the men worked either at the Minnesota and Ontario Paper Company mill or the fiberboard factory. Women also worked at the mill or stayed at home with their children. While some homes had indoor plumbing and appliances, others relied on outhouses, wood heat, and old-fashioned iceboxes. "Drinking problems were ubiquitous," compounding the general disorder, recalls a former neighbor of Tammy's. Nearby in the same neighborhood was the "small, run-down shack" of "Black Bernice," a former prostitute and one of the neighborhood's few black residents. Tammy's stepfather, Fred Grover, was not terribly involved with his children, but then neither were most of the other fathers in that time and place.[28]

Tammy and a friend "functioned as older, uncompensated babysitters for the younger neighborhood kids," remembers Jim Bruggeman, who grew up in the neighborhood from about six years of age through thirteen. "The two of them organized and inflicted on us a variety of 'constructive' activities during the summer, including organizing a neighborhood library and conscripting us into a 'reading club' with assignments to read a certain number of books during the week. They also functioned as moral police, making sure that we 'stayed out of trouble,'" and reporting to their parents when they did not. "'Trouble' meant shooting birds or each other with our BB guns, making and setting off smoke bombs," and other "escapades," according to Bruggeman. He enjoyed the reading, including the *Mr. Popper's Penguins* series.[29]

Apart from their poverty, her mother's divorce dramatically shaped Tammy's childhood, particularly the way she was treated by her church, which viewed divorce and remarriage as a form of adultery. To the people of her Pentecostal church, Full Gospel Assembly, "my mother was just a harlot," Tammy later remembered. "I don't know why she stuck it out." Despite giving more than she could afford and pitching in at church activities, the church refused to let her play the piano or kneel and pray at the altar, which was considered sacred space (she had to pray at her pew instead). "I remember some terrible fights at our house when the pastor and his wife would come over and scream at my mother," Tammy later recalled.

Instead of attending her mother's church as a young child, Tammy went to the Mission Covenant Church with her aunt, Virginia Fairchild. Aunt Gin became her second mother, giving Tammy the attention her own mother could not spare. Tammy spent so much time at Aunt Gin's that Nancy Helland, who also attended Mission Covenant, thought that Tammy was Gin's daughter. Aunt Gin made her dresses, permed her hair, and took her out to eat. Later she got Tammy her first job at Woolworth's, where Aunt Gin worked for forty-four years, when she was fifteen. At about age ten, Tammy returned to her mother's Pentecostal church where she experienced the Baptism in the Holy Spirit and spoke in tongues at a Tuesday night prayer meeting, bringing her more fully into the Pentecostal fold. Shortly thereafter the church became more welcoming to her mother. The church's new pastor saw "potential" in her mother and allowed her to play the piano in church.

Tammy was popular at church and school. Two summers in a row she was elected queen of Bible camp. At school she sang in the choir and got a part in the play *Oklahoma!* Acting and singing on stage seemed almost scandalous, given her conservative church roots, but she was nonetheless delighted (Tammy didn't see her first movie, *White Christmas*, starring Bing Crosby, until after she was married). *Oklahoma!* was also the first time she wore makeup. She occasionally experimented with a little eye makeup after that but never wore lipstick until she was married. "I had been taught if you put on lipstick you are going to hell," she later said.

In high school Tammy was "reserved, shy, and serious," nothing like the "brainless, loquacious bimbo" later portrayed in the media, recalls her former neighbor, Jim Bruggeman. She enrolled in a vocational program in which students went to school in the morning and worked in various businesses in the afternoon. Ironically, Tammy sold makeup at Woolworth's because she was too short to work behind the candy counter. Few young women of her time and place were encouraged to go to college. There was little in Tammy's upbringing that prepared her for television and the pressure of celebrity she would encounter at PTL.[30]

In high school Tammy also began dating the preacher's son from her mother's church, Stanley Kramer. After graduation the two became engaged. But Stanley did not want her to attend Bible College with him, apparently so that he could survey the field and perhaps find someone more attractive. Tammy decided to enroll at North Central Bible College anyway (her Aunt Gin had been secretly saving money for her). Once there, she and Stanley broke up.[31]

Jim Bakker had arrived at North Central the year before, in September 1959. After Tammy broke up with her fiancée they quickly discovered each other. They had a lot in common. Both grew up in Midwestern Pentecostal churches, felt alienated from their families, and loved the stage. "She was absolutely the cutest girl I had ever seen," Bakker later remembered. On their first date they went to a Wednesday night meeting at the Minneapolis Evangelistic Auditorium, where Bakker had become the youth director. Tammy was only four feet ten inches and Bakker five foot four. "He weighed 130 pounds and I seventy-three. We looked great together," Tammy later recalled. They went out the next night and the next. On their third date, Jim asked Tammy to marry him. She said yes. "I had no doubts," she later wrote.[32]

Others were not so sure. When the couple visited Jim's family during a February break, Tammy was "awed" by how "wealthy and prosperous" the Bakkers were. "Their house had two bathrooms, big velvet drapes, curtains, a baby grand piano, and a kitchen with a dishwasher. I mean their house had things I had never seen in my whole life." Jim's parents made it clear that they did not want him to marry until he had finished Bible College. Jim's sister Donna offered to let Tammy try on her wedding dress, but she had "no sooner put the gown on, when Jim's dad walked in. He just gave us a real hard look, turned around and slammed the door." They tried to sneak the dress back to Minneapolis in Jim's brother Norm's car, but when the car broke down and Jim's father came to retrieve it, he also took back the dress.[33]

Back at school, Jim and Tammy's grades plummeted. Since North Central did not permit students to marry during the school term, they either had to wait or drop out. To make ends meet, Tammy worked as a sales clerk at Woolworth's and Jim bussed tables in the fountain room at Young-Quinlan, an upscale department store near North Central. Jim's boss, whom he calls Lena, helped them rent a third-floor walk-up apartment for sixty dollars a month. "Lena was a real classy dame—the long cigarette, big hats, the furs, big diamonds, big car and Este Lauder perfumes poured all over her. I used to smell her and it was just fabulous," Tammy later recalled. Not knowing any better, Tammy planned to wear her favorite red dress at the wedding. "No, no! Honey you can't get married in red," Lena scolded. She helped Tammy pick out a mint-green dress with white gloves instead. Two days before the wedding, Jim and Tammy slipped out of North Central for the last time. They were done with school. On April 1, 1961, Russell Olson married them at MEA.[34]

Shortly after their marriage, the couple visited Tammy's family in International Falls. Up till then, Tammy had been reluctant to discuss her family, and Jim had assumed she was an only child. The big family and the run-down house were a revelation, not to mention the outhouse. When Jim wanted a bath, Tammy brought him two tubs of water. Not knowing any better, he sat down in one and put his feet in the other. Tammy laughed until she cried and then explained that one was for washing and the other for rinsing.

Back in Minneapolis the Bakkers served as youth ministers at MEA. When Jim asked Fern Olson, "What's the key to success as an evangelist?" she replied without hesitation, "Results." "If you want to be a successful evangelist and have churches call you, you must get results. It's nice to have a theory, but only results will demonstrate the value of the theory." It was a lesson Bakker never forgot.

That fall an evangelist spoke at MEA about his ministry in South America. Dr. Samuel Coldstone, as Bakker calls him in his autobiography, planned to buy a yacht formerly owned by the actor Errol Flynn and cruise up and down the Amazon River preaching to the natives. Coldstone was smooth and engaging, and the church contributed "thousands of dollars" to his ministry. The Bakkers were so captivated that they decided to join Coldstone in South America. That meant raising enough money to pay for the trip. When a preacher from Burlington, North Carolina, Aubrey Sara, held a revival at MEA, the Bakkers confided their plan to him. Impressed, Sara invited them to preach a revival at his church and collect offerings for their trip. The Bakkers planned to take the bus to North Carolina, but Russell Olson bought them first-class plane tickets instead.

The South was a culture shock for the Bakkers. They were puzzled the first time they were served hamburgers with coleslaw on top. Tammy sang and Jim preached, but his initial sermons flopped. Instead of results—people streaming to the altar to give their lives to Jesus—the congregation only sat and stared. In a pattern that would become familiar at PTL, Bakker sank into self-pity, collapsing on the floor of Sara's office, sobbing "my heart out into the green carpet." Then, near the end of their allotted two weeks, a young Presbyterian followed his girlfriend to the altar, spoke in tongues, and actually rolled "from one end of the building to the other," according to Bakker (the term "holy roller" comes from antics like this). Soon others were leaving their pews and kneeling down front, getting "saved and filled with the Holy Spirit." The success of this revival convinced Bakker that he could make it as a Pentecostal evangelist.[35]

But they were not going to South America. Word arrived from Minneapolis that Coldstone was a fake. There was no Errol Flynn yacht, no South American ministry. The man, and the money he had collected, up and vanished. Tammy was secretly relieved. "Can you imagine me in the Amazon!" she later wrote. With nowhere else to go, the Bakkers decided to hit the road as traveling evangelists, carrying on a long American tradition that stretched back to Methodist circuit riders of the early nineteenth century, who rode from town to town preaching the gospel instead of settling down with a single congregation, and the big tent evangelists of the early twentieth century. To get them started Sara wrote to other ministers in North Carolina to arrange some meetings. The Bakkers bought a used Plymouth Valiant and they were off.[36]

2

A Show of His Own

JIM AND TAMMY began as small-time Pentecostal healing evangelists, traveling a circuit from church to church in the Bible Belt. For six months they preached across North Carolina, sometimes receiving as little as $30 for a week or two of meetings. Once they were paid with a live chicken, which Tammy turned into a pet, feeding it apples and bread crumbs. They visited Alaska and then broadened their circuit across the South. Tammy's mother had taught her to play the piano, and now she learned to play the organ and accordion as well. After a couple of years they got tired of sleeping in musty churches and taking sponge baths in the church kitchen, or staying in the homes of pastors who complained about how much hot water they used. So they bought a twenty-eight foot Holiday Rambler trailer to tow behind the '59 Cadillac they were now driving. When the hitch on the trailer broke, sending it careening into a utility pole and wrecking it entirely, the manufacturer replaced it for free.

Looking to broaden their appeal, they created a puppet show for the children who attended their meetings. They made the puppets from the caps of bubble bath bottles that were shaped like animal heads, creating Susie Moppet and her family. Soon they added Allie Alligator. Tammy worked the puppets behind a small set, using a "little Susie Moppet voice" and a "big Allie Alligator voice," while Jim stood out front playing the straight man. The puppets were an immediate hit and brought the Bakkers to the attention of Pat Robertson, who had just started a small Christian television station in Portsmouth, Virginia.[1]

Pat Robertson and Jim Bakker were a study in contrasts, beginning with their upbringings. Robertson's father, Absalom Willis Robertson, served six consecutive terms in the US House of Representatives and three in the US Senate from Virginia. He was both a social and fiscal conservative of the Old South. Pat's mother, Gladys, became something of a recluse in their spacious Lexington, Virginia, home and, later in life, a fundamentalist. Robertson had a privileged childhood and was a precocious student, graduating magna cum laude from Washington and Lee University in 1950 at age twenty. He served as a Marine Second Lieutenant in Korea during the war and then enrolled at Yale Law School in 1952. Bakker, in contrast, was raised in a Rust Belt working-class home and attended an obscure Pentecostal Bible college. But religion is one of the great equalizers in America, and in time their paths crossed.

Robertson failed the New York bar examination in 1955, marking the end of a lackluster academic career at Yale. In 1954 he married Dede Elmer, a nursing student at Yale and something of a "party girl," because she was pregnant with their first child. After several failed business ventures, Robertson decided to become a minister. Only after that decision, surprisingly, did he have a born-again conversion experience, initiated through his mother's fundamentalist contacts. Robertson's spiritual transformation was far from over.

In the fall of 1956 Robertson entered The Biblical Seminary of New York (which became New York Theological Seminary in 1965). Biblical Seminary was decidedly fundamentalist, and Robertson pursued his studies with fresh intensity. Not content with a narrow fundamentalism, Robertson was drawn to the "raw, personal, experiential religion" of Pentecostal meetings he attended in New York City. In 1957 Robertson met Harald Bredesen, a pioneer in the charismatic movement, which was only beginning to take shape in the 1950s. Charismatics are mainstream evangelicals who nevertheless accept the Pentecostal theology of the Baptism in the Holy Spirit while remaining in their Protestant, Catholic, and Orthodox churches. The charismatic movement's emergence was yet another sign of Pentecostalism's growing influence in broader American Christianity in the post-war era. Rarely are charismatics fundamentalists. A graduate of a Lutheran seminary, though he never served as a Lutheran pastor, Bredesen received the Baptism in the Holy Spirit with speaking in tongues at a Pentecostal camp meeting in 1946. Under Bredesen's guidance, Robertson himself soon spoke in tongues. Like Pentecostals, Roberston believed that Christ's return was imminent, that divine healing was still available to believers, and that God could speak directly to the faithful through dreams, prophecies, and supernatural impressions.

After graduating from Biblical Seminary in 1959, Robertson briefly served at a rundown Presbyterian church in the Bedford-Stuyvesant neighborhood of Brooklyn before moving his family (which now included three children) to Portsmouth, Virginia. There Robertson intended to buy a defunct UHF "hillbilly" television station, a calling he believed he had received from God. When the owner asked how much the Lord was willing to pay, Robertson offered him $37,000, even though he had no money. His plan was to raise support from viewers. The Christian Broadcasting Network (CBN) was chartered on January 11, 1960, and went on the air in October 1961. The station, WYAH, channel 27, operated from a rundown building on Spratley Street. It had a thirty-by-thirty-foot studio, one camera, and a seventy-foot creosote pole holding up its antenna. Two years later it was still only on for three hours each evening, Tuesday through Saturday, and five hours on Sunday. Robertson came up with a scheme to ask seven hundred viewers to pledge ten dollars a month and the *700 Club* was born. Smoking cost about ten dollars a month at the time, so the campaign was pitched in part as a way to give up cigarettes.[2]

Robertson was still struggling to find an audience in 1965 when he heard about Jim and Tammy and sent Bill Garthwaite to check them out. Garthwaite, who had previously worked at a network television station before Robertson recruited him to be his production manager in 1963, was impressed. Based on Garthwaite's report, Robertson hired the Bakkers to do a kids show called *Come On Over*. The name was eventually changed to the *Jim and Tammy Show* to capitalize on the Bakkers' growing popularity.[3]

The show, launched in September 1965, was a huge success, drawing a large live audience every afternoon. The set, which became more elaborate over time, featured the front of a house, complete with a porch, front door, and picture window. Kids waited up to four weeks for tickets, and Zippy the Mailbox, a fixture on the program, received as many as five thousand letters a week. The Bakkers ad-libbed the show, a pattern they continued for more than two decades of doing live television, giving the show a spontaneous, if sometimes goofy, feel. John Gilman, a director at CBN, did the voice of Zippy. Gilman and the show's crew staged pranks without telling the Bakkers, like spring-loading Zippy so that the mail shot out at Jim when he opened it on air, or rigging Zippy to roll across the set when Bakker approached. Once during "mail time," as Jim and Tammy stood next to Zippy reading letters, Tammy gave a "hint to the mothers" who were watching. After buying bars of soap, they should take them home and unwrap them, so that the soap would dry out and "last twice as long," Tammy said. "And it makes your clothes smell good if you like to put it in your drawers," Tammy added. Everyone in the studio laughed as Tammy looked around, bewildered, until she figured it out. She spent the rest of the show giggling. Sometimes the Bakkers continued off-air arguments during the show, with Tammy using the puppets' voices to say whatever was on her mind. Susie Moppet was the one who got mad at Jim, while Allie Alligator acted as the peacemaker. "I guess it was therapy for me," Tammy later wrote. Tammy never had much of a filter; what you saw was who she was, a quality that endeared her to just about everyone.[4]

The show made the Bakkers local celebrities. They appeared at shopping malls and other events with their puppet cast. A CBN press release described Tammy as "cute as a button," and looking "almost like one of the kids," descriptions repeated in local newspaper stories. Over two hundred children jammed into CBN's small building for a Halloween show in 1965, while their parents waited outside. The show had its own fan club, with more than three thousand members by 1967. Tammy mailed out scores of membership certificates each week with "Jesus Loves Me" rings. Later they sent out decoders so that kids could decode secret messages Susie Moppet read over the air. In 1967 a local reporter wrote that "Jim and Tammy are to Channel 27 what Lucille Ball is to CBS and Ben Cartwright [the lead character on the western *Bonanza*] is to NBC. Their show is the flagship for Channel 27 five nights a week." Another article referred to the show as the station's "anchor program." In October 1967 Bakker was promoted to "Vice President and Television Production Manager," though a CBN press release announcing the move misidentified Bakker as a "graduate of Northwestern Bible School in Minneapolis, Minnesota."[5]

By then Bakker had also proved himself a natural at fundraising, beginning with the November 1965 telethon. The 1964 telethon, before Bakker arrived at CBN, had raised only $40,000. The 1965 effort had a loftier goal of $120,000, but as the week wore on it looked like they would fall woefully short. On what was supposed to be the last night, they were still $40,000 behind. Bakker broke down and began crying on air. "Our entire purpose has been to serve the Lord Jesus Christ through radio and television . . . but we've fallen far short. We need $10,000 a month or we'll be off the air," he pleaded. "Listen people," Bakker continued, still sobbing, "it's all over. Everything's gone. Christian television will be no more. The only Christian television station is gone, unless you provide us with the money to operate it." It was the kind of hard sell that Robertson had always avoided, but it worked. Rather than signing off at 11 p.m. as usual, Bakker stayed on the air until 2:30 a.m. as callers jammed the phone lines. Some who could not get through drove to the station to hand in their donations in person.

Callers not only made pledges, they also asked for prayer and got "saved and filled with the Holy Spirit," according to Garthwaite, something that had not been a part of previous telethons. The next morning the phones were still ringing and "the telethon that wouldn't end" continued all week.[6]

The 1965 telethon raised enough money to pay off all the station's debts and fund operations for the coming year. The 1966 telethon was equally successful, raising more than $150,000 over ten days. As had happened the previous year, people called in not just to give money but also for prayer and counseling.

The success of the telethons led Bakker and Garthwaite to pitch an idea to Robertson that Bakker later claimed had long been on his mind. Why not combine the call-in format of a telethon with a late-night talk show? Back when Jim and Tammy itinerated from church to church, they would unwind in their trailer at night watching the *Tonight Show* with Johnny Carson. Carson, who began hosting the show in 1962, was the king of late-night television, combining monologues, comedy sketches, guest interviews, and a live band. The show was immensely popular, and Bakker wondered why Christian television could not offer something as good. Robertson had his doubts but agreed to give it a try. Building on the success of the telethons, the new show was called the *700 Club*, debuting in November 1966.

The Christian talk show was Bakker's first big breakthrough, though subsequent accounts differ on just how much of its initial success was his doing. Robertson later claimed that the initial shows were "terrible" until he joined as cohost. Eventually they worked out an arrangement, with Bakker hosting the show two or three nights a week and Robertson and other CBN staff picking up the other nights. Six to ten volunteers answered the phones. Bakker had more "personal charisma" than Robertson and the other hosts, remembers cameraman Roger Wilson. "There was a lot more response when Jim hosted the program." With a limited budget, Bakker had to rely on local guests or the occasional "celebrity" preacher who happened to be passing through. Yet at times the results were dramatic. In late 1967 the Cameron Family Singers were performing when "heaven itself seemed to descend into the studio." The show continued until 5 a.m., the phones "ringing to report healings and miracles throughout the Tidewater area."[7]

The Bakkers' success led to conflict between Jim and others on the CBN staff. Jim tended to be a micromanager with little tolerance for strong-willed people who disagreed with him, a tendency magnified with disastrous results later at PTL. In this instance, he was upset by an initiative, led by one of Pat Robertson's young protégés, Scott Ross, to create a new style of programing for CBN aimed at bridging the gap between the church and sixties counterculture, something that the Bakkers' shows were not designed to do. In response, Jim and Tammy pressed Robertson to keep CBN "100% Christian," as Tammy later put it.[8]

Scott and Nedra Ross joined CBN in 1967, bringing with them a wealth of experience in music and broadcasting. Scott emigrated from Scotland to the United States with his family at age nine, settling in Hagerstown, Maryland, where his father barely made ends meet preaching in a tiny Pentecostal church. Ross wanted nothing to do with the hypocrisy he saw among his father's parishioners. Instead, he dreamed of life on the airwaves.

The first time Ross saw the inside of a local radio station in Hagerstown he was hooked. At twenty-one he got a job at WINS in New York City as an assistant director. Working in radio opened up connections in the music world that seemed too good to be true. He partied with the Beatles, the Rolling Stones, and Bob Dylan, and soon parlayed these connections into his own radio show. In an all-too-familiar pattern, his partying reached epic proportions until a drug bust cost him his show and his career in radio.

Nedra grew up in Manhattan and first performed at the Apollo Theater when she was ten years old with five of her cousins, four girls and a boy. By the time she was fifteen, Nedra and two of her cousins had formed the singing group, the Ronettes. They signed with producer Phil Spector in 1963 and had their first big hit, "Be My Baby," that same year. By the time Nedra was eighteen they were performing with the Rolling Stones in England. They toured with the Beatles, and Nedra dated Ringo while one of her cousins dated George Harrison. Eventually Nedra's cousin Ronnie married Spector, and the group broke up. Keith Richards inducted the Ronettes into the Rock & Roll Hall of Fame in 2007.

Scott and Nedra began dating when she was nineteen, while the Ronettes were still together. They married shortly after Nedra turned twenty-one and Scott lost his job in radio. When they visited Scott's mother in Hagerstown, she dragged them to her small Pentecostal church where both Scott and Nedra unexpectedly experienced the kind of powerful spiritual awakening that drew so many people into the Pentecostal and charismatic movement in this period. A few months later, Scott met Pat Robertson and agreed to join the staff of his tiny radio and television station in Portsmouth, Virginia. It was a long way from the music scene in

New York City, but the Rosses had lost none of their show business savvy. They were everything the Bakkers were not. While Scott had mixed with real celebrities in New York City and Nedra had a Billboard number-one hit, Jim and Tammy had preached and sung in small southern Pentecostal churches. The Bakkers pressed the Rosses for "rock 'n' roll stories," according to Scott Ross, and were "enamored," but also intimidated, by their show business connections.

In contrast to the Bakkers' narrower Pentecostalism and preference for southern gospel music, Scott Ross wanted to reach out to the emerging youth culture by playing their music on radio and television and openly debating their philosophies. When Ross brought a rock band into the CBN studio to play Bob Dylan's "Like a Rolling Stone," Bakker led a boycott of the entire camera crew. Bakker likely had this event in mind when, a few years later, in December 1977, he referred to an experience he had had at a Christian station. "Some young people came to the ministry and they said, 'We think you ought to put some rock and roll music on this Christian station.' And I said, 'No, I just don't think so. And it was a battle, because they fought so hard, and they said, 'All you do is babysit the Christians . . . you need to reach out to the unsaved world and play some rock and roll music and then you can tell them about Christ.' And I said, 'Well, that's a new concept for me. I've never heard of trying to be like the world to win the world. I didn't see Jesus being a prostitute to win a prostitute.' " But, of course, Jesus ate with sinners.[9]

Bakker's conflict with Ross was less about cultural accommodation than control over CBN. Later, in the 1980s, Christian rock groups, even heavy metal, performed at Heritage USA with Bakker's blessing. The competitive dynamic between Bakker and Ross extended to Bakker and Pat Robertson, who ended up "competing for audiences," as Ross put it. Bakker had talent, especially when it came to fundraising, but it was Robertson's station.[10]

By 1972 the Bakkers felt ostracized at CBN. Tammy acknowledged that many CBN staffers saw them as "prima donnas." Feeling underappreciated for their role in creating CBN's most successful shows, the Bakkers increasingly found themselves at odds with staffers pushing Robertson to diversify the network's programming. In early 1972 CBN changed its "programming philosophy" to "attract wider audiences," according to a local newspaper story. They were soon airing reruns of "proven network successes," including *The Dick Van Dyke Show, Leave It to Beaver, The Courtship of Eddie's Father, Gilligan's Island*, and *The Bold Ones*. They also aired cartoons before and after school. The Bakkers were losing their battle to keep CBN "100% Christian" and felt ignored by Robertson. "There was constant conflict" and "fighting to see who could get the closest to Pat," Tammy later wrote. With her usual candor, Tammy summed up her feelings for Robertson: "I've sewed on his buttons, mended tears in his clothes. I've loved him with a real deep love of the Lord. But at times when he would do certain things because of other people I built up a terrible, terrible resentment in my heart against him." Jim resigned from CBN in November 1972, a decision that Robertson accepted in an "amazingly calm" manner, according to Bakker. Not long after the Bakkers left, the CBN staff tore down the children's show set. Jim and Tammy were through with CBN, but not with television.[11]

The Bakkers formed a non-profit corporation, Trinity Broadcasting Systems (TBS), to house their now-unaffiliated ministry in November 1972. By the time they left CBN, the network had begun "nationwide distribution" of the *Jim and Tammy Show*, sending tapes from one television station to the next, a practice known as "bicycling." When their house in Portsmouth sold, the Bakkers bought another trailer and hit the road, traveling from station to station that had broadcast their show, holding telethons to help the stations raise money. In Los Angeles they met Paul and Jan Crouch. Paul, who had been assistant pastor at Jim's church in Muskegon, was now the general manager of a Christian television station, Channel 30. Together they hatched a plan to rent, and eventually buy, a Los Angeles area station, Channel 46, under the Bakkers' non-profit, TBS, which was approved to operate in California in June 1973. The plan was for Crouch to run the business end of things while Bakker handled the production side.[12]

SOUTHERN CALIFORNIA WAS an ideal place to start a Christian television station in the 1970s. Not only was it the entertainment capital of the world, it was receptive to new religious movements, as the Azusa Street revival had proved more than a half century before. Between the 1930s and the 1960s, more than six million southerners left the South, a large proportion of them headed for Los Angeles. By 1969 California had more southern-born residents than Arkansas. Many of these people brought their southern-style evangelicalism with them, creating a receptive audience for evangelists like the Bakkers.[13]

Bakker quickly began pulling together a team of talented young people who were fascinated with television and its potential for ministry. Most came from working-class Pentecostal backgrounds. They did not have degrees from prestigious universities, but they were smart and armed with the conviction that with God, all things are possible. One of Bakker's first recruits was Dale Hill. Hill would remain a key member of the television broadcasting team through the mid-1980s, directing much of the technical innovation at PTL, including the implementation of the satellite network. But that was several years in the future. When Hill arrived in Santa Ana in 1973, TBS was about as low tech as you could get and still be on the air.

Hill got a job at CBN in 1966, when he was only sixteen and the station was just starting to produce Jim and Tammy's children's show. At about the same time that the Bakkers left CBN, Hill moved to Greenville, South Carolina, to help Jimmy Thompson start another Christian television station, channel 16. Jim Bakker was in town to appear on Thompson's show one night when he asked Hill to go to California with him. "When?" Hill asked. "Tonight," Bakker replied. The idea seemed absurd. "There's no way I'm going to California," Hill told him. But Bakker kept asking throughout the day. "I'll tell you what," Hill finally said, "if you get Jimmy [Thompson] to agree to let me go, I'll go with you." Hill thought he was safe, since "there was no way Jimmy would agree to that." About ten minutes later Bakker returned, saying, "Okay, Jimmy says you can go." They flew to Los Angeles late that night.

Hill expected to find a working television station in Santa Ana, but that was not exactly the case. Bakker and Crouch had launched their station using a remote truck loaned to them by a large Anaheim church, Melodyland Christian Center. But the church had asked for their truck back shortly before Hill flew to Los Angeles with Bakker. On the flight out Bakker told Hill that they would go on the air at seven o'clock the next night. What he failed to mention was that they had next to no equipment to broadcast with. The building Bakker took Hill to had a set, but as Hill looked around the room he spotted only two old TR-22 two-inch videotape machines, a Sony industrial camera, and an audio console built for a home stereo system. As Hill stared at the makeshift equipment, Bakker said, "we go on at 7, I'll see you later." "Oh, by the way," Bakker added as he walked out the door, "we have two shows that air prior to going on at 7, the tapes are in there." And with that he left.

Someone less resourceful might have followed Bakker out the door, but Hill knew all about low-budget broadcasting. Drawing on his experience at CBN and in Greenville, Hill patched together a system, running the camera output through the two tape machines and then on to the microwave transmitter. He had graphic cards made, identifying the station and the show, to hold up in front of the camera at the appropriate time. After running the two taped shows, he ran a short intro he created that day and then stuck the two graphics cards in front of the camera. As the camera rolled off the second card, there was Bakker and his guest sitting on a sofa, ready to begin.[14]

When Hill returned to South Carolina in August 1973 to move his things to California, Sam Orender went along to help. Orender, a graduate of Bob Jones University, had also gotten his start in Christian television at channel 16 in Greenville, South Carolina. Orender grew up "in the coal fields" of southwest Virginia, attending a Freewill Baptist Church, a fundamentalist denomination that wanted nothing to do with Pentecostals. He first attended the Freewill Baptist Bible College in Nashville, Tennessee, before transferring in the early 1970s to Bob Jones, where he graduated with a degree in broadcast engineering. While working at channel 16 in Greenville, Orender gained a new respect for evangelicals outside of fundamentalism, particularly Pentecostals and charismatics. Once in California, Orender decided "this was where I was supposed to be." The problem was that Trinity could not afford to hire him. Orender started coming to work anyway. A few days later Paul Crouch took him aside. "Sam, you know we haven't hired you," Crouch said, but Orender just kept showing up. Eventually they began paying him one hundred dollars a week, cash. "I never was hired, I never filled out any kind of papers," remembers Orender.[15]

Joining this crew in California was Roger Flessing. Flessing had grown up in Sacramento, California. His father was from Wisconsin and his mother from North Dakota. They met while they were students at North Central Bible College in Minneapolis, the same school that Jim and Tammy attended. After they got married, they moved to California. Roger's father, who died when Roger was eighteen, was a school principal, and his mother was the secretary to the California Senate majority leader.

Flessing accepted Christ after watching a Billy Graham movie at age seven and thereafter wanted to be a youth minister. He attended Sacramento State, majoring in psychology, and then went to Bethany Bible College, an Assemblies of God school in Santa Cruz, California, where he majored in pastoral theology. He was working as a summer camp counselor when a friend told him about a new television station in Phoenix. Flessing started as the sports reporter (he had worked part-time as a sports reporter for the *Sacramento Bee* in college) but soon discovered that he liked working behind the camera better. The station wasn't much, but the experience was like broadcasting "graduate school." A staff of fourteen people produced more than eighty live programs a week. When his shift was over, Flessing would stick around, learning how to run a camera, audio, and all of the technical ins and outs that a director needed to know.

One Saturday Flessing was in the station's tiny audio room when the door opened and Jim Bakker stuck his head in. Bakker was in town to do a telethon for the station, which had carried the *Jim and Tammy Show* when the Bakkers were at CBN. "You're good," Bakker said, something that no one in broadcast had ever told Flessing before. He became a key figure in Bakker's organization for the next decade.[16]

Del Holford was another of the new TBS recruits. Like the others, Holford was looking for a challenge and believed in television's potential for spreading the gospel. He certainly wasn't there for the money. Holford, who would work for PTL longer than just about anyone, started as a volunteer, much as Sam Orender had done. The son of a minister, Holford grew up in Tacoma, Washington, before his family moved to Santa Maria, California, when he was in high school. Holford attended a number of colleges, including Sacramento State, Cal State Long Beach, and Southern California College, a Christian college in Costa Mesa. While traveling with a singing group from Southern California College, Holford became intrigued with running the audio system. After college, a friend told him about a new Christian television station in Santa Ana. Excited, Holford met with Paul Crouch, but Crouch told him that they were not hiring. But before he could leave, Holford ran into Flessing, whom he had met while Holford and Flessing's brother, Greg, were students at Sacramento State. Flessing offered to teach Holford "everything you need to know about running cameras." Holford knew that he could not afford to work for free, but he also knew that this was what he wanted to do. After five weeks Dale Hill simply walked up and handed him a check. His new salary was $125 a week. Holford was elated.[17]

The new television show, launched in late spring 1973, was called the *PTL Club*, reminiscent of the *700 Club*. PTL was meant to be a sort of code, immediately recognizable to evangelicals as short for Praise the Lord, but non-threatening to the "lost." The station broadcasted five hours a night, seven days a week. For a while Bakker had a friend at CBN send him old tapes of the *Jim and Tammy Show* to rebroadcast at Channel 46. Bakker felt that he had a right to the shows, but when Robertson found out, he had all of the *Jim and Tammy Show* tapes erased.[18]

The station's equipment gradually improved but always remained a patchwork of odds and ends. Once, when they lost audio between the studio in Santa Ana and the broadcast tower on Mount Wilson, Roger Flessing had the station's art director, Alex Valderama, make a sign reading, "We're having trouble with the audio portion of the program. We'll be back in five minutes," and place it in front of the camera. When the problem persisted, Valderama simply reached his hand in front of the camera, "scratched out five, wrote in thirty and waved to the audience." "That's the funniest thing I've ever seen," the station's owner later said.[19]

Just prior to going on the air at Channel 46, Bakker received a call from a friend in Charlotte, North Carolina, telling him that a struggling station owned by Ted Turner, WRET, Channel 36, wanted to rebroadcast the *PTL Club*. Bakker already had contacts at Channel 36 from his CBN days. In early 1972 Bill Flint, a Charlotte businessman who had previously worked in Portsmouth and watched the rise of CBN, and Jim Moss, who owned an industrial cleaning business in Charlotte, invited Pat Robertson to speak at a Full Gospel Business Men's Fellowship International (FGBMFI) meeting in Charlotte. Founded in 1952 by California dairy farmer Demos Shakarian, the FGBMFI provided a forum for lay leaders who wanted to spread the gospel in their community. Though non-denominational, the FGBMFI operated from a Pentecostal/charismatic perspective. After the meeting, Flint and Moss took Robertson to dinner and urged him to rebroadcast CBN shows in Charlotte. Robertson was reluctant at first, but by April he had agreed to send tapes of CBN programs. That September Jim and Tammy held a telethon in Charlotte to raise money for the station. A year and a half later, the connection to Channel 36 would provide a lifeline for the Bakkers' ministry.[20]

Initially the Bakkers and Crouches got along "fantastically," as Tammy put it. Tammy and Jan were particularly close. "We both love lots of jewelry. We had the same taste in decorating. We both love to bargain hunt.... Everywhere we went people asked if we were sisters," Tammy later wrote. "It was a beautiful, wonderful relationship, and we thought nothing in the world could ever come between us." But it did not last.[21]

As had happened at CBN, Jim Bakker's inability to share authority soon began to rub Paul Crouch and his backers the wrong way, particularly the pastor of Santa Ana's First Assembly of God church, which supplied much of the start-up funding for Trinity. Even though they were Pentecostals, Crouch's supporters thought that Bakker's demeanor was too flamboyant for Christian television. He emphasized praying for healing and speaking in tongues too much, and his fundraising was too aggressive. He also wanted to spend more on equipment than the more cautious Crouch thought they could afford. In his 1976 autobiography Bakker claimed that Crouch loaded the ministry's board against him and forced his resignation. "On that point you were right and I was wrong," Crouch later confessed to Bakker in July 1976. "We were having some very heavy expenses hit us. . . . We were right on a ledge. . . . I'm afraid I got scared at that point," Crouch admitted.[22]

While Jim and Paul mostly avoided open confrontation (always Bakker's style), Tammy and Jan went at it with a passion. "I told her where to get off and she told me where to get off," Tammy later wrote. By the end of November 1973, the Bakkers were once again unemployed and broke.[23]

Meanwhile, back in Charlotte, Ted Turner had ordered Channel 36 to stop airing CBN programs in the spring of 1973, annoyed over competition from a station CBN had acquired in Atlanta. Deprived of CBN's programming, Robertson's supporters, led by Martha and Sandy Wheeler, the general manager of WRET, made plans to continue airing Christian programs in Charlotte under the auspices of TBS. Initially they hoped to lure the Bakkers back to Charlotte to host a call-in talk show. When Bakker decided to stay in California, they created their own show with a team of rotating hosts that included Tim Kelton, a local Foursquare pastor with radio experience (the Foursquare church was created by celebrity Pentecostal evangelist Aimee Semple McPherson in Los Angeles in the 1920s). They also asked Bakker to send them tapes of the California shows to rebroadcast in Charlotte.[24]

For a while the arrangement worked, but that summer Crouch and his supporters demanded that the Charlotte group send all of the contributions they received to Santa Ana where they would be divvied up. Sandy Wheeler and Larry Hall from the Charlotte group flew to Los Angeles to argue for more independent control over their operation. But Crouch was hostile to the North Carolinians, and Bakker refused to intervene, characteristically sidestepping the conflict. Failing to reach an agreement, the two sides decided to split Trinity in half. The Charlotte group remained Trinity Broadcasting Systems and the California ministry became Trinity Broadcasting Network. When Kelton could not host the Charlotte talk show, Moss filled in, even though he had no experience in television and no theological training.[25]

Back in California, after the split between the Bakkers and Crouches, most of the young Trinity staff left with the Bakkers, including Dale

Hill, Sam Orender, Roger Flessing, Alex Valderrama, and Del Holford. Supporters gave them money and food to stay together. Donations totaled more than $6,000 by the end of the year. Meanwhile Bakker created yet another new ministry, Dove Broadcasting Corporation, and the group schemed to launch another Christian television station in southern California.

Then, in January 1974, Jim and Tammy drove to Charlotte to conduct a telethon. The Charlotte group booked the Ovens Auditorium to kick off the fundraising effort, and an enthusiastic crowd of more than 2,400 people welcomed the Bakkers back. "I don't believe I've ever had as exciting a night as that," Bakker told a reporter from the *Charlotte News*. "The tumors and cancers just dropped off bodies that night as we prayed. It was as if God had said, 'How much clearer can I make it, Jim? Stay here.'" Bakker immediately called Dale Hill and told him to pack up everything they could and head to Charlotte. Bakker sent money to rent a truck, and Hill and Sam Orender organized the move east, cramming as much of their furniture and possessions as they could into the rental, leaving behind Tammy's birds and her two dogs, Biscuit and Fi Fi. The California crew arrived in Charlotte in early February 1974.[26]

By that time the Wheelers had already rented a former furniture store on Independence Boulevard to serve as their studio. Dale Hill remembers driving up to the building and being impressed by the offices in the front of the building. But when Bakker opened the door leading to the new studio "there's a big empty building, just nothing, just a warehouse," remembers Hill. Bakker told them that they would "go live out of this building" in June. "That's why you're here." Initially they had only six employees, though volunteers regularly showed up to help with carpentry and other jobs that the full-timers lacked the skill to handle.

In the morning they did the live show from WRET, broadcasting from 11 a.m. to 1 p.m. Then they would go to "that furniture store," as Orender remembers it, and "work till sometimes midnight," tearing out walls and building the studio. "I think every wall in that building was probably moved by the time they were done with it," recalls Holford. Lack of money pushed them to the cutting edge of broadcast innovation. Television equipment had always been notoriously expensive, but fortunately products were just hitting the market that cost far less and still worked well. In place of expensive monitors, Hill found a guy who was taking Sony Trinitron televisions straight from the factory and modifying them with a new circuit board, turning them into studio monitors. Hill could buy ten of these for the price of a standard monitor. Philips Norelco had just introduced a new industrial camera that used the same basic technology as standard television cameras but cost much less. Hill bought three. They got deals on lighting and an audio console. "There was a lot of innovation going on back then," remembers Hill.[27]

No sooner were they on the air than control of the ministry became an issue, as it had at CBN and in California. The first to go were the Wheelers. The Wheelers had encouraged Bakker to create TBS and had helped him file the paperwork back in November 1972. When the crew from California first arrived, Sandy still worked as general manager at WRET, but Martha now worked for Bakker managing the Trinity office. Martha was forty years old, with a college education and a brisk, confident manner, not the sort of person who would simply give Bakker whatever he wanted. In the summer of 1974, shortly after they began broadcasting from the former furniture store, Sandy Wheeler quit his job at WRET to become the ministry's president and general manager. As had happened in California, and would happen again and again in the future at PTL, Bakker bristled at efforts to control his spending. By January 1975, the ministry was pulling in more than $140,000 a month, but the Wheelers were alarmed at the even more accelerated pace of Bakker's spending.[28]

In his 1976 autobiography Bakker claims that he forced a showdown with the Wheelers because they were mismanaging the ministry's money. He says that up to that point he rarely involved himself in the ministry's "business affairs. I didn't sign checks. I was on the air preaching and praying for people and raising the finances. Others decided where and when the money should be spent." But as the ministry expanded he became aware that its "bills were not being paid." The fiscal irresponsibility "seemed to be a tremendous drag on the Holy Spirit within the work . . . holding back more progress and results." In response, Bakker says that he wrote a letter of resignation and gave it to Jim Moss. Moss asked him to "hold on a few more days, God is working something out." That something was a vote by the board to dismiss the Wheelers. God had moved "another mountain," as Bakker remembered it.[29]

The Wheelers did not see it that way. From their perspective, it was Bakker who was being fiscally irresponsible. Another staffer remembers that Bakker was annoyed that the Wheelers were not aggressive enough about signing up new affiliates in other regions. Sandy Wheeler warned the board that firing him "is a mistake that you'll live to regret. You never let the talent run the business." But the ministry could not survive without the talent. Martha Wheeler was so incensed that she sued, claiming that she had been "wrongfully and unjustifiably terminated." The ministry settled with her out of court.[30]

When Hill and Orender joined Bakker in Charlotte in 1974, Roger Flessing stayed behind in the Los Angeles area, doing freelance work in television and honing his craft. In late 1975 Bakker called him saying, "Things are really starting to take off here in Charlotte and we need another director, would you be interested?" Flessing decided that if Bakker offered $250 a week he would take it. Bakker offered $200. "Close enough," thought Flessing. He and his wife packed their Ford Pinto station wagon, surrounded by their belongings, into a Ryder rental truck and headed to Charlotte in January 1976. By that time PTL had sixty or seventy employees. They were mostly young, energetic, and captivated by the vision of broadcasting the gospel to the ends of the earth. Like Bakker they were risk takers, intent on doing something big. They didn't have money but that was okay. The Lord would provide.[31]

3

Everyday in the USA

PTL'S GROWTH IN the second half of the 1970s was nothing short of spectacular. It was a "wild ride," as one PTL employee put it, including the rapid expansion of the network of affiliate stations, the creation of a satellite network, the purchase of new properties, the launch of overseas ministries in Latin America, Europe, Africa, and Asia, and the continued evolution of the talk show. The staff expanded from half a dozen in 1974 to seven hundred by the end of 1979, and the money poured in.

The first step in building an audience was signing up affiliate stations to carry PTL programming. Jim Moss, who was a better businessman than television personality, took the lead in building the network. Moss commandeered an office in the front of the furniture store, working the phones from morning until late at night, beginning with stations on the east coast and working his way west, following the sun. By the end of 1975 the network included forty-six affiliates. By July 1976 it was up to seventy stations. Many were in small markets, places like Chattanooga, Tennessee, Dothan, Alabama, and Greenwood, Mississippi.

This was only the beginning. Bakker and his staff were determined to have a presence in every major television market in the country. Jim Moss adopted the motto, "PTL everyday in the entire USA." Even in the mid-1970s, many stations, including most ABC affiliates, did not sign on until 11 a.m. Moss would call and pitch them the idea of running the *PTL Club* from 9 a.m. to 11 a.m. Most station managers initially laughed at the idea. The manager in Birmingham, Alabama, laughed so hard he fell over backward in his chair, disconnecting the call. But when the ratings started coming in, most of these managers were pleasantly surprised. Rather than competing for audience share, PTL was creating a whole new market. By November 1979, PTL's network had expanded to 218 stations, the majority of which were not in the Bible Belt. They stretched from Bangor, Maine, to Miami, Florida, to San Diego, California, to Bellingham, Washington, and everywhere in between. Texas led with eighteen affiliates, but California had fifteen and Pennsylvania ten. The network eventually included over six hundred stations, more than 80 percent of them network affiliates of ABC, NBC, and CBS.[1]

The talk show format attracted viewers nearly everywhere, not just the South. The goal was not to be "some down-home, cornpone and chitlins, folksy, skip-dash operation," as one PTL staffer put it in May 1975. Bob Fouracre, the general sales manager of WSMW, Channel 27, in Worcester, Massachusetts, was "leery of putting the program on at first." "I just figured it was another typical Bible Belt religious show, and I didn't know how it would be received from our predominantly Catholic viewing audience of some five million persons living in the metropolitan Boston area." The response surprised him. Within weeks two thousand letters poured into the station. "The results were astounding," according to Fouracre. "Out of all the mail there were only two negative letters. In my 14 years of broadcasting, I'd never seen that kind of response to a program."[2]

Bakker and his staff initially relied on semiannual telethons conducted at the affiliate stations to raise money. Del Holford was part of the first telethon team in the fall of 1974, driving a used twenty-one-foot truck (later replaced by a diesel model) to Montgomery, Alabama, Paducah, Kentucky, Rossville, Georgia, and Columbia, Missouri. Early on, Jim Bakker traveled to many of these sites to host the telethons, joined by board members and staff. At Rossville, the contributions were so lackluster that when they asked for pledges "a call poured in," as the staff later joked. But in general the telethons worked, raising the money needed to drive PTL's initial growth.

As the network expanded, Bakker turned the traveling telethon hosting over to Don Storms, Joey Hamby, and others. They created two telethon teams, sometimes adding a third, which traveled from one affiliate to the next. Within a year the teams were traveling by air, spending five to seven weeks on the road before returning to Charlotte for a week or two and then setting out again. Weekend telethons were a staple of their schedule. Often they arrived at the affiliate station on Friday, held the telethon from 1 p.m. to midnight on Saturday and 4 p.m. to midnight on Sunday, and then packed up and moved on. By January 1976, PTL was holding as many as four telethons a week. Once they added a new station, they usually tried to hold a telethon within eight to ten weeks. Their goal was to get two thousand people to pledge a minimum of $10 a month to defray broadcast costs, which typically ran $10,000 to $15,000 a month per station.[3]

Apart from fundraising, the telethons provided intensive training in how to run broadcast television. After Del and Gail Holford married in April 1975, they spent the next year together on the road with one of the telethon teams. The Holfords each made $150 a week. Del designed traveling sets that could be broken down and fit into two boxes, each 4 feet by 4 feet by 12 inches, suitable to check on commercial flights. He also learned to set up lighting, run cameras, direct shows, and everything else involved in airing a program. Gail kept the team's books. The hours were long and they did not earn much, but they had a feeling they were on the cusp of something big.[4]

Like the Holfords, Lee and Nancy Nagelhout joined PTL to work on one of the telethon teams. Both were graduates of Oral Roberts University (ORU), Nancy in 1975 and Lee in 1976. During Lee's last semester at ORU, PTL held on-campus interviews. Though neither Lee nor Nancy knew much about PTL, it sounded like the kind of ministry opportunity they were looking for. Lee signed up for an interview and was hired as a traveling cameraman. They married three weeks after Lee's graduation, and the next weekend they were in Bangor, Maine, for a telethon. They were PTL employees 125 and 126.

On one occasion they arrived dead tired at 3 a.m. in Thermopolis, Wyoming, and checked into a motel. While Lee went to look for a vending machine, Nancy collapsed on the bed. A few minutes later she heard a knock at the door. When she opened it, there stood Lee, half asleep. They were so groggy they did not recognize each other. Lee stammered out an apology, and Nancy shut the door. A moment later she realized it was her husband and called him back, just as Lee was about to knock on the next door down. In all it was exhausting but also exhilarating. When the traveling telethon teams were eventually phased out, Lee and Nancy both took positions with PTL in Charlotte. They stayed for more than a decade, through the years of spectacular growth all the way to the ministry's collapse in 1988.[5]

Along with newcomers like the Holfords and Nagelhouts, PTL's expansion drew in young veterans of Christian television, some who had worked with the Bakkers at CBN. Roger and Linda Wilson, who went as far back with the Bakkers as anyone, arrived at PTL in March 1974. Back in their days as traveling evangelists, the Bakkers had baptized Linda at age sixteen when they held a revival at her Assemblies of God church. Roger, also raised in the Assemblies of God, was a radar technician in the Navy stationed in Virginia Beach when he and Linda married. After the Navy, Roger went to work at CBN as a cameraman, working with the Bakkers on the *Jim and Tammy Show* and the *700 Club*.

The Wilsons and Bakkers soon became close friends. When the Bakkers' daughter, Tammy Sue, was born in 1970, the Wilsons stepped in to relieve some of the pressure of the Bakkers' hectic schedule. "They were busy with the station so we adopted Tammy Sue. . . . We just about raised her the first two years," recalls Linda. Tammy later wrote, "Linda and I became super close friends. If it hadn't been for Linda, I don't know what I would have done. . . . Linda would shop with me, cook with me, was at our house, or I was at hers. For the first time in my life I had a true friend." The Wilsons left CBN in 1971, a year before the Bakkers' exodus to California.[6]

In early 1974, the Wilsons moved to Charlotte at about the same time the Bakkers returned from California. Roger initially worked at WRET, Ted Turner's small UHF station, and Linda got a job working for the owner of a construction company, a "phenomenally organized" man who used a drawer in his desk as a trash can, so as not to give the appearance of clutter. "Can you come and organize me that well?" Jim Bakker asked her. "Sure," she replied. It was hopeless. "There's no organizing that man," Linda would later conclude. Bakker made decisions on impulse and resisted any attempt to limit his spontaneity, a failing that would become increasingly obvious over time. After a year or two, Linda took another position in PTL. When Tammy started her own television show in 1978, Linda became her assistant, doing everything from designing sets to appearing on the show.

At PTL Roger became "Jim's conscience," as Wilson put it, until Bakker fired him. Roger continually found himself urging Jim to "count the cost" before beginning a project. Instead, whenever PTL fell behind on its financial commitments, Bakker would come up with a new project to pitch to his audience. "We had an inside joke that today's projects pay for yesterday's projects," remembers Wilson. Worse yet, Bakker often invented these projects on the fly, without consulting anyone. The various departments all had televisions so that the staff could watch the show and find out what they were doing next. It was a system with few checks and balances that relied heavily on Bakker's intuition. Still, like just about everyone else who joined PTL early on, the Wilsons were caught up in the possibilities the ministry offered. PTL was a "consuming place" that would "just eat you alive," as Roger Wilson later recalled, but it was doing things that no one else had even thought of.[7]

PTL GOT INTO television at just the right time. Television defined American culture during the 1970s in a way that it never had before and never would again. Most of this cultural weight rested with the three major networks, CBS, NBC, and ABC, which saw their revenues increase from $1 billion to $3 billion over the decade. In 1970 the cost of a sixty-second ad on a primetime program ran about $60,000. By the end of the decade it was up to $200,000. Despite this success, the networks' hegemony was about to be tested by an alternative to broadcast television, the cable satellite network. As with most business transformations, those who got in first had a significant advantage. PTL was there from the start.[8]

Cable television had been around since the late 1940s in the form of Community Antenna Television (CATV). After World War II, it was clear that television had the potential to revolutionize access to news and entertainment, but only if you lived near a city. Television signals travel in a straight line; they do not bounce off the ionosphere and jump over ridges or flow into valleys the way AM radio signals can. This meant that in places like central Pennsylvania, which is divided by wave after wave of ridges and valleys running roughly southwest to northeast, people who lived any distance from Philadelphia, Pittsburgh, or a few other cities were left out. They would just have to wait until someone built a station near them. Then in 1948 the Federal Communications Commission put a four-year freeze on new television station licenses.

To solve this problem, entrepreneurs across the nation began building large antennas on ridges and tall buildings to capture signals from distant cities. They then amplified these signals and sent them to individual customers by coaxial cable, creating cable networks. By 1952 there were thirty-eight such networks in Pennsylvania and another twenty-eight in other states. Some of the men who created these systems had learned radio and radar technology during the war. Others were appliance dealers who wanted to sell more televisions. By the late 1950s, microwave relays, which transmit on a more efficient frequency, extended the reach of CATV systems. The added reach of microwave technology allowed CATV operators to be more selective about which broadcasts to include on their network, picking and choosing among the broadcasters now within range. By 1965 there were 1,570 cable systems connecting nearly 1.6 million subscribers across the United States. By 1972 the number of cable subscribers had grown to 7.3 million, and the number of cable systems had nearly doubled.[9]

Cable offered the possibility of niche programming that, in the minds of activists, could provide richer content and address America's abiding divides, including race and economic inequality. It offered, in short, progress through technology. It inspired, as one writer put it, a "quasi-religious faith" in cable's possibilities.[10]

There was nothing quasi about it at PTL, which represented a niche that secular activists overlooked. PTL had several advantages as it entered the cable market. Its growing staff of young people had a clear sense of why they were there and were willing to work long hours on the cheap. They thought of themselves more as missionaries than upwardly mobile professionals. They were not sophisticated, but they were bright, flexible, and unencumbered by the established practices of network television. PTL also had a well-defined niche audience who would support it financially and a proven method of fundraising, the telethon. Had they tried to produce something like a sitcom, a staple of network programming at the time, they would almost certainly have failed, but there was nothing quite like the *PTL Club* on network television to compete against.

What no one could envision before the 1970s was the extent to which satellites would redefine the distribution of television programming. Satellites were a "historic inflection point, a quantum leap" in the development of television technology, writes one historian of cable television. Futurist and science fiction writer Arthur C. Clarke first envisioned satellite communication in a 1945 essay in *Wireless World*. Clarke proposed placing three manned space stations, enough to receive and transmit radio and television signals from any point on earth, in high geosynchronous orbits of approximately 22,300 miles. At this altitude the stations would orbit the earth every twenty-four hours, meaning they would remain stationary in the sky relative to a fixed location on the ground.[11]

But it was not until the launch of the Soviet Union's Sputnik I that most Americans woke up to the potential of satellite communication. Sputnik's launch on October 4, 1957, followed by the United States' Explorer I on January 31, 1958, inaugurated the Cold War's space race. From there space technology advanced at a dizzying pace. AT&T's Telstar, launched into a low orbit in July 1962, was the first American satellite capable of receiving and retransmitting television signals. The following year Syncom II, built by Hughes Aircraft Corporation, achieved a high geosynchronous orbit. In the summer of 1964, Syncom III reached orbit in time to beam coverage of the Tokyo Summer Olympics to America. At that point all the basic components necessary for satellite television had been demonstrated.[12]

But how to make money from this new technology was still up in the air. Satellites did not turn out to be any cheaper at carrying telephone calls than transatlantic (and eventually transpacific) cables. As the volume of telephone calls from the United States to the United Kingdom increased from 10,000 in 1927 to 4.3 million in 1961, so did the capacity of cables. Fiber optic cables further expanded this capacity in the 1980s. But television was different. Nothing could extend the reach of television signals quite like satellite.[13]

The first proposals for satellite television focused on the elegantly simple idea of beaming signals directly from satellites to homes. But the cost of launching satellites powerful enough to deliver television signals to small home receivers remained prohibitive. During the height of the Cold War, politicians also worried that direct broadcast satellite (DBS) service might spark a television propaganda war with the Russians, as each side vied to beam its message from the sanctuary of space. Less politically risky and more economically feasible was the idea of transmitting satellite signals to domestic cable networks, which would then deliver them to individual homes.[14]

In June 1972, the FCC issued an "Open Skies" order, clearing a path for the launch of commercial television satellites. The first of these satellites, Westar I, was launched on April 13, 1974, four months after the Bakkers left California for Charlotte. Cable operators had to invest in a satellite dish to receive satellite signals, but the size and cost of dishes quickly decreased. The nine-meter dishes approved by the FCC in 1975 cost about $80,000, but in December 1976 the FCC lowered the requirement for receiver-only dishes (TVROs) to 4.5 meters. The cost of these fell from $25,000 in 1977 to as little as $10,000 in 1979 and $3,500 in 1983. The number of cable systems with satellite dishes correspondingly increased from about five hundred in 1977 to nearly five thousand by 1982.[15]

Home Box Office (HBO) was the first independent network to capitalize on the possibilities of cable satellite systems. HBO was the brainchild of Chuck Dolan, a cable entrepreneur, and Jerry Levin, a former divinity school student turned lawyer whom Dolan hired in 1972. In the early 1970s Dolan, who ran a small, struggling cable company servicing lower Manhattan, came up with a scheme for a movie and sports network he could market to other cable operators. HBO launched on November 8, 1972, transmitting the movie *Sometimes a Great Notion* by microwave from New York to a cable network in Wilkes-Barre, Pennsylvania, about one hundred miles west of the city. At about the same time Dolan left and Jerry Levin took over as president of HBO. Levin saw the potential of satellites and in December 1974 rented one of the twenty-four transponders, or channels, on RCA's new Satcom I satellite at a cost of $9.6 million for six years. It was a huge gamble considering that HBO had yet to turn a profit, losing $4 million in 1974 alone. It paid off. Even before Satcom I's launch in December 1975, HBO used Westar I to provide its subscribers live coverage of the September 30, 1975, Muhammed Ali-Joe Frazier fight from the Philippines—the Thrilla in Manila—a feat that the networks could not match. Viewers were stunned by the clarity of the picture. Nine months later HBO had half a million subscribers, and in 1977 it finally turned a profit. By 1979 HBO's network had grown to a thousand cable system affiliates and nearly four million subscribers.[16]

While the networks inexplicably hesitated, a small number of television entrepreneurs followed HBO into space. In 1969 Ted Turner purchased a struggling UHF station in Atlanta. Turner had inherited the family billboard advertising business in 1963 at age twenty-four when his father committed suicide. He bought the television station after its owners took out space on one of his billboards advertising that it was for sale. Stuck with the technical limitations of UHF, the station perennially trailed its network competitors, showing mostly old movies, roller derby, and reruns of *Gilligan's Island*. When Turner heard what HBO was doing with satellite, he realized that he could use satellite distribution to create a national superstation unfettered by the limits of local broadcasting. While the networks had pretty much ignored HBO's satellite launch, they fought Turner's scheme. It didn't matter. WTBS, as Turner later renamed the station, began satellite service in December 1976. It was enormously profitable. Building on the success of WTBS, Turner launched the Cable News Network (CNN), the first twenty-four-hour news channel, in 1980.[17]

No sooner were HBO and Ted Turner's station up on satellite than PTL's television team began wondering how they could do the same. Turner's example was all the more compelling since he owned the small UHF station in Charlotte, Channel 36, that broadcast the PTL show live (Turner bought the station at auction on the courthouse steps, writing a personal check to pay for it, in July 1970). If Ted Turner could do it, why couldn't they? The PTL staff knew that Pat Robertson's crew at CBN was wondering the same thing, another incentive for those who had worked at CBN earlier in their careers. Bakker in particular was always anxious to keep up with whatever Robertson did.[18]

Up to this point, in addition to the live local broadcast out of Charlotte, PTL syndicated its program on a "bicycle," shuttling tapes from station to station around the country. This system allowed PTL to build its network, but it was cumbersome and limited by the speed with which tapes could be moved from one city to the next. It was also one of the reasons PTL relied on telethons for fundraising rather than appeals during the regular show, which no one outside of Charlotte saw live. Since some audiences did not see the "live" show until a month after it was first broadcast, Bakker and his guests had to be careful not to say anything that would date the show.

In the 1970s television shows were generally recorded on two-inch Quadruplex videotape. Each reel was 12.5 inches in diameter, weighed about twenty-five pounds, held an hour of programing, and cost about two hundred dollars. Since the show ran two hours, each daily episode required two reels of tape. At first Roger Wilson created duplicate tapes and sent them to the affiliates. But as the number of affiliates grew, PTL farmed out the duplication process to a company in Michigan with high-speed equipment. Each set of duplicate tapes could service three or four affiliates in a month, depending on how long it took to ship the tapes from one station to the next. If there were 150 affiliates, this required producing forty to fifty copies of each day's show, five days a week. Satellite offered an elegant solution to the daunting logistics of the bicycle.[19]

In his monthly newsletter for May 1977, only six months after Ted Turner's Atlanta station began satellite service, Bakker informed his supporters that PTL had "signed a contract to purchase a Satellite Ground Station." That July Bakker wrote to supporters that sixty "Christian broadcasters have already agreed to supply programming for this Satellite Network." By January 1978 the satellite ground station was nearly complete, and in May 1978 PTL began transmitting programming twenty-four hours a day on an RCA satellite. The dedication of the satellite system included live reports from Guatemala, where a Latin American version of the *PTL Club* was already on the air, and Seoul, Korea, home of the world's largest church, pastored by Paul Yonggi Cho. It took several years before every station had a satellite link and the bicycle was completely phased out, but there was little doubt that satellite would define the network's future. The uplink initially cost about $49,000 a month, which turned out to be a bargain considering the audience and fundraising it opened up.[20]

In setting up its satellite network, PTL did something new. When Ted Turner put his station on satellite his lawyers advised him that he could not own both a broadcast service and a satellite uplink. To get around this, Turner set up Southern Satellite Systems to act as a common carrier for anyone who wanted to link to satellite and sold the business to Tulsa businessman Ed Taylor for $1. But in the rapidly changing world of FCC regulations, Roger Flessing guessed that by late 1977 the same rules might not apply to PTL.[21]

To sort this out Flessing went to Washington, DC, where he and PTL's lawyer walked to the FCC office to discuss starting an integrated satellite network. "You have to go through the common carrier," Flessing remembers one of the FCC staffers telling them. "What if we became our own common carrier?" Flessing asked. "Well, no one's ever done that before," the staffer said. "I think we're onto something," PTL's lawyer replied. In December 1977 the FCC granted PTL its own private satellite network license, the first of its kind. From the start, PTL controlled its own uplink, a pattern other networks followed. "This stupid little Christian television satellite network blazed a whole new trail that everybody followed," remembers Flessing.[22]

NO SOONER HAD PTL's broadcast team got the studio up and running in the former furniture store than it became apparent that it would not be big enough to house the ministry's growing operations. PTL had been broadcasting from the furniture store for little more than a year when they bought a three-story Georgian house on twenty-five acres, located at 7224 Park Road on Charlotte's south side. The mansion, formerly owned by millionaire contractor F. N. Thompson, was modeled on the Carter's Grove plantation house near Williamsburg, Virginia. Anxious to move a property that had been on the market for several years, the owners sold the estate to PTL for $200,000 plus a letter stating that they had donated $150,000 to PTL, presumably to reduce their taxes.[23]

The last day of broadcasting from the furniture store was March 26, 1976, after which Bakker and his crew set up a temporary studio in the mansion. Attractive as it was, the mansion had nothing like the space for an adequate studio and satellite ground station. Even before they began broadcasting from the mansion, Bakker broke ground, on October 30, 1975, on an adjoining 54,000-square-foot studio called the International Counseling and Broadcast Center. The new facility cost $3 million to build, compared to the $1,870 a month PTL had paid to rent the furniture store.[24]

Bakker named the new complex Heritage Village, building on the publicity surrounding the nation's bicentennial, and the front of the broadcast center was modeled after the Bruton Parrish Church at Colonial Williamsburg. The studio had 9,000 square feet of floor space, with 208 theater-style seats for the live audience. The cameras, recording equipment, audio, and lighting were state of the art. Hidden inside the steeple was a broadcast antenna. From design to completion, the project was finished in only thirty-three weeks. Bakker timed the dedication of the new facility for July 4th, a pattern he would repeat for major building projects over the next decade.[25]

Impressive as it was, the twenty-five-acre complex was not nearly big enough to accommodate PTL's continuing expansion, as Jim Moss had warned Bakker when he purchased it. By the end of 1977, some of PTL's four hundred employees were already working off-site in temporary rented facilities. In response, PTL purchased a 1,200-acre wooded tract straddling the North and South Carolina border to develop as the ministry's new headquarters. When Moss took Bakker to the site for the first time, Bakker was immediately captivated by its potential. The two men ruined the new suits they were wearing tromping through the briars as Bakker envisioned where various buildings would be located.[26]

On January 2, 1978, his birthday, Bakker broke ground on the first building at what he was now calling Heritage USA. When the ministry bought the land, most of the staff, including PTL's senior vice president Roger Flessing, initially saw it as a way to support the TV show, which had always relied on counselors working the phones to take prayer requests and contributions. Early on, the counselors used color-coded forms to keep track of calls. The blue "prayer form" recorded what callers needed "to be healed of" or "delivered from." It listed forty-two problems with a box next to each, everything from arthritis to hemorrhoids, along with a line for "other." Even though they were on the phone, counselors often prayed with their eyes closed raising a hand over their head. Callers were urged to call back to report healings and other answers to prayer. This triggered a pink "Praise Report," on which counselors were instructed to "Explain Healing in Detail!!!!" The final form was a "Salvation Report" for those who prayed with a counselor to be saved. This kind of real-time contact with callers was essential to PTL's ministry concept and fundraising.[27]

Syndicating the show made it more difficult to keep an adequate number of people on site to take calls day and night. Expanding to satellite only compounded this problem. In January 1976 about a dozen people (almost all women) answered the phones while the show was on the air. By June the number of phone counselors had increased to about thirty, and by the end of the year there were sixty. A year later PTL received about six hundred calls a day. By late 1978, the number of phones on the set had increased to about one hundred.[28]

The answer to the need for more phone counselors was a campground where people would be available at all hours. Instead of one hundred phone lines, Heritage USA could accommodate one thousand. "We had four things" at the original campsites, remembers Roger Flessing. "We had water, electricity, cable TV, and a phone jack." As far as Flessing was concerned, television remained PTL's central focus.[29]

THERE WAS NOTHING else like the *PTL Club* on television. The daily show was the centerpiece of PTL's programming through the 1970s, broadcast live and recorded on tape five days a week from 11 a.m. to 1 p.m. in front of a studio audience. By the end of the decade, PTL's audience had grown into the millions.

Bakker had a subtle feel for his core audience, even if outsiders had no idea what defined its borders. Unlike other talk show hosts, including Johnny Carson, who worked from a carefully prepared script of questions and jokes, Bakker never used a script and rarely pre-interviewed guests. Members of his staff, including his sister-in-law Dorothy Bakker, sometimes interviewed guests before they went on, but Bakker freely deviated from their notes. He did two hours of live television a day, deciding on the spur of the moment what he and his guests would talk about and for how long, when the music acts would perform, and sometimes what they would sing. Bakker's ability to improvise on the fly was "some of the best I've ever seen," recalls Roger Flessing, who directed the show two or three times a week. "He really did have a talent. . . . It was amazing."[30]

An unscripted format had a particular appeal for Bakker's audience. Since the nineteenth century, evangelicals have been suspicious of preachers who read their sermons or prayers, preferring spontaneous performances that rely on the leading of the Holy Spirit. On television Bakker did just this. "I don't think a format ever came off the way it was written, because it was more like our type of church would be and that would be by inspiration. . . . If the spirit of God was moving, we would stay with whatever was happening," Bakker later said. Better to feel for the Spirit than produce a slick show that excluded it. Of course, this implied that God would not reveal his purposes in advance, but evangelicals were conditioned to believe that there was something about the moment that could not be predicted or discerned before it actually happened.[31]

Making so much up on the fly could be nerve-racking for the production crew, but it was also exciting. People tuned in just to see what would happen next. Once, when Jim and Tammy were hosting the show together, they brought a live camel on the set, which they had just acquired for one of the ministry's dramatic productions. As they discussed how "magnificent" the camel was, it proceeded to pee a river across the stage. On another occasion Tammy did an entire show on a merry-go-round. One of the cast threw up inside the dog costume he was wearing.[32]

Flessing in particular had a way of keeping things light that relaxed Bakker and the television staff without dulling their creative edge. Everyone who was at PTL in the late 1970s remembers the time Flessing climbed to the top of the water tower at Heritage USA, when development at the property was just beginning. Flessing was up there to tape a promo so that the television audience could see the new land. As he described the upcoming development, he leaned precariously over the water tower's railing. What the television audience did not know was that his assistant, Bobbie Garn, had dressed a dummy to look like Flessing and taken it up on the water tower. As the camera cut away Flessing screamed and an assistant pushed the dummy over the railing. A camera on the ground caught its fall and then cut to Flessing (who had meanwhile climbed down) lying on his back on the ground. Flessing groaned, "My back, back," and then, with a smile, said, "back to you Jim." The studio was flooded with calls to find out what had really happened to Flessing. Several callers complained that they had nearly fainted at the sight of Flessing falling. But most people thought it was funny, and everyone remembered it.[33]

Celebrities, who appeared in increasing numbers as the viewing audience grew, gave the show cultural weight. Colonel Sanders, founder of Kentucky Fried Chicken, appeared on the show in December 1979, dressed in his trademark white suit with a string bow tie and carrying a bucket of his fried chicken. Sanders, who was eighty-nine at the time and hard of hearing, described how God had delivered him from the habit of "cussin'" and used an enema to remove a polyp from his colon. The colonel went into considerable detail in describing the blessed event. It was not great television except that he was the colonel, a living legend and an evangelical, which was really the point. At the end of the show the staff passed around chicken to everyone in the studio audience. PTL's magazine for its supporters, *Action*, ran a feature on Sanders soon after.[34]

Astronaut James Irwin also appeared on the show and then in an interview in *Action*, describing his experience aboard Apollo 15 that led him "to put Christ first in my life." Fifty thousand miles out in space he sensed a "deep change taking place inside of me as I felt the undeniable nearness of God." Walking on the moon was a spiritual experience for Irwin, who later wrote, "I can't imagine a holier place." Irwin was subsequently part of several expeditions to find Noah's Ark on Mount Ararat in eastern Turkey, the first in 1982.[35]

Eldridge Cleaver, another guest on the show, was famous for something more earthly: a shootout with Oakland police in April 1968, two days after the assassination of Martin Luther King Jr. After his arrest and bail, Cleaver fled the country in November 1968, first to Cuba, then Algeria and France. Tired of life as an exile, Cleaver returned to the United States in 1975 to face trial. He became a born-again Christian while in jail in 1976. In January 1977 a *PTL Club* regular, George Otis, published a hastily written account of the shootout and Cleaver's subsequent conversion, likening it to the Apostle Paul's experience on the road to Damascus. When Cleaver appeared on the *PTL Club*, shortly after publically declaring his newfound faith, Jim Bakker appealed to viewers for money to defray Cleaver's legal expenses.

Bakker and other evangelicals could not resist the allure of Cleaver's celebrity (a real Black Panther!). If a former badass revolutionary and international fugitive could come to Jesus, anything was possible. But Cleaver was never conventionally evangelical, particularly with regard to his sexuality. He later admitted that he obtained political asylum in France because he and the president of France, Valéry Giscard d'Estaing, shared the same mistress. While living in France, Cleaver was responsible for one of the worst fashion designs ever, a pair of pants with a pouch in the front to show off a man's penis. One observer suggested calling them "meat cleavers." Cleaver continued to promote the pants even after his conversion, though one can hardly imagine that they were a hit with PTL's audience. By 1979 Cleaver had taken up with Sun Myung Moon's Unification Church. He later became a Mormon.[36]

Little Richard appeared on the show in April 1978. At the time, the show's voiceover introduction described it as "the world's most unusual talk/variety show," which the combination of Jim Bakker and Little Richard sitting next to each other seemed to confirm. Little Richard was born Richard Penniman in Macon, Georgia, in 1932. His father, Bud Penniman, was a Seventh Day Adventist preacher, brick mason, and bootlegger who owned a bar called the Tip In Inn, where he was shot to death in 1952 by an unruly customer.

Like so many other black and southern musicians, Richard began singing in church. He was also at times flamboyantly gay, and his sexual appetite seemed insatiable. While touring, he held orgies that were the stuff of legend, even by rock 'n' roll standards. He liked to watch his girlfriend, stripper Lee Angel, have sex with other men while he masturbated. Yet the morning after the wildest party imaginable, friends would find Richard reading the Bible or wake up to him quoting scripture. His Bible was a constant companion amid a lifestyle whose sexual excess seemed to know no bounds.[37]

For two decades before he appeared on the *PTL Club*, Little Richard shifted back and forth between ministry and rock 'n' roll. In 1957, he quit performing after a concert in Sydney, Australia, during which he took off almost all his clothes and threw them into the crowd, a regular part of his show. Toward the end of the concert the remnants of the Russian satellite Sputnik blazed through the night sky. Richard took it as a sign. "It shook my mind. It really shook my mind. I got up from the piano and said, 'This is it. I am through. I am leaving show business to go back to God.' "[38]

Determined to become a preacher and find "peace of mind," Richard enrolled at Oakwood College, a historically black Seventh Day Adventist school in Huntsville, Alabama. But he was never a good student and flouted most of the Oakwood's expectations. He drove his yellow Cadillac to campus, turned up late for class, and once asked a male student to "show himself to me." After that he returned to his old act, including touring Europe, where the Beatles and Rolling Stones opened for him. The orgies were bigger than ever, with "hookers, hustlers . . . and girls. All kinds of girls," as Richard put it. This time around, his partying included lots of drinking, cocaine, sometimes mixed with heroin (a speedball), and angel dust ("there's no angel with it at all," he later told Bakker). After the deaths of several friends and family members, including his younger brother, Tony, Richard once again returned to the ministry in 1977, only months before his appearance on the *PTL Club*.[39]

Richard opened his appearance on the *PTL Club* with the staid gospel song "It Is No Secret (What God Can Do)." He refused to do any of his rock 'n' roll hits. "That's dead, let it stay dead." Instead he wanted to talk about how God had delivered him from alcohol, drugs, and a gay lifestyle. "Any man that participates in homosexuality don't know Jesus. I don't care who he is," declared Richard. His testimony sounded genuine and he looked comfortable talking about his faith, at times quoting the Bible from memory. But Richard's frank discussion of his gay lifestyle made Bakker nervous. Guests on the show generally understood that they were supposed to talk about how hollow and destructive their lives were before their conversions, but only in ways appropriate for a morning talk show aimed at evangelicals. Perhaps Bakker was simply reading his audience, but he had his own secret past that he was not prepared to deal with in front of the camera.[40]

Why, given Richard's history of "backsliding," did the PTL producers invite him to appear on the show? He was the polar opposite of Pat Boone, a regular on the *PTL Club*, who was famous in part for his bland, clean-cut versions of Little Richard's songs "Tutti Frutti" and "Long Tall Sally." What the two had in common was cultural credibility. They demonstrated the reach of PTL's message, all the way to the heart of the entertainment industry. For his part, Little Richard looked uncomfortable by the end of his appearance on the show, as if he realized that, for all the glitz and optimism he projected, Jim Bakker was not particularly interesting or profound. Like a Pat Boone song, the *PTL Club* presented a safe cover of life's grittier realities, something that held little appeal for Little Richard.

At times the show became repetitious and derivative, as Bakker and his guests repeated evangelical truisms about theology, history, and the fate of humanity. But at its best the show became a crossroads of American life, an intersection where evangelicals and non-evangelicals could meet. These moments were more fleeting than constant, mixed as they were with a good deal of half-baked material thrown together on the fly. But when it worked the show transcended entertainment. For millions of viewers the *PTL Club* became a virtual community or church, even family, offering a source of meaning and direction otherwise difficult to find. Short testimonials often aired at the end of the program. In one of these from 1979, a woman in her twenties or thirties smiles at the camera and says that having PTL in her home "was like friends being there. When other people couldn't, I knew PTL would be there everyday." Bakker ended almost every show by looking directly into the camera, smiling, and saying, "God loves you, he really does."[41]

The talk show was innovative, but why stop there? On April 27, 1977, Bakker surprised Roger Flessing by inviting him onto the set as an unannounced guest while the show was live on the air. Bakker then announced that he wanted Flessing to produce "the first Christian soap opera." Flessing did not know this was coming, but he was ready nonetheless. "Many people have the same kind of negative bias against the gospel that they have against communism," Flessing said. To change this perception, Christians needed to present the gospel in new, more culturally interesting ways. "I think the key now is to make the gospel unavoidable through daytime drama, through late night specials, through documentaries. . . .

We have a story and I think we need to be the ones to tell our story rather than everybody else mixing the story up who don't know it, who don't understand it," Flessing said. Bakker agreed. He asked for volunteers—actors, writers and editors—to come to PTL and donate a year of their lives to launch this new vision. Unfortunately for Flessing's vision, over the course of the next year, Bakker would shift PTL's focus away from television to building Heritage USA.

AT THE SAME time that they were creating the satellite network in the United States, PTL's television team was working on expanding the ministry's programming overseas. From the start, PTL saw itself as a missionary organization, dedicated to using television to proclaim the gospel to the ends of the earth. PTL publications devoted as much space to foreign missions as any other topic before 1980, and missionaries were frequent guests on the show.

PTL's first and most enduring foreign outreach was to Latin America. In July 1976, Jim Bakker announced on air that PTL would launch a television program for Latin America. Initially Bakker wanted to use dubbed versions of the American show, which is what Pat Robertson first tried at CBN. Bakker was always anxious to keep up with CBN, but Elmer Bueno, who became the host of the Latin American show, convinced him that to work the show needed to feature native speakers who understood Latin American culture. Bueno was the son of missionary parents who worked in four Latin American countries: Venezuela (where he was born), Cuba, Chile, and Argentina. Vincente Montaño, who had appeared on CBN singing in both Spanish and English, joined as Bueno's cohost. Shooting the show in Spanish gave it an authenticity that it would otherwise have lacked. The result was hugely successful.

In November 1976, Bueno, along with PTL Vice President Jim Moss, Director of Foreign Operations Sam Orender, and International Director of Education Bob Manzano, made a whirlwind trip to Central and South America, lining up contracts in seven countries in just nine days. By January 1977, *Club Alabaré*, or "Praise Club," as the show was first called, was on the air in those seven countries, pulling in good ratings (the name was changed to *Club PTL* a few months later). The show was produced in the Charlotte studio, using a Spanish-speaking cast, on the same set as the American show. Bueno and Montaño, who lived in southern California, flew to Charlotte four times a year to shoot for two weeks, recording two one-hour programs a day. Shooting in Charlotte gave Bueno and his guests access to state-of-the-art equipment, run by PTL's regular camera operators and technical staff.

Bueno and Montaño incorporated short, snappy, six- or seven-minute interviews into their show interspersed with lots of music, a format that was more appealing to Latin American audiences than the talk-heavy American version. The show had a live band from the start, prompting Bakker to form a band for his show, which up to that point had relied on guest musicians and recorded soundtracks. Bueno and Montaño also avoided churchy, Bible Belt language, which would have bewildered their viewers. Even when they adopted the PTL logo (which meant that the they could use the Charlotte set without alteration), they rendered it "Para Total Latino" (For Every Latino). Tapes of the show were sent on a bicycle through Latin America, usually airing for an hour on Saturday in each country. PTL maintained an office in Panama, and Bueno and Montaño made frequent trips to the region to hold crusades. By the end of 1979, the Spanish show was available in seventeen Latin American countries and on the Spanish International Network (later Univision) in the United States.[42]

In February 1977, a month after the Latin American show launched, Korean pastor Paul Yongii Cho appeared for the first time on the *PTL Club*. Cho later played a role in PTL's first run-in with the government, one that would make Bakker the target of an investigation by the Federal Communications Commission (FCC). After suffering from tuberculosis in his teens, Cho had a vision of Jesus and experienced the baptism of the Holy Spirit while fasting and praying one night. After graduating from seminary in Seoul, he started a church with his future mother-in-law. By 1964 Cho's church had three thousand members. Realizing that he could not minister to so many people directly, Cho divided the church up into cells, and the growth continued.[43]

By the time he visited PTL in 1977, Cho's church in Seoul seated ten thousand and membership stood at about fifty thousand, growing by two hundred a week. Twenty-six hundred deacons ran cell groups of eleven to fifteen families each. Cho, who was already responsible for starting one quarter of the Assemblies of God churches in Korea, had visited America thirty-two times since 1964 looking for ways to keep expanding. At the same time, Bakker was eager to extend PTL's reach into Asia. Both had big plans and an expansive vision. It looked like a perfect fit. PTL Senior Vice President Roger Flessing and other key members of Bakker's staff spent the next year working on a plan to start a Korean version of PTL, produced in Korea, before the project unraveled (more about this later).[44]

A month after Cho's first appearance on the show, Bakker promised support for Benson Idahosa's *Redemption Hour* television program, broadcast in Nigeria. Idahosa first appeared on the American *PTL Club* in 1976, quickly becoming an audience favorite. As an infant, Idahosa was rejected by his father. His mother discarded him on a rubbish heap in the rain, only to be overwhelmed by guilt and retrieve him a few hours later. Idahosa craved an education, but his father mostly refused to let him attend school until, as a teenager, he moved to Benin City to live with relatives. There, in 1960, he was converted by a local preacher from another tribe, something almost unthinkable to his relatives and friends. While working at a shoe company, Idahosa started his own church from scratch. By 1975 he was the leader of the largest Pentecostal church in Benin City, with attendance of more than two thousand on Sunday, in addition to a Bible school and a local television program. Donations from PTL viewers helped Idahosa extend his ministry's reach, expanding it to a network of more than six hundred African churches by 1981. Bakker wrote the foreword to a flattering biography of Idahosa published that same year.[45]

International projects continued to multiply at a dizzying pace. In October 1977 Bakker announced that PTL would soon sponsor a Brazilian *PTL Club* in Portuguese, hosted by Bob McAlister, and in July 1978 Bakker offered to support an Australian PTL, hosted by Alan Langstaff. By then the English version of PTL was available in the Philippines, Guam, the Marshall Islands, and Hawaii.

On September 6, 1978, Bakker left on an around-the-world trip to check up on PTL's projects and prospects outside the United States and to escape a wave of bad press in the Charlotte newspapers over PTL's financial troubles. Roger Flessing, Ruth Egert, Bakker's secretary, her husband, photographer Phil Egert, and cameraman Burt Lehman accompanied Bakker on the trip. They flew first to Hawaii then Tokyo and Singapore, where Bakker attended a conference of "Christian leaders" from "35 nations," including Pentecostal statesman David DuPlessis. Leaving Singapore, Bakker and his entourage made their way to Manila and then Seoul, where Bakker met with Yonggi Cho. From Korea the group traveled to Calcutta where they witnessed flooding and appalling poverty. Next was Nigeria, where Benson Idahosa hosted Bakker and his entourage, followed by stops in Brussels, London, the Netherlands, and Paris. Despite all that Bakker saw on the trip, he was already losing interest in foreign missions by the time he returned to Charlotte.[46]

Still, the push to extend PTL abroad continued for several years, propelled by the momentum of the resources already committed to it. By February 1979, PTL Thailand was on the air with a Thai host, and a Japanese host had been selected for the Japanese version of PTL, which was now separate from the Korean initiative. In September 1979 PTL launched a French version of the show under Willard Cantelon, a missionary to Europe for nearly thirty years and a frequent guest on Bakker's show. The French show was hosted by Roland Cosnard and produced in Charlotte. The next month the ministry launched a pilot program for an Italian *PTL Club*, which debuted in 1980. By the end of 1979 various versions of the *PTL Club* were on the air in forty nations.[47]

PTL's international programs were revolutionary, particularly in their commitment to using local hosts and formats that fit with indigenous culture. Had PTL continued to pour resources into these programs, there is no telling how far they might have expanded. As it turned out, 1978 and 1979 were the high point of PTL's overseas initiatives. After that, Bakker's attention shifted to building Heritage USA.

4

Abundant Life

IN ADDITION TO their interest in missions and evangelism, PTL's core audience watched the show to learn the secrets of an abundant life. As much as any group, Pentecostals benefited from the post–World War II prosperity that brought middle-class abundance to millions of Americans. For large numbers of Pentecostals, the good life and the godly life converged for the first time in the 1960s and 1970s. At the same time, people in mainline Protestant and Roman Catholic churches began adopting Pentecostal doctrine and practices in what became known as the charismatic movement.

If the charismatic movement had an Azusa Street moment, it was April 3, 1960, when Episcopal priest Dennis Bennett stepped before his affluent Van Nuys, California, congregation and announced that he had spoken in tongues. *Time* picked up the story, noting that speaking in tongues was "on its way back in US churches—not only in the uninhibited Pentecostal sects but even among Episcopalians."[1] In 1967 the movement caught on among Roman Catholics at Duquesne University in Pittsburgh and the University of Notre Dame. During the 1970s up to one million American Catholics participated in the charismatic renewal. The Full Gospel Business Men's Fellowship International (FGBMFI) proved particularly effective at drawing middle-class Americans into the charismatic movement. By 1975, the FGBMFI had 1,650 chapters, with at least one in every state and fifty-two foreign countries, and a monthly attendance of more than half a million. By that time, it had drawn in so many non-Pentecostals that it had become "a polyglot of denominationalists united only by their experience with the Holy Spirit." Perhaps no one personified the mainstreaming of Pentecostalism more than Oral Roberts, who left the sixty-five-thousand-member Pentecostal Holiness church to join the eleven-million-member Methodist church in 1968.[2]

By the mid-1970s, Pentecostals no longer looked as bizarre as they once had. Now they seemed more attuned to the loosening up of American culture. Pentecostals had always clapped, swayed, shouted, and even danced as they worshipped, all of which seemed more appealing post-1960s. Suddenly, well-educated and affluent Methodists, Episcopalians, and Catholics could be overheard discussing the gifts of the Spirit and worshipping with their hands in the air, swaying from side to side. The charismatic renewal brought Pentecostalism a measure of cultural legitimacy unimaginable before the war. With it came an expansive sense of confidence.

Pentecostals and charismatics used a particular understanding of faith to put this confidence into action. Faith missions emerged in the late nineteenth and early twentieth centuries out of impatience with the failure of denominational mission boards to act quickly in sending out missionaries, often because of limited finances. Faith missions solved this problem by simply ignoring the money. They took the approach that "if it was God's will to reach an unreached area, it was up to God to provide," writes historian William Svelmoe.[3] Millions of evangelicals grew up listening to stories of missionaries who sailed to foreign lands with nothing in their pockets and no secure funding, but with a faith that somehow God would provide. The moral of the story was always the same: faith meant taking risks, extending beyond your resources. God only handed you the parachute after you jumped out of the plane. The most dynamic overseas missions organizations created in the twentieth century ran on this model, including Wycliffe Bible Translators and Youth With a Mission (YWAM).

Requiring missionaries to raise their own financial support made these groups more entrepreneurial. It also meant that faith missions had little reason to remain within established denominations, where they might be hemmed in by administrative inertia. Founded in the 1930s by William Cameron Townsend, Wycliffe Bible Translators (and its affiliated Summer Institute of Linguistics) required its missionaries to raise their own support. From its founding, Wycliffe trained thirty to forty thousand linguists who translated the New Testament into five hundred languages, working in remote locations around the world. A generation later, YWAM followed much the same organizational structure. Founded in 1960 by Loren Cunningham, YWAM broke with the Assemblies of God in the 1960s in order to maintain a more aggressive approach to sending out young volunteers, all of them responsible for their own support. By 1983 YWAM had 3,800 full-time workers and was sending out 15,000 short-term volunteers a year. In that year it operated 113 permanent bases in 40 nations and had sent volunteers to a total of 193 countries. YWAMers went to the ends of the earth, often with just enough money to get there.[4]

Faith missions were central to evangelicals' sense of themselves as dynamic communities committed to reaching the lost. They created a funding model that permitted, even required, organizations to exceed their means, to commit themselves to doing more than they had the money on hand to do. PTL thought of itself as exactly this sort of enterprise. "Some people think you need plenty of money in the bank before you can begin to operate in faith. I never have," Jim Bakker wrote in 1977, just as PTL was taking off. "Are you currently debating over taking a step of faith in the Lord, or are you waiting until it looks safe to move? . . . Remember, facts don't count when you have God's word on the subject." As outrageous as this might sound, millions of Pentecostals and charismatics had grown up hearing missionaries say more or less the same thing. "There's a certain sort of mindset in a lot of Pentecostal theology," says Roger Flessing. People at PTL took the approach, "we're just going to do it. We'll step out, God will meet us." This was at the heart of everything PTL did.[5]

In his first autobiography, written in 1976, Bakker tells the story of how, during the early days at the furniture store, PTL had fallen $70,000 in debt to the station that aired it. The station manager gave Bakker thirty days to pay up, an impossible deadline given that the show only brought in $20,000 a month. Then, as Bakker tells it, God spoke to him: "*Give him what he asks,* the Lord said, *and I'll do the miracle for you.*" That Friday Bakker instructed his vice president, Jim Moss, to write a check for $20,000, even though they were broke and Monday deposits rarely exceeded $7,000. Since it was already Friday, Bakker had no time for a special appeal to his audience. Moss, who had run a successful business before joining PTL, was deeply conflicted about taking a dubious check to Jim Thrash, the station manager. But in the end his sense of business ethics gave way to the imperative of faith. That Monday $30,000 arrived in the mail, enough to cover the check. So the next Friday Bakker told Moss to write another $20,000 check, saying, "God told me to do it again." Moss protested that they were still broke but sent the check anyway. That Monday, "it happened again! Contributions totaling more than $20,000 came in." Here was real faith in action.[6]

Of course, there is another way to describe what Bakker was doing: writing bad checks. The distinction for Bakker and his followers was that God had told him to do it. The checks were not bad because the Lord stood behind them. Bakker told this and similar stories over and over again throughout his career, though at times he omitted and glossed over key details. One element of the $70,000 debt story that might have given Bakker's followers pause, considering his later fundraising techniques, was that, as Bakker tells it, the money came in without a special appeal to his audience. Bakker also left out the fact that they had just conducted a telethon in Ohio. He and Moss did not know how much money to expect, but the Monday morning checks were not exactly a miracle out of the blue. Regardless, the message remained clear for Bakker and his followers. "If you're in need of money, God wants to prosper you," Bakker declared in a short, hastily written book devoted to the topic of prosperity, *The Big Three Mountain-Movers*, published in December 1977.[7]

The prospect for blessings extended not only to those who received and spent the money, but also to those who gave, a concept popularized by Oral Roberts. In 1970 Roberts published *Miracle of Seed-Faith*, declaring, "*Whatever you can conceive, and believe, you can do!*" By 1976 there were nearly two million copies of the book in print.[8] The key to seed faith was realizing that giving to God was like planting a seed: you reaped in proportion to what you sowed. "If you want God to supply your financial needs, then give SEED-MONEY for him to reproduce and multiply," Roberts wrote. Giving became a test of one's faith. When you entered into a "Blessing-Pact" with God, you had to "EXPECT A MIRACLE." The book is full of anecdotes of people giving, despite desperate financial need, only to get back far more in return.[9]

The success of Roberts's ministry certainly seemed to validate his approach. By the mid-1970s, Roberts had reinvented himself from big-tent evangelist to television personality and college president. The Oral Roberts University basketball team became a nationally recognized program and played in the NCAA Tournament for the first time in 1974. Roberts played golf with Bob Hope and appeared on all of the major television talk shows, including the *Tonight Show* with Johnny Carson.[10]

Roberts was a frequent guest on the *PTL Club*, and Bakker copied his model of seed faith. During a telethon in November 1978, Bakker told his audience, "many of you have never given because you really don't trust God." If only they would give in faith, God would return to them "a hundred fold in this world, and . . . eternal life in the world to come. I mean, that is about the best deal I've ever heard in my life," Bakker declared. The live studio audience agreed, applauding enthusiastically. Buoyed by their response, Bakker drove his point home by reinterpreting the biblical parable of the rich young ruler. The parable involves a rich young man who asks Jesus what he must do to gain "eternal life." Jesus tells him to keep the commandments: "Do not commit adultery, Do not kill, Do not steal, Do not bear false witness, Honour thy father and thy mother." When the young man says that he has done all of this "from my youth up," Jesus tells him that he lacks only one thing: "sell all that thou hast, and distribute unto the poor, and thou shalt have treasure in heaven: and come, follow me." When the young man hears this he turns away, unwilling to give up his possessions. The usual interpretation of the parable is that the rich man's love of money and the things of this world kept him from following Jesus. Had he given away his wealth and embraced a life of voluntary poverty, he would have found something far more valuable: eternal life.[11]

Bakker declared that this missed the point entirely. "You know a lot of people misunderstand when Jesus said to the rich young ruler, 'give all you have and give to the poor and come follow me.' They thought Jesus was asking the poor man to get wiped out and . . . live in poverty for the rest of his life. That's what most critics of gospel fundraising [say]." In fact, according to Bakker, Jesus was merely testing the young ruler's faith. "What would have happened if the rich young ruler had given all to follow Jesus?" Bakker asked. "He would have had abundant life. He would have had everything God [had to offer], and he probably would have had a book of the Bible named after him." What could be better than that? By not giving, the rich young man had missed out on his chance for fame and even greater wealth. The studio audience loved it and contributions to the ministry poured in. Bakker often repeated this interpretation of the parable during fundraising events over the course of the next decade.[12]

Faith understood in this way had several consequences. First, it allowed ministries to ignore the normal financial controls that businesses and banks had to follow because God would never fail to supply their need. The facts of accounting applied only to those who lacked faith. Second, it allowed ministries to aggressively raise funds, since by taking their followers' money they were really doing them a favor. The more believers gave, the more God would give them in return. "A rejected opportunity to give is a lost opportunity to receive," wrote Oral Roberts.[13]

Bakker later admitted that he "got most of my sermon ideas from other preachers" without much reflection. "In much of my sermon preparation time, I simply picked out some motivational principles, then scanned through the Bible to find a verse or passage that supported what I wanted to say." He was adept at sensing which ideas audiences were the most receptive to and building his message around those. In this case, "I simply pulled [verses] out of context" and used them "to justify my God-wants-you-rich theology."[14]

The faith mission model mixed easily with the word of faith movement, popularized by Kenneth Hagin, Kenneth Copeland, Frederick Price—all of whom appeared on Bakker's television show—and a host of other prosperity preachers in the 1970s, as historian Kate Bowler has shown. Word of faith proponents believed that through faith believers could speak just about anything into existence, a concept sometimes called "name it and claim it," or "blab it and grab it."[15]

By the late 1970s, Bakker had adopted the basic language of the word of faith movement. "Decide on what you need. Is it a house? A solution to a problem? A healing? Money? Salvation of a loved one? Maybe you just want to lose weight.... So you begin by simply speaking out what you need," Bakker wrote in 1977. A good "confession" could solve any problem. Like many of the abundant life preachers from this period, Bakker asserted that our lives are largely governed by what we say. "We can confess doom or prosperity," Bakker wrote in *Eight Keys to Success*, published in 1980. He told readers that he had seen the power of giving a "good report" in his own life. He had started out as a small-time evangelist trusting God for fifty dollars a week. Now he believed God for "a million dollars a week," and it worked. Putting this idea into action liberated Bakker and his supporters from the notion that God prefers a conservative, methodical approach. Just the opposite. God rewards the daring. The safe, timid approach is an admission that you do not really believe. "When PTL got involved in its massive building project, I never looked at our bank balance," Bakker wrote in 1977. "I didn't have the money to build it, but I knew God did, and that kept my confession positive." If only his creditors had seen it that way.[16]

THE GOSPEL OF abundant life also blended smoothly with American therapeutic culture, particularly as it developed after World War II. Tom Wolfe famously identified the 1970s as the "me decade," a product of "the thirty-year boom" following the war. Post-war prosperity "pumped money into every class level of the population on a scale without parallel in any country in history." The resulting "luxury" created a new "alchemical dream." Rather than changing lead into gold, the new dream sought to change "one's personality—remaking, remodeling, elevating, and polishing one's very *self.*" *Self* magazine began publication in January 1979, and best-sellers of the 1970s included *Winning through Intimidation* (1973) and *Looking Out for Number One* (1977). The titles say it all.

Wolfe likened this focus on self-awareness to a religious revival, "the third great religious wave in American history, one that historians will very likely term the Third Great Awakening," after the First Great Awakening in the 1730s and 1740s and the Second Great Awakening in the first half of the nineteenth century. The me decade was not quite that, but Wolfe had a point, particularly when he identified "charismatic Christianity" as the "leading edge" of the new awakening. For decades the assumption of sociologists and historians had been that the rise of therapeutic culture in the twentieth century came at the expense of religion. As it turned out, the two were easy allies.[17]

PTL had the perfect message for the me decade, a message that lent itself to evangelical fervor. PTL programs featured a steady stream of guests giving advice on how to love yourself, lose weight, improve your marriage, and reach your full potential, including Norman Vincent Peale, Robert Schuller, and Merlin Carothers. Peale was an early guest on the *PTL Club*, and his half-hour television show was one of the first programs added to PTL's satellite network in 1978. Peale started his career as a Methodist preacher in 1922 before becoming a household name with the release of his blockbuster book, *The Power of Positive Thinking*, published in 1952. By the late 1980s the book had sold more than fifteen million copies. Essentially a collection of anecdotes, the book presents upbeat, unpretentious accounts of people overcoming life's demands and setbacks. Peale urged his readers to stop "thinking thoughts of defeat . . . for as you think defeat you tend to get it." Instead, Peale counseled readers to retrain their minds to expect success. "Fill your mind with fresh, new creative thoughts of faith, love, and goodness. By this process you can actually remake your life," Peale wrote.[18]

A broad range of mainline church leaders and evangelicals criticized Peale for his close reliance on New Thought, a movement from the late nineteenth and early twentieth centuries that emphasized the power of the mind to harness the energy of the cosmos. Bakker knew next to nothing about New Thought, but he nevertheless adopted much of Peale's language. "Our minds are so powerful. We were created in the image of God. . . . You can control your whole body by your brain. The organs of our body can heal or die by your mental attitude," Bakker wrote in 1980. As Bakker himself would later write, he "often simply [took] a 'positive thinking' type of message and put a Scripture to it and labeled it 'positive confession.'"[19]

Like Peale, Robert Schuller was an early guest on the *PTL Club*, and the PTL network aired his weekly *Hour of Power* television show, broadcast from Schuller's Crystal Cathedral in Garden Grove, California. In his book *Self-Esteem: The New Reformation*, Schuller argued that the first reformation under Luther and Calvin had gone too far in emphasizing "theocentric communications." What was needed to correct this was a second reformation that emphasized "the deepest needs felt by human beings." Self-esteem was "the single greatest need facing the human race today," Schuller wrote. His scheme fit neatly with Bakker's perspective, and the two remained allies through the 1980s.[20]

Merlin Carothers's fame came and went faster than Peale's or Schuller's, but for nearly a decade his books enjoyed astonishing sales, and he was a favorite at PTL. Carothers burst onto the national stage in 1970 with the publication of his autobiography, *Prison to Praise*, which sold 1.5 million copies in its first year in print. Carothers had joined the Army during World War II looking for adventure. He volunteered for paratrooper training but then got bored and, with a buddy, went AWOL and stole a car. After holding up a store, they were arrested. Pleading that he simply wanted to go to war, Carothers received a suspended sentence and shipped out to Europe. He fought in the Battle of the Bulge and then stayed on in Germany after the war, working the black market. Back in the United States, he reluctantly went to church with his grandparents, got saved, and his whole life changed direction. He became a Methodist preacher and then an Army chaplain, received the Baptism in the Holy Spirit, and saw people healed when he prayed.[21]

Carothers's breakthrough moment came when he realized that God wants people to praise him in every situation. Though circumstances might look dire, God is in control and intends his children nothing but good. "The battle isn't ours, it is God's. While we praise Him, He sends our enemies scurrying," Carothers wrote. *Prison to Praise* is filled with anecdotes of people (mostly soldiers Carothers counseled as a chaplain) who, when faced with sickness, divorce, alcoholic spouses, and battlefield danger, thanked God for their trials. Though Carothers insists that this is not bargaining with God, everyone in the book who follows his formula finds some sort of quick and complete deliverance.[22]

In *Prison to Praise*, Carothers tells the story of a lawyer, Ron, whose wife, Sue, had attempted suicide when he was drafted into the Army as a private. When he received orders for Vietnam she again threatened to kill herself. An adopted child who was now estranged from her adopted family, she had no one else in the world except her husband. The couple came to see Carothers hoping that he could get Ron's orders changed, but instead Carothers advised them to "thank God that Ron is going to Vietnam." Reluctantly they prayed with Carothers, thanking God for their situation. While Sue sat in the waiting room afterward, she met a young soldier distressed because his wife wanted a divorce. "It won't do much good to see *that* Chaplain," she told him. As they talked, the soldier showed Sue his family pictures. Looking at them she suddenly recognized her birth mother, whom she had never met, from another picture she had once seen on an adoption form. The two were brother and sister. As this was happening, Ron ran into a friend from law school who was now a legal officer. He arranged for a transfer so that Ron could stay in the states. Ron and Sue were not separated, and now Sue had the extended family she had always dreamed of. The lesson was clear: praising God inevitably leads to victory; only those who lack faith are defeated. This was essentially the same message as Peale's, only substituting praising God, which no evangelical could object to, for positive thinking, which struck some as relying too much on the human mind. Carothers even wrote in the same anecdotal style as Peale, which both of them no doubt gleaned from the master of self-help advice, Dale Carnegie.[23]

Carothers followed up the success of *Prison to Praise* with five more books on the same theme. By 1976 there were six million copies of his books in print in twenty languages. It is no accident that Jim Bakker named his ministry PTL (Praise the Lord). The confidence and optimism it conveyed captured the mode of evangelicals perfectly. "You can be certain God never made a failure yet. He is a God of success. His word is programmed to succeed," Bakker wrote in 1977.[24]

The abundant life, as Bakker and his guests conceived of it, drew together newer and older themes in Pentecostalism, particularly in the way that it slid easily from divine healing to healthy living. A perfect example is Charles and Frances Hunter. For most of their itinerant career, the Happy Hunters, as they were called, were primarily known as healing evangelists. But by the mid-1970s Frances had developed an interest in healthy eating. On January 12, 1977, the Hunters appeared on the *PTL Club* to promote Frances's latest books, *God's Answer to Fat* and *The Fabulous Skinnie Minnie Recipe Book*. In the former, Frances describes her struggles to lose weight with the kind of quick humor that earned the couple their nickname. She blamed her poor eating habits on her upbringing during the Depression, when she often went hungry and her family lived for long stretches on nothing but potatoes. More than anything she longed for a banana split, the kind she saw through the windows of ice cream parlors she could not afford to enter. As an adult, she was determined to enjoy everything she had been denied as a child.[25]

The result was predictable. For years Frances tried "every kind of diet there is!" without lasting success. Then she met Graham Kerr, "The Galloping Gourmet," famous for his television cooking show, who had become an evangelical Christian. Kerr advised her to get a USDA publication that listed the nutritive values of food. She was shocked to discover just how many calories she was eating. It turned out that God's answer to fat was eating a healthy diet, mostly vegetables, fruit, and lean meat, while avoiding fats, oils, and sweets. A year after publishing *God's Answer to Fat*, Frances followed it up with the *The Skinnie Minnie Recipe Book*, published in 1976, which contained more than 150 of her favorite recipes. By the time she and Charles appeared on the *PTL Club* in January 1977, Frances had lost sixty-five pounds.[26]

When Bakker heard about Frances's approach to eating, he was sold, though it took more than a year before he lost much weight. In their first years in Charlotte, Jim and Tammy both struggled with their weight. Jim appears pudgy on camera and in photos from 1974 through much of 1978, and Tammy's weight ballooned to 130 pounds on her four foot ten inch frame, up from the 83 pounds she weighed when she and Jim got married. "I had gotten so chubby that my tummy stuck out as far as my breasts. I was embarrassed to walk across the bedroom. I couldn't wear nice skimpy and frilly lingerie, because of my bulges. I looked terrible in a swimming suit," Tammy later wrote with characteristic candor.[27]

They finally got serious about diet and exercise in late 1978. In less than six months Tammy lost twenty-four pounds, and her dress size went from an eleven to a five. Jim lost nearly thirty pounds, making his features, if not chiseled, at least more like the television star he wanted to be. They publicized their new looks in a short, hastily written book, *How We Lost Weight & Kept It Off!* published in April 1979 (at which point they had only kept it off for a matter of weeks). Unlike Frances Hunter's diet books, *How We Lost Weight* was as much about exercise and a healthy lifestyle as it was about diet.[28]

By the time *How We Lost Weight* was out, Jim Moss (a former high-school football All-American) had hired a recreation director for PTL,

Melvin Stewart, along with his wife, Myra, who had a longstanding interest in nutrition. The couple were featured in the April 1978 edition of *Action*, photographed while jogging with Jo Jo Starbuck, a former figure skater and bronze medalist at the 1972 World Championships and wife of Pittsburgh Steeler's quarterback Terry Bradshaw.

As the ministry expanded, new construction included recreational facilities. There was an Olympic-size swimming pool, sauna, and hot tub in the basement of the ministry center at Heritage Village. Melvin Stewart's son, also named Melvin, grew up swimming in the pool. He later became a world record holder in the butterfly and won two gold medals and a bronze at the 1992 Summer Olympics in Barcelona. By the late 1970s, PTL's version of the abundant life had evolved to include a holistic approach to physical, mental, and spiritual health that included diet, exercise, and, yes, sex.[29]

Bakker and his guests did not shy away from frank discussions about sex. Among evangelicals there was a new openness toward discussing the pleasures of sex by the 1970s, though they were quick to stress that this only applied to married couples. The best-selling nonfiction book of 1974 was Marabel Morgan's *The Total Woman*, which eventually sold more than ten million copies. Though it is rooted in gender norms of the time, its discussion of sex is hardly stuffy or Victorian. "The Creator of sex intended for His creatures to enjoy it. We need never be ashamed to talk about what God was not ashamed to create," Morgan writes. She advises women to meet their husbands at the door wearing sexy costumes, everything from "pink baby-doll pajamas and white boots" to "black mesh stockings, high heels, and an apron. That's all." When marriage counselor Ray Mossholder appeared on the *PTL Club* in September 1979, he advised couples to talk openly about sex and to work at creating an exciting sex life. "God says get over Victorianism," declared Mossholder. Jim and Tammy, who co-hosted the show that day, heartily agreed. Tammy once did an episode with Dr. Marvin Brooks featuring a demonstration of the "newest type" of inflatable penile implants.[30]

Perhaps nothing better demonstrated the Bakkers' willingness to deal openly with the topic of sex than Jim's interview with Larry Flynt, publisher of *Hustler* magazine. Of all the guests who appeared on the show, Flynt was arguably the most outrageous. Born in poverty in the hills of Kentucky in 1942, Flynt's father was an alcoholic. At age nine Flynt had sex with a chicken, and at eleven his parents divorced. He quit school after the eighth grade, lied about his age to join the Army and later enlisted in the Navy. As a radar technician aboard the USS *Enterprise*, Flynt tracked John Glenn's Mercury space capsule's reentry from orbit in 1962. After leaving the Navy, he bought a series of bars in Dayton, Ohio, before launching *Hustler* in 1974. Three years later, in November 1977, Flynt became a born-again Christian under the guidance of Ruth Carter Stapleton, sister of President Jimmy Carter. Stapleton had a ministry centered on bringing "inner healing" to people wounded by painful childhood experiences, of which Flynt had a bundle.[31]

"I think we have a lot in common," Stapleton told Flynt the first time they spoke. "We both think sexual repression is bad for people." Indeed, in *The Experience of Inner Healing* (1977), Stapleton writes, "There is a solution for those who have found no other resolution for uncontrolled sexual feelings. It is surrender. The first step is to embrace your dark side, your sexual self." Stapleton gives the example of Susan, a devout Catholic who became "horrified by her sexual feelings" as a teenager, so much so that she decided to become a nun. But even as a novitiate she could not overcome her temptation to masturbate. Then she attended a religious conference where a speaker explained that Jesus never said anything on the topic and that "the childhood experience of sexual experimentation" was a healthy part of "self-discovery." Here was a religion that Flynt could relate to.[32]

Flynt's conversion occurred aboard his jet on a flight to Los Angeles with Stapleton. As they prayed, Flynt had a visionary experience in which God appeared to him and he had a "premonition" of "myself in a wheelchair." For the next several months the experience changed the direction of Flynt's life. At the Hustler Christmas party in December 1977, Flynt announced that he was starting a new profit-sharing program for employees and a free daycare center "so working parents could have lunch with their kids." "Many of you have read that I've been born again. It's true," Flynt wrote in the March 1978 edition of the magazine. "Just know that we are working for God. We will try to do what God would approve of in our stories and pictures. . . . My aim is to address my HUSTLER readers in the language they understand best, to answer many of their problems in dealing with deep-rooted religious convictions."[33]

On February 3, 1978, Flynt flew to Charlotte aboard his $4 million jet, formerly owned by Elvis Presley, which he was now calling "God Force One." Flynt and Bakker taped a fifty-minute interview, which ran as part of the *PTL Club*'s regular broadcast on Monday, February 6. After the interview Jim and Tammy drove to the airport to see Flynt's plane. While onboard the two men exchanged gifts. Bakker gave Flynt a Bible, and Flynt, who had become a vegetarian as part of his conversion, gave Bakker books on "natural foods and vegetarian diets."[34]

During his interview with Bakker, Flynt displayed a mixture of bravado and candidness that one might have expected from the king of porn. When Bakker asked what it meant to be born again, Flynt replied, "It means just that. But it means more than just becoming a new person. I've also set a new standard of morality for myself. I've obtained a higher level of consciousness, and a relationship with God." Jesus, Flynt said, was a "renegade rabbi with a police record." He was "not a religious person. He had no religion. He had a philosophy of unconditional love." "Anytime I get mistreated, whether it's by a Christian or non-Christian, I just pray for them. And I think that this love, it's not just total love, but unconditional love.... We have to be able to love our enemies," Flynt added.[35]

Reactions to the Flynt interview were mixed. PTL claimed that immediately after the show aired, 178 callers supported having Flynt on the show and only three were opposed. But critics quickly emerged. The Rev. Garland Faw, pastor of the Truth Temple in nearby Kannapolis, North Carolina, borrowed $1,300 from his congregation to take out three-quarter page ads in the *Charlotte Observer* and *Charlotte News* under the headline: "Pornography Or the Bible, Either/Or—Not Both." Bakker defended the interview in an editorial published in the *Observer*. "I cannot help but wonder what Jesus would do with Larry Flynt.... Are we living in a day when bartenders are permitted to talk with troubled men but not the clergy?" Bakker asked. He invited Ruth Carter Stapleton to appear on the show on February 15 to defend Flynt's conversion story. During the weeks before and after his *PTL Club* appearance, Flynt spent nearly all his time trying to figure out "how we would combine religion with a skin magazine," as he later wrote. Knowing this, Bakker wrote to Flynt offering to give him the entire staff of PTL's *Action* magazine to help turn *Hustler*, which had a circulation of 2.5 million, into a "new magazine for Jesus."[36]

But it was not to be. An assassin's bullet derailed Flynt's conversion only a month after his appearance on the *PTL Club*. A white supremacist serial killer shot Flynt in Lawrenceville, Georgia, where he had gone to face obscenity charges. The shooting left him partially paralyzed in a wheelchair and in nearly constant, agonizing pain. Ruth Stapleton, who had become Flynt's "best friend," visited him in the hospital, and Tammy Faye wrote to him. But Flynt's conversion was not deep enough to survive his injuries. "I didn't have room for God in my pain-ravaged daily existence," he later wrote. "I began to think that I wasn't particularly interested in the kind of God who would let people suffer as I was." In the end, Flynt's association with the Bakkers was only fleeting, but the point is that they met him halfway, in part for the publicity, but also out of a genuine desire to engage American culture at multiple levels, including the sexual revolution.[37]

PTL'S OPENNESS EXTENDED in a measure to race and gender. Reverend Evelyn Carter Spencer was a frequent guest on the show beginning in the 1970s and served on PTL's board of directors beginning in 1985. She was featured in *Action*, and Bakker wrote an endorsement of her book *No Ground*, published in 1978. Spencer grew up feeling unwanted and out of place, with a mother who told her that she would "never amount to anything," and a father who "hated white folks." She had a daughter a month after she turned sixteen despite never having kissed a man. "I thought I would never get in trouble because you only had babies when you kissed people and I hadn't kissed him," Spencer later wrote. Eventually she became a Baptist preacher. The welcoming, upbeat atmosphere at PTL drew Spencer in, as did its message of abundance. "I like the word 'lavish,'" Spencer wrote in her book. "You can just wallow in that. It means overabundant—kinda sloshy." After an episode of the *PTL Club* shot on location in Florida in 1977, Jim Bakker walked up to Spencer and gave her a new car. It was so much nicer than anything she had ever driven that she was reluctant to accept it.[38]

PTL's relaxed attitude toward race often surprised reporters and outsiders who ventured onto the ministry's grounds. Appearing on the *PTL Club* and similar shows was something of a necessity for black preachers since white televangelists controlled the Christian television networks, but it was also a genuine expression of shared beliefs. The prosperity gospel in particular took deep root in the African American community, and Jim and Tammy made racial diversity a priority at PTL. Tom Skinner, a black evangelist and chaplain of the Washington Redskins, hosted the *PTL Club* once a month in the late 1970s. Like Evelyn Carter, Dr. James Johnson, the grandson of a slave and a former Under Secretary of the Navy, became a member of PTL's board of directors. He was also a guest on the show and featured in the December 1977 edition of *Action*. Dozens of black singers and musicians performed on the *PTL Club*, and black preachers, entertainers and athletes were regular guests. Despite their earlier conflicts at CBN, Jim and Tammy maintained a lasting friendship with Scott and Nedra Ross, an interracial couple. The Rosses visited the Bakkers in Charlotte, and their son spent a summer living with the Bakkers when he was fourteen.[39]

PTL was mostly run by men, as was the rest of the entertainment industry at the time, but it stood out for the steady stream of women who appeared on the show and served in leadership positions. The Holiness movement and Pentecostalism had a tradition of female preaching and leadership from the beginning, including Maria Woodworth Etter, the so-called trance evangelist, and Aimee Semple McPherson. Woodworth Etter, sometimes referred to as the grandmother of Pentecostalism, preached to huge crowds across the nation beginning in the 1880s before building her own church in Indianapolis, Indiana. McPherson built the 5,000-seat Angelus Temple, in Los Angeles in the 1920s and founded her own denomination, the International Church of the Foursquare Gospel. Jim and Tammy had direct connections to these kinds of female preachers, beginning with Fern Olson at the Minneapolis Evangelistic Auditorium. "There's good in the women's liberation movement in this country today. There's so much good that it's about 95 percent good," Jim told reporter Frye Gaillard. "I think God is trying to get us to elevate the place of women," Bakker said.[40]

Tammy was a constant presence on PTL's main television program and often hosted her own show in the afternoon. Aimee Cortese, an Assemblies of God pastor from the Bronx, appeared on the *PTL Club* and joined PTL's board of directors in 1979. When Frances and Charles Hunter were guests on the show, it was Frances who dominated the conversation, even with regards to theological discussions, sitting in the wing-back chair next to Jim while Charles sat on the couch by his wife's side. Bible teacher Marilyn Hickey was a regular on the program and taught a series of weeklong seminars on the Bible at Heritage USA. Roman Catholic nuns were occasionally a part of the mix, including Mother Angelica, who founded Our Lady of the Angels Monastery in Irondale, Alabama, in 1962 and the Eternal Word Television Network (EWTN) in 1981.[41]

In the late 1970s, Bakker and his staff were using television in revolutionary ways, attracting an audience in the millions. Oral Roberts or Pat Robertson would not have had Larry Flynt on their shows. But in 1978 and 1979 Bakker began to shift his focus to Heritage USA, a decision that eventually curtailed innovation on the television side of the ministry. Building the park would test Bakker's conception of faith and money to its limits.

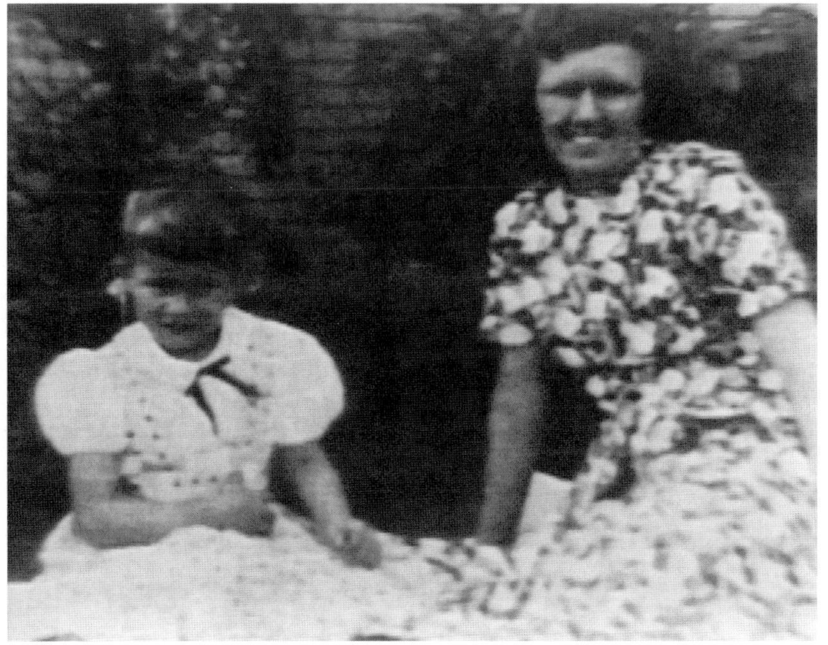

Tammy Faye and her Aunt Gin. Tammy is wearing a dress her aunt made.
Credit: Flower Pentecostal Heritage Center.

A young Jim Bakker.
Credit: Flower Pentecostal Heritage Center.

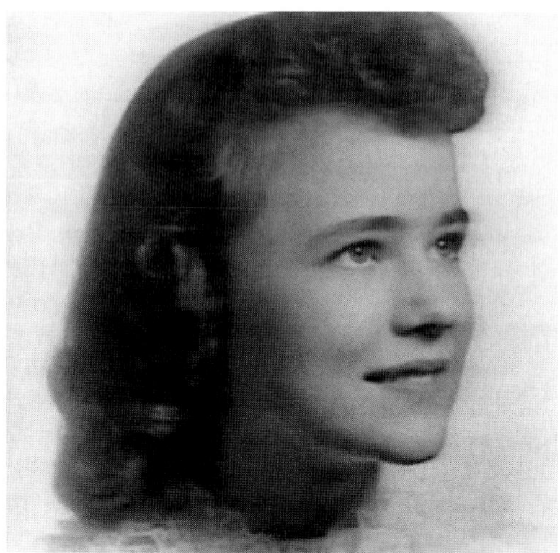

A young Tammy Faye.
Credit: Flower Pentecostal Heritage Center.

On the set of the *Jim and Tammy Show* at CBN.
Credit: Flower Pentecostal Heritage Center.

Susie Moppet and Allie Alligator, Tammy's two favorite puppets.
Credit: Flower Pentecostal Heritage Center.

Bakker and Henry Harrison on the set of the *PTL Club* in 1975.
Credit: *The Charlotte Observer*.

Jim and Tammy on the air in March 1976, with their son Jamie Charles. This was the last show broadcast from the former furniture store on Independence Boulevard.

Credit: Flower Pentecostal Heritage Center.

The Heritage Village Complex in 1977.

Credit: *The Charlotte Observer*.

Roger Flessing discussing the future of Christian television on the *PTL Club*, April 1977.
Credit: Flower Pentecostal Heritage Center.

Gary Paxton on the *PTL Club*, February 1978.
Credit: Flower Pentecostal Heritage Center.

Bakker interviewing Ronald Reagan, November 1979.
Credit: Flower Pentecostal Heritage Center.

Efrem Zimbalist Jr. narrating *Under Investigation*, the 1980 PTL documentary aimed at countering the FCC investigation of the ministry.
Credit: Flower Pentecostal Heritage Center.

John Wesley Fletcher, who arranged Jim Bakker's Florida encounter with Jessica Hahn.

Credit: The Charlotte Observer.

Jim Bakker and John Wesley Fletcher on the PTL set in Hawaii, January 1981, a month after Fletcher introduced Bakker to Jessica Hahn in Florida.

Credit: Flower Pentecostal Heritage Center.

Tammy in Hawaii in January 1981. Her smile belies the tension surrounding the trip.

Credit: Flower Pentecostal Heritage Center.

Bakker interviewing Kevin Whittum during a broadcast of the *PTL Club* in December 1981.

Credit: Flower Pentecostal Heritage Center.

5

The Emperor's New Groove

THE BEGINNING OF PTL's financial troubles can be dated to January 2, 1978, the day Jim Bakker broke ground on the Total Living Center at Heritage USA, and not coincidently his birthday. Through the end of 1977, PTL's accounts were current, and it had enough money coming in to meet its bills despite spectacular growth. In 1974, the Bakkers' first year in Charlotte, the ministry took in $239,670. During the first five months of 1977 it received more than $8 million in contributions. At the time the television show was seen on 165 stations and 2,500 cable systems across the country. Jim's salary that year was a modest $23,740 plus a housing allowance ($260 a month in 1976). Tammy earned an additional $150 a week for singing on the show and other activities. An audit by the Big Eight accounting firm of Haskins and Sells found "no irregularities or major bookkeeping errors," and a professor of accounting at the University of North Carolina at Charlotte gave PTL's bookkeeping practices a "very clean" bill of health.[1]

By early 1979 the network was spending about $1 million a month for airtime on 198 affiliate stations and the duplication of tapes used to distribute the show. At the same time, revenue was about $4 million a month. The television network easily turned a profit, even after accounting for payroll, facilities, and other related expenses. Jim Moss, who ran the affiliate department, later testified that he could not remember a station that did not at least break even. "All of our affiliates were producing. They were doing fine," Moss said. The profitability of the network allowed PTL to keep growing and Bakker to dream big.[2]

The result was Heritage USA. Buying the land for the vacation and retreat center strained the ministry's finances, but it was the pace of construction beginning in 1978 that pushed PTL's cash flow to the breaking point. PTL spent about $1.5 million for the first 1,200 acres straddling the North Carolina–South Carolina border. The cost of the first major project at Heritage USA, the Total Living Center (TLC), which initially included plans for a university, a campground, and a day school, was pegged at $100 million. Bakker wanted the complex dedicated on July 4, 1978, barely six months away. Jim Moss, who was PTL's executive vice president and second in authority to Bakker at the time, pleaded with him to string the project out and aim for July 4, 1979, or even 1980, but Bakker would not listen. "Of all the giddy, improbable developments of the last several years, none has captured Bakker's imagination more completely than the Total Living Center," noted the *Charlotte Observer*. "For sheer scope and opulence, it's tough to equal."[3]

That spring the Bakkers began taking weekend trips to Disney World, in part so that Jim could get ideas for developing Heritage USA. Eventually Bakker planned to add a hospital and nursing home. On the air he and his cohost, Henry Harrison, began saying that PTL stood for "People That Love," reflecting a more local focus on those in need. "This is the greatest project ever in the history of Christianity," Bakker declared as he broke ground on that January day.[4]

In order to push construction along as quickly as possible Bakker looked for a loan of about $50 million. Taking on this kind of debt seemed "ridiculous" to Moss, who argued that with a little patience the ministry could pay for construction out of its surplus revenue. In the end, no bank would loan PTL the kind of money Bakker was looking for. He pushed ahead with his building plans anyway.[5]

PTL hired the same general contractor that had built the Heritage Village complex, the Laxton Construction Company, to oversee construction of the TLC (for a time the ministry referred to it as the Positive Total Learning Center, evidently so that the initials would include PTL). Construction began in earnest in March. Jim Moss asked the Laxton managers how far they would allow PTL to fall behind in its payments during construction. Their limit was $300,000. "What if Mr. Bakker comes to you and pressures you to do more than that?" Moss asked. They could "stretch it" to $500,000 "if we had to," the Laxton representatives replied. By June PTL owed more than $2 million in unpaid construction costs. Bakker pleaded with his television audience that he needed at least $1 million by the end of the month to keep going. When Moss confronted the Laxton project managers as to why they had allowed things to get so out of hand, they replied, "Well, his personality overcomes us, you know, and he talks us into it." That August, Laxton had had enough and halted construction of the TLC until PTL could pay what it owed. Moss thought that Laxton got what it deserved.[6]

PTL not only ran up construction debt, it also fell behind in many of its other accounts as it struggled to pay for the massive building project. Bakker was "reaching out for every dime he could get," as Moss put it, but there just was not enough. The network began to miss payments to affiliate stations for airtime and to the employees' retirement funds. It also reneged on promises to support missions groups operating abroad, a failure that would soon embroil it in an FCC investigation. Bakker had earlier said that he wanted PTL to reach the point where it could give 95 percent of its income to world missions and operate on the remaining 5 percent. In reality, PTL was now giving only about 3 percent to missions.[7]

As PTL slid into financial crisis, the board of directors met on June 20, 1978. Those present included Jim Bakker, Jim Moss, Roger Flessing, James "Johnny" Johnson, a former Under Secretary of the Navy under Richard Nixon, A. T. Lawing, a local business owner, Forbes Barton, a Charlotte surgeon, attorney Q. Harold Caviness, and Herb Moore, PTL's Financial Director. Bakker told the board that he planned to fire sixty employees that week and another forty in two weeks. This was necessary because of "overhiring, duplication of jobs, unskilled people who have been hired with a hasty decision, and others who simp[ly] are unhappy at PTL and not willing to cooperate and be a part of the team," Bakker explained. At the time, the ministry had 690 employees on its payroll. Bakker also announced that they would quit publishing *Action* "because of the heavy expense involved." This was necessary despite the fact that PTL had taken in $3.4 million in May, twice what it had the year before. No one mentioned construction debts or challenged Bakker's reasoning.[8]

At the same meeting James Johnson brought up Bakker's salary, which at $700 a week was, in his opinion, "way too low." In most organizations the size of PTL, Bakker would be making $500,000 a year, Johnson argued. "Walter [C]ronkite makes $750,000 a year and he gives out bad news," Johnson quipped. Despite his misgivings about the budget, Moss agreed that Bakker's salary needed to be increased. Johnson made a motion to raise Bakker's salary to $1,000 a week, retroactive to May 15, 1978. Flessing seconded the motion, and the board unanimously approved. Flessing and Moss also got raises to $600 a week. No one questioned the incongruence of firing one hundred employees and giving board members a raise at the same time.[9]

Near the close of the meeting Bakker made a motion "that we make a policy that we no longer distribute financial information to the Press." The board gave its unanimous consent. Only six months before, *Action* had printed an audit of the ministry and the Bakkers' personal finances by the accounting firm Haskins and Sells. The audit, completed in August 1977, pegged the Bakker's personal net worth at $23,568. After paying $40,000 to Haskins and Sells, PTL abruptly suspended the 1978 audit before it was complete.[10]

After the firings, a number of former employees complained that they had been forced to work overtime without pay. Bakker was unapologetic. "The Lord spoke to me and advised me not to be slothful in business," he told a reporter. Bakker took particular notice of who showed up for unpaid Saturday work sessions at the Total Living Center, arguing that it provided "vivid illustration" of who was truly committed and who was not. A year later, PTL agreed to pay nearly three hundred past and present workers $34,045 in unpaid overtime wages after an investigation by the US Labor Department.[11]

Bakker's own commitment to building Heritage USA remained undaunted. He sometimes woke up at two or three in the morning, fumbled for a sheet of paper and sketched out a design for yet another building. After taping the television show each day "his afternoon is almost invariably spent at the site, slogging through ankle-deep mud and choking cheerfully on the Caterpillar dust," according to the *Observer*. Bakker decided everything, from where the roads should go to which trees to preserve. To his critics in the press, he had become "a Christian egomaniac suffering from an edifice complex."[12]

On July 14, 1978, a few weeks after the June board meeting, Bakker sent a memo to Herb Moore with the "demand" that "you only pay me $600" a week rather than the $1,000 the board had approved in June. PTL "is in no financial condition to pay this additional increase in my salary, and I therefore request that it be accrued on the books . . . until such time that our cash flow is in a positive position," Bakker wrote. Yet, as was so often the case, Bakker's restraint was short-lived. Only three weeks later he used $6,000 of PTL's money for a down payment on a houseboat, a 43-foot Drifter with two bedrooms, a kitchen, bathroom, television, and gas grill. The total price for the houseboat was $30,000. By the time the story broke that summer, local press coverage of PTL had turned decidedly negative.[13]

Allen Cowan, a new reporter at the *Charlotte Observer*, initially set out to write what he told Moss would be "a very positive, constructive article concerning the PTL Television Network." But as Cowan spent day after day at PTL in the early summer of 1978, he realized that all was not right. Cowan teamed up with veteran reporter Frye Gaillard, who had already written about Bakker and PTL, to publish a series of articles reporting on PTL's troubled finances and tensions within the ministry. Charlotte's other newspaper, the *Charlotte News*, likewise began printing a series of hard-hitting stories about the ministry beginning in the summer of 1978.[14]

By that time Bakker was using the emerging financial crisis to plead for more money from PTL's supporters through its mailing list of 700,000 "partners." "Unless God performs a financial miracle, this could be the last letter you will receive from me," he wrote to the partners in his August 1978 newsletter (which was actually written in July). Faced with a "$2,500,000 construction bill . . . Tammy and I are giving every penny of our life's savings to PTL," Bakker claimed. He wrote this at almost exactly the same time he bought the houseboat. In a follow-up "Special Message" Bakker wrote, "PTL is losing $100,000 to $200,000 a week. We cannot afford to go on much longer." Without a financial "miracle," the ministry would be forced to "close up to 95% of our foreign offices at a time when new doors of Gospel outreach are opening to us on five continents."[15]

But when questioned by reporters about the letters, Bakker said that "rather than having a financial crunch," PTL was only "experiencing growth pains." In fact, in early July contributions were running at an all-time high of $1.5 million a week, and PTL had hired back twenty-two of the sixty employees it fired the month before. A guest who had just arrived to appear on the show asked Bakker's brother, Norm, "What happened with that financial emergency?" There was no emergency, Norm cheerfully replied. It was just "a tool for people to rally around."

That summer and fall Bakker continued to portray PTL's financial situation as either a crisis or nothing to worry about, depending on his audience, though sometimes with unintended consequences. He wanted contributors to keep giving, but he also wanted vendors to keep extending credit. When Bakker declared on the air that the network might be forced to close if giving did not increase, the bank that processed its credit card transactions cancelled its contract with the ministry, afraid that it would be left holding bad debts. Bakker quickly backtracked, insisting that the bank did not "understand the stability of contributions."[16]

By the time Bakker left on his around-the-world trip in September 1978, the *Charlotte Observer* was reporting that the ministry had $4 million in bills due immediately. Bakker complained on air that PTL could not get a loan because banks refused to loan money to religious groups. Local lenders denied that this was the case, explaining instead that PTL was simply a "bad risk." Its land and buildings had limited use and would be difficult to sell, thus limiting their value as collateral, its new facilities would not earn enough to cover operating expenses and construction costs, and its "lack of disclosure" and "lack of investments or long-range planning" made PTL unpredictable. Even when PTL had been able to pay its bills, it had never built up a reserve. Between January 1 and May 31, 1977, before purchasing the land for Heritage USA, PTL took in more than $8 million in contributions. But on May 31 it had only $5,808 in cash. Now, with the bills for Heritage USA piling up, it had no reserve at all. "It's like a house of cards," said one analyst. "As long as the millions in pledges keep pouring in, PTL is OK. But that's an emotional issue, which could stop at any time. It's not the kind of sound, stable financial picture that makes lenders confident."[17]

When Bakker returned to Charlotte from overseas he claimed to have traced PTL's $4 million debt to a "computer problem," which left up to 400,000 letters sent by contributors unanswered. Bakker surmised that many had simply given up sending anything more when they did not receive receipts for previous contributions or gifts they had been promised. "There's no doubt about it. This is the problem. I know for sure," Bakker told the *Charlotte Observer*. He transferred employees from other areas of the ministry to help answer the mail, including "60 speed typists." Bakker was confident that the error, which he estimated had cost the ministry $13 million, could be quickly resolved.[18]

Yet PTL's financial problems persisted, pulled down by the cost of building the TLC. On November 3, 1978, PTL announced that it would not be able to meet its payroll, about $500,000 every two weeks for eight hundred employees. By then the *Charlotte Observer* was reporting that PTL "is behind more than $6 million in current bills and has a debt that exceeds $13 million." It owed the company that duplicated its tapes, NET Television of Ann Arbor, Michigan, more than $1 million, jeopardizing its ability to distribute the show nationwide. "We're within days of the network ceasing," Bakker told his television audience on November 3, 1978, wiping tears from his eyes. "I realized when I came to the studio today, this was my last opportunity to see this ministry survive. I'm not crying wolf. I'm facing facts," Bakker said.[19]

A few days after PTL failed to meet its payroll, the Charlotte newspapers reported that the ministry had been given a $195,000 house for the Bakkers to live in rent-free. It would replace a $79,000 house in an "exclusive" development on Lake Wylie that the Bakkers had purchased less than two years before, in July 1977. Harry Ranier, a wealthy supporter who had made a fortune in construction, coal, and real estate and also owned a NASCAR team, donated the house to PTL for the Bakkers' use. He and his wife, Juda, had been house hunting with Jim and Tammy when they spotted the house. "All four of us went out to look one night, saw it and liked it. So we bought it for them," Juda told a reporter. The ten-year-old, 4,500-square-foot home had four bedrooms, 3 ½ baths, a playroom, den, and two fireplaces. The November 14 article pointed out that at the time of the gift, PTL was "$6 million behind in current debts."[20]

In December Bakker pledged that PTL was on its way to putting its financial house in order. He announced that the ministry would begin 1979 by making a "surprise" payment of $1 million to the contractor who stopped work on the Total Living Center when PTL fell $2.5 million behind in its payments the previous summer. Bakker now told his studio audience that "PTL's problems were caused by unexpected growth and department supervisors' lack of managerial skills" and "pledged to control the situation in the new year," according to the *Charlotte Observer*. "We will not build buildings without money in the bank or financing from now on. There's no sense going broke in the middle of a miracle," Bakker said.[21]

Even if the financial crisis was over (and it wasn't), the fallout had long-term consequences for PTL. Conflict over the ministry's finances and its new focus on building Heritage USA "ripped apart the staff," as Jim Moss remembered it. The ministry's organizational structure had always been haphazard, though everyone understood that Bakker was ultimately in charge. PTL's board of directors met half a dozen times a year at most. In theory the board had the power to overrule Bakker, but it never did. There was also an executive committee that met with Bakker several times a week, if not daily. The size and makeup of the committee varied over time, though it usually included those at the top of PTL's leadership and closest to Bakker. While Moss, Flessing, and others sometimes "took issue" with Bakker during these meetings, in the end they did "whatever he determined," according to Moss. Those who objected too strenuously soon found themselves on the outside looking in. By the end of 1978, PTL had about a dozen vice presidents in charge of various aspects of the ministry. Within a year almost all of them would be gone.[22]

Among the first to go was PTL Vice President Bob Manzano, who was forced to resign on October 23, 1978, after more than a week of speculation that he was on his way out. Manzano had joined the ministry in March

1977 as editor of *Action*. His portfolio quickly expanded to include missions, land acquisition for Heritage USA, and the university. A reporter for the *Charlotte Observer* later described Manzano as "gracious, witty, erudite, perceptive, pompous, arrogant, and flamboyant in equal measure." PTL staffers called him Dr. Manzano, and Jim Moss later testified that Bakker "feared Dr. Manzano because Dr. Manzano is an educated man." His PTL bio sheet claimed that Manzano had an undergraduate degree from CCNY and a doctorate from UCLA. In fact, he had attended CCNY without graduating and never attended UCLA at all. Manzano's only advanced degree was from Union University of Los Angeles, a correspondence school targeting non-traditional students.[23]

Manzano represented himself as the grandson of a wealthy New York City developer, and Bakker joked, "He's our token rich boy." In fact, Manzano's parents had emigrated from Puerto Rico, and he was raised in some of New York City's less glamorous neighborhoods, including the Lower East Side and the neighborhood of Jamaica in Queens. Manzano used his allegedly affluent background to wheedle extra compensation from PTL. "I left my former life behind and came down here with a whole different attitude. But they [PTL officials] felt that it was not fair to leave that [his affluent lifestyle] behind," he told a reporter in September 1977. At the time, Manzano's base salary was $13,800 a year, but he had a housing allowance of $1,000 a month. This allowed him to buy a $131,500 home, which he and his wife filled with "Persian rugs, Tiffany lamps and hand-carved antique desks," noted a July 1978 article in the *Observer*.[24]

When PTL began diverting funds to build the TLC, Bakker blamed Manzano for failing to live up to PTL's promises to various missions organizations. Manzano had his allies, Moss among them, but not everyone at PTL trusted him. At the time of Manzano's resignation, another PTL vice president, Bill Perkins, wrote to Bakker that Manzano's departure was a "positive sign" because he had "caused embarrassment around the world and internal problems at home."[25] Manzano had indeed managed to alienate several overseas groups he dealt with, including Cho in Korea and Elias Malki, a missionary to whom PTL had pledged support to build a radio transmitter on Cyprus. Still, Moss concluded, "Bob could do no more than Mr. Bakker would allow him to do. . . . He used Dr. Manzano as his scapegoat."[26]

Bakker called Moss from Singapore in September 1978 during his around-the-world trip and told him to fire Manzano, who, Bakker said, had become "a rascal." Moss refused. "Well, if you won't do it, I will do it when I get back," Bakker replied. Moss "knew he wouldn't do it when he got back here." It was not Bakker's style to confront anyone face to face. Instead, "he assigned the project to Mr. Flessing," according to Moss. Flessing, who distrusted Manzano and had clashed with him over missions projects, complied. Manzano asked for, and apparently received, a severance package of $24,900.[27]

The *Charlotte Observer* characterized Manzano's forced resignation as a symptom of the growing tensions at PTL. On October 14, the newspaper reported that Manzano's "impending departure is symptomatic of management problems that have plagued the Charlotte-based religious television network for much of this year." Ten days later Manzano told the newspaper that the "problems in his department were the result of Bakker's tendency to launch projects PTL couldn't afford." Few at PTL would have disagreed.[28]

Manzano's departure probably helped PTL more than it hurt, but Roger Flessing's was another story. Flessing had joined Bakker at Trinity Broadcasting in California in 1972. When Bakker came to Charlotte in 1974, Flessing stayed in California working in commercial television. Flessing rejoined Bakker at PTL in Charlotte in January 1976, quickly becoming one of the central figures in the network's development. By the end of 1978, he was a senior vice president, a member of the board, and as close to Bakker as anyone.

Flessing brought a creative edge to the ministry, but without Bakker's insecurity. Flessing had been a driving force behind a number of key innovations at PTL, including creating the satellite network, expanding into Korea and the rest of Asia, and developing new programming beyond the talk show. He also had a way of using humor to defuse tense situations and otherwise make his point. "Flessing is the staff iconoclast—part clown, part intellectual; an ambitious political liberal who believes evangelical Christianity has suffered in the past from intolerance and from a basic indifference to the world's social problems," noted a July 1978 article in the *Charlotte Observer*. At the same time, his rise at PTL was "tainted by an atmosphere of anger, suspicion and assorted other un-Christian nastiness—all of which seems at odds with his genial demeanor." Wherever he went, Flessing stirred things up.[29]

As recently as September and October 1978, Flessing had been part of the entourage that accompanied Bakker on his around-the-world trip. That November, Flessing traveled to Japan to "finalize plans for our Asian Network," as Bakker wrote in his monthly newsletter. But when Flessing returned to Charlotte, Bakker informed him that he was diverting funds designated for Korea to a pay for construction at Heritage USA. "I quit," Flessing immediately told him. "I felt strongly that we didn't need another building, we needed to put our money where the real ministry was and that was in international television," which was just beginning to take off. Despite everything that PTL had committed to overseas programming, Bakker was determined to shift as much of PTL's money as he could get his hands on to what was quickly becoming the ministry's primary focus, Heritage USA. Flessing understood that this represented a seismic shift in the nature of PTL's mission and wanted no part of it, though he was initially more circumspect with the Charlotte newspapers, saying only that he wanted to "reassess personal priorities."[30]

Flessing's resignation, dated November 28, took effect December 8, 1978. After quitting PTL, he went to New York City at Christmas to visit a friend and look for jobs. He got an offer to be an associate producer on CBS's *Sports Spectacular*, but his wife did not want to move to New York, so they returned to Sacramento instead, where Flessing took a job as program director for the local CBS station.[31]

As the year drew to a close, the wave of resignations from Bakker's inner circle continued. Alex Valderama, another PTL vice president and at the time an executive producer of the television show, resigned on December 4, 1978, effective at the end of the month. Valderama, thirty-two, had been with Bakker since the Trinity Broadcasting days in California. Like Flessing, he was dismayed at the change in Bakker's priorities, particularly with respect to the arts. "If there is to be communication between culture and counter culture or between the Christian community and the surrounding society, it is imperative that we listen to the voice of the artists and writers who are sensitive to our way of life," Valderama wrote in his letter of resignation. This now seemed less a possibility at PTL than it had only a few months before.[32]

WHAT TROUBLED BILL Perkins was not the arts but the money. Perkins joined PTL in April 1977, leaving a better paying job at Sandia National Laboratories in Livermore, California, where he was only five years away from retirement, to head up PTL's Finance and Accounting Department. Perkins had been treasurer of his Assemblies of God church in California and "already deeply involved in the Lord's work," as he put it, when he accepted Bakker's offer to move to Charlotte. "I had High expectations of making a substantial personal contribution to the ministry," Perkins later wrote. "I was given the charge to make the financial operation 'so clean it squeaks,' and proceeded on that premise."[33]

Bakker got more than he bargained for in Perkins. Perkins combined a keen sense of high moral purpose with the meticulous eye of an experienced accountant. His idea of squeaky-clean and Bakker's were not nearly the same. "He was brilliant," remembers Roger Flessing. "We didn't have financial controls before. . . . He brought in the right kinds of financial accountability and integrity." The result was "tough for Jim," who had been used to spending whatever he wanted, regardless of the ministry's account balances.[34]

As PTL's finances began to unravel in the summer of 1978, Perkins became increasingly alarmed. He was dismayed that PTL had delayed its $35,000 monthly payments to the employees' retirement plan for March, April, and May 1978 until that summer and then discontinued the plan. As of October 9, 1978, it had not made payments to the new retirement plan for June, July, and August 1978. Worse, Herb Moore, PTL's director of finance, whom Perkins had largely been responsible for hiring, kept insisting that newspaper reports about the missed payments were in error. Perkins knew better.[35]

When the story broke about Bakker using $6,000 of PTL's money to buy a houseboat, Perkins confronted Moore. Moore told him that as long as the money was paid back within a year it could be considered a loan and therefore "perfectly legal." Perkins disagreed. He suggested that it would have been better for the board to give Bakker the money outright as a bonus. Moore replied that "there wasn't any way he could have gotten Board approval in one day and Jim wanted the boat that day." Most disturbing from Perkins's perspective, Moore told him "he didn't feel it was wrong to bend ethics a little if it was necessary." He reminded Perkins, "None of us would even have a job at PTL if it wasn't for Jim Bakker." Perkins persisted, telling Moore "someone is going to have to say 'No!' or at least 'Wait!'" when it was for Bakker's own good. But telling Bakker no was not a part of the culture at PTL by this time. "Hero is not too strong a word to use to describe the way the people at the network feel about Bakker," noted an article in the *Charlotte News*. Perkins was one of the few people at PTL who never really understood this.[36]

Moore attempted to fire Perkins on Friday, October 6, 1978, offering him one month's salary as severance. Perkins replied that Moore had no authority to fire him since they were both vice presidents and reported to Bakker. Perkins took his case directly to Bakker the following Monday in the form of a seven-page memo. Bakker tried to appease Perkins by offering him the position of treasurer of the World Missions Division. But before taking the new position Perkins wanted to meet with Bakker personally to discuss his concerns. After waiting nine hours for an appointment one day, an exasperated Perkins sent Bakker another long memo outlining his reservations about how the ministry was being run.[37]

"It would be much, much easier to accept yet another position and remain silent or just leave and pretend the last nineteen months never existed, but God won't let me," Perkins wrote to Bakker on October 17, 1978. PTL was not dealing honestly or honorably with people it owed money to, Perkins bluntly told Bakker. "CREDITORS, SUPPLIERS, AND ANYONE ON STAFF WHO NEEDS MONEY FROM THE ACCOUNTING DEPARTMENT HAVE BEEN LIED TO, AVOIDED, IGNORED, AND TREATED IN ANYTHING BUT A CHRISTIAN MANNER," Perkins wrote.

> I have witnessed suppliers in person and on the phone begging to be paid to save their business only to receive a calloused, unsympathetic response. We have even lied to them! The shifting and maneuvering within the accounting department has made it impossible for any one person to be knowledgeable of the true status of our position with any given creditor. One person will tell the creditor that the check has been prepared, letting them assume it is on the way. When the creditor calls again and says they haven't received the check, they most likely talk to someone else who would then say, "Oh, you must have misunderstood, it was typed but is awaiting signatures."

Perkins told Bakker that he would remain at PTL only if he could be sure that these problems would be fixed. "I await your direct, *personal* response," Perkins wrote to Bakker. After waiting nearly eight weeks for a reply, Perkins had had enough. He resigned on December 11, 1978, and moved to Albuquerque.[38]

In his earlier memo to Bakker, on October 9, Perkins clearly articulated what many were beginning to see as the central problem at PTL. He reminded Bakker that the "last real time of unity among the executive staff" had been at a staff retreat on Kiawah Island, near Charleston, South Carolina, in November 1977, "before we even budgeted for the purchase of the land" for Heritage USA. "Since we have taken on the TLC project with all its diverse applications, we have had conflicts, confusion and total disintegration of executive unity," Perkins wrote. "Why not concentrate on the thing that God called you to do—spreading the gospel by television around the world—and let others do those things that they are best suited to do. If we tackle too many diversified projects, aren't we likely to become mediocre or ineffective in all of them?" This was essentially the same point that Flessing had tried to make when he resigned.[39]

But it was not what Bakker wanted to hear, and he took steps to ensure that no one inside PTL could force him to adopt the more measured approach that Perkins advocated. No sooner had Perkins and Flessing left in early December than Bakker called a meeting of the board on December 14, 1978, to revise PTL's by-laws. The new by-laws made Bakker President, Chief Executive Officer, and General Manager of PTL for life, with the power to appoint his successor. He could be removed only if convicted of a felony, declared mentally incompetent, or for "immoral" conduct "as declared by a competent court of law."[40]

On top of everything else, plans for the university were unraveling. Heritage University had been the centerpiece of Bakker's plans for the new complex from the beginning. A university offered the allure of status and respectability that Bakker and his audience craved and a powerful rationale for fundraising. It also promised to put Bakker in the same league as Oral Roberts, who started Oral Roberts University in 1965, Jerry Falwell, who founded Liberty University in 1971, and Pat Robertson, who was in the process of creating Regent University. As always, Bakker was anxious to keep up with Robertson. Local newspapers reported that PTL's "liberal arts college" would have twelve thousand students and a basketball team. Heritage University would be "the most important project in PTL's history," Bakker told his supporters.[41]

Announcements about Heritage University figured prominently in PTL promotional literature during the first half of 1978. The February 1978 edition of *Action* reported that the university would be "one of the first complexes . . . built" at Heritage USA and would eventually include classroom buildings, dorms, and a football stadium straddling the North Carolina–South Carolina border. By March, Bakker had hired an executive dean of the university, Dr. Brooks Sanders, previously the director of educational technology at Broome Community College in Binghamton, New York. He also hired a dean of the School of Communications, Dr. Donald Barnhouse, a former professor of communications at Drexel University, and a dean of students, Dr. Thurnace York. Sanders predicted that the school would be an accredited four-year university within five years. Someone at PTL convinced Charles Malik, a former Lebanese ambassador to the United States and the United Nations, to join the school's Board of Regents. Malik visited the site that spring to review construction plans. In May Bakker claimed that he had already turned down ten thousand students who were anxious to enroll.[42]

Nevertheless, Bakker's enthusiasm for the school quickly waned. It opened in September 1978 with three hundred students in makeshift facilities. In January 1979 students were told to transfer if they wanted to earn a degree. Bakker was still calling the school "our college" in the fall of 1979, but by then PTL promotional literature and television spots referred to it only as the Heritage School of Evangelism and Communications. Two of the three original deans were also gone. Barnhouse had been fired even before the school opened, and Sanders resigned in January 1979.[43]

Television promos aired at the end of the *PTL Club* in the summer and fall of 1979 offered prospective students internships in eight areas: TV Production, Broadcast Technology, Writing, Graphic Arts, Performance, Music, Counseling, and Missions. This covered most of what PTL was involved in at the time, but it hardly constituted a college education. The internships required only eleven months to complete. By June 1980 there were only about one hundred students left in the internship programs. Only two years before, in early 1978, Bakker had said that students would be able to study topics as diverse as agriculture and medicine at the university, and that dorms for three hundred students were already under construction. He appealed for "1,000 sponsors, who will give $1,000 each to help me build the Heritage University and School of Evangelism." In the end, very little of it was ever completed.[44]

PTL's grade school managed to open on September 6, 1978, with 21 teachers and 250 to 300 students, most of them children of PTL staffers. Delays in the construction of the TLC forced classes to initially meet under shade trees and in trolley cars and tents. Financial pressures forced the school to close in June 1980. The school lacked "appropriate facilities," and PTL did not have the money to build them, according to Ed Stoeckel, PTL's new general manager. Closing the school was part of an "overall reassessment of PTL's priorities," Stoeckel said.[45]

The four-hundred-acre campground, Fort Heritage, part of the original plan for Heritage USA, opened on July 4, 1978, at first without electricity because PTL had yet to secure county and state approval to occupy most of the complex. Bakker opened the campground by cutting a log instead of a ribbon, the first time he had ever used a chainsaw, which was obvious. A twenty-five-foot-tall plastic moose stood next to the general store, and a sign on the winding two-mile drive leading to the campground read "Speed Checked by God."[46]

As Bakker would soon discover, God was not the only one concerned with upholding the law at PTL.

6

Look Me in the Eye

THE NEW YEAR started on a promising note. Jim Bakker celebrated his thirty-ninth birthday on January 2, 1979, "by paying nearly $660,000 in overdue bills and promising financial conservatism for the Charlotte-based religious television ministry in 1979," according to the *Charlotte Observer*. Laxton Construction got $300,000, satisfying their lien against the ministry, though nine other liens remained in place. PTL had spent $10 million on the Total Living Center so far. The current payments reduced the ministry's immediate debts to less than $2 million. "We have a real feeling of maturity and stability greater than we've ever had before," Bakker said. He celebrated on the show that day with guests Pat and Shirley Boone and their four daughters, including Debbie Boone, twenty-two, who the year before had the number one song in the country for two months, "You Light Up My Life."[1]

Then the bottom fell out. On January 18, the *Observer* ran two feature articles by Allen Cowan and Frye Gaillard accusing PTL of deception and fraud. The front-page stories drew on interviews with Roger Flessing, Bill Perkins, and Robert Manzano, all of whom had left PTL within the last three months. Each said that they still considered Bakker a friend and spoke "reluctantly and with anguish." Manzano even sent a retraction the next day, saying that he did not know his comments, made to Cowan on January 2, would be part of a larger story. The *Observer* articles signaled a new level of conflict between Bakker and the press that would eventually draw the attention of federal authorities.[2]

The *Observer* stories attacked Bakker on two levels. More generally, they accused him of deception and poor management. More specifically, they claimed that PTL had diverted "hundreds of thousands of dollars contributed for specific overseas missions programs, using the money to finance other projects and pay its bills at home." The first spoke to PTL's corporate culture. The second potentially broke the law.[3]

What began as a "family-style religious venture" had "burgeoned into a multi-million dollar corporation," noted the *Observer*. PTL's leaders had little experience with the "secular world" and tended to distrust "banks and newspapers." Employees were allowed to write IOUs and borrow money from PTL donations. They took collections home to be counted. The ministry had twenty-four petty-cash accounts, including "one in Bakker's office which his wife, Tammy, used at times for personal expenses." Often these accounts were never reconciled.[4]

But there was more to it than just sloppy accounting. Bakker and other PTL executives liked to say that PTL had twenty million viewers. They claimed that this made it the world's most watched television show and more popular than Johnny Carson, who had 8.5 million viewers. The *Charlotte Observer* itself had routinely repeated the twenty million figure at the bottom of its stories about PTL in 1978, as had the *Charlotte News*. A July 1978 article in *Christian Life*, written by Jeff Park, managing editor of *Action*, pegged PTL's audience at twenty-five million. Manzano, PTL's first public relations director, now admitted that he had simply made the number up. It was a "total fabrication," Manzano said. The television rating agencies Arbitron and Nielsen estimated PTL's audience at no more than 1.3 million.[5]

Bakker initially admitted the mistake, saying that they had relied on the inflated figure, "because we run a very sloppy organization. We have been mismanaged. It will be corrected. It will be corrected." But in a pattern that would become all too familiar, Bakker quickly backtracked and defended PTL's original estimate. In a response printed in the *Charlotte Observer*, he claimed that PTL represented "specialty programming" that Nielson and Arbitron failed to accurately measure. Assuming one thousand viewers for every piece of mail PTL received per month yielded a viewership of two hundred million. Taking a "conservative 10 percent" of that figure indicated an audience of twenty million. Bakker gave no further evidence to substantiate these estimates. By the end of the year, PTL lowered its own estimate of viewers to "3 million to 5 million people daily in all 50 states and 37 countries."[6]

The *Observer* stories pounded away at Bakker's credibility, with example after example adding weight to the notion that he could not be trusted to tell the truth. Readers now learned that at the same time Jim and Tammy were pledging to give "every penny of our life's savings to PTL," in the summer of 1978, Bakker used $6,000 of PTL's money as a down payment on his new houseboat. Bakker had also told the *Observer* that he was taking a pay cut when in fact he was only deferring his recent raise. He further claimed on the air that he could not afford the property taxes on the $195,000 house Harry Rainer had donated to PTL for the Bakkers' use the previous year. At the time, property taxes on the house were $187 a month. PTL gave Bakker a housing allowance of $800 a month. Bakker later said he meant he could not afford the gift taxes. Federal and state laws made paying gift taxes the donor's responsibility, which Rainer said he was happy to do.[7]

Relying on Perkins as its source, the paper reported that PTL had not sent money collected from employees to its retirement fund for "at least six months in 1978" but instead used the money to pay bills. The ministry had also "stalled and misled creditors by postdating checks or mailing them without signatures or stamps on the envelope," reported the *Observer*. "We lied to them, we gave them the runaround," Perkins told the paper. "We're proud of our television show. We should be proud of our business operations. We're not." The overall effect was to make Bakker and the ministry look conniving and dishonest.[8]

As bad as all of this was, legally the more damaging information had to do with diverting contributions. Over the course of eighteen months, beginning in the summer of 1977, PTL reportedly diverted $337,000 in donations earmarked for missions projects in Korea, Cyprus, and Brazil. The biggest failure involved Korea.[9]

When Dr. Yonggi Cho first appeared on the *PTL Club* in February 1977 his church in Seoul had about fifty thousand members and was growing by two hundred members a week. When Cho returned to the *PTL Club* in June 1977, Bakker offered to partner with him to launch a Korean version of the *PTL Club*. In August, PTL Senior Vice President Roger Flessing traveled to Korea to meet with Cho, who agreed to donate a 3,000-seat gym for use as a television studio. Cho also secured airtime from the Korean government and agreed that PTL could place two of its board members on the board of PTL Korea. In return, PTL agreed to supply television cameras, color videotape recorders, and a remote videotape truck, worth a total of $500,000, all to be shipped to Korea.[10]

Meanwhile Bakker was busy soliciting contributions for the Korean initiative over the air and through newsletters. In his August 1977 newsletter, Bakker breathlessly informed PTL's partners that the Korean and Japanese broadcasts would "begin . . . in a matter of days!" This was a considerable exaggeration given what little had actually been done. That November, after Flessing returned from Korea, Bakker informed the partners that he had just signed an agreement with Cho's church. "As I signed the document to complete the television studios for Dr. Cho, who pastors the largest church in the entire world, I knew that you were signing it with me because I could never fulfill the agreement without your support. I need your support so much!"[11]

In fact, PTL never shipped the promised equipment to Korea. By the spring of 1978, Bakker's staff had discovered that television equipment sent to Korea would be subject to a 100 percent tax, effectively doubling the cost. In June 1978, Bakker informed the partners that there had been delays in getting the equipment promised to Cho "out of the country because of international shipping problems. These things happen." As PTL dragged its feet looking for a way to avoid the extra expense, Bakker lost interest in the project as his attention shifted to building Heritage USA. Despite collecting $281,000 for the project, PTL never sent "even a dollar" to Korea, as Cho told the *Observer*.[12]

During his around-the-world trip in September 1978, Bakker was "shaken by the resentment toward PTL he encountered," particularly in Korea, according to Flessing, who accompanied Bakker on the trip. When Bakker met Cho in Seoul he tried to placate the Korean minister, assuring him that the promised equipment "was on the loading dock waiting to be shipped." But Cho had lost patience. "Cho was upset," remembered Flessing. "He told Bakker, 'I don't want your equipment. Send it to Japan . . .' And, of course, there was no equipment on the loading dock." Bakker nevertheless wrote to PTL's partners in October 1978 that he was still "making final arrangements for equipping the Korean studio."[13]

The story in Brazil was much the same. PTL's initiative in Brazil was channeled through Robert McAlister, a missionary to Brazil for the past eighteen years with family ties to Charlotte. His daughter was one of the first students admitted to Heritage University. When McAlister appeared on the *PTL Club* in October 1977, Bakker promised to help launch a Brazilian version the show. As in Korea, the initial plan was for McAlister to build a studio and PTL to provide color cameras and a videotape remote truck worth about $400,000. When Jim Moss and Robert Manzano visited Brazil in late 1977 to make arrangements, McAlister suggested that instead of building and equipping a facility, it would make more sense to rent a local studio and begin production immediately. Moss and Manzano agreed, and PTL promised to send McAlister $50,000 a month for three months to kick-start the show. PTL eventually sent McAlister about $11,000 worth of cameras and equipment and $10,000 cash in the spring of 1978 but nothing close to the promised $150,000. When Moss asked why, he was told that PTL no longer had the money.[14]

While Bakker was on his way to Singapore, he heard that McAlister was also planning to attend the Singapore conference, scheduled for September 11–17. Anxious to avoid embarrassment, Bakker called Manzano at his home in Charlotte and ordered him to immediately fly to Singapore with a $50,000 check for McAlister. Manzano did as he was told, but McAlister never showed, and PTL never gave him the money. When the *Observer* contacted McAlister in January 1979, he said that he had not "heard from PTL since he received the $10,000." Did he expect the rest of the $150,000? "That was eight months ago. I guess I'm not expecting it any more, no," McAlister replied.[15]

After he returned home, Bakker blamed Manzano for PTL's failure to fulfill its commitments to overseas missions. Bakker's contention that he did not know the depth of the problem until he traveled around the world was an "unmitigated lie," according to Manzano.

Finally, there was Cyprus. When Elias Malki appeared on the *PTL Club* on November 28, 1977, he described his plans to build a radio transmitter on Cyprus to broadcast the gospel throughout the Middle East. Bakker immediately offered to help. "Even while this magazine is being printed, we are flying to Cypress at the invitation of the Cypress government to set up an AM transmitter on that island, which will reach the entire Arab-Israeli world with the Gospel through radio (including several hundred million Moslem followers in that area)," Bakker wrote in the January 1978 edition of *Action*. In fact, it was Manzano who flew to the Middle East, where he concluded that Malki's "project was not well conceived" and PTL "should search for an alternative project in the Mideast."[16]

By the time the story about diverted funds broke in the *Observer* on January 18, 1979, PTL had collected $56,000 designated for the Cyprus transmitter but had not sent any of it to Malki. As it happened, Malki was scheduled to appear on the television show the next day. That morning Bakker decided to cancel Malki's appearance, which had been scheduled several months in advance, and have Jim Moss give him a check for $56,000 in private. Malki was not included in the list of guests announced by Henry Harrison during the show's on-air introduction.[17]

But when Moss offered Malki the check back stage, he would not take it. "I don't know what is going on," he told Moss. From the moment he arrived, Malki had been surrounded by PTL security trying to keep him from talking to reporters. "I have been handled around here today like I am some spy or something," Moss remembered Malki telling him. During the break between the first and second hour of the show, Moss worked out a compromise. Bakker agreed to present the check to Malki on the air but gave "instructions to rush him out of the studio as quickly as possible. And believe me, it was done in great fashion. And I don't believe [President] Carter's people . . . could handle it any better," Moss said. Malki's appearance on the show lasted less than ten minutes, and he was gone before the final credits rolled.[18]

As the controversy over diverting funds unfolded, Bakker further consolidated his control over PTL. On February 14, 1979, he fired executive vice president and board member Jim Moss, who had done more than anyone to bring PTL and the Bakkers to Charlotte and build the network. Moss had been trying to convince Bakker to form a "brain trust" of Christian leaders from around the country to help guide PTL, an idea that Bakker had no interest in. With his affable manner and easy ability to persuade others, Moss was the only real threat to Bakker's authority on the board. Indeed, only days before members of the board had tried to convince Moss to fire Bakker while he was out of town and Moss was technically in charge of ministry. Moss refused. "If you want him fired you do it collectively as a board of directors. You're not going to put that on me," Moss told them.[19]

At the February 14 meeting, Bakker countered by demanding that the board fire Moss, but they remained silent, reluctant to act. Moss likewise refused to resign "from the ministry God gave me." "If you all side with Jim Moss today, then I am out of here. I will resign and you will be left with a $16 million debt," Moss remembers Bakker threatening. When it was clear that the rest of the board would not stand up to Bakker, Moss turned to him and said, "Jim, look me in the eye, be a man and ask me to resign like a man." Bakker would not do it. He kept staring "down at the floor behind his desk" refusing to look up until Moss finally left.[20]

By March 1979, PTL was sliding back into financial disarray. In a staff meeting on Wednesday, March 7, Bakker announced that he would lay off as many as two hundred employees, a quarter of PTL's workforce. Contributions, which peaked at $1.6 million a week in 1978, had fallen off after the first of the year following a wave of negative news stories. The ministry now faced $10 million in immediate bills. Along with the prospect of layoffs, the swimming pool in the basement of the Heritage Village complex was boarded up, employee athletic programs were eliminated, the executive dining room was closed, and free busing for children attending the grade school, which had reopened, ended. Bakker declared March "Miracle Month" and redoubled his pleas for money from supporters.[21]

A WEEK LATER news broke that the FCC was launching an investigation into whether PTL had diverted approximately $337,000 raised for missions to pay other bills, as reported by the *Observer* in January. It is against FCC rules to raise money over the air for one purpose and then spend it on something else. The FCC had no jurisdiction over content producers, but it could punish the owners of any station that broadcast offending shows. This included PTL by virtue of its purchase of a television station in Canton, Ohio, the only station it owned at the time. PTL bought the station, WJAN, Channel 17, for $2.5 million in August 1977. WJAN was one of the first three stations to carry PTL programming and remained a center of support for the show. When it went up for sale, Bakker was afraid that he would lose access to its market. Roger Wilson, who had worked with Bakker since the CBN days, warned him that purchasing the station would bring a new level of scrutiny. Wilson had an FCC license and knew what dealing with the agency entailed. "You don't want to get in bed with the FCC," Wilson told Bakker. "You can produce all the programs you want and they can't touch you ... but when you run a TV station, it's a whole 'nother animal." Bakker bought the station anyway.[22]

Bakker responded to the FCC investigation by denouncing "the lies ... propagated by the enemies of the ministry," including the media. "I believe if we are forced off the air it will be the saddest day in the history of this nation," Bakker said. He also refused to hand over tapes of the program. He claimed that agents had arrived unannounced, "accompanied by shouts and threats," and "demanded within twenty-four hours" three hundred hours of tapes, which would take "three months to prepare" and "cost more than one hundred thousand dollars" to produce. It was, Bakker declared, "a major assault against the constitutional rights of PTL." In a newsletter to supporters, mailed that May, Bakker compared the FCC to Hitler and communist Russia. "They gained control because the good people, the Christians, didn't take a stand. There are leaders in our country today that would want to bring all religion under government control and take everything that speaks of morality and decency off of television," Bakker wrote.[23]

Officials at the FCC were dumbfounded by Bakker's "outrageous" behavior. Arthur Ginsburg, chief of the FCC's compliance and complaints division, told reporters that he had sent two staff members to PTL, one a lawyer and the other an agency veteran whose professionalism was "beyond reproach." Neither made demands of the sort that Bakker claimed. After being questioned by the FCC investigators, Robert Manzano told the *Observer* that the agent in question was "a spirit-filled Christian," who was "sympathetic to PTL's goals." From the viewpoint of the FCC, none of its requests were unreasonable. In fact, in a string of twenty-five separate cases over more than forty years, the FCC had clearly established its jurisdiction over stations that broadcast religious programs. "The PTL objections are without merit," concluded a law professor who examined the case as it unfolded. Bakker's belligerence eliminated any possibility of a compromise with the FCC.[24]

Much of Bakker's defiance toward the FCC and the press was designed to motivate his supporters to give more, to convince them that nothing short of heroic action could save Christian television, maybe the nation itself. But behind the scenes Bakker realized that PTL needed help. In April he agreed to step away from day-to-day management and turn PTL's finances over to a new executive vice president and general manager. "I was wearing too many hats," Bakker told reporters at the time. "Every corporation reaches the point when, if the founder-manager doesn't allow others to take over, it will be a disaster." "We were operating above our own managerial capabilities," Bakker added a few months later, in July 1979. "We knew a little about television . . . but we just couldn't run this thing anymore as a mom-and-pop operation."[25]

One of the immediate casualties of PTL's belt tightening was Elmer Bueno, host of PTL's popular Latin American show, who resigned from the ministry in June 1979. Bueno's one-hour weekly show was seen by an audience of up to thirty-five million viewers in thirteen Latin American countries: Guatemala, Honduras, Nicaragua, Costa Rica, Panama, Venezuela, Ecuador, Peru, Chile, the Dominican Republic, Netherlands Antilles, El Salvador, and parts of Mexico, according to the *Charlotte Observer*. In comparison, the American show, available daily on about 200 stations in the United States and Canada, had an estimated audience of 1.3 million people. Fundraising was not allowed on Latin American telecasts, so Bueno had to find other avenues of support.[26]

In early 1979 PTL told Bueno that it could no longer afford the $150,000 he needed to hold rallies in various countries to raise support, nor could it pay $15,000 a month for ten offices he ran in Latin American countries to do follow-up work. Bueno offered to raise this money independently if PTL would continue producing the show in Charlotte and buying air time, services valued at $1.6 million, though the incremental cost of producing the Latin American show alongside the American show was minimal. PTL refused and Bueno resigned, "extremely frustrated" that he had been unable to get an appointment with Bakker for the previous five months. "I don't think I was ever able to completely explain or express where I was coming from. Decisions were made without the full information," Bueno told reporters. PTL eventually hired a new host of the Latin American show, Juan Romero, but Bueno's departure represented another step away from PTL's roots in television evangelism.[27]

Bakker's choice to reorganize PTL was Ed Stoeckel, who was recommended by a new member of the ministry's board, Richard Dortch. Stoeckel, who became PTL's general manager on April 9, 1979, was an excellent choice for the job. Stoeckel, fifty-four, had grown up near St. Louis. He had an engineering background and had worked his way up the corporate ladder during a nineteen-year career at Ralston Purina. Stoeckel promised that he would not be a "yes-man," and he lived up to his own billing. He fired Herb Moore, who had clashed with Bill Perkins over the ethics of PTL's accounting. He suggested selling Heritage USA and leasing back the buildings PTL needed, a proposal that stunned Bakker, but he could not find a buyer.

Under Stoeckel's direction, by July PTL was current on all its bills and operating within the limits of the $3 million it took in in monthly contributions. "We don't begin a new project until we have financing, or until the money is in hand," said John Franklin, PTL's new finance manager and a part of Stoeckel's management team. Stoeckel's no-nonsense approach reduced much of the political infighting among PTL's senior leadership. "Jim's biggest problem as a manager was his tendency to take disagreements personally," said one longtime staffer. "As a result, people were inclined to tell Jim only what he wanted to hear."[28]

Under Stoeckel and Franklin, PTL returned to the practice of releasing financial information. From June through August 1979, the network took in just over $8 million. Its immediate bills totaled nearly $6.5 million, while its short-term assets, those that could be easily converted to cash, were slightly less than $2.2 million, not including uncollected pledges. PTL's total assets, including buildings and property, totaled more than $27 million.[29]

Stoeckel also implemented a new approach to dealing with the FCC and the press. Bakker himself became more "mellow and expansive" in public interviews. The new strategy for dealing with the FCC involved taking a less belligerent stance and marshaling evidence that "PTL's intentions were honorable," even if its follow-through was sloppy. In May, the ministry sent $300,000 to the Assemblies of God foreign missions department to start television ministries in Japan and Thailand, rather than Korea, since Cho was no longer interested in working with PTL. (Bakker nonetheless told 700,000 supporters in his July 1979 newsletter that PTL had sent "a large check to Dr. Yonggi Cho," which Cho denied when contacted by reporters.) This donation, along with the money already disbursed for Cyprus and Brazil, meant that PTL had now given away all of the money it collected specifically for these projects (contributions for Brazil fell far short of the $150,000 PTL had promised for that initiative).[30]

The FCC investigation ground forward all the same. The first witness summoned by the commission on June 22, 1979, was Robert Manzano, who was questioned by FCC attorney Lawrence Bernstein. Bernstein had worked in advertising before earning a law degree and joining the FCC in 1973. Manzano testified that he kept Bakker up to date on PTL's problems, but he also bragged about his background, claiming that he spoke five languages, had visited eighty-six countries, and held a doctorate.[31]

Bill Perkins and Jim Moss followed Manzano. Perkins's testimony reiterated much of what he had written to Bakker in his earlier memos. Moss was more equivocal, painting a picture of good intentions undermined by haphazard management. He told the hearing that Bakker never pre-interviewed guests and that the show was "totally spontaneous." In general Bakker was "totally unfamiliar with the guest that is going to be on if he has never had them before," Moss said. Was it any surprise that Bakker would make spontaneous financial commitments on the air, since everything else was done on the fly? Moss clearly implied it was not.[32]

Moss testified that he and Perkins tried to keep Bakker informed about PTL's financial deterioration, but Bakker would not listen, in part because he did not want to know and in part because he did not completely trust his staff. Bakker "always felt someone was trying to take over" the ministry, Moss said. "He is a very paranoid type personality and even schizophrenic." With regard to funds designated for specific projects, Moss testified that he and Manzano had warned Bakker not to ignore contributors' instructions.[33]

This was the same warning that Bill Perkins had sounded in his October 9, 1978, memo to Bakker, shortly before he left PTL. At the time, PTL accountant Dean Blackburn told Perkins that Herb Moore had instructed his staff "to stop source coding designated contributions and to destroy all the records we had with designations." "If it were me I would not destroy any records," Perkins advised Blackburn. "So long as we solicit contributions on TV and in our letters for specific projects, we should record designated giving and show them in our books as a payable (which clearly shows intent to live up to our commitments)," Perkins wrote to Bakker. This would protect against accusations "of soliciting funds under false pretenses." Perkins account was later corroborated by Sandy Stevens, PTL's head cashier, and Shelby Jeffcoat, head of PTL's correspondence department, both of whom acknowledged that they had been told to stop recording designations.[34]

In the wake of testimony from Manzano, Perkins, and Moss, PTL went to court in July in an attempt to block the FCC's investigation. The ministry's lawyer, John Midlen, argued that the ministry had not committed fraud because it had a good reason to divert the funds in question. US District Court Judge George Hart, Jr. only laughed. "A bank robber might have a good reason, too," Hart told Midlen. The judge dismissed PTL's suit in a proceeding that lasted only forty-five minutes. A week later PTL filed a request to open the FCC hearings to the public, again unsuccessfully.[35]

Bakker's testimony before the FCC began on November 14, 1979, initiating a string of appearances before the commission that would last seven months. Inside the closed hearing room, Bakker admitted his forgetfulness and deficiencies as a manager. He could not remember the year he was ordained or how to spell Paul Crouch's name. To justify PTL's handling of contributions, Bakker leaned heavily on the imperative of faith, the notion that God only supplied your needs after you demonstrated your trust. "Everything we have ever done at PTL, we never had the money in the bank.... You can't measure faith in dollars and cents.... I am not a businessman. I am a minister, and faith is what motivates us, not fact," Bakker told the FCC.

During his testimony, Bakker made it clear that "facts" included more than just the fine points of accounting. When Bernstein read statements Bakker had made on the air that exaggerated or misstated what PTL had accomplished overseas, Bakker replied that at the time he made those statements he believed they were true, even though his staff was telling him the opposite. What Bakker seemed to imply was that faith did not only apply to the future; it could justify altering facts in the present (also known as lying).[36]

In other respects Bakker was able to push back against the FCC attorneys. Having spent more than a decade doing daily live television, he was not helpless in front of an audience. "Even sources close to the FCC said Bakker was persuasive on the witness stand," the *Charlotte Observer* reported. Bakker showed the FCC videotape from November 17, 1978, eight weeks before the initial *Observer* article that precipitated the FCC investigation, in which he announced that Elias Malki would appear on the *PTL Club* in January. Seven days before the *Observer* articles appeared, Bakker announced on the air that PTL had "$56,000 earmarked" for Malki's transmitter. This effectively countered the *Observer*'s assertion that Malki's appearance had been hastily arranged in response to their January article. Bakker also produced at least three tapes from the fall of 1978 in which he announced that Cho had asked that the money he had been promised go to Japan. What the FCC was discovering was that Bakker made a lot of often contradictory statements on the air. There was no simple story line to follow.[37]

Outside the hearing, in front of cameras, Bakker lashed out at the FCC. "It seems like they're trying to trick me," Bakker said on a segment aired on the *PTL Club* on Friday, November 16. After testifying for six and a half hours, he looked exhausted and broke down in tears. "I really think it's a witch hunt, it's a fishing expedition. . . . We'll make it. If I don't every broadcaster and every church that uses the media can then be destroyed through government regulation." In a display of self-dramatization Bakker personalized the entire investigation as a conspiracy against him.[38]

The FCC hearings also weighed heavily on Tammy, who had to host the show in Jim's absence and for which Jim gave her little credit. "Tammy's just not doing it. I've watched some of her tapes and I know she doesn't know how to ask people to respond for finances, so I've told her she just doesn't have to do it," Jim complained on a taped segment aired on November 16. Tammy's makeup that day was thick, a sign of her stress, as she sat before the cameras and listened to Jim's criticism broadcast over the air.[39]

In December Bakker told his television audience that the FCC was after PTL because the government agency was opposed to missions. "The reason we are at the FCC right now is because of missionary fundraising," Bakker said. That month he and his staff worked feverishly to produce a one-hour "documentary," *Under Investigation*, designed to tell their side of the story. The program would "present the facts," and "show if PTL is on the level or on the take," according to PTL ads carried by local newspapers and radio stations. The show, which aired on a local television station on February 12, 1980, was narrated by a new member of PTL's board, Efrem Zimbalist, Jr., who was famous for playing an FBI agent on the TV series, *The F.B.I.*, a fitting choice to counter the feds in real life. Handsome in a silver-haired way, Zimbalist had a magnificent deep voice, at once disarming and authoritative.[40]

The program opened with Zimbalist speaking from the Heritage Village complex and the PTL television set. Zimbalist described PTL's overseas shows in Latin America, Africa, France, Thailand, Brazil, and its pilot programs in Japan and Italy. PTL had sent $4.5 million to missions projects since 1977, Zimbalist said. It also featured testimonials from viewers and a message from Bakker as "The Battle Hymn of the Republic" played in the background. The *Observer*'s TV critic, Ron Alridge, dismissed the program as "textbook propaganda." FCC lawyer Lawrence Bernstein, who saw the program in a congressional office in Washington, DC, was unimpressed, but a number of letters to the *Observer* in the wake of Alridge's review took PTL's side. "Why is *The Observer* pushing, pushing, pushing against PTL, yet never wants PTL to present its story?" asked William O. Montgomery from nearby Shelby, North Carolina. In the court of public opinion, PTL held its own.[41]

PTL's battle with the FCC continued through the spring of 1980. The ministry refused to comply with a November 21, 1979, subpoena from the FCC, asserting that the "information is protected by the First Amendment guarantee of freedom of religion." On January 8, 1980, Bakker refused to appear at an FCC hearing in connection with the subpoena. By April, PTL had agreed to hand over the records. That May, Bakker returned to Washington for three more days of grilling before the commission. The hearings dragged on into September, when Bob Manzano was asked to return to Washington for two more days of testimony.[42]

The "sum and substance" of the FCC's inquiry into PTL had to do with money raised for "world mission projects," as Lawrence Bernstein put it. But, as would be the case a decade later in Bakker's federal criminal trial, a good deal of attention focused on Bakker's lifestyle, on whether he had used funds designated for missions for "personal enrichment." Bernstein believed that there "had been intentional misappropriation of funds," which the Bakkers used to buy "all kinds of luxuries." Bernstein's convictions notwithstanding, at this point the Bakkers' lifestyle did not strike most observers as outrageous. The next time around would be a different story.[43]

As the FCC investigation ground on, Stoeckel continued to work toward meaningful financial controls at PTL. Unfortunately, as with all efforts to reform PTL's finances, once the crisis passed, Bakker could not resist returning to his old habits of spending beyond the ministry's means. Stoeckel worked tirelessly, often putting in twelve- to fifteen-hour days while commuting home to Memphis on weekends. He believed that PTL should focus on television and foreign missions, its core ministries, rather than sink money into Heritage USA. But the latter was Bakker's dream, and he pressed Stoeckel to resume construction. Exhausted, Stoeckel resigned on March 6, 1980. He was replaced by Gary Smith, thirty-three, an engineer and business consultant from Waco, Texas.[44]

As the FCC investigation was winding down, Roger Flessing returned to PTL. After leaving PTL, Flessing had become program director for the CBS station in Sacramento. In November 1979 he got a call from Tink Wilkerson, chairman of the board at Oral Roberts University, offering to triple his salary if he joined Oral Roberts ministry as a television producer. "It's the only time in my life I ever took a job for the money and it was not a good fit," remembers Flessing. When Bakker called Flessing offering to make him the head of PTL's Broadcast Division, Flessing was ready to take it. "You were right. We made some mistakes around here," Bakker told Flessing. Flessing returned to PTL in March 1980, anxious to "try some innovative programming: sophisticated drama with a Christian theme, children's shows that are not simplistic, and perhaps an occasional documentary on a controversial subject." He also had in mind "a Christian equivalent of *Saturday Night Live*," which was then near the height of its popularity.[45]

Churches rarely have a plan for dealing with the kind of growth and income that PTL experienced in the late 1970s. Bakker's theology of the abundant life was typical of most charismatics and Pentecostals of his generation, but the resources he had at his disposal were not. Like a lottery winner, Bakker and those around him were unprepared to handle the prosperity they had so confidently predicted and fervently desired.

By the end of 1980 PTL was not the same place that it had been three years before. Heritage USA created a range of new possibilities, but it also brought unprecedented financial challenges, ripping the staff apart and leading to a wave of bad press and government intervention in the form of an FCC investigation. In front of the camera Bakker remained as buoyant and optimistic as ever, but behind the scenes he became more reclusive. Over the past two years he had lost most of the key people who had helped to keep the ministry grounded and focused, who could still remember what they had set out to do before all the money and glitz. He had also neglected his marriage, leaving Tammy deeply frustrated and resentful, something that would become more apparent in the months ahead. Bakker was in a vulnerable and dangerous place, putting all of PTL at risk.

7

Time Bomb

SHE WORE A close-fitting, wraparound dress, made from a sheer, plum-colored material, with a sash that tied in back, a style popular at the time. Her pastor's wife had bought it for her, and it was her prettiest dress. She was devoted to her church and worked there full-time as the church secretary. It was December 6, 1980, and she had just flown from Long Island, New York, to Tampa, Florida. John Wesley Fletcher, a minister she knew from her home church, purchased the ticket so that she could come to Florida and babysit Jim Bakker's daughter while Bakker and Fletcher did a telethon for WCLF, a local Christian station. She was twenty-one years old, and she watched Bakker everyday on television. He was her "idol," and she could not wait to meet him. By the end of the day her world would be turned upside down and her life set on a course she could never have imagined.[1]

Jessica Hahn first walked into the Massapequa Assembly of God Church on Long Island on June 21, 1974. She was carrying her two-year-old brother, her constant companion. The church was holding a revival under a big yellow and white tent set up next to the building, with a searchlight circling the sky to draw in visitors. From her home, Hahn could hear the music on the breezy night air. Walking into the church "changed my entire life. I felt that it had everything I wanted. I instantly felt complete. I felt I belonged."[2]

The church quickly became the center of Hahn's life. She began to read her Bible every day and attend meetings whenever she could. "It was like falling in love.... I couldn't wait to go to church, I couldn't wait to pray." Between choir practice, Bible studies, and prayer meetings there was something nearly every night of the week. "Nothing else mattered. If it were up to me, I'd never have gone back to school. I wanted to be in that church." It was her "new family," replacing a home life that "wasn't exactly functional." She never knew her real father. Her mother told her he refused to hold her on the day she was born, and her parents divorced before her third birthday. A few years later her mother remarried, and her stepfather moved the family to Long Island. Her parents fought a lot, and her stepfather was an alcoholic who physically abused her mother. She had few friends her own age and rarely socialized with anyone outside her church.[3]

Having been raised Catholic, she was impressed by the Pentecostal energy of the Massapequa Assembly of God, started in 1969 by Gene Profeta. A native New Yorker born and raised in Brooklyn, Profeta had preached on street corners in New York as a young man before attending A. A. Allen's Bible school in Miracle Valley, Arizona.

Allen was the model for what Profeta and Fletcher, who regularly held crusades in Massapequa, hoped to become. One of Pentecostalism's more colorful personalities, Allen had risen to prominence in the 1950s as a faith healer and proponent of the prosperity gospel. Tammy Faye sang at an Allen revival as a child. Allen's religion was, as he put it, "unashamed, old-fashioned, devil-chasing, sin-busting, Jesus-worshipping, Bible-loving, Holy Ghost-Miracle-Restoration-Salvation-Healing-Saving-Revival" religion. Born in 1911 in Sulphur Rock, Arkansas, Allen grew up in grinding poverty surrounded by heavy drinking. For amusement his parents would let their children drink, no matter how young, and then laughed as they stumbled around the room. Armed with only an eighth-grade education, Allen spent time in jail for stealing corn during the Depression and roamed the country looking for work. "If there was a sin I missed, it was only by accident, not design," Allen later wrote, recalling his childhood.[4]

By the time Allen was twenty-three, he and his mother were running a dancehall roadhouse near Carthage, Missouri, selling bootleg alcohol they distilled in their kitchen. One day Allen stumbled into a small Methodist church and heard his first sermon, preached by a local woman dressed all in white. When she invited anyone who wanted to be saved to come forward, Allen got to his feet and his life was never the same. Allen soon became a Pentecostal, preaching his way through rural Missouri. By the 1950s he had established himself as a nationally recognized healing evangelist whose accounts of miraculous healings and casting out demons made Oral Roberts look timid.[5]

Allen maintained his fervor for healing and deliverance up until his death in 1970, but like Roberts he also increasingly promoted prosperity.

Writing in 1963, Allen declared, "GOD IS DOING A NEW THING! God is doing more than giving us power to lay hands on the sick, cast out devils and perform miracles!" Now he was adding the "POWER TO GET WEALTH." Specifically, God had given Allen the ability to lay hands on people to cast out "the demon of poverty," bestowing wealth in its place. He was known to give away Cadillacs at his revival meetings. Though Allen was often surrounded by controversy—he resigned from the Assemblies of God after being arrested for drunk driving and likely died of alcoholism—his message of healing and prosperity deeply influenced both Profeta and Fletcher. Their careers mirrored Allen's in many respects.[6]

By 1975, Profeta's church had a well-established reputation on Long Island. A *New York Times* article in December 1975 noted that the church "has several services a week and is so overfilled that it has to 'bar the doors,' after its capacity has been reached to conform with local fire laws." The *Times* reported that the walls of the church "are lined with the crutches of people who had come for healings. The music is loud, almost deafening. People clap their hands, some literally jump for joy." The congregation was mostly young people, and about 70 percent were former Catholics.[7]

Hahn was awestruck by the confidence and authority of the preachers she heard at the church, particularly John Wesley Fletcher. Like A. A. Allen and many of the healing evangelists, Fletcher came from a humble background. The eighth of ten children, Fletcher was born in 1940 in Durham, North Carolina, where his father worked in a tobacco plant. He dropped out of high school at twenty-one after repeating both the ninth and tenth grades and took a job at a funeral home while moonlighting as a party clown. "He had oodles of personality. . . . He could just persuade anybody to do almost anything," said Hilda Hudson, owner of the funeral home. After leaving the funeral home, he drove an ambulance, helped perform autopsies at Duke University Medical Center, and claimed to have run a topless bar. By the time he left Durham in 1970, he had been convicted five times for writing bad checks and faced four ongoing suits for $3,800 in unpaid debts.[8]

Fletcher first appeared on the *PTL Club* on March 30, 1976, wearing a three-piece suit and sporting a full pompadour to go with a relaxed, almost smarmy, southern gospel manner. He told the story of his conversion while working in the "restaurant business" in Durham in 1969. According to Fletcher, he was in his car when he heard the gospel song "He Touched Me" on the radio. Convicted of his sin, he drove to the radio station broadcasting the song and "silently dared God to make a move."

After a few minutes a preacher walked out a side door and "made a bee-line" for Fletcher's car. "Young man, what you need is Jay-sus," Fletcher remembers him saying. Fletcher fell on his knees and "gave my heart to God" right there in the parking lot. He launched his preaching career shortly thereafter.[9]

By the time Hahn first met him in 1974, Fletcher already had a growing healing ministry and a family. In March 1971 he met a young woman, Shirley Connour, at a revival meeting in Dallas, where she was singing and playing the organ for another traveling evangelist. She had grown up in Keokuk, Iowa, the daughter of a minister. In 1961, less than a year after graduating high school, she married David Connour. A year later they had a daughter, Carmel. In a short book published after her marriage to Fletcher, Shirley recounted two occasions in which she believed that God had miraculously healed her. The first was after a serious car accident in which she broke her back in four places, her pelvis, and "all of my ribs." The second was after a pressure cooker exploded in her face, leaving her with "third degree burns on thirty percent of my body." Miraculously, she recovered without any scarring. A year later her husband died suddenly of "pleurisy." Soon after, she hit the road with the traveling evangelist she was working for when she met Fletcher.

After a whirlwind romance that lasted less than two weeks, most of it conducted over the phone, Fletcher asked Connour to marry him. Unsure of what to do, she sought God's guidance by pulling a "promise card" that a baby had chewed on out of the trash at church. On the front was the verse, "He that dwelleth in love dwelleth in God, for God is love," and on the back, "I am with thee in all that thou doeth." Exactly what these passages contain in the way of marriage advice is difficult to see, but it was good enough for her. The couple married that May, and their son, John Wesley, Jr., was born a little more than two years later in September 1973.

Fletcher set up his headquarters in Peoria, Illinois, and in 1975 began publishing a magazine, *Compassion and Praise*, to keep his supporters up to date on the activities of his ministry, which he called the John Wesley Fletcher Evangelistic Association. Fletcher had an eye for the dramatic, and his magazine was chock-full of accounts of healings from a variety of ailments. In the summer of 1975, *Compassion and Praise* reprinted an article from the Florida *Manatee Times*, dated May 23, 1975, reporting on a Clearwater woman who claimed to have been healed of blindness at a Fletcher crusade. Helen Louise Pelletier had lost more than 98 percent of her vision as a complication of multiple sclerosis. After doctors "sent me home to die," her brother, Norman, took her to a Fletcher healing crusade. As she listened to Fletcher preach and pray that night she thought, "Well, this is really kind of foolish." But with her guide dog Kate leading the way she walked down front to have Fletcher pray for her anyway. When Fletcher laid his hand on her she fell to the floor, like most of people Fletcher touched (Pentecostals and charismatics call this being slain in the spirit).

The next morning she was startled to find that she could read both her large-print Bible and one with a smaller font. Three days later an ophthalmologist told her that she "had gone from about 1 ½ per cent eyesight to almost perfect vision." Another doctor could find no trace of her multiple sclerosis, according to Pelletier. The next month she got a driver's license. "Jesus healed me," she concluded.[10] This was the kind of story that Fletcher hoped would make him famous. Eventually Fletcher's ministry published a short book recounting Pelletier's experience.

In 1975, a year after he first met Hahn, Fletcher was still mostly preaching in Illinois, Oklahoma, and Florida. That summer he made his sixth trip to Gene Profeta's church on Long Island for a six-week crusade. "I can say without a doubt I've never witnessed God use a man such as He does you," Profeta wrote to Fletcher after this meeting. Fletcher continued to hold crusades at Profeta's church every summer. In 1976 a Chicago businessman, Armin Englehardt, president of Englehardt Gear Company, gave Fletcher an eight-passenger twin-engine Cessna 421 airplane. Dan Borgan, a former Air Force pilot with eight thousand hours of flying time, signed on as Fletcher's pilot. In early 1977, Fletcher moved his ministry headquarters to Oklahoma City, and his schedule expanded to include crusades in at least sixteen states. Back home, Fletcher regularly held meetings at Crossroads Cathedral, which billed itself as Oklahoma City's "six thousand seat spiritual center."[11] Fletcher's ministry was growing, but nothing on the scale of Bakker's. PTL was the big time and Fletcher knew it.

Along with the gift of healing, Fletcher claimed that God spoke to him, revealing things about people he prayed for that he could not have otherwise known, what Pentecostals called the gift of knowledge or the ability to speak a word of knowledge. The first time Hahn walked into the church on Long Island, Fletcher told her that her father was "gone" and that she was "very alone," exactly the way she felt. How did he know that? "Nobody knew me in the church" remembers Hahn, and Fletcher had no way of knowing that she would be there that night. Over the next several years Hahn saw Fletcher do this time and again with people he had never met before. "He used to lay hands on people and tell them stuff that there is no way he could have known," recalls Hahn. "I thought that was a huge gift."[12]

At the same time there was always something unsettling about Fletcher, an odd mixture of flamboyance, hucksterism, and grasping ambition. "He was very secretive and very sneaky," remembers Hahn. She soon realized that Fletcher and Profeta went out drinking together, something strictly forbidden among Pentecostals. When she babysat for Fletcher he used gum to try to hide the alcohol smell, but Hahn could still tell. Fletcher also had a "one-track mind" when it came to money and was constantly thinking about how to squeeze more out of an audience. Before preaching he would ask, "Does my suit look cheap enough?" He wanted his listeners to feel sorry for him, so that they would give generously. "He was very money oriented," says Hahn.[13]

Fletcher and Profeta both appeared on the *PTL Club*, but it was Fletcher who caught Bakker's eye. After appearing on the show half a dozen times in 1978 and 1979, Fletcher became a regular in 1980, returning thirty-four times. Bakker seemed intrigued with Fletcher's gifts of knowledge and healing and his ability to work a crowd. Austin Miles, another regular on the show at the time, remembers Bakker imitating Fletcher's delivery and even the way he walked. "Jim was so enamored by him, he . . . idolized him," remembers Miles.[14]

Others were suspicious of Fletcher from the start. "John was the most carnal preacher that I've ever met in my life . . . but for some reason Jim was just enamored with him. . . . It was a strange, strange situation," remembers Sam Orender, who regularly directed the show during the 1970s. "The guy was a sleaze," recalls Scott Ross, who, along with his wife Nedra, had known the Bakkers since the CBN days and occasionally visited them in Charlotte. Fletcher was "a very bad influence on the Bakkers," according to Roger Wilson, who took to calling him John Fleshly Letcher. "I wouldn't have trusted him in any kind of deal: real estate deal, a car deal, let alone this," says Roger Flessing, referring to Fletcher's presence at PTL.[15]

Just about everyone I have talked to from PTL at the time says more or less the same thing. Perhaps to some extent they are projecting later events back into their earlier memories of Fletcher, but this cannot really account for the consistency of their recollections, particularly considering that many of them have not discussed these events together in years. Fletcher was trouble, and just about everyone except Bakker knew it.

Sex was part of the connection between Fletcher and Bakker. After the Jessica Hahn scandal broke in 1987, Fletcher would say that he and Bakker had sex together and that he saw Bakker in bed with another man. But before 1980 this was a secret that Bakker closely guarded.

Tammy had secrets of her own.

DESPITE THE RELATIVE calm that settled over the ministry in the summer of 1980, the turmoil of the last two years and Jim's continuing obsession with building Heritage USA opened up deep rifts between Jim and Tammy. The two frequently alluded to their struggles as a couple on the air and in their publications, something that endeared them to their audience. It made them seem more approachable and connected to the realities of everyday life, even if they rarely shared the truly difficult parts of their marriage. In fact, by the spring of 1980 Tammy had all but decided to leave Jim.

Nearly everyone liked Tammy. She always said exactly what she thought, for better or worse. There was nothing of Jim's secretiveness or distance. Tammy had little in the way of a social filter. She said things that made even her friends cringe, but with a guileless honesty that was difficult to resist. Viewers could not help watching just to hear what she would say next. She was smart but lacked confidence, and often expressed her insecurities in the form of ditzy self-deprecation. She never "thought I was pretty enough, thin enough or talented enough." But she had a shrewd commonsense approach to business and ministry that Jim lacked. If Tammy had been in charge of PTL's finances, things would have turned out differently.[16]

Tammy struggled to find a role at PTL, unwilling to be left at home while Jim devoted all his waking hours to the ministry. Early on she occasionally revived her puppet act. Tammy was brilliant with those puppets. She did not preach through them, did not use them merely as props to convey a message. She gave them personalities. In one episode of the *PTL Club*, Suzy Moppet and Allie Alligator sing a song from Tammy's new album, *Oops! There Comes a Smile*. Tammy does their voices from behind a puppet stage, while the audience claps along, genuinely engaged despite the silliness. Tammy's voice worked perfectly for the puppets, and she was good at working them with her hands, the product of years of practice.[17]

Tammy used the puppets to say things to Jim and the audience that she could not say on her own. The February 24, 1978, episode of the show opens with Jim standing in front of a puppet stage with Susie Moppet and Allie Alligator. "Allie, what have you got on?" Jim asks. Allie begins to sing,

"I feel handsome, oh so handsome, I feel handsome and debonair. I feel handsome because I've got some underwear," which she then shows to the audience. "You embarrass me," says Jim, to which Allie replies, "I can see how I embarrassed you, you're so timid, tender and shy." The message to Jim was clear: lighten up, have some fun.[18]

But puppets are not sophisticated. As the *PTL Club* became slicker and more professional, Tammy had to find other ways to express herself. She launched her own show for women, the *Tammy Faye Show*, in March 1978. "It will be a show for the average American woman, the woman who has to live on a budget, the woman whose children are following her around all day crying 'Mommy,' the woman who washes her own clothes and seldom gets that much-longed-for trip to the beauty parlor, the working woman, the mother, wife, chauffeur, maid and sometimes queen," as Tammy put it. "The show will deal with the real world we live in, real problems, and practical solutions. We will cook, sew, have fashion and make-up classes, decorate the house and a cake, do some canning, make home made bread and ice cream, visit with Moms and their kids."[19]

None of this involved anything that Tammy was particularly good at, other than a desire to create a fun, happy home environment. She clearly intended it to be different from Jim's show. There was almost nothing in the way of overt religious content. While promoting her autobiography, *I Gotta Be Me*, on the *PTL Club*, Tammy said that if she could not be herself she would be Sophia Loren or maybe Dolly Parton. Jim suggested that she should have said Kathryn Kuhlman, the famous healing evangelist, or "someone spiritual," but Tammy disagreed. When Tammy asked Jim who he would like to be, he said Billy Graham. One can hardly imagine Billy Graham with Sophia Loren or Dolly Parton, which summed up much of the divide between Jim and Tammy. Tammy never felt the need to project a religious persona in the same way that Jim did.[20]

Still, for most of the 1970s their marriage seemed resilient. Back in 1970 Tammy had struggled through a bout of post-partum depression after the birth of her daughter, Tammy Sue. "I was just a zombie for about a year," she later recalled. Jim wondered if their marriage would survive, even suggesting at one point, "Maybe we should separate." But after about a year Tammy recovered her balance, and for several years the couple seemed happy together. "Jim is a man who's kept me in a honeymoon stage for 17 years," Tammy told a reporter in July 1978. Jim agreed, claiming their marriage was "the best in America," and suggesting that they would write a book about it.[21]

That book was never written. By the fall of 1978, Jim's relentless campaign to build Heritage USA had driven a wedge between the couple. The staff at PTL began to refer to the Total Living Center as Jim's "mistress," his "dream." But it was not Tammy's dream. Jim often turned to Roger and Linda Wilson, whom he and Tammy had known since the CBN days, for advice. He complained that he had bought Tammy a car, a fur coat, clothes, but none of it helped. They told him that Tammy simply wanted his attention. "The Total Living Center is your mistress as far as she's concerned and if she's not going to get attention from you, she's going to get it somewhere," Roger warned Jim. "Just let her know she's the most important thing in your life," Linda advised him. "I just got tired of saying it," she remembers, but Jim never seemed to listen. On an August 1979 episode of the *PTL Club*, Jim told the audience that he had asked Tammy what ten things she would like most. None of them cost money. She wanted him to say he loved her, or put his arm around her in the middle of the day. "That amazed me," he admitted.[22]

Tammy struggled to stay involved at PTL, her only point of contact with Jim. She hosted the show when he was not in town, as was the case during the FCC hearings. Tammy's most consistent presence on the show was through her singing, which was unfortunate. Nedra Ross, formerly of the Ronnettes, who remained friends with Tammy through the years, describes her voice as "an out of control vibrato, but she loved the Lord and she felt the louder she sang, the more she had the kingdom." What she lacked in talent Tammy tried to make up for by belting out her songs with relentless enthusiasm. Jim encouraged her to sing and it gradually became her identity so far as the *PTL Club* was concerned, though Tammy always doubted her own talent. "I'm not a singer," she wrote in *I Gotta Be Me*, published in 1978. "Many times after singing in front of a large congregation, I would sit down and weep bitter tears," because she did not think she was that good.[23]

Confidence came in the form of a burned out rock 'n' roller turned Jesus People songwriter, singer, and producer, Gary Paxton. Paxton was best known for his hit songs "Alley Oop" (1960) and "Monster Mash" (1962). After more than a decade of sex, drugs, and rock 'n' roll, Paxton hit bottom in Nashville in 1971, wandering up and down music row "trying to sell songs for booze." Struggling with "whiskey, drugs and wild women," Paxton was saved after stumbling into a Nashville church while stoned. A bio on Paxton in *Action* noted that by then he had already "walked away from five wives and four fortunes." Paxton soon became a regular at PTL, writing new theme songs for the *PTL Club* and the *Tammy Faye Show*. "Maybe the craziest part, and the hardest to explain, is the close relationship that has grown between Gary and Jim Bakker," added the profile in *Action*.[24]

Paxton did more than anyone to shore up Tammy's confidence in her singing. He was everything that Jim was not. Paxton first appeared on the *PTL Club* in October 1977 sporting a bushy red beard and wearing a buckskin leather jacket over a light blue polyester jumpsuit with brown boots. A few months later he turned up in tinted glasses wearing the buckskin jacket, a red jumpsuit and shiny red cowboy boots to sing "Blessed Assurance," though not a version that Fanny Crosby could have imagined. Paxton was tall and burly, with an easy, relaxed manner. While Jim was doing his best to look like Johnny Carson, Paxton could have doubled for Grizzly Adams (except for the jumpsuits). They were nothing alike.[25]

Paxton soon began producing Tammy's records at the Sound Stage recording studio in Nashville. He gave her the attention and support she craved. Though Tammy professed to be good friends with Paxton's wife, Karen, she soon became infatuated with Gary. "She was in love with Gary, or thought she was, and she knew I knew it," Karen later said. At one point Tammy asked Karen to give her the pillow that she and Gary slept with. Gary had the same goofy sense of humor as Tammy, evident in "Alley Oop" and "Monster Mash." In the foreword to her book, *I Gotta Be Me*, he wrote, "A lot of people ask, 'Is Tammy really that short?' My answer is, 'No, she just gets caught standing in a hole every time they take her picture.' " The two spent hours alone together in the studio, sometimes all night. Unlike Jim, Paxton did not push Tammy to become more polished or spiritual. "Don't change, Tammy. . . . We all love you!" Paxton wrote in *I Gotta Be Me* foreword. It was exactly what Tammy desperately wanted to hear.[26]

Linda Wilson was Tammy's secretary, associate producer of the *Tammy Faye Show*, and Tammy's best friend at the time. She traveled with Tammy to Nashville for recording sessions and drove Tammy, Paxton, and his wife, Karen, to Denver for a Christian booksellers convention in the fall of 1978 because Tammy was afraid of flying. Linda watched the developing relationship between Tammy and Gary with mounting apprehension. One night Linda called Karen to ask where Tammy was. "In the studio with Gary," Karen said. Wilson was shocked. "Get over there! They shouldn't be left alone together," she told Karen. When Tammy told her that she had fallen in love with Paxton and confessed that they had hugged and kissed, Linda told her that she was making a big mistake. But there was something irresistible about Paxton's outlaw persona. "Knowing her background and how she was raised, it was a real liberation, a different life style. . . . She fell in love with that," Wilson later said.[27]

Paxton always maintained that nothing had actually happened between the two. There was nothing unusual about a hug and a kiss on the cheek in the music business. Years later Linda Wilson saw Paxton across a crowded green room. "I never slept with her," he called out, loud enough for everyone to hear.[28]

Thurlow Spurr was a different story. Spurr joined PTL in February 1978 as Director of Music in charge of the PTL Band and Singers that performed daily on the show. Born in 1934 in Perth, New York, to an evangelist father, Spurr was best known for his ability to assemble and produce musical acts. He had established himself on the gospel music scene in 1959 when he started the musical group, the Spurrlows. In 1963 Chrysler hired the group to present driver education events at high-school assemblies across the country. By the time Spurr joined PTL, he had produced over forty record albums. Jim Moss had seen one of Spurr's groups perform and convinced Bakker that having a live band would improve the show. Bakker liked the idea of adding a component that made the show look more like the *Tonight Show* with Johnny Carson, which had a band under the direction of Doc Severinsen. Spurr soon turned the PTL band into an orchestra. Under his direction the PTL orchestra prepared up to ten songs per day that Bakker could choose from.[29]

At first, Tammy "didn't like Thurlow at all" and "let a lot of people know that," says Linda Wilson. Spurr's slick style and professionalism intimidated her. When Tammy found out that Spurr was coming to PTL she worried, "maybe they wouldn't need me anymore. Maybe I wouldn't be considered good enough to sing, on PTL anymore." Many of the new singers and musicians had music degrees. Tammy could not read music. As weeks went by, "many days I was no longer asked to sing," and when she was she "felt inadequate," pulled down by "deep feelings of inferiority." The other singers and musicians, "didn't understand the old-fashioned, down-home unprofessional style my heart heard," Tammy later said.[30]

From Spurr's perspective, "Tammy was a work in progress." She liked the "simpler, more direct" storylines of country music, which usually contained a clear hook to convey the message. "She felt like she didn't need all of these instruments and all of these voices" to perform, Spurr said.[31] Yet Tammy was his boss's wife, and Spurr wanted to keep her happy. After one disastrous rehearsal, Tammy ran off the set sobbing, "nearly out of my mind." The next day she walked into Spurr's office and "poured out my heart to him." They talked and cried together for an hour. That afternoon as she practiced with the group everything seemed to click. "It was a miracle!!" Tammy later wrote. Eventually it was more than that.[32]

By the end of 1979 Tammy had dramatically transformed her image compared to five years before when she and Jim had arrived in Charlotte. She now wore heavy eyeliner and mascara with short hair "puffed up high or covered by a Dolly Parton-like wig." "Not by any stretch of the imagination does she look like a preacher's wife," wrote a reporter for the *Charlotte News*. She more resembled "a country music singer or a nightclub entertainer." On any given day PTL staffers could tell how she was feeling with one look at her appearance: the heavier the makeup the worse her mood. Tammy now hid behind her makeup much as she had earlier hidden behind her puppets.[33]

In the spring of 1980 Jim Bakker, accompanied by Roger Flessing, stopped by a hospital in Palmdale, California, across the San Bernardino Mountains north of Los Angeles, on their way to a convention in Las Vegas. On the flight from Charlotte, Flessing remembers that Bakker "leaned over to me . . . and he said, 'I think Tammy's having an affair.'" Flessing was surprised. When they landed he called the Palmdale clinic and made the appointment. A few months before, Dr. Fred Gross, who directed the hospital's Christian Therapy Program, had appeared on the *PTL Club* to talk about the value of Christian-oriented counseling. After talking with Bakker and consulting with Flessing, Gross suggested bringing Tammy to Palmdale.[34]

Tammy was reluctant to go. She still hated to fly despite what she had written in her new book, *Run to the Roar*, which was published that year. In the book, which is mostly about overcoming fears, Tammy explained how God had freed her from her fear of flying and the need to take tranquilizers before boarding a plane. She took one anyway as she left for California. Roger and Linda Wilson, who knew that Tammy was thinking about leaving Jim, picked her up and drove her to the airport. Along the way Tammy insisted that they stop so that she could say goodbye to Gary Paxton. The Wilsons watched Tammy's flight takeoff just to make sure she was onboard.[35]

For two weeks the Bakkers met with Gross's team of counselors, airing their grievances. The Bakkers and Flessing had rooms next to each other at the local Holiday Inn, where the walls were "about as thin" as the desert air, so Flessing heard "everything that was going on. And it was pretty messy."

Predictably, the counselors told Tammy that she had committed adultery in her heart with Paxton and needed to repent. Equally predictably, they told Jim that he needed to pay more attention to his wife and spend more time at home. Flessing remained with the Bakkers in Palmdale, trying to keep things on track.[36]

Roger and Linda Wilson flew to Palmdale during the Bakkers' second week of counseling, bringing the Bakkers' children, Tammy Sue and Jamie Charles, with them. The Wilsons had to leave their infant daughter Christy with friends. When they arrived, the first thing Jim said was, "Roger, they told me exactly what you've been telling me." "I could have saved you a lot of money," Roger replied.[37]

Tammy "hated" Linda for sending her to Palmdale. "She barely spoke to me when we got there because we had put her on the plane to go to California." Their relationship was never quite the same. Linda later took a position writing letters for Jim to the ministry's major donors. When she "got so I couldn't honestly answer those letters, I said, 'That's it. I'm leaving.' " She resigned in June 1981. Tammy gave her a necklace and said, "I wish I was leaving instead of you." A few weeks later Roger Wilson was asked to leave PTL. The Bakkers had lost two more trusted advisers who had been there from the beginning, who would look them in the eye and tell them things they did not want to hear.[38]

Paxton later told Jim that he could have slept with Tammy on numerous occasions but instead urged her to reconcile with him. But Bakker kept calling, accusing Paxton of having an affair with Tammy. Finally Paxton had had enough. "You short sonuvabitch, come on down here to Nashville and I'll pound you in the ground," he told Bakker. Paxton never returned to the show. Bakker ordered Spurr to replace the theme songs that Paxton had written with new ones. "Jim was hurt to find out his wife might be even interested in another man, even if it was just a close friendship," Linda Wilson later said.[39]

BY THE SUMMER of 1980, as the Bakkers' marriage threatened to unravel, Jessica Hahn had carved out an identity in the Massapequa church. After high school she became the full-time church secretary, counting the offerings, praying with people on the phone, and doing the many small jobs that keep a church running. She babysat Profeta's children, and when the Fletchers came to town every summer she did the same for them. Her entire life revolved around church.

Then on December 4, 1980, Fletcher called Hahn from Florida, where he and Bakker were holding a telethon, asking her to join the PTL crew as a babysitter for Bakker's daughter. Hahn was thrilled. Here at last was a chance to meet the television preacher she "idolized." She had bought her first black-and-white television specifically so that she could watch Bakker on the *PTL Club* every day. "I hung on every word he said." From her church salary of eighty dollars a week she sent fifteen dollars a month to PTL.

Hahn had read Bakker's new book, *Eight Keys to Success*, "probably two dozen times" over the past several months and was deeply impressed with its promise of an abundant life. "To think that God doesn't want your life to be rich, exciting and full of adventure is the greatest lie that I know," Bakker wrote in *Eight Keys to Success*. Hahn was captivated by Bakker's accomplishments—"I was obsessed with this man. How was he able to do all of this?"—and his formula spoke to her dream of a more fulfilling life. "I think the greatest thieves in all the world are those who steal somebody's dream . . . dream tramplers," Bakker wrote in *Eight Keys*. Having a dream "keeps us alive and vital. It keeps that adrenalin flowing and keeps us young." What Hahn did not know was that at that moment Bakker's life was filled with turmoil and uncertainty, the opposite of what he projected on television and in his book. He was about to become the biggest "dream trampler" she would ever encounter.[40]

Pressure had been building on Bakker for months, both at work and at home. PTL's financial woes, the FCC investigation, the resignation of longtime key staffers, and increasingly negative press coverage all stoked Bakker's insecurity. His relationship with Tammy was still strained. Two years before there seemed to be no limit to what PTL could accomplish. Now all that he had worked for threatened to unravel.

At the same time, Fletcher was struggling to maintain his foothold at PTL. He knew what television had done for Bakker's career, and he had his sights set on cohosting his own show with Bakker. But Fletcher also knew that most of the PTL staff distrusted him. Bakker was Fletcher's only real ally at the network. What he needed was a way to make Bakker feel obligated to keep him on, to put Bakker in his debt, without jeopardizing his own career, as exposing Bakker's same-sex relationships might have done. Jessica Hahn seemed like the perfect solution.

According to Hahn, when she arrived in Tampa on December 6, 1980, she thought it was odd that only Fletcher came to the airport to pick her up. He said that it was because he wanted to talk to her alone. "That's when things started to sound weird," Hahn later told *Playboy*. Fletcher told her about the FCC investigation and how "the newspapers were ripping

[Bakker] apart." He also told her about Tammy's relationship with Gary Paxton, which shocked Hahn. To her, Jim and Tammy "were like Mr. and Mrs. Brady of *The Brady Bunch.*" Fletcher didn't stop there. He went on to say that Bakker was suicidal and to describe difficulties in Jim and Tammy's sex life. Hahn was confused, but she hoped that things would clear up when they reached the hotel, where she expected to see both Jim and Tammy.

Hahn later told her story of what happened at the hotel in great detail to *Playboy* and to reporter Art Harris, who published his story in *Penthouse.* When they arrived at the Sheraton Sand Key Hotel in Clearwater Beach, according to Hahn, Fletcher grabbed her bags and told her to walk behind him through the lobby. "This way, people won't get the wrong idea," Fletcher said. He already had the key to her room, number 538. Once there, Hahn tried to hang her things up but there was something wrong with the closet door. "Fuck the closet," Fletcher said. He had never used that kind of language around her before. He gave her a glass of white wine. She was nervous and had not slept much the night before or eaten all day. She later told her legal adviser, Paul Roper, that she thought the wine might have been drugged because she soon began to feel sick. Fletcher took her onto the balcony, which overlooked a large pool and had a view of the beach and ocean. They waved to Bakker and his daughter, Tammy Sue, who were at the pool.

A PTL producer who accompanied Bakker to Florida remembers Hahn's arrival at the hotel differently. He says that he met Hahn and Fletcher in lobby when she first arrived. The three went up to Hahn's room, where she and Fletcher appeared relaxed and comfortable together, at one point playfully tussling on the bed. He suspected that this was not the first time Fletcher and Hahn had been together in this sort of situation, and he never got the impression that she was nervous or apprehensive. When he left, Fletcher offered to send Hahn to the producer's room later.

While Fletcher went down to get Bakker, Hahn says that she took a quick shower and then got dressed again. When the two men walked into the room Bakker was barefoot and sandy, wearing only an "itty bitty" white terrycloth bathing suit. Hahn was startled that she and Bakker were the same height, five foot four inches, and stood eye to eye. "I didn't know women from New York were so beautiful," Bakker said. When Hahn asked where Tammy was, Bakker told her that she was in California and that they were "going through a separation."

By this time, Hahn said, she was feeling increasingly dizzy, but Fletcher and Bakker kept talking to her anyway. Bakker complained that Tammy belittled him and that when it came to sex, "Tammy Faye is too big and cannot satisfy me." What he needed, he told Hahn, was a woman to help him cope. At first Bakker was "very hyper" and sat on the bed rubbing his thighs. "If I don't get this help, I feel like I'll lose everything," Bakker told her, switching to the same dramatic quiet-but-serious voice he employed in front of the camera. Fletcher chimed in, saying, "Jessica, you're going to be doing something tremendous for God."

Fletcher handed Hahn a bottle of Vaseline Intensive Care lotion, telling her, "Jim Bakker loves back rubs" (she kept the little yellow bottle for years). Then Fletcher left the room. Bakker continued to tell Hahn that without her help he would not "be able to go on," but she pleaded that she didn't "feel right" about what was happening. Bakker then pulled off his bathing suit. "What are you doing?" Hahn demanded. She told him that she was a virgin and asked why he did not "just hire somebody." Bakker replied, "You can't trust everybody." He pulled her onto the bed and undressed her. She tried to push him away, saying, "You have to leave!" Bakker replied, "Jessica, by helping the shepherd, you're helping the sheep."

She was in pain and crying but Bakker just kept going for nearly an hour, moving from one position to another, as Hahn later remembered it. He "just did everything a man could do to a woman." There was no kindness in it at all. She was worried that she would get pregnant. When he had finished, Bakker told her that he wanted to see her again. She was still "crying and trying to tell this man that he destroyed my life." "You'll appreciate it later," Hahn remembers Bakker saying. He told her he had jets at his disposal and could make "arrangements" for her to "be by his side." "You really ministered to me," Bakker said, just before he left.

Hahn stumbled to the shower and threw up. She was "freezing," so she turned the water up as hot as she could stand. She put on a robe and crawled into the room's second bed that was untouched. Fifteen minutes later Fletcher walked into the room. "Jim is so happy. He's lying in a fetal position in his room, saying he's happy," Fletcher said. Hahn begged him to "get me out of here." But Fletcher reminded her that he had to stay for the telethon. "Jessica, you can't believe . . . you just saved PTL."

Realizing that he was not going to help her, Hahn asked Fletcher to leave. "No!" he replied. "And I never, never in my life saw a man's face change like I saw his. It scared the hell out of me. His face was demonic. It was horrible," Hahn later recalled. Fletcher tore off her robe and threw her on the floor. "You're not gonna just give this to Jim Bakker! You're not going to remember Jim Bakker! You're going to remember *me*!" Hahn screamed but Fletcher did not stop. "The guy is just tossing me like I was one of those Raggedy Ann dolls. You know, like, legs are up, legs are down.... I thought, He's going to kill me." Bakker had been brutal but Fletcher was doubly so. Her back burned from rubbing on the carpet and soon began to bleed. When she dug her fingernails into him Fletcher seemed to enjoy the pain. "It wasn't normal. It was just weird, and I was waiting for this man to finish me." When Fletcher was done Hahn crawled back in bed. Blood from her back stained the sheets.

Before he left the room Fletcher turned on the TV to the station broadcasting the telethon. A little while later both Bakker and Fletcher appeared on the show. "Jim, God really ministered to us today, didn't He," Hahn remembers Fletcher saying on the air. "Yeah. He really did," replied Bakker. They smiled broadly and got down to the business of raising money.[41]

When Fletcher returned to the room after the telethon, Hahn begged him again to help her leave. Fletcher gave her $129, the exact amount she needed for airfare home. The ordeal was devastating for Hahn. "They took from me what should have been for somebody I loved. They took from me that first experience—that first time when you love somebody and it's everything good.... They stole that from me. I will never in my life get that back ... no money in the world can pay for that," she told *Playboy* in November 1987.[42]

Fletcher later disputed Hahn's account, saying that they first had sex in February 1980 in a Hilton Hotel in New York City, ten months before the Florida trip. He also claimed that Hahn willingly had sex with him after her encounter with Bakker. Hahn later told reporter Charlie Shepard that she sensed that Fletcher was sexually attracted to her in February 1980 but she ignored it.[43]

Despite all that she had been through, Hahn initially did not want to expose Bakker or PTL. She believed in the church and the ministry too much for that. She also convinced herself that "maybe I did help." "I kept thinking this had to be God's will—maybe I really *did* help Bakker.... There is a scripture that says, 'Touch not Mine anointed.' ... And I was petrified, because I thought, These men are God's anointed." If Bakker had simply come back to the room and apologized, had brought her a flower and said he was sorry "it would have made a huge difference. I would have done anything to not have the story come out," she recently told me. But Bakker did nothing of the sort.[44]

There is a good deal of understandable anger in Hahn's account in *Playboy*. She still sticks to the details of that story, but "I see things differently now," she recently told me. Over the years she has "softened up about Jim Bakker." It now seems clear to her that Fletcher manipulated her and Bakker for his own "vicious" reasons. "I feel like we were set up by John [Fletcher]," Hahn says. She was naïve and overwhelmed by the situation, but to a certain extent so was Bakker. It was not "consensual" and she did not "say yes." "It just happened, it just suddenly happened and I didn't run out of the room because I felt, to be honest with you, that this guy was like my idol and I didn't know what to do. I just thought I should go through with this because it's Jim Bakker. And that's something that I haven't really thought about but that's basically the truth," Hahn says. "I can't call it rape. I just can't. Everybody else does, though, and it bothers me for some reason." Hahn said more or less the same when she appeared on the television show *The View* on February 22, 2011. On that occasion she also said that her encounter with Bakker lasted "fifteen minutes in a hotel."[45]

That version is closer to the story Bakker tells. He had agreed to have sex with Hahn in order to make Tammy jealous and win her back, he later said. Now there's a good idea. Of that December day in Florida, he writes, "We had a fifteen- to twenty-minute tryst, a quick, furtive sexual encounter.... We did not drink wine, as was later reported. Nor did I imply that by having sex with me she was serving God somehow. Most of all, *I did not rape Jessica Hahn.* Foolish and sinful as it was, the sexual encounter for which we are both infamous was completely consensual." Bakker later told the press that Hahn was the one who pressed him to have sex and that she was a "professional who knew every trick of the trade." But, as Hahn pointed out, how did Bakker know what those tricks were?[46]

Whatever actually happened in that Florida hotel room, Bakker miscalculated if he thought that Fletcher and Hahn would be content to keep quiet. The fuse had been lit. Six years later the bomb would go off.

8

Special Math

IN THE EARLY 1980s PTL experienced a resurgence as construction resumed at Heritage USA and Bakker and his staff launched a number of new initiatives. By 1983 Bakker claimed that the PTL satellite network reached six hundred million people in more than forty countries. Though PTL always hovered on the brink of financial ruin, it once again did so in the context of expansion.

For the mostly young staff of PTL's various divisions, the turmoil of 1978 and 1979 seemed little more than a minor distraction. They were young, busy, and wrapped up in the camaraderie of life at PTL. When they had the time to think about it at all, they tacitly accepted Bakker's public explanations of PTL's financial crises and the FCC investigation. They rarely read the *Charlotte Observer* or *Charlotte News*. Since the era of the Scopes trial and the publication of *Elmer Gantry* in the 1920s, evangelicals in general and Pentecostals in particular had learned to distrust the press, which regularly mocked them as poor and ignorant dupes who lived on the wrong side of the tracks. This stereotype continued in the post-war years as the PTL staff was growing up. Both Scopes and Gantry were recast for a new generation as big-budget movies in 1960 (*Inherit the Wind* starred Spencer Tracy, Frederic March, and Gene Kelly; *Elmer Gantry* starred Burt Lancaster and Jean Simmons). The hostility that those at PTL now sensed from the local newspapers seemed nothing more than an extension of a familiar, almost comforting pattern. They knew that PTL was far from perfect, but still believed that it had the potential to accomplish great things for the kingdom of God. They were proclaiming the gospel around the world, seeing the sick healed, saving marriages, reclaiming alcoholics, and giving hope to the hopeless. Was it their problem if the local press didn't like it?

PTL viewers in the United States saw frequent promos celebrating the reach of the ministry's programming abroad. By the end of 1982, PTL programs reached audiences in Latin America, Asia, Africa, and Europe. Juan Romero now hosted the Spanish-language show, which aired in Bolivia, Chile, Ecuador, Paraguay (with some coverage in Argentina), El Salvador, Honduras, Panama, Netherland Antilles, Dominican Republic, and Puerto Rico. The Spanish show was also carried on 137 stations in the United States. The French PTL program, *Entr' Amis* (*Among Friends*), hosted by Roland Cosnard, aired in France, Belgium, Luxembourg, and Haiti. The PTL Redemption Hour, with Nigerian host Benson Idahosa, could be seen in Nigeria and parts of Ghana and Uganda. Japan PTL, with host Kenichi Nagagawa, was broadcast over eleven stations covering about 90 percent of the nation. PTL Thailand, hosted by Thasanapong Suwaratana, had been on the air for three years and reached an audience of twenty million, according to Bakker. The newest foreign television program, *Tra Amici* (*Among Friends*), went on the air in Italy in mid-1982. Hosted by Fred Ladenius, the Italian show was broadcast out of Monaco. With the exception of the Nigerian, Thai, and Japanese shows, all of the programs were produced in Charlotte at the Park Road studio. The American *Jim Bakker* program could also be seen in Liberia, Sierra Leone, the Philippines, the US Virgin Islands, the West Indies, Bermuda, Australia, and Haiti.[1]

Overseas missions were great publicity among evangelicals, who took seriously the mandate to evangelize the world, and PTL relentlessly promoted itself as an organization deeply committed to overseas missions. PTL's new magazine for its partners, *Together*, regularly featured stories about the ministry's foreign-language television programs and its partnerships with missionaries. Bakker assured viewers that by becoming a PTL partner "you will have the best feeling in all the world, knowing that you're part of worldwide evangelism, helping to bring back the King of Kings and Lord of Lords." Yet in terms of where the money was spent, foreign missions never again rivaled Heritage USA as the focus of PTL's energy and resources.[2]

By the summer of 1980, contributions were double what they had been the year before, allowing Bakker to revive building projects put on hold for the past two years. Gary Smith, PTL's new vice president for corporate planning, was more inclined to "let Jim be Jim" than Ed Stoeckel had been and to go along with Bakker's plans to resume construction at Heritage USA. On September 1, 1980, forty thousand people turned out to celebrate the opening of a 3,000-seat Barn auditorium on the Heritage USA grounds.

Reminiscent of the large wooden "glory barns" constructed by evangelists like Billy Sunday in cities across America in the early twentieth century, the Barn provided PTL with a large indoor auditorium. Construction of the Barn, which cost more than $2 million, had been halted in 1978 when PTL could not pay its contractor. For about a year and a half the Barn sat half finished, with puddles of water collecting inside and the wind whistling through its interior. Its completion signaled a renaissance in PTL's development. Oral and Evelyn Roberts and Rex and Maude Aimee Humbard, along with Charlotte Mayor Eddie Knox, attended the "Victory Day" celebration, which included a parade with floats, marking the building's dedication. With his usual hyperbole, Bakker called it "the greatest Victory in the history of PTL."

Only a few months before, Stoeckel had been looking for a way to sell Heritage USA. The turnaround was proof to Bakker that Stoeckel's push for a balanced budget was unnecessarily constraining. "God has a special math that doesn't have anything to do with the mathematical system of the world," Bakker wrote in 1981.[3]

The Barn provided the space to start a church, something PTL had never done before. The PTL Television Network was originally incorporated as Trinity Broadcasting Systems, a nonprofit religious corporation, in February 1973. In November 1976 it changed its name to Heritage Village Church and Missionary Fellowship, but it still remained primarily a television network. Despite the new name, PTL never actually ran its own church until September 1980, when the Heritage Village Church began meeting in the Barn. By March 1981, the church had six hundred members, and Sunday attendance averaged about one thousand, mostly PTL employees. Bakker preached whenever he was in town. To take care of the day-to-day responsibilities of running the church, visiting the sick, counseling the needy, and conducting the Wednesday night meetings, Bakker hired an associate pastor, Aubrey Sara. The two had known each other since the early 1960s, when Sara had been instrumental in launching the Bakkers' career as traveling evangelists in the South. Meeting as a church at the Barn further solidified Heritage USA's identity as a community and the center of PTL's focus. The complex now attracted two hundred thousand visitors a year, making it one of the area's leading tourist attractions. No longer a sideshow, Heritage USA was now the sun around which everything at PTL orbited.[4]

In September 1981, a year after the Barn dedication, another Victory Day celebration and parade marked the dedication of the World Outreach

Center (WOC). The three-story, pyramid-shaped building became the ministry's main administrative headquarters. Construction on the building, originally called the Total Living Center, began in March 1978 during Bakker's initial building spree at Heritage USA. It was halted in August 1978 when PTL ran out of money, though Bakker later blamed the interruption on the FCC investigation. At the time, the building was about 80 percent complete. It stood deserted for two years, with weather and vandals taking their toll, before construction resumed in September 1980. As with the Barn, completing the WOC signaled to many that PTL was back on track, poised to fulfill its destiny.[5]

At about the same time that the WOC was dedicated, Bakker and his staff created a new television program, *Camp Meeting USA*. Initially broadcast live at 8 p.m. every night from the Barn over PTL's satellite network, the show served three purposes. It provided an overflow for musicians and television guests who could not get enough airtime on the *Jim Bakker* show, a nightly event for visitors at Heritage USA to attend, and a vehicle to strengthen connections with PTL's charismatic and Pentecostal base. Bakker rarely appeared on *Camp Meeting USA*, which was instead hosted by other PTL staffers. Uncle Henry and Aunt Susan were regulars. Rather than copying Bakker's talk show format, *Camp Meeting USA* combined a variety show format with a traditional church service, including hymn singing and sermons. The preaching was generally fast and loud, Pentecostal style, camp meeting style.

The name *Camp Meeting USA* was no accident. Bakker would later say that Heritage USA was a modern expression of an old-time camp meeting, but it did not start out as that. Heritage University was at the center of Bakker's original plans for the grounds. The WOC was first intended to house the university before construction was suspended in the summer of 1978. But universities are not cheap, and Bakker's commitment to higher education was mostly derivative, an attempt to copy what Oral Roberts, Pat Robertson, and Jerry Falwell were doing.

As his interest in higher education waned, Bakker began to see Heritage USA as something else entirely. He now envisioned it as a giant Christian theme park, retreat center, and community, a combination of Disney World and an old fashioned camp meeting. As a boy, Bakker had attended camp meetings, which had a long and rich tradition among Pentecostals. "My greatest religious experience as a young man was at the camp meeting in Faholo Park," near Jackson, Michigan, Bakker later said. But by the 1970s camp meetings were mostly relics of the past. "Church people were going to Disneyland [and] Disney World," but "they weren't going to camp meetings anymore," Bakker said. He intended for Heritage USA to revive the spirit of the camp meeting in a modern setting.[6]

While Presbyterians, Baptists, and Methodists all participated in the creation of the camp meeting in the early nineteenth century, it was the Methodists who turned it into a cultural phenomenon. By 1810, less than a decade after the first camp meeting was held, Methodists were holding five hundred camp meetings a year, each one attracting hundreds and sometimes thousands of participants. Attendees brought their tents and wagons, assembling in a carnival-like atmosphere of preaching, praying, singing and fellowship. Early camp meetings were raucous affairs, combining entertainment with wild and sometimes frightening religious fervor. The curious were more likely to attend a meeting outside the walls of the church, and the size of the gathering was limited only by the capacity of the campground.[7]

Camp meetings drew thousands of new converts into the church during the nineteenth century, but by the time of Bakker's youth they had mostly lost their appeal, particularly among upwardly mobile Pentecostals and charismatics. Musty, stained mattresses, cold showers, and outhouses could not compete with newer forms of entertainment and recreation. "I recognized that the drab, outmoded campgrounds I had attended as a child would no longer appeal to a generation accustomed to vacationing at clean hotels and theme parks," Bakker later wrote. His new "vision" was "to build what I called a twenty-first-century, total-living community modeled on the old-time camp meetings, but where the entire family could come and enjoy both a beautiful park and plentiful opportunities for spiritual growth." Heritage would offer a Christian alternative to worldly entertainment. "We don't have to take a backseat to gambling casinos. Why in the world do we think they can spend millions on gambling casinos and we're not supposed to do anything for the King of Kings and Lord of Lords?" Bakker asked his viewers in March 1983.[8] His concept built on both Pentecostalism's heritage and its new middle-class aspirations to experience all that American consumer and leisure culture had to offer. Nothing like it existed anywhere else in America.

On July 4, 1982, in an event staged in a 7,000-seat tent, Bakker dedicated the newest building on the Heritage USA grounds, the Upper Room. The program included television evangelists Maude Aimee and Rex Humbard, Richard Dortch, C. M. Ward, and actors Efrem Zimbalist Jr. and Donna Douglas, "Elly May" from the *Beverly Hillbillies*. Constructed of cinderblock covered with a rough stone façade, the building was modeled after the room in Jerusalem traditionally believed to be the site of the Last Supper and the place where the 120 were filled with the Holy Spirit on the day of Pentecost. Bakker claimed that the vision for the Upper Room came to him in early 1981 when "PTL was going through the most severe crisis of its entire history. Friends and foes alike were predicting the demise of the entire ministry." As he walked the grounds of Heritage USA, Bakker said that Jesus spoke to his "spirit . . . 'If you'll build this for Me,' said the Lord, 'I'll save your ministry.' " The building was open around the clock for anyone who wanted a place to pray or meditate. The ground floor housed a twenty-four-hour-a-day international phone center, where counselors prayed with the needy and took contributions around the clock. The Upper Room was meant to represent PTL's core values and figured prominently in PTL promotional literature.[9]

More central to Bakker's goals for Heritage USA was the Total Learning Center, built next to the Barn Auditorium and opened in January 1983. The center provided a venue for seminars aimed at couples, parents, singles, and young people. Workshops at the center were supervised by Dr. Fred Gross, who had earlier provided marriage counseling for Jim and Tammy in Palmdale, California and now joined PTL as international director of the TLC. Joining Gross's team as resident director of the center was Vi Azvedo, who had also been part of Gross's staff at Palmdale and had been involved in the Bakkers' marriage counseling there. Azvedo initially came to PTL as director of human resources and had earlier run a restaurant. She had no degrees in counseling or anything else but soon became part of the Bakkers' inner circle, eventually eclipsing Gross in influence. Other staffers marveled at her rise to prominence given her lack of sophistication. Outside of Bakker's inner circle she had a reputation as a "viper." But Bakker trusted her and knew that she would keep his secrets. By May 1982, Azvedo was PTL's "vice president of personal counseling" and by 1984 she had a "special arrangement" with Bakker and reported directly to him.[10]

By the summer of 1983, the Total Learning Center offered a range of three-day workshops, including Marriage Enrichment, Communicating, Personal Growth, Sexual Relationships & Problems, Parenting, Teen Years/Relationships & Problems (For Parents, Teens, Peers & Christian Workers), Inner Healing of Memories & Past Traumas, and Christian Counseling for the Church Worker. Each workshop met for four hours a day and required a minimum donation of seventy-five dollars.

The marriage seminar promised "training and practice on how to live together in harmony; to become aware of hidden expectations . . . to resolve differences and bring back romance." The workshop on communicating offered "training . . . to develop or increase . . . sensitivity and listening skills." The Personal Growth workshop was "for any person with a need to develop self-esteem and a personal concept of self which allows for their full potential to be realized." Sexual Relationships was "for adults desiring a Biblical perspective of their sexual capacity and appropriate behaviors for personal growth and satisfaction," including "psychosexual methods for 'working through'" sexual dysfunction. The parenting workshop had an "emphasis on emotionality, learning difficulties and behavior problems." The teen seminar was aimed at "teens with a need to understand their bodies, minds and emotions and to come to grips with such pressures as drugs, alcohol, sex, learning stress and parental demands." Inner Healing promised "psychospiritual insight into mental and emotional hurts" from participants' "childhood or adult history. Deep muscle relaxation coupled with guided imagery exercises will allow for an 'unlearning and relearning' of past events and the necessary transformation of mind to allow for healthy adjustments." The counseling workshop offered "Christian Therapy principles and specific methodology with a psychospiritual basis."[11]

This was only the beginning as Fred Gross saw it. "We've just scratched the surface," he said in August 1983. "Jim and I both want to blanket the country with Christian Therapy Units in hospitals, increase greatly our workshops in many other cities, make available mental health videotapes for church leaders and counselors," Gross said. "All this will be backed by a complete, comprehensive Christian care center here at the home base, Heritage USA, including nursing home care, residential care, urgency and emergency care and hospitals for the acutely ill. In my opinion, we are seeing the dawning of a new age in total Christian treatment," Gross said.[12]

Though most of it would go unrealized, the scope of Gross's agenda for PTL demonstrated the degree to which Bakker embraced therapeutic culture. Bakker had long been attracted to self-help approaches. In 1969 he had a nervous breakdown while working for CBN. After one particularly hard day that May, he came home and collapsed. "My nerves were jangled and I felt as though I was losing all the restraints that held my life together," Bakker later recounted in his 1976 autobiography. He could not sleep or stand to talk with anyone. When he showered, the water felt "like hundreds of tiny needles." Medication only made him more "agitated."

Bakker retold this story throughout his career, telling his television audience in January 1981 that after his breakdown he did not face the camera for thirty days, and it took five years to fully recover.[13]

What finally started him down the road to recovery was not medication but a form of self-help therapy. While alone at home one day, Bakker saw a television interview with Dr. Claire Weekes, an Australian medical doctor who specialized in nervous illness. "When you find yourself getting tense," Bakker remembered Weekes saying, "don't fight to stay calm. Simply accept your condition and imagine you are floating on water or a fluffy cloud." Bakker bought a copy of Weekes's book, *Hope and Help for Your Nerves*, in which she outlined her method of dealing with anxiety that involved four steps: facing, accepting, floating, and letting time pass. Bakker's interest in Weekes's particular methods soon waned, but his overall faith in therapy never did.[14]

Investing in Christian therapy put Bakker on the leading edge of yet another cultural wave. By 1975 Americans were spending $1 billion a year for mental health services, and by the 1980s therapy had gone mainstream. Talking your troubles out with a professional, or at least someone you trusted, rather than "repressing" them, became the cultural norm. Bookstores created a "recovery" section, which soon became the largest section in most major chains. Support groups emerged for just about every problem imaginable, and Americans joined them in droves. In the same way that Oral Roberts hoped to combine faith healing and modern medicine in his giant City of Faith hospital, which opened in 1981, Bakker hoped to combine Christian counseling and modern psychology at Heritage USA. This was a far bigger commitment than he made to any political agenda, demonstrating again Bakker's instinct to gravitate toward cultural engagement rather than politics.[15]

Hiring Fred Gross and his team, along with building the Total Learning Center, gave PTL the staff and facilities to work with people face-to-face rather than just over the air and provided another draw for people to come to Heritage USA. Many in Bakker's audience did not have professional Christian counseling available in their church or community. At Heritage USA, visitors could attend what they were assured were top-notch programs in a safe, accessible environment. Many no doubt felt more comfortable opening up to "professionals" they would never see again rather than people in their home church with whom they had ongoing relationships. Some of PTL's seminars, such as the marriage and parenting courses, were familiar fare among evangelicals. But others pushed the therapy envelope for Bakker's audience, particularly the inner healing seminar, which was closely associated with the work of Ruth Carter Stapleton, the sister of President Jimmy Carter, who had appeared on the *PTL Club* and was instrumental in Larry Flynt's conversion.

Agnes Sanford (1897–1982) pioneered the inner healing movement after World War II. Born in China, the daughter of Southern Presbyterian missionaries, Sanford moved back and forth between China and the United States until 1925 when she and her husband, Edgar Sanford, an Episcopal priest, left China for the last time and settled in Moorestown, New Jersey, where Edgar pastored a church. Feeling constrained by the life of a housewife and mother, Sanford discovered that she had a gift of healing. In 1947 she published *The Healing Light*, which catapulted her into national prominence as a healing evangelist. In 1955, the Sanfords started a School of Pastoral Care in Massachusetts to teach ministers how to heal the "soul, mind, and body through faith and prayer." Among those deeply influenced by Sanford's ideas was Francis McNutt, a Catholic priest who became a leader in the Catholic charismatic movement, and Ruth Carter Stapleton, who sometimes taught alongside McNutt.[16]

What made Sanford's conception of healing different from other faith healers was the emphasis she placed on the lasting effects of childhood experiences. Physical healing was almost impossible without emotional healing, particularly from painful childhood memories stored in the subconscious. "The part of us that reasons is only one-tenth of the consciousness. . . . It is the submerged part of the consciousness—this subconscious mind—that controls our bodies," Sanford wrote in *The Healing Light*. Stored in the subconscious mind was a perfect record of everything that ever happened to an individual. Since the subconscious mind responded to suggestion rather than reason, it had to be gently guided through a process of reprogramming. "We must re-educate the subconscious mind, replacing every thought of fear with a thought of faith, every thought of illness with a thought of health, every thought of death with a thought of life," Sanford wrote.[17]

Stapelton's methods closely followed Sanford's. As an adult, Stapleton thought she had had the perfect childhood until she began to recover memories she had repressed for years. She discovered that her inner child knew only rejection and failure. To deal with her own hurts and those of others, she developed a form of "faith-imagination therapy" that involved recovering painful childhood memories and then reimagining those experiences as they should have happened. "There is a natural law in the universe which says that two things cannot occupy the same space at the same time. Using faith-imagination, the mind fills the emotional space occupied by a negative thought or memory with a new, more powerful, positive thought and image," Stapleton wrote. The result created a new reality. "Faith imagination creates an objective experience. It does not approximate or simulate one." Jesus can change past experiences because he is not bound by time. We "can't go back; but Jesus can . . . every moment you ever lived or ever will live is a present-tense experience for him."[18]

Stapelton's first book on inner healing, *The Gift of Inner Healing* (1976), consists mostly of stories of those healed through this process. One describes a woman, Joyce Joiner, who was literally on her way to a mental hospital when her husband brought her to see Stapleton. Joiner, whose mother had died when she was only four years old, grew up feeling unwanted. As an adult she became "cold, calculating, impersonal." Stapleton had Joiner imagine the day of her mother's funeral and imagine Jesus walking into her house to comfort her in her loneliness. But when Stapleton asked Joiner to imagine Jesus bringing her mother back to life she could not do it; her mother remained "in the box." So Stapleton had her imagine walking into her childhood bedroom with Jesus and then inviting Mary, Jesus's mother, into the room. As Mary entered, "there was a pause, and then Mrs. Joiner broke into deep, wracking sobs. She could barely speak through the flood of emotion. 'Holding me, holding me, Mary is holding me.' " After being comforted by Mary, Stapleton had Joiner return to the living room where her mother now stood, waiting to embrace her. "Her deepest desire had been fulfilled. Her mother's arms held her at last," writes Stapleton. This was exactly the kind of inner healing therapy that PTL now offered its partners. One wonders what would have happened if Bakker had opened himself up to this approach, considering the hidden traumas of his childhood.[19]

Heritage USA also provided the space and facilities to launch programs aimed at those who needed financial and material assistance. On April 26, 1982, PTL opened its first People That Love Center at Heritage USA. By December there were 550 People That Love Centers scattered around the country, from Florida to Texas to California to Wisconsin to New Hampshire and in just about every state in between, each run by a local church and staffed by volunteers. Eventually there were more than eight hundred. The centers distributed food, clothing, and children's toys to those in need and helped the unemployed pay their rent and find jobs. They resembled Salvation Army thrift stores, except that everything was given away for free. The original center at Heritage USA served about two hundred families a week by the end of 1982. The centers provided significant help to those in need, and PTL capitalized on their public relations appeal. People That Love Centers figured prominently in PTL's promotional literature from this period, though the ministry spent only about half a percent of its operating budget on them. The cost was negligible compared to the centers' branding potential.[20]

In late 1983 PTL began construction of a home for unwed mothers at Heritage USA called the People That Love Home. The home, which opened on July 1, 1984, was designed to provide an alternative to abortion. It was intended to accommodate about thirty pregnant women and new mothers in a bright, attractive setting, with a central living room, complete kitchen, laundry facilities, and a supportive staff. Mothers also had access to accredited high-school classes and vocational training. Soon after it opened, the home was at full capacity and had a waiting list. PTL also had its own adoption agency, The Tender Loving Care Adoption Agency. The agency allowed birth mothers to help choose the families for their babies by giving them access to non-identifying information about prospective parents. The goal was to ensure "that the baby went into the best Christian-like family atmosphere for that particular infant," said Vickie Liddell, one of the agency's child placement social workers. "We were very active and vibrant and did a lot of community networking within the state and outside the state as well," Liddell later said. The home represented a principled stand for PTL but, as with the People That Love Centers, it was also good for marketing. Combating abortion was important to evangelicals, and the home figured prominently in PTL literature. At one point Bakker was told that the home could be used to raise ten times more money than it cost to run. Like the People That Love Centers, it only accounted for about half a percent of PTL's operating budget.[21]

Much the same was true of PTL's prison ministry. Tammy had been visiting prisons since the late 1970s and usually made a point of doing so at Christmas time. She visited both men's and women's prisons, mostly in the South, but understandably felt the strongest connection to the women. She was completely uninhibited by the setting and talked to the women in the same way she talked to any other audience, without condescension or judgment. They in turn embraced her. It was perhaps the only audience in front of which Tammy felt sure that she was not being judged for her lack of polish and sophistication, which might explain why she kept going back. Promos on PTL's prison ministry often featured Tammy, but not Jim, who had little direct connection to the outreach. In March 1983, Bakker told his viewers that PTL programming was available in more than one thousand prisons, and that more than thirty-seven thousand prisoners had been won to Christ. The result, Bakker claimed, would save the government millions because "those boys that get saved very few of them will ever go back to prison. A big percentage of crime is conducted by ex-convicts in America. But Jesus changes lives."[22]

In June 1983, PTL completed construction of a 96-room motel, the Heritage Inn, designed to supplement the 325 campsites available to visitors. It also continued the construction of housing developments on the grounds for permanent residents and vacation rentals, beginning with the Dogwood Hills condominiums and then expanding to include the Mulberry Village single-family homes, the Wood Ridge duplexes, and the Lakeside Lodges time-share apartments. Heritage Farm, located on the grounds, had a petting zoo with goats and other small, cuddly animals and horse stables. By spring 1983, the farm had eight horses, which were available for trail rides winding through the wooded and undeveloped portions of the Heritage grounds for only five dollars. There were also three restaurants at Heritage USA at the time, a hamburger stand called McMoose's, the Wagon Wheel Inn cafeteria, and The Little Horse Restaurant, which provided "sit-down dining at its best."[23]

In September 1983, PTL purchased the childhood home of Billy Graham, which was located on Park Road in Charlotte and was about to be demolished to make way for development. Graham was born in 1918, and his family moved into the house in 1928. PTL planned to disassemble the 3,000-square-foot home brick by brick and reconstruct it at Heritage USA. The total cost was over $200,000, but for Bakker this was a small price to pay for the chance to be so closely associated with Graham. When the renovation was finally complete, it became one of Heritage USA's most popular attractions, averaging three hundred to four hundred visitors a day. In essence, Bakker was using the Graham home to buy authenticity.[24]

All of these initiatives represented an expansion of Bakker's vision for Heritage USA. Highlight videos from the period show constant construction, with a new groundbreaking every few months. The complex was fast becoming a self-contained community, a resort, and ministry center designed to draw thousands inside its gates from far and near. Bakker was not nearly finished. The biggest projects were yet to come.

CHANGES TO THE flagship television show, now called *Jim Bakker*, reflected the new expansiveness and confidence that Bakker exuded. In late 1981 and early 1982, the Barn was renovated to create a more attractive television studio that looked less like, well, a barn. The new set was designed to resemble the interior of a home, with a big living room at the front of the stage and a kitchen and dining room opening off the back. Gone was the more imposing *Tonight Show*–style desk. Bakker and his guests now sat at a big L-shaped arrangement of sofas and stuffed chairs. Behind and to the side were more sofas and chairs, at which the PTL Singers or other musical guests sat until it was their turn to perform. Then they would assemble around a piano or in some other casual arrangement as if they just happened to drop by.

It was all very relaxed and informal and represented another innovation. In the 1960s, talk shows like the *Tonight Show* represented the height of cultural cool. But Bakker now sensed that his audience wanted something more intimate and cozy, soft talk, not formal interviews. The new set looked just as professional, if not better than the sets of other daytime talk shows, including *The Merv Griffin Show* and the *Phil Donahue Show*, two of the most popular network talk shows of the early 1980s (Oprah did not go national until 1986).

The redesigned set gave the show a new look, but it did not solve the technical problems with the Barn, which had not really been designed as a television studio. For several years production of shows from the Barn had to be run through a remote truck parked alongside the building, with cables running from the set to the truck. Once, during a telethon in March 1983, PTL lost four hours of airtime when water shorted out the cables. To solve this problem Bakker built a new 1,500-seat Broadcast Center next to the Barn, which opened in July 1983. The new set incorporated the same living room look. In terms of production values, the show was now at the top of its game, and its equipment and facilities were on par with anything the networks had. In 1981, *The Merv Griffin Show* became the first network daily talk show to be distributed by satellite, something that PTL had been doing for years.[25]

The technical and design changes mirrored the new feel of the show. Earlier, in 1981, the show had cut back from two hours a day to one. This saved money, reducing by half the amount of airtime that had to be purchased from affiliates, but it also generally gave the show a more fast-paced, sophisticated look. Gone was the pervasive defensiveness and uncertainty that had accompanied the financial collapse in 1978 and 1979 and the pressure of the FCC investigation. Bakker was now trim, fit, and invariably stylishly dressed. "There is something so psychologically damaging to not finishing your goals. . . . They are like monuments to failure in your life," Bakker told his audience in February 1981. The opposite was true of seeing things through.

But in the process of becoming slicker and more polished, the show also lost some of its edge. It no longer included guests like Eldridge Cleaver, Little Richard, and Larry Flynt. Highlight videos now featured the likes of Pat Boone, Donna Douglas, NBA star Elvin Hayes, *Hee Haw*'s LuLu Roman, former Miss America Cheryl Prewitt, singer Dottie Rambo, Ruth Carter Stapleton, Efrem Zimbalist Jr., Roy Rogers and Dale Evans, actor Dean Jones, NASCAR driver Bobby Allison, and celebrity preachers Robert Schuller, Jimmy Swaggart, and Frederick Price. In February 1983, Jim and Tammy did an interview with Billy Graham. "I love you with all my heart," Graham told them. "I watch you so often, my goodness, I feel like I'm part of your family." No American religious figure of the early 1980s was more respected than Graham. PTL's success made it more mainstream and pulled it more to the center of its religious base, the kinds of people who would happily watch an hour of *Camp Meeting USA* every night in prime time.[26]

NONE OF IT came cheap. From all appearances, PTL was more vibrant and successful than ever, but ramping up construction at Heritage USA required constant fundraising. By the end of 1982, PTL needed about $1 million a week to stay afloat. It was known as a "slow pay" organization and rarely paid vendors on time. On August 13, 1982, during one of PTL's periodic financial crises, Bakker begged his audience to give more, telling them that he needed a $1 million "to get caught up." "I've got to have a miracle. I've *got* to have a miracle," Bakker pleaded.[27]

A week later he read off a list of 155 affiliate stations and how much PTL owed to each one on the air. It took eight minutes, non-stop, for him to read all the stations and the amounts due. The bills ranged from $176,300 in Philadelphia, $150,680 in New York City, and $137,000 in Los Angeles to $688 in Ottumwa, Iowa, $3,100 in Glendive, Montana, and $3,600 in Hazard, Kentucky. The total was $3,717,590, not including Canada and international. "I've set a goal that every one of my affiliates and all my bills are going to be paid. Otherwise I'm not going to spend another penny. I'll keep cutting back until I can pay every bill," Bakker promised his viewers. But of course construction continued at Heritage USA.[28]

To keep people interested and entice them to give, PTL periodically adopted promotional themes and gave away a variety of gifts. For much of 1982 and 1983, the theme of the show was "You Can Make It!" complete with a theme song by the same name. Partners received a "You Can Make It!" lapel pin and placard. There was also a "You Can Make It!" license plate and refrigerator magnet. For a $15 a month pledge, partners got Jim's latest book, *Survival: Unite to Live*, Tammy's book, *Run to the Roar*, a subscription to *Together* magazine, and a membership card that entitled them to 10 percent off everything at Heritage USA when they visited. PTL published annual devotional guides and calendars, available when you sent a donation. For $25, contributors received Bakker's six-cassette tape sermon series, "How You Can Guarantee Success." For $50, donors could get cassettes of Efrem Zimbalist Jr. reading the Psalms and Proverbs in his magnificently rich voice. Earlier, in 1981, Zimbalist had recorded the entire New Testament, which viewers could get for a gift of $120. For a gift of $1,000, donors could have their name engraved on a stone placed in the "Walk of Faith" outside the Upper Room. In 1983 Jim published a new book, *You Can Make It!*, but the ministry continued to give away copies of *Survival: Unite to Live*, which they apparently had a lot of. The same was true of the six-cassette series on success. Various combinations of gifts were promoted on nearly every PTL broadcast from 1981 to 1983.

When this was not enough, Bakker resorted to telethons. PTL held at least one major telethon a year, and the events seemed to energize Bakker, launching him into full huckster mode. For six or seven hours a day of live television, his enthusiasm did not wane. Nearly all of the staff participated in one way or another, often manning phones or tallying up pledges and then racing to Bakker's side to report the results live on the air.

The major telethon for 1983, "You and Us Together," had its own theme song, which began "You and us together, what a winning combination . . . reaching out in love." To supplement PTL's call center in the Upper Room, Bakker contracted with an off-site professional call center for an additional eighty phone lines and operators to take pledges, and a PTL staffer, Brad Lacey, did live on-the-air updates from the contract call center. Part way through the telethon, the phones in the Upper Room were moved onto the set to make them more a part of the action.

Granted, fundraising events are not the best indication of an organization's intellectual depth. Public radio does not sound its best during annual pledge drives (tote bag, anyone?). But fundraisers are a good indication of what organizations think their contributors value and what they will give money to support. Bakker peppered his viewers with statistics on what PTL was accomplishing at home and around the world. He claimed that the 633 People That Love Centers then in operation would serve 24 million people that year. He repeatedly told viewers that PTL was on the air in 39 nations and had a potential audience of 600 million, though he offered no real proof and usually omitted "potential." Once the 600 million figure had been established, he spun off a dizzying array of numbers on what donors' contributions would accomplish. With a $50 million a year budget, PTL was spending only $0.0833 per person to reach 600 million people around the world. Each $15 a month pledge would reach 2,168 people in 39 nations every day for an entire year. No other form of evangelism came this cheap. Of course, these numbers would have been even more impressive had Bakker told his viewers exactly what portion of the budget actually went to television programming, but then he would have had to explain where the rest of the money ended up.[29]

Bakker pressed his supporters to give, preaching what historian Kate Bowler has termed "hard prosperity." Prosperity preachers from the 1970s and 1980s tended to reduce the cause and effect of giving and receiving to something resembling a legal contract or mathematical equation. In fact, Bakker had a number: 23 percent. During the "You and Us Together" telethon he told viewers, "An outside firm that does surveys surveyed the viewers of PTL. And they found out that the people that watched the [PTL] satellite network, actually there was a 23 percent increase in income" over the previous year. "The survey people" could not "figure that out, why there was such a dramatic change that was not evident in the national trends." Bakker knew why: "we knew the principle of giving, and those people that were watching the [PTL] satellite [network] have been fed on the word of God and God has prospered them. Oh, people, you can't beat God giving, no matter how hard you try."[30]

The majority of Bakker's justification for his prosperity message came not from surveys but from the Bible. One of Bakker's favorite Bible verses in this regard (a favorite of every prosperity preacher from this period) was Luke 6:38: "Give, and it shall be given unto you; good measure, pressed down, and shaken together, and running over, shall men give into your bosom. For with the same measure that ye mete withal it shall be measured to you again." Giving obligated God to bless you with a multiple of what you gave. "God always keeps his part of the bargain," Bakker assured his viewers. "So when you give God says I'll give back to you pressed down, shaken together . . . give and you will receive, sow and you will reap . . . a 30-, 60-, or 100-fold blessing."[31]

Likewise, not giving brought a curse. Here Bakker and other prosperity preachers quoted Malachi 3:8–9: "Will a man rob God? Yet ye have robbed me. But ye say, Wherein have we robbed thee? In tithes and offerings. Ye are cursed with a curse: for ye have robbed me, even this whole nation." But the situation could easily be reversed. The next verse in Malachi reads: "Bring ye all the tithes into the storehouse, that there may be meat in mine house, and prove me now herewith, saith the LORD of hosts, if I will not open you the windows of heaven, and pour you out a blessing, that there shall not be room enough to receive it." For Bakker's audience, these verses, presented in this way, were a powerful incentive to give.[32]

Bakker's prosperity teaching was hardly unique, and his guests reinforced his message. On day six of the "You and Us Together" telethon, Richard Roberts, son of Oral, dropped by to preach and sing. More than once during the seven-hour telecast he sang a song entitled, "I Started Living When I Started Giving to God." Part of the chorus reads, "I started living when I started giving to God. Pressed down, shaken together, running over he's blessing me," and one of the verses reads, "There are pages in my life that I truly regret. I lost everything I had, stayed deep in debt. But then one day I happened to read, in Malachi chapter 3, that my release would bring an increase for me." The tune was as simple as the lyrics.[33]

While Bakker waited for his staff to total the pledges during the last hour of that day's show, Richard Roberts and singer Vicki Jamison prayed for healings, using words of knowledge to identify various ailments that they believed God was healing over the air and asking viewers to call in when they had been healed. When Bakker returned to the set he triumphantly announced that they had raised $1,067,402 in the last 100 minutes of the broadcast. "Just think how God is going to multiply it back to everyone that gave," Roberts said. "That could be $100 million in blessing out there all over the country," Bakker agreed. Then Bakker drew a connection between the healings that Roberts and Jamison had been praying for and the money that had poured in. "That's why so many miracles are taking place. I've never seen it to fail that whenever the people give like this we always see an outpouring of healings take place. It's fixed in God's principles of sowing and reaping and giving and receiving," Bakker said.[34]

To convince his audience that God rewarded giving with 100-fold returns (or at least 23 percent), Bakker had to overcome long-standing and deeply held understandings in Christian theology that linked poverty, simplicity, and disregard for the things of this world with holiness. But Bakker had recent trends on his side, not to mention the myriad voices of other prosperity preachers. Consumerism had been on the rise in American culture throughout the twentieth century, but in the 1980s "conspicuous consumption," the buying of luxury items for public display, reached a new level of accessibility and acceptance among the middle class. Between 1963 and 1983 the median price of new homes sold in the United States jumped from $18,000 to $75,300. By 1993 it was $126,500. Adjusted for inflation this represented a 30 percent increase from 1963 to 1983 and a 50 percent increase from 1963 to 1993. The size of single-family homes increased by one-third over the same period, and consumer credit expanded dramatically. Robert Allen's 1980 bestseller *Nothing Down* advised readers on how to buy real estate with little or no cash of their own. "You've got the world to gain and nothing to lose," Allen wrote. "You can become wealthy with as much or as little effort as it takes to be poor."[35]

The status of money and what it could buy worked its way deep into popular culture. By 1980, "citizen" and "consumer" were used interchangeably in discussions of economic policy. A line from Madonna's hit 1984 song "Material Girl" proclaimed "the boy with the cold hard cash is always Mister Right." In the 1987 film *Wall Street,* Gordon Gekko, portrayed by Michael Douglas, utters one of the most memorable movie lines of the decade: "Greed, for lack of a better word, is good." Douglas won an Oscar for Best Actor for the role.[36]

The real-life inspirations for Gordon Gekko—Ivan Boesky and Michael Milken—were every bit as audacious as the screen character. The son of a Russian immigrant, Boesky made millions on Wall Street brokering corporate takeovers. The year before *Wall Street* premiered, Boesky gave the commencement address at the University of California at Berkeley's Business School. "Greed is all right, by the way. I want you to know that. I think greed is healthy. You can be greedy and still feel good about yourself," Boesky told the students, who applauded enthusiastically. A few months later Boesky was arrested for insider trading and eventually sentenced to three years in prison. Michael Milken was even bigger, using junk bonds to raise tens of billions of dollars for startups and entrepreneurs, while making hundreds of millions in profits for himself and his employer, the Wall Street firm Drexel Burnham. Arrested shortly after Boesky, Milken received a ten-year sentence for securities fraud.[37]

American charismatics and Pentecostals would never say that greed was good, but they now had little patience for the notion that restraint, let alone poverty, was any better. Bakker became, in some respects, a religious counterpart to Boesky and Milken. He had none of their financial savvy but every bit as much ambition. Like Milken, Bakker had a grand sense of mission. Milken wanted to get rich, but he also "saw himself on a mission to save the U.S. economy," according to historian Robert Collins. Just as Milken's junk bonds provided financing for struggling startups and entrepreneurs while earning Drexel (and Milken) millions, Bakker's PTL satellite network provided a platform to proclaim the gospel around the world while earning contributors (and Bakker) God's guarantee of a 30-, 60-, or 100-fold blessing. Where could you get a better deal than that?[38]

PTL was bringing in more money than ever, but it was still never enough to keep up with the pace of construction at Heritage USA. On June 20, 1983, Bakker held an impromptu telethon from the unfinished Broadcast Center. The building was originally supposed to cost $2.5 million, but the bill had ballooned to $5 million, and it was still not done. It was scheduled to open the next day, but Bakker had run out of money, and the contractor refused to resume work until they were paid. "Tomorrow I have to have $1 million, and, well, I don't have it," Bakker told viewers. In fact, Bakker did not know the extent of PTL's debts and did not really want to. While on the air Bakker turned to Peter Bailey, PTL's accounting manager and a member of its Finance Committee, and said, "When I say we got needs I'm not stretching." "Not one bit. You probably don't even realize how much there is to pay," Bailey replied. "If I had $10 million you would still owe some bills wouldn't you?" Bakker asked. "Yes, but that would go a long way to keeping us from going so far behind. But even with the $10 million we'd still have a lot to pay," Bailey said. Somehow Bakker managed to get enough money to finish the Broadcast Center in time for its July 4th dedication before immediately moving to his next project.[39]

BAKKER RARELY ENGAGED in politics, and then only in ways that bolstered his celebrity status and abundant life theology. PTL's resurgence made Bakker an attractive ally for politicians, particularly as the 1980 presidential election approached. "The PTL Club is fast becoming a campaign stop for presidential candidates," noted the *Charlotte Observer* in January 1980. That March, President Jimmy Carter invited Bakker and a half dozen other preachers, including Oral Roberts, Rex Humbard, Demos

Shakarian, and Jerry Falwell, to the White House for breakfast to discuss "economic, moral and international problems," according to Bakker. In April Bakker spoke at a "Washington for Jesus" rally on the national mall in front of an estimated half-million people. The day before the event, First Lady Rosalyn Carter invited Jim and Tammy to the White House for a reception. In late August President Carter's liaison to the religious community, Bob Maddox, a Southern Baptist preacher from Georgia, came to Charlotte to meet with Bakker and other church leaders. These efforts notwithstanding, Carter's presidency had been a disappointment to most evangelicals, which is why he hired Maddox in an effort to rebuild his support among evangelicals.[40]

Carter's declaration that he had been "born again" was key to his success in the 1976 presidential election and was one of the main reasons *Newsweek* declared 1976 "The Year of the Evangelical." Carter's Southern Baptist faith was deep and sincere and only intensified as he entered politics in his home state of Georgia. His commitment to human rights and social justice was steadfast throughout his presidency and firmly anchored in a biblical framework. A hastily written campaign biography, *The Miracle of Jimmy Carter*, declared that what made Carter special was his faith: "faith in the Lord Jesus Christ, faith therefore in himself, and faith in the American people." The same press that published Jim Bakker's first autobiography, *Move That Mountain*, also published the Carter biography. In fact, the two books appeared almost simultaneously—Carter's biography on June 25, 1976, and Bakker's nine days later on July 4.[41]

Yet Carter largely failed to engage evangelicals and their concerns directly. For most of his presidency his staff held evangelical leaders at arm's length, refusing to answer their letters or return their calls, and Carter did not appoint any evangelicals to significant government posts. By the time Carter appointed Maddox, two and a half years into his presidency, it was already too late. Carter's interview in *Playboy*, which appeared in November 1976, did not help his image among evangelicals, even though what he said in the interview was unremarkably orthodox. Nor did his sober outlook on the human condition, which did not fit well with the optimistic sensibilities of Bakker and his audience. Carter was an admirer of the theologians Reinhold Niebuhr and Paul Tillich, who tended to emphasize the gulf between faith and culture. Though both appeared on the cover of *Time*, Niebuhr in 1948 and Tillich in 1959, by the 1970s neither was much admired among evangelicals. Carter saw issues such as "abortion, gay rights, prayer in the schools, the Equal Rights Amendment or the spread of pornography" in "complex terms" noted an article in the *Charlotte Observer* about Maddox's meeting with Bakker. But what most clearly separated Carter and Bakker was something more central to the latter's core message.[42]

Carter's so-called malaise speech, given as the nation confronted an energy crisis brought about by decreased oil production in the wake of the Iranian revolution of 1979, was the polar opposite of the "positive confession" that Bakker had always urged his audience to maintain. Though Carter never actually used the word *malaise* in his July 15, 1979 speech, he spoke at length about America's "crisis of confidence . . . a crisis that strikes at the very heart and soul and spirit of our national will." Unlike Bakker, who tended to blame enemies or the devil for his problems, rather than himself, Carter urged Americans to examine their own failings and recent tendency toward "fragmentation and self-interest." "This is not a message of happiness or reassurance, but it is the truth and it is a warning," Carter told the nation. To be fair, Carter acknowledged "the strength of America" and listed "America's confidence" as one of "our greatest resources." But his jeremiad was ill timed to appeal to evangelicals caught up in visions of an abundant life.[43]

Ronald Reagan's theological commitments were murkier than Carter's, but his pervasive optimism was a much better fit with Bakker's prosperity message. Reagan grew up attending a Disciples of Christ church in Dixon, Illinois. The Disciples are part of the Restorationist movement that began in the early nineteenth century, so called because they aimed to restore Christianity as it had been practiced at the time the New Testament was written, without all of the corruptions introduced over subsequent centuries. After high school Reagan attended Eureka College, a Christian Church (Disciples of Christ) school in Illinois before becoming a radio sports announcer in Iowa and then heading to Hollywood in 1937.

In 1940 Reagan married actress Jane Wyman, but the two divorced in 1949 as her career flourished and he became more interested in politics. Three years later Reagan married another actress, Nancy Davis, whom he had met in 1949 while serving as president of the Screen Actors Guild. Fortunately for Reagan, divorce was no longer as important an issue in 1980, when he ran for president, as it had been only a few decades before, as Tammy's mother had so painfully discovered. Reagan also reversed his stance on abortion. Earlier he had supported abortion rights, signing into law the Therapeutic Abortion Act as governor of California, one of the nation's most liberal abortion statutes at the time. By 1979 he had changed his mind and aligned himself with the pro-life movement. Reagan was, in the words of historian Steven Miller, "more of an evangelical's president than an evangelical president." Reagan's tax returns revealed that he gave little to churches and charities. At about the same time that he taped an interview with Jim Bakker in his California office in November 1979, Reagan appeared on stage with Dean Martin and Frank Sinatra.[44]

But none of this mattered to Bakker and his audience as much as Reagan's sunny outlook. Reagan insisted that America was a great nation with a glorious future. While Carter's presidency had become mired in worries about inflation, energy, and the Iran hostage crisis, Reagan told Americans that the best was yet to come. In accepting the Republican presidential nomination in July 1980, Reagan declared that he intended to "renew the American spirit and sense of purpose." He criticized Carter and his party for saying "that the United States has had its day in the sun; that our nation has passed its zenith . . . that the future will be one of sacrifice and few opportunities. . . . I utterly reject that view." Reagan ended his speech by asking delegates to join together in a moment of silent prayer. The words might as well have been Bakker's.[45]

Then there was Reagan's apocalypticism. Like Bakker, Reagan understood that Americans in general and evangelicals in particular were fascinated with the end times. According to a 1984 poll, 39 percent of Americans connected a nuclear apocalypse with biblical prophecies. A few months before Carter invited him to the White House, Bakker taped an interview with Ronald Reagan in Los Angeles. After a brief discussion of his commitment to bring "moral fiber" back to the White House, Reagan turned to the end times. "Do you ever get the feeling that if we don't do this now, if we let this be another Sodom and Gomorrah, that maybe we might be the generation that sees Armageddon?" he asked Bakker.[46]

Decoding Bible prophecy drove enormous book sales among American evangelicals. The best-selling book of the 1970s was Hal Lindsey's *Late Great Planet Earth*, which Reagan read and which eventually sold more than twenty-eight million copies. In 1979 it was turned into a movie narrated by Orson Welles (*Citizen Kane* it is not). Lindsey was a former Mississippi River tugboat captain who preached to Jesus People in Southern California and on the UCLA campus in the late 1960s, developing a series of lectures on the coming apocalypse that formed the structure of the book.[47]

There was nothing particularly original about Lindsey's predictions—books on prophecy jammed the shelves of Christian bookstores at the time—but his account was short, lively, and easy to understand. According to Lindsey's scheme, Russia would trigger humanity's last great battle at Armageddon by invading Israel. This would pull in African countries and the Chinese ("The Yellow Peril," in Lindsey's words), resulting in World War III and Christ's second coming. The end was near, Lindsey assured his readers. Jesus would almost certainly return before the end of the millennium, a conviction that Bakker and many leading evangelicals shared. Gerard Straub worked as a television producer for Pat Robertson at CBN from 1978 to 1980. Once, Straub's boss at CBN approached him with a special project: televising Christ's Second Coming from Jerusalem to every corner of the globe in all the necessary languages. The technical challenges were daunting, but no one seemed to doubt that the event was imminent. Bakker often told reporters and his television audience that he was sure Christ would return during his lifetime.[48]

Reagan understood this conception of history, reflected in his strong support for Israel and deep suspicion of communist Russia. Bakker likewise staunchly supported Israel, in part because it was the land of the Bible, but also because of its prophetic significance. Bakker visited Israel on several occasions, beginning in June 1981 when he and Tammy met privately with Prime Minister Menachem Begin in his office. Despite his clear religious beliefs, Jimmy Carter's worldview was more nuanced and based on a wider reading of the Bible that did not place nearly as much weight on connecting prophecy to current events. After his interview with Reagan was over, but while the camera was still rolling, Bakker assured Reagan that "we can deliver, with God's help . . . fifty million votes." "Wow," responded a cautious, but nevertheless intrigued, Reagan.[49]

Yet Bakker did not endorse Reagan. PTL aired a twenty-minute segment of Bakker's interview with Reagan on January 9 but also extended invitations to appear on the show to President Carter and Democrat Edward Kennedy, as well as Republicans John Connally and George Bush. The day after the Reagan interview aired, PTL announced that Republican candidates Howard Baker, Philip Crane, John Anderson, and Bob Dole had agreed to appear on the show, along with Mississippi Governor Cliff Finch, a Democrat. This pretty much covered the field. On October 31, 1980, Bakker flew from Memphis to Jackson, Mississippi, with Carter aboard Air Force One. Bakker and Carter "spent much of the flight in private conversation," praying and reading the Bible. In Jackson, Bakker rode in Carter's motorcade, though Roger Flessing, who accompanied Bakker, pointed out that this did not constitute "an endorsement of Carter." Bakker later told reporter Frye Gaillard that he voted for Carter in the November

1980 election. Bakker's public support for Reagan only solidified after the election, in which 80 percent of evangelicals voted for Reagan.[50]

After the election, Bakker helped to shore up evangelical support for Reagan, and Reagan's attention bolstered PTL's image. When PTL held a "Victory Day" celebration in July 1983 to mark the completion of the new Broadcast Center, Reagan sent a 245-word telegram congratulating the ministry as it began "a new chapter in your efforts to share the spiritual values and proclaim the faith that are the foundation of your work." Five years earlier it looked like PTL might collapse under the weight of its debts. Now it enjoyed the endorsement of the President, and Bakker was thrilled. His politics were never as well defined as those of Jerry Falwell or Pat Robertson, and he was relatively uninvolved in formulating the Religious Right's agenda. But this was not what he was really after. Reagan's optimism was a better fit with Bakker's prosperity message than Carter's realism, but Bakker had nevertheless been thrilled to ride with Carter on Air Force One and put a photo of himself shaking hands with President Carter on the cover of *Action* in April 1980 and another of himself and Tammy with Rosalyn Carter at the White House on the July 1980 cover. The allure of politics for Bakker mostly boiled down to photo ops, which is why he did not spurn Carter and endorse Reagan before the election. For Bakker, cultural relevance mattered more than political ideology.[51]

After reading Reagan's telegram to a standing-room-only crowd in the Barn auditorium on July 2, Bakker told them that the next year would be a year of "dynamic change." Buoyed by a growing sense of optimism, Bakker's ambition only increased over the next several months. "I'm believing that 1984 is going to be the greatest year of . . . progress this ministry has ever had," Bakker told his viewers in November 1983. "We're planning to do more in '84 . . . than we've ever done. I plan, with God's help, to probably do as much in '84 as I have done in all my life put together." As his plans grew, Bakker ratcheted up his fundraising as well. He now had a new, catchier number for donors to use: 1-800-CALL-JIM.[52]

But off camera the ethical and organizational failings that led to recent crises remained unresolved. PTL's foundation was not strong enough to hold the weight of what Bakker planned to do next. He was poised to launch a new set of projects that would represent his greatest achievements and sow the seeds of PTL's eventual demise.

9

Secret Lives

THERE WAS ANOTHER side to PTL's development in the early 1980s. The divide between the secret lives of PTL's leaders and the ministry that everyone else saw (including most PTL employees) became deeper and wider than it had been only a few years before.

Apart from its paid staff, PTL had a large contingent of volunteers, many of whom had moved to Charlotte so that they could serve at PTL. Their focus was not so much on the Bakkers as the specific ministries they were involved in. Kay Tohline, thirty-two, became a volunteer phone counselor at PTL after she moved to Charlotte from Knoxville, Tennessee. "Jim Bakker is not for me the most important thing about PTL. I'm at PTL because of the beautiful people I meet here," she told the *Charlotte Observer*. Volunteering at PTL changed Bill Appleford's life. After retiring and spending a few years in Fort Lauderdale, Appleford moved to Charlotte to be near his children and grandchildren. "For three years, I just sat around like a vegetable," Appleford told a reporter. Then he volunteered as a statistician for the network. "Life has so much meaning and more fulfillment for me now. There's so much love and compassion here. You want to live for the Lord, and you want others to see Jesus through your daily life. I just wish I could express in words what is in my heart," Appleford said.[1]

At its peak, PTL had more than a thousand volunteers serving in various capacities. Many of the paid staff at PTL began as volunteers. Elaine Sinclair, fifty-seven, moved from Boston to Charlotte after her husband's death. She began answering phones as a volunteer and then was hired to work in food services at Heritage USA. "I wouldn't be anywhere doing anything else," she told a reporter in June 1980. "Every day I come to work, I get a lump in my throat. I get the same feeling that I get when I see the United States flag, because I know all this property is anointed by God."

For staffers and volunteers like Tohline, Appleford, and Sinclair, PTL was a community that extended far beyond the Bakkers.[2]

Most PTL employees saw the Bakkers only in passing and never spoke with Jim or Tammy at any length. They had no way to gauge the deep divides that threatened to tear the Bakkers' marriage apart. In an interview in November 1980, Tammy confessed that when construction began at Heritage USA in 1978, "at first it was fun . . . but as the weeks began to turn into months with Jim gone all the time overseeing every tree that was cut, every road that was put in, my enthusiasm began to sour. Would this never end?" When Ed Stoeckel insisted on putting the property up for sale, Tammy was "happy it was almost over: the days and nights of worry, the horrible extra financial burden, the months of talking to a husband who never heard a word I said, the months of doing things all by myself." This was the most positive spin she could put on the events of the past two years in a column she wrote for the PTL partner magazine. In reality her loneliness and disappointment was much worse.[3]

In the fall of 1979 Jim and Tammy began cohosting the *PTL Club* in an effort to make Tammy feel more a part of the ministry, an arrangement that relegated Henry Harrison to one of the guest chairs or the couch. But hosting an increasingly sophisticated television talk show was not nearly as fulfilling for Tammy as it was for Jim. "We used to be more alike than we are now. Jim's more laid-back and quiet than I am. Sometimes I wish he were more nutty," Tammy confided to the *Saturday Evening Post* in late 1980.[4]

A week after Jim returned from Florida and his sexual encounter with Jessica Hahn, the Bakkers and a large contingent of PTL staff left for Hawaii to shoot a series of shows on location in Honolulu. They were gone for nearly a month. The event was billed as PTL's first international prayer meeting. Hosts of the overseas PTL shows were invited, as were supporters from the mainland and abroad. The setting was paradise, but the escalating tension between Jim and Tammy was anything but. They both looked fit, tanned, and thin, even as their marriage was falling apart.

The show's primary set was on an outdoor lawn overlooking the beach. PTL shipped its own remote truck to Hawaii to handle production (the staff who spent most of their day inside the truck joked that it looked the same in Charlotte as in Hawaii). After each episode was shot, it was sent back to Charlotte that night via satellite uplink and aired the next day. For the January 6 episode, Jim Bakker, Henry Harrison, and their guests all wore white pants and Hawaiian shirts, including Alan Langstaff, host of the PTL show in Australia, and actors Efrem Zimbalist Jr. and Richard Denning, who played the governor of Hawaii in the TV series *Hawaii Five-O*. A few minutes in, John Wesley Fletcher bounded onto the stage to report on healing meetings he had been holding across the islands under the auspices of PTL. Less than a month after the Jessica Hahn affair, Bakker and Fletcher seemed the closest of confidants. Fletcher sat next to Jim while Tammy sat at the other end of the set next to Uncle Henry. In all the irony surrounding the Hawaii trip, perhaps none exceeded Jim Bakker asking Fletcher to pray on the air for God to heal and restore broken marriages.[5]

Jim and Tammy stayed in a $350-a-night suite at the top of the Ilikai Hotel overlooking the beach, but slept in separate rooms and spent much of their time together yelling and arguing. Alan Langstaff remembers that the tension between Jim and Tammy was palpable. "You could cut it with a knife," recalls Lee Nagelhout, who was part of the production team in Hawaii. When Langstaff and a number of others were invited up to the Bakkers' suite, Tammy stayed in her room, too upset to come out and greet her guests. Tammy told Jim that she did not love him and that she was moving out and wanted a divorce (she did not even know about Jessica Hahn at this point). Jim consulted some of his key staff, including Roger Flessing, Sam Orender, and Thurlow Spurr about what to do next. There seemed to be little hope of reconciliation. "We were doomed for divorce, we were doomed for a broken family," Tammy later said.[6]

The PTL staff on location could not help but notice Tammy "running back and forth scantily clothed," recalls Lee Nagelhout. "She was trying to get attention and she was getting it." An article in the *Saturday Evening Post* from January 1981 noted that Tammy had recently lost thirty pounds and was now "a perfect size 5 in clothes, shoes, and rings." She had also had cosmetic surgery, including breast implants, which she seemed determined to show off. The best that the Bakkkers' inner circle could hope for was to contain the fallout. Don Hardister, PTL's chief of security, knew they were in trouble when Roger Flessing pulled him aside. "Got a little wrinkle for you," Hardister recalls Flessing saying. "Jim and Tammy are no longer a couple. We're gonna do this and when we're done with this, she's goin' her way, he's goin' his way. Your job is to make sure that that doesn't happen until it's supposed to," Flessing told Hardister. "That was a miserable, miserable time," recalls Hardister.[7]

When the Hawaii trip ended, Tammy refused to go back to Charlotte. Her initial plan was to move to California and become a nurse. Instead she agreed to rent an apartment in Palmdale and undergo more counseling under the direction of Fred Gross and his team. Back home, Jim and the kids moved out of their house in downtown Charlotte and into a doublewide mobile home at Heritage USA. Jim also changed the name of the show from the *PTL Club* to *Jim Bakker*. Otherwise, PTL officially described Tammy as "under doctor's orders to relax." Bakker told his audience that Tammy had simply been working too hard and needed rest. He also blamed the FCC, his scapegoat for nearly everything that went wrong. "The doctors told me that the FCC problem was almost too much for Tammy to go through," Bakker told viewers on January 26, 1981.[8]

Gary Paxton was long gone by this time, but even in Hawaii Jim was convinced that Tammy was having another affair, he just did not know with whom. He tried to wheedle information out of Joyce Cordell, who did Jim's hair and makeup and Tammy's hair (Tammy insisted on doing her own makeup) before they went on the air. Cordell had seen Tammy and Thurlow Spurr together and suspected what might be happening but remained discreet.[9]

In early 1981 the Bakkers still owned a house on Lake Wylie in the River Hills development. Jim had not been there in months, but he knew Tammy still spent time at the house. In January, shortly after returning from Hawaii, but while Tammy was still in California, Jim spent a day house hunting around Lake Wylie with a real-estate agent. Since he was in the neighborhood he decided to stop by the old lake house. That night he phoned Joyce Cordell to tell her that he knew about Spurr. Bakker had found a letter torn to pieces in a trashcan and painstakingly reassembled it, a process that took "hours" since the letter was several pages long. It was from Tammy to Spurr, who was married, describing how she could not "wait until we can get away and be together." No wonder the Hawaii trip was so tense. While Jim harbored his secret about Jessica Hahn, Tammy was infatuated with Spurr, who was in charge of the music in Hawaii. The Bakkers, Fletcher, and Spurr often sat or stood only a few feet apart on the set as the cameras rolled and everyone smiled.[10]

When Jim confronted Spurr, he apparently made no effort to deny the affair. Instead he told Bakker what any number of associates had been telling him for years, that he should have paid more attention to Tammy. For once Bakker took the advice, flying to California repeatedly, in a jet chartered by PTL, to visit Tammy. "I feel like I'm dating again," Bakker told his television audience on January 26. By the time Tammy returned from California Spurr was gone, replaced by a new director of the PTL orchestra.[11]

Tammy resumed cohosting the show with Jim during the first week of February 1981, though she initially looked tired and pensive, and her makeup was thicker than ever. That same month the Bakkers moved into a new $350,000 home, paid for by PTL, in the stylish Tega Cay development on Lake Wylie, in an attempt to restore their marriage and family life. Home decorating was something that Jim and Tammy both enjoyed, and the Tega Cay house, built in a "Tiki" Polynesian style with cedar wood and pagoda roofs, had character. But it was also in disrepair and needed work. The floor in the kitchen had completely rotted through. The Bakkers did more than simply spruce it up. When they moved in, the house was 7,000 square feet. Over the next six years they continually remodeled it until it sprawled to more than 10,000 square feet at a total cost of $1 million.[12]

Jim and Tammy could never have enough closets. The master bedroom originally had two walk-in closets on either side of the bathroom. They added another 600-square-foot closet for Tammy as part of a new addition. The house eventually had twenty-five closets in all. The redesigned master bedroom had adjoining bathroom suites, with a sunken whirlpool tub between them. They expanded the deck area around the fish-shaped pool and added a hot tub and an outdoor kitchen area with a grill. The house eventually had three kitchens, one with commercial appliances. The living room was remodeled several times, including the addition of a catwalk with a spiral staircase, interior brickwork, and built-in bookcases. The staircase was solid mahogany and built with pegs, not nails. The paneling was one-inch-thick Blonde Honduran mahogany. The Bakkers added a bedroom for Jamie (Tammy's closet was above it) and converted another bedroom into Jim's office, removing two walls and replacing them with windows and glass doors so that Jim could have a view of the water. They also added a safe room, measuring nine by sixteen feet, with a door hidden behind a swing-away bookcase. In case of an attempted assassination or kidnapping, the Bakkers' children were trained to run for the safe room. Supporting the weight of all the renovations required rebuilding the foundation and footings. The electrical system was upgraded to 600 amps. Over the next several years PTL bought half a dozen neighboring homes to create a security perimeter around the Tega Cay house. As in so many other ways, with success Jim and Tammy became more isolated.[13]

NOWHERE WAS JIM'S reclusiveness more evident than in his new entourage. Among the new faces at PTL none would ultimately be more influential than Richard Dortch and the Taggart brothers, David and James. Like Bakker, all three would eventually go to prison for their roles at PTL.

The Taggart brothers came to PTL with Thurlow Spurr. They had grown up in a close-knit family with doting parents. When the boys were in grade school, their teacher, Mrs. Kitchen, asked their parents, Henry and Jane Taggart, to stop by the school to discuss "the artistic abilities of James and the special talents of David in music," according to Jane. Following the suggestion of the teacher, the Taggarts bought a piano and both boys took lessons. David could "make a piano talk," his mother later recalled. Above all, Jane Taggart taught her sons to stick together.[14]

David Taggart graduated from Churchill High School in Livonia, Michigan, in 1975. After high school he attended School Craft College in Livonia and then transferred to Wayne State University in Detroit, where he majored in piano performance. In the spring of 1978 he left college to join Thurlow Spurr's staff at PTL as Spurr's assistant, making about $12,000 a year. Taggart's background in music was helpful in his administrative role, but playing piano "was not his primary talent," according to Spurr.[15]

Jim Bakker spotted David Taggart's administrative skills and efficiency when Taggart was in Los Angeles, helping Spurr produce one of Tammy's records. The Bakkers had been vacationing in Mexico when they decided, on the spur of the moment, to go to Los Angeles so that Tammy could record the album, a project that ended up taking a month. Taggart had the flexibility and resourcefulness to deal with the sort of abrupt and complicated changes that Bakker often sprung on his staff. Bakker invited Taggart to become his personal assistant in September 1980, a few months before his encounter with Jessica Hahn in Florida.

Working for Bakker was exhausting. He was a micromanager who expected his staff to be constantly available. Bakker usually called Taggart first thing in the morning, sometimes as early as 5 a.m., and expected him to be in the office by 7:00 or 7:30. Bakker had a phone in his car that he would use to stay in touch with Taggart throughout the day. Taggart handled Bakker's schedule and correspondence, made travel arrangements for Bakker and his entourage, shopped for Bakker's wardrobe, and picked out the clothes he would wear each day on the show. After a twelve- to sixteen-hour workday, Bakker would sometimes call Taggart in the middle of the night. He was lucky if he got three or four hours of sleep. "I had basically no social life at all," Taggart later said.[16]

Even in junior high James Taggart knew he wanted to be an interior designer. After high school, he attended Lawrence Technological University in Southfield, Michigan, where he earned a degree in business and human resources with a minor in architecture. After college, James went to work for Splendor Productions, one of Thurlow Spurr's companies headquartered in Orlando. In December 1979 he moved to Charlotte as Spurr shifted more of his interests there. When David went to work for Bakker, James took his place on Spurr's Charlotte staff. After Bakker fired Spurr in early 1981, Taggart went to work for Lyn Robbins, a producer for the television show, as an administrative assistant.[17]

At about the same time, in early 1981, the Taggart brothers rented the River Hills home the Bakkers still owned. Shortly after moving in, they hosted an anniversary party for Jim and Tammy. James redecorated the home for the party, painting the beige walls apricot and replacing Tammy's rattan furniture with black lacquered pieces. The result was "very theatrical, very dramatic." Jim loved it. Up to that point he had no idea that James did interior decorating. "Why haven't you told me?" Bakker asked him. Instead of "running around doing paperwork," Bakker assigned James to work for Charlotte Whiting, a PTL vice president whose responsibilities included interior decorating for Heritage USA.[18]

Richard Dortch's association with PTL began with an appearance on the television program in 1977, when the studio was still located at the former furniture store. Born on October 15, 1931, during the Depression, Dortch was raised on a small farm in Illinois, about ten miles from St. Louis. At the start of World War II, the family moved to Granite City, Illinois, so that his father could take a job in a defense factory. Dortch found the Lord in December 1947 while listening to a twenty-nine-year-old evangelist from Oklahoma, Oral Roberts. Though he had dreamed of playing professional baseball, from that point on he wanted to be a preacher.[19]

To prepare for the ministry, Dortch attended North Central Bible Institute in Minneapolis, the same school that Jim and Tammy would later attend, and was subsequently licensed in the Assemblies of God, Jim's denomination. For five years, beginning in 1958, Dortch and his wife, Mildred, served as missionaries in Brussels, Belgium. Returning to the United States in 1963, Dortch took a pastorate in Alton, Illinois. In 1966 he was elected state secretary of the Assemblies of God in Illinois and in 1970 superintendent for Illinois. In 1978, about a year after he first appeared on the *PTL Club*, Dortch joined PTL's board.[20]

Dortch had a reputation as a pastor's pastor. He encouraged churches to increase pastors' salaries and contribute more toward their retirement. He also had an eye for talent and recruited capable young men to join his staff. As superintendent for Illinois, he had over nine hundred ministers under his care. With a big smile and deep voice, a firm handshake, and an outgoing manner, he exuded the warmth and confidence that Bakker lacked away from the cameras.

At the same time, Dortch had a deep personality flaw, a propensity to say things that were literally true, but calculated to deceive. The PTL staff called this "being Dortched." For instance, Pentecostals believe that God still speaks directly to individual believers. But instead of saying "God told me," Dortch would say, "I was made to know." In a sense, this provided a level of deniability. He was not literally saying that God spoke to him, but he knew that this was what fellow believers would assume. If things worked out, he got the credit for discerning the voice of God; if they did not, he could point out that he had not literally claimed to hear from God.[21]

As the Illinois superintendent, Dortch had a full schedule that included lots of time on the road, crisscrossing the state. Like Bakker, Dortch worked his staff hard. Al Cress became Dortch's executive assistant in January 1977 after graduating from Central Bible College in Springfield, Missouri. Born and raised in Trinidad, Colorado, the seventh of nine children, Cress graduated high school in 1967 and two years later joined the Navy, serving in Hawaii, Japan, the Philippines, and Latin America, before eventually enrolling at Central. As Dortch's assistant, Cress often worked seven days a week, dividing his time between the district office, where he answered Dortch's mail and kept his schedule, and traveling with Dortch on weekends. Dortch "was not a theologian, he was not a man of depth, he was basically an ecclesiastical politician," remembers Cress. With little time to study, Dortch got most of his sermons by having tapes of other preachers' sermons transcribed. "He would go somewhere, he would bring back a tape, we'd transcribe it and that became his sermon," remembers Cress. Cress rarely saw Dortch read his Bible.[22]

At times Dortch paid other ministers to write sermons for him, according to Jim Cobble, another member of Dortch's Illinois staff. Cobble, who had a Masters of Divinity degree from McCormick Theological Seminary in Chicago and a PhD from the University of Illinois, was director of continuing education for the Illinois district under Dortch. Cobble occasionally prepared talks for Dortch and on at least one occasion was "stunned by how good a job he did," delivering a talk from Cobble's notes. Dortch was not a "complicated" or "curious person," nor was he a "reader," according to Cobble, though he had considerable "diplomatic skills." From the vantage point of his position in the church, Dortch had watched many ministers face "a very bleak financial existence" once they retired. After he was passed over to become the head of the Assemblies of God, Dortch was determined not to let this happen to him. "I don't think that he would have ever gone [to PTL] other than the fact that the door closed on becoming general superintendent" of the Assemblies and PTL offered "a much higher level of compensation," says Cobble.[23]

At PTL Dortch was also easily pulled in by the allure of television. Almost every time Dortch went to Charlotte for a board meeting he also appeared on the show. "It didn't take long for me to be captivated and enchanted by the experience," he later wrote. On top of financial security, television offered Dortch an opportunity he thought he had missed, the chance to become a celebrity.[24]

The Bakkers' lifestyle became more luxurious after Dortch joined the board and David Taggart became Bakker's personal assistant. The departure of so many of the old hands who had helped to found the ministry in the 1970s, when they had no money, removed much of the restraining influence that had held the Bakkers' spending in check. Jim's new advisers were not inclined to do anything on the cheap.

The Florida condominium is a perfect example. In September 1981, Richard Dortch suggested to the board that the Bakkers ought to have a vacation home in Florida. The topic came up again at the December 1981 board meeting, but nothing happened until David Taggart went to Florida for a weekend vacation in October 1982. Dortch and Bakker instructed Taggart to stay until he found a suitable condominium to buy. Taggart picked out a beachfront condo on the Gold Coast at 2727 South Ocean Boulevard in Highland Beach that was still under construction. The price was $375,000.[25]

Since Bakker wanted to use the condo that Christmas, there was not time to get a mortgage. Instead, PTL paid cash, closing the deal on October 29, 1982. To complete the transaction, Peter Bailey, PTL's accounting manager, transferred $222,000 out of accounts designated to pay the vendors who supplied the gifts that PTL sent to donors. The transfer required the suppliers to wait at least another five or six weeks to be paid for bills that were already overdue, assuming PTL could get financing for the condo at all. The board did not approve buying the condo until its December 17 meeting, nearly two months after the actual purchase. No one objected.[26]

At the time PTL purchased the condo, it was "in essence a shell," with little more than dry wall and concrete floors, according to James Taggart, who Bakker sent to Florida to oversee its completion. The condo was in a brand-new high rise and had three bedrooms and a total of nearly 3,000 square feet. It was about seven stories up, on the more desirable northeast corner of the building, which got morning sun but was shaded from the afternoon heat, and had a wraparound tiled balcony that overlooked the ocean. Bakker told Taggart that he wanted the condo done in white, with "a very glamorous look . . . a very theatrical presentation."[27]

Taggart went to work, sparing no expense. He used lots of beveled mirrors, which were a favorite of Jim's. The carpet in the master bedroom was "very plush" and the wallpaper was made of "white string silk." The foyer was Italian white marble. The draperies were made of silk moire fabric. Bakker hated seams, so the cornice board that stretched the length of the living room, approximately twenty-five feet, was one solid piece. It would not fit in the elevator, so it had to be hoisted up the side of the building. The drapes were motorized, opening and closing with the flip of a switch. The drapes, bedspreads, and headboards cost $40,000 alone. At the last minute, Taggart had a Christmas tree installed with hand-blown glass ornaments at a cost of $5,000. Staffers brought wrapped gifts down from Charlotte to put under the tree so that when the Bakkers walked in everything would be ready for the holidays. They also brought clothes to put in the closets and toys for Jamie's room and stocked the kitchen with groceries. Since Taggart had only five weeks to complete the entire project, he often paid double or triple overtime for labor. In all, he spent more than $150,000 decorating the condo.[28]

Jim loved it, but after a few days Tammy, who had no input on the purchase or decorating, declared that it was "nothing but a hotel suite." They only stayed in the condo for about three weeks. "The Bakkers had a tendency to grow very bored with whatever they had," James Taggart later said.[29]

Under Richard Dortch's direction, Bakker's compensation steadily escalated. At the September 22, 1981, board meeting Dortch proposed raising Bakker's salary to $102,000 a year plus putting 30 percent of that amount into his retirement fund, finding a way to transfer ownership of the Tega Cay house from the ministry to Bakker, while still having PTL pay for "maintenance . . . remodeling, redecorating, payments of utilities, et cetera," providing Bakker a company car, "either a Cadillac or Lincoln," raising Tammy's salary to $1,000 a week, and paying for "a vacation for

Jim and Tammy when they feel they need it." The board approved everything without dissent.[30]

A little more than a year later, at the December 17, 1982, board meeting, Bakker's salary was raised from $102,000 to $195,000 a year and Tammy's was increased from $52,000 to $80,000 a year. At the same meeting the board gave Jim a $75,000 bonus and Tammy a $40,000 bonus. Only the previous July the board had given Bakker a similar $50,000 bonus. On July 4, 1983, the board gave Jim and Tammy bonuses of $100,000 and $50,000, respectively, and the same again on September 26. PTL paid the income taxes on all bonuses, a practice called "grossing up." So, a $50,000 bonus actually cost PTL closer to $100,000, since the Bakkers were in about the 50 percent tax bracket. The board seemed unable to meet without giving the Bakkers a bonus or a raise. Jim's total compensation rose to $290,000 in 1982 and $461,000 in 1983.[31]

There were two ways to look at Bakker's salary, the first of which involved seeing the Bakkers as celebrities. People expected celebrities like athletes, entertainers, and prosperity preachers to live large. In the case of the latter, it served as a validation of their message. From this perspective, Bakker's audience did not mind seeing him dress well, live in a large home, and travel abroad. But running parallel to this expectation was the conviction among Pentecostals and charismatics, the core of Bakker's contributors, that the church's primary responsibility was to save the lost and help the needy. They expected Bakker to spend the money they gave to do just that. Bakker addressed this concern in two ways. First, he never revealed how much he made once his income started to balloon. Second, he assured his audience that his salary did not impede PTL's mission. After the Heritage Village Church began meeting in the Barn in the fall of 1980, Bakker repeatedly told his television viewers that his church paid his salary and that "Jim Bakker and Tammy Bakker don't even get a salary from PTL." But of course Heritage Village Church and PTL were one and the same. It was PTL's board that set Bakker's salary and awarded him bonuses, the same board that, at least in theory, controlled the television network and the development of Heritage USA. The money all came from the same place, but Bakker wanted viewers to believe that his salary came strictly from his local congregation and did not represent a drag on the ministry's finances. If PTL was in financial trouble, and it always was, it was not his fault. In this way he could continue to flaunt a lavish lifestyle while still pleading for money to keep PTL on the air and expand Heritage USA.[32]

The PTL board was ineffective to say the least. Efrem Zimbalist Jr. was a member of the board from December 1979 through 1985. "It at no time functioned as a Board of Directors normally does, which is a regulatory body or a body that controls . . . the budget and the disbursement of funds and programs and so forth," Zimbalist later said. "It was not that kind of a Board. It was a Board of, you might say, approval or a board of affirmation, something like that." When proposals were put before the board, "we would approve them. They were never disapproved," Zimbalist said. Anything involving money was "very loose." "I never assumed that I was responsible for anything, because I wasn't, because the Board didn't do that," Zimbalist claimed. A. T. Lawing, owner of the Charlotte Oil Equipment company, served on PTL's board from 1974 until March 1987. He later testified that throughout his tenure on the board he was unaware of the specifics of PTL's finances and paid little attention to bonuses and salaries paid to the Bakkers or anyone else at PTL. This was exactly what Bakker and Dortch wanted.[33]

ROGER FLESSING LEFT again in early 1982. He had returned to PTL in March 1980 with the hope of creating innovative programming beyond the talk show, including documentaries and dramas. He hoped to turn PTL into a "Christian Hollywood." But by 1982 he had once again decided that PTL was headed in the wrong direction. Flessing lived near the Bakkers in one of the Tega Cay homes that PTL owned, so he had a closer view of the Bakkers than most. "I could see excessive spending, I could see renting jets when we didn't need to, I could see trips to Palm Springs when we didn't need to, I could see Jim and Tammy disintegrating [as a couple], and then going on the air and being hypocritical [about their marriage]. Those kinds of things bugged me," recalls Flessing. He remembers calling his mother one day and telling her, "There's something not right here and I just have this feeling that unless things change someday people could go to jail." When Flessing got an offer to join the Billy Graham organization, "I didn't have to think twice on that one."[34]

By the spring of 1983, David Taggart was exhausted from more than two years of constantly attending to Bakker's needs. It wasn't just the long hours but also the stress of Bakker's unpredictable demands. The Bakkers' first trip to Israel in June 1981 was a classic example of Jim's spur-of-the-moment style. Taggart had no idea they were going until lunch one Sunday afternoon when Jim announced that they were leaving the next day. It was up to Taggart to make all the travel arrangements, including obtaining passports for several members of the approximately ten-person entourage who did not have them. Somehow he managed to pull it off. "Heritage operated on a last minute procedure," Taggart later said.[35]

By March 1983 Taggart had had enough. "I was stressed out. I physically was exhausted." He had lost 20 pounds, down to 140, and was taking six to eight Excedrin a day. His salary at the time was $35,000 a year plus a bonus, but it no longer seemed worth it. They were in Palm Springs, sitting by a pool, when he told Bakker that he was leaving. "I don't want to know your last day. . . . I don't want any goodbyes," Bakker told him. Taggart resigned on April 12. His brother James quit at about the same time. Like David, he was "physically very, very exhausted. The ministry is a very demanding corporation to work for. Jim Bakker himself is very demanding of your time."[36]

Together they moved to Florida where they leased a condo on South Ocean Boulevard, six or seven buildings down from the one James had decorated for the Bakkers. Facing the ocean on the third floor, the apartment had two bedrooms, a large living room, kitchen, and dining room. Florida was attractive to James because he had gotten to know design marts and vendors there while working on the Bakkers' condo and hoped to start his own interior design business. Most of all, "it was somewhere that was not Charlotte. It was somewhere that was not PTL," according to James. When David told Bakker in Palm Springs that he was leaving, Bakker promised him a year's severance pay, but that never happened. Instead, the brothers withdrew their retirement savings from PTL and also borrowed $22,000 from their parents to pay the lease on the Florida condo. David intended to spend about six months practicing piano and preparing to audition for the Juilliard School in New York City.[37]

In August Jim and Tammy started calling David, asking him to return to PTL. Jim promised him a salary of $100,000 a year plus an annual bonus. "David," Taggart remembers Bakker saying during one of the calls, "I'm going to send a Learjet for you. It will come get you in Florida. It will return to Charlotte, and you and Tammy and I will go out to Palm Springs and spend a week or two weeks just on . . . vacation, not necessarily discussing your return to PTL . . . let's just talk . . . we were always family." Taggart declined the offer of the Learjet but did return to Charlotte in October on a commercial flight. They did not go to Palm Springs, but Bakker did offer to give him a house in the Tega Cay compound. Taggart declined. "I didn't want to live that close to the Bakkers. It was bad enough being on 24-hour-a-day call." Taggart did not want a house or a car, but he did want PTL to cover all of his business and personal travel, including vacations, and to have "the same resources [Jim] had, only I wanted to control how I spent my resources." To Taggart's surprise, Bakker agreed. Instead of returning to Florida, Taggart stayed and immediately began work, though he did not go on the payroll until December. His new title was Vice President of the Executive Office. James soon followed David back to PTL.[38]

While Dortch and the Taggarts were settling into their positions at PTL, John Wesley Fletcher was on his way out. Fletcher was a regular on the show during 1980 and was one of the featured speakers at the Barn dedication that September. After Bakker's encounter with Hahn in December 1980 and the Hawaii trip that January, Fletcher continued to ingratiate himself to Bakker. He often appeared as an unannounced guest on the show and preached at Heritage USA on a regular basis. "I have never been as excited and never been as optimistic as I am today about the ministry of PTL, because I sincerely believe that this is the year that all of the flowers are going to bloom that we have planted all these months," Fletcher proclaimed on the show on February 5, 1981, sounding more like a member of the team than a guest. He soon hoped to cohost the show with Jim.[39]

But Fletcher was also becoming notorious at PTL for making sexual advances at young male staffers. "It took a while" for most of the PTL staff to realize what was going on, as Don Hardister, Bakker's chief of security, remembers it. Among evangelicals at the time there was almost nothing in the way of a discussion about gay issues, which they lacked a vocabulary to even talk about. "I'd never seen it before, so it wasn't on my radar screen.... I didn't have any gay friends. I didn't grow up around anybody that was gay. I just didn't know," Hardister recalls. It made him uncomfortable that Jim liked to have other men rub his feet and back, and Hardister never gave Bakker a massage, but it also never occurred to him that the rub downs might have a sexual component.[40]

For those who did notice, the Bakkers' tolerance and openness toward the gay community was remarkable for the time, which might in part explain why Fletcher was able to hold on as long as he did. At other ministries, including Pat Robertson's CBN, gays were actively investigated and forced out, but the Bakkers did not create an environment in which exposing gays was high on anyone's agenda. Among the gay community, PTL was known as a ministry that "was hiring gay people all over the place," according to actor Jim J. Bullock, who would later host a syndicated talk show with Tammy. After Anita Bryant, famous for her 1977 campaign to repeal a Dade County, Florida, ordinance that prohibited discrimination on the basis of sexual orientation, appeared on the show, Jim publically backed away from her stance. "I'm not with Anita (Bryant) on this fight ... I think we ought to welcome them into our churches, because we're not going to reach the homosexual for Christ by segregating them off to one side and preaching hate," Bakker said. He equated homosexuality with alcoholism and said that he would not refuse to hire "a homosexual" who was "asking God for deliverance." Jim and Tammy's audience understood this as a way to reach out to sinners without embracing their sin.[41]

By this time, rumors about Bakker's sexual orientation had begun to surface at PTL, though mostly confined to a relatively small number of staffers. Most of the PTL staff and guests I have interviewed from this period say they never thought to question Bakker's sexuality. He was good at keeping secrets, beginning with his childhood experience of sexual abuse. Not until after the Jessica Hahn scandal broke in 1987 did former employees and television show guests come forward with salacious stories from the late 1970s and early 1980s involving Bakker. One of them was Austin Miles, who claimed to have seen Bakker and three male staff members "frolicking about in the nude" in the sauna room at the Heritage Village headquarters sometime before the spring of 1979, when the pool and sauna were closed.

Miles was a clown. Born during the Depression, he ran away to join the circus at fourteen, where he became Kokomo the Clown and eventually a ringmaster. In 1973 he joined the Royal Lipizzan Stallion Show as narrator. After becoming a born-again Christian at a Full Gospel Businessman's meeting, he was ordained in the Assemblies of God in 1974. Miles first appeared on the *PTL Club* while it was still broadcasting from the former furniture store on only nine stations. After that he was a regular at PTL for more than a decade.[42]

In his 1989 autobiography, and again in a recent interview with me, Miles recounts opening the door to the sauna at the Heritage Village complex to find Bakker and three male staffers "absorbed in playing with and massaging each other.... Jim had one of the naked young men stretch out on the table ... massaging the prone man's legs, working his hands up over the knees and thighs." When Bakker suddenly noticed Miles standing in the doorway, "there was a moment of deafening silence." "Regaining his composure," Bakker covered himself with a towel and "became very professional and formal." He complimented Miles on his part in the show that morning and told one of the young men to schedule him on the program every month. Miles backed away, unwilling to believe what he had just seen.

No sooner had Miles closed the door than he heard footsteps and ducked out of sight. Tammy "was storming across the room, her face flushed with anger. She banged her fist on the steam room door," according to Miles. "Jim Bakker, you come out of there right now! I know you're in there! Now, come out of there—I mean it!" As she pounded on the door one of her eyelashes fell off. "This was the last straw," writes Miles. " 'Dammit!' she screamed while trying to recover the eyelash. 'GODDAMMIT!' She leaned up against the door and started to cry." Jim never did open the door. If Miles's account is accurate, Tammy at least suspected that Jim had other sexual interests at about the same time she formed her attachments to Gary Paxton and Thurlow Spurr.[43]

Gary Smith, who had replaced Ed Stoeckel as PTL's general manager, suspected as well. Sometime between March and October of 1980, when he resigned from PTL, Smith attempted to fire an employee who drank too much. The man told Smith he could not fire him because he had "been with Jim" on his houseboat. Smith did not understand what this meant and proceeded with the termination. Smith later told reporter Charles E. Shepard that at three in the morning he got a call from Bakker. "Gary," Bakker said, "don't fire him."[44]

John Wesley Fletcher later claimed, in a 1989 *Penthouse* article, that he and Bakker first had sex in the Heritage Village sauna, which would have been sometime before the spring of 1979. According to Fletcher, in early November 1980, a few weeks after Smith left PTL and a month before Bakker's encounter with Hahn in Florida, Fletcher, Bakker, and David Taggart flew to Bermuda for an impromptu break. There, Fletcher claimed that he walked in on Bakker and Taggart in bed. Taggart later pleaded the Fifth Amendment when asked under oath whether he had ever had sex with Bakker. Fletcher says that his sexual encounters with Bakker continued until 1981, when he was defrocked by the Assemblies of God and banned from PTL after a security guard complained about his advances. This would have been at almost exactly the same time that Bakker said Jesus spoke to him, telling him to build the Upper Room, in the midst of "the most severe crisis of [PTL's] entire history." Officially the Assemblies of God removed Fletcher for drinking, but everyone close to the situation knew there was more to it than that. According to Shepard, when Dortch met Fletcher at the St. Louis airport to deliver the church's decision, Fletcher asked, "What are you going to do about Jim?" "John," Dortch replied, "you would be a very poor witness against anybody." As with Jessica Hahn, Bakker had not heard the last of John Wesley Fletcher.[45]

Fletcher's departure and PTL's renewed success coincided with an improvement in Jim and Tammy's marriage. They hosted the show together during 1982 and 1983, looking relaxed and confident. Tammy wore her hair short, without a wig, and used only moderate makeup, by her standards, always a sign that she was feeling upbeat. Jim admitted on the air that he had neglected his family in the past as he struggled to build Heritage USA. Now he talked about how comforting it was to know that he and Tammy would grow old together. "We're the happiest we've ever been in our lives," Jim declared on the October 20, 1982, broadcast. "We really are," Tammy agreed. They had just returned from a vacation in Switzerland. "Love is better as we grow old together," Jim said a year later, in December 1983. "I wouldn't trade anything to be back in my twenties. . . . We are the happiest now that we've ever been."[46]

The two books Bakker published in the early 1980s clearly illustrate the change in his outlook. *Survival: Unite to Live,* published in 1980, is a dreary little book. On one level it is a plea for unity in the body of Christ against the forces of the devil in these last days, but it is also filled with complaints about attacks from other Christians. The previous summer Bakker had complained on the air about other Christian broadcasters calling him up, eager to buy PTL's television equipment once it went under. "It is sad, but I must say that in the last two years I have found more Christians lying and being haughty or proud. . . . I wonder very strongly if they are indeed Christians," Bakker wrote. "Oh, dear God, the lies, the lies, the lies that are told in Christendom today."[47]

You Can Make It!, published in 1983, is giddy by comparison. While the cover of *Survival* has a fairly formal picture of Jim standing alone, the cover of *You Can Make It!* shows Jim and Tammy standing together, smiling broadly, his arms around her, on the new living room set of the *Jim Bakker* show. "Christianity is a winning way of life. God intends for you to be successful in every part of your living," Bakker wrote in *You Can Make It!* "I tell you, God is for you, not against you. And with Him on your side, you cannot be defeated. He is thinking good thoughts about you, wanting good things for you—and He'll move heaven and earth to help you make it!" Energized with new confidence, Bakker was set to launch his boldest set of initiatives yet during the next year. It would be his undoing.[48]

10

Four Days and Three Nights

NEAR THE END of 1983 Jim Bakker bought a train, or, more precisely, his supporters bought one. The miniature train cost $133,000, not including the track and stations, and had eight cars and a locomotive. Tracks eventually ran around Lake Heritage on the Heritage USA grounds. The train was similar to the Zooline Railroad at the St. Louis Zoo. In fact, Bakker had gotten the idea after seeing the St. Louis Zoo train. The locomotive was named and modeled after the C. P. Huntington, used during the construction of the Transcontinental Railroad in the 1860s, and looked similar to The Little Engine That Could. Each passenger car carried about twenty-one people. To purchase the train, 133 families in the Heritage Village Church gave $1,000 each, which made them "owners" of the railroad with the right to ride free for life. On November 24, Bakker appealed on the air for another two hundred donors to contribute $1,000 each to complete the construction of the railroad, which would allow them to become owners as well. All they had to do was dial 1-800-CALL-JIM. It was a funding model that Bakker would soon use again in a much bigger way.[1]

By the end of 1983 there were many reasons for the faithful to visit Heritage USA. Fans of the television program could join the live studio audience of the *Jim Bakker* show at 11 a.m. or *Camp Meeting USA* at 8 p.m., or they could serve as phone counselors after a brief training session. In between they could attend a seminar or workshop at the counseling center. In the summer there were plays and events at the amphitheater, including the Passion Play, depicting Christ's death and resurrection. The play had a large cast and included live camels, horses, and sheep. There was also a full range of activities for children and teens, including a swimming pool and playground at Buffalo Park, a petting zoo, horseback riding, a roller rink, and other recreational and religious programs geared just for them.

Or visitors could simply relax in a clean, safe environment without alcohol or smoking. Increasingly it was the allure of leisure and a vacation that drew people to Heritage USA. As the train would suggest, Bakker was keen to further this appeal.

Just as middle-class Americans gained a taste for conspicuous consumption in the middle decades of the twentieth century, they also acquired a taste for what economist and sociologist Thorstein Veblen called "conspicuous leisure." The US gross national product per capita doubled between 1940 and 1970, even when adjusted for inflation. Vacations, which were unheard of for most workers before the twentieth century, became a fixture of American worklife by mid-century. Between 1950 and 1990, the average number of vacation days per year nearly doubled, from 6.5 to 10.5. Americans now had more time for leisure and more money to spend on it. Leisure was largely democratized, and the notion of an elite leisured class lost its meaning. By 1993, "Americans spent $341 billion on recreation and entertainment, or 9.43 percent of all 'non-medical consumer spending,'" according to one analysis. Pentecostals, PTL's core constituency, were as much a part of this transformation as any group, but felt out of place in Las Vegas or Atlantic City. When they heard about Heritage USA, they realized that it was just what they had been looking for.[2]

The problem was that there were just not enough rooms. Not everyone wanted to camp, and the 96-room Heritage Inn and other rentals on the grounds did not nearly meet the demand. The Inn turned away 125,000 people looking for a room in 1983, according to Bakker. In all, PTL estimated that 1.8 million people visited the park in 1983. If Heritage USA was "to bring the camp meeting into the 21st century" and provide "a place where people could come for Bible studies, camp meetings, workshops, seminars . . . a haven of rest for Christians today," as Bakker put it, it needed more lodging.[3]

His answer was to build a Partner Center that included a 500-room hotel, the Heritage Grand Hotel. Bakker later said that the vision for the Partner Center came to him in the middle of the night. "I woke up and it was like a vision or a dream—I don't know what it was—but the concept, God gave me the concept of the Heritage Grand Partner Center and the lifetime partners. And I got up and I began to sketch what I had felt was the dream and the vision for that."[4]

Bakker took his plans to Roe Messner, a general contractor who specialized in building churches. Together they mapped out the next phase of Heritage USA's development. Messner came to regard Bakker as a "creative genius" with an extraordinary ability to look at a plot of land and envision where each building, road, or lake should go. No detail was too small for Bakker, who, as always, took a particular interest in which trees to cut down and which to save.[5]

Bakker first met Messner at an Assemblies of God convention in Anaheim, California, in August 1983, where Messner had a booth advertising his business. Born in 1935, Messner grew up in a poor sharecropping family in Waldron, Kansas, and learned to build houses as a teenager. Since 1956 he had built more than 1,100 churches in forty-seven states, an average of a church every ten days for nearly thirty years. The Assemblies of God (Bakker's denomination) was one of Messner's biggest customers. He had built more than four hundred Assemblies churches, many in Illinois, where he and Richard Dortch had been "very good friends" for thirty years, according to Messner. A decade after he met Jim Bakker, Messner would become Tammy Faye's second husband.[6]

Beginning in September 1983, Bakker and Messner drew up plans that included a 504-room hotel at one end of the Partner Center complex, a mall called Main Street USA in the middle, and a 650-seat Grand Palace Cafeteria and 14,000-square-foot conference center on the other end. Main Street USA was modeled after the Main Street USA attractions at Disneyland and Disney World, except that it was enclosed. Like the Disney complexes, it featured a mix of shops and restaurants, including Victoria's Boutique, for women's fashions, J. Charles Limited, a fashion store for men named after the Bakkers' son, Jamie Charles, Susie's Ice Cream Parlor, named after their daughter, Tammy Sue, Royal Hair Design, Heritage Florist, the Heavenly Fudge Shoppe, Heritage Gift Shoppe, Ye Old Bookstore, Noah's Toy Shoppe, Designer Bags and Accessories, Perry's Jewelry Emporium, the Shutterbug Shoppe, Goosebumps Handcrafted Gifts, Accessories and Stitchery, Grand Promenade Café, Copeland Drugs, PTL Wills and Trusts, and a Nutrition Center. Noah's Toy Shoppe sold $740,000 worth of "Jesus action figures" and other Bible-themed toys in its first year. The Grand Palace Cafeteria offered more than one hundred choices and could "handle 75 diners every 15 minutes." Its most popular items were "carved round of roast, fried chicken, and liver and onions."[7]

Bakker freely copied the look and feel of Disneyland and Disney World. His Grand Palace Cafeteria resembled Disney World's Crystal Palace Cafeteria. Like Disney, Bakker wanted his park to reflect "a quieter time in history," which he generally identified with a Victorian ethos. He originally wanted to put a glass roof over his Main Street, but when he consulted with "the people at Disney," they told him it was impossible to heat and cool such a large glass-ceilinged area, so he decided to cover it with a vaulted roof painted and lit to look like sky. Altogether the Partner Center complex enclosed 500,000 square feet stretching three football fields in length. The hotel's main lobby was four stories tall and had its own swimming pool. The concrete alone cost $2 million. "I just wish Walt Disney were able to come and see that Jim has replaced him," said Art Linkletter, the radio and television personality, after visiting Heritage USA as the buildings and attractions were going up.[8]

At the time Bakker presented his new vision to his staff in late 1983, PTL's finances were stable but there was no room for new major projects. The previous February Peter Bailey, PTL's finance director, wrote a memo to Bakker outlining the ministry's financial condition. Bailey noted that PTL's income was $4 million a month and its operating expenses were $3 million a month, excluding capital expenditures. Leaving aside the cost of construction, Bailey projected that the ministry would have a positive cash flow of $5,641,000 in 1983 and $6,644,000 in 1984. But this would only happen if capital projects were held in check. "I strongly urge that we stop further construction until we can pay as we have money available," Bailey wrote to Bakker a month later.[9]

In fact, PTL never realized the positive cash flow that Bailey projected for 1983 or 1984 because of past construction debts and the cost of new projects. The ministry fell so far behind by June 1983 that it started making guests who appeared on the television program pay their own travel expenses. On September 2, 1983, Bailey wrote to Bakker telling him that over the past three weeks they had received $1,870,000 in contributions but spent $2,921,000 from the general fund. Bills to many of the affiliate stations across the nation were more than ninety days overdue. In November, PTL took in $4.7 million in contributions but spent $6.8 million. More debt was the last thing PTL needed. It was at exactly this moment that Bakker decided to launch his biggest construction project ever, the $25 million Partner Center and Grand Hotel.[10]

How to pay for such a massive project? Bakker certainly did not want a repeat of 1978 when he had been forced to abandon construction of the Barn and Total Living Center for nearly two years when he ran out of money. Instead he came up with a brilliant idea, elegant in its simplicity. If he had stuck to it, it would have nearly paid for the new complex debt free. The plan was to offer 25,000 lifetime partnerships in the Heritage Grand Hotel for $1,000 each. In return for this contribution, each lifetime partner would be guaranteed four days and three nights a year free in the Grand Hotel for life. The partnerships would generate $25 million, enough to completely pay for construction of the new complex under the original estimates. Providing each partner four days and three nights a year would account for slightly less than 50 percent of the hotel's rooms. The other 50 percent would generate enough income from paying guests to cover maintenance and upkeep. What could be simpler than that?

Bakker and his staff broke ground on the Grand Hotel on December 7, 1983, a month before they began to promote it to PTL's supporters. The first brochure announcing the lifetime partnership program went out to 140,282 people on PTL's mailing list on January 7, 1984. "Once every lifetime, an idea is born so filled with potential for good that it must be shared immediately," the brochure read. "For a one time gift of $1,000 you will be able to stay free 4 days and 3 nights, every year, for the rest of your life, in the Heritage Grand Hotel! Think of the thousands of dollars you will save during your lifetime!" Over a forty-year span "the gift value of your room at the Heritage Grand Hotel could be worth $20,000. You will not be able to find a better investment opportunity anywhere!" the brochure claimed. But only if you hurried. "After we hear from 25,000 Lifetime Partners and receive their investment of $1,000, Lifetime Membership in the PTL Partner Center will be closed!"[11]

The day before it was mailed, PTL's lawyer, John Yorke, wrote to Richard Dortch, Bakker's new Senior Executive Vice President, to express concerns about the brochure, which he had been asked to review only two days before on January 4. Yorke worried that the partnership program contained securities violations under the South Carolina Time Share Act and recommended holding off sending it out until these issues could be resolved. Bakker and Dortch sent it anyway. They had already begun construction, and this was the only fundraising plan they had.[12]

Bakker had already done something similar to pay for the train and for the 96-room Heritage Inn. The previous year, in the spring of 1983, Bakker sent a letter to supporters offering memberships in the "Bethany Builders Club." In exchange for a gift of $15,000, club members would have a room named after them in the Heritage Inn. "Your picture will hang in the room and your brass name plate will be displayed on the door," Bakker wrote to prospective donors. Bethany Builders Club members would also be guaranteed seven days and six nights free lodging at Heritage USA. "If you call me far enough in advance and let me know you are coming, I will do my best to see that you can stay in that special room with your name on it," Bakker wrote. The Bethany Builders promotion would only have raised $1,440,000 even if all 96 rooms in the Inn found sponsors, but it and the campaign to pay for the train served as models for the Heritage Grand partnership program.[13]

Bakker began to promote the Grand partnerships on the air in February 1984. At that point PTL had assets totaling $7,834,456 and liabilities of $19,840,011 (assets include anything that can be turned into cash in a year, while liabilities are bills due within a year). Every month PTL spent more than it took in. From June to November 1983, just before groundbreaking for the Grand Hotel, the average shortfall was $758,000 a month. The partnership program had to work to sustain Bakker's plans for Heritage USA and he sold it fervently. During a telethon on February 20, Tammy showed off a mock-up of a room in the Grand Hotel, and Jim urged viewers to snap up one of the partnerships before they were all gone. "If you haven't called you need to do it now, because when the partnerships reach 25,000 all the lifetime partnerships will be gone."[14]

Lifetime partners also received a "masterpiece" sculpture of David slaying Goliath, created for PTL by Yaacov Heller, a sculptor and artist who was born in Cleveland but moved to Jerusalem in 1972. Supporters who did not want to become lifetime partners could get one of the sculptures for a gift of $125. On the air, Bakker claimed that anyone who bought the sculpture in Jerusalem "would pay at least $1,000 for it," a claim he also included in the January 7 brochure. "Do you realize that these are hand poured . . . they're handcrafted individually," Bakker told viewers on February 20. Each had a "beautiful antique pewter finish" and was "hand numbered" and "signed" by the artist. "It's a collector's item," Bakker confidently asserted.[15]

In fact, the sculptures cost PTL $10 each, and they look it. I recently bought one online for $35, number 72,997 of 100,000. The metal is cheap (mine has turned a dull olive green) and the construction flimsy. David's sword slips out of his hand and could easily be lost or broken. The sculpture measures about 7 ½ inches each in length, width and height, including the sword. Bakker later claimed that the inflated value he placed on the sculpture derived from its "spiritual value."[16]

During the February 20, 1984, telethon Bakker predicted that the 25,000 lifetime partnerships would all "be gone in ten days." They did not go that fast, but by July 7, 1984, PTL had received full payment from 25,303 lifetime partners, plus partial payment on an additional 1,568 lifetime partnerships and another 13,102 pledges. At this point the partnership program had already exceeded the limit that Bakker established at the outset in January. But it was not enough.[17]

The more than $25 million the partnership program raised by July fell short of what was needed to build the Grand Hotel and Partner Center for two reasons. First, the cost of the project steadily rose. As early as February 1984, when the foundation was just going in, Bakker admitted that the complex would cost at least $30 million. The final price tag rose to $35 million by the time it was finally done. Second, Bakker used about half of the money raised for the hotel to make up for shortfalls in PTL's monthly budget and to launch new projects. In the end, only 52.8 percent of the money raised through Grand partnerships was actually spent on the hotel complex.[18]

One of the old projects that PTL still owed money on was the People That Love Home for unwed mothers. On May 16, 1984, singer Pat Boone hosted the show in place of Jim and Tammy who were out of town. Boone praised Heritage USA as a Christian version of Disneyland and Disney World, but his main focus was on the People That Love Home. A video clip aired during the program showed Boone in front of the home, which was slated to open on July 4 but was still only 80 percent done. Boone pleaded with viewers to send money to finish the project in time for the dedication.[19]

PTL also continued to aggressively buy land. Between December 1983 and November 1985, the ministry paid nearly $9 million for 793 acres adjoining Heritage USA. The additional land enlarged the park to about 2,300 acres.[20]

As if this was not enough, that spring, when the Grand Hotel was little more than a foundation, Bakker began construction on a massive five-acre waterpark opposite the hotel. He claimed that it would be the largest waterpark ever built, like "nothing the world has ever seen." Building it involved creating a lake, Lake Heritage, with an island in the middle, Heritage Island. Instead of using scaffolding and stairs to reach the top of the water slides, Bakker wanted to build "mountains" on the island out of sand and rock that would look more "natural." Like the hotel, Bakker wanted to open the water park on July 4, 1984.[21]

The waterpark immediately began to suck up money intended for the hotel. In March Peter Bailey wrote to Bakker, "we have borrowed from the hotel $1,226,861 mainly for the water park and television time." This was only the beginning. After a series of cost overruns and lawsuits, the waterpark would end up costing PTL $13 million by the time it finally opened two years later in July 1986.[22]

Through the end of May 1984, PTL spokespersons were still telling viewers that the hotel would be completed by July 4. But on June 1 Bakker admitted that PTL's finances were in desperate shape. He and Tammy cohosted the show that day outdoors at the newly remodeled Buffalo Park recreational area. Every few minutes the train would pass behind the set going forward and then reverse course and pass by going backward since the track around Lake Heritage had not yet been completed. If they quit now, Bakker told his audience, they would be left with a "$16 million pile of rubble." Instead, he urged supporters to dial 1-800-CALL-JIM and take advantage of the lifetime partnerships that he claimed were still available because of people who had signed up but never sent in their money. "What a hedge against inflation. If you gave $2,000 and took two memberships, you would stay a week the rest of your life in luxury surroundings that over a normal lifetime" would be worth "$40,000 to $80,000," Bakker said. And that was based on a room rate of $70 a night. Bakker claimed that "hotel people" had told him that $70 was "way too low." A "world-class hotel" like the Grand "should rent for at least $125 to $150 a night per room." Bakker assured viewers that Heritage USA had recently been appraised "at a market value of $77 million," but in reality PTL's total assets were about 10 percent of that. Tammy urged viewers to use their credit cards to buy a lifetime partnership as an expression of their faith. "Why can't we put one thing on our credit card for Jesus?" she asked.[23]

Through the summer and fall of 1984, Peter Bailey sent Bakker a string of increasingly alarming memos regarding PTL's finances. On June 29 Bailey wrote that during the past week they had received contributions totaling $872,000 but spent $1,979,000. "Unless we quickly and seriously reduce our spending, we will not be able to pay future payrolls," Bailey wrote on July 16. "The payroll this Friday will be $700,000. To date I have been able to set aside $70,000 toward it," he wrote a month later, on Monday, August 20. Bailey met with a representative of the accounting firm Deloitte, Haskins & Sells on September 13 to review their audit of PTL's books for the fiscal year ending May 31, 1984. "The main concern expressed in the report is whether PTL will be able to continue as 'a going concern' based on current assets of only 8.6 million against 28.5 million in current liabilities," he reported to Bakker. Part of the problem, as Bailey saw it, was that the lifetime partnership program had shifted how people gave to PTL. "More and more of our funds were coming from lifetime partnerships" while "monthly contributions dropped off drastically," he later said.[24]

When the number of paid lifetime partnerships in the Heritage Grand reached the target of 25,000, Rich Ball, PTL's Vice President of World Outreach, whose department kept track of the numbers, found Dortch and Bakker in Bakker's dressing room and gave them the news. "They told me not to worry about it . . . not to worry about the number," Ball later said. They were working on a new plan.[25]

To keep construction going, Bakker turned to an old trick that he had used many times in the past: launch a new project and use the funds raised for the new project to pay old debts. It was like getting a new credit card to make payments on an old card that was maxed out. Though the Heritage Grand was still several months away from opening, in September 1984 Bakker announced a new lifetime partnership program for a second hotel, the Heritage Grand Towers. "When in doubt, build something more!" Bakker declared to his viewers on September 17. Partnerships in the new hotel would be capped at 30,000, Bakker told his audience. The 21-story, 500-room Towers would be built adjacent to the Heritage Grand, with a walkway connecting the two. "The windows of heaven have been opened and the blessings are pouring out," read a brochure sent to 596,232 people on PTL's mailing list between September 27 and October 5, 1984. "I want to invite you to be part of the PTL miracle as we build the Heritage Grand Towers and help complete the final phase of the PTL partner center," Bakker wrote in the brochure. The original terms of the deal were the same as for the Heritage Grand partnerships: for a gift of $1,000, lifetime partners would receive four days and three nights free for the rest of their lives in the Towers.[26]

A subsequent brochure, sent out to 596,865 people a few weeks later, in October, further described the new hotel. "The lower level will house a health spa with complete professional health and fitness equipment, a theater featuring Christian and fine family films, lap pool and family bowling lanes." Bakker urged supporters to snap up a Towers partnership, since the program would be capped at 30,000 and "memberships will soon be increased to $1,500."[27]

The Towers Hotel was never completed. It was about 80 percent finished when construction was halted for the last time in July 1987. Today it is a steel and concrete hulk standing on the former Heritage USA grounds, slowing deteriorating under the Carolina sun.[28]

From the beginning it was unclear as to how the money raised for the Grand or Towers would be spent. Tax attorneys advised PTL that because lifetime partners received something of measurable value (a promise of lodging in the hotel), their payments were different from other gifts given to the ministry and should be treated differently for tax purposes. They urged "that we consider putting the hotel operations under the for-profit organization" so as not to jeopardize PTL's tax-exempt status as a religious organization, according to Peter Bailey. A brochure promoting lifetime partnerships in the Heritage Grand, mailed to 570,874 people in March 1984, reflected this reasoning. "Because of the value being invested in exchange for your payment of $1,000, no part of this $1,000 is a charitable contribution and should not be claimed as a tax deduction," it advised prospective donors. Promotional literature also often included a clause stating that lifetime partnerships were "non-transferrable, non-inheritable and non-tax deductible." That seemed to imply that payments for lifetime partnerships were separate from, and different than, other gifts to the ministry and would be used only to build the hotels.[29]

Relying on advice from a different set of lawyers, PTL at other times argued that lifetime partnerships were exactly like any other contribution it received and could be used to support the ministry more broadly. From the beginning, PTL donors were often "returned a gift in one form or another to honor or recognize each contribution." These gifts included books by Jim and Tammy, Tammy's records, pins, magnets, calendars, devotional guides, and so on. The gifts served as "a visible sign to represent the bond of loyalty and faith of the contributor not only to the organization but to the message." The lifetime partnership program was nothing more than an extension of this practice. Lifetime partners were issued "a membership card which is just that, nothing more. It specifies nothing but membership." With regard to lodging, lifetime partners received only "a bare offer that at some indefinite future time, subject to availability, and other conditions, the contributor may be furnished with lodging or accommodations on a limited basis and subject to contingencies. These are gifts, pure and simple, and no more." Indeed, the Heritage Grand was not "a hotel in the commercial sense" because its lobby was used for prayer meetings and its swimming pool for baptisms.[30]

Following this logic, Bakker and his staff often implied that money received for lifetime partnerships would be used to support PTL as a whole, not just build the hotels. Richard Dortch hosted the television show on October 5, 1984, while Jim and Tammy were in Palm Springs. "Remember there is only one week left for you to get a lifetime partnership [in the Heritage Towers] for $1,000, only one week left and then those lifetime partnerships go to $1,500," Dortch told viewers. "And by sending that $1,000 you know what you get?" he asked. "You get the joy of knowing that you're going to share in this ministry because not only are we able to give you a lifetime partnership in the Towers, but with that money we're going to pay off the Heritage Grand . . . and then we're going to build the beautiful Towers. And with the rest of the money . . . we're going to pay off all of the television stations all across the country."[31]

So, were lifetime partners giving only to build the hotels, for which they received lodging in return for their payment, or were they giving to support PTL as a whole, including its domestic and international television programs? PTL's accounting practices made it clear that Bakker and his immediate staff assumed the latter. PTL had about forty-five bank accounts at the time. When Peter Bailey, PTL's finance director, needed money for general operating expenses, he took it from "whatever account of the 45 that had money in it," including the lifetime partnership accounts. On September 28, Bailey wrote to Bakker informing him that they had received almost $1.4 million for Towers lifetime partnerships that week, but only $665,000 in general contributions, down from the $1 million a week average before the partnership promotions began. The only way to make up for the shortfall was by using money raised through the lifetime partnerships to pay other expenses. By October 17, PTL had collected $5.2 million in Towers partnerships. Of that sum, $2.6 million had been spent on the Grand, $1.2 million for television time, $450,000 on the waterpark, and $450,000 on payroll, leaving only $500,000 to build the Towers.[32]

Peter Bailey was not out to fool anyone. Like the character with the same name from *It's A Wonderful Life*, he saw his job primarily as a way to serve others. Bailey was reticent by nature, and PTL was the biggest enterprise he had ever been involved with. Even though he was PTL's finance director, Bailey was not invited to attend board meetings. By this time he did not know how much PTL's top executives received in bonuses or even what their salaries were (more about this later). Bailey believed that PTL would succeed because they were doing the Lord's work. "God has all things in control; His timing is perfect; He is never late, and He never makes a mistake," Bailey wrote at the end of a February 1983 memo to Bakker. "I am not discouraged," he wrote at the conclusion of another otherwise gloomy memo in March 1984. Had his position at PTL been "a secular job, I probably would have left," Bailey later said. But even after PTL fell apart in 1987, Bailey still had "nothing but awe and admiration for the place . . . there is no place like PTL. If you haven't been there, you've missed something." Like Bailey, most PTL employees believed in the ministry's mission and that God would ultimately provide the money to see them through.[33]

Nevertheless, by the end of 1984 Peter Bailey was at his wits' end trying to juggle PTL's books. One of the banks the ministry did business with was bouncing as many as 250 PTL checks a day. "PTL's top management must have the financial integrity to stop approving expenditures that can continually exceed our income. This is the root of our problem," he wrote to Dortch and Bakker on January 5, 1985. Bailey then listed current monthly expenditures totaling $5,108,000, or $1.2 million a week. By that time general contributions were running about $700,000 a week. To make up the difference, Bailey took money from the Towers partnership program. "I agonize daily over this and the lack of action taken by top management to resolve this critical problem."[34]

They had one last chance to fix things, as Bailey saw it. As of January 14, 1985, PTL had used $20 million from the Towers account "for Heritage Grand Hotel construction and expenses, TV time, payroll and the water park." About $2 million remained in the account with approximately 9,000 lifetime partnerships left to sell at the current price of $2,000 apiece. That would leave $20 million to build the Towers if, and only if, all of the money was put aside for that purpose. The current estimated cost to build the Towers was $19.2 million. "What this means is that no longer will we be able to cover payroll, our loan maintenance costs, utilities, television time or partner expenses at the present level. This Friday, I will not issue payroll checks unless there are funds in the general account . . . unless approved in writing by Jim Bakker, David Taggart, or Richard Dortch." Much to Bailey's dismay, the spending continued unabated.[35]

BY THIS TIME, PTL's top leadership had become more secretive, largely through the influence of Richard Dortch. Dortch took over as PTL's Senior Executive Vice President in December 1983, a position previously held by Jim Moss and Roger Flessing. Dortch took Flessing's old office on the third floor of the World Outreach Center, in a corner opposite from Bakker's. Only about a dozen senior staff worked on the third floor. It took a special key to reach it by elevator. Dortch supervised all PTL employees except for Bakker's personal staff, a group that included David and James Taggart, Vi Azvedo, Charlotte Whiting, and Bakker's secretary, Shirley Fulbright.[36]

Staffers soon became aware of Dortch's deceptive nature. Dortch was "a very secretive person," according to Don Hardister, PTL's chief of security.

"Reverend Dortch was probably the only person that would not talk in my presence," Hardister said. "I didn't sense honesty; I didn't sense forthrightness and truth," said Lois Chalmers, who wrote for the ministry's magazine and worked on brochures and other mailings. "I just didn't feel like I trusted him," said Peter Bailey, PTL's Vice President of Finance. "I do not believe that Reverend Dortch is capable of telling the complete truth," said Marisa Matthews, who eventually directed one of PTL's four finance divisions. When Dortch left Illinois to come to PTL, the Assemblies of God gave him a gift of $13,000. Dortch did not report it on his taxes, reasoning that it was from "individuals" who "sent in $10 gifts and $20 gifts and $5 gifts." Even though the check was from the Assemblies of God, Dortch reasoned that it just amounted to friends handing him five, ten, or twenty dollars at a time. Earlier, when Dortch bought his house in Illinois, he signed two contracts on the same day for $48,000 and $68,000. The first was what he paid; the second was what he claimed he paid when he later sold the house, so as to avoid capital gains taxes that applied to home sales at the time. In 1986 Dortch would claim a $15,680 tax-deductible gift to PTL that did not show up in any PTL records.[37]

In April 1982, while he was a member of PTL's board, Dortch instructed Sylvia Watson, who, as assistant secretary to the board, took the meeting minutes, to discontinue recording who made motions at board meetings. Dortch did not want the minutes to reflect that he "always made the motion" to give "bonuses, and raises and perks," according to Watson. She refused and instead resigned. After Dortch arrived at PTL as Senior Executive Vice President, he once again insisted that the board minutes not reflect who made a motion to give bonuses or the amount of the bonuses. At the time, Shirley Fulbright, Jim Bakker's secretary, took the board minutes. John Yorke, one of PTL's lawyers, remembers Fulbright calling him sounding "very panicky" and saying "that Reverend Dortch wanted her to change the minutes and that he was going to fire her if she didn't." When Fulbright persisted in including the names, Dortch personally "deleted them." In October 1983 PTL's lawyers sent a letter to Porter Speakman, then PTL's budget director, reminding him that board minutes could not be changed without subsequent review and approval by the board. "Removal, alteration, or destruction of existing and approved minutes is unlawful under State law as well as Federal Income Statutes," wrote attorney Don Etheridge of the firm Caudle, Underwood, and Kinsey. Regardless, Dortch continued to regularly alter board minutes. "He is not truthful and he is not honest. I think he lies a lot," Sylvia Watson later said of Dortch.[38]

Aside from revising the minutes, Dortch took other steps to make the ministry less transparent. John Yorke remembers a board meeting on December 20, 1982, to which he had been invited. When Dortch saw Yorke in the building, he pulled Bakker aside and told him it was not a good idea to have lawyers at board meetings. Bakker "acquiesced" and sent David Taggart to tell Yorke "that I would not be needed." A year later, in November 1983, Yorke wrote to Bakker expressing his firm's concern over the policy of excluding lawyers from board meetings. "We continue the recommendation ... that a lawyer be present at the Board meetings ... many of the problems of the past could have been avoided with a little advice up front." Bakker and Dortch ignored this advice, and Yorke never attended another board meeting.[39]

Dortch's hostility to lawyers did not stop there. In December 1984 he wrote to Yorke upbraiding him for discussing PTL's finances with a bank that the ministry was trying to get a $10 million loan from. Yorke wrote to his boss, Eddie Knox, that he had only told the truth and represented PTL's best interests. "There is no amount of money that PTL or any other client could offer that would cause me to deceive a prospective lender on their behalf," Yorke wrote. As to Dortch's letter, "it makes me mad as hell. My first inclination was to go down there and stuff it down his throat." He wrote a response to Dortch, but Knox would not let him send it. From there, things only got worse. In November 1985 Knox wrote to Bakker complaining that for years his firm had served as PTL's general counsel, but now they felt increasingly "uninformed and uninvolved" and did not know who was in charge of the ministry's legal representation. Soon thereafter Knox's firm backed away from its relationship with PTL.[40]

Shortly after Dortch arrived at PTL in 1983, he set up a separate Executive Payroll Account. Prior to that, Peter Bailey paid everyone on PTL's payroll, including Jim Bakker. Dortch put the new Executive Payroll Account under an outside accounting firm, Deloitte, Haskins & Sells and later Laventhol and Horwath. After that, even as PTL's finance director, Bailey did not know how much Bakker and his personal staff made in salary and bonuses, a group that included Dortch, Tammy, David Taggart, Shirley Fulbright, and a handful of others who worked on the third floor. Bailey knew the total executive payroll because the outside firm would periodically tell him how much money to transfer into the account, but he did not know the breakdown of who got what. Often the money for the executive payroll came from the lifetime partnership accounts, the money raised to build the hotels. Bailey had nowhere else to get it.[41]

With compensation for Bakker and his senior staff hidden behind the wall of the Executive Payroll Account and lawyers barred from board meetings, bonuses flowed like water. In November 1983 PTL spent $2 million more than it took in. At the next board meeting, on December 16, the board awarded Jim a $100,000 bonus and Tammy a $50,000 bonus. By March 1984, PTL was spending about $7.5 million a month but taking in only about $3.3 million a month. At the March 13 board meeting Bakker received a $195,000 bonus. On June 29, Bailey wrote to Bakker informing him that they had spent twice what they had received during the past week. Bailey implored Bakker "to cut back on our expenses." A few days later, on July 3, the board voted a $100,000 bonus for Jim and a $50,000 bonus for Tammy. On November 16, Bailey wrote to Bakker telling him that he still owed $296,463 on the previous week's payroll and had nothing left for "utility bills, honorariums, employee medical insurance, taxes, travel and daily necessary expenses." "We are in a very serious cash flow position," Bailey warned. Four days later the board gave Jim a $150,000 bonus and Tammy a $50,000 bonus. All of the bonuses were "grossed up," effectively doubling the cost to PTL. "As long as I pay the income tax, I can take what I want," Bakker once told Dortch.[42]

After he was excluded from the board meetings, attorney John Yorke wrote to his boss about a conversation he had had with Bob Brown, who worked for PTL's current accounting firm, Deloitte, Haskins & Sells. Yorke reported that he had told Brown "that the alarming thing to me is that the suspect expenses are growing exponentially. Bob Brown said that he thought Richard Dortch was part of the problem. It was interesting to me that he recognized that. . . . It seems that everyone is thinking the same on that point." The Bakkers spent it all as quickly as they got it. Their income for 1983 was $700,000, but they earned only $600 in interest.[43]

The Bakkers weren't the only ones reaping a windfall. When Jim and Tammy got bonuses, other senior staff usually did as well. At the November 20 board meeting, Richard Dortch got a $50,000 bonus, board members Aimee Cortese, Charles Cookman, Efrem Zimbalist Jr., and A.T. Lawing got $10,000 each, and Ernie Franzone, a new member of the board, got $1,000. Dortch also put his wife, son, and daughter on PTL's executive payroll. Jim and Tammy had seven family members on PTL's payroll at one point, and both Jim and Tammy's parents lived in houses owned by the ministry and drove company cars.[44]

Initially Deloitte, Haskins & Sells sent the executive payroll checks to one of the law firms that represented PTL, where they were signed with a stamp and then sent to PTL for distribution. Eventually the secretary who stamped the checks came to John Yorke, who primarily handled the PTL account, concerned that "the checks are coming more than once a month and the amounts are growing significantly." Yorke went to his boss, Edie Knox. "We had a discussion in the firm," remembers Yorke, after which one of the firm's partners "decided that we would discontinue the practice because they were concerned . . . that PTL would think our stamping the checks was acquiescing the amounts of the checks," Yorke said. After that, the checks were sent directly to PTL, where Bakker's secretary, Shirley Fulbright, stamped them with a signature, bypassing the lawyers.[45]

Early in his career Bakker had advisers who pushed him to be more straightforward and transparent. But Dortch encouraged Bakker's worst tendencies in this regard. With Dortch by his side, Jim could have whatever Jim wanted.

THE HERITAGE GRAND Hotel finally opened with fireworks and fanfare on December 22, 1984, a year after Bakker broke ground but still six months behind schedule. A lavish forty-fifth birthday party was held for Jim on January 2 in the four-story lobby of the hotel with dozens of out-of-town guests. Bakker dressed in black tie and Tammy wore an elegant long white dress. The party ran late into the night. Among the honored guests were Dottie and Arnold Santjer from Bradenton, Florida, who had purchased fifty lifetime partnerships. By June 1985 the Santjers had more or less moved to Heritage USA, though they still owned a $175,000 home in Florida. Eventually they bought a total of seventy-six lifetime partnerships. Like most lifetime partners, Arnold later testified that he remembered "nothing about" Bakker setting a limit of 25,000 on lifetime partnerships in the Grand.[46]

To keep the cash flowing, Bakker and his staff announced yet another membership program on February 19, 1985, the Silver lifetime partnership. For an additional gift of $1,000, Silver partners were entitled to free admission to non-food events, including most recreational activities, free transportation on the park's train, trams, and buses, and two workshops a year. It did not include lodging since it was intended for those who had already purchased a lifetime partnership in the Grand or Towers.[47]

When this did not prove to be enough, the next month Bakker reopened the lifetime partnership program in the Grand Hotel. After a "final tabulation" on the total number of partnerships in the Grand, "we . . . discovered that because of some credit card problems and some who did not follow through on their phoned in membership pledges, there are several hundred original lifetime partnerships left," Bakker wrote in a letter sent to 19,264 supporters on March 28, 1985. "These are not Tower partnerships. They may be used in the Heritage Grand Hotel this year." A month later Bakker sent another letter to 594,794 supporters claiming that because of "checks and credit card payments that did not go through" there were still "over 900 Lifetime Partnerships" available in the Heritage Grand Hotel for the original price of $1,000 each.[48]

In fact, by April 11, 1985, PTL had received full payment on 34,983 lifetime partnerships in the Heritage Grand, almost 10,000 more than the original limit of 25,000. Between April 11 and July 8, when Bakker once again announced that the Heritage Grand partnership program was closed, PTL received full payment for another 23,765 lifetime partnerships, for a total of 58,748 Heritage Grand partnerships. In addition, PTL received partial payment for 2,032 partnerships and pledges for an additional 15,975. At that point Bakker had sold enough lifetime partnerships to fill every room in the Grand every night. But it still was not enough.[49]

Jeff Eggen joined PTL in July 1979 as the supervisor for data research. When the lifetime partnership program began in 1984, Eggen ran the computers that stored the partnership data. One day he saw Dortch on the air offering partnerships in the Heritage Grand after he and Bakker had announced the program was closed. Dortch told viewers he could do this because some of the partners had died, leaving their spots up for grabs. Eggen wondered if this was true, so he ran a report to see how many deaths showed up in their files. The result was "zero." Dortch had simply made it up.[50]

Bakker and Dortch knew the correct figures all along, or at least they should have. Hollis Rule began working at PTL in November 1980 as a computer programmer. One of Rule's tasks was collecting data on the lifetime partnerships. In June 1985, after Bakker had reopened the Grand partnership program, Rule became concerned that the number of partnerships was "going high." On June 7 he wrote to his supervisor, Rich Ball: "Rich, I would like to keep you informed on the latest counts of the lifetime memberships. The total paid Grand lifetime memberships is now 44,375. I am concerned about this because this would require 73 percent occupancy to completely fulfill our obligations." Rule was also concerned because Towers partners were being allowed to transfer their memberships to the Grand.[51]

Three weeks later Rule wrote to Ball telling him that Grand partnerships now accounted for 84 percent occupancy of the Grand. By July 15 Grand partnerships represented 88.2 percent occupancy of the Grand, and Towers memberships accounted for 31.9 percent occupancy of the yet-to-be-completed Towers. Rule's reports were clear and emphatic. There was no misunderstanding his point. On July 29, Rule wrote to his new supervisor, Vice President Steve Nelson, that the number of Grand partnerships now stood at 60,251, or 99 percent of the hotel's capacity, with an additional 19,367 Towers partnerships already sold. Until the Towers was completed (and it never was) there was simply nowhere to put the overflow.[52]

Rule kept sending updates every week or two through the summer of 1985. "I was concerned about the partners. It was my job to keep management informed," he later said. On September 3, Rule wrote to Nelson to say that the total number of paid partnerships was 63,341 for the Grand and 19,100 for the Towers, or 104.1 percent occupancy for the Grand and 31.3 percent for the unfinished Towers. At that point the partnership program was clearly oversubscribed and should have been halted, at least until the Towers was completed.[53]

Instead, on September 4, 1985, Bakker announced yet another new lifetime partnership program, the Silver 7,000. For a gift of $3,000, Silver 7,000 partners were entitled to seven days and six nights in the Heritage Towers plus the same benefits as Silver partners, which included free admission to non-food events, free transportation inside the park, and two workshops a year. These were announced as the last 7,000 partnerships that would be offered for the Towers, hence the name.[54]

Before the promotion launched, Bakker asked Mark Burgund, PTL's budget director, to calculate the value of a Silver 7,000 membership over time. Figuring on a family of four visiting the park every year for thirty years and an annual inflation rate of 6 percent, Burgund calculated that a Silver 7,000 partnership was worth $84,735. But when Burgund showed his results to Bakker he told him to rework the numbers. Burgund had "the general idea," Bakker said, but he wanted to know "how much usage it would have to be for it to be worth a million dollars." With the new target in mind, Burgund redid the math.[55]

Two days later, on July 28, 1985, Burgund had a fresh set of numbers for Bakker. Burgund started with a family of five who used their Silver 7,000 to stay at the park for seven days and six nights every year for fifty years and who used all of Heritage USA's recreational facilities—the waterpark, miniature golf, skating rink, horseback riding, paddleboats, carousel, petting zoo, antique car rides, all night sings, and so on—every day. But this was still far short of $1 million. So Burgund added an additional thirty days each year, for which the family would need to find its own housing if they did not live locally. If they used all of the recreational facilities and transportation each day for an extra thirty days a year and went to the Passion Play, which was performed in the amphitheater, two more times each year, the total combined value, as Burgund figured it, was $1,005,487. It was theoretically possible, but not at all likely. Regardless, Bakker used Burgund's calculations to announce on television that a Silver 7,000 partnership was worth $1 million. "The Silver 7,000 Club is the most exciting thing in all the world. If you use it for a family of five for up to fifty years it could be worth a million dollars to your family, literally," Bakker said.[56]

That November Burgund redid the numbers once again to account for plans to include a bowling alley and health spa in the Towers. Adding in the value of a family of five going bowling ($4 each per day) and visiting the health spa ($10 each per day) every day they were at Heritage USA for fifty years, in addition to all of the other previously calculated activities, yielded a total value of $1,614,262. Finally, in December 1985, Burgund did a similar set of calculations for a Silver partnership, which did not include lodging. He concluded that a Silver partnership alone would be worth $1.4 million for a family of five over 50 years.[57]

Meanwhile, the pattern of giving large bonuses to Jim and Tammy and other senior staff continued even as PTL's finances deteriorated. On January 18, 1985, Peter Bailey wrote to Richard Dortch, who now mostly oversaw PTL's day-to-day operations, reporting that between June 1 and December 31, 1984 the ministry lost $9,704,055. Two months later, on March 28,1985, the board gave Jim and Tammy bonuses of $200,000 and $50,000, respectively. On April 18 Bailey wrote to Dortch that the loss for March alone was $1,685,000. Two days earlier the board had voted Jim and Tammy bonuses of $200,000 and $20,000. On June 30 Bailey reported to Dortch that for the fiscal year ending May 31, PTL lost $20 million. Part of this loss was the result of general contributions declining to $40 million, down from $52 million the year before, as more people shifted their giving to lifetime partnerships. Five days later, on July 5, the board approved bonuses for Jim and Tammy of $200,000 and $50,000.[58]

"At present, our income is one-half of what it takes to operate the ministry at its present pace," Peter Bailey wrote to Jim Bakker on August 19, 1985. The payroll alone was over $1 million per pay period. "Because of this, all other bills are getting further and further behind including television time, product costs, travel expenses, mortgage and lease payments on real estate, maintenance, advertising, road construction, loans on vehicles and equipment, operating supplies, utility bills, insurance bills, medical bills, et cetera," wrote Bailey. A month later, on September 30, 1985, Bailey recommended a 40 percent cut in payroll, about one thousand people, to stave off financial collapse. At the time, PTL owed its affiliate stations $5.5 million for airtime and many were threatening to cancel the show. "It's a religious runaround," said the business manager of the Oklahoma City station. "It's my opinion that a Christian organization pays their bills first and foremost. They shouldn't have gone into this building program if they couldn't pay their bills." Another station manager in Jackson, Mississippi, pointed out that losing stations reduced PTL's ability to raise funds, which could lead to a financial death spiral of even more stations lost and therefore less fundraising. "It's going to come down . . . like a house of cards." Bakker sent an "emergency" message to supporters on September 13 declaring that PTL was "on the brink of a disaster" and urged them to immediately send an extra gift of $100. Two months later, in November, with the same debts still looming, the board awarded Jim and Tammy bonuses of $200,000 and $100,000, respectively. As was their practice, PTL grossed up these bonuses to cover the income taxes.[59]

To manage the Grand, PTL hired the Brock Hotel Corporation, which appointed William Mabrey General Manager of the hotel in April 1984. Mabrey had worked for Brock for a dozen years, mostly running Holiday Inns, before becoming a regional manager for the company. Mabrey was entirely qualified for the job, but the Heritage Grand would test even his resourcefulness.[60]

Brock agreed to make 50 percent of the rooms available to lifetime partners free of charge. Brock's management fee was based on the other 50 percent, the paying guests, and amounted to 5 percent of gross revenues. About three months after the hotel opened Mabrey's senior assistant manager walked into his office with a printout. "Have you seen this?" he asked Mabrey. "What do you have?" Mabrey replied. It was a list of all the lifetime partners. After "doing some calculations," they realized the extent to which Bakker and Dortch had over-promoted partnerships in the Grand. "We would have to run in excess of a hundred percent occupancy 365 days a year just for the lifetime partners," Mabrey concluded.[61]

Mabrey took the printout to Richard Dortch, who told him, "Bill, you have to understand that one of three things may occur, that some people just purchase the lifetime partnerships merely as a donation to the ministry. Others may come once and never use it again and yet others may be deceased before they ever use it. So don't worry about it. Get back to running the hotel." But Dortch was wrong, as Mabrey and his staff soon learned.[62]

For a fee, Brock agreed to expand the number of rooms reserved for lifetime partners to 60 percent, but soon this was not enough. Compounding the problem, as of July 3, 1985, six months after the hotel opened, the third floor was still unfinished, leaving only 418 rooms to rent. By August all of the rooms allotted for partners were booked for the remainder of the year, and Mabrey's reservations department was "beginning to receive many abusive phone calls from many irate lifetime partners who are demanding $1,000 refunds," as he wrote to Bakker and Dortch. Mabrey alleviated some of the pressure by allowing partners to use their 1985 benefits in January and February 1986, but this was only a short-term fix.[63]

A month later, in September 1985, Mabrey wrote to PTL's Partner Research Department looking for help dealing with what by then had become a steady stream of angry partners. "Joy Cole, our Reservation Manager, recently handed me a stack of complaint letters from lifetime partners, most in reference to not being able to make reservations at the Heritage Grand. It is my concern that Joy has essentially been asked to be a complaint department for the lifetime partners," Mabrey wrote. As a result of the "stress" of dealing with "irate partners demanding either accommodations or their money back," turnover in the reservations department was 40 percent in one month alone.[64]

Adding to the difficulty of Mabrey's job, Bakker demanded that the Grand run like a 5-star hotel. When it came to the Heritage grounds and buildings, Bakker was a perfectionist. He and Mabrey stayed up late one night before the hotel opened going over "every minute detail of the design of the [hotel staff] uniforms," Mabrey said. When Bakker noticed people standing in line to check in, he demanded extra staff at the front desk. To deal with a poorly lit hallway leading to the lobby restrooms, Charlotte Whiting, a member of Bakker's personal staff, ordered a $15,000 chandelier. The hotel itself had some elegant touches, such as redwood trim instead of pine, but in other respects the building performed poorly. The rooms lacked sufficient ventilation, leading to "a lot of mildew problems." Mabrey kept a "staff of six painters" to continually repaint hallways and rooms. "It was just a very tough animal to manage," Mabrey concluded.[65]

Bakker and Dortch initially demanded that Mabrey set aside thirty rooms for guests of the television show and other VIPs, including seven of the hotel's nine suites. The only two suites available to the public when the hotel opened were the Adam and Eve suites. Later, as financial pressures mounted, Bakker agreed to rent out the other suites as well, except for the Presidential Suite, which was initially reserved for the Bakker family.[66]

As with the Florida condo, Bakker assigned James Taggart the task of decorating the Presidential Suite, located on the fourth floor. Everything was behind schedule as construction crews rushed to get the hotel ready for opening day. When Taggart first saw the suite in December 1984, "there was nothing up except steel studs ... the floors were still concrete ... some of the plumbing was in," he later recalled. Bakker wanted it finished before the hotel opened in just twelve days so that he and his family would have "a place to relax" over the holidays.[67]

Taggart set about the job with his usual panache. The suite was 4,000 square feet, including a full kitchen, four bedrooms, and 5½ baths with "gold plated fixtures," according to Taggart. As with the Florida condo, he used lots of beveled mirrors with gold accents, the kind Bakker liked. Taggart bought antique brass beds from a local dealer. The living room included a decorative fireplace and a piano Bakker had recently bought in California. The master bedroom had another decorative fireplace and a "solid brass" cabinet that took "four or five men to hand carry it up." Tammy's closet was "ten feet wide and about fifty or sixty feet long," with its own chandeliers. One "entire side" had double racks for hanging clothes, with built-in storage spaces for purses and shoes on the opposite wall. Taggart used whatever workmen he could find, including some of the television set crew. Remarkably, he got it all done before opening day, with the exception of some "temporary draperies."[68]

The Bakkers lived in the Presidential Suite for about six months after the hotel opened. After that, they only stayed there occasionally. Living on the grounds meant that Jim was almost never home, which Tammy hated. A few other celebrity guests were allowed to use the suite—Oral Roberts, Art Linkletter, Pat Boone—but mostly it sat empty.[69]

By the fall of 1985 Bakker believed that the success of the Silver 7,000 partnerships, launched that September, was "our key to survival," as he wrote to two of his assistants, Steve Nelson and Walter Richardson, who bought PTL's airtime on affiliate stations. At about the time the program kicked off, Bakker called a meeting of the President's Club, Partner Research, and Reservations to enlist their support in selling the Silver 7,000 memberships. The President's Club handled PTL's major donors, anyone who gave over $1,000, which included all of the lifetime partners. Among those in attendance were Carol Craddock and J'Tanya Adams.[70]

Adams started working at PTL in June 1984 when she was about twenty years old. She had grown up Presbyterian but began attending a Pentecostal church in her teens. She loved working at PTL. "It was a very warm, very friendly environment . . . like going on vacation to hang out with great people." She started at $4.25 an hour and at times had to choose between gas and food, but she did not mind. "That is what being a servant is all about . . . loving mankind and making yourself available, especially in time of need," Adams said.[71]

Her boss at the President's Club was Carol Craddock. "Carol was the best. She was almost like the mother of the group. . . . She was strong and very kind . . . a wonderful woman to work with," remembers Adams. As manager of the President's Club, Craddock supervised a staff of fourteen women. The department "ran very efficiently, very shrewdly, [a] very exemplary group of godly, professional women. . . . I never worked with a group of women like that," recalls Adams. "The partners, as far as we were concerned . . . came first," Craddock later said. She gave out her home number, and "they were free to call me at any time day or night." If they needed prayer or just someone to talk to, they called. If they needed a ride from the airport, Craddock picked them up in her car, even though PTL did not reimburse her for mileage.[72]

As reservations for the Grand became increasingly difficult to get, partners called the President's Club for help. At times Craddock was able to talk the hotel's reservations department into giving up a paying room to a partner as "a personal favor." But they made it clear that "we can't do this every time." Increasingly Craddock and her staff had to be "just brutally honest" with partners and say, "look, we can't get you in because there are no rooms." When partners began asking for refunds, Steve Nelson, Craddock's supervisor, told her to "discourage giving refunds." But she "did not always follow" this policy "to the letter . . . because my conscience would not allow me to." "At one point we had as much money going out as we had coming in," Craddock later said. PTL eventually paid more than $7.3 million in refunds. At times Craddock discouraged people from buying a partnership in the first place. When a woman in her 70s was going to sell her burial policy to buy a lifetime partnership, Craddock talked her out of it. "It got to a point where you couldn't make sense of it anymore," said J'Tanya Adams.[73]

The meeting with Bakker to discuss promoting the Silver 7,000 partnerships was held in the President's Club lounge at the Grand Hotel over a lunch of chicken salad with grapes. Bakker urged the President's Club staff to sell the Silver 7,000 memberships "as quickly as we could," Craddock said. He told them "that whoever sold the most memberships would receive a Cadillac." Craddock hardly knew what to say. Her department was "overwhelmed . . . trying to accommodate" the partners they already had, "and yet, we were being encouraged to sell even more memberships."[74]

Then J'Tanya Adams stood up. "Mr. Bakker," she said, "how are we going to do this if we're already oversold and we've already got more memberships than we can accommodate; how are we going to do this?" "You could have heard a pin drop," said Craddock. Bakker stood in silence for a moment and then said, "There are going to be people from all over, California, wherever, that buy memberships that are not going to come every year and because they're not going to come every year, I don't think we have to worry about it." But the women who ran the President's Club knew better. "I looked at him . . . his verbal response, his body language, the look in his eye . . . and then I knew, oh my God, we're in trouble," remembers Adams.[75]

Bakker's real response came two or three months later when he disbanded the President's Club. J'Tanya Adams was transferred to partner research, but when she got there they told her they "did not have a place for me." She quit on October 31, 1985. Carol Craddock was simply fired. "Steve, I just want to know why," she asked her boss, Steve Nelson. Nelson leaned back in his chair, "Carol, that's the price you pay for knowing too much and not keeping your mouth shut." "Okay," replied Craddock, "I can understand that because, yes, indeed, I fought tooth and toenail for these partners and, yes, every opportunity that I had to tell Mr. Bakker what the situation was, I took it." But why take it out on the other women in her department? Nelson leaned back again. "That's the price they pay for you knowing too much and keeping them too informed," he said. All Craddock could do was cry. No one ever won the Cadillac.[76]

Despite Bakker's best efforts, sales of the Silver 7,000 partnerships were sluggish in comparison to the earlier Grand memberships, so he turned to another old trick: hold a telethon. The "Brink of a Miracle" telethon kicked off on Monday, October 7, 1985, and ran for the next two weeks. It had its own theme song: "Don't Give Up On the Brink of a Miracle." Satellite coverage on the first day lasted thirteen hours, with "nearly 10,000 callers making new pledges to PTL, or renewing and enlarging" existing commitments, according to the *Heritage Herald*, Heritage USA's full-size newspaper. When Bakker could not be on the set, Dortch and other staffers took over hosting the marathon event.[77]

"The brink of a miracle and the brink of disaster is the same place," Bakker told viewers during the telethon. Early in his career Bakker had learned that he needed to "have one of two things going all the time, either a crisis or a project," as one of his staffers later put it. The Brink of a Miracle telethon had both. The crisis was the $5.5 million PTL owed to its affiliate stations. The projects included all of the construction at Heritage USA and PTL's expanding overseas broadcasts, though in truth most of the money was going to building the park.[78]

Bakker and Dortch offered a range of entry points for donors. Supporters could join the Booster Club for a pledge of $5 a month, the Heritage Club for $10 a month, the PTL Club for $15 a month, the Worldwide Club for $20 a month, the Jubilee Club for $50 a month, the President's Club for $100 a month, the Reaching Out with Love Club for a one-time gift of $1,000 for world missions, the Silver 7,000 Club for $3,000, and the SOS (Save Our Stations) Club for a one-time gift of $100. A big scoreboard on the set kept track of the pledge totals in each category.

To say that the telethon got monotonous is an understatement of biblical proportions. It never really ended, as the fundraising push continued on into November and December. Bakker kept the giant scoreboard on the set through the end of October. By then, 6,646 people had pledged to become Silver 7,000 members for $3,000, but by November 6 PTL had received payment for only 852 of these partnerships. To entice more donors to follow through, Bakker and Dortch arranged for financing through local banks. For $300 down, donors could purchase a Silver 7,000 and then make monthly payments on the balance. "There's a simple application here, just a little thing you fill out . . . it's not even a page, really just half a page," Bakker said. He and Dortch continued to remind viewers that the Silver 7,000 was worth $1 million. "It is a million dollar gift, the Silver 7,000, because stretched out over 40 or 50 years . . . it's worth over a million dollars," Dortch said on the December 6 broadcast. They also assured donors that the Towers would soon be open. "The Towers are going to be built, perhaps in just about, oh, I would say eight, nine, ten months they are going to be ready," Dortch assured viewers on December 6.[79]

Despite Dortch's assurances, construction on the Towers inched along because PTL was chronically late in paying its builder, Roe Messner. "I hesitate to bring up money, Jim, but I am needing to receive a large payment to satisfy my banker," Messner wrote to Bakker on November 12, 1985, as the Brink of a Miracle campaign was just about over. "He is losing confidence in the project. He has advanced me over four million, and we keep getting further behind. I told him after the telethon, I would be able to pay him up to date. The $500,000 check last week bounced, and he about died.... I am laying off 30 men on the Towers to help meet my payroll." Six months later, in May 1986, Messner wrote to Bakker that the "Towers is moving now at a snail's pace," with only twenty men on the job. "It will take six weeks per floor at this pace," Messner told Bakker.[80]

As the Brink of a Miracle telethon was winding down, Bakker introduced new ways to give. On October 29 he and Tammy unveiled a new Susie Moppet doll, modeled on Tammy's original puppet, for a gift of $50. When squeezed, Susie sang *Oops! There Come's A Smile,* or said something adorable. The Susie Moppet dolls eventually raised a reported $4 million. Bakker called Susie his "million dollar baby."[81]

Bakker also announced that Fort Hope, a shelter for homeless men where they could learn a trade, would be completed by the end of the year. A promo, aired at the end of October, showed foundations being poured and some buildings being framed on the Heritage USA grounds. In fact, Fort Hope was one of the projects Messner suggested slowing down until PTL caught up on its bills. On the same show Jim and Tammy and members of the stage crew held an impromptu fashion show, modeling clothes available from one of the retailers on Main Street USA. During the last three months of 1985, marketing and fundraising became an increasingly prominent part of the daily television show.

Richard Dortch pushed the merchandise as hard as anyone, as did a group of PTL regulars who took over when Bakker was not on the set, including Mike Murdock, Sam Johnson, and singer Doug Oldham. "Faith is always in the red. It's never stored up. It's never in the black," Johnson told viewers. They all seemed to realize that their position on the show depended on selling. Dortch and the other guest hosts urged supporters to use their credit cards, which made the money immediately available to PTL.

BY THE END of 1985, PTL was a deeply divided place. Under Bakker and Dortch, PTL's leadership had in many ways abandoned honesty and transparency in order to enrich themselves and build Bakker's dream of a Christian Disneyland. At the same time, sincere and dedicated employees like J'Tanya Adams and Carol Craddock worked tirelessly to maintain the ministry's core mission to evangelize the world, serve the church, and reach out to the needy. J'Tanya Adams always regarded PTL as "a beautiful place.... It was safe.... It was serene.... You got to meet beautiful people from all around the world and I'm glad I got to witness that and be a part of that." But Bakker's duplicity shook her faith to its core. After she left PTL, "I didn't know what to believe, who to believe, what to think, what to trust, because I just didn't expect all of that."[82]

None of this was obvious from the outside. On television, Bakker looked more relaxed and confident than ever. He dressed sharply and seemed to have settled into his role as a Christian celebrity. This was particularly evident when he interviewed other celebrities, everyone from Pearl Bailey to a growing number of Hollywood actors. Many of his guests seemed to crave his approval, rather than the other way around, as had been the case only a few years before. Guest hosts seemed to compete with one another to see who could lavish the most praise on Bakker. Video clips of Heritage USA aired on the *Jim Bakker* show showed a bustling, clean, modern, and happy place where everyone was greeted with a smile and there was something fun for the entire family. At the close of 1985, J'Tanya Adams was part of a relatively small group of people outside Bakker's inner circle who knew just how closely PTL teetered on the brink of disaster, not just financial disaster, but moral and spiritual disaster as well. In a little more than a year everyone would know.[83]

11

Cover-Up

JESSICA HAHN STRUGGLED to make sense of what had happened to her in that Florida hotel room in December 1980 after she returned to Long Island. She lived at home but did not dare tell her parents. She was worried that she might be pregnant. Fletcher told her that he had had a vasectomy, but she was not sure about Bakker.[1]

The details of the cover-up surrounding Hahn and Bakker's encounter are murky because they involve phone calls and clandestine meetings between people who did not want to be found out. For most of these events, there are at least two versions of what happened. Hahn claims that PTL staffers called her repeatedly and spread rumors about her for several years after the events in Florida. Bakker's staff insisted that it was Hahn who kept calling, demanding to talk with Jim Bakker.

Both sides agree that on Monday, December 8, two days after their encounter in Florida, Bakker called Hahn. He says that he called to ask her forgiveness. When she invited him to meet her in Long Island, he told her that they could not see each other again. It was their last conversation, according to Bakker. Hahn tells the story differently. "I don't want you to tell anybody," Bakker said when he called, according to Hahn. "If this becomes public knowledge, it will be devastating not only to me but to my ministry, to the kingdom of God. Millions of people will suffer. I've got a lot more to lose than you do." Bakker told Hahn that she was "blessed" and "special." In time, "you will appreciate it. You will realize that I chose you." When Hahn asked why Bakker had chosen her, he said that he could trust her. She had grown up in the church and "understood the importance of keeping silent." Bakker had kept his own experience of sexual abuse as a child secret for more than twenty years, and he evidently expected Hahn to do the same.[2]

That same week John Wesley Fletcher called to say that Bakker wanted to see her again, according to Hahn. "He's willing to pay your way anywhere to do anything, because he enjoyed you so much." Hahn says she hung up without replying. Within a couple of weeks she says that David Taggart, Bakker's personal assistant, called to say that Bakker was "broken" and worried that she might talk. Taggart reminded Hahn about the tremendous stress that Bakker was under running PTL. No one asked about her. David Taggart later testified that it was Hahn who called him about two weeks after Florida. Taggart had been part of Bakker's entourage in Florida, but he had not met Hahn there. Hahn demanded that Bakker call her back, according to Taggart.[3]

Hahn says that before Florida, she and Gene Profeta, her pastor and boss who was twenty-two years her senior, had "a father-daughter" relationship. But she also told reporter Charles E. Shepard that Profeta kissed her in February 1978 after they went out for a drink, though she maintained that they never had sex before her encounter with Bakker. She cleaned Profeta's home, babysat his kids, and worked as his secretary. Confused about what to do next, she waited a few days after returning from Florida before telling him what had happened. Profeta "actually cried" and was angry with Fletcher and Bakker, but not for the reason Hahn expected. Profeta told her "he should have been first." After that "it really got ugly and abusive. He would smack me around and pulled earrings out of my ears," Hahn told me. Profeta carried a gun, and she was afraid he might kill Fletcher. That July, Hahn and Profeta began a sexual relationship that lasted six years. They met in secret every Tuesday and took trips to Atlantic City, according to later reports. Profeta was indicted for tax evasion in 1988. The charges included using church money to buy Hahn "fur coats, casino trips, hotel stays, [and] jewelry," and to make her rent and car payments. Eventually Profeta became "obsessed" with controlling her life, and the two had a falling out after her encounter with Bakker became public in 1987.[4]

Hahn's parents worried about her, though they knew nothing about what had happened in Florida or her developing sexual relationship with Profeta. She lost weight and they feared she had anorexia. They brought trays of food to her room that she refused to eat. When she went to church the worship did not feel the same. "I cut myself off from everything and everybody," she later said. She struggled to make ends meet on her salary of ninety-eight dollars a week. She eventually found a "Christian psychiatrist" who charged fifty dollars an hour. "Do you know who Jim Bakker is?"

she asked as she was "working up to tell him" about Florida. "Yeah. I've been on his TV show," he replied. Of course. Everyone in her world knew Bakker. Hahn stayed at the church in Long Island for the next six years because "I just didn't know any other life. I really didn't." "It was a sick bunch of years," as she recalls it now.[5]

Several men later told the press that they had affairs with Hahn before and after her encounter with Bakker. Barry Hawkins, who was married at the time, claimed that he had an affair with Hahn in 1984. "Gold and diamonds and silk dresses—she was the most expensive looking woman I've ever seen," Hawkins told reporters. He also said that Hahn told him she was not a virgin when she had sex with Bakker. Hawkins said he broke off his relationship with Hahn after a threatening phone call from Profeta.[6]

According to Hahn, Richard Dortch first called her on March 12, 1984, a few months after he became the second in command at PTL. They talked for two hours during which Dortch tried to reassure her that he cared about her as he did his own daughter. He sounded phony to Hahn. "He kisses Jim Bakker's butt and covers up his dirt," she later told *Charlotte Observer* reporter Charles Shepard.[7]

A few days later, Dortch called again, and Hahn told him that she was considering getting a lawyer. That was the last thing Dortch wanted, so he set up a meeting with Hahn in New York. Dortch arranged for Hahn to meet Aimee Cortese, an Assemblies of God minister from the Bronx and a member of PTL's board since December 1979, in the LaGuardia airport gift shop. Hahn remembers Cortese looking like "a large prison warden, standing there with her arms crossed" (in fact, Cortese was a former prison chaplain). She took Hahn to room 616 at the airport Holiday Inn. When Dortch arrived, he had papers for Hahn to sign that put the blame on her and said, "I had, in effect, raped" Jim Bakker. The documents also stated that she had come to them for money and they had helped her. "If you don't sign these statements, I don't think you're ever going to have any peace," Hahn remembers Dortch saying. He told her that Bakker "really does want forgiveness" and that he was afraid Bakker might have a breakdown or kill himself. "Jessica, how would you feel if Jim Bakker took a gun and put it to his head and shot himself?" Dortch asked. He and Cortese spent "hours and hours" trying to convince Hahn to sign but she refused.[8]

In Dortch's version of the story, he first talked to Jessica Hahn in late fall 1984, at least six months after they actually met at the LaGuardia Holiday Inn. Dortch says that he had no idea who she was when she first called. "I want you to know that Jim Bakker raped me. He's ruined my life," Dortch remembers Hahn screaming, in a "shrill, panicky voice." Outside Dortch's window workers were putting up the lights for PTL's annual Christmas display. Hahn asked for "money to pay for medical and psychiatric bills," according to Dortch. He "did not even consider the possibility that her story could be credible." It did not fit the Jim Bakker he knew. "I knew him as shy, withdrawn, usually fearful of others." Dortch says that he prayed with Hahn. "You can make it," he assured her, repeating PTL's current slogan. She was just a "distressed soul" who would not call again.[9]

But a few days later she did. When the calls continued, Dortch arranged to meet Hahn at the LaGuardia Holiday Inn accompanied by "one of our board members, a pastor living in New York City." After the meeting was over, Dortch remembers Cortese telling him, "without question, this is a New York heist. A con, plain and simple." Still, Dortch gave her $2,000 of his own money to "handle the situation." Cortese in turn handed the money over to Hahn in a Massapequa diner on April 24, 1984 (about six months before Dortch claimed he first talked to Hahn).[10]

According to Dortch, Hahn brought a friend who was a paralegal and used the alias Carla Hammond to the LaGuardia meeting. Hahn says that she only told her friend about the meeting later and that her friend wrote a letter to PTL on Hahn's behalf without telling her. "It later turned out that she was signing my name to things and wasn't very stable," Hahn later said. The five-page letter, which runs more than two thousand words, was evidently sent to PTL in March 1984, addressed to David Taggart. It contains a wealth of details about the events of December 6, 1980, in Clearwater, Florida, that only Hahn could have provided. Either Hahn helped to write the letter or she told the story in full while her friend took notes. As with Dortch, there are elements of Hahn's story that do not quite add up.[11]

According to the letter, Hahn was particularly concerned that people at PTL were talking about her and that she was "being socially disgraced." The "spiritual . . . psychological and emotional damages," of her encounter with Bakker left her without "the usual anticipation of marriage and a happy future." She had four "requests." First, she wanted the leaks to stop. Second, she wanted an apology from Bakker. Third, she wanted her family "protected from any future embarrassment." Fourth, she wanted $100,000 to make a "fresh start." "Miss Hahn will not just walk away, and Mr. Bakker must be made aware of this. She was left broken-hearted. It is unrealistic, unjust, and unwise of him to presume she will walk away empty-handed as well," the letter stated. If Bakker refused, Hahn would go the Assemblies of God and then file a lawsuit, resulting in a "massive

Bakker with Billy Graham in December 1983. PTL played this video as often as they could.

Credit: Flower Pentecostal Heritage Center.

The David and Goliath sculpture that Bakker said was worth $1,000, but only cost $10 to produce.

Credit: Photo by the author.

Aerial view of Heritage USA. The Heritage Grand Hotel, Towers Hotel, and waterpark are in the upper right. The Barn is bottom center, with the amphitheater just above it. The Upper Room is lower right.

Credit: *The Charlotte Observer*.

The World Outreach Center. The executive offices were on the third floor.

Credit: Flower Pentecostal Heritage Center.

The Heritage Grand Hotel, under construction in 1984.
Credit: Flower Pentecostal Heritage Center.

The lobby of the Heritage Grand Hotel.
Credit: Photo by Robin Rayne Nelson/ZUMA Press.

Main Street USA, which connected to the Heritage Grand Hotel.
Credit: Flower Pentecostal Heritage Center.

Heritage Grand Partner Center and unfinished Towers Hotel, as seen from the waterpark.
Credit: *The Charlotte Observer*.

The train at Heritage USA.
Credit: *The Charlotte Observer*.

Richard Dortch on the PTL television set in 1984.
Credit: Flower Pentecostal Heritage Center.

Bakker and his Rolls Royce near Palm Springs in October 1984. He had just driven into the desert to pray, with a film crew.

Credit: Flower Pentecostal Heritage Center.

Tammy interviewing actor Mickey Rooney.

Credit: Flower Pentecostal Heritage Center.

Jim and Tammy during the "Brink of a Miracle" telethon, October 1985. The phones are on the left and the big board gives the membership totals.

Credit: Flower Pentecostal Heritage Center.

The waterpark at Heritage USA.

Credit: Photo by Robin Rayne Nelson/ZUMA Press.

The PTL television set in the mid-1980s.
Credit: Flower Pentecostal Heritage Center.

public scandal." Dortch was convinced that Gene Profeta was behind the letter. By this time he knew about the "romance" between Profeta and Hahn. Dortch later reportedly said that Profeta threatened him, saying that if Hahn did not receive enough hush money "he would come to Charlotte, North Carolina, and when he got finished with Jim Bakker and me, we would never be able to do anything else with a woman for the rest of our lives."[12]

In Dortch's version of events, he says that he did not ask Bakker about Hahn until after he returned from their meeting at LaGuardia. "Oh, by the way, I have been dealing with a woman who says that you raped her," Dortch remembers casually remarking to Bakker at the end of a meeting about something else. "Where is she from?" Bakker asked. "New York," Dortch said. "What's her name," Bakker asked, though he surely knew what was coming. "Jessica Hahn," Dortch said. After staring out the window for a "long" time, Bakker turned to face Dortch. "I never raped anybody," he said, "but there is a problem."[13]

The two sides went back and forth through the summer of 1984, exchanging phone calls. By this time Dortch was worried that John Wesley Fletcher would leak the story to the press, and he wanted Hahn's signature on a document that would contradict whatever Fletcher said. In fact, Fletcher was already talking. Loose ends are the undoing of many a cover-up, and in this case none was more likely to unravel than Fletcher.

Fletcher anonymously called the *Charlotte News*, the *Charlotte Observer*'s sister newspaper, in February 1983, sixteen months after he was kicked out of the Assemblies of God. Fletcher still had an active ministry, drawing more than $900,000 in contributions in both 1983 and 1984, but he knew that his shot at the big time was over. Reporter Terry Mattingly took the call, taking notes as Fletcher talked. Mattingly thought he might be listening to Oral Roberts's son, Richard, whom he had recently seen on Bakker's television show. "My name is synonymous with religion. I don't think there is a household in America that wouldn't know my name. . . . I've got to talk to somebody, somehow, someday. I'm scared to death . . . my nerves are gone," Fletcher said. "I never knew a more corrupt man in my life, period, than Jim Bakker. Now I see him for what he is." Fletcher suggested that Mattingly contact Dortch and ask him about the Florida condo. He also had actor Efrem Zimbalist Jr.'s home number and knew the name of his maid. He asked Mattingly why the Taggarts were living in the Bakker's first home on the lake and suggested that it was because David was Jim's "lover." "Jim is a switch hitter," who liked both men and women, Fletcher told Mattingly. Then Fletcher added a new piece of information to the mix. "Just remember this name: Jessica Hahn," he told Mattingly.[14]

Fletcher called a couple of more times in the next few weeks. Mattingly could tell that he was calling from airports, evidently to keep their conversations secret from anyone on Fletcher's end. Fletcher suggested that they meet out of state, but Mattingly's editors wanted to keep the meeting in North Carolina to save money. Mattingly never got Fletcher's name.[15]

Meanwhile Dortch urged Hahn to sign the confession he had drawn up, arguing that it would protect her against Fletcher's allegations, should they become public. When Dortch called, he referred to Bakker as "J. B.," in case their conversation was taped, and suggested that Hahn use the name Jennifer Leigh when she called.[16]

Hahn finally agreed to meet Aimee Cortese at her church in the Bronx on November 1, 1984. The church was in a "tough neighborhood" and Cortese had "two enormous guys" guarding the door. Her upstairs office was "the size of a bathroom stall." She pushed a confession, written by Dortch, in front of Hahn and told her to sign. Hahn says that they argued but eventually Cortese "talk[ed] me into it." She signed, admitting that she had forced herself on a reluctant Jim Bakker. When she got up to leave, according to Hahn, Cortese tossed her an envelope with $10,000 inside. "Get some counseling," Cortese tersely advised her.

Dortch had borrowed the money from Sam Johnson, who soon became a regular on the *Jim Bakker* show, and sent it to New York with one of his assistants, Mark Burgund. "Just don't ask me any questions about it," Dortch told Burgund before he left for the city. Johnson later told investigators that he could not remember where he got the $10,000, but he denied that it was church money. Five months later, PTL gave Johnson $13,700, presumably to repay the original loan and to cover taxes, since the ministry reported the repayment as income. Johnson was later indicted for lying under oath about the source of the money. That July, PTL gave Cortese's church $50,000 to help pay for a new building in the Bronx.[17]

The next day, Hahn had second thoughts and called Cortese. "I changed my mind. I want to give you this money back. And I want that document." Cortese told her it was too late; the papers were already on their way to PTL. Hahn kept the money, spending it little by little, but she was far from satisfied with the outcome. "She didn't want to live a lie," as one of her legal advisors later put it.[18]

Acting on Hahn's behalf, Gene Profeta contacted Paul Roper, a self-appointed guardian of the faith from Southern California. Roper had been the business manager of the Melodyland Christian Center in Orange County California in the early 1980s. There he uncovered "widespread moral and financial corruption," according to one of his associates at the church. Roper went public with the information and left the church in early 1983 to form "Operation Anti-Christ," an organization intended to expose corrupt ministries and help their victims. Hahn's case fit Roper's agenda perfectly. Roper flew to New York on January 3, 1985, to hear Hahn's story. They met at the church on Long Island. Over a two-hour period, Roper taped Hahn's account of what had happened in Florida as they sat in a church office with Gene Profeta looking on. Listening to Hahn's testimony, Roper was convinced she was telling the truth. "She was sobbing," Roper later told reporter Art Harris. "She kept bowing her head when she got embarrassed so she wouldn't have to look me in the eye."[19]

Hahn was never very astute about picking her advisers in the aftermath of her encounter with Bakker, and Roper was no exception. She thought that he was a lawyer, and he later represented himself as her "attorney in fact," a designation that initially fooled Richard Dortch as well. In fact, Roper, about forty, was a first-year law student at Western State University College of Law in Orange County, California, which at the time was not accredited by the American Bar Association. Roper grew up in eastern Montana, where his parents had a Pentecostal ministry to Native Americans. In 1961 he moved to Southern California to attend Life Bible College, founded in 1923 by Pentecostal celebrity preacher Aimee Semple McPherson. Roper also attended California State University, Fullerton, but did not earn a degree. After business ventures in the Pacific Northwest, Roper returned to Southern California in 1978, where he became the business manager at Melodyland. One of his associates at the church hired Roper to run a bank in Seattle, Washington. The bank's failure led to a criminal investigation and two lawsuits involving Roper.[20]

Roper knew he needed help for what he had in mind with Hahn, so he turned to a friend, John Stewart, who had just completed his final semester of law school at Western State and was studying for the bar exam. "I'm gonna be going back to New York to talk to a young gal and I may need to bring you in on this . . . this could be something big," Stewart remembers Roper telling him before he left for Long Island to meet with Hahn. Stewart was shocked by Hahn's account as he read the transcript of Roper's recording. Together they devised a plan for seeking restitution from Jim Bakker.[21]

To get Bakker's attention, Roper and Stewart decided to draft a lawsuit and send it to PTL with an offer to negotiate a settlement before the suit was filed. "The idea was to try to get some kind of admission and confession out of Bakker and do some kind of reconciliation," says Stewart. He didn't think that Hahn "was interested in publicity, I don't think she was even interested in money, she was interested in some sort of apology and vindication that she had been abused by someone in a position of trust," remembers Stewart. On January 11, 1985, Stewart drove to the Orange County courthouse and law library to research and draft a civil suit against Bakker. When he was finished, he gave his handwritten notes to Roper, who had his wife type them up along with a cover letter, dated January 14, 1985, which they sent as a package to PTL. The letter gave PTL until January 21 to respond.[22]

The suit sought $12.3 million in damages. It charged Bakker with battery, assault, and false imprisonment. It also charged Bakker, Dortch, the Assemblies of God, Aimee Cortese (misspelled Amy Cortize), and her Crossroads Church with inflicting emotional distress, and the Sheraton Hotel with negligence. As a means of getting Dortch's attention, the proposed suit worked perfectly.[23]

On February 10, Dortch landed at the John Wayne airport in Orange County aboard PTL's Sabreliner 75 jet to meet with Roper. PTL had purchased the twin-engine airplane, which seated eight passengers with all the amenities of a corporate jet, including a galley, the previous July for $965,000. Dortch had already stopped by Palm Springs, where the Bakkers were staying, to brief Jim on the situation. Roper suggested that they each choose a Christian leader, who would then select a third person, and let the three of them arbitrate the case after hearing testimony from both sides. Dortch said that he would consult with Bakker and get back to Roper. A few days later Dortch called to say that they would not agree to arbitration. Instead, Dortch hired Howard Weitzman, a celebrity lawyer from Los Angeles, on a $25,000 retainer. Weitzman had recently successfully defended John DeLorean, who claimed to be a born-again Christian, against charges of cocaine trafficking. DeLorean was founder of the DeLorean Motor Company, maker of the car featured in the 1985 film, *Back to the Future*. To Stewart, hiring Weitzman removed any lingering doubt he had about Hahn's story. It only made sense if Bakker was guilty.[24]

There was a David and Goliath quality to Roper's first meeting with Weitzman. The former was a first-year law student at a commuter college. The latter was a lawyer to the stars whose clients eventually included Marlon Brando, Magic Johnson, O. J. Simpson, Arnold Schwarzenegger, and major movie studios. "You haven't got a fucking case," Weitzman told

Roper as soon as he walked in. For starters, the statute of limitations had probably run out on the civil charges Roper and Stewart proposed. The case would probably never make it to trial. But Roper knew that the publicity mattered more to PTL than winning in court. A credible accusation alone could bring down the ministry. "Bakker needs to pay," Roper told Weitzman.[25]

Attorney Scott Furstman handled the case on behalf of Weitzman's firm, but it was Dortch and Roper who worked out a settlement totaling $265,000 "without the benefit of counsel," according to Furstman. Bakker did not want to know the exact details. "I hate to give them anything. I hate to give them a dime, but do what you have to do to get it solved," Dortch remembered Bakker telling him. In exchange for the money, Hahn agreed not to go public with any accusations against Bakker related to their December 1980 encounter. She would receive $115,000 up front with the remaining $150,000 placed in a trust fund in her name for twenty years, from which she would receive monthly dividends. After twenty years the money was hers, unless she breached the agreement, in which case it would revert back to PTL. Before agreeing to the settlement, Dortch flew to Palm Springs aboard the PTL Sabreliner to discuss the details with Bakker. Hahn, Roper, and Furstman signed off on the agreement on February 27, 1985, in front of a retired judge of the Los Angeles Superior Court, Charles Woodmansee, who acted as arbitrator. Neither Bakker nor Dortch attended. The $115,000 up-front payment intended for Hahn was made payable to the Bank of Yorba Linda, California, where Roper had an account. In one of the many ironies surrounding the settlement, Hahn got only $20,000 of the $115,000. Roper gave $12,500 to Stewart in a check dated February 28, 1985, and kept the rest as his fee for representing Hahn and overseeing her trust. PTL paid Furstman $85,000 for his services.[26]

Where did Dortch get the $265,000? Stewart believed that the money came from Bakker himself, from real estate he liquidated for this purpose, which only seemed fair as Stewart saw it. "Bakker is going to pay out of his own pocket, he's owned up to it," Stewart remembers Roper telling him. In fact, despite the Bakkers' rapidly rising income, Jim did not have the money. Instead, the money came from PTL, though Dortch did his best to hide the source. Dortch first asked James Taggart to launder the money through his interior design business, which dealt almost exclusively with PTL, but Taggart refused. Next Dortch turned to Roe Messner, reasoning that his company, PTL's principal contractor, "had the most to lose" if a scandal led to a halt in PTL's construction, with the Grand Hotel still not finished and the Towers barely begun.[27]

Over lunch at Heritage USA on February 21, 1985, six days before the settlement with Hahn was signed in Los Angeles, Dortch told Messner that a woman in New York claimed that Jim Bakker had raped her, without giving him Hahn's name. Dortch said that he was going to take care of the problem, telling Messner that as chief executive officer of an organization that did "over 100 million dollars in business a year," he had "the authority to make a $265,000 decision." He said that he had hired Howard Weitzman and "made a big deal out of telling me who he was," according to Messner. "We've hired the best attorney we can hire . . . we're doing it right and it will forever be over," Dortch said. Messner later testified that Dortch asked him for a $265,000 loan and then told him to create a phony invoice for the same amount for brick, block, and labor used in construction at the amphitheater, where the Passion Play was performed. Messner agreed to launder the money, and an extra $265,000 charge for the "Passion Play Set per Reverend Dortch" appeared on the next month's statement. Dortch had Messner wire the money directly to Weitzman's firm on February 26 to avoid creating a paper trail, though Furstman "assumed that it was coming from PTL." When Dortch tried to tell Bakker how the settlement had been handled he refused to listen. "I don't want to know it. I don't want to hear it," Bakker told him. Neither Bakker nor Dortch told PTL's board, apart from Aimee Cortese, about Jessica Hahn or the payments to her.[28]

Once again, Hahn came away dissatisfied. During the February 27 meeting in Weitzman's office to sign the agreement she "hardly understood what was being said." Roper kept telling her, "You're going to be set for life." She never thought to ask why she was only getting $20,000 of the $115,000. What she really wanted was to get back the document she had signed in front of Aimee Cortese and for Bakker to apologize in person or even over the phone, but none of the men in the room paid much attention to her. "They treated me like I was twelve," she recently told me. From her perspective, "nothing was accomplished." When the story finally broke her bitterness would well up like a fountain.[29]

MEANWHILE TAMMY BAKKER had her own demons to confront. In the spring of 1984, Roger Flessing returned to PTL for another brief stint. After a March 1 meeting with Jim Bakker, David Taggart, and Richard Dortch, Flessing recorded in his notes, "Tammy may be on or near a nervous breakdown. Tammy addicted to --------." Flessing refrained from recording the exact drugs, but others knew. Mike Richardson worked as a security guard at PTL from November 1983 to October 1984, much of the time as Jim's personal bodyguard. "Tammy was taking serious amounts of Valium that year, 'for her nerves,' and we all knew it. She had both blue ones and yellow ones. I personally saw her take Valium more than twenty times—and I wasn't with her all day long the way I was with Jim," Richardson later wrote. At least twice that year, Vi Azvedo took Tammy to California when "the Valium was getting to her and she needed to 'dry out' some." On one of these occasions, in October 1984, while Jim and Tammy were in Palm Springs, Richard Dortch told PTL viewers that Tammy was in the hospital for tests on her heart. For an evangelical audience, a bad heart was far better than drug dependency.[30]

One of the things that everyone loved about Tammy was her openness, but she often revealed more than she intended, or at least more than Jim and others at PTL wished she would. On December 3, 1984, after returning from California, Tammy hosted the *Jim Bakker* show live from the studio while Jim supervised the completion of the Grand Hotel, which would open in less than three weeks. The theme of the show was alcoholism, and all of Tammy's guests were recovering alcoholics. As they described their experiences, Tammy was suddenly overwhelmed with emotion. "Well you know it's the same way you get hooked on pills. . . . Even prescription drugs are so terribly dangerous because you get up and you say, well, I'll just take one, or I'll take half a one, just to help me through this stressful time, and before you realize it, you can't stop taking them," she said as tears welled up in her eyes. Soon "you need more than a half a one, and then you need a whole one . . . to get you through the stress. And then all of a sudden a whole one isn't doing it anymore and you need a whole one plus a half . . . and before you know it there's no way you can get off it yourself," Tammy said.

> And that is drugs the doctor prescribes; it seems so innocent. . . . People be careful, it's that first little bit, it's that first one, that leads to destruction. . . . If you just won't take the first one, you won't have to go through the hell of withdrawal of these things, and that is truly hell. The withdrawal of alcohol, the withdrawal of a little innocent looking pill can be literal hell on earth, you think that your body, the inside of your body is going to destroy itself trying to get off of it.

It is difficult to imagine that many of PTL's senior staff did not understand that Tammy was describing her own experience. She sometimes shared her Valium with Jim, who learned that he could only tolerate a half or a quarter of a pill at a time, to calm his anxiety and help him sleep.[31]

Part of Tammy's anxiety stemmed from her insecurity about her role at PTL. Over the years Tammy had a number of her own television shows, usually taped in the afternoon after Jim's show, all of which ended when she lost interest in them. Her shows were usually less explicitly religious than Jim's. While Jim invariably focused on the religious sensibilities of his audience to the point of pandering, Tammy often seemed to be searching for something else that interested her. She was at ease talking about her faith, but could just as easily leave it out.

In the early months of 1985, Tammy did a series of taped interviews with religious and entertainment celebrities, including Arvella Schuller, wife of televangelist Robert Schuller, and actors Mr. T, Nell Carter, and Lou Ferrigno. Schuller described dealing with trauma and grief after her daughter lost a leg in a motorcycle accident. With Mr. T, who grew up in the housing projects of Chicago, and Nell Carter, who starred in the sitcom *Gimme a Break!* Tammy discussed the challenges of being a Christian in Hollywood. But with Ferrigno, who was famous for his television role as the Incredible Hulk ("It's not easy being green," Ferrigno reminded Tammy), she only talked fitness and nutrition.[32]

Perhaps Tammy's most memorable television moment was her November 1985 interview with Steve Pieters, a gay minister from Los Angeles. Tammy was her most bubbly and exuberant self as she interviewed Pieters on her *Tammy's House Party* show via satellite hook-up. Pieters told her that he first realized what it meant to be gay at eleven or twelve years old. When he told his Congregationalist minister in Massachusetts, where Pieters grew up, he "freaked out." "He told me, 'Don't tell anybody. Never say anything to anybody about it. Keep it to yourself and it will go away.' " But it didn't. Pieters also talked to a psychiatrist who "said it was a phase." He felt ashamed and dated girls in high school and college in an effort to "program myself to be straight, and it never worked." At twenty-four, after joining the Metropolitan Community Church in Chicago, Pieters finally told his parents that he was gay. His mother cried and his father held his hand and "told me I was his son and he loved me no matter what." "Thank God for a mom and dad who will stand with a young person," Tammy said. "That's the way it is with Jesus. . . . Jesus loves us through anything."

Throughout the interview Tammy was more empathy than understanding. "Don't you think that maybe you just haven't given women a fair try?" she asked Pieters. But her empathy was remarkable given the fear of homosexuality and AIDS among evangelicals. Pieters had been diagnosed with AIDS in April 1984. The disease was little understood at the time, and Pieters described the fear that it triggered in others, who refused to touch him and served him food on paper plates, lest their dishes be contaminated. "How sad that we as Christians, who are to be the salt of the earth, and . . . are supposed to be able to love everyone, are afraid so badly of an AIDS patient that we will not go up and put our arm around them and tell them that we care," Tammy said. Here was the openness that everyone loved about her.[33]

By 1985 this was an interview that Jim would not have done. But Tammy did not think in terms of fundraising and maintaining a base. Indeed, she mostly resented Heritage USA and all that it had cost her and her family. "The happiest time of my life was when I was able to be with Tammy Sue and Jamie and be a Mom," Tammy later wrote, reflecting on her life during the PTL years. Among evangelicals in the 1980s, there was no higher calling for a woman than to be a loving wife and nurturing mother. Judy Bycura, Tammy's next-door neighbor at Tega Cay and one of her best friends for nearly thirty years, remembers that Tammy loved to cut hair. When she got out her scissors, everyone from Jim to the Bakker and Bycura children scattered. "We stayed away from her when she had scissors in her hand," says Bycura. She remembers spending Sunday afternoons with the Bakkers either at home or on one of the houseboats that each family owned. On these Sunday afternoons, the Bakkers seemed like any other suburban American family.[34]

After 1983 these suburban moments became increasingly rare, as Jim was more and more preoccupied with building Heritage USA, even on Sundays. For Tammy, the steady erosion of family time was devastating. PTL staff came and went at the Bakkers' house, day and night. They had three maids, all paid for by PTL, including Johnnie Mae Heffney, who did most of the cooking. Tammy "liked having vast quantities of food in the house," but by this time she rarely cooked, except on her television shows. Security guards were a constant presence. Jim, Tammy, and both of their children each had a personal security guard. The security staff kept a file on bomb threats and threats against Bakker and his children, including kidnapping. Don Hardister, Bakker's chief of security, remembers "one morning having to make up my own mind if I was going to ride with him or not," because they had received "threats from a foreign type group over some Israeli programming that we were doing." Hardister took executive protection courses to learn evasive driving techniques. Judy Bycura recalls an incident in which someone left a briefcase in the middle of the Bakkers' driveway. Security guards called the bomb squad at Fort Jackson who arrived by helicopter, landing at the Tega Cay Country Club parking lot. When they opened the briefcase it contained only a Bible.[35]

The Bakkers' security guards did more than just protect the family from outsiders. Every night when the Bakkers returned home, security guards washed and vacuumed their cars. George Gardner, one of the guards at the Bakkers' house, was in charge of buying groceries and cleaning the cages of Tammy's six to ten parrots and other tropical birds that she kept in a twenty-by-twenty-foot atrium next to the pantry. Tammy often complained that he did not do it right. Maids did the laundry and folded clothes. "None of the family lifted a finger around that house," remembers one of the security guards who worked there.[36]

In the morning Jim got up early and ate breakfast alone. He liked his food set out in a specific order: a selection of bran cereals, a small pitcher of milk, juice, and yogurt or fresh fruit. If it wasn't right, "it put him in a bad mood for the day." Tammy usually did not eat breakfast, except for perhaps a Tab soda. When Coca-Cola changed the formula for Tab in 1984, replacing saccharin with a NutraSweet mixture, Tammy had a meltdown. She demanded that David Taggart call Coca-Cola and have them make special batches of the old formula for her. Instead, the security guards "scurried around the area's stores" looking for old-formula Tab, and eventually "squirrel[ed] away forty cases." In the evenings Jim and Tammy often went out to eat. When the kids stayed home a maid fed them. When the kids came along, David Taggart called ahead to have the maids get them ready. At times one of the security guards or Vi Azvedo, who spent a lot of time at the Bakkers' home, put the kids to bed, even when the Jim and Tammy were home.[37]

It was not a family that spent a lot of time together after 1983. Tammy rarely went anywhere with her children unless Jim was along. Once Tammy Sue became a teenager, she and her mother had an increasingly tense relationship. They "fought a lot over how much freedom and independence Tammy Sue could have—whether she could be out on the PTL grounds late at night, or whether she could attend this or that party," according to Richardson. After the fall of PTL, Jim Bakker told his daughter that he missed "the good old days of family life." "Dad, get a grip," she replied. "We *never* were a family. We all were doing our own things. We came out of our rooms for meals and then went back to doing our own things." "My dad was a workaholic," remembers Jay, as he now prefers to be called, who was born in 1975. "I never saw my dad and mom before school. A security guard named George would usually wake me up, make me breakfast—my favorite was pancakes with Mickey Mouse ears and a syrup smile—drive me to school, and then pick me up. But I thought that was normal." Even the children's religious instruction was left to others. "I don't remember my parents talking to me about religion or even reading me stories from the Bible," recalls Jay.[38]

Wherever Jim Bakker went on the Heritage USA grounds he carried a tape recorder to make notes of anything he saw amiss. His office staff transcribed these notes, creating checklists of items that needed attention. If Bakker saw a burnt-out light bulb or a flowerbed that needed weeding, he made a note of it. "Have housekeeping go through all of the elevators and have the doors opened and vacuumed down into the crevices where the doors open please," he noted on July 12, 1985. The park was never far from Bakker's mind, and no detail was too small to escape his notice.[39]

Bakker also used these checklists to direct his staff to care for his personal needs and those of his family. "Please notify the housekeepers to not put any of my good suits on metal hangers. Please put them on good wooden hangers," he noted on June 12, 1985. "Tell Joyce [Cordell] I need some shampoo at home, please. I need someone to pick up some . . . Fanciful Rinse Number 12, Black Rage, and also some Steel Gray," he noted on June 25, 1985. "Make sure that they [the security guards at the Bakkers' house] are putting flea powder on our dogs, all the dogs, and taking care of the cats. . . . Also, tell [security guard] George [Gardner] if Jamie goes out stinking so bad anymore, he can just find another job. With all the people at that house, if they can't see to it that Jamie has fresh clothes on, I don't understand." In the summer of 1985, Bakker had a tree house built for Jamie. Constructed on posts that were eight feet tall on the uphill side and twenty feet on the downhill, it had two stories "complete with glass windows that opened and shut, a mini-refrigerator, window air conditioner, and ladder escape hatch," Jamie later remembered. One of the security guards estimated that it cost $20,000. "Find out why they took the air conditioning out of Jamie's tree house and get them to put it back in immediately," reads Bakker's memo for July 7, 1985. In Bakker's mind, PTL's staff existed as much to care for him and his family as it did to run the ministry.[40]

Jim and Tammy had grown up in the boom years of American consumer culture, and shopping remained one of the constants in their lives. They loved to shop, whether it was for houses, boats, cars, or clothes. In

January 1984, the Bakkers bought a home in Palm Desert, California, for $449,000 after Jim and the Taggart brothers looked at several houses in the area. At the next board meeting in March, Bakker received a $195,000 bonus, grossed up to $390,000, to cover the down payment. The house, which had a pool and a large patio, was on Greenbriar Lane in the new Summit subdivision, ten miles southeast of Palm Springs. Unlike the condo in Florida and the suite at the Grand Hotel, Tammy loved the Palm Desert home. In her mind it had nothing to do with PTL. When she walked in she threw "her arms wide, saying, 'I'm so glad we bought this house! This is the first house we've gotten to be our very own—the first that's really ours.' "[41]

North Central Bible College, where Jim and Tammy had attended but not earned degrees, decided to give Jim an honorary doctorate in May 1984. For the Bakkers it was a triumphal return. "Jim was happy as could be about that, laughing and cheerful as we made plans to go to Minneapolis for the ceremony. Tammy was tickled too," remembers Mike Richardson. The Bakkers stayed in a hotel suite in downtown Minneapolis, and their entourage, including Richardson, Vi Azvedo, Richard and Mildred Dortch, Shirley Fulbright, and David Taggart, had their own rooms. After the ceremony they went shopping for a couple of days. Tammy bought "eight or ten pairs of shoes, and a lot of jewelry—rings and necklaces," and Jim purchased "six suits, and about a thousand dollars worth of leisure clothing—summer jackets, summer shirts, white pants." David Taggart "didn't buy much in Minneapolis; I don't think the things were elegant enough for him," according to Richardson. This was only a warm-up.[42]

After a brief stop in Detroit, the entourage moved on to New York City for four or five days, minus Shirley Fulbright and the Dortches. They stayed at the Waldorf Astoria, where the Bakkers' suite cost $1,400 to $1,600 a night. It had a baby grand piano, a fireplace, and antique furniture. "The dining room had a long, Queen Anne style table, big windows, and a very high ceiling," remembers Richardson, who stayed in the "maid's room" attached to the suite. The next day the Bakkers started shopping and continued for the rest of the week. Jim bought five or six St. John suits at Saks Fifth Avenue for about $5,000 to $6,000. Tammy Faye, Vi Azvedo, and Tammy Sue bought clothes, Louis Vuitton handbags, and accessories. Jamie wanted leather pants and a Michael Jackson red coat and glove for one hand. They "went all over New York" and finally found a set for $200. David Taggart bought a pair of leather pants for $400 and leather shorts for $200. But the purchase that floored Richardson was a pair of linen pajamas with short bottoms that Taggart purchased for $700. When the Bakkers traveled and shopped, David Taggart usually paid the bills, which meant that PTL covered everything in one way or another. The shopping for clothes and jewelry did not end in New York. At the end of 1984, the Bakkers added $24,500 in furs, including a "natural full length Blackglama mink coat," and $27,500 in jewelry, including a $6,800 "ladies diamond watch," to their homeowners' insurance policy. This was at exactly the same time that Bakker was scrambling to fund the Heritage Grand Hotel and pleading with viewers to buy lifetime partnerships. Eventually the Bakkers' insurance policy covered $158,590 in jewelry. "David Taggart was constantly preparing envelopes of large sums of cash for Jim," Richard Dortch later recalled. "How can they spend this much money?" Dortch remembered Taggart wondering.[43]

The Tega Cay house had a dock on Lake Wylie, and the Bakkers owned a series of houseboats and other boats. In 1982 they bought a new Summerset houseboat, fifty-eight feet long and fourteen feet wide, with two bedrooms, a sleeper sofa, two heating and air conditioning units, a full kitchen, and a wet bar with an icemaker. As with the Bakker cars, PTL staff cleaned and maintained the houseboat, which was appraised at $93,250 in 1983. That year Don Hardister, Bakker's chief of security, arranged for some repairs to the houseboat. When the work was finished, the service company put the houseboat in the water at the Lake Wylie marina. Between the marina and the Bakkers' house stood the Buster Boyd Bridge, which the houseboat was too tall to fit under. Hardister could not call the repair company back to move the boat on a trailer because PTL had not yet paid them and probably would not anytime soon. Bakker demanded that Hardister call Duke Power and have them lower the water level of the lake, which has more than three hundred miles of shoreline. Hardister knew they would not do it, but he called anyway. Finally, Hardister had the railings and air conditioners removed and loaded the houseboat with "a ton of people" to serve as human ballast. The houseboat slid under the bridge with only inches to spare.[44]

On June 6, 1984, not long after returning to Charlotte from New York, the Bakker entourage, including Jim and Tammy and the kids, Vi Azvedo, Johnnie Mae the maid, David Taggart, and Mike Richardson, decamped for the Bakkers' new home in Palm Desert. They flew to California in a chartered Gulfstream jet at a cost of $101,786 round trip. A few days after they arrived, Jim decided that he wanted to buy a Rolls Royce, but not just any Rolls Royce. Bakker wanted a vintage Rolls. Since the dealer in Palm

Springs only had new ones, David Taggart located a dealer near Santa Ana, California, that dealt in antique Rolls Royces. Instead of driving the ninety-three miles from Palm Springs to Santa Ana, on June 11 Taggart rented a Learjet for $3,000. Learjets are the sports cars of business jets, known for their speed, high cruising altitudes, and skittish handling. The Lear's fuselage is narrow, with only one seat on either side of the center aisle, so Tammy refused to go. In Santa Ana Jim wanted to buy a Rolls that had belonged to Walt Disney, but it was already sold. Instead, Bakker bought a 1953 Silver Dawn Rolls Royce for $58,884. He also bought a second Rolls, a 1939 Phantom III, for $35,000, and paid another $27,438 to have it restored. Bakker wanted to put the 1939 Phantom on display at Heritage USA. The next day, back in Palm Desert, Jim bought Tammy a new Mercedes 380SEL for $48,525. Two months later, on August 14, Bakker bought a new Jeep for $14,671 after driving one that Eddie Azvedo, Vi's husband, had rented and deciding he liked it.[45]

Despite all of the new purchases, Jim had a hard time relaxing in Palm Desert. Every morning he and Tammy watched the *Jim Bakker* show and critiqued Richard Dortch's performance as guest host. Jim was particularly concerned that Dortch, who lacked Bakker's charisma, was not selling the lifetime partnerships hard enough, even though Dortch promoted the memberships with giddy enthusiasm.[46]

One afternoon Vi Azvedo sent Mike Richardson to the liquor store to buy vodka and orange juice. Richardson returned carrying the bottle of vodka by the neck in a brown paper bag and put it on the kitchen counter in front of Jim, Tammy, Vi Azvedo, and David Taggart. Everyone knew what it was. "A bottle of booze that's been carried that way doesn't look like anything but a bottle of booze," Richardson later wrote. Azvedo mixed a drink for Jim and herself, all the while making a "big game that she was pouring Jim a simple orange juice, that she was hiding the stuff from Jim." Jim played along, grinning and saying, "Ooh, this is good! What'd you put in it, Vi?" Richardson thought that the charade was for his benefit. Drinking among Assemblies of God preachers was strictly forbidden. When he did not object, Bakker drank in front of him on other occasions without pretending.[47]

By August 1984 the *Charlotte Observer* had gotten wind of the Bakkers' new home in Palm Desert and was planning to run a story. On September 26, the paper contacted Richard Dortch and requested an interview. Dortch stalled while he and Bakker figured out what to do. On October 2, at four o'clock in the afternoon, Bobbie Garn, one of PTL's talented young directors, rushed home to pack her bags and hurry to the Charlotte airport by 5:30 p.m. She had not been told where she was going, only that the trip was secret and urgent. At the airport Garn joined a cameraman and engineer aboard PTL's Sabreliner jet, the same airplane that Dortch used to negotiate the Jessica Hahn settlement in California.[48]

Garn and her companions were handed brown bags full of cash to pay for fuel at a stop in Amarillo, Texas. The money had been hastily pulled from cash registers at Heritage USA stores. To throw off anyone who might be trying to track their movements, the pilot filed a flight plan for Arkansas. In fact, they were headed for Palm Springs, where they met Jim and Tammy the next morning at the Palm Desert home. Jim, who had also been at Heritage USA the previous day, had taken a commercial flight to divert attention away from the Sabreliner and its passengers. Garn and her crew filmed the Bakkers at their "home in the desert" and then filmed Jim taking a drive in the 1953 Rolls into the desert to pray. Back at their hotel someone tried to steal the videotapes, which were stacked near the door of Garn's room, by pushing the door open as far as the chain would allow and then reaching through the opening. Garn slammed the door on the thief's fingers. She never found out who it was. That evening they boarded the Sabreliner and flew home to Charlotte.[49]

The next morning the *Charlotte Observer* reporters who had been working on the story and waiting to talk to Dortch were startled to see a segment on the *Jim Bakker* show featuring a relaxed and smiling Jim and Tammy welcoming viewers to their desert hideaway, "a place where we come occasionally," said Jim, though "not as often as we would like, and not as often as Tammy's doctors would like us to." Tammy offered to make fudge while Jim talked about the pressures of running PTL and the difficulty of staying at hotels, where there were always "so many hundreds of people around." "So we found this house in the desert, and it's just a marvelous hideaway. . . . It's not really a secret," Jim said. By breaking the story first, Bakker eliminated the newspaper's element of surprise, spinning the story to his advantage.[50]

The segment featuring Jim and the Rolls aired the next day on the *Jim Bakker* show, with Richard Dortch sitting in as guest host. It opened with Jim and Tammy standing next to the car, which Jim described as "my pride and joy," without ever revealing the make or model. Tammy refused to ride in this "old car," so Jim drove out to the desert without her, with the camera crew filming over his shoulder. Sitting on a rock, Jim told viewers that he first prayed in the desert after the death of his brother Bob. The experience changed his life, Bakker said. Who could begrudge him a car that he used for such a wholesome purpose? He seemed as relaxed and genuine as ever, a man at peace with the world.[51]

The *Charlotte Observer* ran its story on the Bakkers' Palm Desert home on October 5, but it did not generate the outcry that the newspaper had hoped for. The Bakkers' emphasis on the spiritual and healing value of their home in the desert mitigated the *Observer*'s report on how much it cost. Besides, abundance was a sign of God's approval, not a moral failing. Bakker preached that God blessed those who had faith in him, and as far as supporters could see everything that Bakker touched was an unmitigated success. The house and the Rolls Royce were not a problem; they were proof that Bakker was on the right track. It made supporters feel good to know that the Bakkers' lifestyle was possible for those who believed.

THE BAKKERS WERE not the only ones with secrets to keep. After returning to PTL in 1983, David and James Taggart led an increasingly flamboyant lifestyle. They spent lavishly on clothes, food, travel, and real estate. The brothers told their colleagues at PTL that their money came from their father, who owned as many as seven Cadillac dealerships in Detroit. They also said that their grandparents had owned a large parcel of land in Detroit that they sold to developers, leaving a sizeable inheritance. David told colleagues that he and James each had a trust fund worth $3 million. Everyone at PTL believed them.[52]

It was all a lie.

Henry James Stevenson Taggart, David and James's father, emigrated from Belfast, Ireland, in 1948. He married David and James's mother, Jane Margaret, in 1952. Henry worked as an auto mechanic for General Motors dealerships in Detroit that sold Pontiacs, Oldsmobiles, Chevrolets, and Cadillacs, eventually working his way up to body shop manager at the Cadillac dealer. He was injured on the job in 1981 and retired in 1982. For a time he and his wife worked as janitors in their church. Jane Taggart's father had indeed owned a "big, big parcel of land" in Detroit that would have eventually been "worth millions," according to Jane, but he lost it during the Depression. There was no trust fund, no large family inheritance. Still, the myth of the Taggart family fortune allowed the brothers to live large without raising suspicion.[53]

By 1984 David Taggart's control over PTL rivaled Bakker's and Dortch's. Bakker hated to be confined to his office. When he was not out of town he was at the television studio or somewhere else on the Heritage USA grounds. "If you wanted to get a message to Jim Bakker, you called David Taggart and you told David what you needed to know or what needed to be decided and he would communicate that to Jim," recalled John Yorke, one of PTL's lawyers. After his first few months at PTL, Richard Dortch also spent relatively little time in his office. In the competition for Bakker's favor, Dortch plied his boss with bonuses that he orchestrated at board meetings and lavish praise in front of the television camera, but he did not attempt to usurp Taggart's control over the executive staff. Al Cress, who, as Dortch's personal assistant had an office in the executive suite, "never" remembered Dortch questioning Taggart's authority.[54]

On the third floor of the World Outreach Center, Taggart spoke for Bakker, and no one questioned his decisions. "He had the same authority that Mr. Bakker and Mr. Dortch had," said Pat Harrison, who maintained the executive accounts on the third floor. "Everyone on the third floor answered to David," said Maxine Raudebaugh, who assisted Shirley Fulbright, Bakker's personal secretary. "When David gave me instructions ... it was Jim's instructions," said Don Hardister, PTL's head of security. "David was more important to me [than Bakker or Dortch] because he was there," concluded Peter Bailey, PTL's Vice President of Finance. "David, I felt, cared more about what was going on." Bailey talked with Bakker "once every couple of weeks" and Dortch "a couple of times a week," but with Taggart nearly every day.[55]

Everyone who worked for Taggart liked him. No one worked longer hours or with more energy than he did. Co-workers described him as "loyal," "efficient," "dedicated," "compassionate," and "honest." They also described both brothers as "generous," and no wonder. When David and James invited friends out to eat or to travel with them, they invariably paid for everything. They also liked to buy extravagant gifts for friends, particularly single women. What no one apparently realized was that it was all on PTL's dime.[56]

PTL had financial controls in place to monitor how the ministry's money was spent, but the rules did not apply to David Taggart. From 1984 to 1987, Taggart obtained cash advances of $740,769 using PTL credit cards and $622,042 through PTL checks. "It was not uncommon" for Taggart to take out $10,000 at a time, according to Peter Bailey. PTL employees who received a cash advance were required to submit receipts or return the remaining cash within ten days of returning from their travel. If they failed to do so, accounting would withhold their next paycheck, even if the amount in question was only ten dollars. Anyone who did not adequately account for a cash advance was prohibited from obtaining another. Except for David Taggart, who never turned in receipts or accounted for how he spent his cash advances and who had the authority to sign his own cash advance checks. The accounting department could not have gotten to Taggart's pay even if they had wanted to because it was hidden behind the wall of the Executive Payroll Account. Indeed, Taggart often took advances from the executive office account, which was also hidden from accounting. Pat Harrison, who worked on the third floor, was responsible for maintaining the executive account, but her supervisor was David Taggart.[57]

By November 30, 1985, Taggart had $215,578 in outstanding cash advances. With no way to account for this money, Peter Bailey simply wrote it off to travel expense on PTL's general ledger. This tidied up the books but did not explain where the money had gone. After that, Taggart told Bailey that he would keep all of his receipts on the third floor. Bailey "had to take his word" that the money was being spent for legitimate purposes.[58]

In addition to the cash advances, David Taggart charged another $298,530 to PTL credit cards that he never accounted for. In all, David and James Taggart, who maintained a joint banking account, obtained $1,661,341 from PTL from 1984 to 1987. Some of this money was used on behalf of the Bakkers, but the brothers also spent extravagantly on their own. Prosecutors in their 1989 trial for income tax evasion claimed that they diverted $1.1 million in PTL money for their personal use. They had no other significant source of income.[59]

Wherever the brothers went they seemed to have a female friend along. Penny Hollenbeck worked at PTL from 1981 to 1984, first as a set designer, then in makeup and wardrobe. Eventually she did Jim Bakker's makeup and wardrobe for his television show. For about four years she dated James Taggart, going out with the brothers two or three times a week. She traveled with them to Palm Beach, Florida, and New York City, usually flying first class. In New York they stayed at the Waldorf Astoria and The Pierre, facing Central Park, before the brothers bought a condo in Trump Tower (more about that later). One of their stays at The Pierre in 1985 cost $9,000. They shopped at expensive clothing and jewelry stores and ate at trendy restaurants. The brothers paid for it all.[60]

Lucinda McLellan worked at PTL briefly from December 1984 to June or July 1985. Her father, Vern McLellan, worked at PTL for about ten years, part of the time as Vice President of World Missions. Lucinda dated James Taggart for "several months" and remained friends with both brothers. From 1984 to 1987 she traveled with the Taggarts to New York City "at least

15" times to shop and enjoy the city's restaurants. The tab for one meal at the Petrossian restaurant on W 58th St ran $617. Over the 1985 Christmas holiday, the brothers took McLellan to London for a week, flying on the Concord and staying at the Savoy Hotel. At Escada, a woman's fashion store in London, the Taggarts bought McLellan clothes and accessories totaling $5,925. In February 1987, McLellan visited the Taggarts in Palm Springs, where the brothers were staying with the Bakkers. One evening the three chartered a jet to fly to Laguna Beach, California, for dinner, a distance of 102 miles. Dinner cost $282, not including the jet. Five or six hours after they left, they were back in Palm Springs. The brothers paid for everything.[61]

In December 1985 David and James took their parents to Paris, Belfast, and Monte Carlo for nine days, flying on the Concord from New York to Paris and back. "They stayed at superior deluxe hotels . . . amongst the best hotels that a person can stay at," their travel agent later recalled. The airline tickets alone cost $8,200. They also bought their father a Rolex watch and a Cadillac and their mother a fur coat and jewelry.[62]

In the fall of 1984 the Taggarts bought Darlene Peterson a mink coat for $2,595 from a Manhattan furrier and a ring for $1,000. Both were Christmas presents. Peterson had become friends with the brothers in the mid-1970s in Detroit and briefly worked at PTL from September 1984 to September 1985. She traveled with the Taggarts to Florida and New York City on several occasions, where they stayed at the Waldorf, the Plaza Hotel on 5th Avenue, and, eventually, the Trump Tower condo.[63]

In December 1984 Shirley Fulbright, Jim Bakker's secretary, accompanied the Taggarts to New York, where they bought her a mink coat for $3,795, one of approximately four trips she took with the brothers to the city. In New York they also bought her clothes and jewelry. On one occasion they chartered a Learjet for the flight from Charlotte to New York. In Charlotte, Fulbright ate out with the Taggarts once or twice a week from 1984 to 1987. She never paid for anything.[64]

David Taggart and Shirley Fulbright's close working relationship on the third floor of the World Outreach Center allowed them to take advantage of the secrecy of the executive accounts. Taggart authorized loans from PTL to Fulbright totaling $45,000, which were later converted to bonuses and "grossed up" so that PTL covered the income tax. He had Fulbright sign Jim Bakker's name to the memo authorizing the conversion of the loans to bonuses, so that Bakker knew nothing about it. Along with Peter Bailey and David Taggart, Fulbright signed a contract obligating PTL to pay

$250,000 to JHT Limited trading as Panache Designs, James Taggart's interior design business, again without discussing it with Bakker. In the fall of 1986, James Taggart redecorated Fulbright's condo in Charlotte, running the $5,599 cost through his interior design business and then charging PTL the same amount against an account used to maintain the Bakkers' Tega Cay home. In September 1986, at David Taggart's direction, Fulbright signed Bakker's name to an agreement obligating PTL to pay James Taggart's corporation $100,000 for design work at the Heritage Grand Hotel, again without asking Bakker. A month later, in October 1986, again at David Taggart's direction, Fulbright signed Jim Bakker's name to a memo placing James Taggart's business on PTL's executive payroll at $10,000 per month. Bakker did not know anything about that agreement either. James Taggart never turned in documentation to PTL's accounting department specifying how the money was spent.[65]

The brothers were as generous with themselves as they were with others. Everyone noticed how stylishly they dressed. They liked fur coats. During 1984 and 1985 they bought a number of furs for themselves from Miller and Berkowitz in Manhattan. David bought a longhair beaver jacket and a coyote reversible vest jacket for $2,590, and James purchased a coyote parka for $2,100 on October 31, 1984. That December James bought a custom-fit coyote coat for $3,750, and in February he purchased a coyote reversible vest jacket for $1,095. David bought a mink jacket and a silver-hair raccoon coat for $10,690 on November 16, 1985, and James bought a custom-fit mink coat and a longhair beaver coat for $8,395. Counting the mink coats they purchased for Darlene Peterson and Shirley Fulbright, the brothers spent $35,000 on furs from Miller and Berkowitz in just over a year. By November 1985, they owned $52,000 worth of furs.[66]

The brothers liked clothes and shoes. They shopped so often at Gianni Versace on Madison Avenue in New York City that the sales staff "considered them our best client at the time." They kept the store open late—"however long it took"—to accommodate the brothers "because we knew that they would probably spend a good deal of money." On one visit in August 1985, the brothers spent $13,815 at Versace. On another visit the following summer, July 18, 1986, they spent $21,175. From February 1985 to February 1987 they spent a total of $138,769 at Versace. At Barney's in New York City, the brothers looked "for the best of the Italian manufacturers that we carried," said a store manager. From May 1984 to August 1986 the brothers spent $46,124 on Giorgio Armani suits and accessories at Barney's. Another of the Taggarts' favorites was a Palm Beach, Florida, store that specialized in handmade Italian suits costing $1,200 to $2,000. They also sold trousers for $200 to $500, shoes for $200 to $600, and socks for $20 to $25 a pair. "The person purchasing in our shop doesn't ask the price," said the storeowner, who remembered the brothers as "very good customers."[67]

For shoes the brothers shopped at Susan Bennis Warren Edwards in New York City, a store that specialized in handmade Italian shoes. They stopped in "every four months, five months," according to the store's assistant sales manager. On February 16, 1985, they bought five pair of shoes for $4,085. That June they bought another four pair for $3,352. On January 7, 1986, they bought two pair of black baby crocodile shoes for $3,036. On August 30, 1986, David bought nine pairs of shoes, mostly alligator and lizard, for $12,555. From 1982 to 1986 the brothers spent $98,368 at this shoe store alone. Penny Hollenbeck remembers that the brothers owned fifty to one hundred pairs of shoes between them.[68]

From the exclusive men's haberdasher A. Sulka and Company on 5th Avenue in New York, the brothers purchased a $3,500 smoking jacket with 18-carat gold thread, a $1,500 smoking jacket, a $500 silk robe, a $175 nightshirt, and other items. At Beltrami, also on 5th Avenue, they bought two leather jackets for $4,800 each and a third leather jacket for $2,800, three pair of leather pants for $1,000 each, and other items of men's and women's clothing. Between March 1985 and December 1986, they spent $49,837 at Beltrami.[69]

The brothers' jewelry was stunning. Cartier, on 5th Avenue in New York City, was one of their favorites for jewelry and accessories. James bought a platinum and diamond pin for $85,000 on July 29, 1985. The pin consisted of a 3-carat emerald-cut sapphire, two 2-carat emerald cut diamonds, and more than one hundred other diamonds approximating 9.3 carats. It was about three inches long and "very, very attractive," according to Lucinda McLellan, who remembered James wearing it. On January 6, 1986, James purchased a 12.5-carat starburst diamond ring for $96,900 and an antique platinum sapphire bracelet, circa 1930, with a 1.75 carat sapphire and diamonds totaling 28 carats for $64,600. That July David bought a platinum and sapphire diamond bracelet with a 3.15 emerald-cut diamond, 156 baguette diamonds totaling 17 carats, and thirty emerald-cut sapphires totaling 25 carats for $75,000. Colleagues at PTL remembered the brothers wearing the bracelets. They also purchased from Cartier a five-by-seven silver picture frame for $425, eight demitasse cups for $880, clocks for $725, $395, $575, and $5,500, the last an onyx and deco style, an

18-carat diamond bezel Vondon watch with an 18-carat bracelet for $5,400, and a solid 18-carat gold lighter with forty rubies for $3,750. David also bought a Rolex 18-carat gold watch from Fred Joaillier on 5th Avenue in New York City for $10,025 on November 23, 1985. The brothers wore their diamond rings, including diamond pinkie rings, watches, bracelets, and other jewelry "all the time," according to Penny Hollenbeck.[70]

The brothers' biggest purchase was a condo in the Trump Tower, located in Midtown Manhattan at the corner of 5th Avenue and 56th Street. They first rented the condo, situated on the 57th floor, for $4,000 a month starting in May 1985. The apartment itself was relatively small, one bedroom, two bathrooms, a kitchen, and living room, but it had a marble fireplace and big windows with panoramic views. In March 1986 David bought the condo for $640,000, and James co-guaranteed the loan. For the down payment, David borrowed $72,000 from his brother's interior design company, JHT, and then arranged for PTL to write a check for $75,000 to JHT. To obtain a loan for the remaining amount of the purchase, David had his lawyer, Robert Gunst, draft an employment agreement between Taggart and PTL that referred to him as the President of PTL with an annual salary of $150,000. Taggart's actual salary was $90,736 a year, and of course he was not the President of PTL. The document was signed by Peter Bailey, PTL's Vice President of Finance and attested by Shirley Fulbright at David Taggart's direction.[71]

"It was always a desire of David's to live in New York," remembered Darlene Peterson, who had known the brothers since the mid-1970s. The brothers developed a circle of New York friends who knew nothing about their connection to PTL. When they shopped or dined in the city they rarely discussed the ministry. One of their New York friends, actor and musician James Allen Nichols, believed that the brothers lived in the city and had never "even heard of PTL," even after socializing with them for a year. Despite frequently going out with them, stopping by their Trump Tower condo, meeting them in Fort Worth, and traveling with them to Charlotte, Nichols only "knew that James was an interior decorator and that David had a very stressful executive position with a company in one of the Carolinas."[72]

The brothers spent liberally to decorate the Trump Tower condo and their townhouse in Charlotte. At Morano Jewelers on 5th Avenue in New York, they bought two Kuan Yin rose quartz statues and a French crystal ice bucket for $16,250 on December 9, 1985. A few days later they purchased a pair of ivory incense burners for $25,000 from the same shop. From Joneil, a jewelry and art store on 5th Avenue, they purchased a pair of rose quartz figurines, a jade incense burner, an ivory figure, a French crystal vase and Lalique crystal bookends, caviar dish, and flower for $37,000 on December 8, 1985. They charged $25,000 of this purchase to a PTL Visa card. Visitors to their New York condo remembered the ivory and quartz pieces. From Asprey, a London jeweler and retailer of luxury goods with a store in Manhattan, the brothers bought a replica of a George I tea set made of silver and ivory for $2,273, leather-bound collectors' editions of the poems of Robert Frost and Walt Whitman for $1,088, and a miniature set of Shakespeare's plays for $368.[73]

From the Mecklenburg Design Center, a Charlotte furniture store that did $300,000 worth of business with PTL in the mid-1980s, the brothers bought a sofa, loveseat, cocktail table, two brass curio cabinets, a glass desk, six dining room chairs, and other furnishings for $24,111. They paid approximately $15,350 of the bill with a PTL MasterCard and the rest with a PTL check. Then they created a receipt showing that the furniture went to the Heritage Grand Hotel even though it was actually delivered to their Trump Tower condo. They also purchased an armoire, canopy bed, and mattress and box springs for their Charlotte townhouse from the same store for $6,243. They paid with a PTL Visa card and then created documents showing that the items had been delivered to the Presidential Suite at the Heritage Grand.[74]

In October 1986, five months after David purchased the Trump Tower condo, Peter Bailey helped him obtain another loan for $75,000. Taggart needed the money quickly; he did not say why. Bailey called Rock Hill National Bank, where PTL had accounts, and arranged for the loan over the phone. Bailey secured the loan with a $75,000 certificate of deposit from PTL, which he and Shirley Fulbright signed. Neither Bailey nor Fulbright discussed the loan or CD with Bakker or Dortch. When Taggart missed a payment, the bank seized the CD in June 1987 and closed out the note. Though Bailey had earlier been an outspoken critic of PTL's financial irresponsibility, even he was not immune to the allure of the money sloshing around the third floor. From 1985 to 1987 he received a $30,000 loan from PTL, later converted to pay, bonuses of $30,000 and $50,000 (grossed up), and a car.[75]

Much of this information comes from the Taggart brothers' 1989 criminal trial for income tax evasion. Undoubtedly there was a lot more spending that the prosecutors did not have records to substantiate. The brothers drove Jaguars and Mercedes and ate out at good restaurants nearly every night. In September 1983 they filled out a financial statement that listed their net worth at $171,075. Two years later, in November 1985, they claimed a net worth of $431,000, including artwork, $95,000 in cars, $75,000 in jewelry, and two Baldwin pianos worth $80,000, one in the Trump Tower condo and one in their Charlotte townhouse. By July 1986, their net worth had climbed to $1,128,000, and by September 1987 it was $1,695,837. The money came from PTL in one way or another. James Taggart's business income from his interior decorating company derived almost entirely from PTL and the shops on Main Street USA in the Heritage Grand complex. David in particular increasingly led a double life, divided between his duties as Jim Bakker's loyal and tireless assistant and the life he coveted in the city that never sleeps.[76]

Bakker and Dortch should have known what was happening in the executive office. Beyond that there were only about a dozen people who had access to enough information to figure out what was going on. The secrecy of the executive accounts, put in place by Richard Dortch, assured that. By 1985 PTL had become a place divided between a corrupt leadership isolated on the third floor of the World Outreach Center and thousands of employees diligently working to build the kingdom of God. While they scrimped and sacrificed, PTL's leaders spent recklessly to gratify their own desires and ambitions. Bakker's abundant life message did not sanction what David and James Taggart did, but it made it possible. They could not have lived so extravagantly except in an organization that approved of wealth and its display. Things would get worse before the end.

Not everyone was willing to stick around and watch it happen. Al Cress had been Dortch's executive assistant in Illinois before Dortch accepted the position as Senior Executive Vice President at PTL. Cress did not want to come to PTL, but Dortch talked him into it. Cress arrived in Charlotte on December 31, 1983. From the start "I just hated the place," he later said. He immediately sensed that PTL's senior staff was divided between "the David and James Taggart camp," the "Jim and Tammy camp," and the "Richard Dortch camp." "I just felt lost," says Cress. PTL seemed like a "juggler" with too many "balls in the air." Dortch, in particular, was in "over his head," according to Cress. "He did not have an MBA. He didn't even have a high school" diploma, "he had a GED . . . never finished college. We're talking about a corporation. . . . You needed somebody in there with business management skills. He just did not have that."[77] The same, of course, was true of Bakker.

More than that, Cress was troubled by the lack of integrity at the top. As Dortch's assistant, Cress became aware of the situation with Jessica Hahn shortly after he arrived at PTL, and he was deeply troubled by its implications. In May or June of 1985, Cress was sitting in David Taggart's office with Taggart and Shirley Fulbright at the end of the workday. Cress knew that things were not going well at PTL and was worried about his job security. "We'll never get fired," Taggart said. "Why?" asked Cress. "We know too much," Taggart replied. "You mean like the Jessica Hahn deal?" Cress asked. Taggart and Fulbright both laughed. "Al, we know stuff a lot worse than that."[78]

"That moment is forever etched in my mind," says Cress. It all began to make sense to him, the Taggart brothers' lifestyle (regardless of where the money came from), the perks available to Fulbright and other third-floor staff. "PTL was basically a place where every day was Saturday and every night was Saturday night," says Cress. "If you live in that kind of atmosphere, Saturday night kind of stuff is going to happen." Cress resigned in July 1985.[79]

12

Saturday Night

BAKKER'S FOLLOWERS LOVED Heritage USA and for good reason. Heritage USA was often described as a theme park, but it was more than that. The closest analogy in American religious history is the Chautauqua Institution, founded in 1874 by Methodist minister John Heyl Vincent and Methodist inventor and businessman Lewis Miller. Located on 750 acres along Chautauqua Lake in western New York State and rooted in nineteenth-century camp meetings, Chautauqua became a self-contained community, combining summer educational and cultural enrichment programs with privately owned homes, a grand hotel (the Athenaeum Hotel built in 1881), shops, restaurants, and recreational activities. A century later, Heritage USA expanded this concept, combining worship, education, service, shopping, leisure, and lodging in an all-inclusive community. It was unlike any place else in America.[1]

It was also more than a southern phenomenon. PTL had partners in every state and around the world where its programs were broadcast. By January 1987 nine states accounted for more than half of PTL partners. California led with 9.5 percent of the total, followed by Texas with 6.2 percent. Pennsylvania, Ohio, Florida, Michigan, North Carolina, New York, and Illinois each contributed from 4 to 6 percent.[2]

Greeters smiled and waved at everyone who entered the park, and hosts manned the Welcome Center to answer questions and give directions. There were more than a dozen restaurants and places to eat, from full-service dining to ice cream parlors and hot dog stands. None served alcohol, and smoking was banned at the park. In July 1986 PTL announced that it would build the world's largest Wendy's at Heritage USA. Designed to resemble a sand castle with a ten-story turret, the restaurant would seat two hundred people and cost $1.2 million to build, a sort of prosperity gospel version of a medieval cathedral.[3]

There was something for every age group, morning to night. The Upper Room offered prayer, anointing, and communion services around the clock. A variety of Bible studies and seminars were offered at 9:00 a.m. or 9:30 a.m., weekdays. Visitors could join the studio audience and watch a live production of the *Jim and Tammy* show at 11:00 a.m. Monday through Friday. Tammy usually had her own television show in the afternoon, produced in front of a live audience, the latest version of which was called *Tammy's House Party*. The afternoon and early evening featured four or five more seminars, including the "Lookin' Good" seminar on health and personal appearance at 6:00 p.m., and the New Vine Fellowship for alcoholics and their families at 7:00 p.m. *Camp Meeting USA* was produced live with a studio audience at 7:30 p.m., Monday through Friday. Childcare was available 6:30 a.m. to 6:30 p.m., and the buses and trams ran from 7:00 a.m. to 1:00 a.m. The railroad, carousel, paddleboats, bicycle rentals, antique cars, miniature golf, and tennis courts were available midday until about sunset. Sunday mornings featured Heritage Village Church services in the Barn Auditorium, preceded by Sunday School "for all ages." In the evening there were concerts and meetings geared for teens and young adults and dinner theater for the older set.[4]

"There was no way anybody in their right mind could have been bored while they were there visiting because there was something available almost any hour of the day. Even if you wanted to go volunteer on the prayer lines in the night, you had that opportunity," remembers Ron Kopczik, who became associate editor of the *Heritage Herald* newspaper in 1981, just after finishing college, and editor the next year. He stayed on until 1988 and in the process chronicled much of the park's expansion. At first the paper was an eight-page weekly, then a longer bi-weekly, and eventually a full-sized monthly of thirty-five to forty pages. It was intended to keep visitors informed about what was happening at the park and was given away for free. Enough people wanted to keep up with the park's activities after they left that the paper developed a paid subscription mailing list of 10,000.[5]

In 1986 Jim Bakker used PTL's annual July 4 celebration to dedicate three new projects at Heritage USA: the Heritage Island Water Park, Fort Hope, and Kevin's House. Bakker had originally planned to open the five-acre waterpark two years earlier, but the project was plagued by cost overruns and PTL's inability to pay contractors. In the end it cost $13 million to complete. Despite the delays, once it opened the waterpark became one of the most popular attractions at Heritage USA. Its signature ride, the Typhoon, consisted of twin sixty-foot-high slides where swimmers reached speeds up to thirty miles per hour before plunging into a pool at the bottom. Guests could also tube down the Raging Canyon Rapids through eleven whirlpools, waterfalls, and slides or the more relaxing Lazy River, a winding twenty-minute ride at 3 mph. They could play in the Breakers, a three-hundred-foot-long, ninety-six-foot-wide wave pool up to ten feet deep or ride the Rushing River, two fiberglass slides that twisted down the mountain. A large sand beach with 1,400 pieces of beach furniture offered a break from the water, and two restaurants, the Sea Cave Café and Dock Side Restaurant, offered refreshments. The waterpark "brought the ocean to Charlotte," Bakker said. The combined pools contained 1.6 million gallons of water covering 52,000 square feet. During peak periods over one hundred lifeguards watched over the bobbing, splashing sea of humanity. Daily attendance peaked at 2,000 guests during the summer months, and total attendance for the 1986 season was 185,000. It was, as Bakker had promised, an impressive venue.[6]

Kevin Whittum first appeared on Bakker's television show in December 1981, when he was twelve years old. Whittum suffered from brittle-bone disease (osteogenesis imperfecta), and at seventeen, in 1986, he was twenty-nine inches tall and used an electric wheelchair. Bright and articulate, he was the adopted son of David and Ione Whittum, who had also adopted two other disabled children. On April 2, 1986, as the Whittums were preparing to leave Heritage USA at the end of one of their regular visits, Kevin broke into tears at the thought of leaving the park. Bakker spontaneously promised Whittum that he would build a house for him and other disabled children so that they would never have to leave again. Two months later, Bakker broke ground on a 13,260-square-foot home only 32 days before its scheduled dedication. The three-story Victorian-style house was designed with a wraparound porch seven feet four inches wide, few corners, and six-foot-wide halls so that two wheelchairs could pass.[7]

Kevin's House was a perfect example of Bakker's fundraising and management style. The project connected with PTL's base. Supporters could readily identify with Kevin Whittum's needs and those of other disabled children. But a month was not enough time to complete construction and the house was not hooked up to water or sewer at its dedication. To get the necessary permits in time, PTL had to certify the house as a home for only

Kevin and his family and not the group home it was advertised as. Roe Messner, the builder, tried to include features that would be needed later to get it approved as a group home, including sprinklers and space for an elevator shaft, but it never met all the requirements. The ministry claimed that the project would cost $700,000, but in the rush to get it completed by July 2 the final price tag rose to $1.3 million. Bakker continued to promote the project into the fall, eventually raising more than $3 million. The excess was siphoned off for other projects.[8]

Fort Hope, dedicated a day after Kevin's House, was intended to function as a rescue mission and vocational job-training center for homeless men with a history of substance abuse. The first four buildings—two bunkhouses sleeping eighteen men apiece, a senior counselor's home, and a dining and administrative hall—were under construction by May 1986. Plans called for adding two greenhouses and two training facilities, one for auto mechanics and body repair and the other for woodworking and cabinetmaking. The expectation was that men would stay in the program from eight to twelve months. "Fort Hope is a little different from other programs," said Manley League, Fort Hope's director. "Most programs just try to take the person off the street, while we're trying to take the street out of the person. We're going to help people renew themselves through Jesus Christ." Fort Hope took in its first residents that fall while construction continued on its facilities. It was originally projected to cost $580,000, but as the project expanded it wound up costing about $1.5 million.[9]

Fort Hope was relatively small, and it never accounted for more than half a percent of PTL's budget, but it nevertheless succeeded in helping a number of men who were down on their luck. Lee Stillwell grew up in an impoverished family and quit school after the fifth grade. His father was an alcoholic and Lee "drank since I was a little bitty fellow." He lived on the street for twenty years, except when he was in jail. After his last stint in prison, while he was in a halfway house, someone from PTL came and invited him to join the recovery program at Heritage USA. "When I got to PTL . . . they was waiting for me, open arms, just loving me right on in there," Stillwell later said. He learned to run a bulldozer, front-end loader, excavator, and other equipment. "There's not a doubt in my mind that if the Lord hadn't used Mr. Bakker, give him a vision for people like me on the street, where nobody don't want, don't care for anyway . . . I know for myself I'd have been dead." Eventually he was able to support himself laying rock, stone, and brick and doing cement work.[10]

Standing on the grounds of Heritage USA in the summer and fall of 1986, PTL partners could look with pride and gratefulness at just about everything they saw. If they were lucky enough to get a room in the Grand Hotel, the park offered a wide range of possibilities. And everywhere they went they met smiling, happy staffers and fellow visitors who shared their religious values. It was an oasis in a parched land.

If all of that was not enough, each winter PTL staged one of the biggest light shows anywhere. Christmas City 1986 was bigger and better than ever, with more than 1.5 million sparkling lights in a rainbow of colors. It included a nativity scene with live actors and animals near the park's entrance and a thirty-two-foot Christmas tree in the lobby of the Grand Hotel. Heritage Island, the mountain at the center of the waterpark, was transformed into the North Pole. The holiday display kicked off with an "electric light parade" of floats and marching bands on November 1. The grand marshals of the 1986 parade were Gavin MacLeod, captain of TV's *Love Boat*, and his wife Patti. A "floating light parade," was held every night from 7 to 9 p.m. on Lake Heritage. The lake floats included a giant whale fashioned out of lights, from the biblical story of Jonah and the Whale, and Noah's Ark. Helicopter rides offered a bird's-eye view of the lights for fifteen dollars a person. By Christmas more than a million visitors had come to marvel at Christmas City. More than 1.5 million were expected before the lights went out on January 31.[11]

PTL did not fail for lack of interest from Bakker's constituency. Just the opposite. Had most of the lifetime partners not followed through on using their four days and three nights, the way many people sign up for gym memberships but never go, Bakker's plan probably would have worked even as he oversold the rooms he had available. But come they did.

OUTSIDERS WERE LESS impressed. On January 26 and 27, 1986, the *Charlotte Observer* published a collection of a dozen articles written by reporter Charles E. Shepard on the FCC investigation of PTL, which ran from March 1979 to December 1982. "Bakker Misled PTL Viewers, FCC Records Show," declared the front-page headline. The FCC investigation had been sparked by January 1979 stories in the *Observer* alleging that PTL had diverted $350,000 donated for programming in Korea, Brazil, and Cyprus to construction at Heritage USA. After the FCC declined to hold full public hearings on the matter in 1982, the *Observer* spent the next three years seeking access to the 4,500 pages of FCC transcripts, which it finally obtained through the Freedom of Information Act, anxious to prove that it had been right all along. The January 1986 articles broke little new ground, but they demonstrated that the newspaper's reporting at the time of the investigation had been accurate and that Bakker and PTL had misrepresented the facts in significant ways. Though the FCC investigation was old news—some of the events in question had occurred more than eight years before when PTL was a much smaller operation—the *Observer*'s tenacious digging created a new level of hostility between Bakker and the local press.[12]

Three days after the initial story ran, on Friday, January 31, Bakker lashed out at the *Observer* on the air. "Tammy and I are undergoing the most vicious attacks in the history of this ministry," Bakker said. He painted a picture of relentless persecution by the enemies of God. The FCC investigation had ended on a contentious 4–3 vote, which allowed PTL to sell its television station in Canton, Ohio—the only station PTL owned and the basis of the FCC's jurisdiction—and avoid further scrutiny. The three commissioners in favor of full public hearings wrote an angry dissenting opinion, and the FCC's lead attorney in the case, Lawrence Bernstein, resigned from the agency, disgusted by its inaction. Many inside and outside the FCC saw the agency's decision as a reflection of the new political climate under President Ronald Reagan, who had publically praised Bakker and PTL. After voting not to proceed, the FCC referred "relevant information" to the Department of Justice, which four months later decided not to pursue the case. But the *Charlotte Observer* refused to let go. "We were tried in the press once. We were tried by the FCC. We were tried by the Justice Department and we were cleared. And now they said, 'We're not satisfied with what two agencies of government have done, we're going to try you again this time by public opinion,' " Bakker complained. "Somebody said, 'enough is enough.' And I think this ministry has had enough." "Enough is Enough" became PTL's new slogan, appearing on bumper stickers and in a new song that Tammy belted out on the air: "Watch out, Satan, I'm calling your bluff . . . enough is enough."[13]

Never one to miss a fundraising opportunity and knowing that viewers were more likely to give in response to a crisis, Bakker created a telethon around the controversy, the "Enough is Enough" telethon, which ran from April 14–25. "Having gained new strength from the Lord in the midst of recent vicious media attacks, Jim is eager to tell all God's people everywhere that they can take a positive, victorious stand, declaring to His enemies, 'Enough is enough!' " read an article in PTL's newspaper, the *Heritage Herald*. Two weeks in, Bakker declared the fundraiser "one of the greatest telethons we've ever had," with nearly 150,000 calls taken by PTL's bank of one hundred toll-free telephones manned twenty-four hours a day. An article in the *Heritage Herald* compared Bakker's "declaration of *Enough is Enough* to the enemies of God" to Ronald Reagan's "stand against global terrorism."[14]

The battle between PTL and the *Observer* continued for months and some of its stories were picked up by the national press. In response, PTL partners phoned the newspaper "by the thousands," wrote angry letters, and "a thousand" canceled subscriptions. The ministry hired a Charlotte private detective to investigate former PTL executive Robert Manzano, the source of some of the most damaging testimony during the FCC investigation. Bakker also commissioned a book about the controversy by author Doug Wead. The year before, Wead had co-authored *The Courage of a Conservative*, with Jim Watt, the US Secretary of the Interior from 1981 to 1983 and a member of PTL's board. Wead never finished the PTL book, but the ministry picked up support from other Christian writers.[15]

Jamie Buckingham, an influential voice among Pentecostals and charismatics and a former guest on Bakker's show, wrote supportive pieces for his *Buckingham Report* newsletter and *Charisma* magazine after traveling to PTL at his own expense in January 1986 to evaluate the *Observer*'s criticisms. "If I were the devil," a PTL vice president told Buckingham, "I would destroy this ministry by spreading lies about our integrity. Our partners believe in us. If that trust is destroyed, we'll go under."[16]

Buckingham saw no cause for alarm. "The problems I unearthed at PTL have to do with differences in style—not ethics," he wrote. "I wince over Bakker's emotive behavior on TV. I shudder at his fund-raising techniques. And I have a hard time trying to sort out the mixture of God, commercialism, high fashion, and entertainment at Heritage USA." Yet, "as my wife pointed out, 'What's wrong with having a first-class, decent family park where Christians can come at reasonable prices for clean, wholesome fun and entertainment?' She's right. Jim and Tammy are doing a good thing. . . . PTL has grown—and Jim Bakker has grown with it. He no longer makes snap decisions on the air. He has learned to submit to wise men." It was time to "unite our forces against the common enemy who wants to divide us into little chunks so he can easily devour us," Buckingham wrote. "If the bell tolls for Jim Bakker, it also tolls for me." Buckingham spoke for a large and important constituency, Pentecostals and charismatics who generally supported PTL and other ministries like it, but who knew next to nothing about the inner workings of the ministry. He allowed that PTL operated "on the thin ice of monthly contributions," but did not understand just how thin that ice had become. Buckingham, like many others, would soon have reason to rue his credulity.[17]

THE FCC AND the Department of Justice might have been leery of pursuing PTL, but not the IRS. In August 1982, as the FCC investigation was winding down, PTL and one of the law firms that represented the ministry, Caudle and Spears, hired CPA James Guinn to look over PTL's books and advise the ministry about potential violations of IRS rules. Guinn, whose office was in Irving, Texas, was an expert in the IRS rules pertaining to religious and tax-exempt organizations. After his initial visit, Guinn returned to PTL in September 1982 to do a more thorough review of "high risk areas" for tax-exempt organizations, including travel expenses, entertainment, and the use of credit cards and petty cash. "I found . . . significant problem areas," Guinn later recalled. Particularly worrisome were "bonuses that were not on tax returns" and "many personal items [that] were charged to the organization and paid by the organization." Guinn wrote a letter to PTL's lawyers and also discussed his concerns with Jim Bakker and David Taggart. Employees of tax-exempt organizations may be paid a fair wage for their work, but they may not receive excessive compensation or use the organization's money for personal benefit, what the IRS refers to as inurement. After only a brief investigation Guinn was concerned that PTL's senior staff had crossed the line. Bakker was also warned about the danger of inurement by Guy Forcucci, who worked for the accounting firm Deloitte, Haskins & Sells and prepared the Bakkers' personal tax returns for 1982 and 1983.[18]

Guinn's and Forcucci's warnings went unheeded until the IRS began an audit of PTL's tax-exempt status with regard to fiscal years 1981–1983. Guinn attended J. Don George's church in Irving, where Ernie Franzone was also a member. Both were on PTL's board. George convinced Richard Dortch to bring Guinn back to PTL in February 1985 to deal with the IRS audit on PTL's behalf. Bob Gunst, the lawyer with Caudle and Spears who was assigned to handle the audit for PTL, had assured David Taggart and Peter Bailey that "there was no problem and that there was not going to be any consequences of this audit." Guinn was not so sure.[19]

For legal advice Guinn called in attorney Michael Wigton, a fellow Texan with an office in Fort Worth. Wigton was an ex-IRS attorney who, like Guinn, specialized in religious and tax-exempt organizations. Wigton and Guinn concluded that although the IRS "hadn't beat anybody up" yet, there was serious trouble ahead. "My conclusion was ... that PTL would lose its tax-exempt status unless there was a vigorous battle started," Guinn said. Wigton "thought they were going to get a proposed letter of revocation" from the IRS, an initial step in removing the ministry's tax-exempt status. Guinn wrote a letter to Richard Dortch summing up their conclusions. After that, Dortch essentially fired Guinn, at least for the time being.[20]

PTL retained Wigton, but he got little cooperation from Gunst until the IRS sent the proposed letter of revocation that Guinn and Wigton had warned about. Wigton returned to PTL in September 1985 to begin working on a response. That January he insisted on rehiring Guinn as part of his team over Dortch's objections. For Wigton, the PTL audit "was a full-time endeavor." He rarely returned home, even on weekends. Guinn likewise worked for an entire year on the case. Even so, they could barely keep up. The IRS had been working on the case for two years and had essentially opened a branch office in Room 110 of the Heritage Inn. "It was a huge case," remembers Wigton. Compounding the challenge, PTL "was not a model of organization," as Wigton put it. The audit involved an enormous number of loosely organized documents. "It was not a snow storm of them, it was a blizzard. It was incredible. Never seen anything like it and all disorganized too. It was incredible. It was just a mammoth job," Wigton later recalled with evident exasperation.[21]

David Taggart's cash advances figured prominently in the IRS's case against PTL, along with the Bakkers' compensation. Taggart's documentation was fragmentary at best, particularly with regard to his use of a PTL American Express credit card. No one at PTL seemed to know where Taggart's American Express receipts were. "It was like pulling teeth out of an alligator sometimes to get documents out of anybody because everybody seemed to have other things to do," Wigton said. When Wigton and Guinn could not locate the receipts at PTL, they ordered copies from American Express. But before they could look them over "they just disappeared," according to Wigton. So they reordered the copies. Again, as soon as they arrived at PTL they disappeared. Wigton and Guinn also asked Taggart to provide a log of his business travel on behalf of PTL. He never did. Wigton told Dortch that he and Bakker should fire Taggart. Dortch, who knew that Bakker would never do that, only smiled.[22]

Instead, it was Wigton and Guinn who left, quitting in July of 1986 (Guinn ended up staying until February 1987). They had just started working on a new IRS audit of PTL for 1984 and 1985 when Dortch decided to "resist" handing over documents to the IRS, which led to a "disastrous relationship" between PTL and the agency, according to Guinn. By then Wigton and Guinn had succeeded in getting about $600,000 in IRS adjustments against PTL for 1981–1983 overturned. But the 1984 and 1985 audit promised to be much tougher to deal with. David Taggart's undocumented cash advances and issues of inurement surrounding the Bakkers for 1981–1983 were nothing compared to what happened after that. Wigton and Guinn had only begun to work on the 1984–1985 audit when they discovered that once again key records, particularly Taggart's credit card receipts, were missing. They had not yet figured out what Taggart was doing with the money, and neither, apparently, had the IRS, but Wigton was beginning to have his suspicions. Guinn continued to ask for the credit card statements after Wigton's departure. Peter Bailey and his secretary "both said they had been there but they were gone now and had no explanation for where they were," according to Guinn. He never did find the credit card documents.[23]

When reporters at the *Charlotte Observer* found out about the IRS audit, PTL refused to discuss any of the details, other than to say that the ministry's finances were sound. "As we have indicated on the air, PTL has instituted the finest and most demanding budgetary process in its history," said spokesman Neil Eskelin. "The income during the past year represented an all-time high. With our costs under control, we are very optimistic about the future." On December 16, 1986, Dortch reassured PTL's board "that the [IRS] investigation was going smoothly and that he had every hope that the investigation would be completed satisfactorily to the ministry and that everything was progressing on a positive note," according to board member J. Don George. Things probably would not have gone well for PTL had the IRS's audit for 1984–1985 run its course. As it turned out, the investigation was subsumed under the larger scandal that erupted in the spring of 1987.[24]

Bakker put his own spin on the IRS audit, telling supporters that he "had learned that the world glorifies the 'underachiever.'" "As you grow up and you begin to try out your wings, you find out society doesn't really want you to achieve. You'll find out that as you become big, the IRS is very interested in you. And they're going to do everything they can to stop you and they're going to take every loophole where a man can make money in America and close it up quick if they can," Bakker said on the air. "We find out the IRS is not in favor of success." In typical Bakker fashion he also portrayed the IRS audit as an attack of Satan. "The larger a ministry grows the more you become an enemy of Satan," he declared on the air. Satan's tool was "government agencies" that were "anti-Christ and anti-God," Bakker said. "You find out that your enemy is your own government, that if you make one mistake as a ministry they will close you down, if you don't dot every i and cross every t."[25]

JIM BAKKER DID not carry his own wallet. Bakker's Chief of Security and his main bodyguard, Don Hardister, usually carried Bakker's wallet, making sure that it always contained about $1,000 in $100-bills. On Thursdays, Hardister "would check to see how much he had and I would call David Taggart and tell him how much money was there and then David would replenish so that going into the weekend, Jim had his normal amount." John Aiton, who worked security at PTL and also occasionally carried Bakker's wallet, remembers David Taggart telling him to make sure there was plenty of money in it. If not, Aiton was to find Taggart so that he could replenish its supply. This reflected Bakker's larger approach to money. It was abstract, something that should always be at hand, but not something he wanted to be directly responsible for.[26]

Bakker also did not pay his own bills or write his own checks. "He normally did not handle his affairs. He left that to his staff," remembers Hardister. Pat Harrison, who kept the books for the executive accounts from December 1983 on, balanced Bakker's checkbook, and his secretary, Shirley Fulbright, "signed his checks for him, his monthly expenses." Fulbright practiced so that she could sign Bakker's name almost exactly as he did.[27]

Bakker was also reluctant to sign contracts on behalf of PTL. He "didn't want to be called as a witness in cases and didn't want to be made to give his deposition," remembers John Yorke, one of PTL's lawyers. A partner in Yorke's firm advised Bakker "on several occasions that he should let other officers in the corporation sign the contracts and he shouldn't sign them himself," Yorke said. The board of directors authorized Shirley Fulbright, Bakker's secretary, to sign contracts on behalf of PTL in her own name. "I assumed I could sign everything," Fulbright later said.[28]

Increasingly during the mid-1980s Bakker fired or marginalized everyone inclined to maintain effective financial controls over the ministry. Of the three men running the ministry by 1986—Jim Bakker, Richard Dortch, and David Taggart—none had the ability or desire to keep PTL's fiscal house in order. As Bakker started one new construction project after the next, the only solution was more aggressive fundraising.

Bakker spontaneously launched the Victory Warriors fundraiser in the spring of 1986 without consulting his senior staff. The entire campaign was done over the air since there was no time to produce mailings. The timing was particularly odd since the "Enough is Enough" telethon had ended only weeks before. On May 24, Bakker pleaded for five hundred people to give $1,000 each and become Victory Warriors. Two days later he announced that the new program had miraculously raised $7 million practically overnight, prompting him to extend the offer. God had "opened the windows of heaven," Bakker said. He told his audience that 60 percent of the pledges from the most recent telethon were "phony," which justified adding more lifetime partners to programs that he had previously announced were closed. For $1,000, Victory Warrior members were promised four days and three nights in the Towers Hotel plus admission to nonfood events, general transportation, and two workshops a year, essentially combining the Towers and Silver memberships for half the price. Bakker told viewers that this was the last opportunity to become a Towers member for all "eternity."[29]

The Victory Warriors campaign caught nearly everyone off guard. Richard Dortch had just returned from giving a commencement address at a college in New England over the Memorial Day weekend when the staffer who met him at the airport told him about the new promotion. Dortch rushed "directly to the studio and walked on the set and heard for the first time the term Victory Warrior." The Victory Warrior promotion ran for less than two months, pulling in $34,908,076 by July 9, 1986. Within days there was "nothing" left, according to Peter Bailey, PTL's Vice President of Finance. The money had all been spent on operating expenses and debt. Nothing was set aside to finish building the Towers, where the Victory Warriors had been promised lodging.[30]

Lifetime partnerships in the hotels were a "gold mine," Bakker had once told Dortch. There was "no limit to the amount of money that we could raise," Bakker said. "You get what you ask for," Bakker once told his chief of security, Don Hardister. "If you ask for $15 a month, you'll get $15 a month; if you ask for $1,000, you'll get $1,000." But this was only the case if they had something to sell. Desperate to keep the money flowing, after the Victory Warriors promotion Bakker launched a series of hastily conceived lodging projects in the second half of 1986 for which he could offer new memberships.[31]

"We have just started construction on the Bunkhouse Hotel, the newest and most unique lodging facility at Heritage U.S.A.," Bakker announced in a brochure sent to 510,874 supporters in mid-August 1986. "The new Bunkhouse Hotel will be comprised of dozens of western style bunkhouses . . . amid the unspoiled splendor of the Carolina countryside," read the brochure. For five hundred dollars contributors could join the Family Heritage Club, entitling them to three days and two nights lodging each year for the rest of their lives, plus free admission to a wide range of activities. The brochure promised that 50 percent of the bunkhouse beds would be reserved for Family Heritage Club members. Evoking an odd mixture of historical settings, a subsequent article in the *Heritage Herald* promised that "the ultimate frontier vacation in the Bunkhouse Hotel will allow families to relive the excitement, romance, and adventure of the Victorian era." Bakker planned to build more than thirty bunkhouses with sixteen units each that slept six people per unit.[32]

One of the virtues of the bunkhouses, from Bakker's perspective, was that they were cheap, costing only $400,000 each to build. "This means that approximately $2 of every $3 raised from the Bunkhouses may be used for ministry needs, while $1 of every $3 raised is needed for construction," Peter Bailey, PTL's Vice President of Finance, wrote to Bakker on September 9, 1986. But Bakker did not set aside even the $1. September's total contributions, including lifetime partnerships, totaled only $3,588,640. "Except for 1983, this is the lowest September since 1981 for total contributions," Bailey informed Bakker. By October 30 the balance in the Bunkhouse account was $75,000. Most of the rest had been spent on "operating expenses." A few days later, on November 3, the board voted a $500,000 bonus for Jim and a $100,000 bonus for Tammy. By November 17, the balance in the Bunkhouse account was zero. On December 16, Jim and Tammy received bonuses of $100,000 and $50,000, respectively. Only one of the bunkhouses was ever completed.[33]

On September 26, a month after announcing the bunkhouse program, Bakker broke ground on his biggest project yet, a new condominium and golf course development at Heritage USA. The first two seven-story buildings, known as Mulberry Towers, would have 111 units each, ranging in price from $59,000 for a one-bedroom unit to $145,000 for a three-bedroom "penthouse." The units would have "all the amenities that you would find in a luxury type condominium," said Roe Messener, whose company Messner Enterprises was supervising the construction on behalf of PTL. Plans called for an eventual total of 130 high-rise condominium buildings on a 6,800-yard "championship" golf course at a cost of $1.5 billion. Each building in the Villages of the World complex would be constructed around a different international theme. The clubhouse would feature a twelve-story, 500-room hotel with an Aztec design. By March 1987 the exterior walls of the first building reached four stories. "We are moving into the 21st century with a 21st century Christian retreat center," Bakker said.[34]

Bakker and Dortch hoped to bring in $15 million a year in sales from the Villages of the World condos, using the profits to help sustain PTL for years to come. But this was a long-term project, and PTL needed money now, as Peter Bailey reminded Bakker in a January 13, 1987, memo. It owed Messner Enterprises, PTL's principle contractor, $10,281,461 and still needed another $14 million to complete the Towers Hotel and recreation center. "We also, on average, are spending $1,500,000 a month more than we take in on contributions to operate the ministry," Bailey wrote. The only solution seemed to be offering more lifetime partnerships, even though the existing partnership programs were substantially oversold.[35]

In late 1986, Bakker created the 1,100 Club, a new membership program involving lodging in the Farmland section of Heritage USA, where the bunkhouse development was planned. For a contribution of $1,100, members would receive free lodging in a bunkhouse or in one of the new housing projects that Bakker planned to add to the development: the Country Inn, the 1,100 Club Mansion, and the 1,100 Club Campground. "Your vacation dream come true. Now, as an 1,100 Club member, you can enjoy an American tradition plus the comfort of charming lodging facilities nestled in the Carolina countryside every year for the rest of your life," read a brochure sent to prospective lifetime partners. "Take your pick of lodging at any of the brand new lodging facilities in Farmland USA as an 1,100 Club member," read a subsequent mass-mailing letter. "Choose the rustic bunkhouse, the charming Country Inn Farmhouse, the elegant 1,100 Club Mansion and stay four days and three nights each year for the rest of your life." Members could also choose seven days and six nights in the 1,100 Club Campground. The letter implied that all of these facilities were currently available, or soon would be, but apart from the one bunkhouse none were ever built. A subsequent article in the *Heritage Herald* laid out plans to add an Old Grist Mill restaurant, a Farm Village Country Chapel, and a Heritage Village shopping center, featuring "200 unique shops" and "1,000 permanent arts and crafts booths." None of these ever materialized either.[36]

The deception continued on the air. "You told the people that we were going to build the Heritage Grand, and we built it, and now the memberships are gone. You told the people we were going to build the Towers, and we built it, and now the memberships are closed," said Dortch, facing Bakker during a December 3, 1986 telethon. "You said if we can just build this bunkhouse and now it's built and all the memberships are gone. Everything you've said you were going to build you've built it," Dortch said. Bakker only smiled.[37]

With each new project Bakker dug the ministry further into debt. PTL raised $66,938,820 from lifetime partnerships in the Grand Hotel and Partner Center, of which it spent $35,365,201 to build the facility, or 52.8 percent of the total collected. The ministry took in $74,292,751 from Towers Hotel partners, spending $11,422,684 on construction of the never-completed hotel, or 15.4 percent. Through May 31, 1987, PTL received $17,382,228 from Bunkhouse and 1,100 Club members, of which it spent $864,911, or 5 percent, on construction, most of it on one completed bunkhouse and a second that was nearly finished. The rest of the money went to prop up other projects and for general operating expenses. By the end of 1986 PTL's finances were a house of cards. The slightest breeze would blow it down.[38]

As PTL's debt spiral deepened, its board of directors remained as docile as sheep. They did not understand the extent of the ministry's financial crisis or how much Jim and Tammy's compensation had increased in recent years, in part because Richard Dortch only added the amounts of bonuses and raises after the fact, recording them on separate sheets of paper from the rest of the minutes. Dortch was later asked how the board was supposed to know PTL's true financial condition from the information he and Bakker gave them. They "couldn't have known," he admitted. J. Don George, senior pastor of a large church in Irving, Texas, joined the board in November 1985. George was no stranger to PTL. He had appeared on the *Jim Bakker* and *Camp Meeting USA* television programs and had spoken at various seminars at Heritage USA. Bakker, in turn, had spoken at George's church in Texas. Yet George never knew how much Jim Bakker made. "It was my feeling that Mr. Bakker lived on a rather meager salary," he later said.[39]

At the July 3, 1986, board meeting, just after the conclusion of the Victory Warriors fundraiser, George remembered "a glowing report given to the Board concerning the financial condition of the corporation," including "a 15 million dollar surplus of funds in corporation accounts." It did not concern George that board members were not allowed to keep financial reports or board meeting minutes. "I trusted Richard Dortch. I believed that he was watching over things and had absolute confidence in his managerial ability," George said. He later claimed to have no recollection of giving Jim and Tammy bonuses totaling $750,000 on November 3, 1986, and December 16, 1986, though he did remember hearing an "upbeat, encouraging, positive" report on the ministry's status at the January 2, 1987, board meeting. George finally resigned from the board on February 18, 1987, after he became aware that most of the money raised in connection to the Farmland USA development "was, in fact, being spent to complete the Towers project." But while he was a member of the board he did little to intervene in PTL's financial chaos.[40]

If anyone should have understood the complexities and risks of hotel construction and management, it was Ernie Franzone, who joined PTL's board in August 1984. Franzone spent thirty years in hotel and restaurant management, eventually supervising the "southeast United States" for Brock Hotels. "I was always under the impression that everything was under control financially," Franzone later said. He did not know that there were not enough rooms to accommodate all of the lifetime partners nor how much Bakker and Dortch made. At board meetings, Franzone recalled being given "maybe five minutes, ten minutes, something like that" to review financial reports. "We never did take the time to ask for more financial information." After his first board meeting he "folded the minutes up, I was going to put them in my lapel pocket" until "I was told that the minutes were not to be taken out of the room." Yet Franzone went along with it all because of the "many good things happening at PTL." "When I walked the grounds and talked to the people that were at PTL, whether it was at the show or in the hotel or where it was, there was a lot of positive, good things" going on. Franzone bought two lifetime partnerships himself. "I trusted Mr. Bakker and Mr. Dortch."[41]

Evelyn Carter Spencer said more or less the same thing. Spencer first appeared on the *PTL Club* in the late 1970s and joined the board of directors in November 1985. She did not know Jim Bakker's salary or the exact amount of the bonuses given to Jim and Tammy at board meetings. Like Franzone, she later recalled being told that she could not keep meeting minutes. A.T. Lawing, who owned the Charlotte Oil Equipment Company and served on PTL's board for thirteen years, through March 1987, later said that he would not have approved bonuses for Jim and Tammy had he known PTL was in debt. But as he walked the grounds, Lawing had no doubt about how much good the ministry was doing. "Oh, I'll tell you, that was hog heaven. I went through that place, and I'll bet I hugged a thousand people a day. I enjoyed that. I was blessed by it, the testimonies of the people," Lawing said. No one thought to ask if it was all too good to be true.[42]

PTL tried to obtain long-term financing in the range of $50 million but could not find a bank willing to make a loan of that size. The best that budget director Mark Burgund could do was a $2 million loan from a bank in Maryland and a smaller loan from a bank in Rock Hill, South Carolina. PTL might have been able to issue a bond, but that would have required creating a prospectus disclosing executive salaries, which Bakker and Dortch were unwilling to do. In one of the more bizarre episodes in PTL's search for money, in the summer of 1986 Burgund and Sam Johnson, PTL's director of foreign missions, traveled to Switzerland to try to borrow money through a Swiss broker. When they discovered that they would need to set up a Swiss corporation and transfer PTL's assets into that corporation, they gave up and returned home.[43]

Despite public assurances about the soundness and transparency of its finances, in December 1986 PTL abruptly quit the Evangelical Council for Financial Accountability (ECFA), which it had been a member of since 1981. PTL had been on shaky ground with the ECFA for more than a year before cutting its ties to the organization. In October 1985 the ECFA voted to terminate PTL's membership but reversed that decision in February 1986 after ECFA representatives, including Art Borden, executive director of the ECFA, visited Heritage USA on January 27, 1986. The ECFA's reprieve came with a warning. Borden wrote to Bakker expressing the organization's "deep concern regarding PTL's apparent precarious financial condition."

> The Board believes it would be remiss to ignore signs of apparent persistent and substantial financial difficulties such as chronic under capitalization, over spending or cash-flow shortages. PTL's current liabilities are significantly in excess of liquid assets.... From a strict accounting standpoint, the organization is technically bankrupt. In other words, the organization's continued financial viability is largely dependent upon the forbearance of its lenders.[44]

As Borden's warning made clear, PTL's books were in no condition for the kind of outside scrutiny that the ECFA required. ECFA rules called for members to submit to an independent audit each year and have oversight from a board of directors made up mostly of outsiders. It also stipulated that fundraising "clearly identify the purposes and programs to which the donations will be applied" and "ensure that these donations are used for the purpose for which they are raised." In March, Richard Dortch claimed that PTL was "in compliance with" ECFA "criteria," but the ministry nevertheless refused to continue making its audits public, leading to its break with the ECFA that December. PTL would still release a "financial report," Dortch said, but not the complete audit, which the year before had brought the IRS audit to the attention of the press. Dortch insisted that the ministry was still accountable to the Assemblies of God denomination and the 1,200-member National Religious Broadcasters (NRB), but of course neither organization required detailed financial reporting from its members. From the outside looking in, PTL's break with the ECFA did not seem as ominous as it would later prove. All but two television ministries had recently dropped out of the ECFA, including those of Jerry Falwell and James Robison. Most of the ECFA's remaining three hundred members were big churches and Christian colleges, camps, and relief agencies.[45]

As PTL's financial condition deteriorated, Jim and Tammy spent more time away from Charlotte. In August 1986, two and a half years after acquiring their Palm Desert home, they bought a mountainside house on two acres above Gatlinburg, Tennessee, for $148,500. The purchase of the two-story, 2,300-square-foot home overlooking Gatlinburg in the exclusive Greystone Heights neighborhood was covered by $200,000 in bonuses (grossed up to $400,000) that the Bakkers received at the July 3, 1986, board meeting. "This summer the doctors told me, If Tammy Faye does not begin taking regular time off, her present heart condition will worsen and could prove fatal," Bakker said in a statement released by PTL. "I love the serenity of the mountains, and Tammy loves the shopping."[46]

The Bakkers immediately made plans to remodel the Gatlinburg home, enlisting Roe Messner to help them assess the new property's possibilities. In September they began construction of a stone wall that ran 390 feet around the property. The two-foot-thick wall was topped with a wrought iron fence that stood twelve feet. Locals called it the Great Wall of Gatlinburg. The wall, with the accompanying security system that included a gate staffed by guards twenty-four hours a day, cost $87,946. They also added a swimming pool, a deck with a spa, a new heating system, an additional room, and a log guesthouse. Altogether the renovations cost $341,000. At the November 3, 1986, board meeting, Richard Dortch recommended that PTL pay for the security fence, to ensure that Bakker would "obtain the rest that he needs to escape the pressure of his duties at the Church," and for the cost of maintaining guards at the home. The board readily agreed. At the same meeting, according to the minutes, the board also awarded Jim and Tammy bonuses "to pay for the addition on the home in Gatlinburg, Tennessee." The total amounts—$500,000 for Jim, $100,000 for Tammy, and $100,000 for Dortch—were recorded on a separate memo, which the board did not see.[47]

When the purchase of the Gatlinburg house became public in November 1986, Bakker claimed that he planned to sell "our California home, which we are seldom able to use because of the distance." Instead, the Bakkers bought a second California home in Palm Springs for $600,000 in February 1987. The house sat on about half an acre and was surrounded by a high wall, as the Bakkers preferred. The main house had five bedrooms and five baths, with an adjacent 700-square-foot guest cottage and 46-foot swimming pool. The Bakkers used some of their recent bonuses and also borrowed $150,000 from PTL for the down payment. James Taggart had found the home and David Taggart arranged the closing. That same month David received a $120,000 bonus, grossed up to $225,000.[48]

Palm Springs fit Jim's sense of himself as a celebrity and his growing isolation inside the bubble created by his entourage. Mirroring the rise of Hollywood in the 1920s and 1930s, Palm Springs became the "desert playground" for a generation of Hollywood celebrities, many of whom owned homes there, including Frank Sinatra, Dean Martin, Sammy Davis Jr., Bob Hope, Bing Crosby, Kirk Douglas, and Cary Grant. Johnny Carson, Bakker's role model, vacationed there, as did Marilyn Monroe. By 1987 Bakker had become, like so many of the stars with a home in Palm Springs, the "intimate stranger" that modern celebrity demanded, constantly in view but rarely accessible.[49]

When asked about the nearly $1 million in real estate that the Bakkers had acquired since 1983, PTL spokesman Neil Eskelin replied, "They've never pretended to live in poverty." From November 1985 through February 1986, PTL laid off 283 people, an annual savings of $3,613,780. Bakker's total compensation for 1985 and 1986, as calculated by the IRS, was $3,946,229.[50]

ON JANUARY 2, 1987, his forty-seventh birthday, Jim Bakker unveiled his most ambitious project yet. Balloons danced in a biting winter wind as he broke ground on the 1.25 million-square-foot Crystal Palace Ministry Center in front of a crowd of four hundred onlookers, the PTL board of directors, an eleven-piece band, and two dozen singers. Tammy was there to belt out a song, and dignitaries in attendance included John Spratt, US Representative for South Carolina's 5th congressional district. "Jim and PTL have exceeded everyone's expectations, except possibly their own," Spratt said. Plans called for the center to seat 30,000 people and have a counseling center, seminar rooms, offices, chapel, restaurant, and 5000-seat television studio. Construction was expected to take three years at a cost of $100 million. The complex would be located on a forty-acre site between Farmland USA and the Heritage Grand Ministry Center. The corners of the massive structure were marked with giant red banners so that the crowd could appreciate its size. "This is probably the greatest birthday present I've ever had," Bakker told the crowd.[51]

The new ministry center was intended to be a "replica of London's famed Crystal Palace," which Bakker admired for its grandeur and what he saw as its Disneyland Victorianism. Originally erected in Hyde Park, London, for the Great Exhibition of 1851, the Palace was dismantled and moved to Sydenham, a suburb of London, where an expanded and redesigned version was completed in 1854. It was constructed with a slender cast iron frame covered almost entirely in glass, using a new method for casting large sheets of plate glass. The vast expanses of the glass walls and ceilings amazed visitors. Destroyed by fire in 1936, the Palace's nave measured 1,608 feet by 312 feet and was crossed by three transepts with domed glass ceilings, the largest rising to 168 feet. Bakker promised that his palace would be just as grand, and the drawings he presented looked remarkably similar to the London palace. They showed a glass structure 916 feet by 420 feet, crossed by transepts with domed glass ceilings, the largest rising to 176 feet, much like the original. "I've fallen in love with this building. It's an obsession. I will either build this building or I will die trying," Bakker declared on that cold January day.[52]

Bakker assured the audience gathered for the groundbreaking that the day "we march into the Crystal Palace, I believe it will be totally paid for and it will be dedicated debt free." He could make this promise, he told his listeners, because "everything else that God has spoken to us and led us to build, has been built and paid for as it was finished." No one outside of PTL's senior management knew just how far from the truth that was.[53]

The groundbreaking was preceded by several days of celebration, adding to the sense that PTL was on the cusp of something great. On New Year's eve PTL threw a gala celebration that went on half the night, featuring dozens of singers and musical groups. The next day Bakker and a collection of the *Jim and Tammy* show regulars reminisced on the air about the ministry's recent struggles. They acknowledged that 1985 and 1986 had been difficult years but predicted that 1987 would bring a wave of blessings and prove that they had been right all along. If nothing else, they proved that they were no prophets.[54]

The next day, January 2, the board of directors and the television crew threw Jim a birthday party on the *Jim and Tammy* show, a few hours before the Crystal Palace groundbreaking. Tammy was exuberant and Dortch as anxious to please as ever. In front of the live studio audience, Dortch asked Bakker what his favorite animal was. "A giraffe," Bakker replied. Dortch then revealed that the ministry had bought Bakker two one-year-old giraffes, a male and a female, to keep as pets in the Heritage zoo. Dortch had intended to have the giraffes on stage, but they had been delayed on the freeway in a snowstorm. Bakker also received a spring-wound music box made in Germany in 1875 and an 1890 Symphonion music box.[55]

In retrospect, the Crystal Palace was the height of hubris. To commemorate the event, Bakker had the muddy shoes he had worn at the groundbreaking preserved in an $1,800 custom-made acrylic box. But at the time Bakker's confidence did not strike many observers as entirely misplaced. Other ministries had also taken on projects of similar scope. In 1981 Oral Roberts dedicated the City of Faith, a massive medical complex next to Oral Roberts University in Tulsa, Oklahoma, that included a 600-foot-tall clinic, a 300-foot-tall hospital, and a 200-foot-tall research center. Roberts raised more than $100 million to build the City of Faith, which also housed medical and dental schools. Plans called for an eventual total of 777 hospital beds. Despite the enormous financial burden of building and operating the City of Faith, which never broke even, in January 1985 Roberts announced plans to build a $14 million healing center adjacent to the complex. In time the City of Faith would prove to be Roberts's Achilles heel, but in January 1987 this was not yet evident. If Roberts could build a $100 million project, why not Bakker? "You wait and see," Bakker told the crowd assembled for the Crystal Palace groundbreaking. "The best is yet to come."[56]

Local community leaders were convinced. On January 12, 1987, ten days after the Crystal Palace groundbreaking, Bakker took the York County Council on a five-hour tour of Heritage USA to present his vision. Bakker outlined plans for a thirty-six-acre Bible theme park, which would include a ride through "heaven and hell," a monorail transportation system, a village called Old Jerusalem, which would offer visitors the "sights and sounds of Biblical times without having travelled halfway around the world," the

Crystal Palace development, which would include a thirty-one-story condominium tower, and a five-story Greek-style mausoleum. "I think it was real eye-opening," said council Chairman Murray White after the tour. "Every time I come out here, I'm never ceased to be amazed at what all is going on." A number of the proposed buildings would need a variance because they violated a new zoning ordinance limiting the height of buildings in a four-hundred-foot buffer around Heritage USA. White and planning commission Chairman Frank McCarthy did not think that would be a problem. Bakker convinced them that PTL needed to build up, rather than out; even with 2,300 acres it would soon run out of space. He projected that the Heritage complex would eventually have a resident population of 30,000.[57]

TAMMY DID NOT attend the January 12 tour because, as Bakker told his guests, "she's the sickest she's ever been in her life." The next day, January 13, Tammy was admitted to the Eisenhower Memorial Hospital in Rancho Mirage, California, near Palm Desert, where the Bakkers still owned a home. She was hospitalized "for pneumonia and for complications caused by medications," according to a PTL statement. Ministry spokesman Neil Eskelin speculated that the complications might have resulted from drugs Tammy was taking for bronchitis. By the time PTL announced Tammy's hospitalization, Jim had joined her in California. He would never return to Heritage USA as the president of PTL.[58]

Tammy's journey to Eisenhower Hospital was more harrowing than the PTL statements let on. After the Crystal Palace groundbreaking the Bakkers and their entourage had gone to the Gatlinburg house, where Tammy began to run a fever. When Jim returned to Charlotte to conduct the York County Council tour he left Vi Azvedo behind to look after Tammy, along with their eleven-year-old son, Jamie Charles. As Tammy's symptoms worsened, she mixed Ativan, a tranquilizer prescribed to help her cope with her fear of flying, with Aspergum and Valium and "promptly overdosed," as her son later recalled. He knew something was wrong when Tammy went out on the balcony to dry her freshly washed hair in the below freezing winter air. The next morning she started hallucinating. She saw pink elephants falling from the sky and panicked. "Black demons" lunged at her with "huge pitchforks." "There's something in the closet!" she screamed. Jamie, who was sitting by her bedside, jumped up and "rebuked" the devil and Tammy temporarily calmed down. But later Jamie realized that he could hear the television show Tammy was watching from across the house. The drugs had made her temporarily deaf.[59]

Azvedo called Jim who had her call Lester Nichols, a California physician and former owner of the Palmdale hospital whose wife, June, was part of PTL's counseling ministry team. Nichols, who took the call while driving on a freeway in Los Angeles, caught a flight to Knoxville without even stopping to pack a bag. He took one look at Tammy and immediately advised taking her to a hospital. Instead of choosing a local facility, they chartered a business jet to fly from Knoxville to California at a cost of $36,920. (PTL no longer owned the Sabreliner jet, having sold it the previous year to cut costs. Dortch, who used the jet to attend Cardinals baseball games in St. Louis and for vacation trips to Florida, had wanted to keep it.)[60]

As they were leaving, Azvedo gathered up all of Tammy's medications that she could find, enough to fill "half a grocery bag." The flight was a nightmare. Once airborne, Tammy "shrieked" when Jamie stretched out on the floor of the jet to relax. "Jamie, get up! You've got bugs crawling all over you." Next she saw an orchestra on the plane's wing and then a cat. She put on her coat and tried to open the jet's door to leave. At the hospital, doctors "loaded her system with Valium" in order to calm her down and wean her off the other drugs. "We gave her enough Valium to kill a truck driver," one of the doctors later told Jim. She was put on a respirator and her blood pressure went "through the roof." Had they waited "one more day, Tammy would probably have died in the mountains," doctors told Jim. As it was, brain damage was still a possibility.[61]

On January 23, PTL issued a press release to combat rumors that Tammy had died. It added little that was new, other than a statement by Neil Eskelin that Tammy had been treated for a rapid heartbeat for "the past few years," prompting doctors to "remove her from caffeine." A week later, sixteen-year-old Tammy Sue, who had stayed behind in Charlotte to host the *Jim and Tammy* show, announced that Tammy had left Eisenhower and was resting at the Bakker's California home. "She can't shop, she can't go out and do anything," said Tammy Sue.[62]

It had taken three weeks to detox Tammy at Eisenhower. After her release, she expected to go home to the house in Palm Desert, but instead Jim and the PTL entourage checked her into the Betty Ford Center next door. Tammy felt "horribly betrayed" and could not stand the confinement. "She screamed and cried throughout the night," according to Jim, and called him in the "early hours of the morning," begging to get out. The next day the Betty Ford staff reluctantly agreed to treat Tammy as an outpatient. To support Tammy, the whole family went through a twelve-step program with her, as did David Taggart and Vi Azvedo. It was at this point that the Bakkers bought the house in Palm Springs, with its high walls. "We'd soon need those walls, because we'd be surrounded by hundreds of press, who rented these big U-Haul trucks so they could stand on the roofs and shoot down into your home," Jamie later recalled. Much of the drama of the break-up of PTL would be played out in this house in the weeks to come.[63]

Living in California exacerbated Bakker's isolation from everyone outside his entourage. Donna Chavis worked at PTL from 1978 to 1979 as an assistant director and then returned to PTL in 1984. During her first stint at PTL, she saw Bakker "every day" and felt free to talk with him whenever she needed. "Everybody felt like family," as she remembered it. But by 1984 Bakker was "kept isolated in this bubble of people that moved with him," creating an "invisible wall" between Bakker and everyone outside his inner circle, says Chavis. "It was as different as night and day." Richard Dortch, who joined PTL's senior staff in late 1983, was responsible for much of the new isolation among PTL's senior management. After Dortch's arrival, he and Bakker were "surrounded by security guards," even when they went to church on the PTL grounds. "They never mingled with the people or prayed with the people," said Sam Johnson, who later pastored the Heritage Village Church. Al Cress, Dortch's executive assistant at PTL, remembers seeing a letter from Eric Watt to Dortch describing how cabinet members in Washington were treated. Eric's father, James Watt, was the Secretary of the Interior under Ronald Reagan and later served on PTL's board, and Eric was a member of the Heritage Village Church staff. After reading Watt's letter, Dortch had someone from security carry his briefcase from the executive suite on the third floor of the World Outreach Center to his car in the parking lot. "He had this perception of himself that he had arrived, he was actually a celebrity," recalls Cress. Dortch once compared himself and Bakker to the Pope in a meeting with PTL's lawyers and accountants.[64]

Working from his house in Palm Springs in March 1987 as Tammy continued her recovery, Jim desperately pushed for more fundraising. Once again he turned to lifetime partnerships, which by that time accounted for about 40 percent of PTL's revenue. Despite having announced that Towers partnerships were closed for "eternity" at the end of the Victory Warriors campaign, Bakker reopened memberships in the Towers with the Family Fun package. For $1,000 members would get four days and three nights lodging, plus admission to non-food events and one workshop per year. Promotional literature for the Family Fun membership was mailed to

524,003 prospective contributors. Bakker justified the new round of memberships by claiming that after previous fundraisers some of the partners had not followed through with payments for their memberships. "I am very disappointed in some of those partners who have pledged to be a part of the Towers [but] have not followed through on their commitment. I believe God will provide partners who will stand in the gap . . . [and] say, Jim, I will take one of those lifetime partnerships that was not followed through on." It was a typical Bakker ploy, blaming his mismanagement on the failure of others to live up to their commitments.[65]

For more than two months Jim and Tammy were absent from Charlotte and their daily television show. Then, on March 8, they used a videotaped message, televised before a broadcast of the Sunday Heritage Village Church service, to refute persistent rumors that Tammy was dead or that they had divorced. Instead, they disclosed that Tammy was being treated for "drug dependency." The thirty-five-minute video opened with the Bakker family—Jim, Tammy, and their two children—sitting on a white sofa in the elaborately decorated sitting room of their California home. Tammy was noticeably thinner than in her last television appearance in early January. After recounting the story of her illness in Gatlinburg and the emergency flight to Eisenhower they got to the crux of the matter. "We had to face some realities that Tammy Faye had been taking a lot of medications for a long, long time," Jim said. "We found out as we began to talk and research, that she really started probably 17 years ago." Tammy might be gone from the show for up to a year, they told viewers. She had already quit hosting what turned out to be her last television show at PTL, *Tammy's House Party*, in the fall of 1986. The good news was that she had been drug free for thirty days and the whole family had benefited from the Betty Ford program. It turned out that once Tammy was off drugs there was nothing wrong with her heart. As with the breakdown of their marriage seven years before, God had turned a crisis into a miracle. "We're the happiest we've ever been," Jim said. Most of the calls to PTL in the aftermath of the announcement were supportive, as was an editorial in the *Charlotte Observer*, PTL's longtime adversary, which concluded that "whatever the flaws of her organization or personal life, Tammy Bakker deserves . . . compassion."[66]

The compassion ended about a week and a half later, on March 19, 1987, when all hell broke loose.

13

Scandal

CHARLIE SHEPARD WAS determined to expose what was really going on at PTL. Shepard, thirty-two, joined the *Charlotte Observer* in 1977 after graduating from Harvard University with a history degree. By 1986 he was the newspaper's lead reporter covering the ministry. Shepard, who had written the spate of January 1986 stories about the FCC investigation that led to Bakker's "Enough is Enough" campaign, often bridled under what he saw as the newspaper's timid approach to PTL. Like many reporters who learned their craft in the shadow of Watergate, Shepard's instinct was to follow the money. He had little interest in, or sympathy for, the Pentecostal or charismatic message that inspired Bakker's followers.[1]

In April 1986 Shepard tracked down Al Cress, Dortch's former executive assistant who had left PTL the previous July, at the home of friends in Robinson, Illinois. But when Shepard rang the doorbell Cress refused to talk. Despite Cress's disaffection with PTL, "Charlie Shepard was like the devil calling.... I dodged him all day," recalls Cress. After a fruitless day of sitting in his car by the curb, Shepard returned to Charlotte. But his visit spooked Cress enough that he called David Taggart and told him that Shepard "was hunting me down, he had found me in Robinson, Illinois." Taggart arranged for Cress to fly to Charlotte at PTL's expense, where Dortch's wife and daughter met him at the airport. That night Cress stayed at a friend's condo on the Heritage USA grounds, and a few days later Richard Dortch picked him up and took him to a restaurant. As they talked, Cress's respect for Dortch dwindled further.[2]

Convinced that he needed to confront Dortch, Cress wrote a letter to his former boss with the help of Jim Cobble, who, like Cress, had been part of Dortch's staff back in Illinois before they all moved to PTL. "There are serious ethical, moral, biblical, and legal implications regarding the Jessica

Hahn scandal," which threatened to become a "religious 'Watergate,'" Cress wrote. "First Jessica Hahn was paid to sign a document recanting that the event took place. In essence, PTL paid her to lie. Second, when that didn't work, a very large sum (over $200,000) was laundered in a covert way to 'compensate her.' The true motive was to keep Jim Bakker's public image clean." Cress asked Dortch how he would have "handled a matter like this involving a pastor in the Illinois District?" back when Dortch was the district superintendent. "Do we use one set of cards to deal with those less prominent and without access to large amounts of money and influence, and then use another set of cards to deal with those who can pay their way to cover up sin?" Cress asked.[3]

Cress delivered his letter to Dortch's wife, Mildred, on May 14. Three days later, Dortch called Cress and invited him to have coffee at a Marriott next to the interstate. There, Dortch tried "to pull these crocodile tears on me, 'Oh, Al, I can't believe that somebody who worked with me as long as you did feels this way about me' and starts to cry," remembers Cress. Dortch gave Cress two hundred dollars and offered to take him to Florida the next day for a vacation aboard his boat. But Cress no longer trusted the man he had served for almost ten years and declined the invitation.[4]

Jim Cobble had also lost confidence in Dortch. Like Cress, Cobble had followed Dortch from Illinois to PTL in January 1984, though he had reservations about the move from the start. "The day I arrived, I [was] still thinking to myself that this was a 50–50 judgment call," that "it's very possible that I had made a major mistake." Cobble quickly came to see PTL as a dysfunctional organization, with leaders who "were in over their heads," and growth that "exceeded their organizational skills." The turmoil of PTL's finances and constantly changing plans induced a kind of "motion sickness" among employees. It was "like getting on a big boat that was rocking pretty violently at times," remembers Cobble. He found it "bizarre" that Dortch could not "see through a lot of that." Cobble was already planning to leave PTL when Cress told him about Bakker's encounter with Hahn and Dortch's role in covering it up. Even if it was not technically illegal, "it certainly was a violation of everything that I thought Richard Dortch believed in," says Cobble. He left PTL shortly thereafter.[5]

By July 1986 Shepard's editors at the *Charlotte Observer* had decided to pull back on their coverage of PTL. The paper had received a good deal of pushback from readers over its recent stories about the FCC investigation, which struck many as digging up old controversies to little purpose. Shepard's managing editor concluded that "we were writing the same story—mismanagement, shoddy business practices, pricey executive lifestyles," and that "it was time to move on." Shepard argued that "just because someone's committing the same crime doesn't mean you ignore it," but even he was "tired of PTL too." "I had arguably lost a measure of . . . perspective after nearly a year of intense PTL reporting," he later wrote. Still, he "winced at our daily stories about PTL. . . . Our reports seemed too trusting. I began to hear whispers that the newspaper had been co-opted." The détente would not last long.[6]

LIKE JIM BAKKER, Jimmy Swaggart operated one of the biggest ministries in the Assemblies of God. Swaggart's ministry, based in Baton Rouge, Louisiana, employed about 1,500 people and reported $142 million in revenues in 1986, while PTL had about 2,000 employees and $129 million in revenues. Swaggart's focus was more evangelistic than Bakker's and openly contemptuous of abundant life theology. While Bakker's therapeutic "you can make it" message appealed to charismatics and upwardly mobile Pentecostals, Swaggart's fire and brimstone approach connected with the church's old-line Pentecostal base.[7]

Bakker often claimed to have grown up in poverty, but Swaggart actually had. He was born and raised in Ferriday, Louisiana, along with cousins Jerry Lee Lewis, the pioneering rock 'n' roll pianist, and Mickey Gilley, the country singer whose Gilley's club in Pasadena, Texas, inspired the film *Urban Cowboy*. Even in Louisiana, Ferriday had "the reputation of being one of the darker and more Gothic pockets of humanity," notes author Lawrence Wright. Jimmy Lee touted his connection to Jerry Lee throughout his career, later writing, "we were actually as close as brothers. At times it seemed as if we were twins." If twins, they were also mirror images of each other. Jerry Lee was brash, restless, and hell-bent on doing whatever he was told not to. Jimmy Lee was sanctimonious, cautious by comparison, and determined to subdue the darkness that raged inside him. Neither finished high school. They learned to play the same honky-tonk-style piano from a local player named Old Sam, with his "walking left hand," and by sneaking into Haney's Big House, a black nightclub on the edge of town. They won local talent contests so often they were barred from entering any more, and they had the same dream of escaping Ferriday. Both grew up attending the local Assembles of God church, where Jimmy created a stir by appearing to predict the atomic bomb in a prophecy he uttered at age nine in 1944. When Jerry Lee left to make it big in music, Jimmy stayed behind to preach.[8]

Despite growing up in the church, as Elvis Presley and many other pioneers of rock 'n' roll had, there was a dark side to Swaggart's family history, characterized by poverty, drinking, failed business ventures, carousing, and tumultuous marriages that began at a young age. Jimmy's grandfather, W. H. Swaggart, married Ada Lewis when he was twenty-one and she was eighteen, already her second marriage. Jimmy's father, W. L. Swaggart, nicknamed Sun, married Minnie Bell Heron when he was eighteen and she was sixteen. They fought constantly until they were saved and filled with the Holy Spirit, and sometimes after that. Jerry Lee Lewis famously married his cousin Myra Gale Brown, his third marriage, when she was barely thirteen. She later revealed that she had been raped at age twelve by a man who lived next door. Jimmy married Frances Anderson in 1952 when she was fifteen and he was seventeen. He had to lie about their ages to get the license. When a relative suggested that Frances was only fourteen when they married, Jimmy asserted that she was fifteen "and not pregnant," revealing more than he intended about the expectations of his kin. They were so poor starting out that the best they could do was a twenty-eight-by-eight-foot trailer parked in Aunt Irene Gilley's front yard.[9]

In 1954 Jerry Lee recorded "Crazy Arms," his first hit song, at Sun Records, the same Memphis studio that had launched Elvis Presley's career. Jimmy was taking a break from his job draining swamps at a diner in Winnsboro, Louisiana, when he first heard the song on the jukebox. "My thoughts drifted back to the times Jerry Lee and I had played piano together, the times we had talked about making lots of money, the times we had planned to leave Ferriday for the big time. Now it looked as if Jerry Lee had finally realized his part of the dream," Swaggart later wrote. It was a "dark" moment for Jimmy, who feared he would "never do anything but preach in little backwoods churches."[10]

But Jimmy was a magnetic preacher, with a power and energy in the pulpit that Pentecostals often referred to as an anointing, and Frances was ambitious for him to succeed. In 1969 Jimmy launched his first radio show, *Camp Meeting Hour*. At the time his ministry had a budget of five hundred dollars a day, which seemed overwhelming. It turned out that even over the radio Jimmy could captivate an audience like few other preachers. By the early 1970s it became increasingly difficult to find churches big enough to hold his meetings, and he began to book city auditoriums and sports coliseums. Then in 1981 the ministry made a quantum leap. "All of a sudden somebody pulled open the blinds, the light hit us, and we just exploded across the nation," recalled Jimmy's son Donnie, who worked for the ministry. In 1982 Swaggart's ministry took in $60 million. By then he had sold twelve million record albums and his monthly magazine, *The Evangelist*, had a circulation of eight hundred thousand, rivaling many major newspapers. CBS anchorman Dan Rather called him "the most effective speaker in the country." By 1986 Swaggart's Baton Rouge headquarters had its own zip code and handled more mail—forty thousand letters a week—than any other organization in Louisiana. His television program was translated into at least sixteen languages, and Swaggart claimed that he was on the air in 145 countries. Unlike Bakker, Swaggart spent much of his time on the road, preaching crusades across the United States and increasingly in Latin America, India, Africa, and elsewhere.[11]

Despite the parallel trajectory of Swaggart's and Bakker's ministries in terms of growth, there were significant differences between the two. Swaggart's quarrel with Bakker went back to the 1970s when they were both still relatively small. In April 1978 a Swaggart supporter from West Virginia, Jim Dunbar, wrote asking that his name be removed from Swaggart's mailing list. He had seen Swaggart on the *PTL Club* and was upset about the range of guests who appeared on the show, including Hank Snow, Johnny Cash, Pat Boone, Bob Harrington ("the chaplain of Bourbon Street"), and Ruth Carter Stapleton, "who claims that her brother's beer is delicious." Swaggart wrote back, "I have been on the P.T.L. Show one time in my life and that was about three years ago. Apparently, you saw a re-run of that particular program." He assured Dunbar that he did "not agree with many of the practices there," and wanted nothing further to do with PTL. "They have repeatedly tried to get me to come back since then. I have refused to do so," Swaggart wrote.[12]

Swaggart was particularly critical of the therapeutic elements of Bakker's message. The March 1987 cover of Swaggart's monthly magazine, *The Evangelist*, featured a drawing of a frowning Jim Bakker in a hardhat, a not very subtle swipe at Heritage USA and all that it represented. Worked into the contours of the sketch were phrases—"Self-Esteem," "Freudianism," "Marxism," "Darwinism," "Inner Healing," "Communist Manifesto"—implying a link between Bakker's theology and modernity's most corrosive ideas. Inside, Swaggart blasted "the gospel of self-esteem" as "man-made and man-oriented" and "totally unscriptural." If the self-esteem gospel was right, "we should then *stop* telling people they're sinners who need Jesus Christ as a Saviour. We must no longer convince them of their sin. . . . We must never speak of hell, nor warn of the terrible, eternal consequences of rejecting the wonderful offer of salvation as an unmerited gift from God,"

Swaggart wrote. "Tragically," those who "listen to these philosophies . . . end up on a road that leads nowhere. God have mercy on the souls of preachers who lead such astray." Especially Jim Bakker.[13]

The gulf between Bakker and Swaggart widened over the case of Marvin Gorman, who, like Swaggart, was a rising star in the Assemblies of God. Born in 1933, Gorman began preaching at eighteen, shortly after graduating high school, and in 1955 he married Virginia Adams, when she was about twenty. In 1965 Gorman became the pastor of the First Assembly of God Church in New Orleans, which at the time had about one hundred members. Over the next decade the church grew to five thousand members with a budget of $8 million a year, and Gorman began to branch out into radio and television.

As Gorman's ministry grew, so did rumors of infidelity. About 1973, Gail McDaniel, who babysat Gorman's three children, came to him for counseling, worried about rumors in the church that she was a lesbian. According to McDaniel, Gorman advised her that the only way to settle the matter was for the two of them to have sex on the floor of his office. About five years later, in 1978, Lynda Savage, whose husband David was an Assemblies of God minister, came to Gorman for marriage counseling. One day she called Gorman from a New Orleans motel threatening to kill herself. Gorman rushed to her side and the two ended up having sex, though Gorman claimed that he was immediately overcome with guilt. He always maintained that it was a one-time encounter, but Savage later testified that the affair continued for three years.[14]

Two years later, in 1980, Lynette Goux went to a motel room where Gorman was staying for advice on how to deal with her troubled marriage. Later they would disagree on what happened that day. Goux claimed that Gorman made sexual advances toward her and she fled, while Gorman told his wife that Goux took off her blouse and he fondled her breasts, but no more. Goux's husband, Ronnie, was the Executive Vice President of the Jimmy Swaggart Evangelistic Association. He later claimed that he had secretly recorded his wife's phone conversations with Gorman and had seen letters from Gorman suggesting that he had a sexual interest in her. When Goux confided in Frances Swaggart, she sent her to Jimmy, who confronted Gorman, first in the Dallas airport and then in his office. Gorman admitted to meeting Goux in his motel room, but claimed that he was the one who left and that there was little truth to the rest of her story. At the time, Jimmy decided to let it be and did not press the matter.[15]

Through the mid-1980s Gorman's career blossomed. He became one of the Assemblies of God's thirteen Executive Presbyters and in 1985 was a frontrunner to become the next General Superintendent, the church's top post, before withdrawing his name. Gorman was a regular on Jim Bakker's television show, and by 1986 the Inspiration Network, as PTL's television network was now called, carried Gorman's show, *Marvin Gorman Live*, five days a week. Swaggart kept close track of ministers he considered competitors, and none was more prominent within the Assemblies of God or closer to home than Marvin Gorman.[16]

In the summer of 1986 Swaggart decided to take Gorman down. On July 15, 1986, David Savage confronted Gorman at his church about his affair with his wife, Lynda, nearly eight years before. Gorman admitted having had sex with Lynda and agreed to meet with Michael Indest, the pastor of another New Orleans area Assemblies of God church. Bill Treeby, Jimmy Swaggart's lawyer and a board member of Jimmy Swaggart Ministries, was a member of Indest's church. When Gorman and Savage met with Indest, he said that the matter was "too big for him to handle alone" and insisted that they go to see Jimmy Swaggart. Gorman did not know it, but this was all part of a plan that Swaggart, Treeby, and Indest had arranged several days in advance. That night an entourage from New Orleans that included Gorman, David Savage, Indest, and Treeby drove to Swaggart's mansion in Baton Rouge.[17]

Seated in Swaggart's immense study, Gorman was stunned as Indest, with Swaggart and the others looking on, accused him carrying on a series of affairs over a period of years. Swaggart brought up the Goux incident, implying that Gorman had lied to him back in 1980 about his philandering. The stakes were high because Gorman was supposed to close on a $20 million loan the next day to buy two Louisiana television stations and pay for a satellite uplink and construction of a new 3,000-seat auditorium at one end of a shopping center that his church owned. But Swaggart refused to back down, and the next day Gorman resigned from the New Orleans First Assembly of God. He was expelled from the Assemblies of God, and a local television documentary portrayed him as an embezzler and sexual predator. Gorman declared bankruptcy, and his career was in ruins.[18]

Among those dismayed by Gorman's fall was Jim Bakker. "One of the great ministers of this country in a church of six-thousand people, by evil devices, this man has just been destroyed. He has resigned his church. He is a man who is one of my dear friends," Bakker said in a sermon broadcast from the Heritage Village Church on July 20, just days after Gorman's resignation. "I want to tell you who destroyed him. You say, himself? No. The church. The church. The church," Bakker declared. By which, of course, he meant Jimmy Swaggart. "We drive our preachers until they break and then we kick them out," Bakker said. "Woe unto you that cast the first stone . . . because honey, you got something in your life." Bakker continued to defend Gorman, and the Inspiration Network carried Gorman's television show through October. PTL also loaned Gorman $75,000, putting up a Certificate of Deposit as collateral, which it later forfeited when he failed to repay the loan. "If he gets Gorman, he'll get me," Bakker told Don Hardister, his chief of security, referring to Swaggart. Hardister, who knew nothing about Jessica Hahn at that point, did not understand what Bakker "was making such a big deal about." Months later, David Taggart would break the news to Hardister, telling him simply that his boss had been "a bad boy."[19]

Swaggart remained undeterred by Bakker's protests. When a fellow minister wrote to him implying that he was going too far in his vigilantism, Swaggart used the pages of *The Evangelist* to defend the course he was pursuing against Gorman and Bakker. "Just last week a report came to me that you had remarked, in some setting, that you had taken care of one minister, now you were going after the other," the unnamed minister wrote. "If a man in a bank is caught stealing and someone outside the bank finds out, are you telling me that he should just go to the brother and tell him to quit stealing, and say nothing to the bank officers about it?" Swaggart replied. After outlining the Assemblies of God's policy for ministers caught "in an immoral situation," which included a two-year period of rehabilitation, Swaggart went after Bakker directly. "On some television programs, it has been strongly advocated that this is improper, unforgiving, and filled with hate instead of love. And, irrespective of what a leader does, he is to be smiled at, forgiven, and allowed to remain in his same position. In other words, business as usual. Of all the things to hit the church of the living God in the last few years, my brother, this is the most destructive," wrote Swaggart.[20]

It was at about this same time that Jim and Tammy bought the house in Gatlinburg and surrounded it with a high wall. They began to spend less time in Charlotte as Swaggart, the *Observer*, and the IRS, which had just extended its investigation of PTL's books into 1984 and 1985, closed in on them.

As it turned out, the evidence against Gorman was not as clear as Swaggart and his supporters claimed. It was difficult to see Lynda Savage as much of a victim. She later acknowledged having affairs with her brother-in-law and other staff members at churches where her husband was a pastor. Paul Dunn claimed that he and Lynda Savage carried on a torrid affair in late 1985 and early 1986, while Dunn was the music director at the Assemblies of God Church in Kenner, Louisiana, where David Savage was the pastor. Dunn later testified that he and Savage had sex in a motel, in her bedroom, at his house, in a church hallway up against the wall, and in his office while her husband was working down the hall.[21]

Two of the other women who accused Gorman of sexual impropriety had close ties to the Swaggart family, according to Gorman's lawyer. Gail McDaniel attended a church in Shreveport, Louisiana, pastored by Rodney Duron, whose wife, Frances, wrote articles for Swaggart's monthly magazine, *The Evangelist*, and was a close friend of Frances Swaggart. When she gave a deposition, and later in court, McDaniel was uncertain about times or dates and could not remember details about Gorman's office or their purported sexual encounter. After the deposition, Frances Duron gave McDaniel, who worked as a waitress in a restaurant owned by the church, a new 300ZX sports car. Lynette Goux and Frances Swaggart were also close friends. After Lynette and her husband, Ronnie, divorced, she moved into the Swaggarts' home. Later Ronnie could not produce the recordings he claimed to have made of Lynette's phone conversations with Gorman or the purported letters he wrote to her.[22]

Eventually Swaggart and his allies accused Gorman of having hundreds of affairs, misappropriating money from his church, and fathering an illegitimate child. A month after Gorman resigned from his church, Michael Indest, who worked closely with Swaggart to spread these allegations, brought the Reverend Tom Miller to a sectional meeting of Assemblies of God ministers in New Orleans. Miller told the ministers that while casting a demon out of a deaf-mute woman, Rosary Ortego, at his Canal Street Assemblies of God Church, the demon spoke through Ortego in the unmistakable voice of Marvin Gorman. Later, a woman who attended Miller's church told him that Ortego's real name was Troy Lynn McGee and that she had a music degree from Loyola University and had sung opera in New Orleans. Miller stuck to his story anyway.[23]

By 1987 Gorman had had enough and decided to sue "anybody who'd ever eaten crawfish," according to a Swaggart associate. Gorman sued Jimmy Swaggart, Jimmy Swaggart Ministries, Michael Indest and his church, the Lakeview Christian Center, the Louisiana District Council of the Assemblies of God, Cecil Janway, the district superintendent, Bill

Treeby, Swaggart's lawyer, and a number of others. Most settled out of court before Gorman won a $10 million settlement against Swaggart for defamation and intentional infliction of emotional distress. But this did not happen until 1991. In the closing months of 1986 it looked like Swaggart had succeeded in crushing Marvin Gorman. Bakker had ample reason to fear Jimmy Swaggart. There were eerie similarities between his case and Gorman's.[24]

Bakker was also upset by Swaggart's support for *The Seduction of Christianity*, a book critical of the prosperity gospel, Christian psychology and counseling in general, and a number of Bakker's regular guests on his television show in particular, including Robert Schuller, Norman Vincent Peale, Ruth Carter Stapleton, and Paul Yonggi Cho. Cho, who had a television program on the PTL network, was a particular target of the book. He and Bakker had long since patched up their differences over PTL's earlier failure to send television equipment it had promised to Cho's ministry, which had sparked the FCC's investigation of PTL. PTL gave Cho its "Merit Award" in March 1986, and he was a featured speaker at PTL's "International Church Growth Conference" during the first week of March 1987.[25]

Despite their long-standing differences, PTL carried Jimmy Swaggart's television show, *A Study in the Word*, at 9:00 a.m. weekdays and at ten other times during the week, for which Swaggart paid $50,000 a month. PTL needed the cash, but as Bakker fumed over Swaggart's role in the Gorman affair and his enthusiasm for *The Seduction of Christianity*, he decided to pull Swaggart's show from the 9:00 a.m. time slot in mid-September, replacing it with a PTL program. Soon after, Swaggart cancelled his remaining time slots on the PTL network, further widening the gulf between the two sides.[26]

As Bakker feared, Swaggart was indeed ferreting out information on Jessica Hahn. On July 30, Swaggart met with the Assemblies of God presbyters in Springfield, Missouri, where he warned them that he had heard "all kinds of rumors. Some of them I know are true, others I cannot substantiate." If the church did not act quickly, it would be "dragged through the mud," Swaggart warned. Then, after his return from Springfield, John Wesley Fletcher called with more of the evidence Swaggart was looking for, including details about Bakker's encounter with Hahn and rumors of the subsequent payoff. Fletcher later claimed that Swaggart promised him "a safe haven" if he would inform on Bakker. Fletcher also said that once, when he was a houseguest in Louisiana, a Swaggart friend inadvertently taped an incriminating phone conversation he had with Bakker while trying to capture evidence of his wife's infidelity, which sounds very much like Ronnie Goux's phone taps of his wife, Lynette, at about the same time. Fletcher felt as though he had no choice but to tell Swaggart what he knew. The more Swaggart learned, the more determined he became. "Jimmy took on Jim Bakker like a pit bulldog taking on a French poodle," a Swaggart aide later said.[27]

That September, Charles Cookman, the Assemblies of God district superintendent for North Carolina and a member of PTL's board, and his counterpart in Louisiana, Cecil Janway, district superintendent for Louisiana and a member of Swaggart's board, tried to arrange a meeting between Bakker and Swaggart to defuse the tension. Bakker, always reluctant to face conflict directly, refused, sending Richard Dortch to Baton Rouge with Cookman instead. The meeting took place on September 22 in the Baton Rouge Hilton. Flanked by Frances and Donnie, Swaggart was aggressive from the start as he questioned Dortch about Bakker's rumored indiscretions. "Dick, what about the girls?" he asked Dortch, as Cookman later remembered it. "I don't know what you're talking about," Dortch replied. "Well, what about the boys?" pressed Swaggart. Again, Dortch demurred. "Well, what about the lawsuit?" Swaggart asked. "If there's a lawsuit against PTL, I don't know it," Dortch replied, according to Cookman. Dortch acknowledged hearing about a lawsuit against a Jim Baker, with one *k*, but not against Jim Bakker. Of course, no lawsuit had actually been filed.[28]

Dortch remembered the conversation differently. When Swaggart asked him about "Jim Bakker with the boys," he claimed to know nothing about it. When Swaggart asked him about "the girls," Dortch also denied knowing what he was talking about because the question was too "broad-based." There had been only one "girl." When Swaggart asked him if Bakker "had paid off a woman for a sexual encounter for $250,000" he "looked at Jimmy and said, 'If Jim Bakker paid off a woman with $250,000, I don't know about it.'" In Dortch's mind he had given Swaggart "an honest answer," since the amount was $265,000, not $250,000. "Technically, I told him the truth," Dortch later wrote. Though he did not realize it at the time, Swaggart had just been Dortched. The two had known each other since the 1970s, and Swaggart was still inclined to respect Dortch's word as a minister and church leader. Only later would he realize how badly he had been deceived. "I actually believed that Richard Dortch was telling me the truth. Sad to say, he wasn't," Swaggart later wrote in a newsletter to his followers.[29]

Of course, what no one realized at the time was that even as Swaggart went after Bakker he was cruising the cheap motels along New Orleans' Airline Highway in his Lincoln Town Car, looking for twenty-dollar prostitutes.

DURING THE FIRST week of January 1987, while Tammy was being rushed to California for treatment for drug dependency, reporter Charlie Shepard was finally putting together all of the pieces connecting Dortch, Bakker, and PTL to the Hahn payments, relying initially on information from Al Cress. Cress confirmed that, while still at PTL working for Dortch, he had wired $25,000 from PTL to a bank account of Howard Weitzman's law firm, which brokered the Hahn settlement in 1985. Cress had also told what he knew to the Assemblies of God general superintendent, Raymond Carlson, and an Assemblies lawyer, Rich Hammar, who had flown to Denver in July 1986 to meet with Cress. But the Assemblies leadership was more cautious about confronting Bakker than Shepard.[30]

Two weeks after talking with Cress, Shepard flew to Los Angeles to meet with John Stewart, who had drafted the proposed lawsuit against PTL at Paul Roper's direction back in January 1985. Stewart confirmed much of what Shepard now knew about the Hahn cover-up. He showed Shepard a photocopy of the $115,000 check from Weitzman's firm, dated February 27, 1985, which represented PTL's upfront payment as part of the settlement. By this time Shepard had also obtained a copy of a July 2, 1985, letter from Scott Furstman, a partner in Weitzman's firm, to Richard Dortch. In it, Furstman asked Dortch to contact him "at your earliest convenience so we can discuss who to designate as the Trustor of the Jessica Hahn Trust." After meeting with Stewart, Shepard tracked down Jessica Hahn and John Wesley Fletcher during the first week of February 1987 at their respective homes on Long Island and in Oklahoma City, adding two more layers of confirmation to what he knew. Only a few missing links now stood between him and the story he wanted so desperately to write.[31]

In early February 1987, at the National Religious Broadcasters (NRB) convention in Washington, DC, John Stewart met John Ankerberg, who had a TV ministry headquartered in Chattanooga, Tennessee, and whose show had recently been dropped by PTL. As with Swaggart, Bakker had been annoyed by Ankerberg's enthusiasm for *The Seduction of Christianity*. PTL had the largest and most elaborate booth at the NRB, but Bakker decided to stay in California with Tammy and skip the convention, cancelling the address he was scheduled to deliver before its 4,200 attendees. Stewart remembers walking by the PTL booth, staffed by "nice smiling people," and thinking, "these people very soon are going to have the rug pulled out from under them." On February 3, Stewart had lunch with Ankerberg and Walter Martin, the original host of a nationally syndicated radio talk show, the *Bible Answer Man*, that Stewart now hosted. Stewart had told Martin about the Hahn affair, and at lunch Martin let slip that Bakker had been involved in a sex scandal. Ankerberg was shocked. That night, he asked Jimmy Swaggart, the meeting's keynote speaker, if the allegations were true. Swaggart confirmed that he had heard a similar story.[32]

Richard Dortch also attended the NRB convention, where he was initially flattered to be elected one of the organization's directors, and where he met George Bush, who had been invited to give an address, and his wife Barbara. Dortch sat on the platform with Jerry Falwell, Charles Stanley, and other celebrities of Christian television. But the satisfaction of the moment "lost all meaning," Dortch later wrote, when one of the Assemblies of God executive presbyters pulled Dortch aside in a hallway and asked if Bakker had an affair and then paid the woman off. "Did PTL pay her $250,000?" the man asked. "No one has been paid $250,000 to my knowledge," Dortch replied. "*That's an honest answer*," he later remembered thinking at the time, falling back once again on the rationalization that $250,000 was not the exact amount. But even Dortch could feel things slipping.[33]

Jimmy was the talent behind his ministry, but his wife Frances was its driving force. Unlike Tammy Bakker, Frances Swaggart knew every detail of what the ministry was doing. She supervised much of the day-to-day operations, and members of her family, not Jimmy's, held most of the key management positions. She had few friends. "I'm not the type of person who gets close to anyone," she admitted in 1991. Nicknamed the "Dragon Lady" by the ministry's staff, Frances was known to make employees take lie detector tests to find out who was talking to the press. By the mid-1980s she was running six miles a day and pushed the ministry's employees to get fit. In 1985 she instituted a weight policy, similar to the "Pounds Off" program at Oral Roberts University, requiring all employees to line up in the basement and have their weight recorded monthly or quarterly. Once, when asked how she dealt with obstacles, she replied, "knock the door down." "I've seen her do things so cruel and cold-hearted," said her brother, Bob Anderson, who worked for the ministry for fourteen years. Frances could be "as cold as ice water. I don't care about your Christian this or Christian that," her brother said. "The only time I had a problem working with Jimmy was when I had to go through Frances or Donnie . . . and Donnie doesn't know enough to come in out of the rain." No one tangled with the Dragon Lady if they could help it.[34]

After Jimmy's conversation with John Ankerberg at the NRB convention, Frances set her sights on Bakker, determined not to let him wriggle out of the Hahn scandal. She tasked Jerald Ogg Jr. with covertly contacting the *Charlotte Observer*, preferring to work behind the scenes this time, worried that an open attack on Bakker so quickly on the heels of the Gorman affair would make Jimmy look vindictive. The Swaggarts had known Ogg's parents, Jerald Sr. and Janett Ogg, since 1963. Jerald Sr. served as Jimmy's crusade director, and Janett was the first editor of the ministry's magazine. Jerald Jr., who had a law degree and bachelor's degree in journalism, often handled the press for the Swaggarts. Ogg was a reluctant mole, but he did as Frances told him. He had his secretary call the *Observer* anonymously on February 9 to get the name of the reporter investigating the Hahn story. Ogg called Shepard two hours later, using the pseudonym Joe. Over the next several weeks, Joe, who claimed to be a lawyer from Tennessee representing a concerned group of Assemblies of God ministers, relayed information from Frances to Shepard, sometimes copying down questions that Shepard had and then calling back with answers.[35]

As he continued taking calls from Ogg, Shepard also reached out to anyone else he could think of who might be able to help confirm the Hahn payments: Paul Roper, who had represented Hahn in her settlement with PTL, Charles Cookman, the Assemblies of God district superintendent for North Carolina, Roe Messner, who had laundered the PTL money used to pay Hahn, Sam Orender, who had accompanied Bakker to Florida back in December 1980 when the incident with Hahn had taken place, J. Don George, who had recently resigned from PTL's board in part because of the rumors, Raymond Carlson, the Assemblies general superintendent who had recently talked to Al Cress, and of course Richard Dortch. As he did so, the network of people connected to the story steadily expanded, and the room for doubt disappeared.[36]

On March 6, Oral Roberts appeared on the *Jim and Tammy* show as Dortch's guest. By then, Roberts was embroiled in a controversy of his own. Back on January 4, two days after Bakker broke ground on the Crystal Palace, Roberts stood in front of the City of Faith and told his television viewers that he needed $4.5 million in "quick money" to pay debts incurred in building and running the medical center or "God would take him home." "I'm asking you to extend my life. Let me live beyond March,"

Roberts begged. His plea, which portrayed God as an unforgiving loan shark, became the butt of endless jokes on late-night television and created an even more unfavorable frame of reference for televangelists, the last thing that Bakker would need when his own troubles became public. Fortunately for Roberts, Jerry Collins, an eccentric Florida dog-track owner, bailed him out with a $1.3 million donation a few weeks after he appeared on *Jim and Tammy*. But the damage had already been done. "I think he needs psychiatric treatment," Collins said of Roberts, after making his gift. The number of people who wondered how anyone could take these guys seriously steadily expanded.[37]

Two days after Roberts's appearance, on Sunday, March 8, PTL broadcast the video in which Jim and Tammy announced Tammy's drug dependency to their supporters. Toward the end of the video, Jim engaged in a bit of preemptive damage control. "Seven years ago Tammy and I went through a very severe marriage problem. Our marriage collapsed, our lives collapsed," Jim said. "During that time . . . we both made terrible mistakes. But we're so thankful that we serve a God who forgives and forgets." If only Swaggart, the *Observer*, and everyone else pursuing the Hahn story would do the same.[38]

BY MARCH 10, 1987, Ankerberg and Swaggart had contacted Jerry Falwell to work out a plan to confront Bakker, which Ankerberg hoped to do before the *Observer* published its story. The initial goal was to enlist a group of prominent ministers to guide Bakker through a process of public confession and restoration. But none of the other ministers they had in mind—Pat Robertson, Charles Stanley, a television preacher from Atlanta and a former president of the Southern Baptist Convention, or D. James Kennedy, pastor of the Coral Ridge Presbyterian Church in Florida—were willing or available. The next day, John Stewart, who had just returned from New Zealand, drafted a letter on behalf of the group to Bakker, designed to confront him without exposing Jessica Hahn. The draft referred to "the payment of sums in excess of $100,000 through a well-known California attorney" to "an unmarried woman from New York" to "cover up" certain "sexual improprieties by Jim Bakker." The letter closed by urging Bakker to "tell the truth about the offenses, and publically repent of your offenses against God and the body of Christ."[39]

Falwell and Swaggart had reservations about signing the letter. It was idealistic at best, and they doubted that Bakker would submit to public discipline from a group that included ministers he saw as hostile to PTL. Falwell said he wanted to show the letter to his lawyer. Swaggart wrote to Ankerberg outlining his misgivings: "John, I know how the minds of Bakker and Dortch work. They will take that letter and show it over television, deleting the part they do not want read. They will say, 'We had to take these two men off television, and then they went on a 'witch hunt' to hurt us.' " Swaggart reminded Ankerberg that Dortch had already lied to him and that the *Observer* and Assemblies of God leadership were about to take action on their own. Any attempt to convince Bakker to confess before the scandal became public was futile. "Please believe me there is absolutely no chance of Bakker and Dortch stepping down for any type of rehabilitation," Swaggart wrote.[40]

Meanwhile, Falwell broke off communication with the rest of the group, though it would be several crucial days before Ankerberg, Stewart, and Swaggart understood why. As Falwell and his staff debated what to do next, Warren Marcus suggested they reach out directly to Richard Dortch. A few months earlier, Dortch had tried to recruit Marcus, a former producer at CBN, for a position at PTL. Marcus declined and instead went to work for Falwell. Marcus reached Dortch in Florida, where he had gone with his assistant, Gene Shelton, to escape from the media, watch the St. Louis Cardinals baseball team in spring training, and spend some time on his boat. "I already know all about it," Dortch said when Marcus explained why he was calling. "Jimmy Swaggart is trying to take over our ministry. He's been after us for months. It's horrible." Dortch also acknowledged that he knew about the pending *Observer* story, but he was wary of Falwell's intentions until Marcus mentioned the letter from Swaggart to Ankerberg. That intrigued Dortch.[41]

At the same time Shepard was working feverishly to get his story published. In early February, Roper had stonewalled Shepard, denying that PTL had set up a trust fund for Jessica Hahn. By March 11, Roper was ready to confirm the settlement meeting with Howard Weitzman and the retired California judge as well as the $115,000 check on Hahn's behalf, though he still wanted to keep her name out of the story. Shepard now had what he thought was irrefutable on-the-record evidence that PTL had paid for a cover-up. But over the next several days his editors dragged their feet, reluctant to publish the story over worries about legal liability. Shepard groused to colleagues that it would take a signed confession for the newspaper to publish. After a heated argument with one of his editors, he threatened to resign.[42]

On March 12, Falwell's aides Jerry Nims and Mark DeMoss took Falwell's jet to Tampa, Florida, where they met Dortch in a conference room at the executive aircraft terminal. Nims and DeMoss were typical of the mix of smart, capable assistants that Falwell tended to surround himself with. Nims was referred to in newspaper stories from the late 1980s as both a "millionaire businessman" and a "hot-tub Baptist." He spoke in run-on, elliptical sentences that reflected his eclectic professional background. The son of a Baptist preacher, Nims grew up in Northern California where he became a beatnik and played piano in a blues band. He studied social sciences at San Francisco State University before his conversion at a Campus Crusade for Christ retreat in 1967. Later Nims made his way to Francis Schaeffer's L'Abri community in the Swiss Alps. Founded in 1955 in the village of Huemoz, L'Abri welcomed a generation of mostly young people who showed up to experience ample hospitality and vigorous intellectual debates about the connections between Christianity and culture. "By 1970, it was not unusual to have 130 people staying at L'Abri on any given weekend," writes Schaeffer's biographer. During the 1970s and early 1980s, Nims and a partner, Allen Kwok Wah Lo, invented and marketed the Nimslo 3-D camera. Television commercials hailed the Nimslo as "a miracle in photography" and "the most important new camera in your lifetime." The cameras were originally made at a Timex factory in Scotland, and by 1982 the company's stock traded for $4.81 a share. But the Nimslo did not live up to its promise and by 1987 the stock had plunged to 16 cents. Nims was later sued and settled out of court. While developing and marketing the camera, Nims met Falwell, who was recommended to him by Schaeffer. By 1987 Nims was chairman of the Executive Committee for Falwell's *Old Time Gospel Hour* show.[43]

Mark DeMoss, Falwell's personal assistant, was as close to Falwell as anyone outside his family. DeMoss's father, Arthur DeMoss, was an insurance executive and founder of National Liberty Corporation, which pioneered the direct marketing of insurance. Arthur DeMoss had been on the board of one of Falwell's ministries, but died suddenly in 1979, just before Mark's senior year of high school. Mark enrolled at Falwell's Liberty University in 1980, graduated in 1984, and immediately went to work in Falwell's office. A year later he became Falwell's chief aide. "I was running his office, handling his schedule, I traveled with him everywhere. . . . I was the guy he called before he went to bed to see what his schedule was the next morning. . . . He almost became a second father to me," remembers DeMoss.[44]

Falwell's tendency to retain bright, talented assistants even when their religious beliefs did not match up with his fundamentalism is reflected in his upbringing, which was divided between a hard-driving father and pious mother. Born on August 11, 1933, in Lynchburg, Virginia, Falwell was the first preacher in his family. His grandfather was an avowed atheist and his father, Carey Falwell, hated preachers and refused to darken the door of a church. A self-made man, Carey Falwell built an empire of gas stations, bus lines, restaurants, dance halls, and other businesses in Lynchburg during the 1920s and 1930s. He also sold bootleg alcohol during Prohibition. On December 28, 1931, Carey shot and killed his younger brother Garland in self-defense, as Garland tried to shoot him in a drunken rage. He never forgave himself, becoming an alcoholic in his grief. "Dad had a mean streak," Falwell later wrote. He always carried a gun and slept with a pistol next to his bed. "Nobody came close to Daddy when he was resting. They were afraid that if disturbed he might wake up shooting." He also kept a bear in a cage outside one of his restaurants. Once, when a young drunk started to cause trouble, the elder Falwell threw him into the bear cage and waited until the bear had "scared the life out of that poor unsuspecting drunk" before dragging "him from the cage screaming and pretty well mauled."[45]

Jerry Falwell's mother, Helen, was the saint of the family. It was through her influence that Falwell was converted in 1952 and attended Baptist Bible College in Springfield, Missouri. After graduating in May 1956, Falwell returned to Virginia where he started a rival Baptist church to the one he had been saved in. Like his father, Falwell was a relentless entrepreneur. In the summer of 1956, he and a small band of supporters bought an old building that had recently housed the Donald Duck Bottling Company on Thomas Road. That year Falwell started a daily thirty-minute radio program and weekly local television show. No other preacher in the area was on television at the time. By 1976 the Thomas Road Baptist Church had more than ten thousand members and a budget of $12 million. A decade later Falwell's ministry had a budget of nearly $100 million, membership at Thomas Road had swelled to twenty-two thousand, and Liberty University, founded in 1971, had 7,500 students on a 4,700-acre campus. Falwell's *Old Time Gospel Hour* appeared on the PTL television network at 6 p.m. on Sundays. In Matthew 10:16, Jesus instructed his followers to be "wise as serpents and innocent as doves." Falwell learned the first from his father and the second from his mother.[46]

During the four-hour meeting in Tampa on March 12 with Nims and DeMoss, Dortch said that he did not know why Swaggart was after Bakker and blamed many of the recent rumors on Al Cress. He broke down and sobbed, which startled Falwell's associates. "Sort of set us back a little bit because we are the non-weeping crowd," Nims later recalled. Despite his tears, Dortch won over Nims and DeMoss. "If you were outside and it was raining, those guys could almost convince you the sun was shining," Nims later said, referring to Dortch and Bakker. Together Dortch, Nims, and DeMoss speculated that James Guinn, the CPA who had worked for PTL on the IRS audits, might also be a source of leaks. PTL had just pulled Guinn, who had also worked for Swaggart, off the tax case the month before. Nims suggested that PTL needed a tough lawyer to intimidate the *Observer* and keep the paper from publishing the story until something could be worked out. Dortch "was all over that," remembers DeMoss. "That was the best news I'd heard so far," Dortch later wrote. The attorney Nims had in mind was Norman Roy Grutman.[47]

Grutman was famous for his flamboyant style and larger-than-life presence in court and in interviews. Born in the Bronx in 1930, Grutman graduated *magna cum laude* from Yale in 1953 and from Columbia Law School in 1955. He had "a melodious basso voice and a rotund Sydney Greenstreet bearing" that could dominate a courtroom, according to one legal scholar. His wit and combativeness are apparent in the opening lines of his book, *Lawyers and Thieves*: "My mother has sued everyone in our family but me. I used to take that as a compliment, in view of her high principles and low tolerance for losing, but something tells me she must be busy building a case." For eighteen years he represented Robert Guccione, publisher of *Penthouse* magazine, against charges of libel and obscenity. When Jerry Falwell sued *Penthouse* in 1981, Grutman grilled him for two hours on the stand. He won the case and Falwell's respect. "Counselor, if I ever get in serious trouble, be assured I will call you first," Falwell told him afterward. "It will be my great honor to represent you, Doctor," Grutman replied. Over dinner they established a friendship that would last for years.

A life-long New Yorker, Grutman converted from Judaism to Christian Science, hardly a background compatible with Falwell's southern fundamentalism. But Falwell respected talent and hard work wherever he found it, calling Grutman "the most intelligent man I've ever met, and a brilliant attorney." Falwell once wrote of his father, "He was tough. He was sarcastic. He could ridicule and scorn." He might well have been describing Roy Grutman. In 1983 Falwell sued *Hustler* magazine and its publisher, Larry Flynt, for $45 million for defamation after the magazine published a parody of a Campari Liqueur ad featuring Falwell. Grutman won a $200,000 verdict, though it was later overturned by the United States Supreme Court. Always impressed by celebrity, Bakker was delighted to have Grutman's services, though he would learn the hard way that Grutman was Falwell's lawyer, not his. If Bakker saw the irony in employing a lawyer who had spent nearly two decades representing *Penthouse*, he never said so.[48]

The morning after the meeting at the Tampa airport Grutman called the *Observer* and threatened legal action if the story about Bakker and Hahn was published. He also promised the *Observer* an interview with Bakker and Dortch, something Shepard and his editors had been after for weeks. Together, this was enough to convince them to hold off for a few more days.[49]

After meeting with Falwell's representatives in Tampa, Dortch called Bakker, who was still in Palm Springs. On Friday, March 13, Dortch let Falwell know that Bakker was willing to meet. That Monday, Dortch flew to Lynchburg, where Grutman had also arrived. At the airport in Lynchburg, Dortch and DeMoss happened to be in the restroom together. Dortch thanked him for Falwell's willingness to go to Palm Springs and then said, "I don't know which half of the kingdom Jerry wants, but whichever it is, he's got it." "It was a strange comment at that juncture," remembers DeMoss. "It caught me off guard." As far as he knew, "Jerry was going out to see if he can help Jim Bakker . . . whose world is . . . caving in around him and Dortch is talking about dividing up the kingdom. It was a very bizarre comment." Later, as things evolved, it would become evident what Dortch had in mind. PTL had two major components: the television network and Heritage USA.[50]

On the flight to Palm Springs, Dortch sat next to Falwell and across from Grutman and Nims (business jets often have seats facing each other). For two hours Falwell and his associates questioned Dortch about Hahn and the state of PTL. But Dortch avoided telling them about the out-of-court settlement. After they had eaten, Dortch asked Grutman to step to the front of the plane where they could talk in private. PTL had written Grutman a $50,000 check, and Dortch apparently assumed that he and Grutman enjoyed an attorney-client relationship. Dortch told Grutman everything about the Hahn trust and the money laundered through Roe Messner. Grutman later described Dortch as "Bakker's somewhat inept secretary of state."[51]

While Falwell and his team settled into a hotel, Dortch went to see Jim and Tammy. Dortch gave Jim a rosy picture of PTL's finances, telling him that giving was up 15 percent, but for once his boss did not seem to care. Jim had just told Tammy about Jessica Hahn the day before and they were both emotionally exhausted. "I will never forget the moment I found out about Jessica Hahn," Tammy later wrote. They were in a sitting room off the bedroom of their Palm Springs house, on a plush white couch, where two weeks before they had shot the video describing Tammy's drug dependency and rehabilitation. When Jim told her about Hahn, Tammy flew into a rage, screaming at him for his selfishness and stupidity and reminding him that she had never denied him anything, including sex. "I wanted to wring Jim Bakker's neck," she later wrote. As he typically did when faced with conflict, Jim "withdrew and became quiet, deathly still." Finally she told him to "get out of my sight." Jim "shuffled out of the room, leaving me weeping. I don't think there were two more wretched human beings on the face of the planet that day." If Bakker was emotionally vulnerable at the time of the incident with Hahn, as he always claimed, he was doubly so now.[52]

If that was not enough, earlier that week the Bakkers' daughter, Tammy Sue, had secretly flown back to Charlotte. For much of January and February she had remained in Charlotte, filling in as host of the *Jim and Tammy* show while her parents were in California. In February she became engaged to her twenty-four-year-old boyfriend, Doug Chapman, who worked at PTL as a lifeguard at the waterpark. At about the same time the PTL security staff caught Chapman with marijuana and suspected him of dealing drugs, including cocaine. As Tammy Sue was whisked to California, the local Sheriff's Department raided the trailer where Chapman lived and found a small quantity of marijuana. Now, at age seventeen, Tammy Sue had returned to Charlotte where she and Chapman would be married within a month.[53]

The next morning, Tuesday, March 17, Dortch met Jim and Tammy at Maxim's Hotel in Palm Springs, where they joined Falwell and his entourage in a suite. Jim, Tammy, and Jerry Falwell talked privately in the bedroom for about fifteen minutes before Tammy emerged and left the hotel. Bakker and Falwell continued to talk privately for about an hour. Bakker told Falwell about his encounter with Hahn, which he said lasted only fifteen minutes. Falwell later told reporters that Bakker said Hahn was the "aggressor," undressing Bakker and frightening him so badly that "he couldn't have sex." After the incident he wept in the shower and moaned, "Oh God, I've been with a whore." Falwell also claimed that Bakker assured him "no PTL funds were used to pay the 'hush money' to Miss Hahn."[54]

According to Bakker, they then discussed Jimmy Swaggart's plot to take over PTL. Bakker later claimed that Falwell pressed him to give up control of PTL. "For the next hour, Jerry Falwell outlined how I should resign from all three of my positions at PTL, as president, chairman of the board, and pastor of the church. After thirty to ninety days, when the furor over the Hahn disclosure would have dissipated, I could then return to my positions," Bakker later wrote. "You stay here in Palm Springs and take care of getting Tammy Faye completely well. . . . You'll still be in charge of the ministry. We'll work to protect you and save PTL from Jimmy Swaggart." Bakker remembered Falwell saying, "Jim, I'll never even go to PTL!"

Falwell remembered it differently. According to him, it was Bakker's idea to relinquish control of the ministry. A few days later, Falwell told reporters that after they had rejoined the group in the suite, "Jim turned to me for the first time and said, Jerry, I want you to take the chairmanship. . . . I believe God has led you to take this ministry." Bakker's surprise request, which Falwell said they had not discussed in private, left him "slightly stunned." "I stared in disbelief as Jim revealed his plan," he later wrote.[55]

At best, both men heard only what they wanted to hear. It is unlikely, as Bakker claimed, that Falwell would have agreed to such a short period of rehabilitation or put his own reputation on the line only to serve as a front for Bakker's continuing control of PTL. It seems equally unlikely that Falwell came to Palm Springs only to hear Bakker's confession in private and was shocked at the prospect of stepping in to oversee PTL. Grutman later wrote that it was Falwell who "announced that Bakker was resigning and had requested him to assume the leadership of PTL" when the two emerged from their private conversation in the bedroom. Falwell had done something similar the year before, taking control of a church in Bangor, Maine, whose pastor had been caught in an affair. It was DeMoss's impression that Falwell would only be at PTL for about six months. In any event, "there wasn't time to hatch a conspiracy," says DeMoss. The whole thing was concluded in a few minutes without anything written down. "This stuff was going at lightning speed. It was a blur. It was an utter blur." The contradictions between Bakker's and Falwell's accounts would form the core of what the press later called the "holy war" for control of PTL.[56]

After Bakker and Falwell were done, Jim and Roy Grutman went to see Tammy. "I never understood why Falwell didn't go to Jim and Tammy's house. To this day I don't know why Roy went alone," Mark DeMoss has since told me. Perhaps it was because Falwell knew that Tammy would take some convincing, that she would have to be "steam-rolled," as DeMoss put it, in a way that only Grutman could accomplish in a hurry. "Grutman was a tough, tough New York lawyer," says DeMoss. "I could see Grutman scaring the crap out of Tammy Bakker." Still, Tammy resisted. She "smelled a rat" and "adamantly insisted that I not resign," according to Jim. She sensed that resigning meant leaving for good. Standing in the yard of their Palm Springs home, Grutman pressed them to agree, saying that he only had a few minutes before he had to be at the airport to join the others for the flight back to Lynchburg. He brushed aside Tammy's concerns, and, as Bakker remembered it, promised to give Jim signed resignations for all the new board members, including Falwell, which Bakker could cash in at any time. "You can bring back your old board members or do as you please, it will be your prerogative," Bakker recalled Grutman saying. In the end, Jim heeded Grutman's advice rather than Tammy's. Grutman later denied pressuring Jim. "I didn't tell him to resign," Grutman told reporters. "He made that decision."[57]

Singer Doug Oldham, a regular on the *Jim and Tammy* show, and his wife Laura Lee were staying with the Bakkers at the time. Oldham had worked for Jerry Falwell and assured Bakker that he could be trusted. "Jim, Jerry Falwell will never hurt you," Bakker remembered Oldham saying. Later, as they discussed placing the ministry in Falwell's hands, Oldham recalled Bakker saying, "I might not have been able to keep her afloat beyond March, anyhow." Don Hardister, Bakker's chief of security, later said that his boss had "boxed himself into a corner" by allowing associates who knew about his sexual activities, including his homosexual trysts with other employees, to syphon off ministry funds. "Really, the jig was up," Hardister said. "I think he knew that he already had bitten off more than he could chew, and that he wouldn't be able to pull things out."[58]

As Falwell was meeting with Bakker on Tuesday, March 17, Ankerberg, Stewart, and Swaggart were wondering why Falwell had not returned their calls. They were still under the impression that they were working together as a team. That Wednesday, Stewart learned that Bakker had agreed to give the *Charlotte Observer* a statement the next day. Why Bakker would turn to his old nemesis, the *Observer*, was a mystery to Stewart. Despite the uncertainty, he made plans to meet with Roper and Swaggart in Palm Springs on Friday, March 20. Only after Bakker had resigned would Stewart understand what had happened: Falwell had done "an end run" around the rest of them.[59]

To put the Falwell takeover into motion, Richard Dortch called an emergency meeting of the PTL board for Wednesday, March 18, at 9:00 p.m., with Roy Grutman present. Dortch began by describing the story that the *Observer* was set to publish and its potential to do "irreparable harm" to the ministry. He and Grutman told the board members that they needed to resign, emphasizing that they might be exposed to lawsuits and financial jeopardy if they refused. In fact, board members of nonprofits have fiduciary responsibilities on par with their counterparts in for-profit corporations. They can be held personally liable if they fail in their duties. A few weeks later, board member Ernie Franzone wrote to the Assemblies of God complaining that Dortch and Grutman had exerted "maximum pressure" that "frightened" him into accepting their demand in the heat of the moment. Though Franzone had heard rumors about Bakker's infidelity, he did not know that they were true until that night. As the meeting unfolded, "it seemed like everything hit me at one time," Franzone wrote. Later, "upon securing some legal counsel," he realized he should not have acted "in such haste." But of course the board had never exerted itself beyond what Bakker and Dortch instructed them to do, and there was little chance that they would do so now. As he had done with Tammy Faye, Grutman steam-rolled the board while Falwell waited in the wings to take control.[60]

Grutman also told the board that he had "absolute proof" that the Assemblies of God planned to takeover PTL and give it to Jimmy Swaggart. In response, before resigning, the board rescinded a resolution passed on December 10, 1980, four days after Bakker's encounter with Hahn, which gave the Assemblies of God control of PTL in the event that Bakker could no longer serve as president. This removed the threat from Swaggart, but it also raised the question of why they needed Jerry Falwell. Jim and Tammy had been in Palm Springs for nearly three months, during which time Dortch and others had hosted the television show and largely run the ministry. Why not continue with that arrangement, sheltering in place until the storm blew over?[61]

The answer was money. PTL was on the verge of financial collapse. Once the scandal broke, it would take someone with a great deal of visibility and a strong television presence, a celebrity, to keep the contributions rolling in. Saving PTL would require expanding its base, since they were bound to lose supporters in the wake of the Hahn story. Dortch later wrote that prior to turning to Falwell he and Bakker "had talked extensively about turning PTL over to another prominent evangelist we both knew very well. His integrity and reputation were outstanding. This other ministry could provide an umbrella for us and for six months our friend could manage PTL. That's the amount of time we thought it would take for the Jessica Hahn storm to blow over." Three weeks before they were ready to contact this person, "complications developed" when the evangelist's name "surfaced in the press." This might well have been Oral Roberts, whose plea that God would kill him if he did not raise millions had become news in January. When Warren Marcus called Dortch on behalf of Jerry Falwell shortly thereafter, it must have seemed like a gift from heaven.[62]

Talking by speakerphone from Palm Springs, Bakker resigned as his board listened. After hanging up, he went to the couch in his living room and "curled up in a ball and hoped the world would go away." Falwell then joined the meeting in Charlotte via speakerphone from Lynchburg, announcing his new board. It consisted of Richard Dortch, Charles Stanley, Rex Humbard, the old-time televangelist from Akron, Ohio, and a frequent guest on Bakker's show, James Watt, former US Secretary of the Interior under Ronald Reagan, Ben Armstrong, executive director of the National Religious Broadcasters, Sam Moore, president of the Thomas Nelson Publishing Company, and Falwell's associate, Jerry Nims. A week later Stanley stepped aside and was replaced by Bailey Smith, another former president of the Southern Baptist Convention.[63]

Up to this point the Jessica Hahn incident and its implications for PTL had remained the province of a few local reporters and a handful of ministers who had known one another in various capacities for years. In twenty-four hours it would be anything but. The public had been growing increasingly wary of televangelists and their fundraising for several years. According to a Gallup survey at the time, 40 percent of American adults had "less confidence in the ethics or honesty of Christian fundraising than they once did." The PTL scandal would provide an event on which this skepticism could be focused. In the process, it would undermine the glitzy, hard-sell prosperity gospel of the 1970s and 1980s, while at the same time affirming the deep connection between religion and American culture.[64]

14

Holy War

BEFORE 1987, THE national media paid scant attention to Pentecostals and charismatics, often dismissing them as another variety of fundamentalism. Since the 1976 presidential race, evangelicals had become a familiar component of national politics, but they were frequently reduced to the Religious Right, a featureless monolith that only popped into view at election time. For many reporters, covering the Bakker scandal was like being dropped into a foreign country whose customs and cultural divisions were nearly impossible for outsiders to understand. Most New York and Washington, DC based journalists did not know that the Assemblies of God national headquarters was in Springfield, Missouri, or that the church had 2.1 million members and almost 11,000 congregations and 17,000 ministers in the United States. That was about to change, though not in the way the church would have chosen.[1]

At 2:00 p.m. on Thursday, March 19, Charlie Shepard and the *Charlotte Observer*'s senior staff gathered in editor Rich Oppel's office, waiting for Bakker to call in for the interview Grutman had promised. Shepard knew that it would be "momentous," but he had no idea what Bakker would say. At 2:30 Grutman called from the Presidential Lounge at the Heritage Grand Hotel, saying that he was accompanied by Richard Dortch and Neil Eskelin, PTL's vice president for public relations. David Taggart, Shirley Fulbright, and Roe Messner were also there, though Grutman did not say so. Grutman then introduced Bakker, who was speaking by phone from Palm Springs, and asked that he be allowed to read a statement without interruption.[2]

"As you know, for many years, Tammy Faye and I and our ministries have been subjected to constant harassment and pressures by various groups and forces whose objective has been to undermine and to destroy us," Bakker began. As a result, their "physical and emotional resources" had been "so overwhelmed that we are presently under full-time therapy at a treatment center in California." After listening to Bakker thank friends and supporters, "time froze" for Shepard, who suddenly realized what was about to happen. "I have decided that for the good of my family, the church, and of all our related ministries that I should resign and step down immediately from PTL. I have also today resigned from the Assemblies of God," Bakker said. "I am not able to muster the resources needed to combat a new wave of attack that I have learned is about to be launched against us by the *Charlotte Observer*, which has attacked us incessantly for the past twelve years. I am appalled by the baseness of this present campaign to defame and vilify me."

Of course, the newspaper's past reporting did not explain why Bakker was resigning now. For that, Bakker obliquely described his encounter with Jessica Hahn, and in the process blamed just about everyone but himself.

> I categorically deny that I've ever sexually assaulted or harassed anyone. I sorrowfully acknowledge that seven years ago, in an isolated incident, I was wickedly manipulated by treacherous former friends and then colleagues who victimized me with the aid of a female confederate. They conspired to betray me into a sexual encounter at a time of great stress in my marital life. Vulnerable as I was at the time, I was set up as part of a scheme to co-opt me and obtain some advantage for themselves over me in connection with their hope for position in the ministry.

Bakker said that Jesus and Tammy had forgiven him, but his adversaries were still determined to bring him down.

> Now, seven years later, this one time mistake is seized upon by my enemies to humiliate and degrade me to gratify their envious and selfish motives. They have falsified, distorted, and exaggerated the facts so as to make the occurrence appear many times worse than it ever was. Anyone who knows Jim Bakker knows that I never physically assaulted anyone in my life.
>
> In retrospect, it was poor judgment to have succumbed to blackmail. But when extortionist overtures were made, I was concerned to protect and spare the ministry and my family. Unfortunately, money was paid in order to avoid further suffering or hurt to anyone, to appease these persons who were determined to destroy this ministry.

Pointing to the future, Bakker subtly hinted at his return: "I cannot undo the past, but must now address the future. I have no doubt that God has a redemptive plan for PTL and for Jim and Tammy."

Finally, Bakker introduced "my friend, Jerry Falwell," whom he had asked "to help me in my crisis." The PTL board had accepted his resignation, appointed Falwell chairman, and asked him to designate a new board of directors. "He has done this and the old board has accordingly resigned," Bakker said.

Without taking questions Bakker hung up and Grutman took over, introducing Falwell, who said that he would release PTL's financial records and meet with the new board in a week. Shepard and Oppel tried to follow up with questions about where the money for the Hahn settlement had come from, but Grutman brushed them aside. Regardless, they had the biggest story the paper had seen in years.[3]

Bakker later claimed that Roy Grutman wrote the entire statement, "taking kernels of the truth and twisting them together with his own interpretations." Grutman faxed the statement to his home in Palm Springs only "shortly before I was to read it publicly," Bakker claimed. There are certainly passages that sound too erudite and lawyerly for Bakker. It seems unlikely that he came up with "I am appalled at the baseness of this present campaign to defame and vilify me" on his own. But the self-pity, the insistence on blaming others, and the convenient rationalizations all sounded exactly like Bakker. If Grutman wrote the confession, he did so only after thorough consultation with his new client. It was a masterpiece of deception and self-indulgence, a microcosm of Bakker's failings as a leader.[4]

The morning after Bakker resigned, people lined up as early as 4 a.m. to buy a copy of the *Observer*. Not since the death of Elvis had the newspaper sold as many copies. The presses had to be restarted three times that day to keep up with the demand, eventually churning out an extra twenty thousand copies. Lead stories appeared in *USA Today*, the *Washington Post*, the *Los Angeles Times*, and in papers across the nation. The *Charlotte Observer* covered the story relentlessly for the next year and won a 1988 Pulitzer Prize for its reporting on PTL. But it was on television that the scandal and its aftermath played out most dramatically, drawing in record audiences for *Nightline*, *Larry King Live*, and other news shows. Television made the Bakkers celebrities, and it now presided over their fall. As Roy Grutman put it, "In the electronic age, those whom the gods would destroy, they first make TV stars."[5]

John Stewart, who had drafted the lawsuit that brought Dortch to the bargaining table, remembers where he was when he heard that Jim Bakker had resigned. He was just about to go on the air to do his nationally syndicated radio show, the *Bible Answer Man*, when Charlie Shepard called with the news. A few minutes later Paul Crouch, founder of Trinity Broadcasting Network and Bakker's former partner, called Stewart to confirm the news. "I said, 'Yeah, Jim Bakker has acknowledged he was involved in sexual immorality and he's turned over his ministry to Jerry Falwell,'" Stewart remembers saying. "His next question to me was, 'Was it heterosexual?'" Stewart did not pursue the matter further, but he would later wonder why Crouch had asked. Crouch had been a youth pastor in Bakker's church in Muskegon when he was a teenager, and the two had been business partners in the early 1970s.[6]

Roger Flessing was in Paris, France when he heard the news. Without knowing the details of why Bakker resigned, his first thought was "they got the wrong guy." The guy "that should have gone down was Dortch."[7]

Bakker's supporters were immediately confused as to why he had turned to Falwell, a fundamentalist Baptist. Pentecostals and fundamentalists both fall under the broad umbrella of evangelicalism. They agree that salvation comes only through Jesus Christ, that the Bible is the word of God, and that Christ will come again. But as with many close competitors, it is their differences that often matter most (think Protestants and Catholics in nineteenth-century America or Sunni and Shia Muslims). Fundamentalists argue (always they argue) that miracles such as divine healing and gifts of the Holy Spirit, including speaking in tongues, ended with the passing of Christ's original apostles. The written word, in the form of the Bible, eliminated the need for any other form of revelation, including prophecy and words of knowledge, which were common among Pentecostals and charismatics. Falwell once said that modern speaking in tongues was the result of eating "too much pizza last night."

The differences were cultural as well as theological, which is why Nims and DeMoss were so surprised to see Dortch weep at their first meeting. "We non-charismatics, particularly Baptists, go more heavily on doctrine and the teaching of principles and values," said Falwell, the day after Bakker resigned. "We evoke a less emotional response. It's a different style." Historian George Marsden has argued that fundamentalists are most prominently defined by their militant anti-modernism, a specific response to cultural developments in the late nineteenth and early twentieth centuries, including Darwinism, Marxism, and Freudian psychology.

This is why many fundamentalists insist on using only the King James Bible, published in 1611 before the influence of modern literary criticism, which they claim taints more modern translations. Pentecostals tend to be less confrontational and more culturally flexible, reflected in their easy adoption of the twentieth century's therapeutic and consumer culture. When asked about the difference between fundamentalists and other evangelicals, Falwell liked to say, "a fundamentalist is an evangelical who is mad about something."[8]

The differences between Bakker and Falwell were further reflected in their organizations and broader connections. Two of Bakker's most outspoken supporters after the scandal broke were Oral Roberts, by this time a United Methodist, and television preacher Robert Schuller. PTL's board under Bakker included women and African Americans. Falwell's new board members were all men, "most graying or balding," as the *Observer* pointed out.[9]

Like most fundamentalists, Falwell never adopted the full scope of the prosperity gospel. He was a relentless entrepreneur, and at times his ministry had lived "on the financial edge," as he later wrote. "We spent money believing that God would provide before He had provided it." In the early 1970s the Securities and Exchange Commission sued Falwell's ministry for improperly selling $6.5 million in bonds. Aggressive fundraising aside, Falwell never adopted the flashy look or conspicuous consumption of the prosperity gospel. "Jerry was far from the Jesus Cadillac theory," as Nims put it. "He was more fundamentalist austere. . . . He didn't think you prayed to God to get rich." Falwell drove a Suburban and often wore "suits badly in need of dry-cleaning and maybe a little rip in them somewhere," remembers his personal assistant at the time, Mark DeMoss. "I think this prosperity theology—what some call health and wealth theology—is the most damnable heresy being preached in the world today," Falwell told reporters.[10]

When Bakker resigned from PTL, he and Richard Dortch also resigned from the Assemblies of God and pulled the Heritage Village Church and Missionary Fellowship out of the Assemblies. To explain why he had done this, rather than submit to discipline and rehabilitation within the church, Bakker insisted that he was thwarting a "hostile takeover" by Jimmy Swaggart, a fellow member of the Assemblies. Only days after resigning, Bakker accused Swaggart of carrying out a "diabolical plot" to seize control of PTL. Roy Grutman, acting as Bakker's attorney, told reporters, "I have seen unmistakable evidence that . . . Jimmy Swaggart was attempting to orchestrate the ouster of Jim Bakker" in order to take over the ministry. Oral Roberts backed up Bakker's assertion that Swaggart and the *Observer* were acting "in collusion." Robert Schuller asserted that "a hostile takeover was in the works" and that Bakker "was encouraged by Jerry Falwell to give it up" in order to block Swaggart's scheme. Swaggart responded that talk of a takeover was "pure fabrication and outright lie." Swaggart never wanted to take over PTL; he wanted to destroy it. PTL "was a cancer that needed to be excised from the body of Christ," Swaggart said in an interview on *Nightline* on Tuesday, March 24. "It was painful, but it needed to be done."[11]

It took less than a week for the hostile takeover story, which Bakker and Dortch pushed in a clumsy attempt to divert attention away from PTL's finances and the Hahn settlement, to fall apart. Aside from Swaggart's vehement denials that he was after PTL—"What in the world would I do with a waterslide?" he famously quipped—it made no sense legally. PTL's assets were owned by the tax-exempt Heritage Village Church, which in turn was controlled by the board of directors. Once the old board revoked the provision granting the Assemblies of God control if Bakker stepped down or was removed, there was little that Swaggart or the church could do to intervene, even if they had been so inclined. The real battle for PTL would not be between Swaggart and Bakker, but between Bakker and Falwell; not a hostile takeover, but a friendly one gone bad.[12]

Initially, Falwell appeared confident that PTL's financial situation was manageable. The day after Bakker resigned, he described the ministry's finances as "neither critical nor comfortable." He expressed surprise when asked about the reported $10 million PTL owed contractor Roe Messner. "My goodness," Falwell said. He also acknowledged that PTL was preparing an application for a $50 million loan. For a week after Bakker's resignation, coverage of the Hahn settlement focused on the initial $115,000 payment. By March 26 the *Observer* had uncovered the additional $150,000 set aside in the trust fund. It reported that Hahn had received monthly payments of $800 to $1,200 from the trust, a total of $10,045 in 1985 alone. But the source of the money remained elusive. Bakker told writer Jamie Buckingham it had come from an "anonymous donor" and "was not laundered through PTL." "He doesn't know where it came from," Buckingham told a reporter from the *Washington Post*. Falwell stood behind Bakker's version of the story, adding that he did not know how much Jim and Tammy earned, but that PTL would continue to cover their salaries indefinitely. "This ministry would not be here without Jim and Tammy Bakker," Falwell said in a news conference. "It would be less than Christian to terminate and cut off the life supply of the person responsible for this ministry. It was never even considered." It soon would be.[13]

On the day the *Observer* reported the full $265,000 settlement, the new PTL board ordered an audit to determine the source of the money. The next day Falwell learned the truth, telling reporters that the payment "could lead to a criminal investigation." "When you get to paying extortion money, that's real close to the edge, especially if it's not your money," Falwell said. His first two weeks at PTL had brought one surprise after another. "If in the next two weeks comparable information comes out—and today would indicate maybe that's what's happening—the people [at PTL] may be in serious trouble," Falwell said.[14]

The surprises were far from over. On April 18, the *Charlotte Observer* reported that Jim and Tammy had been paid $1.6 million in 1986 and that between January 1984 and March 1987 they drew $4.8 million in salary and bonuses. No one outside of Bakker's entourage was prepared for these kinds of numbers. The Bakkers had last divulged their salaries in 1979, when they earned a combined total of $72,800. Equally shocking was the recent compensation of Bakker's inner circle. Richard Dortch received $350,000 in 1986, $220,000 of it in bonuses, and David Taggart about $360,000, including $275,000 in bonuses. For Christmas, David and James Taggart gave each other matching black Jaguars, costing a total of $87,765. Bakker's secretary, Shirley Fulbright, received $160,000 in 1986, $110,000 of it in bonuses, and Peter Bailey, PTL's finance director, received $110,000 in 1986, including $60,000 in bonuses. At the end of 1986, Dortch had $680,873 in his PTL-funded retirement account, and Bakker had $793,684. More troubling were the payments for the first three months of 1987, during which time the Bakkers pocketed $640,000, Dortch $270,000, David Taggart $220,000, Fulbright $50,000, and Bailey $70,000, most of it bonuses. None were approved by PTL's board. Between June 1986 and March 17, 1987, Jim and Tammy Bakker, Richard Dortch, and David Taggart received a total of $2.2 million in bonuses alone. Other executive perks included Mercedes-Benzes and other luxury cars, the use of PTL-owned houses, maids, groundskeepers, and security guards. Speaking on April 19, Falwell called the compensation of the Bakkers and their inner circle "horrendous" and "indefensible." "There seems to have been an acceleration of bonus payments these first three months of this year, almost in anticipation of some dramatic happening," Falwell said. Indeed, in early 1987 Taggart called Shirley Fulbright from

Palm Springs, where he was staying with the Bakkers, to arrange for some of his bonus payments, which Fulbright rushed through without consulting Bakker or Dortch. Between February and April 1987, Taggart also used PTL checks to pay off $125,000 on his personal American Express card.[15]

The focus on PTL's finances gave new life to past charges of financial impropriety against other televangelists. The April 27, 1987, edition of ABC's *Nightline* featured a segment with Tim Waisanen, an Assemblies of God pastor from southern California who once worked as Robert Schuller's director of marketing and planning. Waisanen recounted sitting in Schuller's living room in Orange, California, in 1981, watching him dictate an "urgent" fundraising letter supposedly sent from China. "I am writing to you today from Peking, China," the letter read. Accompanying the letter was a photograph of Schuller on the Great Wall, with the caption, "Here I am standing on the Great Wall in China." In fact, the photo was shot in a studio in southern California, with a photograph of the wall as a backdrop. Schuller used the letter to raise $1.6 million.[16]

Nor did Falwell escape the collateral damage. Michael Korpi attended Liberty University and then worked as a cameraman for Falwell's television ministry in 1978 and 1979. One of his first assignments was shooting footage of refugees in Thailand for a fundraising campaign. Of the $6 million raised, only $150,000 went to the refugees, Korpi told *Nightline*. Korpi also filmed Vietnamese boat people, refugees fleeing the country by the thousands in the wake of unrest following the Vietnam War. Falwell's ministry used the footage to raise about $4 million, of which only $200,000 went to repair the boat shown in the footage and another $150,000 to boat people programs. In a press conference the next day, Falwell claimed that "every penny" raised for refugee programs "was applied just as it was raised." He also denied that Korpi had ever worked for his ministry, but Korpi had his W-2 statements to prove otherwise. A story in *U.S. News & World Report* bolstered Korpi's allegations. In April 1987, the news magazine reported that Falwell had raised between $740,000 and $3.2 million for famine relief in Sudan, but spent only $300,000 for that purpose.[17]

Meanwhile Jessica Hahn faced a media storm that she did not want, but had nevertheless helped to create. Two years earlier, Hahn had moved into an upper-floor apartment in a house in West Babylon, on Long Island, sensing that the story would soon break. "I knew that, through the grapevine, too many people were asking too many questions," Hahn said. "I just wanted to be away and not have my parents and my family open to this." When the scandal broke, reporters and satellite trucks surrounded her small house day and night. Despite Bakker's allegations, Hahn still did not want to be responsible for the collapse of his ministry. "I don't want Jim Bakker to leave PTL. I don't want to live with that," she told Charlie Shepard the day Bakker resigned. Hahn also denied that she had tried to blackmail Bakker or that she had violated the terms of her trust agreement by talking to the press. PTL nevertheless stopped making payments to her from the trust account as soon as the scandal became public.[18]

As the story unfolded, the media was brutal, referring to Hahn as a harlot and "the whore of West Babylon." Monica Lewinsky has recently spoken about how she was cyberbullied in the wake of her affair with President Bill Clinton. "Overnight I went from being a completely private figure to a publicly humiliated one worldwide.... I was branded as a tramp, tart, slut, whore, bimbo, and, of course, that woman," Lewinsky has said. The internet added an instantaneous dimension to Lewinsky's story, but Hahn experienced much the same thing on television and in magazines and newspapers. She was not skilled at presenting herself in public. "I didn't know how I was supposed to look, what I was supposed to say," she later admitted, making it easy for reporters to mold her into a figure that would sell: the other woman who had shamelessly plied her charms on a powerful older man. "People will always consider me a cartoon character, a bimbo," Hahn later said. "They will always consider that I brought down an empire." The church did not treat Hahn any better than the media, choosing for the most part to either blame or ignore her. "Most of them turned out to be the ones who hurt me most," Hahn said. After the tape of her interview with Paul Roper got out, she was distressed at the number of church leaders who seemed to take a voyeuristic interest in its details without reaching out to her in any way, including Swaggart, Ankerberg, and just about every church leader who spoke out in public. "I've been alone through all of this," she said six weeks after the scandal broke. Yet Hahn never lost her faith. "I realize that God has been by my side, even if no one else has.... All I have is God and he's been very faithful to me. I believe he's going to bring me through this." After running out of money and options, Hahn sought solace in a more forgiving environment: Hollywood.[19]

Dortch had brokered Falwell's intervention in PTL in the hopes of maintaining his own position, but in one of the many ironies surrounding PTL's collapse, it was Falwell who ousted Dortch. The day Bakker resigned, Dortch stood before four hundred employees gathered in the Barn and declared, "I have a very awesome responsibility." Falwell appointed Dortch PTL president in Bakker's place and kept him on as host of the flagship television show, which changed its name from *Jim and Tammy* back to the *PTL Club*. But as information seeped out regarding Dortch's role in the Hahn settlement and the escalation of salaries and bonuses, his position steadily eroded. On April 21 Dortch announced on the air that he would forgo his salary and benefits for twelve months, but it was too little, too late.[20]

THE REVELATIONS WERE not all about money. On April 22 four former PTL insiders, Al Cress, Roger Flessing, Gary Smith, and Ed Stoeckel, met with John Ankerberg in Chattanooga, Tennessee. Ankerberg wanted to hear exactly what they knew about Bakker's misdeeds beyond what had already appeared in the press. The next day the group flew to Nashville to meet with Falwell and Nims, who had just finished meeting with G. Raymond Carlson, general superintendent of the Assemblies of God and three other church officials. The Assemblies representatives were reluctant to take Falwell into their confidence, but he could easily guess where their investigation was headed. Ankerberg and the PTL four confirmed Falwell's suspicions. The most sensational testimony came from Gary Smith, who repeated his story about trying to fire a man with a drinking problem who claimed to have "been with Jim" on his houseboat, only to have Bakker call him in the middle of the night and tell him not to. Smith also said that Bakker had once invited him to go for a swim in the old Heritage Village pool. When Bakker emerged from the shower completely nude and tumescent, Smith was shocked. Before anything else could happen, a PTL staffer and his wife walked in and Bakker scurried back to the shower. After Falwell listened to the four PTL alums, Ankerberg said that he was going to appear on CNN's *Larry King Live* the next day and accuse Bakker of homosexual activity. Falwell would later deny knowing this, but some of those present remembered him enthusiastically endorsing Ankerberg's plan.[21]

Bakker had apparently heard about the meeting in Nashville and suspected what would be said. That day he sent Falwell a telex message, telling him that it was time to "turn the PTL ministry over to charismatics," and suggesting that Falwell appoint James Watt chairman of the board in Falwell's place. Once the new leadership was in control, "I will return to PTL," Bakker said. Refusing, Bakker warned, would ignite a "holy war." It was a desperate ploy by someone who knew that the worst was yet to come.[22]

During his interview with Larry King on Friday, April 24, Ankerberg accused Bakker of visiting prostitutes, engaging in homosexual acts, and condoning wife swapping at PTL. It was one thing to forgive Bakker of adultery, "but that was only part of the evidence against him, and he has not confessed or repented of the other things," Ankerberg said. He told King that his evidence was based on interviews with PTL staff, letters written to PTL officials, and interviews with the prostitute "who serviced him on three separate occasions. And the sad thing is, she knew it was Jim Bakker. She had seen him on television." After the interview aired, Falwell professed shock, saying that he had known nothing about this part of the story. But Jim Cobble, another former PTL employee who had talked to Falwell in recent months, remembers getting a call from Falwell the night before Ankerberg's appearance on *Larry King* urging him not to miss the show.[23]

The day after Ankerberg's interview with Larry King, Bakker denied everything. "I have never been involved with wife-swapping. I am not a homosexual and I've never been to a prostitute," he said. But Ankerberg's charges were soon backed up by other reports. A local Charlotte television station aired a story about a Wilkinson Boulevard prostitute who claimed that Bakker visited her in the late 1970s. "I really did recognize his face, but I couldn't place him until they told me," the woman said, sitting sideways and holding her hand on the side of her head to hide her face from the camera. "I remember how shocked I was. And then after that, you know, I seen him two other times." *Penthouse* magazine later published an interview with another Wilkinson Boulevard prostitute who claimed that Bakker paid for her services five times, beginning in early 1980. Bakker would show up in a white Oldsmobile wearing an ill-fitting blond wig as a disguise. The two discussed biblical prophecy as she gave him her special "peppermint French." He always left a generous tip on his way out, she said.[24]

The charge of wife swapping dated from the chaotic period in the late 1970s and involved two couples who were PTL employees, but not Jim and Tammy. The trysts occurred at the Heritage Village pool, which was one reason it was shut down. But since Jim and Tammy were not directly involved, this part of the story quickly lost traction.[25]

The most damaging and best documented allegations against Bakker involved gay sex. For evangelicals broadly in the 1980s, this was a sin that defied comprehension, particularly for a pastor. Like most Americans, evangelicals at the time lacked a vocabulary for understanding gay issues. Heterosexual affairs and financial mismanagement could be forgiven, but homosexuality left an indelible mark on a minister's record, after which restoration was nearly impossible. The career of Charles F. Parham, one of the founders of Pentecostalism, had been undermined in 1907 when he was arrested in San Antonio, Texas, for committing sodomy with a twenty-two-year-old man. Though the charges were dismissed, Parham's ministry never recovered. More recently, fundamentalist preacher Billy James Hargis had been forced to resign the presidency of American Christian College when *Time* magazine reported that he had had sex with both male and female students. Hargis rose to fame in the 1950s and 1960s, eventually preaching on more than 500 radio stations and 250 television stations, and founded his college in Tulsa in 1970. *Time* reported that in 1974 five students confessed to having sex with Hargis, four of them men. One couple that Hargis married confessed to each other on their wedding night that they were not virgins, only to discover that they had both had sex with the same person: Hargis. Though evangelicals generally recoiled from discussing homosexuality in the ministry, Bakker's case was not without context.[26]

Along with Gary Smith's stories, Austin Miles's account soon surfaced. Miles was the former circus clown and frequent guest on the television show in the early days who claimed to have stumbled upon Bakker and three male staffers "frolicking" in the nude in the sauna room at the Heritage Village complex. Spurred on by the openness of others, another former PTL executive told reporters about an incident in April 1984 in which Bakker summoned him to his Tega Cay home to discuss the network's programming. Inside the house, Bakker lay down on his bed and asked for a backrub. The man complied, awkwardly massaging Bakker's leg and nervously "talking a mile a minute." Then Bakker turned over and, as the man told *Newsweek*, "he takes my hand and pulls it and plants it on his organ. I just freaked, honestly freaked. I had no idea. I broke into an absolute cold sweat. I stood up, and he reached for my zipper." Stammering out something about needing to get home for dinner, the man bolted from the room. Bakker never mentioned the incident, and the executive soon left PTL.[27]

Another PTL staffer told reporters that he and Bakker had a long-running sexual relationship that began in mid-1983. Jay Babcock had moved to PTL in September 1979 to attend the Heritage School of Evangelism and Communication. After finishing his studies in May 1980, Babcock took a job as a groundskeeper at the park. That September he moved to the television production department as a writer. By mid-1983 Babcock had divorced his wife and worked his way up to producing Bakker's show, with a staff of forty or fifty people working under him. One evening when Tammy and the kids were out of town, Bakker invited Babcock to his home and, in a familiar pattern, asked for a backrub as he lay on his bed. Apparently satisfied with Babcock's compliance, a few weeks later Bakker invited him to join the family on a trip to Hilton Head, South Carolina. One night, after Tammy had returned to Charlotte, Bakker asked for another massage. As Babcock rubbed him down, Bakker suddenly turned over and began pulling off the younger man's clothes. In silence, the two masturbated each other. Bakker had found what he was looking for. "I probably always knew I was gay," Babcock now says, though at the time he had not told anyone at PTL, including Bakker. He was, in his own words, "an impressionable young man with no experience," who initially thought he was in love with his boss.[28]

For the next three years Babcock and Bakker worked closely together on the set of the television show. They often met in Bakker's dressing room after the show, where they traded sexual favors in secret on at least thirty occasions. Bakker told Babcock that he did not think having sex with other men amounted to cheating on Tammy. At the time, Babcock and Tammy did not get along, and he suspected the she knew about his relationship with Jim. Once, after Babcock refused Jim's advances, he demoted Babcock from producer to a job as a direct-mail writer, working out of a four-by-four-foot cubicle. After three or four months Bakker brought him back as a producer. By then Babcock was "too beaten down to resist" and their sexual relationship resumed. Bakker warned Babcock that if he tried to reveal their relationship, no one would believe him. Bakker also manipulated Babcock and others by telling them that they were not good enough to make it in television outside of PTL. Only after he left PTL did Babcock realize that was not true.[29]

In November 1986 Babcock had finally had enough and ended his sexual relationship with Bakker. By then he knew of at least five other men at PTL who had been sexually involved with Bakker. Later, when asked by a reporter about Bakker's assertion that he had never participated in a homosexual relationship, Babcock called his former boss a "liar." Taken together these stories painted a picture of Bakker as not just bisexual, but also a sexual predator, taking advantage of employees who depended on him for their livelihood.[30]

ALARMED AT THE new revelations about money and sex, Falwell called a meeting of the PTL board for April 28. About 270 reporters, six satellite trucks, thirty photographers, and forty-four television cameras descended on the Heritage Grand Hotel for what promised to be a momentous event.

Jim and Tammy at the Crystal Palace groundbreaking, January 2, 1987.
Credit: Flower Pentecostal Heritage Center.

Bakker and Roe Messner, with shovels, at the Crystal Palace groundbreaking.
Credit: Flower Pentecostal Heritage Center.

Drawing of Bakker's Crystal Palace.
Credit: Flower Pentecostal Heritage Center.

Jim and Tammy explain her drug addiction and treatment from their home in Palm Springs, March 1987.
Credit: Flower Pentecostal Heritage Center.

The Charlotte Observer's take on Jerry Falwell's takeover of PTL.
Credit: The Charlotte Observer.

Falwell takes questions from the press, April 1987.
Credit: The Charlotte Observer.

Roy Grutman and Falwell at a press conference, April 1987.
Credit: The Charlotte Observer.

James and David Taggart at the time of the scandal in 1987.
Credit: The Charlotte Observer.

Jerry Falwell goes down the PTL waterslide, September 1987.
Credit: The Charlotte Observer.

The Bakker's famous air-conditioned doghouse, which was nothing more than a shed.

Credit: Bettmann/Getty Images.

Jim and Tammy with Melvin Belli in 1987.

Credit: *The Charlotte Observer*.

The sofa in Harold Bender's office that Bakker wedged himself under.
Credit: Photo by the author.

U.S. marshals lead Bakker away from Harold Bender's office, August 31, 1989.
Credit: *The Charlotte Observer*.

Jessica Hahn in September 1987, holding the issue of *Playboy* in which she first appeared.
Credit: The New York Post/Getty Images.

Jim and Tammy leaving the Federal Courthouse in Charlotte during Jim's trial, September 1989. Harold Bender is behind them.
Credit: The Charlotte Observer.

They were not disappointed. Over the course of five hours, the board dismantled what was left of Bakker's inner circle at PTL, cutting the threads that still connected him to the ministry. The first to go was Rex Humbard, one of Bakker and Dortch's few remaining allies on PTL's board, who resigned and then hurried out a side door, getting into a limousine without talking to reporters. Jim and Tammy's salaries were cut off and Dortch was fired, as were David Taggart and Shirley Fulbright. The Taggart brothers "ran out the hotel's front door," according to a reporter who tried to chase them down, and sped away in one of their black Jaguars without comment.[31]

"The business at hand right now is to keep the ship floating," Falwell told the press following the meeting. To get to the bottom of PTL's financial position he appointed Harry Hargrave chief operations officer. Hargrave, thirty-eight, described as "graying and well groomed," was well qualified for the job. A native of Austin, Texas, he had attended Southern Methodist University, earning a business degree in 1970 and an MBA in 1973, and now lived in Dallas's fashionable University Park neighborhood. For the past decade he had worked as a real estate and financial consultant for a company that operated theme parks in several states, including the Silver Dollar City attraction in Branson, Missouri, and Dollywood in Pigeon Forge, Tennessee. He had also managed a water park in Dallas in the mid-1980s.[32]

Hargrave faced a difficult task and he knew it. "The books are a mess," he said, the day after Falwell appointed him. Hargrave announced plans to sell the five Tega Cay houses the ministry owned, including the ones Bakker and Dortch occupied. A week later Hargrave laid off two hundred PTL employees in order to save $1.2 million a month. By the middle of May, Hargrave had determined that PTL was $65 million in debt and losing $2 million a month. From 1984 to 1986, the ministry spent $40 million more than it took in. On Wednesday, May 13 workers boarded up the unfinished twenty-one-story Heritage Grand Towers Hotel. Prior to halting construction, workers had been completing interior and exterior finish work on the lower levels of the hotel, with the hope that the first nine floors could be opened soon. PTL had paid less than $12 million of the $30 million needed to complete the hotel and recreation center, despite raising more than $74 million for the project. Construction was also slowed or halted at the Mulberry Towers condominiums and the Wendy's Sand Castle restaurant. "We have no cash," Hargrave said. "We had no idea the cash flow was this bad—none at all." That same day Falwell announced a

"May Emergency" campaign to raise $7 million by the end of the month and $25 million by the end of August. "We either do it, or we shut down," Falwell said.[33]

The "May Emergency" turned into a "May miracle," as supporters gave $8.5 million by the end of the month. But giving needed to remain at that level if PTL had any hope of meeting the demands of its 1,400 creditors. Above all, the ministry needed to pay off its $8 million debt to the television stations that aired the *PTL Club*. If they dropped the television show, as many were threatening to do, the ministry's fundraising would collapse and it would go under. Though it had been overshadowed by Heritage USA in recent years, PTL still operated the largest all-religious network in America, covering about 80–85 percent of the nation. The network included 160 television stations and 1,700 cable systems serving 13 million subscribers.[34]

The May miracle saved PTL in the short term, but Falwell never succeeded in defining the ministry's direction for the future. Under Falwell, PTL became more respectable, but at the expense of just about everything that had drawn viewers and visitors in. After firing most of Bakker's old team, Falwell pledged to stop selling airtime to the more outrageous faith healers and prosperity gospel preachers and to scrutinize the "lifestyle and quality of Christian testimony" of guests on PTL's programs. "In the past several years, the conduct of some persons appearing on the show . . . was atrocious," Falwell said. He also promised to institute a dress code at the water park aimed at banning skimpy swimsuits. The first host of the *PTL Club* after Dortch was fired was Chuck Millhuff, who had a small ministry in Kansas City that included a thirty-minute talk show on a local television station. No one would have confused Millhuff with Jim Bakker. Millhuff, forty-nine, liked to work on old cars in his spare time, and his wife, Jeanne, preferred to stay out of the limelight. He was so nervous at his first news conference that he could not smile. Falwell succeeded in making the television show seem less like a soap opera, but in the process it became boring.[35]

Without the Bakkers, most of what was unique and revolutionary about the television show disappeared. Jim had never done much scripting, giving the show the feel of reality TV before the concept was invented, a schlock and awe approach that was unlike anything else at the time. What it lacked in polish it made up for in entertainment. PTL became "a continuing daytime drama that evolved to its own art form," said Roger Flessing, who directed the show for several years. "It was part music, part talk show, part telethon, and a major part continuing daytime drama." People tuned in because they came to feel that they knew Jim and Tammy on an intimate level. Their flaws only made them seem more genuine. "Friends came and went, theologies came and went, crises came and went with increasing frequency, building projects came and went," but underneath it all was the sense that viewers were sharing Jim and Tammy's "real lives." On television, they appeared transparent, which in Tammy's case was often true and in Jim's case a talent he could harness in front of the camera. "He had sort of a wide-eyed child's sense of fascination with television," said Flessing. "He was able to look and communicate directly into the camera in a very sincere manner so the person at home knew he was really talking to that one person instead of talking to millions of people." Falwell never understood that connection, and none of his replacement hosts came close to replicating it.[36]

While Falwell and the media pressed forward on all fronts, the Assemblies of God dithered. Just as the press was unprepared to cover the Assemblies, the church was unprepared for the media onslaught it now faced. Unlike Bakker and Falwell, Assemblies officials were unaccustomed to speaking in front of crowds of reporters and banks of cameras and microphones. Juleen Turnage, Director of Public Relations for the Assemblies of God, remembered the sight of satellite trucks parked day and night outside the church's headquarters in Springfield, Missouri, as a jarring and deeply unsettling experience for church leaders, who had never seen anything like it. Turnage handled the press with openness and skill, but church leaders were clearly overwhelmed.[37]

It was initially up to the North Carolina district of the Assemblies of God and its superintendent, Charles Cookman, to determine the church's response to Bakker's resignation and the allegations against him. But even more so than the national leaders in Springfield, Cookman was ill prepared for the challenge he now faced. "I'm just a nobody doing my job, trying to help people know the Lord," he told the *Charlotte Observer*. PTL was the biggest ministry in his district, and for years Cookman had lived in awe of what Bakker and Dortch had accomplished. He had been a member of PTL's board from 1979 until the scandal broke, at which point he resigned to avoid a conflict of interest. At first, Cookman simply tried to sidestep responsibility. Less than a week after Bakker resigned, he declared that his inquiry had ended, since Bakker had confessed to adultery and there was nothing left to investigate. Cookman told reporters that any payments to Hahn were not a "question of morality" and therefore did not fall "under my purview." Church officials at the national headquarters in Springfield begged to differ. They reminded Cookman that ministers could not simply resign under a cloud. Charges of misconduct, including financial wrongdoing, had to be investigated, after which ministers found guilty were usually offered a two-year program of rehabilitation and restoration. Those who refused were dismissed, but not before an investigation into the extent of their failure.[38]

Forced to reconsider the matter, the sixteen-member North Carolina district presbytery met for eleven hours on April 8 in the small town of Dunn, North Carolina. In the meantime, the national presbytery conducted its own investigation, meeting with John Wesley Fletcher and Paul Roper, among others. On May 6, a month after the meeting of the North Carolina presbytery, the Executive Presbytery in Springfield dismissed Bakker over the Hahn affair and for "alleged misconduct involving bisexual activity." Raymond Carlson, the Assemblies general superintendent, said he used "alleged" because Bakker refused to appear to answer questions. But another official said that the church's investigation had turned up "firsthand evidence of homosexual acts." At the same time, Dortch was dismissed for concealing Bakker's encounter with Hahn and using "deceit" to arrange the cover-up. For Bakker the accusation of homosexuality was far more serious under Assemblies of God rules. A minister might eventually be reinstated after a heterosexual affair, but never after homosexual acts.[39]

By June, the patience of PTL's partners with Falwell's new approach was wearing thin. A June slump followed the May miracle, with supporters giving only $2.5 million, as compared to the $8.5 million they contributed in May. At its peak PTL had a pool of 120,000 monthly contributors. In June that number shrunk to 17,000. Unable to pay its bills, PTL filed for Chapter 11 bankruptcy on June 12. "Buildings have been constructed to pay for prior buildings and to pay for negative cash flow, and the game has ended," Harry Hargrave said. "We can't build any more buildings large enough to cover the past fiscal sins. So it has to come to a stop somewhere." The Heritage Grand Hotel was losing $85,000 a month, largely because two out of every three guests were lifetime partners who stayed for free. PTL eventually cut the price of a room from $75 to $49, but the occupancy rate never recovered. In June, only 16,656 out of 44,345 guests at the water park paid to get in. As a result, the water park was losing $23,000 a month. The provisions of Chapter 11 bankruptcy protected PTL from creditors until the court approved a reorganization plan. In particular, it prevented television stations from cancelling the show over unpaid bills. Falwell and his team hoped that bankruptcy would provide breathing room to restructure PTL's operations, but they still had to convince supporters that the new PTL was worth saving.[40]

AS PTL FLOUNDERED and his relationship with Falwell deteriorated, Bakker stepped up his campaign to regain control of the ministry. The day after Bakker resigned, Falwell claimed that when he and Bakker first met in Palm Springs there had been "no discussion" of Bakker's return "at all." Two months later, Falwell admitted that they had discussed Bakker's return after a period of rehabilitation at their initial meeting in Palm Springs. But that was before he discovered the extent of Bakker's financial mismanagement and other accusations against Bakker surfaced. New revelations notwithstanding, Bakker clung to his story that Falwell had promised to give PTL back after a few months, repeating it tirelessly to reporters and anyone else who would listen.[41]

For most of April and May, Jim and Tammy holed up in their Palm Springs home, surrounded by gawkers and reporters. The latter rented delivery trucks so that they could stand on the top and use telephoto lenses to peer into the Bakkers' pool area and windows. Their private space shrunk "to the size of a postage stamp," according to Jim. Celebrity bus tours of Palm Springs added the house to their route, to go along with the homes of the late Liberace, Bing Crosby, and other perennial favorites. By May the traffic had slowed to a car every two or three minutes. One woman drove all night from Arizona. Dressed in white with her hair in a "tight bun," she wore plastic bags over her hands to guard against AIDS. "The Lord told me to come here to speak to Tammy," she said. A man from Michigan arrived at dawn to read Psalm 51 while facing the rising sun. Others rang the doorbell (it was disconnected) or took pictures. Tammy occasionally appeared to talk to reporters, and the Bakkers' security team was unfailingly polite. If there was one part of the scandal they were prepared for, it was demands of celebrity.[42]

As the Bakkers hunkered down, the charges against them mounted, and the publicity turned increasingly negative. Ironically, the story that came to define the Bakkers' extravagance, the famous air-conditioned doghouse, was almost entirely a media creation. Jim and Tammy spent millions on chartered flights, vacation homes, luxury hotel suites, and expensive cars and clothes, but nothing else captured the public imagination in quite the same way. No "artifact better symbolized the excesses of Bakkerdom than the air-conditioned doghouse," noted *Time* magazine more than a decade after the scandal. In fact, the nine-by-eleven-foot structure resembled nothing more than a flimsy tool shed. It had no floor and stood about four feet high, with a used window air-conditioner sticking out one of the sides. The Bakkers' dogs never cared for it, and the doghouse eventually sold at auction for $600, considerably more than it was worth. By July it had found its way to Toledo, Ohio, where a county humane society was offering fifty-cent tours. But pictures of the doghouse rarely appeared in news stories, leaving people to imagine a doggie mansion of ostentatious opulence.[43]

In an attempt to turn the tide of public opinion, on May 26 Jim and Tammy appeared on ABC's *Nightline*, hosted by Ted Koppel. More than twenty million viewers tuned in, giving the show its highest rated episode ever. Koppel reminded Jim that earlier that day Falwell had accused him of a history of homosexual relationships "from 1956 to the present" and of "effectively" raping Jessica Hahn. But Koppel's unfamiliarity with Pentecostalism led him to err on the side of caution. Afraid that he might appear insensitive to their brand of faith, Koppel treated the Bakkers gently, leading one reporter to complain that he "showed all the ferocity of an overweight house cat." Koppel's reserve allowed Jim and Tammy to turn the table on their critics. No one had more experience selling a message on live television than the Bakkers. Having Tammy planted firmly by Jim's side was clearly intended to counter charges of homosexuality. As Koppel wavered, the Bakkers seized the narrative, directing it toward the part of the story in which they were the victims. Jim claimed that it was Falwell who told him about Swaggart's "hostile takeover" plot and Falwell who "said he would be a caretaker and would never even be on the air." "I am totally convinced they came here with the motive to steal Heritage USA and my ministry," Bakker said. "I made a terrible mistake."[44]

Koppel may have been inclined to handle the Bakkers gently, but by this time Falwell had no such scruples. The next day an angry Falwell held a ninety-minute news conference in which he said that Bakker "either has a terrible memory or is very dishonest or he is emotionally ill." To say that he stole PTL was "like saying somebody stole the Titanic just after it hit the iceberg," Falwell said. He repeated Gary Smith's story about Bakker making sexual advances in the nude at the Heritage Village swimming pool. "He needs to acknowledge these homosexual problems dating from 1956 to the present," Falwell said.

The centerpiece of Falwell's rebuttal was the Bakkers' list of severance demands, hand-written on Tammy's pale yellow stationary, which he held aloft for all to see. These included lifetime salaries of $300,000 a year for Jim and $100,000 a year for Tammy, title to the PTL-owned house at Tega Cay, health insurance and legal fees, two cars, security guards, rights to books and records, and a maid and secretary for a year. "I don't see any repentance there," Falwell declared. "I see the greed, I see the self-centeredness, I see the avarice that brought them down." The hand-written note had come to Falwell by way of Roe Messner. After the PTL board cut off the Bakkers' salaries on April 28, Falwell sent Messner to Palm Springs to discuss a financial settlement. Bakker later claimed that it was Falwell, acting through Messner, who had "encouraged us to put down everything we could think of." Expecting further negotiations, they had started "at the top." Messner later confirmed Bakker's version of the story, saying that Falwell instructed him to offer Bakker "a $300,000 salary, a maid for one year, a security guard for one year, health insurance, telephone expense." At the bottom of the note Bakker wrote, "I'm not making any demands of PTL whatsoever, I'm not asking for anything," according to Messner.[45]

Despite wave after wave of damaging revelations, Jim and Tammy were determined to reclaim PTL. "Our goal is to be on the air in 30 days," Bakker told the *Observer* during a layover at the Dallas airport on June 10, as he and Tammy were returning to Charlotte for the first time since the scandal broke. They stayed at their PTL-owned Tega Cay house and drove through Heritage USA, where a crowd of several hundred supporters, alerted to their arrival, surrounded the car. "These are our people!" declared Tammy, as she waded into the crowd. Falwell accused the Bakkers of holding "nightly, alleged prayer meetings" in which followers entered into "blood covenants . . . pledging to-the-death loyalty to the Bakkers to start a new ministry." Jim's new lawyer, the flamboyant Melvin Belli, arrived on June 20, proclaiming, "It's good to be on the side of the Lord," and handing out copies of his autobiography. "Had we been in at the beginning of this, Jimmy never would have resigned," Belli told reporters. He later referred to Bakker as the "best damn Christian I know."[46]

Celebrity was the last card Bakker had left to play, and Belli, who made Roy Grutman look dull by comparison, fit the role perfectly. Belli had begun practicing law in the middle of the Great Depression and is credited with revolutionizing personal injury law, earning him the nickname the King of Torts. "I am not an ambulance chaser, I'm usually there before the ambulance," he once said. His clients included the actor Errol Flynn, with whom he partied in Europe for months at a time in his younger days, Jack Ruby, who shot Lee Harvey Oswald, President Kennedy's assassin, and the victims of the 1984 Union Carbide chemical leak in Bhopal, India, and the 1983 Soviet downing of Korean Air Flight 007. Belli made and spent millions and appeared in movies and on television, including an episode of *Star Trek*. He was married six times and hired and fired beautiful young secretaries with the same abandon with which he did everything else. Those who lasted more than a few days had a high tolerance for chaos, bizarre clients, and an even more eccentric boss. One of Belli's trademarks was his affinity for strippers and prostitutes, both as his clients and he theirs. A few weeks after their appearance in Charlotte, Jim and Tammy met with Belli aboard his 105-foot ocean-going yacht, the "Adequate Award," in San Francisco. Hours later Belli celebrated his eightieth birthday with five thousand "close friends" at the landmark Belli Building in San Francisco, where he had his office. Belli's parties were legendary for their wild abandon and excess, but Jim and Tammy did not seem to mind. Belli was a star.[47]

Meanwhile Richard Dortch's fortunes continued to decline. In early June, Dortch demanded that PTL pay him through 1988 and give him the PTL-owned Lake Wylie house he lived in, under the terms of an undated, unsigned memo from late 1983. A week later the Florida state attorney's office filed a complaint against Dortch's wife, Mildred, for taking a homestead tax exemption on a Winter Haven, Florida, home the couple owned, claiming it as their primary residence. The state also began investigating the couple for claiming a second homestead exemption on another Florida house. A month later PTL quit paying Dortch his $13,500-a-month salary after someone remembered that he had pledged on the air to forgo his compensation for twelve months. "I will not accept any salary whatsoever, nor pension benefits or any other benefits," because "God has spoken to my heart," Dortch told viewers of the *PTL Club* on April 21. Falwell's staff was more than happy to help him obey the Lord's command. With nowhere else to turn, Dortch did what most fallen celebrities do: he launched a lecture tour, beginning with an appearance at American University in Washington, DC on September 9, 1987. When a student asked Dortch if "Jesus would ask for $2 million to go on television," he replied, "No, I think he would ask for hundreds of millions of dollars to do it."[48]

By the summer of 1987, there were two groups of PTL partners organized against Falwell's control of the ministry. The first, the Association of PTL Partners, began in a room at the Heritage Grand Hotel in May.

By June 15 the group claimed ten thousand members, divided into three camps: those who simply wanted to support PTL, those who wanted the Bakkers to return, and those who wanted Falwell out. Over time the hostility toward Falwell increased as members came to believe that he had no interest in their concerns, particularly in preserving Heritage USA. "Its our investment," said Joe Haviland, president of the Association, on July 4. "We're the ones who by blood, sweat and toil have built this place, and nobody has the right to take it away." By September, Haviland estimated that 90 percent of the Association's members had turned against Falwell, but they had also backed away from calling for the Bakkers' return.[49]

That cause was taken up by the Bring Bakker Back Club, formed in mid-June under the leadership of Vicki Goodman Meadows. Her parents, Howard and Vestal Goodman, were Bakker insiders who lived in one of the PTL-owned houses at Tega Cay. Howard and Vestal had married in 1949 and enjoyed considerable success in the 1960s and 1970s, touring with the Happy Goodman Family, a gospel music group. But by the late 1970s their old-time gospel sound had largely lost its appeal, and the group disbanded. In 1985, after regularly appearing on the *Jim Bakker* show for several years, they moved to Tega Cay, where they became "part of the people [Jim Bakker] listens to," according to another PTL staffer. In June, Falwell's staff demanded that the Goodmans vacate the Tega Cay house (they refused), and in July Vestal was banned from the television studio after shouting to the audience that Falwell had stolen Jim Bakker's ministry. Their daughter ran the Bring Bakker Back Club, working out of a room at a nearby Holiday Inn. But by then it was already too late. The multiple stories about sex and money had undermined the Bakkers' reputation with all but a small contingent of die-hard loyalists.[50]

As support for the Bakkers dwindled, PTL's financial position also collapsed, indicating a clear link between the two. Giving rebounded from \$2.5 million in June to \$4.7 million in July, but this was barely enough to cover payroll after meeting the ministry's other obligations, and another one hundred employees were laid off. More cost cutting followed. Falwell's team announced that free admission for lifetime partners to the Heritage Grand Hotel, the water park, and other Heritage USA attractions would end in September. PTL returned the merry-go-round and one of its miniature trains to the company that leased them. It also closed the farm at the center of the Farmland development, one of the park's most popular attractions, and dismissed the couple that ran it. The things that had made

Heritage USA fun steadily disappeared. "The place wasn't built for what they're using it for," said one visitor.[51]

Perhaps the saddest spectacle of PTL's collapse was the battle over Kevin's House. The eleven-bedroom home that Bakker had built for Kevin Whittum and other disabled children never met the necessary fire codes to qualify as a group home. As a result, Kevin and his immediate family were the only ones to live in the house. On August 11, Falwell's staff informed the Whittums that they had thirty days to leave and that David Whittum, Kevin's father, would no longer be paid as caretaker of the home. Jerry Nims, PTL's chief executive officer, was particularly annoyed that the Whittums were collecting mail for the Bakkers and delivering it to the PTL-owned Tega Cay house that the Bakkers still occupied. "We just discovered that recently, and that's the reason they were dismissed," Nims said. Once the Whittums were gone, PTL planned to convert the house into a bed-and-breakfast.[52]

Kevin Whittum, nineteen, who suffered from brittle bone disease and weighed just twenty-two pounds and used a wheelchair, fought back, suing PTL to prevent the eviction. The ministry offered to provide a smaller house for him and his family, but Kevin wanted to stay in the house Bakker had promised him. Kevin and his house had become a symbol of PTL's ability to reach the needy without regard for cost, to do what most religious groups say they would like to do if only they had the resources. Nevertheless, on September 9 a judge ordered the Whittums to vacate the home, closing the door on yet another of Bakker's signature projects. "That's life," Roy Grutman remembered Kevin saying to him after the verdict was handed down, as he turned his wheelchair to leave. Kevin died at his home in Grand Rapids, Michigan, on August 11, 1992. Falwell's team may have prevailed in court, but at the price of appearing vindictive and further tarnishing what was left of the PTL brand.[53]

On September 10, the day after Kevin Whittum's case was decided, Falwell declared financial victory for PTL by plunging down the water park's 60-foot-high, 163-foot-long water slide in a navy blue suit, tie and dress shoes, with his hands crossed over his chest, looking more like a corpse than someone out for a good time. In May, he promised to ride the slide if one thousand people gave $1,000 each to his Resurrection Committee by Labor Day, as part of the $20 million fundraising goal for the summer. With both goals met, Falwell kept his promise. "I may break my fool neck, but I'm going down that water slide," he announced on the air the day before taking the plunge. "I invite you to watch this idiot do it." A crowd cheered as paramedics stood by. One spectator held up a sign reading "Don't Backslide, Jerry." Spectacle aside, the late summer rebound in donations was more of a reprieve than a new beginning. Enough contributors had been willing to give Falwell a chance, but without Jim and Tammy, PTL quickly lost its appeal. Attendance at Heritage USA dropped steadily, down 8 percent in June, 15 percent in July, and 24 percent in August. Occupancy at the Heritage Grand Hotel fell to 66 percent in September 1987, versus 95 percent the year before. "The place seems like a ghost town," said one visitor.[54]

The final straw for Falwell came in bankruptcy court. Falwell's initial bankruptcy filing had been spurred in part by Roe Messner's threat to sue PTL for the $14 million he claimed the ministry owed him. For several months after Bakker's resignation, Falwell had supported Messner's claims against PTL. "Right now I believe that Roe Messner, with a $14 million tab owed him by this ministry, is the man most hurting of all around here," Falwell said on April 28, the day he fired Dortch and cut off the Bakkers' pay. But by September, Falwell and his staff had concluded that Messner cheated PTL out of millions of dollars by overcharging for much of the $60 million in construction work his company had done. They also accused Messner of shoddy construction on the Grand Hotel, including leaks in the roof and exterior walls, cracks in the concrete balconies, bathrooms and hallways that did not meet code requirements for people with disabilities, and plumbing leaks and poor ventilation throughout the building. Messner fired back that Falwell had kept him working through June 1987 as a "pretense" for the May emergency fundraising campaign. Like Bakker, Falwell realized that donors would give more if they saw buildings going up. But Messner said that he never saw any of the money raised that May. What was once an amicable relationship quickly turned hostile.[55]

At the same time, Falwell's relationship with US Bankruptcy Judge Rufus Reynolds began to unravel. Reynolds, who turned eighty in August, had been a bankruptcy judge since 1946. He swam for half an hour every morning and took a no-nonsense, hands-on approach to the cases he decided. For years he refused to let debtors keep a color television because he did not own one. After he was assigned the PTL case, Reynolds began watching televangelists to get a feel for how they operated. "What puzzled me was why people were interested in that little sawed-off runt," Reynolds later said, referring to Bakker. When a woman called the court wanting to know if Reynolds was a Christian, he said, "You tell her I was when I started this case, but now I plead the Fifth Amendment."

But Reynolds's reservations about Bakker did not make him automatically sympathetic toward Falwell. In July he appointed an independent examiner, William Robinson, a Columbia, South Carolina, lawyer, to evaluate PTL's finances. Robinson's appointment was a victory for Bakker and a setback for Falwell, who had argued that he was PTL's only legitimate voice and that his staff did not need additional supervision. As Falwell feared, Robinson concluded that PTL's 114,000 lifetime partners remained "key" to the "survival of the PTL ministry in its present form," and therefore deserved a voice in its reorganization. Robinson's report, filed with the court in September, contradicted Falwell's assertion that PTL was now supported primarily by a new set of donors, with no connection to the ministry under the Bakkers. Robinson was misinformed, Falwell claimed, because he was "spending so much time with a few lunatic fringe dissidents."[56]

Falwell's thirty-six-page reorganization plan, filed on September 30, forced a showdown with Judge Reynolds. Despite prodding from Robinson, Falwell's staff insisted that they would leave rather than work with the lifetime partners or anyone else connected to the Bakker regime. "I do what I say I'm going to do," said Harry Hargrave, PTL's chief operating officer. But Reynolds was not one to be pushed around. On October 8, he announced that he would allow PTL's creditors and lifetime partners to submit a competing plan, remarking that the Falwell proposal contained "no input from any of the creditors, partners, anything."

The next day Falwell and his entire staff quit. Falwell may have been glad to have a reason to leave, and may have forced the showdown for that reason. The day he resigned, he claimed that during his stint at PTL he had salvaged the reputation of televangelists, which had been his main goal all along. "I believe we are going to find our credibility going straight up," Falwell said.[57]

The reputation of televangelists aside, Falwell had also apparently come to the conclusion that the valuable parts of PTL could no longer be extricated from its debt. The satellite network, in particular, now seemed beyond his grasp. Despite the visibility of the Moral Majority and the success of Liberty University, Falwell had missed the cable and satellite revolution of the 1970s and 1980s. His television show, *The Old Time Gospel Hour*, was only on once a week, but distributing the show to less than four hundred stations cost $14 million in 1986. In contrast, PTL's network generated $13 million in revenues that year. When the Bakker crisis emerged, PTL offered Falwell a chance to make up for a missed opportunity. Six months later, that opportunity had disappeared, buried under an avalanche of debt.[58]

By October, PTL had also fallen beyond the grasp of Jim and Tammy. As their options diminished and their income evaporated, the Bakkers decided to launch a nineteen-city "Farewell for Now" tour, beginning in Nashville on November 17 and ending in Atlanta on December 21. Jim would emcee the concerts, with songs from Tammy Faye and special guests, including Lulu Roman from the television show *Hee Haw*. But the Bakker formula was not meant for the big stage. Jim and Tammy had built a following based on the daily drama of their lives, which viewers seemed to realize could not be reduced to a musical. It did not help that the tickets were twenty dollars, expensive for concerts at the time. Ticket sales were sluggish at best. By October 21 only 20 of 9,900 tickets had been sold for Nashville, 19 of 15,781 tickets for Greensboro, and 25 of 11,300 tickets for Norfolk. The entire tour was cancelled a couple of weeks before it was scheduled to begin. By that time Jim and Tammy were living in the Gatlinburg house, which they had deeded to Roe Messner, who claimed that PTL owed him money for remodeling the home. The Bakkers' Palm Springs house sold for $600,000 on September 4. But nothing had quite the sense of finality as the loss of their Tega Cay home. On the advice of the Goodmans and other friends, the Bakkers battled PTL for control of the Tega Cay house until October 26, when they finally turned over the keys to the home. Their ties to PTL had now been almost entirely severed.[59]

AS THE SCANDAL unfolded in the spring of 1987, Jessica Hahn felt used not only by Bakker, but also by Falwell. She tried to arrange a televised meeting with Bakker and Falwell, but both refused. Bakker was only willing if she denied that they had sex, and Falwell did not want to participate in anything that might serve to rehabilitate Bakker's image. Instead, Falwell urged her to go on *Nightline* and describe how Bakker had raped her. Hahn called Ted Koppel, host of *Nightline*, who, to his credit, suggested that it might not be in her best interest. "The ratings would go through the ceiling," Koppel admitted, but not for the reason Hahn hoped. She gratefully declined. Despite Falwell's "pushing," she "just wasn't ready."[60]

Desperate, Hahn turned to the only people who seemed concerned with her side of the story. One of the first outsiders who talked to Hahn "like a human being" was Howard Stern, the radio shock jock. She took his calls while hiding out in her apartment because he did not ask about Bakker; he just wanted to know, "are you all right?" After hearing Robert Guccione, publisher of *Penthouse*, say on television that she was being manipulated, Hahn called him and they met at his house in New York. Guccione was anxious to get the story, suggesting that Hahn meet with Bakker and Falwell while wearing a wire to record their conversations. He also offered her $350,000 to pose for pictures. The whole thing scared Hahn, and she left feeling like "I was leaving some dark place." She was reluctant to get involved with Guccione but gave an interview to the *Washington Post* reporter, Art Harris, who sold the story to *Penthouse* anyway. Harris's story was detailed and broad ranging, but it also questioned Hahn's honesty and integrity at several points. "Is she Victim or Vixen? Is she a Hester Prynne for the eighties . . . or is she a sultry sophisticate sashaying about in tight jeans, boots, and aviator shades?"[61]

Down to her last forty dollars, Hahn signed a contract with a Long Island divorce attorney and headed to Hollywood to discuss book and movie deals. A week later Hahn signed a $1 million contract with *Playboy* to tell her story and appear topless in the magazine. "It's not the kind of story you can tell in *Good Housekeeping* but you could open up here," Hugh Hefner told her. The story was written by *Los Angeles Times* reporter Robert Scheer, who did the 1976 *Playboy* interview with Jimmy Carter, and *Playboy* Executive Editor Barry Golson. As part of the deal, Hahn remained in seclusion until the November edition of the magazine appeared. It had just hit newsstands when she arrived in Charlotte on September 21 to testify before a federal grand jury convened to investigate allegations of tax, mail, and wire fraud at PTL. In fact, a local distributor released the magazine a week early to take advantage of Hahn's Charlotte appearance. Hahn autographed dozens of copies of the magazine for fans, scribbling "Stay sweet," "Keep smiling," "Always look up," on the cover. "She sure doesn't look like any church secretary I've ever seen," one bystander said. *Playboy*'s investment in Hahn proved lucrative for the magazine. By October 2 nearly 5.7 million copies had been sold, 2 million more than usual. Hahn described doing *Playboy* was a form of "therapy." "Now, don't laugh, but I believe this experience has brought me closer to God," she later said. Before the photo shoot she had asked God for a sign while out on a walk and the next thing she knew there was a rainbow in the sky. "That was enough for me . . . I didn't have a church or a preacher to run to. I had just me and God walkin'."[62]

Not everyone agreed. The *Playboy* story and pictures compounded the anxiety that had gripped Hahn's mother, Jessica Moylan, since the scandal broke. She was furious with her daughter for posing topless for *Playboy*, and the two ended up screaming at each other over the phone after the article and pictures appeared. "I don't sleep, I don't eat, it's a wonder I'm not down to 90 pounds," she told the *Charlotte Observer* on September 22. "My mom got sick of it. She stopped eating. . . . All the news crews, she couldn't accept it," Hahn later recalled. Jessica Moylan died of anorexia in 1989, according to her daughter.[63]

PTL PASSED THROUGH the hands of a number of administrators after Falwell's resignation, but as a major ministry it was finished. Immediately after Falwell stepped down, Judge Reynolds temporarily turned the ministry over to his adviser, attorney William Robinson. Less than two weeks later, David W. Clark, vice president of marketing for Pat Robertson's Christian Broadcasting Network (CBN), replaced Robinson. Clark, forty-seven, was ordained in the Assemblies of God and was a former assistant professor of communication at Bowling Green Sate University in Ohio with a PhD from the University of Iowa. He had been at CBN since 1977 and understood Christian television and the scale of PTL's operations. But the ministry needed $20 million above operating expenses over the next six months to survive, and Clark lacked the visibility to pull in that kind of response. Nor was he willing to consider bringing Jim and Tammy back. "Their future is not at Heritage USA," he said when he took the job. On December 10, the IRS filed a $55.7 million claim against PTL, effectively revoking PTL's tax-exempt status from 1981 on and potentially nearly doubling the $60 million the ministry still owed its creditors. The IRS claim also called into question whether future contributions would be tax deductible. Between Christmas 1987 and the end of February 1988, PTL lost more than $15,000 a day. A March telethon fell more than $2 million short of its goal, and the Heritage Grand hotel lost $361,000 that month. By April it was clear that the ministry could not pay its bills. "It looks like it's the end of the road," Judge Reynolds said on April 15 as he ordered PTL to begin pursuing liquidation. David Clark resigned as PTL trustee on May 20, joining a string of former leaders who underestimated the depth of the ministry's troubles.[64]

The fall of PTL rocked the world of television preachers. "That scandal has hit the evangelical world like a bombshell," Pat Robertson said on June 5, 1987. He reported that revenue for the CBN was down $12 million for the year, forcing him to layoff 470 employees. Robertson's frequent absences from his flagship show, *The 700 Club*, as he prepared to run for the 1988 Republican presidential nomination, were likely also a factor, but the fallout hit other religious broadcasters too. A nationwide poll in August found that 53 percent of Americans no longer believed that money sent to televangelists went to a good cause. Closer to home, a public opinion poll covering the Carolinas found that only one in ten had a favorable opinion of Bakker. The numbers were low for other televangelists as well: 27 percent for Oral Roberts, 36 percent for Rex Humbard, 38 percent for Pat Robertson and Jimmy Swaggart, and 45 percent for Robert Schuller. By August, donations to Oral Roberts's ministry were down by one-third.[65]

Only a year after he triumphantly broke ground on the Crystal Palace, Bakker's dream world was gone. Jim and Tammy's early success at PTL had been driven by innovation, including the talk show format, the integrated satellite network and the concept for an all-inclusive community that was Heritage USA. Later, as key staff quit and financial struggles took hold, the Bakkers relied more and more on their celebrity, particularly their status as TV stars at the height of television's power. Flowing under all of this, and mostly out of sight of the media, was the Bakkers' deep religious connection to their constituency and their powerful manipulation of American consumer culture. The gospel of the abundant life was more nuanced than the crass version of the prosperity gospel that emerged in the media in the wake of the Jessica Hahn scandal, but it did not have the power to do what the Bakkers claimed it could. It could not create its own special math, disgorging money whenever they needed it, and it could not turn deception into reality, no matter how hard anyone tried to believe.

Jim and Tammy may have been done with PTL, but PTL was not quite done with them. Judgment day awaited.

15

Judgment Day

JIM BAKKER CURLED up in a fetal position under his lawyer's couch sobbing uncontrollably, tears streaming down his swollen face. He had wedged himself into the approximately ten-inch space between the floor and the bottom of a maroon leather camelback sofa. As his psychiatrist tried to calm him down, Bakker babbled incoherently about giant bugs coming to get him. It was day four of his criminal trial for wire and mail fraud, and Bakker's world was collapsing around him.

The previous day, August 30, 1989, Steve Nelson had taken the stand for the prosecution, offering some of the most damaging evidence of the trial against Bakker. Nelson, thirty-nine, had joined PTL in the fall of 1985 as Vice-President of World Outreach and was responsible for coordinating the telethons. During an October 1985 telethon Nelson learned that PTL had already oversold the number of lifetime partnerships, making it nearly impossible to accommodate all of the partners who had been promised lodging in the Heritage Grand Hotel. Upset by this discovery, he tracked down Dortch, who told him "not to worry about it." Bakker told him the same thing when Nelson found him in his dressing room. But Nelson, who also supervised the departments responsible for hotel reservations and partner relations, knew that the problem would not fix itself. Things only got worse after the Victory Warriors campaign in the spring of 1986, which raised $34 million by offering more than 30,000 additional partnerships at $1,000 apiece, with the promise of three nights free lodging every year for life. "Someone could go to jail for this," Nelson told Dortch. But neither Dortch nor Bakker would listen. "The Lord's done a miracle for us here and there's not anything for you to be worried about," Bakker told him.[1]

In order to keep from appearing to have sold out the available lifetime partnerships during telethons, Nelson testified that Bakker and Dortch had him keep two sets of tallies on the number of partnerships sold. One set was posted on television for all to see and the other set, "the real numbers," were only given to a handful of Bakker insiders. The numbers posted on the air "were a lot lower" than the actual figures, creating the illusion that the partnerships were not all gone. Two or three weeks before Falwell took over at PTL, David Taggart and Richard Dortch told Nelson to destroy all of his reports on the lifetime partnerships. "They thought there was an IRS agent on the property, they wanted to make sure to get rid of all that," Nelson said. Nelson's testimony made Bakker look deliberately deceitful, rather than just sloppy or misinformed. It set the tone for much of what would follow.[2]

During his cross-examination, Harold Bender, one of Bakker's attorneys, did his best to chip away at Nelson's credibility. Nelson admitted that he had called the Heritage Village Church services "stupid" and referred to Norm Bakker, Jim's brother, as "the assistant to the village idiot." Nelson also admitted that he had sworn under oath that he received a $10,000 bonus from PTL, when the actual amount was $20,000, and that he received an additional $30,000 loan that Dortch told him "I would never have to worry about paying" back because it would be converted into a bonus.[3]

As Bender's questions became more aggressive, Nelson suddenly "turned a disgusting sallow color," according to one of the jurors. "His eyes rolled back into his head" and he slumped over, banging his head against the judge's bench. Spectators gasped in "horror." "He's just died," someone murmured. It looked like he was having a heart attack or a stroke. Bender "drew his hands to his face and staggered backward, stunned that his questioning might be responsible for the collapse," the *Charlotte Observer* reported. One of the jurors, Nancy Summey, a Charlotte nurse, "rushed" to Nelson's side, as did Sue Patterson, another nurse who was in the courtroom working as a sketch artist. Urged forward by his other lawyer, George Davis, Bakker joined them moments later, kneeling by Nelson's side to pray. After half an hour Nelson was loaded onto a gurney and taken to a local hospital. Judge Robert Potter told the attorneys for both sides that he had apparently had a heart attack.[4]

As it turned out, Nelson was only suffering from dehydration, the result of the flu. He was given intravenous fluids and released from the hospital three hours later. But the events in the courtroom shook Bakker to his core. Bakker's lawyers called the psychiatrist who had been treating him for the past nine months, Dr. Basil Jackson, who operated a clinic with a staff of fifty at Milwaukee's St. Francis Hospital. Jackson caught the first flight to Charlotte, arriving that evening. After examining Bakker, Jackson prescribed Xanax, an anti-anxiety drug, in an "infinitesimal" dosage, because Bakker had a history of reacting badly to similar medications. By the next morning Bakker had lost touch with reality and was "actively hallucinating," in Jackson's words, hiding under Harold Bender's sofa.[5]

Bakker had had similar episodes in the past, beginning with his 1969 nervous breakdown at CBN, which lasted for more than a month. John Wesley Fletcher said that he had found Bakker curled up in a fetal position after his sexual encounter with Jessica Hahn in 1980, and Don Hardister had discovered Bakker curled up on a couch in Palm Springs in March 1987 after turning PTL over to Jerry Falwell. "He did that when he was in trouble," Hardister said. "It could last hours, or days. He used to spend days on the couch, not eating or drinking." During the March 1987 episode Hardister hid kitchen knives and stayed up with Bakker for three nights, afraid that he might try to kill himself. Employees at every level of PTL were warned not to bring Bakker bad news, an offense that could cost them their jobs. Priscilla Sherrill, who worked in the Correspondence Department answering Bakker's mail, remembered being told "not to approach Jim, we were not to tell him anything." Mary Yeary, who also worked in Correspondence, recalled that when Bakker stopped by her department, "We were not supposed to tell Mr. Bakker anything negative." In recent years his entourage had carefully controlled what Bakker heard, but now there was no one to shield him.[6]

Jackson and Bakker's lawyers tried to convince Judge Potter to send Bakker to a private hospital for evaluation, but Potter was not about to coddle Bakker. As an expert witness, Jackson was less than persuasive. One of his specialties was jury selection, and earlier he had sat in the courtroom and helped the defense select jurors most likely to side with Bakker. Under cross-examination he also admitted that he had published an article entitled "Catnip and the Alteration of Consciousness" in the *Journal of the American Medical Association*. After listening to both sides, Potter ordered that Bakker be evaluated at the psychiatric hospital in the Butner federal prison, two and a half hours northeast of Charlotte. At 11 a.m. on the morning after Nelson's collapse, five US marshals arrived at Bender's office in a Chevrolet Caprice to seize Bakker. The moment produced one of the iconic photos of the PTL story. With a grim-faced marshal on either side,

Bakker emerged from Bender's office, a suit coat covering his hands to hide the handcuffs, "his body slumped as though a powerful force had sucked something vital from him," in the words of the *Charlotte Observer*. He had gained weight over the past two years and his face was "puffy and contorted" with tears. His shoulders shook as he sobbed and his clothes and hair were disheveled. "Please don't do this to me," he kept imploring the crowd of reporters who stared back in silence. Even for Bakker's critics, it was a heart-wrenching moment. And the trial had only just begun.[7]

TWO YEARS AFTER Jerry Falwell and his associates quit PTL, the fate of the ministry and its assets remained in limbo. Heritage USA was unlike any place else, and the search for a buyer produced a range of potential offers from dreamers, schemers, ministries, and business mavericks. The court received bids from an Australian businessman who claimed that he could come up with $200 million in cash but turned out to be an imposter, a man serving time in Oregon for forgery, and a convicted con artist from Florida. Among the more serious prospective buyers were Charlotte sports entrepreneur George Shinn, majority owner of the NBA Charlotte Hornets, Peter Thomas, a Canadian real estate tycoon who wanted to turn Heritage USA into "a Disneyland-style theme park, without its current religious overtones," and Stephen Mernick, a Toronto real estate investor and ordained Orthodox rabbi with an interest in returning "Jewish young people to their religious roots." In June 1988 Jim Bakker claimed he had "strong" financial backing to buy PTL. "Just today, a major firm with multimillions of dollars is very interested in financing the whole package for us," he told reports on June 11. That September Bakker claimed that he could put together an offer worth $172 million, including $70 million in cash. But Bakker's contact with a group of "unidentified Greek financiers," Louis Pihakis, had been to federal prison at least twice for swindling investors, and Bakker's bid fizzled when he was unable to come up with a promised $3 million deposit. That November the Catawba Indians filed an objection to any sale, claiming that Heritage USA's land rightfully belonged to them. A year later Roe Messner, the Kansas contractor who built most of Heritage USA, tried to put together a $55 million bid for the park, but by March 8, 1990, Messner had filed personal and corporate bankruptcy, blaming much of his financial trouble on the $15 million he claimed PTL still owed him. By the end of 1989, none of the prospective buyers had ponied up an adequate down payment, and PTL remained unsold.[8]

In the meantime Heritage USA steadily deteriorated. By the summer of 1988 weeds choked the once meticulously maintained flowerbeds and poked up through cracks in the pavement, and the water park's wave pool no longer worked. "It's getting pretty ragged around the edges," one visitor said. Despite the peak summer season, occupancy at the Heritage Grand Hotel was down to 35 to 45 percent. By December the park was "virtually deserted." The hotel and the Main Street USA shopping mall shut down on September 25, 1989, after which the four hundred families who lived at Heritage USA were the only ones allowed into the 2,300-acre complex. "We went to East Berlin on May Day one time," said a woman who lived at Mulberry Village. "This is almost like that."[9]

For most of 1988, Jim and Tammy drifted from one scheme to the next. In January 1988, before his attempt to bid on PTL, Bakker announced that he would build a $2 billion Christian retreat center, Heritage Springs International, in the California desert. But the project had no financial backing, and by April his plan to buy 1,600 acres fifty miles south of Palm Springs had evaporated. By July 1988 the Bakkers had formed a new Charlotte-based organization, Jim and Tammy Ministries, as part of their effort to retake PTL. As that plan fizzled, Bakker moved his ministry to the three-hundred-acre estate of Amway tycoon Dexter Yager, near Pineville, North Carolina, just south of Charlotte in Mecklenburg County. With Yager's backing, Bakker set up a television studio on the grounds, and on January 2, 1989, Jim and Tammy launched a new show on a small network of cable stations. During their first broadcast, Jim blamed his troubles on Satan, particularly the devil's opposition to the Crystal Palace, Bakker's last major project at PTL. "That was the last straw for Satan," he told viewers. "When we broke ground for the largest church ever built in the history of the world, I think the devil said: This is it. I've got to smash Jim and Tammy Bakker." The devil aside, in May 1989 Mecklenburg County ordered Bakker to stop broadcasting because the studio violated a county zoning ordinance. By then Bakker had bigger problems to worry about.[10]

Jim and Tammy often decried their treatment by Hollywood, but in early 1988 they sold their story to NBC for $90,000, giving up the right to approve the script. The resulting made-for-television movie, *Fall From Grace*, starred Bernadette Peters as Tammy (Tammy wanted Sally Fields) and then-little-known Kevin Spacey as Jim. It is not a great movie. Peters and Spacey said that they wanted to avoid caricatures and portray Jim and Tammy as real people with complex personalities, and at times Peters managed to capture Tammy's zaniness and vulnerability, but otherwise the script had little depth. The movie predictably opens with the 1980 Florida encounter between Jim and Jessica Hahn, during which Hahn spills a glass of wine across a white Bible as she falls into bed. Oh, the symbolism. The real Hahn complained that the movie made her look "like a high-priced call girl," which it did, perpetuating the idea that a woman in her position had to be either a bimbo or an opportunist. Tammy is depicted in much the same way, while Jim is presented as Elmer Gantry-light, a one-dimensional figure defined by smugness, greed, and anger. In one of the movie's many simplistic dichotomies, Richard Dortch is depicted as the voice of reason, attempting to curb Jim's excessive spending and grandiosity. Much of the movie focuses on Jim and Tammy's naïve adoption of wealth and celebrity and the intimate details of their marriage, though even here Tammy complained that they got it wrong. Jim "never turned me down sexually," Tammy said, despite several scenes in the movie implying otherwise. In only one respect did the movie characters exceed the people they portrayed: Peters had a better voice than Tammy Faye. Tammy called the movie "trash, nothing but trash."[11]

Despite the movie's shortcomings, viewers tuned in. *Fall From Grace* did not air until Sunday, April 29, 1990, three years after the scandal broke and Bakker resigned from PTL, but it finished eighth in the ratings that week, ahead of *The Simpsons* and a movie about the Beach Boys. The PTL story proved resilient, a cultural touchstone that intrigued audiences long after Jim and Tammy left the air. Fittingly, the movie received Emmy nominations for best makeup and hair.[12]

THE WORLD OF PTL's former leaders was rocked again on December 5, 1988, when Jim Bakker, Richard Dortch, and David and James Taggart were indicted. The Taggart brothers were accused of evading $494,440 in income taxes and misappropriating about $1.1 million of PTL money for personal use. Bakker and Dortch were each charged with eight counts of mail fraud, fifteen counts of wire fraud (a category that includes telephones and television), and one count of conspiracy to commit mail and wire fraud. The indictments were the result of a sixteen-month grand jury investigation in which about one hundred witnesses were called, including Jessica Hahn, John Wesley Fletcher, and most of PTL's top executives from 1984 to 1987. "I assure you I am going to defend myself with every fiber of my being," Bakker told reporters following his indictment. He did anything but.[13]

A week after the indictments were handed down, Bakker had a new aging celebrity lawyer, George Davis. Born in 1907, Davis earned philosophy and law degrees from the University of California, Berkeley, and spent most of his career in San Francisco. He won his first big case in 1935 and was a long-time opponent of the death penalty. His clients included a Nazi war criminal convicted at Nuremberg and a perpetrator of the My Lai massacre in Vietnam. A "mesmerizing cross-examiner," Davis never shied away from publicity. Spectators packed courtrooms just to hear him argue, and he once played himself in a 1956 movie, *The People Against McQuade*, starring Tab Hunter and James Garner. Davis was semi-retired in Hawaii when he agreed to take Bakker's case. Unfortunately for Bakker, despite his larger-than-life image, Davis was past his prime and never really engaged in preparing for Bakker's trial.[14]

For that, Davis hired Harold Bender as his local counsel. Bender was a self-described "small-town lawyer," with an easy but effective manner. Born in 1942, he earned his law degree from the University of North Carolina, Chapel Hill, after which he worked as a federal prosecutor for several years and served as the US Attorney for the Western District of North Carolina in 1981. Following his federal service, Bender set up private practice as a criminal defense attorney in Charlotte. He was in the Atlanta airport, on his way to see a client, when Davis called and asked him to join Bakker's defense. Bender first met the Bakkers a day or two later at Dexter Yager's estate where they were living. What initially grabbed his attention were the half dozen men and women who were "catering" to Jim and Tammy's "every need," almost as if they were "servants." Even in exile the Bakkers retained an entourage that shielded them from the realities of the outside world.[15]

Davis was called in to replace Melvin Belli because some of Bakker's inner circle were upset by a plea deal that Belli and his Charlotte area associates, attorneys Jim Toms and Ryan Hovis, were pursuing with federal prosecutors. The local assistant US Attorney told Toms that he had "one ticket on the train" available for either Bakker or Dortch, whoever cooperated first. The deal that Toms was working on would have involved Bakker admitting to two counts of tax evasion in exchange for an eighteen-month "active sentence." But Bakker was "despondent over the prospect" of admitting to a felony, and at the last minute some of his supporters convinced him to switch lawyers. Davis, a rival of Belli's in San Francisco, took "one look at the winsomeness" of Jim and Tammy and "their sad story" and urged them to fight.[16]

With no prospects for reclaiming Heritage USA, Bakker's comeback in Charlotte stalled. "He's not making it here," said a former PTL employee. "The money's just not coming in the way they thought it would. I think he thought he could raise $30 million in a week, like he did at Heritage." But apart from a small group of loyalists, no one in Charlotte was willing to go "down that road again," as another former Bakker employee put it. So Jim and Tammy decided to move to Florida, where "God is going to build a new Heritage USA," Jim declared on March 28, 1989. "I already can see it. . . . God has given me a plan." By April 3 they were back on the air from Florida, and by May 9 they had relocated to a "nearly deserted" shopping mall on the outskirts of Orlando. Their new show was carried on about eight stations.[17]

A federal indictment is a serious matter, to say the least. If convicted on all counts, Bakker faced a maximum of 120 years in prison and $6 million in fines. He should have devoted all of his energies toward crafting a defense. Instead, he figuratively curled up in a fetal position and did his best to ignore what was coming. Once, shortly after the Bakkers moved into their new home in Florida, Bender visited them to convey some information about the trial "that wasn't particularly good." As Tammy unpacked dishes in the kitchen, Bender gave Jim the news. In "typical Jim fashion . . . he just sort of clammed up, he didn't respond," Bender later recalled. Finally, Jim looked up and said, "Tammy, did you hear what Harold had to say?" "Yes I did," said Tammy. The next thing Bender knew Tammy had hurled a teacup past his head that shattered against the wall. At times Bender did not even get that much of a response from Jim. "He just would not speak, would not engage in conversation at all," Bender later said.[18]

The Taggart brothers' trial for tax evasion began on July 5, 1989, a prelude to Bakker's trial, scheduled for August. If convicted, David and James each faced up to twenty-five years in prison and fines of more than $1 million. This was on top of the $1 million that US Bankruptcy Judge Rufus Reynolds had ordered David Taggart to repay the previous November and a bill for $456,208 the IRS sent to David for 1981 and 1982, years not covered in the criminal indictment, which focused on 1984 to 1987. The brothers knew they were in trouble, admitted their lawyer, Ben Cotten.[19]

For the first two weeks of the trial, the prosecution presented a parade of witnesses who described how the brothers obtained money from PTL and how they spent it. The details were stunning: jewelry, furs, expensive clothes and shoes, matching black Jaguars, first-class travel, including getaways to Europe, and of course, the Trump Tower condominium. The expenditures were like a jigsaw puzzle, as one of the prosecutors told the jury in his opening statement. Considered individually, the importance of each receipt and credit card statement was not readily apparent, but assembled together they created a picture of astonishing irresponsibility and arrogance. Despite the intricacies of financial records, the prosecution had no difficulty pointing out the extravagance of many of the brothers' purchases, particularly the jewelry: a $97,000 diamond ring, an $85,000 platinum and diamond pin, a $75,000 sapphire and diamond bracelet, a $65,000 antique platinum and sapphire bracelet. The brothers' lawyer, Ben Cotten, tried to argue that much of the money was spent for Jim and Tammy and their entourage, but the records made it clear that most of the purchases in question were for things the Taggarts bought for themselves. As if to prove the prosecution's point, they came to court "well draped in finely tailored and smartly pleated suits ... looking suave and coolly sophisticated," the *Charlotte Observer* reported.[20]

On the trial's second day, the prosecution called Henry Taggart, the brothers' father. The elder Taggart did his best to defend his sons, but for the first time many former PTL employees and others associated with the ministry learned that the brother's money did not come from a family fortune, as they had led them to believe. Their father did not own "seven Cadillac dealerships"—he only worked at one. Members of Bakker's inner circle, including his personal secretary, Shirley Fulbright, were compelled, often reluctantly, to described David Taggart's unchecked power at the highest levels of the ministry. Peter Bailey, PTL's former finance director, testified about the secrecy surrounding the third floor, where PTL's executives had their offices, and his inability to pry financial records loose from the ministry's leaders. In dealing with Taggart, Bailey simply "had to take his word" that everything was legit. In four years, the brothers' net worth increased from $171,000 to $1.7 million, almost all of it from PTL. For years the *Charlotte Observer* had been reporting on PTL's inept management, but now the public got a view behind the curtain from those directly involved. It was worse than the *Observer* had generally claimed. The Taggart trial was not about Jim Bakker, but it had the effect of further chipping away at his credibility.[21]

After two weeks of witnesses for the prosecution, everyone waited to see how the defense would respond. The brothers' lawyer called a number of witnesses who described them as generous, thoughtful, kind, and, particularly in David's case, incredibly hard working. "Only a Vietnam veteran can understand and know a Vietnam veteran.... Only the people at PTL could understand the type of dedication and sacrifice it took to perform the duties that we had," said Don Hardister, PTL's former head of security. No one gave more of his time and energy than David Taggart. But beyond that the defense had little to offer. It had no reasonable explanation as to why the brothers had spent so much PTL money on themselves and then tried to cover it up, and called no witnesses who could contradict the receipts and statements the prosecution presented. The best the defense could come up with was an assertion that PTL had agreed to pay the taxes on anything the brothers spent, in effect converting it into income, but that through sloppiness no one had gotten around to it. Jim Bakker took the Fifth Amendment, refusing to testify in support of his long-time friends.[22]

Both brothers took the stand, but their testimonies did them more harm than good. James claimed that most of the items that ended up in the Trump Tower condo, including a pair of hand-carved ivory vases costing $25,000, were purchased for the Heritage Towers Hotel. He was only storing them at the condo until the hotel was finished, though no one else at PTL seemed to know this. In the fast-paced world of PTL finances, money was money; it could be grabbed from any account to buy just about anything. As the prosecution peppered James with questions about specific transactions, he could only offer vague replies about how busy he had been and how informal PTL's accounting practices were. Really, what did it matter who signed a check or what account it went into? "I don't equate expense with style," James explained.[23]

David Taggart testified that when he returned to PTL in 1984, he struck a "deal" with Jim Bakker, giving him the same financial freedom to spend PTL money without oversight that Bakker enjoyed. Whatever he spent, including "all travel, whether it was personal or vacations or whatever, to be paid by the corporation," as Taggart put it. He repeatedly referred to the money he took from PTL as "loans," which he made to himself without anyone else's approval. Though he never bothered to document these loans, he testified that he expected them to later be converted into bonuses, which would be grossed up to cover the income taxes. Bakker had already denied striking this sort of deal with Taggart under oath. Unfortunately for the latter, none of it was in writing.[24]

It took the jury less than five hours to find the brothers guilty on all nine counts of tax evasion and conspiracy. After the verdict, the jurors who talked to the press said that the evidence against the Taggarts had been overwhelming and they were surprised that the defense did not offer a plausible explanation for their use of PTL money. By the end of the trial, none of the jurors had much of a doubt. "They was hiding something. . . . There was no way I could walk out of that jury room and not find them guilty," one juror said. "There was a snake in the firewood," concluded another juror. Maybe more than one. The outcome did not bode well for Bakker.[25]

Bakker's lawyers tried unsuccessfully to get his trial moved out of Charlotte, just as the Taggart brothers' lawyer had. Instead, both cases were heard in Charlotte before US District Judge Robert Potter, who was widely respected by the lawyers who appeared before him for his "impeccable ethics." Potter was known as one of the nation's toughest federal judges, earning him the nickname "Maximum Bob." His average prison sentence was one and a half times the national average, and he was particularly tough on drug dealers and white-collar crime. He was also a devout Roman Catholic who had little sympathy for PTL-style religious shenanigans. The Charlotte courthouse had a large grand courtroom upstairs—an "absolutely beautiful courtroom, what you would imagine a courtroom should be," as Harold Bender put it—but Potter insisted on holding the trial in his usual, much smaller courtroom downstairs. Of the twelve rows of seats, four were reserved for reporters and artists, and only twenty-eight seats were available for the public. Reporters, including those from the *New York Times*, the *Washington Post*, *USA Today*, the *Los Angeles Times*, the *Chicago Tribune*, and the *Atlanta Journal-Constitution*, had to get there before 6 a.m. if they wanted a seat on most days and as early as 4 a.m. when star witnesses testified. Potter tried his best not to allow the trial to turn into a circus, though even he could not control what happened outside the courthouse.[26]

Bakker's prospects took another turn for the worse on August 8 when Richard Dortch pleaded guilty to two counts of wire fraud and one count each of mail fraud and conspiracy to commit wire and mail fraud. As part of his plea deal, Dortch agreed to testify against Bakker. The agreement was "catastrophic" for Dortch's former boss, according to Ben Cotten, the Taggart brothers' lawyer. "Having pleaded to conspiracy—with Jim Bakker being the alleged co-conspirator—it will be very difficult for Bakker to convince the jury that at least on the charge of conspiracy he's innocent," Cotten said. Dortch, in typical Dortch fashion, later denied that he had agreed to testify against Bakker. He had only "consented" to appear in court and "give truthful answers whenever called upon," he later wrote. Three days before Bakker's trial began Judge Potter sentenced Dortch to eight years in prison and $200,000 in fines.[27]

Bakker and his lawyers were up against two federal prosecutors, Jerry Miller and Deborah Smith, who had been diligently preparing their case for two years. Miller, forty-one, had played defensive end on North Carolina State's football team and then worked as a fingerprint technician for the FBI and a cop in Washington, DC before going to law school. He had seen Bakker's show on a satellite channel before he got the case. "This has got to be a Ponzi scheme. It's just got to be a scam," he later remembered thinking at the time. Deborah Smith had been a reporter in Florida before earning her law degree from Northeastern University in Boston in 1978. She began her legal career in Alaska, eventually serving as the chief assistant US attorney for the state. Neither Miller nor Smith was inclined to talk to the press. Their case files eventually required a 5,000-square-foot warehouse full of file cabinets, and they presented more than 5,000 numbered exhibits in the trial itself. While Bakker lived in denial, the prosecution methodically built its case.[28]

Outside the courthouse a carnival atmosphere prevailed, reminiscent of the Scope's Monkey Trial in 1925. Journalists and spectators, sometimes numbering in the hundreds, milled about in the summer heat, unable to get seats in the small courtroom. Vendors sold food and Jim and Tammy novelty items. Satellite trucks and equipment tents lined the street. "I had never experienced anything like that and haven't since," Harold Bender later told me. On the first day of the trial, a fake Jim and Tammy arrived just before the real Jim Bakker in a Cadillac limousine that the Bakkers had once used. Reporters and onlookers swarmed the car until they realized it was a ruse. The fake Tammy "flashed her dazzling fake diamonds and held out an empty straw purse for money" while the fake Jim "held up two fingers in a V for victory," reported the *Charlotte Observer*. After Bakker's psychiatric breakdown, a local radio station set up a sofa on the sidewalk and challenged spectators to stick their heads under it, as they supposed Bakker had done in Bender's office. The winners got a Tammy Faye album. Every day crowds lined the entryway as Bakker arrived and left to heckle or shout encouragement. "People would shout and yell . . . 'I hope you fry,'" Bender later recalled.[29]

The weekend before the trial started, the *Charlotte Observer* published "Down the Tube," a spoof on the board game Chutes and Ladders. The caption invited readers to "Play the PTL Water Slide Game: It's Cool and Refreshing." Players moved along the board by throwing a die and answering questions. The game was illustrated with cartoon characters looking panicked as they plunged down the water slide. There are more questions dealing with Tammy Faye than with Jim, and six questions about Jessica Hahn. One of the caricatures shows Jimmy Swaggart crying profusely. The intent was clearly to make the Bakkers and PTL look ridiculous.[30]

In his opening statement, George Davis laid out the basic elements of Bakker's defense. With regard to the $1,000 lifetime partnerships, Davis argued that these were donations to the ministry, not purchases of a product. Millions of Americans gave to their churches without expecting anything tangible in return or an exact accounting of how their money was spent. The same was true of the lifetime partnerships. "Now, I think that religious-minded people probably understand what it means to make gifts or donations to a church, and this was a church," Davis said. Offering lifetime partners four days and three nights free lodging for life was PTL's way of saying thanks, but it was not a strict obligation.

Unfortunately for Bakker, most of Davis's eighty-five-minute statement was rambling and imprecise. "It was something about the devil and the righteousness of Jim. . . . It just did not have anything to do with what we were there for," as Harold Bender later recalled. At one point Davis said that everyone agreed that Bakker's sexual encounter with Jessica Hahn lasted "less than fifteen minutes." Since Hahn's representatives later drew up a proposed lawsuit for "ten million dollars," she was, in effect, charging Bakker "almost a million dollars a minute" for her services. As Davis was speaking, Bakker leaned over to Bender and said, "Harold, I thought I was hiring Perry Mason. I think I got Gomer Pyle."[31]

The prosecution's case rested on two primary arguments. The first was that Bakker was firmly in control of PTL's organization and management and that he used his authority to deliberately deceive supporters and his own board of directors by "telling untruths, half truths, and hiding the truth," as Jerry Miller put it in his opening statement. Second, the prosecution argued that Bakker's "motive was extravagant lifestyle." He committed fraud so that he could buy houses, luxury cars, and expensive clothes and travel first class. The details of the Bakkers' lifestyle provided the shock value that the ministry's financial statements would otherwise have lacked.[32]

After his opening statement, Davis contributed little to Bakker's defense other than frequent objections, almost all of which were overruled by Judge Potter. Prosecutor Deborah Smith believed that most of Davis's antics were designed to disrupt damaging testimony against Bakker. By the end of the trial Potter was threatening to have Davis removed from the courtroom. But Potter's bias extended beyond Davis and was evident on the first day. After overruling an objection by Harold Bender, Potter added, "If you have something else, you can take [it] up with the Fourth Circuit" on appeal. "If we're convicted," Bender reminded him. "If you're convicted," Potter agreed, though it already seemed like a forgone conclusion.[33]

The prosecution's first witness was David Taggart, who acknowledged that he was testifying in hopes of getting a lighter sentence. The portrait that emerged of Bakker as Taggart spoke was of a workaholic and micromanager who had access to every detail of PTL's operations and who always demanded the best. Taggart worked as closely as anyone with Bakker during the time period in question, and his testimony took two days as Smith walked him through item after item: the huge bonuses, the Florida condo, the Palm Springs houses, Rolls Royces, chartered jets, plastic surgery paid for by PTL, luxury vacation rentals, one of which came with a butler, shopping sprees in New York City, and on and on. On one occasion Bakker told Taggart that he wanted to own "ten homes," just for their investment value.[34]

David Taggart was followed by Lois Chalmers, who, under Bakker's direction, wrote most of the brochures and promotional literature related to the lifetime partnerships; Hollis Rule, a computer programmer who tracked the number of lifetime partnerships and reported the figures to management; his supervisor, Rich Ball, who also oversaw the production of the David and Goliath statues, the ones that Bakker said were worth $1,000 and which he offered to donors for $125, but which actually cost $10 to make; and Jeffrey Eggen, who was in charge of data collection and tried to warn Bakker and Dortch that the partnerships were overextended. Collectively, their testimony demonstrated that Bakker continued to aggressively promote the lifetime partnership programs even after he knew they were oversold. One of the jurors, who later made her notes available to the press, described Hollis Rule as a "very honest man, eager to set the record straight." The next day Steve Nelson collapsed on the stand, but not before he testified that Bakker and Dortch had kept two sets of numbers, a deliberate act of deception. After that, the defense never really regained its footing.[35]

The week that Bakker spent at Butner was humiliating, particularly for someone used to pampering and constant attention from subordinates. He was confined to a locked ten-by-fifteen-foot concrete cell and wore a prison jumpsuit. His meals were passed through a slot in the cell door on a plastic tray, and he was brought to the visitors' room in handcuffs and strip-searched afterward.[36]

The psychiatrist who examined Bakker at Butner, Sally Cunningham Johnson, had also examined John Hinckley Jr. after he shot President Ronald Reagan in 1981. It was her opinion that Bakker had not actually been hallucinating when he had his breakdown in Bender's office. He had never lost sight of the fact that the reporters and photographers from the previous day were actually people and not animals or bugs, and he was not psychotic. His breakdown was also not the result of taking Xanax. Rather, he had had a panic attack, which was understandable considering the stress of the situation. Johnson suggested that Bakker suffered from a "panic disorder with some mild agoraphobia" and "some dependent and passive aggressive features to his personality." Agoraphobia is "the fear of being in places or situations from which escape might be difficult (or embarrassing)." Johnson also suggested that Bakker's personality had "narcissistic features," characterized by a grandiose sense of self-importance. Otherwise, he was "pretty stable" and competent to stand trial. None of this would have surprised anyone who knew Bakker. After his evaluation he summarized his experience for Tammy as they spoke in the courthouse: "I was in a mental institution. Everybody was crazy. They said I wasn't."[37]

In the meantime, Judge Potter sentenced David and James Taggart on September 8. "I could never really understand the mental workings of the mind of the defendants in this case," Potter said, particularly the way "they went wild" in spending PTL's money. He was also convinced that they had given "untruthful testimony," which violated Potter's deep sense of integrity. Maximum Bob lived up to his reputation, giving David the maximum sentence: eighteen years and five months. James got seventeen years and nine months. The brothers were also fined $500,000 each. Potter hoped that the sentences would send a message about the seriousness of white-collar crime. "I feel like if we don't stop this sort of conduct here and now, just like any other criminal conduct, it's going to continue with other people doing the same thing," he said. It was another bad omen for Bakker.[38]

The trial resumed a week after Nelson's collapse with testimony from J'Tanya Adams, who worked in the President's Club and who confronted Bakker at the "Cadillac meeting" about overselling partnerships, and her boss, Carol Craddock, who broke down in tears as she described her department's struggles to accommodate PTL's partners. Don Hardister testified that even though no alcohol was allowed at Heritage USA, Bakker had him purchase vodka for the Presidential Suite and "some things I'm not proud of." In other interviews Hardister said that Bakker "occasionally had asked him to buy X-rated movies and sex toys." Once, after they had eaten at a restaurant in California, Tammy sent Hardister back to purchase one hundred dollars worth of cinnamon rolls, just because she liked the smell. It took three security guards to carry them back to the hotel. Every morning Hardister heated the rolls up in the room's microwave to coax out the just-baked smell. After four or five days he threw them out. None had been eaten. Cinnamon rolls had little to do with the charges against Bakker, but it was the sort of story that stuck with spectators, journalists, and presumably jurors. It made the Bakkers seem frivolous and arrogant in the face of PTL's mounting financial woes. After Hardister's testimony, a local radio station gave away cinnamon rolls as air fresheners. Tammy appeared on Phil Donahue's television show claiming that the incident never happened. "It's not true at all," she said. "I hate to say this, but Tammy's lying," Hardister said in response.[39]

Two of the prosecution's strongest witnesses were Peter Bailey and Richard Dortch. Bailey was PTL's finance director beginning in 1984. He was diffident and unassuming, but he had a sharp eye for numbers and knew exactly where the ministry's finances stood. Though he was never invited to board meetings, during his testimony Bailey read from more than seventy memos he wrote to Bakker from 1983 to 1987, which gave exact details about PTL's accounts, debts, and obligations. Bailey was a true believer who usually closed his memos with an expression of his faith in God to provide. "I know Jesus will see PTL through," he wrote at the end of an otherwise gloomy memo in June 1985. He still had "deep feelings" for PTL and was reluctant to speak ill of Bakker even now—"he put his life's blood into that place," Bailey said—but his testimony was nevertheless devastating. It demonstrated that Bakker had ample opportunity to understand PTL's precarious position had he only listened to the man in charge of paying the bills.[40]

Dortch's testimony made it clear that he and Bakker tracked PTL's finances and the number of lifetime partnerships "on a constant basis." They "frequently" discussed the likelihood that some partners would die, opening up new memberships, though they never asked anyone to check on how many members had actually passed away. They also speculated on how many partners from California, the state with the highest percentage of lifetime partners, would actually come to Heritage USA. Dortch admitted that they oversold the partnerships because "we needed the money." The most egregious example was the Victory Warriors campaign, which Bakker spontaneously launched without consulting anyone. Dortch also confirmed Steve Nelson's testimony that there had been two sets of partnership numbers, and that Bakker had told him "not to announce" the "real numbers." As with the Towers Hotel, when Bakker created the Bunkhouse partnerships and the 1,100 Club, no one attempted to set aside money to build the projects. Dortch acknowledged that he and Bakker often projected a sense of crisis to entice supporters to give more. They also knew that people would "give more to building" than for general overhead. The lifetime partnerships were "the easiest money that we could raise," Bakker told Dortch. They could "control" the number of people who came to Heritage USA by making "daily" announcements on television "when we don't want them to come." But Dortch knew that it was "impossible" to accommodate all of the partners and that it had been "shameful" to continue offering lifetime partnerships. Despite the wealth of financial information available to Bakker and Dortch, they told the board next to nothing.[41]

Over the course of nearly five hours on the stand, during which he only looked at Bakker once, Dortch made it clear that if there was fraud at PTL, Bakker knew about it. He was the ultimate micromanager. "Not a blade of grass at Heritage USA was not known to Mr. Bakker," Dortch said, and it was Bakker alone who set "the overall direction of policy and what we were going to be doing." When Bakker needed money for a house or some other large purchase, Taggart would tell Dortch, who would then arrange for a board member to make the necessary motion. One of the reasons PTL had difficulty getting loans was because Bakker and Dortch refused to disclose how much the ministry's top five executives received in compensation. Even Dortch did not know how much the Taggart brothers and Shirley Fulbright made. Bakker also encouraged Dortch and others to destroy records whenever possible, a lesson he had learned from the FCC investigation. "Someday they will be in here snooping around and I don't want them to find anything," Bakker told Dortch, referring to government officials in general.[42]

In his cross-examination, Harold Bender tried to shift the focus away from money and to portray Dortch as an opportunist and a liar. Heritage USA was primarily a religious retreat, a place of ministry that people loved. Employees were generally "happy" and had a "good" attitude. Dortch admitted that he was testifying in hopes of getting a sentence reduction, and that certain elements of his testimony contradicted his earlier sworn statements. He had previously denied under oath that he and Bakker ever discussed withholding the actual number of partnerships sold. Now he said that they had agreed to do exactly that. Dortch also changed his testimony about whose decision it was to exclude lawyers from board meetings and alter the meeting minutes. Previously he had said that these were his decisions. Now he said that Bakker had approved the changes. Regardless, Dortch was a compelling witness. He and Bakker had worked closely together. If Dortch was guilty of fraud and conspiracy, and he had already admitted he was, then it was difficult to see how Bakker was not as well.[43]

In the fourth week of the trial, the prosecution played eight hours of composite videos, mostly of Bakker selling the lifetime partnerships on the air. "I would not lie to you about anything," Bakker was shown saying. Prosecutor Deborah Smith frequently stopped the tape to allow FBI agent John Pearson to contrast what Bakker said on the air with what was really happening behind the scenes. Time and again Pearson was able to demonstrate that what Bakker had said was simply not true, particularly with regard to overselling the partnerships. Bakker was shown frequently mentioning the limit of 25,000 partners in the Grand Hotel, saying that when they reached the cutoff they would refuse to accept further gifts. "To be honest, we can't offer more memberships than we can physically handle," Bakker said in one of the segments. Yet that is exactly what he did. Harold Bender argued that the tape segments were taken out of context, a few minutes here and a few minutes there from thousands of hours of live television, but the visual impact was devastating. "I cannot see a way out for them, a way out of the indictment, a way out of the enormous sums of money that were not used properly," one of the jurors wrote in her notes after watching the videos.[44]

Both sides presented testimony from a selection of PTL's more than one hundred thousand lifetime partners. The prosecution called fifteen lifetime partners, all of whom predictably testified that they sent in their partnership payments with the expectation that they were purchasing guaranteed lodging in one of the hotels, not making a general donation to the ministry. Two were coal miners who were retired with disabilities, one with black lung disease; three lived on social security; two were ordained ministers; two were schoolteachers; and one was a divorced mother of five. None could remember Bakker setting a limit of 25,000 partnerships for the Grand, a key element in the prosecution's case. All said that they had never gotten to use their memberships or had had difficulty making reservations. Several tried to get their money back, but only one claimed to have done so before Bakker resigned, and even she could not produce correspondence to that effect. Prosecutor Deborah Smith later remembered the partners' testimony as the most poignant aspect of the case. They felt betrayed by someone they had trusted deeply and foolish and embarrassed for having been taken in.[45]

Yet the moral outrage of the lifetime partners who testified for the prosecution was limited. Those who wrote angry letters to PTL only did so after Bakker resigned, and all who had visited Heritage USA said that they enjoyed it and would have gone back if they could. What upset them about Heritage USA was that it was no longer available. In dealing with other aspects of the case the prosecution presented a flood of numbers and exhibits to buttress its case, but they had no similar data with regard to the lifetime partners, just a small collection of anecdotes.[46]

The lifetime partners called by Bakker's lawyers were more zealous. They loved Heritage USA. "My kids, they couldn't sleep for a month before we came down here. That's all they could think about," said Ricky Baumann. Louise Grimes lived about one hundred miles from the park but visited at least once a month with her family. She eventually had six lifetime partnerships in Bakker's various hotel projects and stayed at the Grand on several occasions. Her grandchildren "just loved to go to Heritage USA," Grimes said. There was so much to do, and she was grateful that she could turn the kids loose and let them explore. "I didn't have to worry about my children, my grandchildren being harmed. They went swimming and roller skating, and they just utilized the whole thing." It was about as close to heaven "as you could imagine," Grimes said. "You could feel the presence of the Lord when you rode on the grounds, there's no doubt in my mind about that." All of the partners called by the defense said more or less the same thing. They considered their partnerships a gift to the ministry, not something they purchased. None reported difficulties making reservations, so long as they called far enough in advance, and a few asked for and received a refund of their lifetime partnerships. They loved being in the studio audience for a live broadcast of the television show, attending the various workshops and seminars, volunteering as phone counselors, spending an afternoon at the water park, watching their kids play in a safe, fun-filled environment, riding the train, attending a performance of the Passion Play or a dinner theater, and just strolling the grounds meeting friendly people at every turn. They took pride in the home for unwed mothers, Kevin's House, and Fort Hope. For them, PTL was a happy place, full of music, laughter, prayer, and the sounds of people having a good time. "It was more than I hoped for," said Harriet Burns. "I felt that Mr. Bakker bent over backwards to see that his staff treated you with great courtesy and great hospitality." "It was the most wonderful place in the world," added Dorothy Taylor.[47]

The person they blamed for PTL's collapse was Jerry Falwell, "that fat man . . . from the north that wasn't Santa Claus," as one Bakker supporter put it. In their minds the story was simple: Jim Bakker built a vibrant, beautiful Christian retreat and ministry center and then Falwell took it over and ran it into the ground. "If Falwell had stayed out of our business, we'd still have a ministry going today and we'd still have been helping the poor," said Celeste Montgomery, a lifetime partner. When "Jerry Falwell came in with his people, I felt like I lived in Communist Russia," said Betty Sacco, who had worked as a research writer for Bakker and whose father was a lifetime partner. Bakker's supporters either did not know or refused to acknowledge the depth of PTL's financial woes at the time Bakker resigned.[48]

For all of their fervor, the partners who testified for Bakker did him more harm than good. "I am in total shock that the admiration has reached this level. It is not unlike a cult of people unable to stand on their own," one juror wrote in her notes. The prosecution did everything it could to encourage that perception. Celeste Montgomery, who said she had been raised in "something like an orphan's home," testified that she had been a PTL supporter since 1972 and believed Bakker to be "a real man of God." When prosecutor Miller asked her about Jim Bakker's lifestyle, she responded that "Jesus" had also "been good" to her. "Praise God, He's been good to me," she said. "Can you answer that question? Okay. If you're through with acting, can you answer the question for me?" Miller snapped. Montgomery was offended but the jurors sided with the prosecution. "It was like they were brainwashed," another juror said after the trial.[49]

Judge Potter agreed. Bakker's lawyers might have called more lifetime partners, but after four days of testimony, Potter began to lose patience. "It's getting so cumulative. How much more do you plan on having?" Potter asked Bender during a late afternoon recess. "The jury knows and everybody in the courtroom knows what they're going to say before they get up here. They love the place and it gives them the spirit of the Lord and they just think it's great," Potter said, with evident sarcasm. "It's getting ridiculous now," he added. In the end, the defense called forty-nine lifetime partners, including about a half dozen who were also former employees.[50]

Unfortunately for Bakker, the testimony of the lifetime partners was the best that his team had to offer. Bakker's lawyers called twenty-two former middle-level employees, a number of whom recalled Bakker's genuine concern for PTL's partners. The one sure way to get fired was to be rude to a partner, Bakker often told them. Several suggested that Dortch and other PTL executives had kept vital information from Bakker, but none were senior enough to have seen this up close and consequently could provide few specifics. Most said that Bakker was overworked and, if anything, underpaid. "Jim was PTL," said Bea Martin, who worked as a nanny and housekeeper for the Bakkers. "He's more than made his salary at PTL. He's not even paid what he's worth."[51]

But the heart of the prosecution's case went unchallenged. None of the defense's witnesses could dispute the financial numbers or deceptive marketing statements presented by the prosecution. It was telling that the prosecution called all of the senior PTL employees who testified. A disproportionate number of the defense's witnesses were from PTL's early days, before most of the questionable fundraising began. Peggy Johnson testified that after Bethel AME Zion Church in Charlotte burned in 1976, Bakker gave $35,000 to help the congregation rebuild, and John Stallings said that in 1978 Bakker gave $50,000 to open a school for deaf children in Bolivia, but Bakker's lawyers presented nothing similar from the 1980s.[52]

The defense also faltered in its cross-examination of some of the prosecution's witnesses, suggesting a confusing range of explanations for what had gone wrong at PTL. Maybe it was incompetent associates, maybe it was the devil. Was it possible that Bakker "didn't know about" PTL's financial problems "because no one ever told him about it?" George Davis asked former board member Aimee Cortese. "It's hard to believe," Cortese replied. Davis next asked Cortese if she believed in the devil. "Yes," she replied, though she seemed puzzled by the question. Did she believe that demons "could take possession of mortal human beings . . . and cause them to act in ways that even they can't explain?" Davis asked. "Yes," replied Cortese. "No further questions," Davis said, as if he had just settled an important point. Judge Potter "rolled his eyes heavenward" and "held his head in both hands." "Do you want to redirect on that?" Potter asked Jerry Miller when Davis had finished, as the courtroom "erupted in laughter." In his opening statement, Davis had suggested that they might not call Bakker at all. As the trial drew to a close it was clear that Bakker was his own last hope.[53]

Unlike the Taggart brothers, Bakker was used to performing in front of an audience. As George Davis guided him, Bakker recounted his call to the ministry, his commitment to live by faith, his vision for Heritage USA, and his understanding of the lifetime partnership program. He said that the Towers Hotel was only weeks away from completion, and he insisted that the number of lifetime partnerships was "never a secret." If all of the facilities he had planned at the time he resigned in 1987 had been built, Heritage USA would have had 211,062 rooms or campsites available for its approximately 150,000 lifetime partners, Bakker said. His figures included the old Heritage Inn, Heritage Grand Hotel, Heritage Grand Towers, Mayor's House, Crystal and Grand Mansions, Jerusalem Inn, 1,100 Club Mansion, Country Farm Inns, Bunkhouses, and various campsites. When Bakker resigned, only the Heritage Inn, Heritage Grand, one bunkhouse, and some of the campsites had actually been completed. No money had been set aside to build the rest.[54]

Under cross-examination by Prosecutor Deborah Smith, the alternate reality that Bakker had created began to crumble. Bakker's theology of living by faith had allowed him to ignore facts, substituting what he believed "by faith" to be true at the time. PTL took out a $10 million loan to complete the Heritage Grand Hotel, but Bakker persisted in telling his supporters that it had been constructed debt free. "I absolutely believed that," Bakker said when Smith questioned him about the discrepancy, even though it was clear that he knew about the loan. Smith challenged Bakker to explain how he could tell donors that a statue of David and Goliath that he knew cost $10 to produce was worth $1,000. "A bit of an overstatement . . . wouldn't you say, Mr. Bakker?" Smith asked. "I believed that when I said it," Bakker replied. He repeatedly denied that PTL's expenses ever exceeded its income, despite being shown statements and memos that demonstrated as much. "I had to speak faith because that's what I am, a minister of the gospel. . . . When we don't have anything, we say, by faith God is going to supply the need," Bakker said. "How about truth, Mr. Bakker?" Smith shot back. Unfortunately for Bakker, under the steely eye of a federal prosecutor the facts did count. There was no special math that could miraculously alter the books.[55]

It was also obvious that Bakker was woefully unprepared. He approached the trial in the same way he did a live broadcast of his show, with only the bare outline of a script, hoping to feel for what his audience wanted. Time and time again he was unable to give dates or specific information in response to Smith. "I don't remember" was all that he could say in answer to many of her questions. He could not recall receiving a $390,000 bonus in 1984. "So many of these figures that I am hearing, I'm hearing them for the first time in these sessions," Bakker said at one point.

When he said that he was "sure" he had told his viewers that he planned to exceed the limit of 25,000 partnerships in the Grand, Smith asked, "can you give me a date?" "No. There [are] so many tapes, I couldn't—I don't know what day I did anything," Bakker replied.[56]

After two days of deliberations, the jury found Bakker guilty on all twenty-three counts of wire and mail fraud and one count of conspiracy. The verdict was front-page news across the nation and the opening story on every network news program. After the trial, several jurors said that they connected with Bakker's description of his early years as he struggled to launch his ministry, but believed little he said after that. When he first took the stand Bakker was relaxed and made eye contact with the jury, but as his testimony continued he looked away and "we started to see the deceit in the telling of the story," as one juror put it. After the verdict, reporters were surprised that Smith and Miller were not more jubilant, having won a major case. But to Smith the whole thing was just too sad for celebration, so much religious devotion gone so wrong. "This case has a lot of tragedy in it," Miller said after the verdict.[57]

Maximum Bob once again lived up to his billing, sentencing Bakker to forty-five years in prison and a fine of $500,000. Under the sentencing guidelines at the time, Bakker would have been eligible for parole after ten years. Immediately after the verdict Judge Potter said that Bakker's followers had "the Jim Jones mentality," referring to the preacher who led a mass murder-suicide of more than nine hundred followers in Guyana in 1978. At Bakker's sentencing on October 24, 1989, Potter went further. Bakker "had no thought whatever about his victims and those of us who do have a religion are ridiculed as being saps from money-grubbing preachers or priests," Potter declared. Eventually those words would come to Bakker's aid, but for now his future looked bleak. Potter received his share of letters in response to the long sentence, including one from "Mrs. Jesus Christ" predicting the destruction of Charlotte.[58]

Potter ordered Bakker transported immediately to the federal prison at Talladega, Alabama. From there Bakker was moved to the Federal Medical Prison at Rochester, Minnesota, a medium-security prison that featured four-man cells, but no armed guards or steel bars. Bakker served the majority of his sentence at Rochester, where one of his cellmates was Lyndon LaRouche, the political activist, conspiracy theorist, and frequent presidential candidate who had also been convicted of mail fraud.[59]

Was Bakker guilty of fraud? Yes, when it came to making deceptive fundraising statements and not always using money in the way that he said he would. He exceeded the limits on lifetime partnerships that he initially set without adequately informing his contributors. He raised money for one project and then used it for another, or to pay general operating expenses. Whether Bakker deliberately conspired with Dortch to deceive donors seems less certain, given Dortch's shaky grasp of the truth. But Bakker and Dortch clearly manipulated the board of directors to their personal advantage. At times Bakker told viewers that he and Tammy had given nearly everything they had to the ministry, when in fact they were continuing to syphon off large bonuses. Much of the prosecution's case rested on arguing for a direct connection between Bakker's appeals for money and Jim and Tammy's extravagant lifestyle, which they argued was the real motive for all the fundraising.

Did the punishment fit the crime? No. Even Bakker's critics generally thought not, including Jerry Falwell and the *Charlotte Observer*. The prosecution was more successful at demonstrating fraud than at identifying the victims. "The people who were defrauded, some of them don't realize it to this day. They just won't accept it," Miller told the jury during his closing argument. But Heritage USA was not Jonestown. None of the lifetime partners lost their life savings or had to dramatically alter their lifestyle as a result of PTL's collapse. None could remember the exact limits that Bakker set on the number of partnerships. All who had visited Heritage USA enjoyed it and most absolutely loved the place. Though the Heritage Grand was full during peak periods, there were rooms available at other times during every year. Bakker's supporters were unconcerned with his salary, arguing that other television celebrities made more and did less good. They brushed aside the prosecution's persistent claim that ministers should make do with less than other celebrities, indicating their firm embrace of the prosperity gospel. Besides, as Harold Bender pointed out in his closing, the charge of fraud had little to do with how the money was spent, only how it was acquired. From 1984 to 1987, the years covered in the indictment, Bakker raised about $158 million through the lifetime partner programs. During that same period the Bakkers' total compensation was $4.7 million, or 3.0 percent of the partnership total. Almost all of the rest was plowed back into the ministry in one way or another. If general contributions are added in, Bakker raised more than $400 million for PTL. In her closing argument, Deborah Smith said that Bakker's testimony "was a remarkable performance that only an accomplished con man . . . would probably have the nerve to try." But the image of Bakker as nothing but a con artist is difficult to square with his devotion to the ministry. He worked eighteen-hour days, living and breathing PTL. If he was a con man, he was also a true believer.[60]

RICHARD DORTCH AND the Taggart brothers got off easy compared to Bakker. On the same day that Bakker arrived at Talladega in irons, the Taggart brothers arrived by taxi at the prison camp at Maxwell Air Force Base in Montgomery, Alabama, carrying one piece of luggage each. Dortch reported to prison at Elgin Air Force Base on February 2, 1990. Both Maxwell and Elgin were minimum-security prisons known as "Club Feds." A national magazine rated them as two of the top five places to do time. Inmates lived in dormitories rather than cells, and the prisons had amenities including fishing lakes, walking trails, and tennis courts. Judge Potter reduced Dortch's sentence to two and a half years in April 1990, and he was released on parole on July 9, 1991 for medical reasons. Citing their cooperation with prosecutors, in October 1990 Potter reduced David Taggart's sentence to thirteen years and five months and James Taggart's to twelve years and nine months. James was released on July 22, 1994, and David on January 15, 1995.[61]

PTL's assets remained on the market after Canadian businessman Stephen Mernick dropped his bid in September 1989. On May 10, 1990, Oral Roberts offered to pay $6 million in cash for the PTL satellite network. Three weeks later, San Diego healing and prosperity evangelist Morris Cerullo offered $52 million to buy PTL, including $7 million for the satellite network and $45 million for the 2,200-acre Heritage USA complex. Cerullo, who was raised in an Orthodox Jewish orphanage in New Jersey, was once ordained in the Assemblies of God, Bakker's former denomination, but now operated an independent international crusade ministry. He had a television show, "Victory with Morris Cerullo," that was carried on PTL's satellite network. Cerullo's vision was to reopen Heritage USA "as a family-oriented, Christian destination resort." The deal closed in December 1990, allowing PTL's trustee to distribute about $37 million to the ministry's secured creditors.[62]

In the fall of 1990, a $757 million class-action lawsuit, *Teague v. Bakker*, on behalf of about 145,000 PTL lifetime partners went to trial. The suit alleged that Bakker, David Taggart, Aimee Cortese, and the accounting firms Laventhol & Horwath and Deloitte, Haskins & Sells conspired to defraud the partners by misusing their money. The case was heard before US District Judge James McMillan. A month into the trial, Laventhol & Horwath, the nation's ninth largest accounting firm, was dropped from the case after filing for bankruptcy, largely as a result of the adverse publicity. On December 14, 1990, the jury found Bakker guilty of common-law fraud, and ordered him to pay $129.7 million in damages, but absolved the other defendants, including Deloitte, Haskins & Sells, of any liability. The result was largely symbolic, since Bakker had no assets and made eleven cents an hour cleaning toilets in prison. "The only asset Mr. Bakker has that I know of is a 45-year lease on a 5-by-7-foot room at a federal prison in Minnesota," quipped one of his lawyers. The deep pockets belonged to the accounting firms. By 2003 the lifetime partners had received $6.54 each, while their lawyers got $2.5 million.[63]

As it turned out, Cerullo did not purchase Heritage USA, which he renamed New Heritage USA, on his own. A group of Malaysian partners with offices in Vancouver and a background in hotel management held 51 percent of the new ministry. While Cerullo spent most of his time on the road holding crusades, Yet-King Loy, one of the Malaysian partners, served as the president and oversaw day-to-day operations at New Heritage. Loy and Lawrence Chai, another of the Malaysian partners, joined Cerullo and Cerullo's son David to form New Heritage's executive committee. Morris Cerullo was the face of the ministry, but it soon became clear that on the ground the Malaysians were in charge.[64]

Even before the sale was final, Cerullo's relationship with his business partners soured. In March 1991 they sued him for fraud after they discovered that he had sold $4 million worth of "gold" and "platinum" memberships in New Heritage USA, promising members half off on hotels and attractions at the park. Cerullo sold more than 14,000 memberships, channeling the money to his ministry, not New Heritage, his partners alleged. Cerullo offered to refund the partnerships, though in practice he made it difficult and cumbersome for donors to get their money back, and the rift with the Malaysians grew. In April they sued Cerullo again, alleging that he continued to divert funds raised for New Heritage directly to his ministry. "Perhaps God brought us here to help instill in him a sense of accountability," said Yet-King Loy. By January 1992 Cerullo had turned over his stake in New Heritage to the consortium run by the Malaysians, though he retained control of the satellite network, renaming it the New Inspirational Network.[65]

New Heritage USA finally reopened with "a rainbow of balloons, orchestra music, ice sculptures and international food," on June 27, 1992, after $8 million in renovations. Pat Robertson gave the dedication address, a symbol of Heritage's broader connections beyond the Bakkers.

"Christians, we believe in resurrection. . . . We believe in a second chance," Robertson declared to a smaller-than-expected crowd. Without the intensity of Jim Bakker's vision or the strong sense of community that had made Heritage USA unique, the park lost its appeal. In 1994 the Heritage Grand Hotel was taken over by Radisson hotels and renamed the Radisson Grand Resort. The next year the Malaysians spun off 1,450 acres of New Heritage's remaining 2,200 acres to create a golf course and housing development called Regent Park. The Radisson Grand began serving alcohol in 1996, but the crowds never returned. New Heritage USA closed on November 30, 1997, becoming a ghost town once again.[66]

In February 1991, an appeals court threw out Bakker's sentence, concluding that Judge Potter's statement about "money-grubbing preachers" was "too intemperate to be ignored" and amounted to punishing Bakker for offending the judge's "personal sense of religiosity." Bakker's resentencing hearing took place that August in Charlotte before US District Judge Graham Mullen. Jim and Tammy recruited Harvard law professor Alan Dershowitz to join Harold Bender in representing Bakker. Dershowitz told reporters that he took the case "because I was outraged at the sentence. It's 10 times greater than any other case like this. Judge Potter takes a one-year case and makes it a decade. He just adds zeros." He also hoped that a reduced sentence would send "a very firm message that judges can't inject their religious biases into religious opinions." At the hearing, Dershowitz argued that Bakker had started out believing that Heritage USA would succeed, but eventually "found himself with a tiger by the tail." Dershowitz had seen the tapes presented by the prosecution at the trial. "What I saw on these tapes, with all due respect, was an extremely unsophisticated man, a man who frankly talked too much, too often, often in an unrehearsed way. I did not see on those tapes a calculated, carefully planning, conniving, manipulative human being," Dershowitz said. His arguments swayed Judge Mullen, who reduced Bakker's sentence to eighteen years. But on one point Dershowitz was wrong. "He simply will not do it again," Dershowitz promised during the hearing. Bakker "would never again be involved in the kinds of activities or even close to the line of the kinds of activities that the Government has claimed led to this problem."[67]

Though the resentencing hearing was not the place to reargue Bakker's conviction, Dershowitz has since told me that he does not think that Bakker should have been found guilty of fraud in the first place. Bakker never had "the Hamlet moment, where he looked at himself in the mirror and said, 'to be or not to be a felon.'" He never sat down and said, "now

I'm going to defraud people who love me. He was not a Madoff," according to Dershowitz, referring to Bernie Madoff, the Wall Street financial advisor who bilked thousands of investors out of some $18 billion. While not specifically referring to Bakker's theology, Dershowitz concluded that he "put hope over reality." Desperation led Bakker to do things that he knew were not right, but he still "honestly believed it was going to work." Testimony about the Bakkers' lifestyle "should not have been allowed in this trial," Dershowitz said. "It's a moral argument, not a legal argument. It's an argument that should have been directed at his parishioners." At most Bakker was guilty of fraud "on the low end of the scale in terms of culpability."[68]

The reduction in Bakker's sentence was not enough to save his marriage. Most couples divorce if one of them is in prison for more than two years, and Jim and Tammy were no exception. In March 1992 Tammy announced that she was ending her marriage to Jim in a letter to supporters of her ministry in Orlando, Florida, which she had continued after Jim went to prison. Tammy blamed the pressures of ministry. "Somewhere along the way, we got our priorities mixed up," placing PTL before family, she wrote. The divorce became final on March 13, 1992. For Jim, it was "worse than losing Heritage USA." That December Judge Mullen reduced Bakker's sentence to eight years, saying that his previous sentence of eighteen years had been "unduly harsh."[69]

Tammy married Roe Messner, the contractor who built most of Heritage USA, in Palm Springs in October 1993. Jim had known about the romance between the two for about a year. Roe had divorced his wife of thirty-six years, Ruth Ann, at about the time that Jim and Tammy's divorce became final. Roe was everything that Jim was not. He was athletic, a winner of the Kansas senior amateur golf championship in 1986, and projected a relaxed confidence that put people at ease. "When I think of Roe, I think of peace. When I think of you, I think 'high energy, big, no stopping,'" Tammy wrote to Jim shortly before she remarried. After years of living on the emotional edge, the contrast was irresistible. Jim and Tammy's divorce broke the last link in the chain that held the PTL vision together, scattering to the winds the lives and careers of the thousands of people who had nurtured it.[70]

Epilogue

APOCALYPSE CHOW

JIM BAKKER'S PRISON sentence ended sooner than anyone first expected. In July 1993 he was transferred to a minimum-security work camp in Jesup, Georgia, a facility with no fences and air-conditioned dormitories. A year later, on July 1, 1994, he moved to a Salvation Army halfway house in Asheville, North Carolina, and five months after that he was freed from custody.[1]

Prison changed Bakker, or so it appeared as he neared release. Writing to friends from prison in Minnesota in September 1992, Bakker said that he now realized that wealth was not a measure of God's blessing. "If that be the case, then gambling casino owners and drug kingpins and movie stars are blessed of God," Bakker wrote. "I have asked God to forgive me and I ask all who have sat under my ministry to forgive me for preaching a gospel emphasizing earthly prosperity." "I'd say God has changed him in prison," said Franklin Graham, son of evangelist Billy Graham and a former guest on Bakker's PTL television show. Once he was out, Bakker wanted nothing to do with fundraising, Graham said. "He doesn't want to be involved in running anything. He doesn't want that headache." About three months before he was released to the halfway house, Bakker's lawyer, Jim Toms, predicted that once he reentered public life he would preach an entirely different message. "There will be a strong core of calling for justice and equity as part of the gospel," Toms said. Bakker agreed with these assessments. "I wouldn't go back now to my life as it was, if I could."[2]

Bakker renounced the prosperity gospel in his lengthy post-prison autobiography, *I Was Wrong* (1996). As he studied the Bible closely in prison, something he "rarely took time to do" at PTL, he was "crushed to think that

I led so many people astray.... How could I have taught and even written books on the subject of 'how to get rich' when Jesus spoke so clearly about the dangers of earthly riches?" He confessed that he had become "obsessed with building Heritage USA." In the process, "money [became] more important than ministry." He sometimes wore a disguise at Heritage USA so that he could move about the park without having to interact with visitors and low-level employees. But he defended the lifetime partnership fundraising program and how the money was spent. He always believed that God would pull them through, even when their bank accounts said otherwise. "To those of us who had worked in Christian ministry," financial chaos "was just normal, everyday life."[3]

Bakker went even further in denouncing the prosperity gospel in *Prosperity and the Coming Apocalypse,* published two years later in 1998. During his PTL days, "I had presented a Disneyland gospel, in which the good guys always get rich, the bad guys are defeated, and everyone lives happily ever after ... a spiritual fantasyland, where God's people are always blessed materially, physically, and of course, spiritually," Bakker wrote. "Like a car salesman, I did not want anyone to see any defects in our 'product.'" He also admitted the moral failure of his salary and lifestyle at PTL. "Were the salaries and bonuses legal? Absolutely. Were they right? Absolutely not. They allowed me to live out the errors of the prosperity gospel I was preaching." Bakker's about-face seemed as plain as it could be. "Never again do I want to be associated with anything that even hints at impropriety," he wrote.[4]

A year and a half after he was released from custody, Bakker went to trial one more time. In 1990 he had been convicted of common-law fraud and ordered to pay $129 million. At that trial the judge ruled that people who had paid for lifetime partnerships at Heritage USA had done so primarily for the free lodging, not as a financial investment. In September 1994 a federal appeals court reversed that ruling, reinstating securities fraud charges against Bakker. Before the new case went to trial in July 1996, the former PTL partners, represented by California attorney Tom Anderson, stipulated that they would no longer seek to collect the earlier $129 million judgment against Bakker. Instead, they now sought to collect $121 million from the insurance company that had covered PTL against acts of negligence, but not against fraud.[5]

The case turned on the relatively narrow question of whether the lifetime partnerships were securities or investments, not just the promise of free lodging. For the first time, Bakker engaged with his lawyers in preparing a defense. They hired Ron Heacock, a fourteen-year police veteran, to review two hundred hours of videotape from PTL telethons. Much as the prosecution had done at Bakker's criminal trial in 1989, Heacock put together excerpts from the telethons in which Bakker explained that money given for the lifetime partnerships would also be used to fund PTL as a whole. Of course, at other times Bakker left this out, but from the standpoint of whether he was selling securities the evidence was convincing. After two and a half hours of deliberation, the jury sided with Bakker and the insurance company. Bakker would later claim that the verdict vindicated him of fraud in the sale of lifetime partnerships, but the case was never about that. The plaintiffs had forfeited the $129 million fraud verdict against Bakker simply because he had no money for them to collect.[6]

Still, Bakker had a point. For the first time a jury saw him not as a coolly calculating con artist, working a carefully orchestrated scam, but as someone who was making it up as he went, who genuinely did not understand the finances of his own organization and often contradicted himself within the space of a few minutes of live television. He spoke "by faith," not as a flimflam man or an investment banker. Had the jury at Bakker's criminal trial seen the same video, it might have created enough reasonable doubt to get him off.

AS JIM BAKKER worked to rehabilitate his image, Heritage USA continued to dwindle, carved up as Charlotte's suburbs spread south. In September 2004, Rick Joyner's MorningStar Fellowship Church bought fifty-two acres of the old Heritage USA grounds from developer Earl Coulston. Coulston eventually purchased nearly one thousand acres, most of which were turned into subdivisions and shopping. The waterpark was demolished, though remnants of the old Heritage USA—the Upper Room, the Barn, one of the bunkhouses—remain scattered across the original grounds. At the time of MorningStar's purchase, Joyner, a friend of Bakker's, said that his goal was to "redeem and restore" the property. He renamed MorningStar's parcel, which included the Heritage Grand Hotel and the uncompleted Towers Hotel, "Heritage International Ministries," or "H.I.M." The ministry has refurbished the Grand, reopening it as a retreat and conference center, but the Towers remains unfinished.[7]

In the weeks after Bakker's trial ended in 1989, John Wesley Fletcher was twice arrested for drunk driving in Durham, North Carolina and then indicted for lying about his role in Bakker's encounter with Hahn to the

US grand jury that indicted Bakker. By that time, he had filed for bankruptcy and his ministry had folded. In March 1990 Fletcher underwent a psychiatric evaluation to see if he was competent to stand trial at Butner Federal Correction Institute, the same facility where Bakker had been evaluated the year before. Two months later Fletcher pleaded guilty to perjury and got off with only eight months probation. In September he received more probation and had his license revoked after pleading guilty to driving while impaired. Fletcher avoided prison, but his life continued to spiral down. He died in Durham in 1996, reportedly of AIDS.[8]

Jessica Hahn was part of what one writer called the "Bimbonic Plague" that swept across America in the late 1980s and early 1990s, and included the likes of Donna Rice, Fawn Hall, and Gennifer Flowers. The scandals pushed the nation toward "the Jim-and-Tammyfication of America—the shameless willingness of almost anyone to discuss almost anything in public." Hahn was no bimbo, but she spoke her mind and became both famous and infamous.[9]

Hahn had dreamed of becoming a preacher, with a ministry to teens, but it did not work out that way. After *Playboy*, she moved to Phoenix in 1988 to host a radio show at a pop music station. In November 1989 she emceed a pay-per-view event, "Thunder and Mud," that combined female mud wrestling with a heavy metal concert. "I wasn't always thinking straight," Hahn says of those years. In 1991 she auditioned for the television show *Married With Children*, where she met Ron Leavitt, the show's co-creator. The two fell "deeply in love," according to Hahn. "I pretty much had everything a girl could ever want." For a time she "got involved in cocaine," she later said. Hahn and Leavitt were together until February 2008, when he died of cancer. Hahn is now married to Hollywood stuntman Frank Lloyd. "She is truly happy now," Lloyd says.[10]

IT TURNED OUT that Tammy Faye had a knack for marrying men who then went to prison. Even before she married church builder Roe Messner, he was in trouble with the law. In March 1990 Messner's construction company, Commercial Builders of Kansas, filed for Chapter 11 reorganization bankruptcy, owing about $27.7 million to more than 300 creditors. Messner and his wife, Ruth Ann, had personally guaranteed some of his company's biggest loans, which meant that they stood to lose their home and other assets. Messner submitted a reorganization plan a year later, but his company was eventually forced into liquidation. He blamed many of his problems on the $15 million he never collected from PTL for work at

Heritage USA. In November 1995, after divorcing Ruth Ann and marrying Tammy Faye, Messner was convicted of hiding about $400,000 in assets during bankruptcy proceedings and sentenced to twenty-seven months in federal prison. He was released on May 21, 1999.[11]

By that time Tammy had branched out on a new career of her own. Beginning in December 1995 she co-starred with openly gay actor Jim J. Bullock in the *Jim J. and Tammy Faye Show*, a nationally syndicated daytime talk show. Bullock's big break in television was the role of goofy Monroe Ficus on the sitcom *Too Close for Comfort*, which ran for six seasons starting in 1980. Bullock grew up in a conservative Southern Baptist home in West Texas, where his father ran an oil field drilling company. He went to Oklahoma Baptist University on a music scholarship, hoping to become an "evangelist-singer." A part in a school production changed his mind, and after his sophomore year he dropped out and moved to Los Angeles. When a producer approached Bullock about doing a show with Tammy and asked if he would meet her, Bullock replied, "Of course I will meet her, I'm gay." By that time Tammy had become an icon in the gay community. She was a survivor who was ridiculed for her flamboyance. "She was odd and different and did not fit into any mold and I think gay people relate to that," Bullock recently told me. She was also one of the first public figures in the 1980s to reach out to gay men who were dying of AIDS. She not only visited them, she hugged them and told them that she loved them at a time when there was a great deal of fear and suspicion surrounding the disease. Tammy was "all about acceptance," Bullock said. "That's truly how she lived her life, whether you were gay, or you were an ex-porn star, had been in prison, whatever you did, she really did approach everyone with a great deal of love and understanding."[12]

But Tammy was reluctant to embrace gay advocacy in the way Bullock hoped she would. "Why can't it just be two people that are funny that want to do a show together? Why do we have to talk about that?" Bullock remembers Tammy asking him. He wanted to pitch their show to a "younger ... hipper audience, the college crowd, gay people, for sure, hands down." But Tammy simply wanted the show to be uplifting, wholesome and fun, the sort of program "where you don't have to chase the kids out of the room" to watch it, as she told a reporter. They taped fifty episodes before Tammy was diagnosed with colon cancer in March 1996 and left the show.[13]

Of all the PTL figures, in the end it was Tammy Faye whom people came to love. She became the "Judy Garland of televangelism" and a celebrity who needed no last name. In 1999 she was the subject of a documentary film, *The Eyes of Tammy Faye*, narrated by RuPaul Charles. For many it was a revelation to see Tammy as something other than the wife of a disgraced preacher, and her candor and resilience won her new admirers. During and after the PTL years Tammy Faye often lamented the toll that celebrity had taken on her and her family, but given every reason to walk away she still sought out the camera. It was the only life she knew. In 2004 she appeared on season two of the reality television series, *The Surreal Life*, which pulled together a group of washed-up celebrities to live together in a Los Angeles mansion. Along with Tammy, the cast that season included Erik Estrada, Traci Bingham, Vanilla Ice, Trishelle Cannatella, and porn-star Ron Jeremy.

Tammy died on July 20, 2007, after her cancer spread to her lungs and spine. When asked what she wanted to be remembered for shortly before she died, Tammy replied, "my eyelashes," and then, "my walk with the Lord." She was right about both.[14]

DESPITE HIS POST-PRISON promises to stay clear of fundraising and empire building, it was not long before Jim Bakker returned to his roots. Back when Bakker was still in prison, Don Hardister, his former chief of security, predicted that he would come back in a big way. Prison had only made Bakker "more determined," Hardister told a reporter in 1991. "I know this sounds weird, but I expect him one day to be as big as ever. The little guy's a fighter, and when he's the underdog, that's when he's at his best." Hardister, who had spent years at Bakker's side, sensed something that most of Bakker's post-prison acquaintances missed.[15]

By 1998 Bakker's focus had shifted from the prosperity gospel to the apocalypse. "In a nutshell, the new message [is] this: the era of prosperity is over; perilous times are upon us, the end of the age is at hand," Bakker wrote that year. Before Christ's return the world would face perils from floods, volcanoes, tsunamis, hurricanes, earthquakes, economic chaos, disease, and asteroids, he predicted. The new mission of the church was to prepare for these calamities. "In the days ahead, the only place you will find the help you need will be the community of believers, the church, the *refuge*," Bakker wrote in 2000. In *Time Has Come* (2012), Bakker reiterated his doomsday predictions and claimed that in 1999 he had a "night vision" of the September 11, 2001, attacks and Hurricane Katrina. He also wrote that God had revealed to him that a major earthquake would hit Japan just before the 2011 earthquake and tsunami that destroyed the Fukushima nuclear reactor. He predicted that a major earthquake would hit southern

California, and did so again after the release of the action movie *San Andreas* in 2015. "Hollywood has been fascinated by stories about the end of the world, but the judgment about to fall upon the earth is far beyond anything the most creative scriptwriter could conceive," Bakker wrote in 2012.[16]

Bakker has built a new ministry called Morningside around his prepper message, which urges followers to gather supplies in preparation for the coming apocalypse. Morningside is located about a dozen miles from Branson, Missouri, a vacation destination for seniors and a place where has-been and never-were entertainers go to make one last stand. Branson is Vegas without the gambling, booze, and prostitutes, where stars live on even after they are dead. Located on seven hundred acres outside the tiny town of Blue Eye, Missouri, on the border with Arkansas, Morningside is a miniature version of Heritage USA. Its façade looks remarkably similar to the partner center of the Heritage Grand Hotel complex, and it has an indoor Grace Street that closely resembles the old Main Street at Heritage USA. Grace Street has condominiums overlooking the current television set, a restaurant, chapel, beauty salon and spa, general store, and cinema.

In exchanging the prosperity gospel for doomsday apocalypticism, Bakker has found a way to turn a profit by selling freeze-dried survival food and gear, including water filters, solar generators, and camping supplies. It is brilliant, in a way. Just as the abundant life gospel fit the 1980s, a survivalist message resonates in post-9/11 America. Once again, Bakker has proven himself adept at detecting shifting patterns in the cultural currents. The ministry has a large warehouse to stock and ship the items Bakker and his guests sell on the show. My family and I have used a lot of this kind of food and gear canoeing and backpacking in the backcountry. The equipment Bakker sells might be fine for a weekend campout at a local park, but most of it would not hold up for long in a real emergency, and much of it is overpriced. It is obviously aimed at people who want to be prepared for disaster but do not know what they are buying.

I have been to Morningside on several occasions to watch a taping of Bakker's show and talk with the staff, who are always gracious and kind. In May 2015, I was there with my former graduate student, Jonathan Root. Bakker and his guests spent the first hour talking biblical prophecy, including predicting a worldwide economic collapse in the fall of 2015, the rapture a few months later, and Christ's second coming by 2019. They spent the second hour of the show selling survival food. Viewers could purchase a forty days and forty nights bucket of freeze-dried food for $140. In a pinch, the bucket could be used for a toilet, a necessity after the grid goes down and you are left hiding out in your basement. As part of the show, Bakker and his guests sampled the potato soup and pasta with marinara sauce included in the bucket, and samples were passed out to the audience. As Bakker and his guests oohed and aahed over how tasty the food was and assured viewers that the day was coming when it would be worth its weight in gold, Bakker blurted out, "And it's low in cholesterol!" Perfect. One less thing to worry about as civilization crumbles.

Improbably, Bakker's comeback seems to be working. When I first started visiting Morningside I did not think that he had much of a chance of recapturing his relevance. But the ministry recently opened a series of new projects, including the Big Red Barn and Lori's House. The barn is six stories tall and has a space for horses, essential once gasoline is no longer available. It also currently stores one million servings of survival food, with plans to add "a few million more," according to Bakker. Near the barn are a greenhouse and the beginnings of a farm. Lori's House, named after his new wife, Lori Bakker, is a larger version of the home for unwed mothers at Heritage USA. It provides free housing, food, and other services to pregnant women in need. The live band for Bakker's new television show is bigger and better than it was a year or so ago. Bakker once again appears in nicely tailored suits, and he and his family vacation on St. Kitts. He sounds more confident than he has in years. "You ain't seen nothing yet," he said during a recent episode recorded at the barn.

Bakker now broadcasts his one-hour program, the *Jim Bakker Show*, co-hosted with Lori, whom he married in 1998, on satellite and online. "The PTL Club was lost but now it's found," Bakker recently told his audience. He has also reclaimed the name PTL Television Network and put together a lineup of shows under the network's umbrella. Most episodes of the *Jim Bakker Show* deal with biblical prophecy and looming disaster, and Bakker has a steady stream of guests who have written books on the subject. Some are more mainstream than others. Former Governor of Arkansas Mike Huckabee appeared on the show in 2015 to launch his new book, *God, Guns, Grits and Gravy*. Guests in 2016 have included James Rickards, author of *The New Case for Gold* (2016) and two previous *New York Times* bestsellers, *The Death of Money* (2014) and *Currency Wars* (2011), and Peter Vincent Pry, who served on the congressional electromagnetic pulse (EMP) commission, the House Armed Services Committee, and with the CIA. Pry has written extensively on the danger of an EMP attack.[17]

Guests on Bakker's show in 2016 also included Tom Horn and Chris Putnam, Jonathan Cahn, Joel Richardson, William Forstchen, and Steve Quayle. Horn and Putnam's recent books include *Exo-Vaticana: Petrus Romanus, Project L.U.C.I.F.E.R., and the Vatican's Astonishing Plan for the Arrival of an Alien Savior* and *The Final Roman Emperor, The Islamic Antichrist and the Vatican's Last Crusade.* In these and other books, Horn and Putnam claim that the Vatican is preparing to welcome extraterrestrials to earth and controls several portals by which "immortal" beings can move between dimensions, and that the current pope is the last pope before Christ's return. Cahn is the author of the *New York Times* best-seller *The Harbinger: The Ancient Mystery That Holds the Secret of America's Future,* a post-9/11 themed novel. Richardson's *The Islamic Antichrist,* a book about Islamic eschatology, is also a *New York Times* best-seller. Forstchen's breakout best-selling novel, *One Second After,* describes the aftermath of an EMP attack. Quayle is a talk-radio host who has appeared on *Survive2thrive* and *Coast to Coast* and authored books on ancient giants, aliens, and a secret Nazi base beneath the ice in Antarctica. The strength of book sales by these and other guests demonstrate that they are tapping into a large subculture, as was the case with PTL in its heyday. During the show, Bakker intersperses interview segments with extended advertisements for the products he sells, often giving the show an infomercial feel. He has also revived the concept of "partners" in a new PTL Club, for a pledge of fifty dollars a month, and recreated a "President's Club" for those who give one hundred dollars a month.[18]

Bakker has always had a talent for identifying cultural trends and crafting a message to fit. Had his role at PTL been limited to this, the ministry might have fulfilled more of its promise. But religious groups have a way of elevating prophets beyond their abilities, a tendency made worse by our modern fascination with celebrity. Don Hardister remembers standing with Bakker next to his car one day before the scandal, looking out over Heritage USA. "Who built this?" Bakker asked, as if he could not believe what he had done. It was as though he had built it just to prove that he could, to rid himself of the sense of inadequacy, doubt, and shame that had haunted him since his youth. Success bred arrogance. Hardister would later feel guilty for buying into the idea that "we were so important [that] God would not allow this to fail, no matter what we did." He should have done more to rein Bakker in, to make it less about Jim and more about others, he says. "I pretended a lot. I let a lot of things go that I shouldn't have. . . . I regret that deeply."[19]

Millions of Americans think about and organize their lives primarily around their religious convictions. But how to connect those beliefs to the world they live in is not always obvious. The intersection between faith and culture is constantly shifting, involving every aspect of the human experience. Almost by definition, ministries like PTL exist in the in-between spaces where belief and popular culture intersect, pulled and shaped by the best and worst of both sides. The bigger the potential for success, the greater the risk of failure.

Nowhere was this more apparent than at PTL. Nearly all of the former PTLers I talked to told me that the ministry started with pure motives but was corrupted by its own success. In its early days PTL became a virtual family for millions of viewers, helping them to connect to a larger world and cope with life's challenges. The same was true for the ministry's employees and volunteers, many of whom remember their time at PTL as the best years of their lives. But along the way the money and celebrity that had been tools to reach the lost became goals in their own right. The ministry's leadership was not sufficiently grounded in its own religious convictions to resist the darker temptations it rubbed up against.

Regardless of PTL's fall, the connection between religious innovation and popular culture remains a powerful force in American life. PTL will not be the last of its kind.

Notes

The federal criminal trials of Jim Bakker and David and James Taggart, conducted in the US District Court, Western District of North Carolina, yielded a wealth of information on PTL in the 1980s. They are referred to in the notes as U.S. v. Bakker and U.S. v. Taggart and Taggart. The Flower Pentecostal Heritage Center, located at the Assemblies of God headquarters in Springfield, Missouri, holds most of the existing videotape from PTL's television shows, as well as extensive print material. The center is referred to in the notes as FPHC. Jim Bakker's flagship television show went by several names in the 1970s and 1980s, including the *PTL Club, Jim Bakker*, and *Jim and Tammy*. Except where noted, access to PTL videos was generously provided by the Flower Center. The most consistent and extensive reporting on PTL during the 1970s and 1980s was done by the *Charlotte Observer*, designated as *CO* in the notes.

INTRODUCTION

1. Many of the topics discussed in this introduction are developed more fully in the subsequent chapters. See the index for specific references.
2. Jim Bakker with Ken Abraham, *I Was Wrong* (Nashville: Thomas Nelson, 1996), 442–450.
3. Kathleen McClain, "Falwell Deluged With Questions, Calls of Support," *CO*, Mar. 21, 1987; Frye Gaillard, "Judge May Have Given Falwell a Welcome Cue to Exit," *CO*, Oct. 9, 1987.
4. Harry S. Stout, *The Divine Dramatist: George Whitefield and the Rise of Modern Evangelicalism* (Grand Rapids, MI: William B. Eerdmans, 1991), xiii–xxiv; Thomas Kidd, *George Whitefield: America's Spiritual Founding Father* (New Haven, CT: Yale University Press, 2014).
5. Josh McMullen, *Under the Big Top: Big Tent Revivalism and American Culture, 1885–1925* (New York: Oxford University Press, 2015); Jennifer Wiard, "At Home in Babylon: Billy Sunday's Revival Team and Evangelicalism in Secular

America" (PhD diss., University of Missouri, 2016); Matthew Avery Sutton, *Aimee Semple McPherson and the Resurrection of Christian America* (Cambridge, MA: Harvard University Press, 2007), 78–80; Edith L. Blumhofer, *Aimee Semple McPherson: Everybody's Sister* (Grand Rapids, MI: William B. Eerdmans, 1993), 266–268.

6. Michael Freeman, *ESPN: The Uncensored History* (Dallas: Taylor Publishing, 2000), 4–5.
7. U.S. v. Bakker, vol. 9, 1491.
8. Jim Bakker with Ken Abraham, *Prosperity and the Coming Apocalypse* (Nashville: Thomas Nelson, 1998), 22; Jim Bakker, *Survival: Unite To Live* (Harrison, AR: New Leaf Press, 1980), 103; Jim Bakker with Robert Paul Lamb, *The Big Three Mountain-Movers* (Plainfield, NJ: Logos International, 1977), 115.
9. Jim Bakker, *Eight Keys to Success*, ed. Jeff Park (Charlotte: PTL Television Network, 1980), 30; Bakker, *Prosperity and the Coming Apocalypse*, 4; Jonathan Root, "Total Salvation: The Gospel of the Abundant Life and American Culture, 1947–1989" (PhD diss., University of Missouri, 2015); Kate Bowler, *Blessed: A History of the American Prosperity Gospel* (New York: Oxford University Press, 2013); David Edwin Harrell Jr., *All Things Are Possible: The Healing and Charismatic Revivals in Modern America* (Bloomington: Indiana University Press, 1975).

CHAPTER 1

1. Jim Bakker with Paul Lamb, *Move That Mountain* (Plainfield, NJ: Logos International, 1976), 1–5; Charles E. Shepard, *Forgiven: The Rise and Fall of Jim Bakker and the PTL Ministry* (New York: Atlantic Monthly Press, 1989), 1–13; U.S. v. Bakker, vol. 9, 1599; "Father of Famous Bakker Dies at 91," *Muskegon Chronicle*, Apr. 23, 1998; "Obituaries: Bakker, Raleigh," *Muskegon Chronicle*, May 26, 1998; Mary Flanery, personal email, Dec. 15, 2012; Lizabeth Cohen, *A Consumer's Republic: The Politics of Mass Consumption in Postwar America* (New York: Alfred A. Knopf, 2003); David M. Potter, *People of Plenty: Economic Abundance and the American Character* (Chicago: University of Chicago Press, 1954). The world economy grew at a faster rate in the second half of the twentieth century than at any other time. See Angus Maddison, *The World Economy* (Paris: OECD, 2006), 1:125.
2. Bakker, *I Was Wrong*, 135, 156, 443.
3. Interview with George Bakker, Nov. 18, 2016.
4. Bakker, *Move That Mountain*, 2; interview with Sandy Tyers McMillan, Nov. 18, 2016; interview with George Bakker, Nov. 18, 2016.
5. Bakker, *I Was Wrong*, 442–450.
6. Bakker, *I Was Wrong*, xiv; Roberto Maniglio, "The Impact of Child Sexual Abuse on Health: A Systematic Review of Reviews," *Clinical Psychology Review* 29 (2009): 647–657; Judith A. Cohen, Anthony P. Mannarino, and Esther Deblinger, *Treating Trauma and Traumatic Grief in Children and Adolescents* (New York: Guilford Press,

2006), 3–19; "Child Sexual Abuse in the U.S.," accessed May 30, 2016, http://www.naasca.org/StopTheSilence/PDFs-DOCs/FactSheets/CSA_SurvivorForce-fact-sheet-long.pdf; Elizabeth Oddone Paolucci and Claudio Violato, "A Meta-Analysis of the Published Research on the Effects of Child Sexual Abuse," *Journal of Psychology* 135, no. 1 (2001): 17–36; Emily M. Douglas and David Finkelhor, "Childhood Sexual Abuse Fact Sheet," accessed May 30, 2016, http://www.unh.edu/ccrc/factsheet/pdf/CSA-FS20.pdf; Howard N. Snyder, "Sexual Assault of Young Children as Reported to Law Enforcement: Victim, Incident, and Offender Characteristics," US Department of Justice, July 2000, accessed May 30, 2016, http://www.bjs.gov/content/pub/pdf/saycrle.pdf; Rebecca M. Bolen and Maria Scannapieco, "Prevalence of Child Sexual Abuse: A Corrective Metanalysis," *Social Service Review* 73, no. 3 (Sept. 1999): 281–313; Robin Malinosky-Rummell and David J. Hansen, "Long-Term Consequences of Childhood Physical Abuse," *Psychological Bulletin* 114, no. 1 (1993): 68–79; Kristin Hawley, personal email, Feb. 12, 2013.

7. Frye Gaillard, "PTL Club: A Wealth of Controversy and Faith," *CO*, July 9, 1978.
8. "Keyholers Set Up 15 Variety Acts," *Muskegon Chronicle*, Dec. 19, 1956. Kinnucan was apparently also known as Marlene Way. See Shepard, *Forgiven*, 17.
9. "Former 'Miss' To Be on MHS Show," *Muskegon Chronicle*, Dec. 6, 1957; Bakker, *Move That Mountain*, 4–7; Shepard, *Forgiven*, 16–18.
10. Interview with George Bakker, Nov. 18, 2016; interview with Sarah Wickerink Russell, Nov. 16, 2016.
11. Susan Harrison, "High School Memories: Shy and Failing or Promoter?," *Muskegon Chronicle*, Apr. 20, 1986.
12. Bakker, *Move That Mountain*, 8–16.
13. Shepard, *Forgiven*, 23.
14. U.S. v. Bakker, vol. 9, 1599–1600; "North Central History," accessed Nov. 12, 2012, http://www.northcentral.edu/academics/general/north-central-history.
15. Gastón Espinosa, *William J. Seymour and the Origins of Global Pentecostalism: A Biography and Documentary History* (Durham, NC: Duke University Press, 2014), 1–37; Randall J. Stephens, *The Fire Spreads: Holiness and Pentecostalism in the American South* (Cambridge, MA: Harvard University Press, 2008), 15–185; Edith L. Blumhofer, *The Assemblies of God: A Chapter in the Story of American Pentecostalism, Volume 1—to 1941* (Springfield, MO: Gospel Publishing House, 1989), 17–64; Edith L. Blumhofer, *Restoring the Faith: The Assemblies of God, Pentecostalism, and American Culture* (Urbana: University of Illinois Press, 1993), 11–42; Edith L. Blumhofer, "Restoration as Revival: Early American Pentecostalism," in *Modern Christian Revivals*, ed. Edith L. Blumhofer and Randall Balmer (Urbana: University of Illinois Press, 1993), 143–160; Donald Dayton, *Theological Roots of Pentecostalism* (Grand Rapids, MI: Francis Asbury Press, 1987), 35–113; Augustus Cerillo, "The Beginnings of American Pentecostalism: A Historiographical Overview," in *Pentecostal Currents in American Protestantism*, ed. Edith Blumhofer, Russell P. Spittler, and Grant A. Wacker (Urbana: University

of Illinois Press, 1999), 229–259; David Bundy, "Keswick and the Experience of Evangelical Piety," in Blumhofer and Balmer, *Modern Christian Revivals*, 118–144; W. J. Hollenweger, *The Pentecostals: The Charismatic Movement in the Churches* (Minneapolis: Augsburg Publishing House, 1972), 3–46. On the connections between Methodism, the Holiness movement, and Pentecostalism, see the fine collection of essays in Henry H. Knight, ed., *From Aldersgate to Azusa Street: Wesleyan, Holiness, and Pentecostal Visions of the New Creation* (Eugene, OR: Pickwick, 2010).

16. Acts 1:8 and 2:2–4.
17. James R. Goff Jr., *Fields White unto Harvest: Charles F. Parham and the Missionary Origins of Pentecostalism* (Fayetteville: University of Arkansas Press, 1988), 15–16, 23–86; Leslie D. Callahan, "Charles Parham: Progenitor of Pentecostalism," in Knight, *From Aldersgate to Azusa Street*, 210–217.
18. Espinosa, *Seymour*, 49–51; Steven J. Land, "William J. Seymour: The Father of the Holiness-Pentecostal Movement," in Knight, *From Aldersgate to Azusa Street*, 218–226; Goff, *Fields White unto Harvest*, 106–111; Cecil M. Robeck Jr., *The Azusa Street Mission and Revival: The Birth of the Global Pentecostal Movement* (Nashville: Thomas Nelson, 2006), 4–5, 17–52.
19. Espinosa, *Seymour*, 53–58; Robeck, *Azusa Street*, 53–76.
20. "Weird Babel of Tongues," *Los Angeles Daily Times*, Apr. 18, 1906.
21. Grant Wacker, *Heaven Below: Early Pentecostals and American Culture* (Cambridge: University Press, 2001), 197–216; Robert Mapes Anderson, *Vision of the Disinherited: The Making of American Pentecostalism* (New York: Oxford University Press, 1979).
22. *Like As of Fire: (A Reprint of the Old Azusa Street Papers)*, collected by Fred T. Corum (Wilmington, MA: n.p., 1981); Frank Bartleman, *Azusa Street* (Plainfield, NJ: Logos, 1980), 153; Robeck, *Azusa Street*, 6–7; Espinosa, *Seymour*, 72–95. Bartleman says he burned all of the letters he received to keep himself humble.
23. Blumhofer, *Assemblies of God*, 2:137; Stephens, *Fire Spreads*, 193–265; Grant A. Wacker, "Travail of a Broken Family: Evangelical Responses to the Emergence of Pentecostalism in America, 1906–16," in Blumhofer, Spittler, and Wacker, *Pentecostal Currents*, 23–49.
24. *The 1961 Archive*, North Central Bible College, 130; "New Staff Appointed," *Northern Light*, Oct. 19, 1960; "Play Cast Chosen," *Northern Light*, Nov. 4, 1960.
25. Jim Bakker, *Move That Mountain*, 18–19; Shepard, *Forgiven*, 26–27.
26. Interview with Sarah Wickerink Russell, Nov. 16, 2016; interview with George Bakker, Nov. 18, 2016.
27. *The 1961 Archive*, North Central Bible College; Bakker, *Move That Mountain*, 18–19; Shepard, *Forgiven*, 26–27.
28. Jim Bruggeman, personal email, Mar. 17 and 18, 2013.
29. Jim Bruggeman, personal email, Mar. 17, 2013.
30. Jim Bruggeman, personal email, Mar. 17 and 18, 2013.

31. Tammy Bakker with Cliff Dudley, *I Gotta Be Me* (Harrison, AR: New Leaf Press, 1978), 13–41; interview with Nancy Helland, Oct. 3, 2011; *Jim Bakker*, Dec. 16, 1983. This was a "best of" show that featured a rebroadcast of Tammy's fortieth birthday party in 1982. Aunt Gin was one of the guests on the show.
32. Bakker, *Move That Mountain*, 19–22; Bakker, *I Gotta Be Me*, 43–44.
33. Bakker, *I Gotta Be Me*, 45–46; interview with Dorothy Bakker, Dec. 14, 2016.
34. *PTL Club*, Jan. 11, 1977; Bakker, *I Was Wrong*, 207.
35. Bakker, *Move That Mountain*, 33–34.
36. Bakker, *Move That Mountain*, 23–35; Bakker, *I Gotta Be Me*, 43–55.

CHAPTER 2

1. Bakker, *I Gotta Be Me*, 56–58, 60–61; Bakker, *Move That Mountain*, 37–47; Cynthia Robins, "Tammy Talks About Her Fall From Grace," *San Francisco Examiner*, July 19, 1987.
2. David Edwin Harrell, *Pat Robertson: A Life and* Legacy (Grand Rapids, MI: William B. Eerdmans, 2010), 1–31; interview with Bill Garthwaite, Aug. 29, 2012; "Generosity Called God's Work," *Virginian Pilot*, Nov. 17, 1965; undated CBN press release, Regent University Archives.
3. Interview with Bill Garthwaite, Aug. 29, 2012.
4. *Jim Bakker*, Dec. 16, 1983; Shepard, *Forgiven*, 37–38; Harrell, *Pat Robertson*, 31–32; Bakker, *I Gotta Be Me*, 61–65; Bakker, *Move That Mountain*, 65–67; interview with Roger and Linda Wilsson, Jan. 4–5, 2011; "Whimsey Parade by Wilkie," undated newspaper clipping, Regent University Archives.
5. "Generosity Called God's Work"; "Channel 27 Expanding," *Ledger-Star*, Sept. 30, 1967; Paul Williams, "Home Viewers Have Best Laugh as Critics Cringe," undated newspaper clipping, Regent University Archives; "WYAH Names 6," undated newspaper clipping, Regent University Archives; undated CBN press releases, Regent University Archives; Bakker, *I Gotta Be Me*, 60–63.
6. Bakker, *Move That Mountain*, 57–58; Harrell, *Pat Robertson*, 31–32.
7. Bakker, *Move That Mountain*, 70; Harrell, *Pat Robertson*, 32–33; interview with Roger and Linda Wilson, Jan. 4–5, 2011; U.S. v. Bakker, vol. 9, 1602–1604.
8. Bakker, *I Gotta Be Me*, 85.
9. *PTL Club*, Dec. 26, 1977, reel 2; interview with Scott and Nedra Ross, June 16, 2011; "Scott Free, Chapter 1&2," accessed Nov. 1, 2012, https://www.cbn.com/700club/scottross/scott_who/scottfree1_2.aspx.
10. Interview with Scott and Nedra Ross, June 16, 2011.
11. Janet Hastie, "CBN Adds Variety to Fall Schedule," *Ledger-Star*, Sept. 1, 1973; Bakker, *Move That Mountain*, 105–108; Bakker, *I Gotta Be Me*, 70, 83–90.
12. "Tidewater Network Expands to Atlanta," undated CBN press release, Regent University Archives; Bakker, *Move That Mountain*, 109–118; Bakker, *I Gotta Be Me*,

91–94; Jane Lee Lisenby, "PTL: Kitchen Table to 'Modern Miracle,'" *Charlotte News*, Sept. 1, 1977; U.S. v. Bakker, vol. 9, 1605.

13. Darren Dochuk, *From Bible Belt to Sunbelt: Plain-Folk Religion, Grassroot's Politics, and the Rise of Evangelical Conservatism* (New York: W. W. Norton, 2011), xv–xviii.
14. Interview with Dale Hill, June 7, 2012.
15. Interview with Sam Orender, May 10, 2010.
16. Interview with Roger Flessing, July 20, 2010.
17. Interview with Del Holford, June 7, 2012.
18. Bakker, *Move That Mountain*, 122–123; Bakker, *I Gotta Be Me*, 94; Shepard, *Forgiven*, 53.
19. Bakker, *Move That Mountain*, 123.
20. Interview with Jim Moss, Aug. 28, 2012; Bakker, *Move That Mountain*, 122; Shepard, *Forgiven*, 48–49; Demos Shakarian, with John and Elizabeth Sherrill, *The Happiest People on Earth* (Old Tappan, NJ: Chosen Books, 1975), 117–136; Matthew William Tallman, *Demos Shakarian: The Life, Legacy, and Vision of a Full Gospel Business Man* (Lexington, KY: Emeth Press, 2010), 137–159.
21. Bakker, *I Gotta Be Me*, 94–95.
22. *PTL Club*, July 5, 1976, reel 2; Shepard, *Forgiven*, 54–55; interview with Roger Flessing, July 20, 2010; interview with Dale Hill, June 7, 2012; interview with Sam Orender, May 10, 2010.
23. Bakker, *Move That Mountain*, 125–128; Bakker, *I Gotta Be Me*, 95–98, 102.
24. Mike Cloer, "Before Bakker: 5 People Started the PTL Dream in 1973," *CO*, Nov. 16, 1978.
25. Shepard, *Forgiven*, 57–59; interview with Jim Moss, Aug. 28, 2012.
26. Bakker, *Move That Mountain*, 135–137; Shepard, *Forgiven*, 60; "PTL Television Network 'Dream' Becomes Reality in Brief 3-Year Period," *Charlotte News*, July 3, 1976; interviews with Jim Moss, Aug. 28, 2012, Jan. 14, 2014; interview with Dale Hill, June 7, 2012; interview with Sam Orender, May 10, 2010; Bakker, *I Gotta Be Me*, 100.
27. Interview with Dale Hill, June 7, 2012; interview with Sam Orender, May 10, 2010; interview with Del Holford, June 7, 2012.
28. Shepard, *Forgiven*, 62–63.
29. Bakker, *Move That Mountain*, 151–152; Jane Lee Lisenby, "PTL: Kitchen Table to 'Modern Miracle,'" *Charlotte News*, Sept. 1, 1977. Tammy corroborates Jim's story, identifying the Wheelers by the fictitious names Stu and Carol. Bakker, *I Gotta Be Me*, 103–104.
30. Shepard, *Forgiven*, 64.
31. Interview with Roger Flessing, July 20, 2010.

CHAPTER 3

1. Interview with Jim Moss, Aug. 28, 2012; Jim Moss testimony, FCC transcript, "WJAN, Canton Ohio," Docket No. 79-64, Washington, DC, July 26, 1979, vol. 7,

766, 791; interview with Del Holford, June 7, 2012; "PTL Broadcast Affiliates," *Action*, Nov. 1979, 14; *PTL* Club, July 5, 1976, reel 2; Shepard, *Forgiven*, 67–68.

2. "PTL Reaches TV Sales Manager," *Action*, Vol. 1, Issue 1, 12; Bob Wisehart, " 'PTL Club'—Another Kind of Talk Show," *Charlotte News*, May 13, 1975.
3. "PTL's Telethon Teams," *Action*, Vol. 1, Issue 1, 6.
4. Interview with Del Holford, June 7, 2012; Del Holford, personal email, Apr. 19, 2013; Bakker, *Move That Mountain*, 147–148.
5. Interview with Lee and Nancy Nagelhout, July 12, 2011.
6. Bakker, *I Gotta Be Me*, 76–77; interview with Roger and Linda Wilson, Jan. 4–5, 2011.
7. Interview with Roger and Linda Wilson, Jan. 4–5, 2011.
8. James L. Baughman, *The Republic of Mass Culture: Journalism, Filmmaking and Broadcasting in America since 1941* (Baltimore: The Johns Hopkins University Press, 2006), 143–144.
9. Brian Lockman and Don Sarvey, *Pioneers of Cable Television: The Pennsylvania Founders of an Industry* (Jefferson, NC: McFarland, 2005), 1–8; Megan Mullen, *The Rise of Cable Programming in the United States* (Austin: University of Texas Press, 2003), 32–38; Timothy Hollins, *Beyond Broadcasting: Into the Cable Age* (London: BFI Publishing, 1984), 114–117; Brian Winston, *Media Technology and Society: A History: From the Telegraph to the Internet* (London: Routledge, 1998), 305–311.
10. Ralph Lee Smith, *The Wired Nation: Cable TV: The Electronic Communications Highway* (New York: Harper & Row, 1972), 1–2; Mullen, *Rise of Cable Programming*, 73.
11. Arthur C. Clarke, "Extra-Terrestrial Relays: Can Rocket Stations Give World-Wide Radio Coverage?," *Wireless World*, October 1945, reprinted in J. R. Pierce, *The Beginnings of Satellite Communications* (San Francisco: San Francisco Press, 1968), 37–43; Patrick R. Parsons, *Blue Skies: A History of Cable Television* (Philadelphia: Temple University Press, 2008), 321.
12. Parsons, *Blue Skies*, 321–322; Winston, *Media Technology and Society*, 280–287.
13. Winston, *Media Technology and Society*, 290–294.
14. Parsons, *Blue Skies*, 322–331.
15. Parsons, *Blue Skies*, 331–333, 356–357; Hollins, *Beyond Broadcasting*, 123.
16. Mair, *Inside HBO: The Billion Dollar War between HBO, Hollywood, and the Home Video Revolution* (New York: Dodd, Mead & Company, 1988), 3–33; Hollins, *Beyond Broadcasting*, 122; Parsons, *Blue Skies*, 335–340.
17. Mair, *Inside HBO*, 27–28; Parsons, *Blue Skies*, 378–383; Sidney Pike, *We Changed the World: Memoirs of a CNN Global Satellite Pioneer* (St. Paul, MN: Paragon House, 2005), 30–67.
18. Interview with Roger Flessing, June 20, 2013; Parsons, *Blue Skies*, 380; Pike, *We Changed the World*, 40. CBN began satellite distribution in April 1977.
19. Del Holford, personal email, June 24, 2013; interview with Jerry Foreman, June 24, 2013.

20. Bakker newsletters, May 1977, Jan. 1978, May 1978; interview with Allen McCarty, May 16, 2013; interview with Jerry Foreman, June 24, 2013; interview with Roger and Linda Wilson, Jan. 4–5, 2011; "Broadcasting the Gospel Until Jesus Comes," *Action*, May 1978, 4. At the end of April 1977, Bakker told his television audience that PTL would begin satellite broadcasting "within 90 days," a ridiculously optimistic timeline. *PTL Club*, Apr. 27, 1977.
21. Parsons, *Blue Skies*, 382; Pike, *We Changed the World*, 64.
22. Interviews with Roger Flessing, July 20, 2010 and June 20, 2013; Jim Bakker, "Editorial," *Action*, Feb. 1978, 2.
23. Frye Gaillard, "PTL Club: A Wealth of Controversy and Faith," *CO*, July 9, 1978.
24. *PTL Club*, Mar. 26, 1976, July 5, 1977; *Heritage Village* (Winston-Salem, NC: Hunter Publishing Company, 1977), 10–11; Moss testimony, FCC transcript, July 26, 1979, vol. 7, 778; Shepard, *Forgiven*, 66.
25. "PTL Television Network 'Dream' Becomes Reality in Brief 3-Year Period," *Charlotte News*, July 3, 1976.
26. Interview with Jim Moss, Jan. 14, 2014.
27. Bob Wisehart, "'PTL Club'—Another Kind of Talk Show," *Charlotte News*, May 13, 1975.
28. "PTL's New Counselling Director Persues the Lost," *Action*, Dec. 1977, 2, 20.
29. Interview with Roger Flessing, July 20, 2010.
30. *PTL Club*, July 5, 1977, reel 2; interview with Dorothy Bakker, Dec. 14, 2016; Laurence Leamer, *King of the Night: The Life of Johnny Carson* (New York: William Morrow, 1989); Paul Corkery, *Carson: The Unauthorized Biography* (Ketchum, ID: Randt, 1987); interview with Roger Flessing, July 20, 2010.
31. U.S. v. Bakker, vol. 9, 1647.
32. Interview with Lee and Nancy Nagelhout, June 13, 2011.
33. Interview with Del Holford, June 7, 2012; interview with Bobbie Garn, June 7, 2012.
34. Hope Lippard, "People Touching Your Life Through The PTL Club," *Action*, Apr. 1980, 17; *PTL Club*, Dec. 3, 1979, accessed Feb. 4, 2014, http://www.youtube.com/watch?v=ttdTGPQer-o.
35. Lippard, "People Touching Your Life," *Action*, Apr. 1980, 21; James B. Irwin, with Monte Unger, *More Than an Ark on Ararat: Spiritual Lessons Learned while Searching for Noah's Ark* (Nashville: Broadman Press, 1985), 15; James B. Irwin, with William A. Emerson, *To Rule the Night: The Discovery Voyage of Astronaut Jim Irwin* (Philadelphia: A. J. Holman, 1973), 22. "We didn't find a shred of evidence of the ark, not a trace" on Ararat, Irwin later admitted.
36. *PTL Club*, Feb. 1, 1977, reel 2; George Otis, *Eldridge Cleaver: Ice and Fire!* (Van Nuys: Bible Voice, 1977); Eldridge Cleaver, *Soul on Fire* (Waco, TX: Word Books, 1978); Kate Coleman, "Souled Out," *New West*, Apr. 19, 1980, 17–27; Kathleen Rout, *Eldridge Cleaver* (Boston: Twayne Publishers, 1991), vii–x, xiii–xiv, 182–183, 252–256; Mark Stillman, "Eldridge Cleaver's New Pants: Every Revolution Needs

a Haberdasher, Right?," *The Harvard Crimson*, Sept. 26, 1975, accessed Nov. 1, 2013, http://www.thecrimson.com/article/1975/9/26/eldridge-cleaver-new-pants-peldridge/cleavers/. Otis was a former general manager of Learjet. Otis's book is entirely favorable toward Cleaver, barely mentioning, for example, Cleaver's earlier admission that he had been a serial rapist.

37. Charles White, *The Life and Times of Little Richard: The Quasar of Rock* (New York: Da Capo Press, 1994), 31–33, 72–73, 84, 89, 93, 181.
38. White, *Little Richard*, 92.
39. David Kirby, *Little Richard: The Birth of Rock 'N' Roll* (New York: Continuum, 2009), 155; White, *Little Richard*, 94, 100, 156; *PTL Club*, Apr. 6, 1978, reel 1.
40. *PTL Club*, Apr. 6, 1978, reel 1.
41. *PTL Club*, Sept. 20, 1979, reel 2.
42. Interview with Vincente Montaño, Nov. 12, 2013; *PTL Club*, Jan. 7, 1977, Mar. 15, 1977, July 6, 1977, reel 1; Dec. 12, 1979, reel 1; "Latin American Breakthrough," *Action*, Jan. 1977, 14; "The PTL Miracle Moves South," *Action*, Aug. 1977, 4; "PTL World Report," *Action*, Dec. 1977, 14–15. When Pat Robertson first showed Montaño a *700 Club* episode dubbed into Spanish, Montaño politely told him it was not "something the Hispanic world would embrace."
43. http://english.fgtv.com/a1/a1_03.asp, accessed Nov. 11, 2013.
44. *PTL Club*, Feb. 21, 1977, reels 1 and 2.
45. Ruthane Garlock, *Fire in His Bones: The Story of Benson Idahosa* (Plainfield, NJ: Logos, 1981).
46. *We Win: John 17:21, Go into All the World* (n.p.: Heritage Village Church and Missionary Fellowship, 1978); Frye Gaillard, "Bakker Going around the World," *CO*, Sept. 6, 1978; Jane Lee Lisenby, "Bakker Going around World," *Charlotte News*, Sept. 5, 1978; Shepard, *Forgiven*, 102–103; interview with Burt Lehman, July 11, 2013.
47. *PTL Club*, Dec. 12, 1979, reel 1; Frye Gaillard, "PTL Television to Produce Talk Show for Brazilians," *CO*, Jan. 14, 1980.

CHAPTER 4

1. Dennis Bennett, *Nine O'Clock in the Morning* (Plainfield, NJ: Logos, 1970), 61; "Speaking in Tongues," *Time*, Aug. 15, 1960, 55.
2. Harrell, *Roberts*, 287–299; Richard Quebedeaux, *The New Charismatics II: How a Christian Renewal Movement Became Part of the American Religious Mainstream* (San Francisco: Harper & Row, 1983), 72–80, 120.
3. William Lawrence Svelmoe, *A New Vision for Missions: William Cameron Townsend, the Wycliffe Bible Translators, and the Culture of Early Evangelical Faith Missions, 1896–1945* (Tuscaloosa: University of Alabama Press, 2008), 60.
4. Svelmoe, *New Vision for Missions*, 252, 315–316; Loren Cunningham with Janis Rogers, *Is That Really You, God? Hearing the Voice of God* (Seattle: YWAM Publishing, 1984), 64–66, 154–155.

5. Bakker, *Big Three Mountain-Movers*, 49, 114, 115; interview with Roger Flessing, July 20, 2010.
6. Bakker, *Move That Mountain*, 152–153; interview with Jim Moss, Aug. 28, 2012.
7. Interview with Jim Moss, Aug. 28, 2012; Jim Bakker with Robert Paul Lamb, *The Big Three Mountain-Movers: Trust, Delight, Commit* (Plainfield, NJ: Logos International, 1977), 3.
8. Oral Roberts, *Miracle of Seed-Faith* (Tulsa: Oral Roberts, 1970), 7.
9. Roberts, *Seed-Faith*, 21, 29.
10. Harrell, *Roberts*, 303–308.
11. Matthew 19:16–23; Luke, 18:18–23; Mark, 10:17–22.
12. *PTL Club*, Nov. 1, 1978, reel 2. Nov. 1, 1978 was day eight of a telethon. Bakker also expounded on his interpretation of the parable of the rich young ruler in *Big Three Mountain-Movers*, 13–15, and repeated it on the *Jim Bakker* show on October 31, 1981. This interpretation of the parable was not original to Bakker. Gordon Lindsay had said the same thing as early as 1965, according to Jonathan Root. See Root, "Total Salvation," chapter 1.
13. Roberts, *Seed-Faith*, 110.
14. Bakker, *Prosperity*, 35, 43, 46.
15. Kate Bowler, *Blessed: A History of the American Prosperity Gospel* (New York: Oxford University Press, 2013), 46, 65, 67, 79–89.
16. Bakker, *Big Three*, 48–49, 117, 137; Bakker, *Eight Keys*, 11, 30, 34, 42.
17. Tom Wolfe, "The Me Decade and the Third Great Awakening," in *Mauve Gloves & Madmen, Clutter & Vine* (New York: Farrar, Straus and Giroux, 1976), 126–167; Eva S. Moskowitz, *In Therapy We Trust: America's Obsession with Self-Fulfillment* (Baltimore: Johns Hopkins University Press, 2001), 218–244; Robert J. Ringer, *Winning Through Intimidation* (Los Angeles: Los Angeles Book Publishers, 1973); Robert J. Ringer, *Looking Out for Number One* (Los Angeles: Los Angeles Book Corp., 1977). Historian T. J. Jackson Lears argues that in the early twentieth century a "Protestant ethos of salvation through self-denial" gave way to "a therapeutic ethos stressing self-realization in this world." As the older Victorian outlook collapsed, Americans replaced "salvation" with "an almost obsessive concern with psychic and physical health" divorced from religious belief. Lears argues persuasively that the rise of consumerism and therapeutic culture was one of the most important developments of the twentieth century. But it did not necessitate leaving faith behind, as Bakker and many of his guests on the *PTL Club* were determined to prove. T. J. Jackson Lears, "From Salvation to Self-Realization: Advertising and the Therapeutic Roots of Consumer Culture, 1880–1930," in *The Culture of Consumption: Critical Essays in American History, 1880–1980*, ed. Richard Wightman Fox and T. J. Jackson Lears (New York: Pantheon Books, 1983), 1–38. Also see Philip Reiff, *The Triumph of the Therapeutic: Uses of Faith after Freud* (1966; repr., Chicago: University of Chicago Press, 1987); T. J. Jackson Lears, *No Place of Grace: Antimodernism*

and the *Transformation of American Culture, 1880–1920* (New York: Pantheon Books, 1981).

18. Norman Vincent Peale, *The Power of Positive Thinking* (New York: Prentice-Hall, 1952), 108, 173; Carol V. R. George, *God's Salesman: Norman Vincent Peale and the Power of Positive Thinking* (New York: Oxford University Press, 1993), 101, 128–139; "PTL Satellite Network Schedule," *Action*, Apr. 1978, 15.
19. Bakker, *Eight Keys*, 33; Bakker, *I Was Wrong*, 231.
20. Robert Schuller, *Self-Esteem: The New Reformation* (Waco, TX: Word, 1982), 19. Peale wrote the introduction to Schuller's *Self-Love: The Dynamic Force of Success* (New York: Hawthorne Books, 1969).
21. Merlin Carothers, *Prison to Praise* (Plainfield, NJ: Logos International, 1970). Bakker quoted Carothers in his 1977 book, *The Big Three Mountain-Movers*, 17.
22. Carothers, *Prison to Praise*, 97.
23. Carothers, *Prison to Praise*, 83–88. On Carnegie see Steven Watts, *Self-Help Messiah: Dale Carnegie and Success in Modern America* (New York: Other Press, 2013).
24. Carothers's other books were *Power in Praise* (Plainfield, NJ: Logos, 1972); *Answers to Praise* (Plainfield, NJ: Logos, 1972); *Praise Works!* (Plainfield, NJ: Logos, 1973); *Walking & Leaping* (Plainfield, NJ: Logos, 1974), and *Bringing Heaven into Hell* (Old Tappan, NJ: Fleming H. Revell, 1976).
25. Frances Hunter, *God's Answer to Fat: Loose It!* (1975; repr., Houston: Hunter Ministries, 1976), 27–41; R. Marie Griffith, *Born Again Bodies: Flesh and Spirit in American Christianity* (Berkeley: University of California Press, 2004), 172, 219, 231.
26. Frances Hunter, *God's Answer to Fat*, 9, 43–56; Frances Hunter, *The Fabulous Skinnie Minnie Recipe Book* (Houston: Hunter Ministries, 1976); *PTL Club*, Jan. 12, 1977.
27. Jim and Tammy Bakker, with Dr. Stephen Gyland and Jeffrey Park, *How We Lost Weight & Kept It Off!* (Charlotte: Jim Bakker, 1979), 25.
28. Jim and Tammy Bakker, *How We Lost Weight*, 14; Jim Bakker, newsletter [c. 1979], FPHC.
29. "Getting Fit For the Race," *Action*, Apr. 1978, 12–13; interview with Jim Moss, Jan. 14, 2014.
30. Marabel Morgan, *The Total Woman* (Old Tappan, NJ: Fleming H. Revell, 1973), 94, 97, 104; *PTL Club*, Sept. 18, 1979, reel 1.
31. Larry Flynt with Kenneth Ross, *An Unseemly Man* (Los Angeles: Dove Books, 1996), 7, 12, 17, 26, 38, 51, 88, 163–169.
32. Flynt, *Unseemly Man*, 163–166; Ruth Carter Stapleton, *The Experience of Inner Healing* (Waco, TX: Word Books, 1977), 57–60. Stapleton was an admirer of Marie N. Robinson's *The Power of Sexual Surrender* (Garden City, NY: Doubleday, 1959), which Stapleton cited in her own work. See Ruth Carter Stapleton, *The Gift of Inner Healing* (Waco, TX: Word Books, 1976), 36, 113. In *The Power of Sexual Surrender*, Robinson writes, "I believe that the problem of sexual frigidity

in women is one of the gravest problems of our times" (7). This frigidity, according to Robinson, "is always rooted in incomplete knowledge gained in childhood and adolescence" (17).

33. Larry Flynt, *Hustler*, Mar. 1978, 5; *Hustler*, Apr. 1978, 5.
34. Wayne Nicholas, "Repentant Porn King Visits 'PTL Club,'" *CO*, Feb. 4, 1978.
35. Vanessa Gallman, "PTL Callers Say Flynt 'Born Again,'" *CO*, Feb. 7, 1978; Wayne Nicholas, "PTL Workers Stop to Pray for Flynt," *CO*, Mar. 7, 1978.
36. "Jim Bakker Discusses Larry Flynt Interview," *CO*, Feb. 6, 1978; "Pornography or the Bible, Either/Or—Not Both," *CO*, Feb. 10, 1978; Wayne Nicholas, "Minister Spent $1,300 to Denounce Flynt's PTL Interview," *CO*, Feb. 11, 1978; Wayne Nicholas, "A Talk about Larry Flynt: Ruth Carter Stapleton, on 'PTL Club,' Says Born-Again Pornographer Needs Love," *CO*, Feb. 16, 1978; Vanessa Gallman, "Will PTL Workers Help 'Save' Hustler?" *CO*, Feb. 23, 1978; Flynt, *Unseemly Man*, 168.
37. Flynt, *Unseemly Man*, 170, 176.
38. Evelyn Carter with Leona Choy, *No Ground* (Plainfield, NJ: Logos International, 1978), 53–54, 83, 107, 108–109; Ev Carter, "No Ground," *Action*, Mar. 1978, 22–23.
39. Bowler, *Blessed*, 118–126; Jonathan L. Walton, *Watch This! The Ethics and Aesthetics of Black Televangelism* (New York: New York University Press), 85; interview with Scott and Nedra Ross; *CO*, Nov. 10, 1978; Bakker, *I Was Wrong*, 278–279.
40. Frye Gaillard, "The Child Who Would Be King: Why Jim Bakker Didn't Know When to Stop," *Southern Magazine*, July 1987, 37; Leah Payne, *Gender and Pentecostal Revivalism: Making Female Ministry in the Early Twentieth Century* (New York: Palgrave Macmillan, 2015), 39–80, 95–121; McMullen, *Big Top*, 42–43, 169, 184–185; Blumhofer, *McPherson*, 232–280; Sutton, *McPherson*, 7–89.
41. *PTL Club*, Apr. 27, 1977; *PTL Club*, Aug. 1, 1979.

CHAPTER 5

1. Jane Lee Lisenby, "PTL's Finances—A Story of Rags to Riches," *Charlotte News*, Sept. 3, 1977; Jane Lee Lisenby, "Bakker's $23,740 Tops PTL Pay," *Charlotte News*, Sept. 3, 1977; Frye Gaillard, "PTL Took in $8 Million up to May, Audit Says," *CO*, Sept. 4, 1977.
2. FCC transcript, July 26, 1979, vol. 7, 781, 783, 829, 837, 854.
3. Vanessa Gallman, "PTL Digs Into Work on Center," *CO*, Jan. 3, 1978; Frye Gaillard, "The PTL Club," *CO*, July 9, 1978.
4. FCC transcript, July 26, 1979, vol. 7, 851–852; Gallman, "PTL Digs Into Work"; Gaillard, "The PTL Club."
5. FCC transcript, July 26, 1979, vol. 7, 851–852.
6. FCC transcript, July 26, 1979, vol. 7, 855–856; *PTL Club*, June 21, 1978, reel 2; Cathy Packer, "PTL Debt Halts S.C. Construction," *Charlotte News*, Aug. 17, 1978.
7. FCC transcript, July 26, 1979, vol. 7, 854, 857, 878, 909, 921–922, 935, 955.

8. Minutes of Special Meeting of Board of Directors of Heritage Village Church and Missionary Fellowship, Inc., June 20, 1978, 3, copy from Jim Moss; Frye Gailllard, "PTL Fires At Least 60," *CO*, June 23, 1978.
9. Minutes of Special Meeting of Board of Directors, June 20, 1978, 5.
10. Minutes of Special Meeting, 6; "James O. and Tammy F. Bakker Statement of Assets and Liabilities," July 31, 1977, *Action*, Dec. 1977, 18; Bill Perkins to Jim Bakker, Oct. 17, 1978, copy from Jim Moss; Allen Cowan and Frye Gaillard, "PTL Officials Divided Sharply Over Publicizing Annual Audit," *CO*, Sept. 25, 1978.
11. Frye Gaillard, "PTL's Rapid Growth Led to Money Woes," *CO*, June 25, 1978; FCC transcript, Jim Moss testimony, vol. 7, 959–961; Charles E. Shepard, "PTL Has Overtime Settlement," *CO*, Sept. 30, 1979.
12. Frye Gaillard, "PTL Club: A Wealth of Controversy and Faith," *CO*, July 9, 1978.
13. James O. Bakker to Herbert M. Moore, July 14, 1978, copy from Jim Moss; Shepard, *Forgiven*, 110–111; "Jim Bakker Selling His Houseboat," *Charlotte News*, Dec. 1, 1978. Bakker decided to sell the houseboat in December 1978 because it no longer provided a "refuge."
14. FCC transcript, July 26, 1979, vol. 7, 923–924.
15. Jim Bakker, Aug. 1978 newsletter, FPHC; Jim Bakker, "Special Message," Aug. 1978, FPHC; FCC transcript, July 26, 1979, vol. 7, 912.
16. Jane Lee Lisenby, "Bakker: PTL Woes Just 'Growing Pains,'" *Charlotte News*, July 28, 1978; Allen Cowan, "The Business of Giving to PTL," *CO*, Nov. 18, 1978; interview with Austin Miles, Jan. 21, 2014.
17. Frye Gaillard, "Bakker Going around the World," *CO*, Sept. 6, 1978; Allen Cowan and Frye Gaillard, "PTL Can't Get a Loan, but Not Because of Religion," *CO*, Sept. 11, 1978; Gaillard, "PTL Took in $8 Million."
18. Allen Cowan, "PTL Money Problem Linked to Computer," *CO*, Sept. 25, 1978.
19. Allen Cowan and Vanessa Gallman, "PTL: We Can't Pay Workers," *CO*, Nov. 3, 1978; Phil Whitesell, "Bakker: PTL 'Within Days' of Dying," *Charlotte News*, Nov. 3, 1978; Allen Cowan, "PTL Seeks Way Out of Debt," *CO*, Nov. 4, 1978.
20. Allen Cowan, "PTL's President, Family Will Live in $200,000 House," *CO*, Nov. 14, 1978; Allen Cowan, "Bakkers' New Friends Buying New Home," *CO*, Nov. 15, 1978; "'Two Little People' Gave PTL a House," *Charlotte News*, Nov. 18, 1978; George Stein, "PTL Host's 'Dream Home' for Sale; He Has Another," *Charlotte News*, July 20, 1977.
21. Allen Cowan, "Bakker: I'll Start 1979 with $1-Million Payment," *CO*, Dec. 16, 1978.
22. FCC transcript, July 26, 1979, vol. 7, 804–807, 909.
23. Shepard, *Forgiven*, 105–106; FCC transcript, July 26, 1979, vol. 7, 926; Frye Gaillard, "PTL Vice President Leaves Network," *CO*, Oct. 24, 1978; Frye Gaillard, "Bakker's Faith Rests in Benevolent God." Johnny Johnson's doctorate was also from Union University.
24. Jane Lee Lisenby, "Bakker's $23,740 Tops PTL Pay," *Charlotte News*, Sept. 3, 1977; Gaillard, "Bakker's Faith Rests in Benevolent God."

25. Bill Perkins to Jim Bakker, Oct. 17, 1978. The *Observer* reported that Manzano's resignation was imminent on October 14. See Allen Cowan and Frye Gaillard, "PTL Faces Problems in Personnel," *CO*, Oct. 14, 1978.
26. FCC transcript, July 26, 1979, vol. 7, 957.
27. FCC transcript, July 26, 1979, vol. 7, 957; Bob Manzano to the Executive Committee, Oct. 19, 1978, copy from Jim Moss.
28. Allen Cowan and Frye Gaillard, "PTL Faces Problems in Personnel," *CO*, Oct. 14, 1978; Frye Gaillard, "PTL Vice President Leaves Network," *CO*, Oct. 24, 1978.
29. Gaillard, "Bakker's Faith Rests in Benevolent God."
30. Bakker newsletters, Nov. and Dec. 1978, FPHC; interview with Roger Flessing, July 20, 2010; Allen Cowan and Wendy Fox, "PTL Loses Another Executive," *CO*, Dec. 1, 1978; Jane Lee Lisenby, "PTL Vice President Flessing Resigns," *Charlotte News*, Dec. 1, 1978.
31. Interview with Roger Flessing, July 20, 2010.
32. Alex Valderama to the Board of Directors, President, Executive Committee, Vice Presidents, Dec. 4, 1978, copy from Jim Moss; "4th PTL Exec Resigns," *CO*, Dec. 6, 1978.
33. Bill Perkins to the Board of Directors, Dec. 11, 1978, copy from Jim Moss; Shepard, *Forgiven*, 80.
34. Interview with Roger Flessing, July 20, 2010.
35. Bill Perkins to Jim Bakker, Oct. 9, 1978.
36. Bill Perkins to Jim Bakker, Oct. 9, 1978; Bob Wisehart, "'PTL Club'—Another Kind of Talk Show," *Charlotte News*, May 13, 1975.
37. Bill Perkins to Jim Bakker, Oct. 17, 1978; Bill Perkins to Jim Bakker, Dec. 11, 1978.
38. Perkins to Bakker, Oct. 17, 1978; Perkins to Bakker, Dec. 11, 1978.
39. Perkins to Bakker, Oct. 9, 1978.
40. "Proposed Amendments to By-Laws of Heritage Village Church and Missionary Fellowship, Inc., December 14, 1978," copy from Jim Moss.
41. Shepard, *Forgiven*, 92; Jane Lee Lisenby, "His Dream: Worldwide PTL Club," *Charlotte News*, Sept. 6, 1977.
42. "New Beginnings in 1978," *Action*, Feb. 1978, 2; "Heritage University to Begin This September," *Action, Mar.* 1978, 4–5; "Building for Total Living," *Action*, Apr. 1978, 7; Vanessa Gallman, "PTL School Will Open This Fall," *CO*, Mar. 23, 1978; Jim Bakker newsletter, May 1978, FPHC.
43. "Heritage University to Begin This September," *Action*, Mar. 1978, 4–5; "Pass On the Good News: Heritage School of Evangelism," *Action*, Nov. 1979, 8; Frye Gaillard and Allen Cowan, "PTL School Trims Plans; Dean Quits," *CO*, Jan. 28, 1979; Shepard, *Forgiven*, 104.
44. Jim Bakker, "Editorial," *Action*, Feb. 1978, 2; "Heritage University to Begin This September," *Action*, Mar. 1978, 4–5; Nov. 1979, 8; *PTL Club*, Aug. 1, 1979, reel 2; Sept. 17, 1979, reel 1; Louise Hickman Lione, "Vacationland for Pilgrims of PTL Club," *CO*, June 22, 1980.

45. Frye Gaillard, "PTL Closing 300-Student School for Lack of Money," *CO*, June 6, 1979; Jane Lee Lisenby, "School Opened by PTL," *Charlotte* News, Sept. 6, 1978; LaFleur Paysour, "Open School at PTL," *CO*, Sept. 8, 1978.
46. Jane Lee Lisenby, "PTL Unveiling 'Fort,'" *Charlotte News*, July 4, 1978; Louise Hickman Lione, "Vacationland for Pilgrims of PTL Club," *CO*, June 22, 1980.

CHAPTER 6

1. Allen Cowan, "PTL Pays Bills, Praises 'Miracle,'" *CO*, Jan. 3, 1979; Doug Waller, "Bakker: 'Miracle' Solves PTL Cash Crisis," *Charlotte News*, Jan. 2, 1979.
2. Allen Cowan and Frye Gaillard, "Insiders' Story: Former PTL Executives Go Public after Attempts to Change Bakker Fail," *CO*, Jan. 18, 1979; R. Whitney Manzano, "Manzano: PTL Story Fell Short," *CO*, Jan. 19, 1979. The *Charlotte News* also began reporting on the diverting of funds at PTL, beginning on January 18, 1979, though its stories largely followed the *Observer* reporting. Doug Waller, "PTL Denies It Diverted Donations," *Charlotte News*, Jan. 18, 1979.
3. Allen Cowan and Frye Gaillard, "PTL Donations for Foreign Missions Used at Home," *CO*, Jan. 18, 1979.
4. Cowan and Gallaird, "Insiders' Story."
5. Cowan and Gaillard, "Insiders' Story"; Jeff Park, "Jim Bakker, Mountain Mover," *Christian Life*, July 1978, 16–17, 39–40.
6. Cowan and Gaillard, "Insiders' Story"; "PTL Responds to Observer Stories," *CO*, Jan. 18, 1979; Sharon Bond, "Preacher's Wife? Yes, But Typical? No," *Charlotte News*, Dec. 3, 1979. According to Jim Moss, Bakker actually expected the *Observer* articles to be worse after Flessing called him to say he had talked to the reporters. FCC transcript, July 26, 1979, vol. 7, 927–928.
7. Cowan and Gaillard, "Insiders' Story"; Jim Bakker newsletter, Aug. 1978, FPHC.
8. Cowan and Gaillard, "Insiders' Story."
9. Cowan and Gaillard, "PTL Donations for Foreign Missions Used at Home."
10. *Action*, Aug. 1977, 3; "PTL World Report," *Action*, Dec. 1977, 12–13.
11. Jim Bakker newsletters, Aug. 1977, Nov. 1977, FPHC.
12. Roger Flessing to Dr. Paul Y. Cho, Aug. 3, 1977, copy from Jim Moss; *PTL Club*, Feb. 21, 1977, reel 1; Jim Moss testimony, FCC transcript, July 26, 1979, 840–850; Cowan and Gaillard, "PTL Donations."
13. Cowan and Gaillard, "PTL Donations."
14. "PTL Comes to Brazil," *Action*, Jan. 1978, 10–11; FCC transcript, Moss testimony, July 26, 1979, vol. 7, 863–887.
15. Cowan and Gaillard, "PTL Donations"; Moss testimony, FCC transcript, July 26, 1979, 863–887.
16. Jim Bakker, "Editorial," *Action*, Jan. 1978, 2.
17. Allen Cowan and Frye Gaillard, "PTL Gives Missionary $56,000," *CO*, Jan. 19, 1979.
18. FCC transcript, Moss testimony, July 26, 1979, vol. 7, 894.

19. Interviews with Jim Moss, Aug. 28, 2012, Nov. 14, 2013.
20. Interviews with Jim Moss, Aug. 28, 2012, Nov. 14, 2013; Allen Cowan and Frye Gaillard, "Jim Bakker Fires PTL Executive," *CO*, Feb. 16, 1979.
21. Frye Gaillard and Allen Cowan, "PTL Plans Large-Scale Layoffs in an Urgent Cost-Cutting Move," *CO*, Mar. 8, 1979; Frye Gaillard and Allen Cowan, "Up to 200 Losing Jobs with PTL," *CO*, Mar. 9, 1979; Allen Cowan and Frye Gaillard, "PTL Club Is Target of Probe," *CO*, Mar. 17, 1979.
22. Cowan and Gaillard, "PTL Club Is Target of Probe"; "PTL Gets OK to Buy TV Station in Ohio," *CO*, Aug. 23, 1977; Mary Bishop and Robert Hodierne, "PTL Network Offers $2.5 Million for Station," *CO*, Mar. 21, 1977; interview with Roger and Linda Wilson, Jan. 4–5, 2011; FCC transcript, July 26, 1979, vol. 7, 813–822.
23. Jim Bakker, newsletter, May 1979, FPHC.
24. Allen Cowan and Frye Gaillard, "PTL Denies It Misused Donations," *CO*, Mar. 20, 1979; "Bakker Predicts PTL Will Be out of Debt within 30 to 60 Days," *Charlotte News*, Mar. 22, 1979; Cheryl Mattox Berry, "Bakker Sends Wife, Kids Away," *Charlotte News*, Mar. 23, 1979; Allen Cowan and Frye Gaillard, "PTL Won't Help Federal Probe, Bakker Says," *CO*, Mar. 24, 1979; Frye Gaillard and Allen Cowan, "FCC Will Subpoena PTL Records, Official Says," *CO*, Apr. 1, 1979; James A. Albert, "Federal Investigation of Video Evangelism: The FCC Probes the PTL Club," *Oklahoma Law Review* 33 (1980): 782–823.
25. Allen Cowan and Frye Gaillard, "Jim Bakker Steps Out of PTL's Management," *CO*, Apr. 5, 1979; Frye Gaillard, "PTL Begins to Climb Out of Financial Quicksand," *CO*, July 22, 1979.
26. Allen Cowan, "PTL Figure Quits Show over Funds," *CO*, June 16, 1979.
27. Cowan, "PTL Figure Quits."
28. Gaillard, "PTL Begins to Climb Out."
29. Frye Gaillard, "PTL Releases '78 Audit, Promises More Openness," *CO*, Sept. 26, 1979.
30. Jim Bakker, newsletter, July 1979, FPHC; Frye Gaillard, "PTL President: An Air of Calm Amid FCC Storm," *CO*, July 23, 1979; Allen Cowan and Frye Gaillard, "PTL Gives Money to a U.S. Church for Asian Ministry," *CO*, June 23, 1979.
31. Shepard, *Forgiven*, 129–130; interview with Lawrence Bernstein, Aug. 6, 2010.
32. Shepard, *Forgiven*, 130; FCC transcript, July 26, 1979, vol. 7, 796.
33. FCC transcript, July 26, 1979, vol. 7, 823, 831, 833, 913.
34. Bill Perkins to Jim Bakker, Oct. 9, 1978; Frye Gaillard, "Bakker, PTL Haven't Heard the Last of FCC," *CO*, Jan. 13, 1980.
35. Robert Hodierne, "PTL Can't Stop FCC's Investigation into Its Money-Raising Tactics," *CO*, July 10, 1979; Frye Gaillard, "PTL Wants FCC Probe to Be Open," *CO*, July 18, 1979.
36. Shepard, *Forgiven*, 133, 134, 137, 138.
37. Gaillard, "Bakker, PTL Haven't Heard the Last of FCC"; "Under Investigation," PTL Network, Dec. 19, 1979, FPHC.

38. *PTL Club*, Nov. 16, 1979.
39. *PTL Club*, Nov. 16, 1979.
40. Frye Gaillard, "PTL Ad Might Be Misleading," *CO*, Feb. 8, 1980.
41. *PTL Club*, Dec. 10, 1979, reel 2; Ron Aldridge, "'Under Investigation' Program Tells PTL's Side of Controversy," *CO*, Feb. 14, 1980; "Alridge Unfair," *CO*, Mar. 5, 1980; interview with Lawrence Bernstein, Aug. 6, 2010.
42. Frye Gaillard, "PTL President to Defy FCC's Order," *CO*, Jan. 8, 1980; "U.S. Sues For PTL Papers," *CO*, Mar. 12, 1980; "PTL, Bakker, Sue to Block FCC Subpoena," *CO*, Mar. 14, 1980; "Bakker, FCC Reportedly Settle Dispute," *CO*, Apr. 10, 1980; Shepard, *Forgiven*, 144–146; Robert Hodierne, "PTL Agrees to Give FCC Memos on Its Finances," *CO*, Apr. 11, 1980.
43. FCC transcript, July 26, 1979, vol. 7, 943; interview with Lawrence Bernstein, Aug. 4 and 6, 2010.
44. Shepard, *Forgiven*, 147–149; Frye Gaillard, "General Manager of PTL Network Has Resigned," *CO*, Mar. 7, 1980.
45. Flessing interview, July 20, 2010; Frye Gaillard, "Former Aide Returning to Bakker," *CO*, Mar. 27, 1980; Frye Gaillard, "PTL's New Broadcast Head Plans Innovative Programs," *CO*, Apr. 14, 1980.

CHAPTER 7

1. Interview with Jessica Hahn, Feb. 5, 2014; Robert Scheer and Barry Golson, "The Jessica Hahn Story: Part One," *Playboy*, Nov. 1987, 82–89, 178–198.
2. Scheer and Golson, "Jessica Hahn Story: Part One," 82–89, 178–198.
3. Interview with Jessica Hahn, Feb. 5, 2014; Scheer and Golson, "Jessica Hahn Story: Part One," 82–89, 178–198; *Larry King Live*, CNN, July 14, 2005; Roddy Ray, "Hahn Confused but Not Ashamed about Encounter," *CO*, Apr. 19, 1987.
4. A. A. Allen, with Walter Wagner, *Born to Lose, Bound to Win: An Autobiography* (Garden City, NY: Doubleday, 1970), 1, 39.
5. Allen, *Born to Lose*, 65–71, 142–143.
6. A. A. Allen, *Power to Get Wealth: How You Can Have It!* (Miracle Valley, AZ: A. A. Allen Revivals, 1963), 3, 27; Harrell, *All Things Are Possible*, 66–74, 194–202.
7. Dudley Dalton, "Charismatics Alive and Well on L.I.," *New York Times*, Dec. 14, 1975. John Wesley Fletcher reprinted this article in *Compassion and Praise*, Vol. 1, No. 7, 8–9.
8. Shepard, *Forgiven*, 162; Austin Miles, *Don't Call Me Brother: A Ringmaster's Escape from the Pentecostal Church* (Buffalo: Prometheus Books, 1989), 145; John Wildman, "Fletcher: From Ambulance Driver to Faith Healer," *CO*, Sept. 26, 1987.
9. *PTL Club*, Mar. 30, 1976; Art Harris, "The Devil's Disciple," *Penthouse*, Jan. 1989, 46–50, 172, 177, 192, 194.
10. Christina K. Cosdon and Susan Denley, "Clearwater Woman, Blind Nine Years, Regains Sight," *Manatee Times*, May 23, 1975; reprinted in *Compassion and*

Praise, Vol. 1, No. 4, 10–11; "She Couldn't See . . . But She Did!" *Compassion and Praise*, Vol. 1, No. 12, 2–4.

11. *Compassion and Praise*, Vol. 1, No. 5, 14; Vol. 1, No. 6, 14–15; Vol. 1, No. 8, 12–13; Vol. 2, No. 1 (Mar. 1977), 16; Vol. 2, No. 2 (June 1977), 16. Ads for Fletcher's meetings at Evangel Temple appeared in *The Oklahoman*, Apr. 19, June 10, and Aug. 20, 1975; Mar. 20 and 27, 1976; Mar. 4 and Nov. 4, 1978; and Aug. 18, 1979. Ads for Fletcher's meetings at Crossroads Cathedral appeared Mar. 13, June 13, Sept. 19, and Dec. 11, 1980; Feb. 21 and Aug. 1, 1981; and July 3, 1982.
12. Interview with Jessica Hahn, Feb. 5, 2014; Scheer and Golson, "Jessica Hahn Story: Part One," 82–89, 178–198.
13. Interview with Jessica Hahn, Feb. 5, 2014; Shepard, *Forgiven*, 162.
14. Interview with Austin Miles, Jan. 21, 2014.
15. Interview with Sam Orender and Donna Chavis, May 10, 2010; interview with Roger Flessing, July 20, 2010; interview with Roger and Linda Wilson, Jan. 4–5, 2011; interview with Scott and Nedra Ross, June 16, 2011.
16. Cynthia Robins, "Tammy Talks About Her Fall From Grace," *San Francisco Examiner*, July 19, 1987.
17. *PTL Club*, Nov. 5, 1976.
18. *PTL Club*, Feb. 24, 1978, reel 1.
19. "Tammy's Column," *Action*, Mar. 1978, 9.
20. *PTL Club*, Sept. 17, 1979, reel 1.
21. Frye Gaillard, "PTL Club: A Wealth of Controversy and Faith," *CO*, July 9, 1978.
22. Interview with Roger and Linda Wilson, Jan. 4–5, 2011; *PTL Club*, Aug. 1, 1979.
23. Interview with Scott and Nedra Ross, June 16, 2011; Bakker, *I Gotta Be Me*, 107.
24. Steve Bransford, "Lord, You've Been Good to Me!" *Action*, Jan. 1978, 5; Art Harris, "Tammy Bakker's Country Crush: A Singer's Friendship with the Evangelist's Wife and the Pain That Followed," *Washington Post*, Apr. 2, 1987.
25. *PTL Club*, Oct. 13, 1977, reel 2; *PTL Club*, Feb. 24, 1978, reel 1.
26. "Signs of Revival in Nashville," *Action*, Mar. 1977, 14; Bransford, "Lord, You've Been Good to Me!" *Action*, Jan. 1978, 5, 7; Gary S. Paxton, foreword to Bakker, *I Gotta Be Me*, 9, 10; Harris, "Tammy Bakker's Country Crush."
27. Interview with Roger and Linda Wilson, Jan. 4–5, 2011; Shepard, *Forgiven*, 154–155; Harris, "Tammy Bakker's Country Crush."
28. Interview with Roger and Linda Wilson, Jan. 4–5, 2011; Shepard, *Forgiven*, 154–155.
29. Hope Hunter, "Thurlow Spurr Adds New Dimension to PTL Television," *Action*, Feb. 1978, 10; "Meet the Man Who Gave the Spurrlows Its Name: Thurlow Spurr," *Charisma*, Aug./Sept., 1975, 6–7, 10–11, 29–31; interview with Thurlow Spurr, Mar. 11, 2015.
30. Interview with Roger and Linda Wilson, Jan. 4–5, 2011; "Talking With Tammy," *Action*, Apr. 1980, 31.
31. Interview with Thurlow Spurr, Mar. 11, 2015.

32. "Talking With Tammy," *Action*, Apr. 1980, 31.
33. Sharon Bond, "Preacher's Wife? Yes, but Typical? No," *Charlotte News*, Dec. 3, 1979.
34. Interview with Roger Flessing, July 20, 2010; Shepard, *Forgiven*, 156; Bakker, *I Was Wrong*, 16.
35. Tammy Bakker with Cliff Dudley, *Run to the Roar* (Harrison, AR: New Leaf Press, 1980), 22–24, 96–103; interview with Roger and Linda Wilson, Jan. 4–5, 2011; Shepard, *Forgiven*, 156, 158–159.
36. Interview with Roger Flessing, July 20, 2010; Shepard, *Forgiven*, 157–158.
37. Interview with Roger and Linda Wilson, Jan. 4–5, 2011.
38. Interview with Roger and Linda Wilson, Jan. 4–5, 2011.
39. Interview with Roger and Linda Wilson, Jan. 4–5, 2011; Harris, "Tammy Bakker's Country Crush"; Bakker, *I Was Wrong*, 17.
40. Jim Bakker, *Eight Keys*, 11, 30, 32, 34, 42; Scheer and Golson, "Jessica Hahn Story: Part One," 86–87.
41. Scheer and Golson, "Jessica Hahn Story: Part One," 82–89, 178–198; Art Harris, "The Jessica Hahn Story," *Penthouse*, Oct. 1987, 109–113, 152; Art Harris, "The Jessica Hahn Tape: Adviser Recalls Her Tearful Testimony of the Episode with Jim Bakker," *Washington Post*, Apr. 9, 1987.
42. Scheer and Golson, "Jessica Hahn Story: Part One," 188, 198.
43. John Wesley Fletcher and Jessica Hahn on *Geraldo*, accessed June 27, 2016, https://www.youtube.com/watch?v=3hyd1Ai_o2w; Shepard, *Forgiven*, 278.
44. Interview with Jessica Hahn, Feb. 5, 2014; Scheer and Golson, "Jessica Hahn Story: Part One," 188.
45. Interview with Jessica Hahn, Feb. 5, 2014.
46. Bakker, *I Was Wrong*, 19, 20; Harris, "Jessica Hahn Tape."

CHAPTER 8

1. "A New Beginning . . . Italian Style! *Together*, Sept. 1982, 3; "PTL Hosts Around the World," *Together*, Dec. 1982, 21; "Foreign Missions," *Together*, Jan.–Feb. 1983, 13. In 1982, PTL produced pilot shows of a program aimed at Great Britain. PTL had also been supporting the work of missionary Mark Buntain in India for five years. See Marlene Floyd, "Mending the City With a Broken Heart," *Together*, Sept. 1982, 4–5; "One Step Closer to the Miracle," *Together*, Sept. 1982, 7.
2. *Jim Bakker*, Aug. 13, 1982.
3. Jim Bakker newsletter, Oct. 1980; Frye Gaillard, "PTL Celebrates Completion of Auditorium," *CO*, Aug. 30, 1980; Shepard, *Forgiven*, 167; Jim Bakker, *Survival: Unite to Live* (Harrison, AR: New Leaf Press, 1980), 103; U.S. v. Bakker, vol. 9, 1622–1623.
4. "Victory Day at Heritage USA," *Action*, Nov. 1980, 11–15; Jane Lee Lisenby, "The 'PTL Club' Format: A Flow of Guests, Salvation," *Charlotte News*, Sept. 6, 1977;

Louise Hickman Lione, "Vacationland for Pilgrims of PTL Club," *CO*, June 22, 1980; Frye Gaillard, "PTL with a Personal Touch," *CO*, Mar. 16, 1981.

5. *PTL Club*, Sept. 7, 1981.
6. U.S. v. Bakker, vol. 9, 1612, 1625.
7. Wigger, *American Saint*, 318–320, 365.
8. Bakker, *I Was Wrong*, 467; "You and Us Together" telethon, *Jim Bakker*, Mar. 6, 1983; U.S. v. Bakker, vol. 9, 1613.
9. Bart Green, "A Place of Agreement: The Upper Room," *Together*, May 1982, 14; Aug. 1982, 2–9; U.S. v. Bakker, vol. 5, 1933; vol. 8, 1029; vol. 9, 1705. When Aubrey Sara died unexpectedly on August 26, 1982, he was buried just outside the Upper Room. Jim Bakker, *You Can Make It!* (Charlotte: PTL, 1983), 4–5.
10. "A Place to Start," *Together*, May 1982, 5; Jan./Feb. 1983, 16; interview with Al Cress, Jan. 15–17, 2010; interview with Jim Cobble, Apr. 21, 2010; U.S. v. Bakker, vol. 6, 7; Shepard, *Forgiven*, 196–198.
11. "Total Learning Center," *Together*, Aug./Sep. 1983, 14.
12. "Total Learning Center," *Together*, Aug./Sept. 1983, 15.
13. Bakker, *Move That Mountain*, 78–79; *PTL Club*, Jan. 26, 1981, reel 1.
14. Claire Weekes, *Hope and Help for Your Nerves* (New York: Hawthorn Books, 1969), 22. Bakker retold the story of his 1969 breakdown in *You Can Make It!* (1983), but left out any reference to Weekes or her method. See Bakker, *You Can Make It!*, 106–107.
15. Nathan G. Hale, *The Rise and Crisis of Psychoanalysis in the United States: Freud and the Americans, 1917–1985* (New York: Oxford University Press, 1995), 302, 380–384; Moskowitz, *In Therapy We Trust*, 245–259.
16. Pavel Hejzlar, *Two Paradigms for Divine Healing: Fred F. Bosworth, Kenneth E. Hagin, Agnes Sanford, and Francis McNutt in Dialogue* (Leiden: Brill, 2010), 29–35, 37–38.
17. Agnes Sanford, *The Healing Light* (Plainfield, NJ: Logos International, 1972; first published by Macalester Park Publishing Company, 1947), 25, 27; Hejzlar, *Two Paradigms*, 162–163, 192–193.
18. Ruth Carter Stapleton, *The Gift of Inner Healing* (Waco, TX: Word Books, 1976), 50; Ruth Carter Stapleton, *The Experience of Inner Healing* (Waco, TX: Word Books, 1977), 10. Stapleton was also influenced by Maxwell Maltz's *Psycho-Cybernetics* (Englewood Cliffs, NJ: Prentice-Hall, 1960); Marie Robinson's *The Power of Sexual Surrender* (New York: Doubleday, 1959); and W. Hugh Missildine's *Your Inner Child of the Past* (New York: Simon and Schuster, 1963).
19. Stapleton, *Gift of Inner Healing*, 39–54.
20. "PTL Recently Unveils People That Love Centers," *Together*, May 1982, 2; "People That Love Centers . . . Helping Families in Need," *Together*, Dec. 1982, 16–17; "People That Love Centers," *Together*, Jan.-Feb. 1983, 15; U.S. v. Bakker, vol. 5, 1745; vol. 8, 1030; vol. 9, 1402, 1405, 1655, 1704.

21. "PTL In Action . . . The People That Love Home," *Together*, Nov./Dec. 1983, 3; "People That Love Home Opens!" *Together*, Fall/Winter 1984, 4; U.S. v. Bakker, vol. 5, 1745; vol. 7, 629–640.
22. PTL video of Tammy at Georgia Women's Correctional Institution, Dec. 5, 1980, FPHC; "You and Us Together" telethon, *Jim Bakker*, Mar. 5, 1983.
23. "A Place Where People Can Know God Better," *Together*, Oct. 1982, 7, "Following a God-Given Plan to Reach the World," *Together*, Jan.–Feb. 1983, 5; "Heritage USA Update," Apr. 20 and 26, 1983, PTL video, FPHC.
24. PTL press conference at the Graham home, Sept. 1983, *Heritage Herald*, Sept. 1986, 3.
25. Bernard M. Timberg, *Television Talk: A History of the TV Talk Show* (Austin: University of Texas Press, 2002), 111; Shepard, *Forgiven*, 230.
26. *PTL Club*, Feb. 9, 1981; "You and Us Together" telethon, Mar. 3, 1983.
27. *Jim Bakker*, Aug. 13, 1982; Richard Dortch, *Integrity: How I Lost It, and My Journey Back* (Green Forest, AR: New Leaf Press, 1992), 70.
28. *Jim Bakker*, Aug. 18, 1982.
29. "You and Us Together" telethon, Mar. 5, 1983.
30. "You and Us Together" telethon, Mar. 5, 1983.
31. "You and Us Together" telethon, Mar. 5, 1983.
32. Bakker repeated this exegesis of Malachi 3 in his 1983 book, *You Can Make It!*, 84–86.
33. "You and Us Together" telethon, Mar. 5, 1983.
34. "You and Us Together" telethon, Mar. 5, 1983.
35. Robert G. Allen, *Nothing Down: How to Buy Real Estate With Little or No Money Down* (New York: Simon & Schuster, 1980; rev. ed. 1984), 243; www.census.gov/const/uspriceann.pdf, accessed Feb. 18, 2015. Thorstein Veblen coined the term "conspicuous consumption" at the end of the nineteenth century. See Veblen, *Theory of the Leisure Class*, 49–69.
36. Lizabeth Cohen, *A Consumers' Republic: The Politics of Mass Consumption in Postwar America* (New York: Alfred A. Knopf, 2003), 386.
37. Robert M. Collins, *Transforming America: Politics and Culture in the Reagan Years* (New York: Columbia University Press, 2007), 95–99; Jeff Madrick, *Age of Greed: The Triumph of Finance and the Decline of America, 1970 to the Present* (New York: Alfred A. Knopf, 2011), 86–95, 202–221.
38. Collins, *Transforming America*, 98.
39. *Jim Bakker Telethon*, June 20, 1983.
40. Frye Gailllard, "Charlotte's PTL Club Is Becoming a Stop for Presidential Candidates," *CO*, Jan. 11, 1980; Jim Bakker, "Dear Friends," *Action*, Apr. 1980, 2–3; Jim Bakker, "Call to Commitment: Washington For Jesus," *Action*, July 1980, 2–3; Robert L. Maddox, *Preacher at the White House* (Nashville: Broadman Press, 1984), 164–165; Gary Scott Smith, *Faith and the Presidency: From George

Washington to George W. Bush (New York: Oxford University Press, 2006), 309; Randall Balmer, *Redeemer: The Life of Jimmy Carter* (New York: Basic Books, 2014), 122–124.

41. Howard Norton and Bob Slosser, *The Miracle of Jimmy Carter* (Plainfield, NJ: Logos International, 1976), 2.
42. Maddox, *Preacher*, 136; Steven P. Miller, *The Age of Evangelicalism: America's Born-Again Years* (New York: Oxford University Press, 2014), 40–49; Balmer, *Redeemer*, 20, 28, 58, 125–126; Randall Balmer, *God in the White House: A History: How Faith Shaped the Presidency from John F. Kennedy to George W. Bush* (New York: Harper Collins, 2008), 79–107; Andrew S. Finstuen, *Original Sin and Everyday Protestants: The Theology of Reinhold Neibuhr, Billy Graham, and Paul Tillich in an Age of Anxiety* (Chapel Hill: University of North Carolina Press, 2009), 1, 14–15, 189–196.
43. Robert Maddox, Carter's liaison to the religious community, largely wrote the "Crisis of Confidence" speech. See Maddox, *Preacher*, 71–72. Jonathan Root points out the disjunction between Carter's malaise speech and the optimism of the prosperity gospel in his dissertation. See Root, "Total Salvation." The text of Carter's speech is widely available online.
44. Doug and Bill Wead, *Reagan: In Pursuit of the Presidency—1980* (Plainfield, NJ: Haven Books, 1980), 21; Maddox, *Preacher*, 165; Miller, *Age of Evangelicalism*, 64; Smith, *Faith and the Presidency*, 326–338; Balmer, *God in the White House*, 111–114.
45. Ronald Reagan, Address Accepting the Presidential Nomination at the Republican National Convention in Detroit, July 17, 1980, accessed Feb. 28, 2015, http://www.presidency.ucsb.edu/ws/?pid=25970; Root, "Total Salvation," 46–49.
46. Jim Bakker, "Dear Friends," *Action*, Apr. 1980, 2; *PTL Club*, Nov. 5, 1979.
47. Lawrence Jones, "Reagan's Religion," *Journal of American Culture* 8, no. 4 (Dec. 1985): 59–70; Matthew Avery Sutton, *American Apocalypse: A History of Modern Evangelicalism* (Cambridge, MA: Belknap Press of Harvard University Press, 2014), 345–348, 354–360; Miller, *Age of Evangelicalism*, 67; Smith, *Faith and the Presidency*, 334; John Herbers, "Religious Leaders Tell of Worry on Armageddon View Ascribed to Reagan," *New York Times*, Oct. 21, 1984; Paul Boyer, *When Time Shall Be No More: Prophecy Belief in Modern American Culture* (Cambridge, MA: Harvard University Press, 1992), 5–7, 126–128; Frederic J. Baumgartner, *Longing for the End: A History of Millennialism in Western Civilization* (New York: Palgrave, 1999), 220; Eugen Weber, *Apocalypses: Prophecies, Cults, and Millennial Beliefs through the Ages* (Cambridge, MA: Harvard University Press, 1999), 204; Stephen D. O'Leary, *Arguing the Apocalypse: A Theory of Millennial Rhetoric* (New York: Oxford University Press), 134–171.
48. Hal Lindsey, with C.C. Carlson, *Late Great Planet Earth* (Grand Rapids, MI: Zondervan, 1970); Frye Gaillard, "Bakker's Faith Rests in Benevolent God," *CO*, July 9, 1978; Gerard Thomas Straub, *Salvation for Sale: An Insider's View of Pat Robertson's Ministry* (Buffalo, NY: Prometheus Books, 1986), 161.

49. *PTL Club*, Nov. 5, 1979; "*Jim Bakker* Special, Israel, Day One, *Jim Bakker* June 4, 1981"; Frye Gaillard, "Carter Aide Reaches Out for the Christian Vote," *CO*, Sept 1, 1980; Frye Gaillard, "PTL Moves Cautiously Among Vocal, Political Evangelicals," *CO*, Sept. 1, 1980; Timothy P. Weber, *On the Road to Armageddon: How Evangelicals Became Israel's Best Friend* (Grand Rapids, MI: Baker Academic, 2004), 191, 200–201; Mark R. Amstutz, *Evangelicals and American Foreign Policy* (New York: Oxford University Press, 2014), 6, 118–119, 123–124.
50. Frye Gaillard, "Bakker Joined Carter for Prayer, Not Politicking," *CO*, Nov. 1, 1980; interview with Frye Gaillard, Oct. 25, 2016; Miller, *Age of Evangelicalism*, 68.
51. "All Night Gospel Sing," July 2, 1983, PTL video, FPHC.
52. *Jim Bakker*, Nov. 23, 1983.

CHAPTER 9

1. Vanessa Gallman, "'People That Love': The Ministry's Heart Beats behind the Camera," *CO*, July 10, 1978.
2. Louise Hickman Lione, "Vacationland for Pilgrims of PTL Club," *CO*, June 22, 1980.
3. "Talking With Tammy," *Action*, Nov. 1980, 22–23.
4. Holly Miller, "Will the Real Tammy Bakker Please Stand Up?," *Saturday Evening Post*, Jan./Feb. 1981, 20, 22, 116.
5. *PTL Club*, Jan. 6, 1981, reel 2; Del Holford personal email, Nov. 7, 2014.
6. Interview with Alan Langstaff, Nov. 17, 2014; *Jim Bakker*, "Brink of a Miracle" telethon, Oct. 21, 1985; interview with Lee and Nancy Nagelhout, July 12, 2011; interview with Sam Orender, June 14, 2016; Shepard, *Forgiven*, 172–173.
7. Miller, "Real Tammy Bakker," 20, 22, 116; interview with Lee and Nancy Nagelhout, July 12, 2011; interview with Don Hardister, June 5, 2012.
8. LaFleur Paysour, "Tammy Bakker Leaves PTL Show 'Temporarily,'" *CO*, Jan. 16, 1981; *PTL Club*, Jan. 26, 1981, reel 1; Shepard, *Forgiven*, 176–177; Bakker, *I Was Wrong*, 193.
9. Interview with Joyce Cordell, July 31, 2014.
10. Interview with Joyce Cordell, July 31, 2014; Bob Dennis, "Bakkers Leave Charlotte for Home at PTL Complex," *CO*, Feb. 7, 1981; Shepard, *Forgiven*, 178–179.
11. Interview with Thurlow Spurr, Mar. 11, 2015; Shepard, *Forgiven*, 179; Bakker, *I Was Wrong*, 195; *PTL Club*, Jan. 26, 1981, reel 1. When I talked with Thurlow Spurr, he refused to confirm or deny his alleged affair with Tammy, saying only that he and Jim mutually agreed that it was time for him to leave PTL.
12. *PTL Club*, Feb. 6, 1981, reel 1; Bakker, *I Was Wrong*, 197–200; Shepard, *Forgiven*, 180–181.
13. U.S. v. Bakker, vol. 4, 1223–1224, 1254–1268; John Vaughan and Jeri Fischer, "Jim & Tammy's Lake Hideaway," *CO*, Mar. 12, 1988; Gary L. Wright, "Businessman's

Bid Lands Bakkers' Former Home," *CO*, July 7, 1988; John Vaughan, "A Bakker House Revisited," *CO*, Mar. 25, 1989; Tidwell, *Anatomy of a Fraud*, 308.

14. U.S. v. Taggart and Taggart, vol. 4, 539, 541.
15. U.S. v. Taggart and Taggart, vol. 5, 147–148; U.S. v. Bakker, vol. 1, 16.
16. U.S. v. Taggart and Taggart, vol. 5, 151, 160–161; U.S. v. Bakker, vol. 1, 20; interview with Thurlow Spurr, Mar. 11, 2015.
17. U.S. v. Taggart and Taggart, vol. 4, 541.
18. U.S. v. Taggart and Taggart, vol. 5, 8–9.
19. Dortch, *Integrity*, 20–21, 29–30.
20. Dortch, *Integrity*, 21–26, 34–35.
21. Dortch, *Integrity*, 22–23, 32; Shepard, *Forgiven*, 210.
22. Interview with Al Cress, Jan. 15, 2010.
23. Interview with Jim Cobble, Apr. 21, 2010.
24. Dortch, *Integrity*, 39.
25. U.S. v. Bakker, vol. 1, 89, 91, 258–261; vol. 9, 1521–1522.
26. U.S. v. Bakker, vol. 5, 1600, 1621–1622; vol. 6, 284.
27. U.S. v. Bakker, vol. 4, 1235–1237.
28. U.S. v. Bakker, vol. 4, 1240–1254.
29. U.S. v. Bakker, vol. 1, 104; vol. 4, 1259; vol. 9, 1715.
30. U.S. v. Bakker, vol. 1, 254–257.
31. U.S. v. Bakker, vol. 1, 119–120; vol. 4, 1504–1505, 1571, 1574; vol. 6, 308; vol. 10, 1861.
32. Bakker repeated the claim that his church paid his salary on the November 16, 1981, episode of the *Jim Bakker* show and the first hour of the "You and Us Together" telethon, Mar. 6, 1983.
33. U.S. v. Bakker, vol. 6, 317–333, 338, 339; Tidwell, *Anatomy of a Fraud*, 169.
34. Interview with Roger Flessing, July 20, 2010; *Jim Bakker*, Jan. 4, 1984.
35. U.S. v. Bakker, vol. 1, 20–21.
36. U.S. v. Bakker, vol. 1, 20–21; U.S. v. Taggart and Taggart, vol. 5, 12–14, 162–163.
37. U.S. v. Taggart and Taggart, vol. 1, 381–382; vol. 5, 12–14, 19, 165–167.
38. U.S. v. Taggart and Taggart, vol. 5, 168–175.
39. "Victory Day at Heritage USA," *Action*, Nov. 1980, 13; *PTL Club*, Feb. 5, 1981, reel 2.
40. Interview with Don Hardister, June 5, 2012.
41. Interview with Jim J. Bullock, May 13, 2010; "PTL's Jim Bakker Speaks His Mind," *CO*, July 10, 1978. Also see Jane Lee Lisenby, "Homosexuals File Complaint against Station," *Charlotte News*, June 16, 1977; Frye Gaillard, "PTL Moves Cautiously among Vocal, Political Evangelists," *CO*, Sept. 1, 1980; Shepard, *Forgiven*, 175; Straub, *Salvation for Sale*, 108.
42. Miles, *Don't Call Me Brother*, 28, 85, 111, 120, 126–127.
43. Miles, *Don't Call Me Brother*, 12–13; interview with Austin Miles, Jan. 21, 2014.
44. Shepard, *Forgiven*, 175–176.

45. Art Harris, "The Devil's Disciple," *Penthouse*, January 1989, 46–50, 172, 177, 192, 194; Shepard, *Forgiven*, 176, 188; Frye Gaillard, "Bakker Joined Carter for Prayer, Not Politicking," *CO*, Nov. 1, 1980; Gary L. Wright, "Grand Jury Wants to Know if PTL Money Bought Sex," *CO*, Sept. 21, 1988. Gaillard's article confirms that Bakker was vacationing in Bermuda on November 1, 1980.
46. *Jim Bakker*, June 14, 1982; Oct. 20 and 21, 1982; Dec. 19, 1983.
47. *PTL Club*, Aug. 1, 1979, reel 2; Jim Bakker, *Survival: Unite to Live* (Harrison, AR: New Leaf Press, 1980), 38–39.
48. Bakker, *You Can Make It!*, 18, 37.

CHAPTER 10

1. *Jim Bakker*, "Thanksgiving Day Special," Nov. 24, 1983; Michael Richardson, *The Edge of Disaster* (New York: St. Martin's Press, 1987), 194.
2. David George Surdam, *Century of the Leisured Masses: Entertainment and the Transformation of Twentieth-Century America* (New York: Oxford University Press, 2015), xiv, 2, 46, 85; Veblen, *The Theory of the Leisure Class*, 53; Cindy S. Aron, *Working at Play: A History of Vacations in the United States* (New York: Oxford University Press, 1999).
3. U.S. v. Bakker, vol. 9, 1613, 1618; *Jim Bakker*, June 1, 1984.
4. U.S. v. Bakker, vol. 9, 1625.
5. U.S. v. Bakker, vol. 7, 819.
6. U.S. v. Bakker, vol. 7, 809–815; vol. 9, 1623; Linda Brown, "High-Volume Church Builder Views Business as His Ministry," *CO*, Oct. 5, 1986.
7. "Two Restaurants Serve Around the Clock," *Heritage Herald*, Oct. 12–25, 1985; Ashley Barron, "Each Day, Utopian Dreams Fade Away," *CO*, Sept. 5, 2004.
8. U.S. v. Bakker, vol. 9, 1626, 1627; "Heritage Summer '84: The Greatest Ever!" *Together*, summer 1984, 2; *Jim Bakker*, Dec. 3, 1984, Oct. 9, 1985; Charles E. Shepard, "$75 Million, 24,000-Seat Center Planned at PTL's Heritage USA," *CO*, Aug. 1, 1985; Steven Watts, *The Magic Kingdom: Walt Disney and the American Way of Life* (Columbia: University of Missouri Press, 2001), 112; Gary S. Cross and John K. Watson, *The Playful Crowd: Pleasure Places in the Twentieth Century* (New York: Columbia University Press, 2005), 167–202.
9. U.S. v. Bakker, vol. 5, 1623, 1625.
10. U.S. v. Bakker, vol. 5, 1626, 1627, 1631.
11. U.S. v. Bakker, vol. 1, 341–342; Gary L. Tidwell, *Anatomy of a Fraud: Inside the Finances of the PTL Ministries* (New York: John Wiley & Sons, 1993), 293.
12. U.S. v. Bakker, vol. 4, 1511–1519; vol. 7, 824; Tidwell, *Anatomy of a Fraud*, 297.
13. U.S. v. Bakker, vol. 1, 336–338.
14. U.S. v. Bakker, vol. 5, 1633; vol. 6, 173; *Jim Bakker*, telethon hour 3, Feb. 20, 1984.
15. *Jim Bakker*, telethon hour 3, Feb. 20, 1984; U.S v. Bakker, vol. 1, 343–344.

16. U.S. v. Bakker, vol. 1, 343–344, 431–433; vol. 5, 1644; vol. 9, 1743; Tidwell, *Anatomy of a Fraud*, 299.
17. U.S. v. Bakker, vol. 7, 502–503.
18. U.S. v. Bakker, vol. 6, 379. Newspaper stories pegged the final cost of the Partner Center at $42 million. Charles E. Shepard, "PTL Appeals for Donations to Ease $5.5 Million TV Debt," *CO*, Sept. 14, 1985.
19. *Jim Bakker*, May 16, 1984.
20. Charles E. Shepard, "PTL's Drive to Buy Land Purchases Near Heritage USA Approach $9 Million in 2 Years," *CO*, Nov. 24, 1985.
21. *Jim Bakker*, June 1, 1984; U.S. v. Bakker, vol. 3, 1015; vol. 9, 1691.
22. U.S. v. Bakker, vol. 3, 1015; vol. 5, 1639. PTL eventually took out a $2 million loan to complete the waterpark. See U.S. v. Bakker, vol. 4, 1467.
23. *Jim Bakker*, June 1, 1984.
24. U.S. v. Bakker, vol. 5, 1640, 1644, 1646, 1650; Tidwell, *Anatomy of a Fraud*, 337.
25. U.S. v. Bakker, vol. 1, 429.
26. U.S. v. Bakker, vol. 1, 329, 350; Charles E. Shepard and Gary L. Wright, "Jury Sees Bakker on Video," *CO*, Sept. 20, 1989; Tidwell, *Anatomy of a Fraud*, 46.
27. U.S. v. Bakker, vol. 1, 329, 350, 352, 360.
28. U.S. v. Bakker, vol. 7, 825, 872.
29. U.S. v. Bakker, vol. 1, 347, 391; vol. 3, 1046–1050; vol. 5, 1748; vol. 9, 1732; Tidwell, *Anatomy of a Fraud*, 294.
30. U.S. v. Bakker, vol. 5, 1777–1780.
31. *Jim Bakker*, Oct. 5, 1984.
32. U.S. v. Bakker, vol. 5, 1603, 1611, 1650, 1652.
33. U.S. v. Bakker, vol. 5, 1781, 1782, 1784; Tidwell, *Anatomy of a Fraud*, 114.
34. U.S. v. Bakker, vol. 5, 1661–1662; Tidwell, *Anatomy of a Fraud*, 125–126, 213.
35. U.S. v. Bakker, vol. 5, 1666–1667.
36. U.S. v. Bakker, vol. 6, 5–8.
37. U.S. v. Bakker, vol. 1, 324, 390; vol. 4, 1353; vol. 6, 137–140; vol. 7, 743–744; U.S. v. Taggart and Taggart, vol. 2, 574.
38. U.S. v. Taggart and Taggart, vol. 2, 225–226; vol. 4, 144–145, 150–153, 167, 232, 238–239, 250; U.S. v. Bakker, vol. 1, 143–144; vol. 5, 1823–1824; vol. 9, 1521, 1523.
39. U.S. v. Bakker, vol. 4, 1498–1500, 1508–1509; U.S. v. Taggart and Taggart, vol. 4, 152.
40. U.S. v. Bakker, vol. 4, 1539, 1554.
41. U.S. v. Bakker, vol. 5, 1607–1611; vol. 9, 1569; U.S. v. Taggart and Taggart, vol. 2, 228, 429–430. After Dortch became PTL's Senior Executive Vice President, one of PTL's lawyers, John Yorke, recommended that he resign from the Board of Directors. Dortch ignored his advice. See U.S. v. Bakker, vol. 4, 1526–1529.
42. U.S. v. Bakker, vol. 1, 132; vol. 5, 1631, 1632, 1636, 1637, 1640, 1641, 1656, 1657; Tidwell, *Anatomy of a Fraud*, 304, 310.
43. U.S. v. Bakker, vol. 4, 1504–1505, 1521.
44. Shepard, *Forgiven*, 294–295; U.S. v. Taggart and Taggart, vol. 2, 396–397; U.S. v. Bakker, vol. 4, 1501.

45. U.S. v. Taggart and Taggart, vol. 1, 31; vol. 4, 155–156, 407.
46. *Jim Bakker*, Jan. 11, 1985; U.S. v. Bakker, vol. 8, 1355–1365.
47. U.S. v. Bakker, vol. 1, 330; vol. 9, 1700–1706.
48. U.S. v. Bakker, vol. 1, 357, 360; Tidwell, *Anatomy of a Fraud*, 295.
49. U.S. v. Bakker, vol. 7, 510–515.
50. U.S. v. Bakker, vol. 2, 449.
51. U.S. v. Bakker, vol. 1, 398–403.
52. U.S. v. Bakker, vol. 1, 409–412.
53. U.S. v. Bakker, vol. 1, 417–418; Tidwell, *Anatomy of a Fraud*, 317.
54. U.S. v. Bakker, vol. 1, 331; "Folks Encouraged to Join Silver 7000 Club & Help Finish Towers," *Heritage Herald*, Oct. 12–25, 1985.
55. U.S. v. Bakker, vol. 3, 998, 1000, 1001.
56. U.S v. Bakker, vol. 3, 1003–1008; *Jim Bakker*, Oct. 18, 1985.
57. U.S. v. Bakker, vol. 3, 1009–1010, 1014–1015.
58. U.S. v. Bakker, 1672, 1673, 1674, 1675, 1676; Tidwell, *Anatomy of a Fraud*, 311.
59. U.S. v. Bakker, vol. 1, 215; vol. 5, 1682, 1684, 1685; vol. 9, 1813–1814; Shepard, "PTL Appeals for Donations."
60. U.S. v. Bakker, vol. 3, 783–785.
61. U.S. v. Bakker, vol. 3, 817–818.
62. U.S. v. Bakker, vol. 3, 818.
63. U.S. v. Bakker, vol. 3, 788–804, 825–827.
64. U.S. v. Bakker, vol. 2, 722–723; vol. 3, 829–830.
65. U.S. v. Bakker, vol. 3, 803, 805, 806, 807, 808, 814.
66. U.S. v. Bakker, vol. 3, 809–813.
67. U.S. v. Bakker, vol. 4, 1271.
68. U.S. v. Bakker, vol. 4, 1272–1275, 1360–1369.
69. U.S. v. Bakker, vol. 3, 811, 839; interview with Judy Bycura, June 6, 2012.
70. U.S. v. Bakker, vol. 2, 637, 642; vol. 10, 1861. By the time of Bakker's criminal trial in 1989, Craddock had married and changed her name to Carol Price.
71. Interview with J'Tanya Adams, Sept. 12, 2011; U.S. v. Bakker, vol. 2, 655.
72. Interview with J'Tanya Adams, Sept. 12, 2011; U.S. v. Bakker, vol. 2, 661–662, 663–664.
73. Interview with J'Tanya Adams, Sept. 12, 2011; U.S. v. Bakker, vol. 2, 664, 670–672; Charles E. Shepard and Elizabeth Leland, "PTL Dug Itself into a Hole with Burgeoning Partnerships," *CO*, July 5, 1987.
74. U.S. v. Bakker, vol. 2, 673.
75. Interview with J'Tanya Adams, Sept. 12, 2011; U.S. v. Bakker, vol. 2, 674.
76. Interview with J'Tanya Adams, Sept. 12, 2011; U.S. v. Bakker, vol. 2, 703–704. Judy Rutliff, who became Adams's supervisor in partner research, testified that Adams was fired for insubordination. See U.S. v. Bakker, vol. 8, 1126–1127.
77. "PTL Telethon Has a Rousing Start!" *Heritage Herald*, Oct. 12–Oct. 25, 1985.
78. *Jim Bakker*, "Brink of a Miracle" telethon, Oct. 21, 1985; Charles E. Shepard, "Broadcasting the Bible," *CO*, Jan. 27, 1986.

79. *Jim Bakker*, Oct. 18, 1985; *Jim Bakker*, Dec. 6, 1985; U.S. v. Bakker, vol. 7, 520–523.
80. U.S. v. Bakker, vol. 6, 274, 276.
81. U.S. v. Bakker, vol. 8, 1191, 1192, 1197.
82. Interview with J'Tanya Adams, Sept. 12, 2011.
83. Pearl Bailey appeared on the *Jim Bakker* show on January 31, 1984.

CHAPTER 11

1. Robert Scheer and Barry Golson, "The Jessica Hahn Story: Part Two," *Playboy*, Dec. 1987, 196.
2. Bakker, *I Was Wrong*, 23; Scheer and Golson, "Jessica Hahn Story: Part Two," 196.
3. Scheer and Golson, "Jessica Hahn Story: Part Two," 196–197; U.S. v. Bakker, vol. 1, 98.
4. Interview with Jessica Hahn, Feb. 5, 2014; Shepard, *Forgiven*, 287; Robert Bellafiore, "Hahn Minister Indicted for Tax Evasion," Associated Press, Oct. 27, 1988; Art Harris and Michael Isikoff, "Jessica Hahn, on the Defensive," *Washington Post*, Sept. 30, 1987. Hahn described Profeta more favorably in her 1987 *Playboy* interview.
5. Interview with Jessica Hahn, Feb. 5, 2014.
6. Daily News Wire Services, "Tax Probe Targets Hahn Ex-Lovers," *Philadelphia Daily News*, Sept. 28, 1987.
7. Shepard, *Forgiven*, 281.
8. Shepard, *Forgiven*, 281–282; U.S. v. Bakker, vol. 6, 3 (insert); Scheer and Golson, "Jessica Hahn Story: Part Two," 198; Charles E. Shepard, "NYC Church Got $50,000 after Hahn Settlement," *CO*, June 5, 1987.
9. Dortch, *Integrity*, 13–16.
10. Dortch, *Integrity*, 79–82; Shepard, *Forgiven*, 283.
11. Dortch, *Integrity*, 80; Scheer and Golson, "Jessica Hahn Story: Part Two," 204; Shepard, *Forgiven*, 284–286; Bakker, *I Was Wrong*, 26. Dortch reprints the letter almost in its entirety in his autobiography. Shepard gives excerpts from the letter that match Dortch's version.
12. Dortch, *Integrity*, 87–93; Sarah Peasley, "Personalities: Hahn Says Bakker Was Threatened," *Washington Post*, Feb. 1, 1988.
13. Dortch, *Integrity*, 82–83.
14. Shepard, *Forgiven*, 216–217; Tim Chavez, "City Evangelist Files Bankruptcy Petition," *The Oklahoman*, June 11, 1988; interview with Terry Mattingly, June 16, 2016.
15. Shepard, *Forgiven*, 217.
16. Scheer and Golson, "Jessica Hahn Story: Part Two," 200.
17. Scheer and Golson, "Jessica Hahn Story: Part Two," 200; U.S. v. Bakker, vol. 6, 76–77; Shepard, *Forgiven*, 284; Shepard, "NYC Church Got $50,000"; Gary L. Wright, "PTL Pastor Can't Recall How He Raised Loan," *CO*, Feb. 26, 1988; Gary

L. Wright and Charles E. Shepard, "2 More Indicted in PTL Case," *CO*, Dec. 6, 1989. Dortch either dictated or wrote out the confession that Hahn signed, and Shirley Fulbright, Jim Bakker's secretary, typed it, according to David Taggart. See U.S. v. Bakker, vol. 1, 99–100. The charges against Johnson were dismissed at trial in April 1990. See Gary L. Wright, "Johnson Charges Dismissed," *CO*, Apr. 11, 1990.

18. Scheer and Golson, "Jessica Hahn Story: Part 2," 200, 202; Jay Mathews, "The Jessica Hahn 'Confession,'" *Washington Post*, Mar. 28, 1987.
19. John Stewart, *Holy War: An Inside Account of the Battle for PTL* (Enid, OK: Fireside Publishing, 1987), 24; Scheer and Golson, "Jessica Hahn Story: Part Two," 202; Art Harris, "The Jessica Hahn Tape: Adviser Recalls Her Tearful Account of the Episode with Jim Bakker," *Washington Post*, Apr. 9, 1987.
20. Scott Fagerstrom, Cheryl Downey, "Roper Crusades for Accountable Ministry," *Orange County Register*, Mar. 29, 1987.
21. Scheer and Golson, "Jessica Hahn Story: Part Two," 202; Dortch, *Integrity*, 95; Stewart, *Holy War*, 24–26; interview with John Stewart, May 10, 2010.
22. Stewart, *Holy War*, 31–36; interview with John Stewart, May 10, 2010; Dortch, *Integrity*, 96; Bakker, *I Was Wrong*, 27.
23. Interview with John Stewart, May 10, 2010, and copies of notes provided by Stewart; Dortch, *Integrity*, 97–104.
24. Interview with John Stewart, May 10, 2010; Stewart, *Holy War*, 40–41; U.S. v. Bakker, vol. 1, 101–102; vol. 3, 941, 1093–1094; vol. 6, 235–237.
25. Interview with John Stewart, May 10, 2010; Stewart, *Holy War*, 43; U.S. v. Bakker, vol. 6, 219.
26. U.S. v. Bakker, vol. 1, 102; vol. 6, 79, 221–224, 246–247; Dortch, *Integrity*, 104–111; Shepard, *Forgiven*, 306; interview with John Stewart, May 10, 2010; Charles E. Shepard, "New Total in Bakker-Hahn Case Reaches $265,000," *CO*, Mar. 26, 1987; Henry Eichel, "PTL Spent $363,700 on Hahn," *CO*, Jan. 3, 1988. Stewart gave me a photocopy of the $12,500 check he received from Roper and of the $115,000 check from Howard Weitzman to the Bank of Yorba Linda, dated February 27, 1985.
27. Interview with John Stewart, May 10, 2010; Stewart, *Holy War*, 46; U.S. v. Taggart and Taggart, vol. 2, 301–302, 640.
28. U.S. v. Bakker, vol. 6, 81–82, 84, 249–250; vol. 7, 847.
29. Scheer and Golson, "Jessica Hahn Story: Part Two," 204.
30. Shepard, *Forgiven*, 243; Richardson, *Edge of Disaster*, 113; *Jim Bakker*, Oct. 5, 1984.
31. *Jim Bakker*, Dec. 3, 1984; U.S. v. Bakker, vol. 2, 530.
32. "Tammy and Mr. T," PTL video, Feb. 28, 1985, FPHC; *Jim Bakker*, Mar. 27, 1985 [excerpt of Nell Carter interview]; "Tammy Interviews," PTL video with Arvella Schuller and Lou Ferrigno, May 22 and 23, 1985, FPHC.
33. "Steve Pieters Interview with Tammy Bakker on PTL/Tammy's House Party," accessed Sept. 20, 2015, https://www.youtube.com/watch?v=GjXXdQ6VceQ.

34. Tammy Faye Messner, *I Will Survive . . . And You Will, Too!* (New York: Jeremy P. Tarcher/Penguin, 2003), 27; interview with Judy Bycura, June 6, 2012.
35. U.S. v. Bakker, vol. 1, 69–70; vol. 4, 1349; Richardson, *Edge of Disaster*, 10, 159; interview with Judy Bycura, June 6, 2012.
36. Richardson, *Edge of Disaster*, 159–160, 170.
37. Richardson, *Edge of Disaster*, 158, 171, 172.
38. Richardson, *Edge of Disaster*, 163, 166; Bakker, *I Was Wrong*, 613; Jay Bakker, *Son of a Preacher Man: My Search for Grace in the Shadows* (New York: HarperCollins, 2001), 9, 16, 17.
39. U.S. v. Bakker, vol. 1, 63, 66.
40. U.S. v. Bakker, vol. 1, 64, 65–66, 67–68; Richardson, *Edge of Disaster*, 167; Jay Bakker, *Son of a Preacher Man*, 17.
41. U.S. v. Bakker, vol. 1, 131; vol. 6, 366–367, 422; Richardson, *Edge of Disaster*, 157; Shepard, *Forgiven*, 257–258.
42. Richardson, *Edge of Disaster*, 124, 125; U.S. v. Bakker, vol. 1, 132.
43. U.S. v. Bakker, vol. 1, 133–134; vol. 3, 1143–1144; Richardson, *Edge of Disaster*, 175–177; Tidwell, *Anatomy of a Fraud*, 304.
44. U.S. v. Bakker, vol. 3, 1135–1137; vol. 4, 1343; vol. 8, 1354; author interview with Don Hardister, June 5, 2012; Shepard, *Forgiven*, 192–193.
45. U.S. v. Bakker, vol. 1, 135–142, 200; vol. 3, 944; vol. 6, 423–424; Richardson, *Edge of Disaster*, 186–189.
46. Richardson, *Edge of Disaster*, 184.
47. Richardson, *Edge of Disaster*, 112–113.
48. Interview with Bobbie Garn, June 10, 2015; Shepard, *Forgiven*, 260; U.S. v. Taggart and Taggart, vol. 4, 515. The plane was purchased on July 11, 1984.
49. Interview with Bobbie Garn, June 10, 2015.
50. Shepard, *Forgiven*, 261–262.
51. *Jim Bakker*, Oct. 5, 1984.
52. U.S. v. David Taggart and James Taggart, vol. 1, 116; vol. 2, 85, 555; vol. 3, 137, 172; vol. 4, 228–230.
53. U.S. v. Taggart and Taggart, vol. 1, 378–388; vol. 4, 539–540.
54. U.S. v. Taggart and Taggart, vol. 2, 248, 372, 376; vol. 4, 156–157, 217.
55. U.S. v. Taggart and Taggart, vol. 1, 112, 333, 375; vol. 2, 425, 428; vol. 4, 221, 226.
56. U.S. v. Taggart and Taggart, vol. 2, 302, 422; vol. 3, 141; vol. 4, 169–170, 203–204, 223–224, 469.
57. U.S. v. Taggart and Taggart, vol. 1, 18, 23, 68, 74, 76, 78, 81, 122, 126, 246–247, 363–373; vol. 2, 57–59, 462.
58. U.S. v. Taggart and Taggart, vol. 1, 80; vol. 2, 465, 469, 474, 479, 489, 492, 503, 510.
59. U.S. v. Taggart and Taggart, vol. 1, 27, 41, 42, 202; vol. 4, 260.
60. U.S. v. Taggart and Taggart, vol. 3, 115–135.
61. U.S. v. Taggart, vol. 3, 13–46.
62. U.S. v. Taggart and Taggart, vol. 1, 384–385; vol. 2, 641–646.

63. U.S v. Taggart and Taggart, vol. 3, 57–80, 101.
64. U.S. v. Taggart and Taggart, vol. 2, 67, 80–81; vol. 3, 102.
65. U.S. v. Taggart and Taggart, vol. 1, 301; vol. 2, 86–90, 164–189; vol. 2, 284–285, 513, 519, 621–623.
66. U.S. v. Taggart, vol. 1, 192; vol. 3, 97–102.
67. U.S. v. Taggart and Taggart, vol. 1, 531–539, 546; vol. 2, 649–656, 678–697; vol. 3, 445, 447.
68. U.S. v. Taggart and Taggart, vol. 3, 104–114, 128; vol. 3, 447.
69. U.S. v. Taggart and Taggart, vol. 2, 342–350, 351–360; vol. 3, 445; Tidwell, *Anatomy of a Fraud*, 316.
70. U.S. v. Taggart and Taggart, vol. 1, 117; vol. 2, 84–85, 124–126, 131–138; vol. 3, 43, 129, 130, 161, 162; vol. 4, 228; John Wildman and Charles E. Shepard, "Highly Paid Bakker Aide Unknown to PTL Viewers," *CO*, Apr. 28, 1987.
71. U.S. v. Taggart and Taggart, vol. 1, 182, 196, 205, 272; vol. 2, 77–78, 141–144, 148–151, 154–158, 268–271, 526–532; vol. 3, 19, 67, 124–125, 285–292; vol. 4, 114, 272–273, 318–320, 349, 351, 354, 429–430, 448–452. The employment contract was dated December 10, 1985. The lawyer who drafted the employment agreement, Robert Gunst, later testified that he actually believed that David Taggart was the President of PTL, even though he had been representing PTL for more than a year and had prepared the brothers' tax returns starting with 1984. See U.S. v. Taggart and Taggart, vol. 1, 245–249. David Taggart later testified that he did not read the document before signing it. See U.S. v. Taggart and Taggart, David Taggart testimony, 212–214.
72. U.S. v. Taggart and Taggart, vol. 1, 393–408; vol. 2, 651–652; vol. 3, 68.
73. U.S. v. Taggart and Taggart, vol. 1, 514–530; vol. 3, 2–9, 51–52, 90–91, 203.
74. U.S. v. Taggart and Taggart, vol. 2, 308, 340–341; vol. 3, 204–206, 215, 229–231, 232–238, 252–253, 261, 265–266.
75. U.S. v. Taggart and Taggart, vol. 2, 532–538, 593–604, 607–609; vol. 4, 556–561. David Taggart also bought Bailey about $10,000 worth of clothes so that he would look "like a Madison Avenue banker." Bailey later had to report the $10,000 as income. See U.S. v. Taggart and Taggart, vol. 4, 193.
76. U.S. v. Taggart and Taggart, vol. 1, 192; vol. 2, 554; vol. 3, 430–435.
77. Interview with Al Cress, Jan. 15–17, 2010.
78. U.S. v. Taggart and Taggart, vol. 2, 202–203, 387–389; interview with Al Cress, Jan. 15–17, 2010.
79. Interview with Al Cress, Jan. 15–17, 2010.

CHAPTER 12

1. "Our History," Chautauqua Institution, accessed July 29, 2015, ciweb.org/about-us/history; Jeffrey Simpson, *Chautauqua: An American Utopia* (New York: Harry N. Abrams, 1999), 31–37.

2. "PTL's Pillars of Support," *Heritage Herald*, Jan. 1987, 1.
3. "Wendy's Will Open at PTL," *Heritage Herald*, Aug. 1986, 20; "'Friendly People' Make Everyone Feel at Home while Visiting PTL," *Heritage Herald*, Sept. 1986, 8; Keith Williams, "Tall Wendy's to Join Heritage Community," *CO*, July 10, 1985.
4. "Heritage USA Daily Schedule, Weekend Schedule," *Heritage Herald*, July 1986, 12; "Heritage USA Daily Schedule, Weekend Schedule," *Heritage Herald*, Sept. 1986, 12; "Heritage USA Info," *Heritage Herald*, Mar. 1987, 14. The same basic schedule is repeated in each edition of the *Heritage Herald* from April 1986 to March 1987.
5. Interview with Ron Kopczik, May 2, 2011.
6. "Heritage Island Is Full of Thrills," *Heritage Herald*, Aug. 1986, 1–2; "Heritage Island's Initial Season Exceeded Expectations," *Heritage Herald*, Nov. 1986, 12; Lawrence Toppman, "Making a Splash!," *CO*, July 4, 1986; U.S. v. Bakker, vol. 9, 1691.
7. "For Kevin: A Miracle of Love," *Heritage Herald*, June 1986, 1; "PTL Celebrates Its Victory!," *Heritage Herald*, July 1986, 1; "Kevin's House Is an Actual Dream Come True," *Heritage Herald*, Nov. 1986, 3; Will Parrish, "Kevin's House Pops Up," *CO*, July 3, 1986; "Kevin's House: Compassion and Credibility," *CO*, July 6, 1986.
8. Shepard, *Forgiven*, 415–421; James A. Albert, *Jim Bakker: Miscarriage of Justice?* (Chicago: Open Court, 1998), 37; U.S. v. Bakker, vol. 7, 839.
9. "Fort Hope Closes in on Its Opening," *Heritage Herald*, May 1986, 3; "Fort Hope Prepares for Its Dedication," *Heritage Herald*, June 1986, 1, 13; "Fort Hope Reaches Full Operation," *Heritage Herald*, Sept. 1986, 2; U.S. v. Bakker, vol. 7, 910.
10. U.S. v. Bakker, vol. 8, 1158–1163.
11. "Christmas City Coming," *Heritage Herald*, Oct. 1986, 1–2; "Christmas City 1986 Begins," *Heritage Herald*, Nov. 1986, 1–2; "Christmas City '86 Continues," *Heritage Herald*, Dec. 1986, 1; Linda Brown, "Beat the Traffic and Get a Bird's-Eye View of Lights," *CO*, Dec. 7, 1986; "PTL Lights Up Visitors' Christmas," *CO*, Dec. 21, 1986.
12. Charles E. Shepard, "Bakker Misled PTL Viewers, FCC Records Show," *CO*, Jan. 26, 1986. The related articles written by Shepard follow in the January 26 and 27 editions of the paper.
13. Charles E. Shepard, "PTL's Bakker Rebuts News Reports of FCC Allegations," *CO*, Feb. 1, 1986; Shepard, *Forgiven*, 366; Jamie Buckingham, *Buckingham Report*, Mar. 19, 1986.
14. "Telethon Set," *Heritage Herald*, Apr. 1986; "PTL's Telethon Is a Success," *Heritage Herald*, May 1986.
15. Shepard, *Forgiven*, 369–372; Jamie Buckingham, *Buckingham Report*, Mar. 19, 1986.
16. Jamie Buckingham, *Buckingham Report*, Mar. 19, 1986.

17. Jamie Buckingham, *Buckingham Report*, Mar. 19, 1986.
18. U.S. v. Taggart and Taggart, vol. 3, 331–347; U.S. v. Bakker, vol. 4, 1571–1576. Tax-exempt religious organizations were generally classified as 501C3 organizations under the IRS code.
19. U.S. v. Taggart v. Taggart, vol. 3, 348–350. George later testified that he did not know that PTL was in danger of losing its tax-exempt status as a result of the IRS audit. See U.S. v. Bakker, vol. 5, 1924.
20. U.S. v. Taggart and Taggart, vol. 1, 449; vol. 3, 351–354.
21. U.S. v. Taggart and Taggart, vol. 1, 460, 491, 507; vol. 3, 357–361.
22. U.S. v. Taggart and Taggart, vol. 1, 463, 464, 469, 488–492, 507; vol. 2, 494; vol. 3, 372–373, 405.
23. U.S. v. Taggart and Taggart, vol. 1, 483, 498; vol. 3, 364, 367–378, 380–381, 406–414, 415–416.
24. U.S. v. Bakker, vol. 5, 1940; Charles F. Shepard, "PTL in Tax Dispute with IRS, S.C. Agency," *CO*, Mar. 24, 1986. Also see Charles E. Shepard, "IRS Audits of Nonprofits Often Focus on Deductions," *CO*, Mar. 24, 1986.
25. Shepard, "PTL in Tax Dispute with IRS, S.C. Agency."
26. U.S. v. Bakker, vol. 4, 1329; U.S. v. Taggart and Taggart, vol. 4, 212; interview with John Aiton, Feb. 17, 2010.
27. U.S. v. Taggart, vol. 1, 349; vol. 2, 21, 40, 161, 291; vol. 4, 212; U.S. v. Bakker, vol. 9, 1570–1573.
28. U.S. v. Taggart and Taggart, vol. 2, 214, 222, 255; vol. 4, 154.
29. *Jim and Tammy*, May 26, 1986; U.S. v. Bakker, vol. 1, 332, 363; vol. 2, 473.
30. U.S. v. Bakker, vol. 5, 1705–1717; vol. 6, 28–29; Tidwell, *Anatomy of a Fraud*, 61–65, 313.
31. U.S. v. Bakker, vol. 6, 55, 56; Henry Eichel, "July Surge in Contributions Puts PTL over the Top, Falwell Says," *CO*, Aug. 5, 1987; Tidwell, *Anatomy of a Fraud*, 302.
32. U.S. v. Bakker, vol. 1, 364; vol. 6, 35; vol. 7, 901; "Bunkhouse Construction Started," *Heritage Herald*, Sept. 1986, 1.
33. U.S. v. Bakker, vol. 1, 333; vol. 5, 1725, 1726, 1727, 1728, 1729; vol. 6, 36, 277; vol. 7, 901. A second bunkhouse was mostly finished when Bakker resigned in March 1987. See U.S. v. Bakker, vol. 7, 827; vol. 9, 1547, 1689.
34. Linda Brown, "Ground Broken on Complex of High-Rises," *CO*, Sept. 27, 1986; "Plans Revealed For New Community," *Heritage Herald*, Nov. 1986, 24; "Construction Continuing Every Day on First of the Mulberry Towers," *Heritage Herald*, Mar. 1987, 24.
35. U.S. v. Bakker, vol. 5, 1732; vol. 6, 124; vol. 7, 830–831.
36. U.S. v. Bakker, vol. 1, 334, 368, 369; vol. 6, 37, 115; vol. 7, 828, 860–861; "Great Response to 1100 Club," *Heritage Herald*, Jan. 1987, 1; "Work Progresses on Next Phase of Farmland," *Heritage Herald*, Jan. 1987, 3.
37. *Jim and Tammy*, Dec. 3, 1986.
38. U.S. v. Bakker, vol. 6, 380–383.

39. U.S. v. Bakker, vol. 5, 1911, 1915; vol. 6, 66; Charles E. Shepard, "PTL Board Minutes Include No Bonus Figures," *CO*, May 30, 1987.
40. U.S. v. Bakker, vol. 5, 1917–1926. George had also heard rumors about Bakker's encounter with Jessica Hahn at about the same time he resigned from PTL's board. Charles E. Shepard, "Dortch May Face Scrutiny over Role in Bakker Case," *CO*, Mar. 22, 1987.
41. U.S. v. Bakker, vol. 3, 847, 849, 852, 855, 860, 877, 881, 889.
42. U.S. v. Bakker, vol. 6, 183, 184, 188, 321, 333.
43. U.S. v. Bakker, vol. 3, 1019–1023.
44. U.S. v. Bakker, vol. 5, 1859; Charles E. Shepard, "PTL's Membership in Watchdog Group Renewed by Board," *CO*, Mar. 6, 1986; Charles E. Shepard, "PTL Severs Links to Financial Council," *CO*, Dec. 25, 1986; Shepard, *Forgiven*, 381.
45. Shepard, "PTL's Membership in Watchdog Group"; Shepard, "PTL Severs Links."
46. U.S. v. Bakker, vol. 1, 176–178; vol. 6, 369; vol. 10, 1878–1879; Charles E. Shepard, "PTL's Bakkers Buy Home outside Gatlinburg," *CO*, Nov. 20, 1986; Shepard, *Forgiven*, 431.
47. U.S. v. Bakker, vol. 3, 864; vol. 4, 1339; vol. 5, 1920, 1935; vol. 6, 194, 195, 299, 301, 310, 422; vol. 7, 887, 889; Shepard, *Forgiven*, 432; Tidwell, *Anatomy of a Fraud*, 325, 326.
48. U.S. v. Bakker, vol. 1, 93, 181–184; vol. 3, 1116; vol. 6, 371; Shepard, *Forgiven*, 471–472; Associated Press, "Bakkers Trying to Sell Home in Palm Springs," *CO*, June 21, 1987.
49. www.visitpalmspings.com, accessed Sept. 19, 2015; Richard Schickel, *Intimate Strangers: The Culture of Celebrity* (Garden City, NY: Doubleday & Company, 1985).
50. Lew Powell, "Undeterred by the Drought of '86," *CO*, Dec. 28, 1986; U.S. v. Bakker, vol. 9, 1806–1807; U.S. v. Taggart and Taggart, vol. 4, 518.
51. *Jim and Tammy*, "Crystal Palace Ground Breaking," Jan. 2, 1987; Dale Albright, "Ground Broken for Crystal Palace!," *Heritage Herald*, Feb. 1987, 1.
52. *Jim and Tammy*, "Crystal Palace Ground Breaking," Jan. 2, 1987; Dale Albright, "Ground Broken for Crystal Palace!," *Heritage Herald*, Feb. 1987, 1–2; Brian Melton, "Bakker Breaks Ground on Crystal Palace," *CO*, Jan. 3, 1987; J. R. Piggott, *Palace of the People: The Crystal Palace at Sydenham, 1854–1936* (Madison: University of Wisconsin Press, 2004), 40; Ian Leith, *Delamotte's Crystal Palace: A Victorian Pleasure Dome Revealed* (Swindon: English Heritage, 2005), 1; John McKean, *Crystal Palace: Joseph Paxton and Charles Fox* (London: Phaidon Press, 1994).
53. *Jim and Tammy*, "Crystal Palace Ground Breaking"; Albright, "Ground Broken for Crystal Palace!"
54. *Jim and Tammy*, Jan. 1, 1987.
55. *Jim and Tammy*, Jan. 2, 1987.

56. *Jim and Tammy*, "Crystal Palace Ground Breaking"; Albright, "Ground Broken for Crystal Palace!"; U.S. v. Bakker, vol. 6, 442; Jonathan Root, "Total Salvation," 2015.
57. Liz Chandler, "Council Gets 5-Hour View of Future Heritage USA," *CO*, Jan. 13, 1987; Liz Chandler, "PTL's Heritage USA Reaching For the Sky," *CO*, Jan. 25, 1987; "Lodging to Grow," *Heritage Herald*, Aug. 1986, 4; Shepard, *Forgiven*, 310–311; U.S. v. Bakker, vol. 9, 1689; Bakker, *I Was Wrong*, 39.
58. Kathi Purvis, "T. Bakker Ill, Hospitalized in California," *CO*, Jan. 17, 1987.
59. Jay Bakker, *Son of a Preacher Man*, 25–26; Bakker, *I Was Wrong*, 38–39.
60. U.S. v. Bakker, vol. 3, 1093–1098.
61. Jay Bakker, *Son of a Preacher Man*, 26–27; Bakker, *I Was Wrong*, 40–41; Shepard, *Forgiven*, 452; Bakker, *Telling It My Way*, 171–173; PTL "Special Presentation" videotape, Mar. 8, 1987.
62. John Wildman, "Hospitalized with Pneumonia: Tammy Bakker Ill, Not Dead," *CO*, Jan. 23, 1987; "Tammy Bakker Leaves Hospital," Jan. 30, 1987.
63. Bakker, *I Was Wrong*, 42–43; Bakker, *Son of a Preacher Man*, 27–28; Bakker, *Telling It My Way*, 175–179; U.S. v. Bakker, vol. 1, 184–186.
64. Interview with Sam Orender and Donna Chavis, May 10, 2010; interview with Al Cress, Jan. 15–17, 2010; U.S. v. Taggart and Taggart, vol. 2, 390; U.S. v. Bakker, vol. 4, 1524; Kathleen McClain, "PTL's Board Scrutinizing All Who Buy Network's Time," *CO*, May 24, 1987.
65. U.S. v. Bakker, vol. 1, 334–335, 371, 372–373; Shepard, "PTL Severs Links." Bakker later claimed that he had nothing to do with the Family Fun program, which he said was created by Richard Dortch. See U.S. v. Bakker, vol. 9, 1717.
66. PTL "Special Presentation"; Charles E. Shepard and Linda Brown, "Bakker Treated for Drug Dependency," *CO*, Mar. 7, 1987; Elizabeth Leland, "Viewers of PTL Call In to Support Tammy Bakker," *CO*, Mar. 10, 1987; Jane McAlister, "Tammy Deserves Compassion," *CO*, Mar. 11, 1987.

CHAPTER 13

1. Shepard, *Forgiven*, 400; Dannye Romine, "Charles Shepard Writing PTL Book," *CO*, Aug. 6, 1987.
2. Interview with Al Cress, Jan. 15–17, 2010; Shepard, *Forgiven*, 397–398, 405.
3. Interview with Al Cress, Jan. 15–17, 2010; Shepard, *Forgiven*, 405, 406.
4. Interview with Al Cress, Jan. 15–17, 2010; Shepard, *Forgiven*, 407–408.
5. Interview with Jim Cobble, Apr. 21, 2010.
6. Shepard, *Forgiven*, 418–419.
7. Elizabeth Leland, "Falwell Defends Swaggart's Motives, Denies Conspiracy," *CO*, Mar. 25, 1987.
8. Ann Rowe Seaman, *Swaggart: The Unauthorized Biography of an American Evangelist* (New York: Continuum, 1999), 82–86, 108–109; Jimmy Swaggart and

Robert Paul Lamb, *To Cross a River* (Plainfield, NJ: Logos International, 1977), 2, 52; Lawrence Wright, *Saints & Sinners: Walter Railey, Jimmy Swaggart, Madalyn Murray O'Hair, Anton LaVey, Will Campbell, Matthew Fox* (New York: Alfred A. Knopf, 1993), 49–69; Lawrence Wright, "False Messiah," *Rolling Stone,* July 14–28, 1988, 103, 106.

9. Seaman, *Swaggart,* 28, 37, 119, 133, 371; Swaggart, *To Cross a River,* 65; Wright, "False Messiah," 109; Wright, *Saints & Sinners,* 56–69.
10. Swaggart, *To Cross a River,* 85–87; Wright, "False Messiah," 109; Wright, *Saints & Sinners,* 68.
11. Seaman, *Swaggart,* 178, 201, 219, 226, 235, 245; Swaggart, *To Cross a River,* 197, 215, 219, 231–232; Wright, "False Messiah," 99.
12. Jimmy Swaggart to Jim Dunbar, May 2, 1978, FPHC; Jimme Dunbar to C. M. Ward, Feb. 16, 1978, FPHC.
13. Jimmy Swaggart, "The Gospel of Self-Esteem," *The Evangelist,* Mar. 1987, 4–9. Swaggart also used the November 1986 issue of *The Evangelist* to attack Christian psychology, psychotherapy, and counseling. See Jimmy Swaggart, "Christian Psychology," *The Evangelist,* Nov. 1986, 4–10.
14. Seaman, *Swaggart,* 216, 221; Hunter Lundy, *Let Us Prey: The Public Trial of Jimmy Swaggart* (Columbus, MS: Genesis Press, 1999), 57–60, 111–112, 167–170; "Jury Is Told That Swaggart Spread Rumors," *New York Times,* July 17, 1991; "The Preacher's Trysts: Marvin Gorman Denies Other Swaggart Claims," *Washington Post,* Aug. 13, 1991; Susan Finch, "Gorman Affair Lasted Three Years, Preacher Says," *Times-Picayune,* July 18, 1991; Elizabeth Mullener, "The Preachers' Wives," *Times-Picayune,* Aug. 11, 1991; Susan Finch, "Woman: Gorman and I Had Sex Several Times," *Times-Picayune,* Aug. 21, 1991.
15. Seaman, *Swaggart,* 240–241; Lundy, *Let Us Prey,* 170–172; Susan Finch, "Gorman's Wife: He Had One Affair," *Times-Picayune,* Aug. 6, 1991; Susan Finch, "Husband: Gorman's Calls Taped," *Times-Picayune,* Aug. 27, 1991.
16. Seaman, *Swaggart,* 268, 271. The *Heritage Herald* carried a daily programming schedule in each edition, which listed Gorman's show in the 1 p.m. slot through October 1986. Gorman later said that he withdrew his name from consideration to become the next general superintendent of the Assemblies of God after Swaggart spread rumors that he had fathered a child by a preacher's wife in Arkansas. See Susan Finch, "Fell Only Once, Gorman Claims," *Times-Picayune,* Aug. 13, 1991.
17. Lundy, *Let Us Prey,* 26–28.
18. Seaman, *Swaggart,* 276–278; Lundy, *Let Us Prey,* 15, 30, 211–213; Ronald Smothers, "Sex, Demons and TV Ratings Fight Enliven Court Battle of 2 Evangelists," *New York Times,* July 21, 1991; Susan Finch, "Agent: Gorman Lost Deal Due To Allegations," *Times-Picayune,* Aug. 9, 1991.
19. Seaman, *Swaggart,* 278–279; Shepard, *Forgiven,* 424, 480; Art Harris, "Jimmy Swaggart and the Snare of Sin," *Washington Post,* Feb. 25, 1988.

20. Jimmy Swaggart, "Two Points of View," *The Evangelist*, Dec. 1986, 46; Seaman, *Swaggart*, 280.
21. Lundy, *Let Us Prey*, 173–174, 230–232; Susan Finch, "Witness: Alleged Lover Slept Around," *Times-Picayune*, Aug. 2, 1991; Susan Finch, "Savage: Gorman Behind 'Door No. 2,'" *Times Picayune*, Aug. 22, 1991.
22. Lundy, *Let Us Prey*, 169, 170–172, 214–215; Seaman, *Swaggart*, 376; Susan Finch, "Witness: Gorman Pressured Me Into Sex," *Times-Picayune*, Sept. 4, 1991. At one point McDaniel claimed that she was eighteen when the incident with Gorman occurred, but she would have been twenty-one in 1973.
23. Lundy, *Let Us Prey*, 39, 194–195, 224–225; Susan Finch, "Preacher: Pastor's Wife Admitted Affair," *Times-Picayune*, July 17, 1991; Susan Finch, "Gorman Affair Rumors Common in Swaggart's Offices, Aide Testifies," *Times Picayune*, July 19, 1991; Susan Finch, "Witness: Swaggart Said Gorman Had 15 Affairs," *Times-Picayune*, July 23, 1991; Susan Finch, "Missionary Says He Heard of 100 Affairs," *Times-Picayune*, July 25, 1991; Susan Finch, "Gorman Aide: Story about Women Grew," *Times-Picayune*, July 30, 1991; Susan Finch, "Swaggart: Affairs Go Way Back," *Times-Picayune*, Aug. 7, 1991; Susan Finch, "Gorman Witness Contradicts Pastor," *Times-Picayune*, Aug. 20, 1991; Susan Finch, "Mrs. Swaggart: No Plot against Gorman," *Times-Picayune*, Aug. 29, 1991; Susan Finch, "Demon Spoke Gorman's Name During Exorcism, Pastor Says," *Times-Picayune*, Aug. 30, 1991.
24. Lundy, *Let Us Prey*, 46, 270–271; Seaman, *Swaggart*, 312; Steve Cannizaro, "Partial Settlement Paid in Gorman Slander Suit," *Times-Picayune*, May 16, 1991; Susan Finch, "Televangelists Take Feud to Court," *Times-Picayune*, July 7, 1991. During the trial, Gorman testified that another woman, Jane Talbot, also made sexual advances toward him. See Susan Finch, "Another Woman Made Advances, Gorman Says," *Times Picayune*, Aug. 14, 1991. Talbot and Cheryl McConnell testified that Gorman kissed and caressed them during counseling in his office. See Susan Finch, "Women: Gorman Always Kissed," *Times-Picayune*, Aug. 23, 1991; Susan Finch, "Gorman Jury Must Sort Contradictions," *Times-Picayune*, Sept. 9, 1991; Susan Finch, "Jurors: Swaggart Defamed Gorman—$9 Million Goes to Ministry," *Times-Picayune*, Sept. 13, 1991; Susan Finch, "Jury: Swaggart Should Have Been Discreet," *Times-Picayune*, Sept. 14, 1991.
25. Dave Hunt and T.A. McMahon, *The Seduction of Christianity: Spiritual Discernment in the Last Days* (Eugene, OR: Harvest House Publishers, 1985); Seaman, *Swaggart*, 279–280; Shepard, *Forgiven*, 427; "Award Given," *Heritage Herald*, Apr. 1986, 1; "Pastors & Leaders Gather for International Church Growth Conference," *Heritage Herald*, Mar. 1987, 1.
26. Seaman, *Swaggart*, 281–282; Shepard, *Forgiven*, 426–427, 428; Dortch, *Integrity*, 144.
27. Shepard, *Forgiven*, 426–427; Wright, "False Messiah," 110; Art Harris, "The Devil's Disciple," *Penthouse*, Jan. 1989, 194; Lloyd Grove, "The Paper Trail and

the Fallen Evangelicals," *Washington Post*, Mar. 26, 1987; Charles E. Shepard, "Swaggart Denies He Schemed to Take Over PTL," *CO*, Mar. 24, 1987.

28. Shepard, *Forgiven*, 428; Seaman, *Swaggart*, 283.
29. Dortch, *Integrity*, 147; Jimmy Swaggart, newsletter, Apr. 1987; Shepard, "Swaggart Denies He Schemed."
30. Shepard, *Forgiven*, 430, 454–457.
31. Shepard, *Forgiven*, 458–459, 464–468; Stewart, *Holy War*, 58–62.
32. Interview with John Stewart, May 10, 2010; Stewart, *Holy War*, 65–68; Shepard, *Forgiven*, 427, 468–469; Dortch, *Integrity*, 148–149; Shepard, "Swaggart Denies He Schemed."
33. Dortch, *Integrity*, 123–127.
34. Seaman, *Swaggart*, 201, 202, 255, 292–293, 294–295; Elizabeth Mullener, "The Preachers' Wives," *Times-Picayune*, Aug. 11, 1991.
35. Shepard, *Forgiven*, 469–471, 485; Seaman, *Swaggart*, 190, 232, 235, 241, 305, 306.
36. Shepard, *Forgiven*, 473–487.
37. Root, "Total Salvation,"160–163; Jay Hamburg, "Millionaire a Mix of Flash, Bounty," *Orlando Sentinel*, Mar. 30, 1987; "Dog-Track Owner Gives $1.3 Million to Oral Roberts," *Los Angeles Times*, Mar. 23, 1987; Dan Tracy, "Florida Track Owner 'Saves' Oral Roberts," *Sun Sentinel*, Mar. 22, 1987.
38. "Jim and Tammy from California," PTL video, Mar. 8, 1987.
39. Stewart, *Holy War*, 73, 76–77; Shepard, *Forgiven*, 492–493; Jerry Falwell, *Strength for the Journey* (New York: Simon and Schuster, 1987), 402; interview with John Stewart, May 10, 2010. Stewart showed me his hand-written draft of this letter when we met, which he says he drafted on March 12, 1987.
40. Shepard, *Forgiven*, 495–496; Shepard, "Swaggart Denies He Schemed."
41. Shepard, *Forgiven*, 496–497; Dortch, *Integrity*, 138–139. Marcus, thirty-seven years old in 1987, was a Brooklyn-born Jew who converted to Christianity in his twenties. He left a career in Madison Avenue advertising to work in Christian television. See Jeff Borden, "Refining, Redefining TV Missions Is the Job of Warren Marcus," *CO*, June 16, 1987.
42. Shepard, *Forgiven*, 473–474, 494–495, 498–502; Stewart, *Holy War*, 74, 75, 80–81. Stewart showed me a photocopy of the $115,000 check when we met on May 10, 2010.
43. Bill Lohmann, "From Beatnik to Religious Right Figure," *Los Angeles Times*, Feb. 6, 1988; Barry Hankins, *Francis Schaeffer and the Shaping of Evangelical America* (Grand Rapids, MI: William B. Eerdmans, 2008), 69; Larry Martz with Ginny Carroll, *Ministry of Greed: The Inside Story of the Televangelists and Their Holy Wars* (New York: Weidenfeld & Nicolson, 1988), 162; DL Cade, "Blast from the Past: Vintage Commercial for the Nimslo 35mm 3D Camera," accessed Dec. 15, 2015, petapixel.com/2013/10/02/blast-past-vintage-commercial-nimslo-35mm-3d-camera; "Nimslo," accessed Dec. 15, 2015, en.wikipedia.org/wiki/Nimslo; interview with Jerry Nims, Feb. 9, 2010. Nims and Allen Kwok Wah Lo filed

ten patents related to the 3-D camera from 1974 to 1976. See patft.uspto.gov, accessed Dec. 17, 2015. Nims told me that before joining Falwell's team he was working with Fred Olsen & Co., a shipping company based in Norway. In newspaper interviews in the late 1980s, Nims said that he "collaborated" with Francis Schaeffer on his 1981 book, *A Christian Manifesto*.

44. Interview with Mark DeMoss, Feb. 9, 2010; Peter Donald, "Sermons & Soda Water: A Rich Philadelphia Widow Wants to Save New York Society," *New York Magazine*, Nov. 7, 1988, 55–58.
45. Falwell, *Strength*, 4, 5, 32, 50, 72, 74. Falwell published a slightly revised version of his autobiography in 1997. See Jerry Falwell, *Falwell: An Autobiography* (Lynchburg: Liberty House Publishers, 1997).
46. Falwell, *Strength*, 63, 130, 142, 179, 202, 205–206, 208, 302, 332; Ed Martin, "Falwell's Own Base Powerful," *CO*, Mar. 20, 1987.
47. Interviews with Mark DeMoss and Jerry Nims, Feb. 9, 2010; Shepard, *Forgiven*, 497–498; Dortch, *Integrity*, 139–142, 149, 151; Kathleen McClain, "Falwell Details Events Leading to Job at PTL," *CO*, Mar. 23, 1987.
48. Roy Grutman and Bill Thomas, *Lawyers and Thieves* (New York: Simon and Schuster, 1990), 9, 34–50; David Margolick, "Roy Grutman Is Dead at 63; Lawyer for Celebrity Clients," *New York Times*, June 28, 1994; Eleanor Randolph, "Blood-and-Guts Courtroom Showman," *Washington Post*, June 20, 1987; Rodney A. Smolla, *Jerry Falwell v. Larry Flynt: The First Amendment on Trial* (New York: St. Martin's Press, 1988), 11; "Norman Grutman," *Los Angeles Times*, June 29, 1994; Douglas O. Linder, "The Falwell v. Flynt Trial (1984)," accessed Dec. 5, 2015, law2.umkc.edu/faculty/projects/ftrials/falwell/trialaccount.html; Falwell, *Strength*, 199.
49. Interview with Mark DeMoss, Feb. 9, 2010; Grutman, *Lawyers and Thieves*, 192; Shepard, *Forgiven*, 502; Dortch, *Integrity*, 152.
50. Interview with Mark DeMoss, Feb. 9, 2010; Shepard, *Forgiven*, 504.
51. Dortch, *Integrity*, 152–155; Grutman, *Lawyers and Thieves*, 192; Bakker, *I Was Wrong*, 47; interview with Mark DeMoss, Feb. 9, 2010; U.S. v. Bakker, vol. 9, 1578.
52. Dortch, *Integrity*, 155; Bakker, *I Was Wrong*, 45; Tammy Faye Messner, *Tammy: Telling It My Way* (New York: Villard, 1996), 188–190.
53. Bakker, *I Was Wrong*, 46; Shepard, *Forgiven*, 506; interview with Roger and Linda Wilson, Jan. 4–5, 2011. In July, Chapman would plead guilty to simple possession and pay a $216 fine. See Liz Chandler, "PTL Partner Charged with Assault," *CO*, July 10, 1987.
54. John Wildman, "Falwell Rejects Bakkers' Return," *CO*, May 22, 1987.
55. Dortch, *Integrity*, 157–159; Bakker, *I Was Wrong*, 49, 50, 51; Falwell, *Strength*, 406–408; Shepard, *Forgiven*, 504–505; Ed Martin, "Falwell's Own Base Powerful," *CO*, Mar. 20, 1987; McClain, "Falwell Deluged with Questions"; McClain, "Falwell Details Events."
56. Interview with Mark DeMoss, Feb. 9, 2010; Grutman, *Lawyers and Thieves*, 193; Carol Horner, "Falwell Begins a Rescue Mission in Bangor, Maine," *Philadelphia*

Inquirer, Jan. 15, 1986; Michael Coakley, "Falwell Becomes Church's Pastor to Break Its Fall from Grace," *Chicago Tribune*, Jan. 26, 1986; William Plummer, "Their Pastor an Adulterer, Some Maine Baptists Call on Jerry Falwell to Pinch-Preach," *People*, Feb. 3, 1986; Martin, "Falwell's Own Base Powerful."

57. Interview with Mark DeMoss, Feb. 9, 2010; Bakker, *I Was Wrong*, 53–54; Gary L. Wright, "Bakkers Sue Roy Grutman, Claim Trickery," *CO*, Mar. 16, 1988.
58. Bakker, *I Was Wrong*, 55; Shepard, *Forgiven*, 506–507; "Bakker Was 'Boxed In,' Ex-Aide Says," *Washington Post*, Aug. 11, 1987.
59. Stewart, *Holy War*, 85–88; interview with John Stewart, May 10, 2010.
60. Bakker, *I Was Wrong*, 56; Shepard, *Forgiven*, 507; Charles E. Shepard, "Ex-PTL Board Member Says Directors Pressured to Resign," *CO*, Apr. 16, 1987; Tidwell, *Anatomy of a Fraud*, 165–166.
61. Bakker, *I Was Wrong*, 56; Shepard, *Forgiven*, 507; Shepard, "Ex-PTL Board Member."
62. Dortch, *Integrity*, 160.
63. Falwell, *Strength*, 411, 416; Bakker, *I Was Wrong*, 57; Shepard, *Forgiven*, 508.
64. Kathleen McClain, "Falwell to Tell Home Church Why He Took On PTL Rescue," *CO*, Mar. 22, 1987.

CHAPTER 14

1. Associated Press, "Bakker the Common Topic as Assemblies of God Meet," *CO*, Aug. 7, 1987.
2. Shepard, *Forgiven*, 509; Bakker, *I Was Wrong*, 57–58.
3. Bakker, *I Was Wrong*, 58–60; Shepard, *Forgiven*, 509–512; Charles E. Shepard, "Jim Bakker Resigns from PTL," *CO*, Mar. 20, 1987.
4. Bakker, *I Was Wrong*, 58.
5. John Vaughan, "Resignation Made Headlines in Many U.S. Newspapers," *CO*, Mar. 21, 1987; Shepard, *Forgiven*, 515; Roy Grutman and Bill Thomas, *Lawyers and Thieves* (New York: Simon and Schuster, 1990), 198; Karen Garloch, "Observer Wins Pulitzer Prize for Coverage of PTL, Bakkers," *CO*, Apr. 1, 1988.
6. Interview with John Stewart, May 10, 2010.
7. Interview with Roger Flessing, July 20, 2010.
8. George M. Marsden, *Fundamentalism and American Culture*, 2nd ed. (New York: Oxford University Press, 2006), 4; McClain, "Falwell Deluged with Questions"; Falwell, *Strength*, 360; Marjorie Hyer, "Pentecostals and Fundamentalists: The Backgrounds of Belief," *Washington Post*, Mar. 28, 1987.
9. Kathleen McClain, "Charismatic: Falwell Has Started War," *CO*, Mar. 24, 1987; Elizabeth Leland, "PTL Continues to Pay Bakkers," *CO*, Mar. 27, 1987.
10. Falwell, *Strength*, 313–314, 326–331; interview with Jerry Nims, Feb. 9, 2010; interview with Mark DeMoss, Feb. 9, 2010; Frye Gaillard, "The Faces of Jerry Falwell," *CO*, June 14, 1987; Kathleen McClain, "PTL's Board Scrutinizing All Who Buy Network's Time," *CO*, May 24, 1987.

11. Charles E. Shepard, "Swaggart Denies He Schemed to Take Over PTL," *CO*, Mar. 24, 1987; Charles E. Shepard, "Denomination Will Press Bakker Inquiry," *CO*, Mar. 25, 1987; Elizabeth Leland, "Falwell Defends Swaggart's Motives, Denies Conspiracy," *CO*, Mar. 25, 1987. Appearing on CBN's *700 Club* on March 24, 1987, Swaggart claimed that he had "no idea" where the *CO* "got their information, but they did not get it from me, my wife, my son, or anyone connected with me."
12. Jay McIntosh and John Wildman, "PTL's Structure Rules Out Risk of Hostile Takeover," *CO*, Mar. 25, 1987.
13. Charles E. Shepard, "Departure May Crimp PTL Future," *CO*, Mar. 21, 1987; Charles E. Shepard, "New Total in Bakker-Hahn Case Reaches $265,000," *CO*, Mar. 26, 1987; Leland, "PTL Continues to Pay Bakkers"; Charles E. Shepard, "Dortch Used PTL Money to Pay Hahn," *CO*, Apr. 28, 1987; Art Harris, "Uncertainty over Hahn Trust Fund," *Washington Post*, May 1, 1987. Hahn says that she "never saw a dime" of the monthly payments, which she believes went to Gene Profeta. Interview with Jessica Hahn, Feb. 5, 2014.
14. Cox News Service and Staff Reports, "Falwell: Case Could Lead to Criminal Investigation," *CO*, Mar. 29, 1987.
15. Charles E. Shepard, "PTL '86 Payments to Bakkers: $1.6 Million," *CO*, Apr. 18, 1987; Charles E. Shepard, "Falwell: '87 PTL Bonuses Shocking,'" *CO*, Apr. 19, 1987; Wildman and Shepard, "Highly Paid Bakker Aide Unknown to PTL Viewers"; U.S. v. Taggart and Taggart, vol. 2, 192–195, 307–308, 547–552; U.S. v. Bakker, vol. 4, 1419, 1421; Tidwell, *Anatomy of a Fraud*, 80, 300.
16. *Nightline*, Apr. 27, 1981; Steve Emmons, "Schuller Accused of Deceit in Fund-Raising Letter," *Los Angeles Times*, Apr. 29, 1987.
17. Interview with Michael Korpi, May 23, 2016; Michael Korpi, personal email, May 25, 2016; *Nightline*, Apr. 27, 1987; Falwell news conference, Apr. 28, 1987; Steven A. Emerson and Gordon Witkin with Robert A. Manning, "For Falwell: New Job, New Questions," *U.S. News & World Report*, Apr. 6, 1987, 60. Thanks to Michael Korpi for sending me the *Nightline* and news conference videos.
18. Shepard, *Forgiven*, 514–515; Shepard, "Jim Bakker Resigns from PTL"; Charles E. Shepard, "PTL Lawyer Halts Payments to Hahn," *CO*, Apr. 9, 1987; Roddy Ray, "Hahn Confused but Not Ashamed," *CO*, Apr. 19, 1987; Jody Jaffe, "Hahn: I Never Once Spoke to the Press," *CO*, Apr. 29, 1987.
19. Monica Lewinsky, "The Price of Shame," accessed Feb. 24, 2016, www.ted.com/talks/monica_lewinsky_the_price_of_shame/transcript?language=en; Jaffe, "Hahn: I Never Once Spoke to the Press"; Scheer and Golson, "The Jessica Hahn Story: Part Two," 205, 206.
20. PTL, "PTL Fallout Staff Meeting," video, Mar. 19, 1987; Charles E. Shepard, "3 PTL Directors Didn't Know What Bakker Was Paid," *CO*, Apr. 22, 1987.
21. Shepard, *Forgiven*, 535–536; Martz, *Ministry of Greed*, 147–148.
22. Shepard, *Forgiven*, 536; Martz, *Ministry of Greed*, 144; Bakker, *I Was Wrong*, 65–66.
23. Art Harris, "Evangelist Levels Accusations at Bakker," *Washington Post*, Apr. 26, 1987; "Bakker Issues Denial of Rival TV Minister's New Sex Allegations,"

Los Angeles Times, Apr. 26, 1987; Stewart, *Holy War*, 150–151; interview with Jim Cobble, Apr. 21, 2010.

24. Elizabeth Leland and Charles E. Shepard, "Falwell Warns of Bakker Plan," *CO*, Apr. 28, 1987; Ted Mellnik, "Bakker, Dortch Dismissed," *CO*, May 7, 1987; Joyce Wadler, "Breaking Faith: Two TV Idols Fall," *People*, May 18, 1987, 81–82, 85–86, 89; *Nightline*, Apr. 27, 1987; "Looking for 'Mr. Baby': Jim Bakker's Secret Hooker," *Penthouse*, Jan. 1989, 48, 184.
25. Martz, *Ministry of Greed*, 154–155.
26. Goff, *Fields White unto Harvest*, 136–142; "The Sins of Billy James," *Time*, Feb. 16, 1976, 68; Robert D. McFadden, "Billy James Hargis, 79, Pastor and Anticommunist Crusader, Dies," *New York Times*, Nov. 29, 2004.
27. Shepard, *Forgiven*, 539; Martz, *Ministry of Greed*, 148.
28. Interview with Jay Babcock, Nov. 1, 2016; Shepard, *Forgiven*, 223–224.
29. Interview with Jay Babcock, Nov. 1, 2016; "Jim Bakker Blackmailed Me to Be His Gay Lover," *National Enquirer*, Oct. 24, 1989; Martz, *Ministry of Greed*, 149–150.
30. Interview with Jay Babcock, Nov. 1, 2106; Gary L. Wright, "Grand Jury Wants to Know if PTL Money Bought Sex," *CO*, Sep. 21, 1988.
31. Elizabeth Leland, "Judgment Day: Dortch, Bakker Cut, Falwell Tightens Control over PTL Ministry," *CO*, Apr. 29, 1987; Elizabeth Leland, "PTL's Dortch Out," *CO*, Apr. 29, 1987; Lisa Pullen, "Fate Unfolds as Tourists Watch, Pray," *CO*, Apr. 29, 1987; Jeff Borden, "PTL Meeting Drew Swarm of Reporters," *CO*, Apr. 29, 1987. David Taggart later testified that he did not know he had been fired when he left the hotel. See David Taggart Testimony, U.S. v. Taggart and Taggart, vol. 5, 216.
32. Leland, "Judgment Day"; Jeri Fischer and Ed Martin, "PTL Names New Chief of Operations," *CO*, Apr. 29, 1987.
33. David Perlmutt, "PTL Records a Mess, Says Operations Chief," *CO*, Apr. 30, 1987; Ed Martin and Charles E. Shepard, "PTL Dismisses 200 Employees in Belt-Tightening," *CO*, May 9, 1987; Ed Martin and Charles E. Shepard, "Workers Board Up Unfinished Towers at Heritage USA," *CO*, May 14, 1987; Michael Isikoff and Art Harris, "Falwell: PTL Needs $20 Million," *Washington Post*, May 15, 1987; Charles E. Shepard, "Government Brings Up Possible Criminal Violations," *CO*, May 15, 1987; Ed Martin, "PTL Declares Fundraising Emergency," *CO*, May 15, 1987; Elizabeth Leland and David Perlmutt, "PTL Overspent Regular '84–'86 Gifts," *CO*, May 30, 1987; "Towers Work Progresses," *Heritage Herald*, May 1987, 3; U.S. v. Bakker, vol. 7, 876, 899.
34. Elizabeth Leland, "Falwell: PTL Got the Money," *CO*, June 2, 1987; "Send More Money to PTL, Falwell Pleads," *CO*, June 6, 1987; "U.S. Probes Intensify, Falwell Says," *CO*, June 11, 1987; Jeff Borden, "PTL Adjusts Its Set," *CO*, June 16, 1987.
35. Linda Brown, "PTL Show Guest Host Debuts," *CO*, May 5, 1987; McClain, "PTL's Board Scrutinizing."
36. Shepard, "Departure May Crimp PTL Future."
37. Interview with Juleen Turnage, Oct. 14, 2009.

38. Charles E. Shepard and Valerie Reitman, "Denomination Will Press Bakker Inquiry," *CO*, Mar. 25, 1987; Charles E. Shepard and Valerie Reitman, "National Church to Push for Answers," *CO*, Mar. 25, 1987; Charles E. Shepard and Valerie Reitman, "N.C. Church Official Drops Bakker Inquiry," *CO*, Mar. 25, 1987.
39. Charles E. Shepard and Kathleen McClain, "N.C. Church Officials Defer Bakker Decision," *CO*, Apr. 9, 1987; Ted Mellnik, "Bakker, Dortch Dismissed," *CO*, May 7, 1987; Shepard, *Forgiven*, 529; Laura Sessions Stepp, "The Bakker Witness: Church Links Unfrocking to Claims of Homosexual Involvement," *Washington Post*, May 8, 1987.
40. Charles E. Shepard, Elizabeth Leland, Ed Martin, and John Monk, "PTL in Bankruptcy Court, Ministry Petitions Under Chapter 11 for Reorganization," *CO*, June 13, 1987; Charles E. Shepard and Elizabeth Leland, "PTL Dug Itself into a Hole with Burgeoning Partnerships," *CO*, July 5, 1987; Ed Martin and Elizabeth Leland, "Awful June Donations Put PTL on Shaky Ground, Falwell Says," *CO*, July 8, 1987; Henry Eichel, "July Surge in Contributions Puts PTL over the Top," *CO*, Aug. 5, 1987; Henry Eichel, "PTL Losses Run $15,000 a Day, Trustee Tells Court," *CO*, Feb. 18, 1988.
41. McClain, "Falwell Deluged with Questions"; Charles E. Shepard, "Bakker Claims on TV Falwell Stole PTL Ministry," *CO*, May 27, 1987.
42. Associate Press, "Bakker Hopes People Will Want Us Back," *CO*, Mar. 31, 1987; Ed Martin, "Bakkers' Calif. Home Popular Tourist Stop," *CO*, May 4, 1987.
43. Elizabeth Leland, "PTL Mementos Thousands of Items Auctioned to Raise Money," *CO*, May, 24, 1987; "Pay 50 Cents, See Dog House," *CO*, July 25, 1987; Richard N. Ostling, "Of God and Greed," *Time*, June 24, 2001.
44. Shepard, "Bakker Claims Falwell Stole PTL Ministry"; W. J. Speers, Knight-Rider Newspapers, "Koppel, Credibility among Reasons for Nightline Success," *CO*, May 30, 1987; Jeff Borden, "Koppel Gets Tough with Bakker on Return Visit to Nightline," *CO*, Oct. 29, 1987; Ted Koppel and Kyle Gibson, *Nightline: History in the Making and the Making of Television* (New York: Random House, 1996), 172–178; Stewart, *Holy War*, 167–172.
45. Michael Isikoff and Art Harris, "Falwell Hits Back—Bakkers Respond as 'Holy War' Intensifies," *Washington Post*, May 28, 1987; Elizabeth Leland, with Charles E. Shepard, Linda Brown, and Liz Chandler, "Falwell: Bakker Dishonest," *CO*, May 28, 1987; Charles E. Shepard, "Bakker Says He Wants PTL Ministry Back," *CO*, May 29, 1987; Russell Watson with Ginny Carroll, Lynda Wright, Daniel Pedersen, and Rich Thomas, "Heaven Can Wait," *Newsweek*, June 8, 1987, 58–65; Bakker, *I Was Wrong*, 72; U.S. v. Bakker, vol. 7, 855.
46. Mark B. Sluder and Ed Martin, "Bakkers Home, Want New TV Show," *CO*, June 11, 1987; Ed Martin, "It Was Old Home Week for Bakkers at Tega Cay Residence," *CO*, June 13, 1987; "Bakker 'Blood' Pacts Alleged," *Washington Post*, June 19, 1987; Mark B. Sluder, "Lawyer Melvin Belli to Help Bakkers," *CO*, June 21, 1987;

Ed Martin with Rachel Stiffler, "Lawyer's Goal: Bakker in Ministry," *CO*, June 22, 1987; Bakker, *I Was Wrong*, 266.

47. Melvin M. Belli with Robert Blair Kaiser, *Melvin Belli: My Life on Trial* (New York: William Morrow, 1976); Mark Shaw, *Melvin Belli: King of the Courtroom* (Fort Lee, NJ: Barricade Books, 2007), 59; "PTL Partners Group Mounts Network Buyout Poll," *CO*, July 12, 1987; Cynthia Robins, "Tammy Talks About Her Fall From Grace," *San Francisco Examiner*, July 19, 1987.
48. Charles E. Shepard, "Dortch Wants Some of His Salary, Lake Wylie Home," *CO*, June 6, 1987; "Florida Files Complaint in Dortch Tax Case," *CO*, June 12, 1987; Elizabeth Leland and Henry Eichel, "Dortch's PTL Salary of $13,500 Monthly Cut Off This Week," *CO*, July 23, 1987. Charges were filed against the Dortches on both homestead exemption cases on July 31, 1987. See Associated Press, "Florida Charges Dortches Tax Break Obtained by Fraud, DA Says," *CO*, Aug. 2, 1987; Bill Arthur, "Dortch Says He's Now Out of Crying Mode," *CO*, Sept. 11, 1987.
49. Ted Mellnik and Ed Martin, "Ex-Bakker Spokesman Will Resign," *CO*, June 15, 1987; Ed Martin, "New Factions Clash on PTL," *CO*, June 17, 1987; Liz Chandler, "Marching PTL Partners Confront Hargrave," *CO*, July 5, 1987; Henry Eichel, "Bankruptcy Case Could Decide Falwell's Fate as PTL Leader," *CO*, Sept. 10, 1987.
50. Ed Martin, with Linda Brown, Elizabeth Leland, and Lane Thomasson, "Bakkers: Goodbye to It All," *CO*, June 12, 1987; Mark B. Sluder, "Friends Influenced Change of Plans," *CO*, June 18, 1987; "Bakkers Trying to Sell Home in Palm Springs," *CO*, June 21, 1987; Vestal Goodman with Ken Abraham, *Vestal!* (Colorado Springs: Waterbrook Press, 1998), 75, 229–230; Ken Harrell, "The Other Woman in Jim Bakker's Life," *Globe*, July 21, 1987, 8–9; Elizabeth Leland, "Bankruptcy Judge Picks PTL Examiner," *CO*, July 16, 1987.
51. Linda Brown, "Former PTL Worker May Lose Farm," *CO*, May 17, 1987; Henry Eichel, "PTL Manages to Pay Its 1,100 Employees," *CO*, Aug. 1, 1987; Eichel, "July Surge in Contributions"; Henry Eichel, "PTL Proposal Considers a 2nd Heritage USA," *CO*, Aug. 12, 1987; Stan Brennan, "PTL Returns Amusement Park Items," *CO*, Aug. 13, 1987; Bruce Henderson, "Bakker's Daughter Helps Partners Group Take Off," *CO*, Apr. 10, 1988.
52. Henry Eichel, "Bakker Knew Kevin's House Didn't Meet Codes," *CO*, Aug. 11, 1987; Dan Huntley and Henry Eichel, "Kevin, Family Forced Out of Kevin's House," *CO*, Aug. 12, 1987.
53. Liz Chandler, "Kevin's House Namesake Sues PTL over Eviction," *CO*, Aug. 22, 1987; John Monk, "Whittum Ordered Out of PTL House," *CO*, Sept. 10, 1987; Grutman, *Lawyers and Theives*, 195; Sophie Smith, "Inspiration for PTL's Kevin's House Dies," *CO*, Aug. 12, 1992.
54. "Falwell Will Take the Plunge," *CO*, Sept. 9, 1987; Henry Eichel, "Bankruptcy Case Could Decide Falwell's Fate as PTL Leader," *CO*, Sept. 10, 1987; Linda

Brown, "PTL Reports Steady Attendance Drop Since Court Filing," *CO*, Sept. 19, 1987; Dale Albright, "Chairman's Slide Was Fal-Well Done," *Heritage Herald*, Oct. 1987, 1.

55. Leland, "Judgment Day"; Michael Isikoff and Art Harris, "PTL Accuses Builder of Conspiracy," *Washington Post*, Sept. 9, 1987; Eichel, "Bankruptcy Case Could Decide Falwell's Fate as PTL Leader"; Henry Eichel, "Messner Details Claim of $14.9 Million at PTL," *CO*, Sept. 15, 1987; Gary L. Wright and Henry Eichel, "Jessica Hahn Scheduled for Appearance Monday before PTL Grand Jury," *CO*, Sept. 20, 1987; U.S. v. Bakker, vol. 7, 862; vol. 8, 1315.
56. Henry Eichel, "Bankruptcy Judge, 79, Prepares for PTL, Watches Evangelists," *CO*, July 12 1987; Leland, "Bankruptcy Judge Picks PTL Examiner"; Henry Eichel, "Partners Impact on PTL Disputed," *CO*, Sept. 16, 1987; Rich Oppel, "Falwell Set to Quit if PTL Board Shifts," *CO*, Sept. 17, 1987; Elizabeth Leland, "PTL: A View from the Bench," *CO*, Jan. 1, 1989; Gary L. Wright, "PTL Judge Won't Issue Gag Order," *CO*, Jan. 25, 1989.
57. Henry Eichel, "PTL Creditors Gather Privately for First Official Meeting," *CO*, July 3, 1987; Henry Eichel, "PTL's Plan Would Split TV Ministry," *CO*, Oct. 1, 1987; "Judge Orders Competing Plan for PTL," *CO*, Oct. 8, 1987.
58. Jonathan Alter with Rich Thomas, "TV Time: Eyes on the Prize?" *Newsweek*, June 8, 1987, 72; Martz, *Ministry of Greed*, 113.
59. Elizabeth Leland with John Wildman, "Bakkers Should Return '87 Bonuses, PTL Officials Say," *CO*, May 23, 1987; "Bakkers' House in California Sells for $600,000," *CO*, Sept. 5 1987; Ed Martin and Gary L. Wright, "Bakkers Ready to Return," *CO*, Oct. 9, 1987; "Bakkers Plan Farewell for Now Tour," *CO*, Oct. 15, 1987; Ed Martin, "Ticket Sales Sluggish for Bakkers' Appearances," *CO*, Oct. 22, 1987; Ed Martin, "Bakkers' Tour Tickets Not Selling Well," *CO*, Oct. 23, 1987; Elizabeth Leland, "Bakkers Say Farewell to 19-City Singing Tour," *CO*, Nov. 3, 1987; Chuck Conconi, "Bakkers Cancel Nationwide 'Farewell' Tour," *Washington Post*, Dec. 3, 1987; Henry Eichel, "Bakkers Turn House Over to PTL Chiefs," *CO*, Oct. 27, 1987.
60. Scheer and Golson, "Jessica Hahn Story: Part One," 196.
61. Scheer and Golson, "Jessica Hahn Story: Part Two," 206; Art Harris, "The Jessica Hahn Story," *Penthouse*, Oct. 1987, 108–113, 152; "Fling Said to Be First for Hahn," *Washington Post*, Apr. 2, 1987.
62. Scheer and Golson, "Jessica Hahn Story: Part Two," 206; Associated Press, "Trip to Hollywood Left Hahn Lukewarm," *CO*, July 6, 1987; "Hahn Telling Magazine Her Story, Lawyer Says," *CO*, July 14, 1987; Gary L. Wright and Henry Eichel, "The Testimony Begins—Hahn to Continue Telling Her Account," *CO*, Sept. 22, 1987; Diane Suchetka and Jody Jaffe, "Hahn's Mother Bitter Over Playboy Poses," *CO*, Sept. 23, 1987; Polly Paddock, "These Lawyers Hardly Fit Mold of Charlotte's Low-Key Bar," *CO*, Sept. 23, 1987; Lawrence Toppman, "Was Hahn's Playboy Fee Worth It?," *CO*, Oct. 3, 1987; Scheer and Golson, "Jessica Hahn

Story: Part One," 198; Scheer and Golson, "Jessica Hahn Story: Part Two," 208, 209; interview with Jessica Hahn, Feb. 5, 2014.

63. Suchetka and Jaffe, "Hahn's Mother Bitter"; "Fletcher at PTL Hearing," *Washington Post*, Sept. 24, 1987; Larry King interview with Jessica Hahn, *CNN Larry King Live*, July 14, 2005, accessed Feb. 22, 2016, www.edition.cnn.com/TRANSCRIPTS/0507/14/lkl.01.html.
64. Elizabeth Leland, Gary L. Wright, and Henry Eichel, "Judge Turns PTL Over to Adviser," *CO*, Oct. 13, 1987; Henry Eichel and Elizabeth Leland, "Trustee for PTL Chosen," *CO*, Oct. 24, 1987; Henry Eichel, Elizabeth Leland, and Gary Wright, "PTL Plan to Require $20 Million," *CO*, Oct. 24, 1987; Henry Eichel and Elizabeth Leland, "Return of Bakkers Dismissed," *CO*, Oct. 29, 1987; Elizabeth Leland, "Portrait of New PTL Trustee: Intense but Compassionate," *CO*, Nov. 1, 1987; Henry Eichel and Tex O'Neill, "PTL Owes U.S. $55.7 Million in Back Taxes, IRS Tells Court," *CO*, Dec. 11, 1987; Henry Eichel, "Time's Up for PTL, Judge Says," *CO*, Apr. 16, 1988; Liz Chandler and Henry Eichel, "PTL Trustee David Clark Steps Down," *CO*, May 21, 1988; "New Trustee Directs PTL," *Heritage Herald*, Nov. 1987, 2; Eichel, "PTL Losses Run $15,000 a Day"; John Monk, "Contributors Could Face Back Taxes," *CO*, Feb. 26, 1988; "PTL Short of Goal," *CO*, Apr. 3, 1988; Henry Eichel, "Looking for a Miracle at PTL," *CO*, Apr. 24, 1988.
65. Bill Arthur, "Bakker Fallout on TV Religion: Varied, but Picture's Fuzzy," *CO*, May 25, 1987; "Pat Robertson Lays Off 470 CBN Workers," *CO*, June 6, 1987; "Poll: PTL Scandal Hurt TV Ministries," *CO*, Aug. 4, 1987; Elizabeth Leland, "Most Say Bakker Not to Be Trusted," *CO*, Aug. 9, 1987; "Roberts Apologizes to Swaggart for Remarks in Defense of Bakker," *CO*, Aug. 22, 1987.

CHAPTER 15

1. U.S. v. Bakker, vol. 2, 461–462, 477, 478.
2. U.S. v. Bakker, vol. 2, 489, 493.
3. U.S. v. Bakker, vol. 2, 515–519.
4. U.S. v. Bakker, vol. 2, 520; John Vaughn, "Diary Shows Bakker Trial as Juror Saw It," *CO*, Oct. 28, 1989; Charles E. Shepard and Gary L. Wright, "Witness Collapses on the Stand," *CO*, Aug. 31, 1987; Art Harris, "The Faint and the Faithful," *Washington Post*, Aug. 30, 1989; Bakker, *I Was Wrong*, 76. Later in the trial, other witnesses who had worked with Nelson were critical of him. Marisa Matthews, who eventually directed one of PTL's accounting divisions, said that Nelson was "selfish" and focused on his own advancement. Priscilla Sherrill, who worked as Nelson's administrative assistant, said she "felt like he was very self-centered, ambitious, and I did not think he was an honest person." Barbara Brewer, who worked under Nelson, said the she "didn't have a lot of respect for Steve Nelson." Judy Rutliff, who worked in partner information under Nelson, said that he

referred to her department as "dumb country girls" and that he "made fun of most everybody." See U.S. v. Bakker, vol. 7, 745, 776; vol. 8, 1073, 1125.

5. Shepard and Wright, "Witness Collapses on the Stand"; John Vaughan and Charles E. Shepard, "Bakker Psychiatrist Highly Experienced," *CO*, Sept. 1, 1989; John Drescher and Charles E. Shepard, "Bakker Better, May Return for Trial, Wife Says," *CO*, Sept. 2, 1989; U.S. v. Bakker, vol. 2, 625, Aug. 31, 1989 transcript of testimony of Dr. Basil Jackson (transcript inserted).
6. U.S. v. Bakker, vol. 7, 780; vol. 8, 1347; Art Harris, "Bakker Mental Tests Ordered," *Washington Post*, Aug. 31, 1989.
7. U.S. v. Bakker, vol. 2, Jackson transcript, 581; Bakker, *I Was Wrong*, 81–83; Harris, "Bakker Mental Tests Ordered"; Gary L. Wright and Charles E. Shepard, "Bakker in Prison Hospital," *CO*, Sept. 1, 1989; "Jim Bakker: You Could Not Look at Him and Not Feel Compassion," *CO*, Sept. 1, 1989.
8. Henry Eichel, "Suitors Push Plans to Buy Heritage USA," *CO*, June 3, 1988; Henry Eichel, "Jim Bakker Says He Has Backing to Buy PTL," *CO*, June 11, 1988; Gary L. Wright, "Australian Offers to Buy Heritage USA," *CO*, July 2, 1988; Henry Eichel, "Australian PTL Bid Questioned," *CO*, July 19, 1988; Henry Eichel, "Canadian Confident of PTL," *CO*, July 31, 1988; Henry Eichel, "PTL Gets $1 Million Deposit," *CO*, Aug. 19, 1988; Henry Eichel, "Canadian's Bid for PTL Is Withdrawn," *CO*, Sept. 8, 1988; Henry Eichel, "Canadians Top PTL's Bidder List," *CO*, Sept. 28, 1988; Henry Eichel, "Likely New Owner of PTL Assets Ordained Rabbi," *CO*, Oct. 6, 1988; Associated Press, "Catawbas: Don't OK PTL Sale," *CO*, Nov. 11, 1988; Henry Eichel and Gary L. Wright, "Benton Has Doubts about Bakker Deal," *CO*, Sept. 3, 1988; Gary L. Wright and Henry Eichel, "PTL Deposit Awaited," *CO*, Sept. 7, 1988; "Bakker Contact Reportedly Was Jailed in Fraud," *CO*, Sept. 8, 1988; Elizabeth Leland and Gary L. Wright, "PTL Trustee: Bakker's Time Has Expired," *CO*, Sept. 10, 1988; Henry Eichel, "From Dreamers to Schemers, PTL Bidding Had It All," *CO*, Nov. 21, 1988; John Monk, "Messner Submits Bid to Buy PTL Retreat," *CO*, Nov. 16, 1989.
9. Polly Paddock, "Heritage USA's Decline," *CO*, July 30, 1988; Linda Brown, "Once Hectic, Heritage USA Stands Quiet," *CO*, Dec. 6, 1988; Ken Garfield, "Isolation Settles In at Heritage USA," *CO*, Oct. 29, 1989.
10. "New Bakker Retreat? Officials Don't Know," *CO*, Jan. 26, 1988; Henry Eichel, "Bakker Backing Denied," *CO*, May 20, 1988; Linda Brown, "Jim and Tammy Ministries Moves into Larger Offices," *CO*, July 28, 1988; Linda Brown, "Bakkers Move Ministry to Mecklenburg," *CO*, Oct. 7, 1988; Linda Brown, "Bakkers May Be Violating Zoning Regulations," *CO*, Oct. 19, 1988; Jim Morrill, "Live From Pineville the Bakkers Return to TV with New Show," *CO*, Jan. 3, 1989; Gary L. Wright, "Bakker's Broadcasts Violate Zoning, Board Says," *CO*, May 22, 1989.
11. Jeff Borden, "Tammy Bakker Has Star Picked to Portray Her," *CO*, Feb. 25, 1988; Tim Funk, "Filming Starts on TV Movie about PTL," *CO*, Feb. 6, 1990; Tim Funk, "It's the PTL Movie," *CO*, Mar. 11, 1990; Tim Funk, "Everybody's a Critic

(Even Jessica)," *CO*, Apr. 28, 1990; Joan Hanauer, "Stars of 'Fall From Grace' Go Beyond Caricature in Portrayal of the Bakkers," *Los Angeles Times*, Apr. 23, 1990; "Today's Quote," *CO*, Apr. 30, 1990; U.S. v. Bakker, Resentencing Hearing, Aug. 22 & 23, 1991, 69.

12. Deborah Hastings, "Fall From Grace Ranks 8th in Nielsen Ratings," *CO*, May 2, 1990; Tim Funk, "Bakker Movie Nominations Make Your Hair Stand On End," *CO*, Aug. 10, 1990.
13. Gary L. Wright, "Jim Bakker, Dortch Indicted," *CO*, Dec. 6, 1988; Gary L. Wright and Tex O'Neill, "We Will Win Case, Bakker Says," *CO*, Dec. 16, 1988.
14. Marianne Costantinou, "George T. Davis—Top Death Penalty Lawyer," *San Francisco Chronicle*, Feb. 16, 2006; Douglas Martin, "George T. Davis, 98, a Celebrated Criminal Lawyer, Dies," *New York Times*, Feb. 19, 2006; Adam Bernstein, "George T. Davis, a Lawyer Who Took On Notable Cases and Clients," *Washington Post*, Feb. 17, 2006.
15. Interview with Harold Bender, Feb. 17, 2010; "Harold J. Bender Obituary," *Wilmington Star-News*, Mar. 26, 2013.
16. Interview with Jim Toms, Feb. 18, 2010.
17. Gary L. Wright, "Bakker's Plan Uncertain," *CO*, Mar. 30, 1989; Joe Sovacool, "Carolina Watch—Jim and Tammy Show Makes Debut From New Location," *CO*, Apr. 4, 1989; Ben Perkowski, "News Note—Bakkers Relaunch Ministry in Florida," *CO*, May 9, 1989; Vinny Kuntz, "Carolina Watch—Distance Separates Jim, Tammy Bakker as His Trial Looms," *CO*, Aug. 21, 1989.
18. Interview with Harold Bender, Feb. 17, 2010; Gary L. Wright, "The Bakker Trial: Jim and Tammy," *CO*, Aug. 20, 1989; Bakker, *I Was Wrong*, 79.
19. Gary L. Wright, "Question of Lifestyle: Taggarts' Case Opens Today," *CO*, June 22, 1989; Gary L. Wright, "Charge Dropped against Former PTL Aides," *CO*, June 24, 1989.
20. U.S. v. Taggart and Taggart, vol. 1, 136–138; Charles E. Shepard and Gary L. Wright, "Taggart Case Hinges On Use of Money," *CO* July 6, 1989; Polly Paddock, "Trial Is Tale of 2 Brothers," *CO*, July 6, 1989.
21. U.S. v. Taggart and Taggart, vol. 1, 388; vol. 2, 510; vol. 3, 431–435.
22. Charles E. Shepard, "James Taggart Says, 'I Trusted My Brother,'" *CO*, July 20, 1989; Charles E. Shepard and Gary L. Wright, "Taggarts Found Guilty," *CO*, July 26, 1989.
23. U.S. v. Taggart and Taggart, vol. 5, 69–73, 136.
24. U.S. v. Taggart and Taggart, vol. 5, 327, 331, 373, 379.
25. Gary L. Wright, "Jurors Sensed a Snake in the Firewood," *CO*, July 26, 1989.
26. Interview with Harold Bender, Feb. 17, 2010; Gary L. Wright, "Bakker's Attorneys Seek Move," *CO*, Aug. 15, 1989; Gary L. Wright, "The Bakker Trial: Jim and Tammy," *CO*, Aug. 20, 1989; Art Harris, "Jim Bakker, Driven by Money or Miracles?" *Washington Post*, Aug. 28, 1989; Elizabeth Leland, "Tough, but Just," *CO*, Sept. 17, 1989.

27. Linda Brown, "Dortch's Guilty Plea Saddens PTL Faithful," *CO*, Aug. 9, 1989; Gary L. Wright and Tex O'Neill, "PTL's Dortch: I Plead Guilty," *CO*, Aug. 9, 1989; Dortch, *Integrity*, 246; Gary L. Smith and Elizabeth Leland, "Judge Gives Dortch 8 Years in Prison," *CO*, Aug. 25, 1989.
28. Interview with Jerry Miller, Feb. 15, 2010; Wright, "Bakker Trial."
29. Interview with Harold Bender, Feb. 17, 2010; Karen Garloch, "Spoofs, Sellers Hold Court Outside," *CO*, Aug. 29, 1989; Gail Smith, "TV Crew Camping Out for Coverage," *CO*, Aug. 28, 1989; Harris, "Jim Bakker, Driven by Money or Miracles?"; Bakker, *I Was Wrong*, 100.
30. "Down the Tube," *CO*, Aug. 19, 1989.
31. Interview with Harold Bender, Feb. 17, 2010; U.S. v. Bakker, George Davis opening statement, 9, 33.
32. U.S. v. Bakker, Jerry Miller opening statement, 7, 13.
33. U.S. v. Bakker, vol. 1, 193; interview with Deborah Smith, May 16, 2016.
34. U.S. v. Bakker, vol. 1, 15–224.
35. U.S. v. Bakker, vol. 1, 323–434; vol. 2, 435–452.
36. Foon Rhee, "Bakker Eats Alone in His Sparse Cell," *CO*, Sept. 3, 1989; "Followers Shocked to See Bakker Treated as Prisoner," *CO*, Sept. 5, 1989.
37. U.S. v. Bakker, vol. 2, 546, 548, 551, 554; *Diagnostic and Statistical Manual of Mental Disorders*, 3rd rev. ed. (Washington, DC: American Psychiatric Association, 1987), 238, 349, 358; Art Harris, "Fit to Be Tried, Prison Psychiatrist Says Preacher Had 'Panic Attack,'" *Washington Post*, Sept. 6, 1989.
38. U.S. v. Taggart and Taggart, Sentencing hearing, 9, 29, 30; Gary L. Wright, "Taggarts Given Prison, Stiff Fines," *CO*, Sept. 9, 1989.
39. U.S. v. Bakker, vol. 2, 654–706; vol. 4, 1340–1341, 1346–1347; Art Harris, "The Roll Not Taken?: Tammy Faye Bakker Denies Bun-Buying Binge," *Washington Post*, Sept. 12, 1989; Albert, *Jim Bakker*, 222.
40. U.S. v. Bakker, vol. 5, 1664, 1720, 1777, 1784, 1789; Charles E. Shepard and Gary L. Wright, "Memos Warned Bakker of PTL's Financial Crisis," *CO*, Sept. 14, 1989.
41. U.S. v. Bakker, vol. 6, 20, 22, 24–25, 26, 29, 31, 36–38, 48, 57, 65–66, 95, 112–113.
42. U.S. v. Bakker, vol. 6, 68–69, 70, 88–89, 90, 93; Tidwell, *Anatomy of a Fraud*, 303.
43. U.S. v. Bakker, vol. 6, 104, 135; vol. 10, 2087.
44. U.S. v. Bakker, vol. 6, 480–497, vol. 7, 499–611; "PTL Tapes Show Bakker Fund Pitches," *Washington Post*, Sept. 19, 1989; John Vaughn, "Diary Shows Bakker Trial as Juror Saw It," *CO*, Oct. 28, 1989; Charles E. Shepard and Gary L. Wright, "Jury Sees Bakker on Video," *CO*, Sept. 20, 1989.
45. U.S. v. Bakker, vol. 3, 892–934, 953–978, 1066–1089, 1100–1109; vol. 4, 1171–1195, 1205–1216, 1370–1418, 1424–1438, 1478–1495; vol. 5, 1883–1911; interview with Deborah Smith, May 16, 2016.
46. U.S. v. Bakker, vol. 4, 1178, 1184.
47. U.S. v. Bakker, vol. 7, 686–694; vol. 8, 1308, 1385; vol. 9, 1466.

48. U.S. v. Bakker, vol. 7, 670; vol. 8, 1245; Gary L. Wright, "Bakker's Witnesses Tell a Very Different Story," *CO*, Sept. 22, 1989.
49. Nancy Webb, "Verdict Follows Tense 10 Hours," *CO*, Oct. 6, 1989; Vaughn, "Diary Shows Bakker Trial"; U.S. v. Bakker, vol. 8, 1240, 1243, 1245.
50. U.S. v. Bakker, vol. 8, 1117, 1119.
51. U.S. v. Bakker, vol. 8, 1201.
52. U.S. v. Bakker, vol. 7, 918, 923; vol. 8, 1002, 1005.
53. U.S. v. Bakker, vol. 6, 32–33; Art Harris, "The Devil Defense?: Bakker's Attorney Raises the Specter," *Washington Post*, Sept. 16, 1989.
54. U.S. v. Bakker, vol. 9, 1688, 1690, 1707; Charles E. Shepard and Gary L. Wright, "Bakker Challenges Charge He Oversold Partnerships," *CO*, Sept. 30, 1989; Tidwell, *Anatomy of a Fraud*, 306.
55. U.S. v. Bakker, vol. 9, 1718, 1743, 1757, 1801; vol. 10, 1856, 1866.
56. U.S. v. Bakker, vol. 9, 1738, 1793, 1811–1812.
57. Webb, "Verdict Follows Tense 10 Hours"; Art Harris, "Jim Bakker Gets 45-Year Sentence," *Washington Post*, Oct. 25, 1989; interview with Deborah Smith, May 16, 2016.
58. U.S. v. Bakker, Sentencing Hearing, Oct. 21, 1989, 32; Charles E. Shepard and Gary L. Wright, "Ex-PTL Leader Faces Possible 120-Year Sentence," *CO*, Oct. 6, 1989; Joseph Menn, "Judge Offers Verdicts on Society's Ills," *CO*, Apr. 20, 1990.
59. Much of Bakker's 1996 autobiography, *I Was Wrong*, deals with his time in prison.
60. Gary L. Wright and Charles E. Shepard, "Bakker's Fate Rests with Jury," *CO*, Oct. 4, 1989; "Fleecing the Faithful in Retrospect, 45-Year Sentence for Bakker Too Long," *CO*, Feb. 13, 1991. Including general contributions to PTL drops the Bakkers' share to about 1 percent of the total. General contributions to PTL were $42,056,000 in 1985 and $43,691,000 in 1986. Partnership donations were about $50 million in 1985 and $57,610,000 in 1986. See U.S. v. Bakker, vol. 10, 2018, 2088, 2126.
61. Nancy Webb, "Where Will He Serve?," *CO*, Oct. 6, 1989; Nancy Webb and Gary L. Wright, "Bakker in Good Spirits after First Day in Prison," *CO*, Oct. 26, 1989; Gary L. Wright, "Dortch's Sentence Reduced," *CO*, Apr. 26, 1990; Gary L. Wright, "Judge Cuts Taggarts' PTL Jail Terms," *CO*, Oct. 16, 1990.
62. Harrell, *All Things Are Possible*, 206–208; Henry Eichel, "Preacher May Buy Network," *CO*, May 11, 1990; Charles E. Shepard, "Pastor Commits to Buying PTL," *CO*, May 31, 1990; Kathleen McClain, "Faith Healer Casts Line to Land PTL," *CO*, June 12, 1990; Allison Salerno, "Some PTL Creditors Are Paid $37 Million, Others Likely to Get Nothing," *CO*, Dec. 18, 1990; Morris Cerullo, *Portrait of a Prophet: The Amazing Life Story of Morris Cerullo* (San Diego: World Evangelism, 1965), 29–32.
63. Jennifer French Parker, "9th Largest Accounting Firm Dissolves," *CO*, Nov. 20, 1990; Diane Suchetka, "Firm Dropped as Defendant in PTL Suit," *CO*, Nov. 27, 1990; Gary L. Wright, "PTL Partners Awarded Millions," *CO*, Dec. 15, 1990;

"Bakker Lawsuit Nets $6.54 Per Plaintiff," *CO*, Aug. 1, 2003; Tidwell, *Anatomy of a Fraud*, 192–203; Albert, *Jim Bakker*, 507.

64. Linda Brown Douglas and Laura Zelenko, "Foreign Partners Own 51 Percent," *CO*, Feb. 23, 1991; Linda Brown Douglas, "New Heritage Chief Takes Humble Approach to Success," *CO*, June 21, 1992.
65. Laura Zelenko and Linda Brown Douglas, "Business Partners Sue Cerullo," *CO*, Mar. 14, 1991; Laura Zelenko and Linda Brown Douglas, "Cerullo Calls Off Card Sales, Hoping to Settle Lawsuit," *CO*, Mar. 17, 1991; Linda Brown Douglas and Laura Zelenko, "New Owners to Refashion Heritage Park," *CO*, Apr. 14, 1991; Laura Zelenko and Linda Brown Douglas, "Cerullo's Business Partners Sue Evangelist Again," *CO*, Apr. 25, 1991; Linda Brown Douglas, "Cerullo's Stake in New Heritage USA Comes to an End," *CO*, Jan. 29, 1992; Ken Garfield, "Old PTL Network Gets New Name," *CO*, Apr. 1, 1992; Tidwell, *Anatomy of a Fraud*, 270–286, 343–344.
66. Linda Brown Douglas, "Sound of Gong Opens New Heritage USA," *CO*, June 28, 1992; Associated Press and Ken Garfield, "Old PTL Resort Now Is Called Radisson," *CO*, Oct. 16, 1994; David Enna, "UDC Pioneers in Regent Park," *CO*, Apr. 8, 1995; John Reinan, "Old Heritage USA No Longer Dry," *CO*, Dec. 4, 1996; Dan Huntley, "Echoes of PTL in Its Heyday," *CO*, Nov. 30, 1997; Ken Garfield, "The Shell of PTL Is Left to Its Ghosts," *CO*, Dec. 1, 1997.
67. U.S. v. Bakker, Resentencing Hearing, Aug. 22 and 23, 1991,124, 128, 130–131, 149; Kevin O'Brien, "Bakker Arrives at New Prison," *CO*, Nov. 4, 1989; Art Harris, "Jim Bakker's Sentence Overturned," *Washington Post*, Feb. 13, 1991; Nancy Webb and David Perlmutt, "Freedom Is Years Closer for Bakker," *CO*, Aug. 24, 1991.
68. Interview with Alan Dershowitz, Sept. 5, 2012.
69. Ken Garfield, "Bakkers, PTL's First Couple, Divorcing," *CO*, Mar. 13, 1992; Ken Garfield, "Bakkers' Marriage Ended without Tears in Fla. Court," *CO*, Mar. 14, 1992; Tommy Tomlinson, "Bakkers' Daughter Carries On Ministry," *CO*, Mar. 16, 1992; Nancy Webb and Ken Garfield, "Bakker Eligible for Parole after Term Cut to 8 Years," *CO*, Dec. 23, 1992; U.S. v. Bakker, Rule 35 Hearing, Nov. 16, 1992.
70. Linda Brown, "High-Volume Church Builder Views Business as His Ministry," *CO*, Oct. 5, 1986; Nancy Webb, "Son Pleads for Bakker's Release," *CO*, Nov. 17, 1992; Ken Garfield, "Tammy Bakker, Roe Messner Wed in Calif.," *CO*, Oct. 5, 1993; Karen S. Schneider, "Tammy's In Love," *People*, Apr. 6, 1992, 79; Bakker, *I Was Wrong*, 336, 373–376, 380, 389.

EPILOGUE

1. Ken Garfield, "Bakker Moved to Low-Security Camp in Georgia," *CO*, July 1993; Ken Garfield, "Former TV Evangelist Jim Bakker to Leave Prison for Halfway House," *CO*, June 30, 1994; Ken Garfield, "Bakker Free as House Arrest Ends," *CO*, Dec. 1, 1994.

2. Ken Garfield, "Ministry of Prosperity Was Mistake, Bakker Tells Friends," *CO*, Sept. 10, 1992; Ken Garfield, "Friend Finds Jim Bakker a Changed Man," *CO*, Dec. 25, 1993; Ken Garfield, "Bakker May Again Preach," *CO*, Apr. 10, 1994; Garfield, "Former TV Evangelist Jim Bakker to Leave Prison."
3. Bakker, *I Was Wrong*, 316–318, 450, 466, 469, 533.
4. Bakker, *Prosperity*, 5, 33, 71.
5. Larry O'Dell, "Appeals Court Reinstates Claims in Bakker Case," *CO*, Sept. 24, 1994; Jack Horan, "Investors' Suit against Bakker Fails," *CO*, July 23, 1996.
6. Albert, *Jim Bakker*, 508–518; Horan, "Investors' Suit against Bakker Fails."
7. Sarah Jane Tribble, "Work Begins at Heritage," *CO*, Oct 24, 2004; Sarah Jane Tribble, "Former PTL Land Goes to Ministry," *CO*, Sept. 29, 2004.
8. Tex ONeill, "PTL Figures Released on Bond," *CO*, Dec. 21, 1989; Rob Urban, "PTL Figure Gets Psychiatric Evaluation at Butner," *CO*, Mar. 16, 1990; Gary L. Wright, "Gavel Falls on Final PTL Figure," *CO*, May 23, 1990; "Elsewhere in North Carolina," *CO*, Sept. 15, 1990.
9. Jeffrey A. Frank, "Bimbonic Plague: Are All Our Sex Scandals Alike?" *Washington Post*, Feb. 2, 1992.
10. Lew Powell, "Good Morning, I'm Jessica Hahn," *CO*, Aug. 25, 1988; Nancy Brachey, "Film Institute Honors Gregory Peck," *CO*, Mar. 11, 1989; Jeff Kaye, "Sex, Mud and Rock 'n' Roll," *Los Angeles Times*, Nov. 9, 1989; *The View*, Feb. 22, 2011; *Larry King Live*, July 14, 2005.
11. Frank Garofalo, "PTL Builder May Lose His Property," *CO*, Feb. 22, 1990; Associated Press, "Messner's Firm to Be Liquidated," *CO*, Oct. 12, 1990; Michael Bates, "Messner's Trial Gets Under Way," *CO*, Nov. 15, 1995; "Messner Convicted in Fraud Case," *CO*, Nov. 23, 1995.
12. Author interview with Jim J. Bullock, May 13, 2010.
13. Author interview with Jim J. Bullock, May 13, 2010; Steven Cole Smith, "Don't Look for Sleaze on the Talk Show," *CO*, Jan. 9, 1996.
14. Tim Funk, "Tammy Faye Upbeat amid Ravages of Cancer," *CO*, July 20, 2007.
15. Art Harris, "Jim Bakker's Sentence Overturned," *Washington Post*, Feb. 13, 1991.
16. Bakker, *Prosperity*, 6; Jim Bakker and Ken Abraham, *The Refuge: A Look into the Future and the Power of Living in a Christian Community* (Nashville: Thomas Nelson Publishers, 2000), 35; Jim Bakker with Ken Abraham, *Time Has Come: How to Prepare Now for Epic Events Ahead* (Brentwood, TN: Worthy Publishing, 2012), 28, 29, 32, 197.
17. Lori Graham Bakker, *More Than I Could Ever Ask* (Nashville: Thomas Nelson, 2000).
18. Books by Tom Horn and Chris Putnam include *The Final Roman Emperor, the Islamic Antichrist, and the Vatican's Last Crusade* (Crane, MO: Defender, 2016); *On the Path of the Immortals: Exo-Vaticana, Project L.U.C.I.F.E.R., and the Strategic Locations Where Entities Await the Appointed Time* (Crane, MO: Defender, 2015); *Exo-Vaticana: Petrus romanus, Project L.U.C.I.F.E.R., and the Vatican's*

Astonishing Plan for the Arrival of an Alien Savior (Crane, MO: Defender, 2013); *Petrus Romanus: The Final Pope Is Here* (Crane, MO: Defender, 2012). Also see Jonathan Cahn, *The Harbinger: The Ancient Mystery That Holds the Secret of America's Future* (Lake Mary, FL: FrontLine, 2011); Joel Richardson, *The Islamic Antichrist* (Washington, DC: WND Books, 2009); William Forstchen, *One Second After* (New York: Forge, 2009); http://www.stevequayle.com.

19. Interview with Don Hardister, June 5, 2012.

Index